Nile Valley Civilization

A 10,000-Year History

NILE VALLEY CIVILIZATION

A 10,000-Year History

Charles S. Finch III

First printing, 2023

Cover Design by Marc Hamm, Pro Web Firm.

ISBN 978-0-9629444-4-4

Library of Congress Control Number: 2022914789

Printed in the United States of America

DEDICATION

This book, **Nile Valley Civilization: A 10,000-Year History,** is my most ambitious undertaking to date, covering 10,000 years of ancient Nile Valley History where African civilization first bloomed, spread to the rest of Africa, and then to the world. A couple of years ago, I remember walking across the desert from the excavation site of the tomb of Karakhamun, Chief Priest of Amun in the 25th Dynasty, co-directed by Dr. Elena Pischikova and Mr. Anthony Browder, and stopping half-way to the road. As I looked down at the ground, it dawned on me that there was a whole world of ancient archaeological treasures beneath my feet waiting to be unearthed. I further understood that all of Egypt is like that. This book is dedicated to the peerless archaeological explorers and historians who have re-constituted ancient Egypt – Kemit – in its African context, to wit:

Dr. Cheikh Anta Diop
Dr. Theophile Obenga
Dr. Ivan Van Sertima
Mr. J. A. Rogers
Mr. John G. Jackson
Gerald Massey
Dr. Elena Pischikova
Mr. Anthony Browder
Dr. Asa G. Hilliard

These are the individuals who have profoundly influenced my own journey of Nile Valley exploration. Nor would this dedication be complete without a bow of thanks and admiration to my wife **Ellen Nixon Finch**—mother of seven Finch children—who has been behind me all the way when she was not shoulder-to-shoulder with me in my explorations. And though I have also thanked my mother, **Louise Antoinette Finch,** in Dedications to previous works, my deep appreciation for her immense influence on my life must be repeated again and again.

One further realization: if the excavation of all the archaeological remnants of ancient Egypt could be attempted it would require 300–500 years of unrelenting effort to unearth it all. It is a heady thought but Egypt has been too widely urbanized and the population has exploded to such an extent it is something that can only be dreamed of…

Charles S. Finch III
November 1, 2022

Table of Contents

Introduction

> Those piles of ruins…in that narrow valley watered by the Nile, are the remains of opulent cities, the pride of the ancient kingdom of Ethiopia. Behold the wrecks of her metropolis, of Thebes with her hundred palaces, the parent of cities, and monuments of the caprice of destiny. There a people, now forgotten, discovered, while others were yet barbarians, the elements of the arts and sciences. A race of men now rejected from society for their *sable skin and frizzled hair*, founded on the study of the laws of nature, those civil and religious systems which still govern the universe.
> —Count Volney, **Ruins of Empires**

> …never…underestimate the power of the human mind to believe what it wants to believe despite any amount of evidence.
> —Robert K.G. Temple, **The Sirius Mystery**

A Perspective of the African Past

Much has been written about African history and culture and yet one will comb this vast literature nearly in vain for a complete and comprehensive survey of African civilizations by a single author. The multi-volume **UNESCO General History of Africa**[1] is, in effect, an anthology and while valuable and wide-ranging, suffers the limitations that all works of collective authorship do. Not all the essays are of comparable quality, different 'schools of thought' contend with one another, and a consequent lack of consistency and a unifying thread

1 **UNESCO's General History of Africa**, vols. I-VIII, Berkeley: University of California Press.

compromises the impact of the grand sweep of civilization on the world's second largest continent, the original home of humankind. A single author, with the requisite scholarly foundation and literary skills, could bring a certain seamlessness to the topic.

The reader will notice that the present writer does not list 'objectivity' as an indispensable criterion for good history writing. It has been my experience that objectivity is a mirage never attained by even the most rational and sober-minded of authors. Put another way, I have never read a book of history where total objectivity prevailed; preferences and biases show through even the most neutral prose. Where Africa is concerned, objectivity has been an ideal honored in the breach. European writers, for the most part, have endeavored to recast the history of Africa in their own image. The occasional scholar of good faith, a Count Volney[2] (see epigram at the beginning of the **Introduction**) or a Basil Davidson[3], have modified this tendency but little. Writers of African descent, on the other hand, can almost never avoid engaging in the process of 'setting the record straight' as a conscious or unconscious anti-colonialist exercise. Even a black Eurocentric writer such as Frank Snowden, author of **Blacks in Antiquity**[4], by demonstrating the pervasiveness of the Black presence in ancient Greece and Rome, is engaging in a kind of special pleading that can hardly be said to be objective. Though he detested Afrocentricty and Afrocentric writers, Snowden too was motivated by the need to set the record straight.

No, we cannot require absolute objectivity as a categorical measure of scholarly validity or merit nor is it necessary for the authentic and accurate reconstruction of an abandoned history. Perhaps the real tests of scholarly merit are accuracy and authenticity rather than objectivity; the first two are not necessarily implied by the latter. Africa's greatest 20th century scholar, the Senegalese polymath Cheikh Anta Diop, perhaps did more than any other single individual to reconnect modern Africa to its civilized beginnings in the Nile Valley with a sweep, an insight, a precision, and an erudition that amounted to genius. And while it is difficult to make the case that Diop was neutral or

---

2 de Volney CFC., **Ruins of Empires**, New York: Peter Eckler Publishing Company (1791), 1926.

3 Davidson B, **The Lost Cities of Africa**, New York: Little, Brown and Co., (1959), 1987.

4 Snowden, F, **Blacks in Antiquity**, Cambridge: Harvard University Press, 1970.

'objective' about his life's work, few could match him in the authenticity and accuracy of his writings.

Cheikh Anta Diop—20th Century African Polymath

Certainly in the discipline of Egyptology, the rule of objectivity in no way abides. The very fact that the study of Egypt is considered separate from African history and usually listed under 'Near Eastern Studies,' removes from Egyptologists any claim to objectivity. That Egypt was born and came into the fullness of its civilization on African soil is treated by them as an unhappy accident, best minimized when it cannot be ignored. Indeed, there is within the European antiquarian two opposing tendencies concerning Egypt: he wants desperately to 'claim' Egypt but because such a claim is empty, tries to 're-adjust' the public perception of Egypt's stupendous cultural achievements. For example, the dynastic chronology has been fudged downward by nearly 1,200 years, from c. 4,268 BC to c. 3,100 BC, to give (non-African) Sumer pride of place as the 'first' civilization. Moreover, Egyptian achievements in philosophy and science are routinely disparaged by comparison to the Babylonians and, even more so, the Greeks. It doesn't matter that the ancient writers on the subject, almost to a man, acknowledged the incalcuable debt owed by Greek civilization to Egypt (and Ethiopia); indeed, northeast, Nilotic Africa stands behind ancient Greece in exactly the same way that ancient Greece stands behind Rome and Renaissance Europe. The modern classicist is locked into the incongruous position of asserting that in this one area—their own history—the Greeks simply didn't know what they were talking about. Armed with the tools (and weapons) of 'higher criticism,' the contemporary antiquarian claims to know more about the Greeks and the Egyptians than either of these peoples knew about themselves. The modern classicist is said to be so much better endowed than ancient Greek writers because he is so much more objective than they were. Martin Bernal has even found a German term for this mentality—*besserwisserei*—defined as 'knowing the ancients better than the ancients knew themselves.'[5] Modern 'objectivity' admits no room for a view of Greek civilization that places Egypt at its source.

But the desperation of the modern antiquarian really shows itself in the relentless attempts to classify the Egyptians as anything other than the black African people they indubitably were. Herodotus—an eyewitness—2,450 years ago, while speaking of the Colchian inhabitants of the Black Sea, had this to say regarding the Egyptians:

> The Egyptians did...say that they thought the original Colchians were men from Sesostris's army. My own idea on the subject was based first on the fact that they have black skins and woolly hair (not that that amounts to much, as other nations have the same), and secondly...on the fact that the Colchians, the Egyptians, and the Ethiopians are the only races which from ancient times have practiced circumcision.[6]

Elsewhere, Herodotus embarks on an extended discussion of the origin of the oldest and most famous oracle in Greece, the Oracle of Dodona, which, by common affirmation, was brought to Greece from Egypt. One tradition says that a black dove flew to Dodona from Egypt and began to make utterances in human speech. About this dove Herodotus says,

> As to the bird being black, they [the Greeks] merely signify by this that the woman was an Egyptian.[7]

5 Bernal M, **Black Athena Writes Back: Martin Bernal Responds to His Critics**, Durham: Duke University Press, 2001, p. 57)

6 Herodotus, **The Histories**, New York: Penguin Books, (1954), 1972, p. 167.

7 Ibid., p. 152.

Modern Representative
of the Ancient Ethiopians

The Eurocentric critic has spent the last two hundred years trying to discredit Herodotus as a result of these unequivocal statements. Though Herodotus saw the Egyptians he described, his presumed credulity and lack of objectivity are said to make him an unreliable witness. Of course a thing is either black or it isn't by the evidence of the eyes; such a description is about as objective as it ever gets. For Herodotus the blackness of the Egyptians was to be considered a mere commonplace, so self-evident to as to be hardly worth mentioning ('not that that amounts to much, as other nations have the same'). For him, the real tell-tale piece of evidence tying the Colchians to the Egyptians and the Ethiopians was the common practice of circumcision from 'ancient times.' Again, Herodotus *saw* the people he was describing; on this matter, his is not hearsay evidence but hard, eye-witness proof.

Modern scholarship is also frequently embroiled in questions of who is qualified to write 'legitimate' history. Mostly, the professional, academically-trained scholar, top-heavy with methodology, claims for himself the exclusive prerogative of writing legitimate history. But clearly there is room for the 'auto-didact.' The auto-didact, literally the 'self-taught,' usually implies that he lacks formal training in methodology and/or access to the primary data essential for reconstructing the past. However, since he is under fewer constraints than the professional academician, the auto-didact is far more willing and able to consider lines of evidence outside the normal academic purview. He can ask questions the academician can't or won't and 'push the envelope' into realms of learning conventional scholars have never considered. Moreover, there is no academic—

or scientific—discipline that has not been profoundly impacted by the work of an inspired amateur. Darwin, after all, was an amateur and through the work undertaken during his five-year voyage around the world, in effect, created modern evolutionary biology. So were Copernicus, Kepler, and Newton, in effect 'amateurs'. Modern Egyptology itself was crafted out of the methods devised by William Flinders Petrie in the latter half of the 19th-century, a surveyor by training, who never set foot inside a university as a student. Here are examples of the development of methodologies that gave birth to entirely new disciplines accomplished by amateurs, or 'auto-didacts,' a class of scholars usually chided for their lack of methodology and formal training! The intellectual history of the world is filled with similar contributions. One might even say that every field requires the occasional input of the talented auto-didact.

With this book, **Nile Valley Civilization—a 10,000 year history,** we are trying to weave a tapestry of African history upon which the ancient civilizations of the continent embroider the fabric of human life in Africa. Human origins go back 6.8 million years in Africa and *Homo sapiens sapiens,* i.e., anatomically modern human beings, appeared in Africa 300,000 years ago.[8] Human culture in Africa began to develop almost simultaneously with the appearance of modern human beings so that human culture has a history in Africa that spans nearly 300 millenia. It isn't surprising that we would find the first traces of civilization—the highest phase of cultural evolution—in Africa, it would be surprising if we did not. Since archaeology has only sporadically explored Africa outside the Nile Valley, what we have are mere fragments from deep in the past, but these fragments are profoundly instructive. Iron ore mining is evident in Swaziland 43,000 years ago, manganese mining was practiced in Zambia 28,000 years ago, and the proto-mathematics evident on the Ishango Bone found in modern-day Congo is 25,000 years old.[9] Other findings in Africa presaging civilization include evidence of agriculture there 15,000 years ago or more and the domestication of animals 18,000 years ago.[10]

8 Finch, CS, **The Star of Deep Beginnings**, Decatur: Khenti Publications, Inc., 1998, pp.23-4.

9 Ibid., pp. 3-6.

10 See Webster B, *African Cattle Bones Stir Scientific Debate*, in Van Sertima I, editor, **Blacks in Science: Ancient and Modern**, New Brunswick: Transaction Publishers, 1983/1998, p. 65.

In recent years, new ways of looking at and approaching data have begun to force a reassessment of ancient Nile Valley chronology. In 1980, Bruce Williams caused a stir by his analysis of artifacts found at Qustul, once part of ancient Nubia but now lying beneath Lake Nasser behind the Aswan Dam.[11] Materials recovered from 12 tombs showed a wealth, abundance, and diversity of material goods that, in Williams's opinion, meant that these tombs were royal. They represented a line of pre-unification Nile Valley pharaohs that ruled the kingdom of Ta-Seti, e.g., the place where pharaonic civilization in the Nile Valley first emerged. They were the immediate forerunners of the line of First Dynasty pharaohs that began with Aha-Mēnēs and were therefore the progenitors of dynastic Egyptian civilization itself. Thus, pharaonic civilization, as we understand it, begins in Nubia.

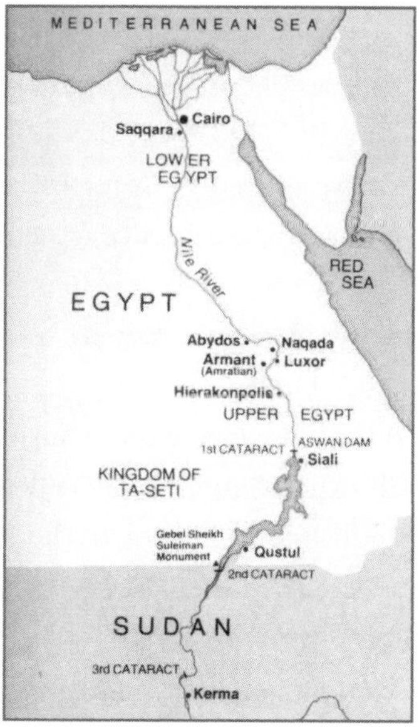

Egypt, Ta-Seti, and Cush

However, the rumbling that Williams caused in academic circles with his analysis dwindled to a murmur under the outraged howls in the face of data brought to light in the 1990s by John Anthony West and geologist Robert Schoch.[12] Examining the walls of the quarry in which sat the Sphinx, West and

11 Williams B, *The Lost Pharaohs of Nubia*, **Archaeology** (33)5, September/October 1980.

12 *Civilization Rethought*, **Conde Nast Traveler,** February 1993, pp.100-5; 168-77. Also, Schoch RM and McNally RA, **Voices of the Rocks**, London: Thorsons, 1999

Schoch showed that the deep, erosive fissures present were the result of heavy run-off from rain, a startling realization considering that it had not rained heavily enough in Egypt to cause such fissuring for 7,000 years. Moreover, the pattern of sub-surface water penetration into the bedrock beneath the Sphinx suggested to Schoch that the Sphinx could not have been built later than 7,000 years ago or earlier than 12,000 years ago. Even if the most conservative date only is allowed, the Sphinx is, minimally, 2,500 years older than the date of 2,500 BC conventionally given for its construction. It would be tantamount to discovering that the Eiffel Tower or the Washington Monument had been erected at the time of the Babylonian Captivity (586 BC) instead of a few generations ago. Several 19th century Egyptologists thought that the Sphinx was already in existence by the beginning of 4th Dynasty and that it was in fact undatable.[13] Nonetheless, the geologist Schoch thinks that the most likely building date for the Sphinx is 7,000 BC (9,000 years ago) and West thinks it is realistic to propose a date of 10,000 BC (12,000 years ago). The predictable snarls of scorn from Egyptologists have indeed been forthcoming but for the first time since early in the 20th century, hard evidence is calling conventional Egyptian chronology into serious question.

We can say this about the study of ancient Egypt: since the discovery of Tutankhamen's intact tomb by Howard Carter in 1922, academic Egyptologists have made comparatively few dynamic contributions to their own discipline. Most of the startling and compelling new developments have come from outsiders, that is to say non-Egyptologists. In the 19th century, the forerunners of these investigators were men like Piazzi Smyth and Norman Lockeyer, two eminent astronomers who demonstrated the unexpectedly advanced knowledge of the Nile Valley sky watchers. In the 20th century, R.A. Schwaller de Lubicz did extraordinary work pushing back the perceived limits of Egyptian mathematical and philosophic knowledge. More recent independent investigators such as John Anthony West, Robert Schoch, Graham Hancock, Robert Bauval, Adrian Gilbert, and Thomas Brophy—none of them trained Egyptologists—are forcing a serious re-consideration of the remote age of Egyptian civilization and its level of accomplishment in

13 Vid. **Budge EAW, A History of Egypt,** The Netherlands: Anthropological Publications, Vol. 2, (1902)1968, pp. 50-1.

all fields of human endeavor. Even the Senegalese polymath, Cheikh Anta Diop, though trained in Egyptology, was always considered an outsider because of his radical use of evidence to prove the African origin of Egyptian civilization. As a group, Egyptologists have become narrow, hide-bound reactionaries who, for all their command of massive amounts of data, don't seem to understand in any fundamental way the mind and spirit of the ancient civilization of the Nile. Moreover, they are ever ready to use their collective leverage to marginalize anyone writing about Egypt who is not a member of the fraternity. They are reminiscent of the French Academy of the 19th century that was content to preserve established artistic conventions while pretending that the Impressionists didn't exist. What is increasingly evident is that engineers, geologists, astronomers, and physicists—all of them Egyptological auto-didacts—are now the ones making the radical discoveries and pushing the frontiers of the discipline outward. They are having the same effect—and provoking even more extreme reactions—as the molecular biologists who, beginning in 1966, 'invaded' the terrain of human paleontology and revolutionized the study of human origins. Clearly the 'New Egyptology' is an emerging discipline that, while not supplanting conventional and established Egyptology, does amplify, change, and steer it in unexpected directions. It is what is supposed to happen in any valid science and, not surprisingly, it is 'outsiders' who are forcing the paradigm shift.

Egypt, or, more precisely *Kemit*, i.e., 'The Black Land,' holds a special position in African history. Gerald Massey asserted that ancient Egypt was the mouthpiece of African wisdom; that all the genius of inner Africa flowed into the lands of the Nile Valley and flowered brilliantly there in the pharaonic civilization of Kemit. But Africa, particularly the Great Lakes region, was the source and taproot of Nile Valley civilization and everything about Egypt proclaims it. There were no fewer than four African origination points for the migrations that terminated in the Nile Valley producing the people that formed ethno-cultural matrix of ancient Kemit: the Great Lakes region, the Horn of Africa, the Sahara, and the Sudan. Africa was the Mother, the Nile the Father, and Kemit the Nursling. But after dynastic Kemit grew to maturity and flourished for four thousand years, there came a time when a kind of 'repatriation' back into Africa occurred. When the major invasions from outside

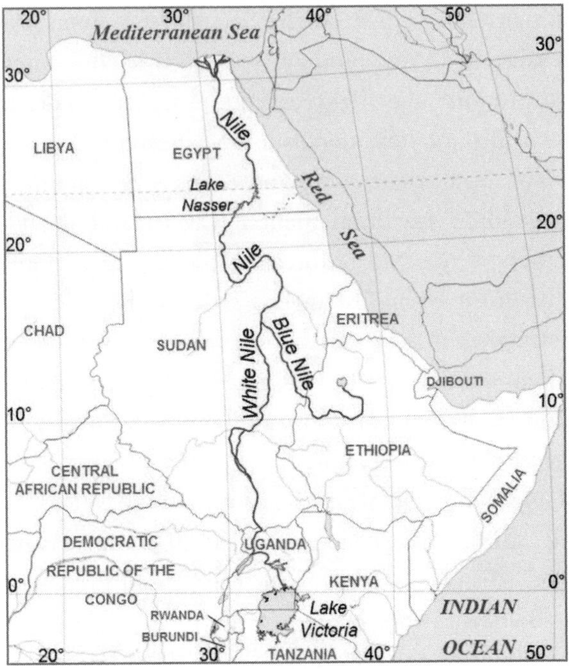

The Nile—Egypt's Umbilical Link to Inner Africa

of Africa into Egypt and the Nile Valley were launched in the seventh century BC—there were to be five in the 1,300-year period between 670 BC and 642 AD—out-migrations from the Nile Valley westward across the Sahara began. There were no fewer than six of these migrations in the period, largely coinciding with the major invasions,[14] the final one (c. 550 AD) involving the people who eventually settled in Mali and became known as the Dogon. A dozen or more major West African ethnic groups can trace their origins to the lands of and around the Nile Valley but of these, the Dogon are among the most remarkable for having preserved so many of the ancient cultural traits and spiritual ideas intact. At least one Egyptologist publishing in the last 20 years has acknowledged the striking similarities between the ancient Egyptian and Dogon cosmic systems.[15] However, the definitive work in the study of the trans-Saharan links

14 See Lam AM, **Les Chemins de Nil**, Paris: Présence Africaine, 1997 for a systematic examination of the evidence for east-west trans-saharan migrations out of the Nile Valley.

15 Cf. Grimal N, **A History of Ancient Egypt**, translated by Ian Shaw, Cambridge (USA): Blackwell, 1988; 1992, p.45.

of West African cultures to the Nile Valley was begun by Cheikh Anta Diop whose comparative linguistic studies uncovered unsuspected links between many West African groups and those of the lands bordering the ancient Nile. His work was taken up and extended by a younger Senegalese colleague Boubacar Lam who has demonstrated the ancient east-west migratory routes of the Peul and Tucolor.[16] The Lebu, one of the largest ethnic groups in Senegal, preserve traditions that trace their origins back to Libya and it is a fact that the ancient Egyptian name for the lands and people west of the Nile was *Lebu*, from which the toponym *Libya* is derived via the Greek language. Parenthetically, *Libya* became the Greek name for all Africa.

There is indeed a continuum in African cultural history, so much so that Diop was moved to write a book entitled **The Cultural Unity of Black Africa**[17] on this theme. Why this discussion is pertinent is that the largest number of Africans carried to the New World on the Middle Passage was taken from that stretch of coast in western Africa—from the Senegal River in the north to the Congo River in the south—whose peoples in many instances could trace their origins to the Nile basin. There is therefore a definite link, though seemingly attenuated by time, between diasporic Africans in the Americas and the cultures and peoples of the ancient Nile Valley. Thus to re-establish the connection linking ancient Nile Valley civilization to West Africa and thence to the diasporic West African communities in the Americas is critical to the process of recovering the *cosaan* of people of African descent. The word *cosaan* in Wolof (Senegal) combines in one word the meanings of 'history,' 'tradition,' 'cultural lore,' and 'spiritual heritage.' It has become an article of faith that the recovery of *cosaan* must undergird any substantive rehabilitation of 'global Africa.'

But civilization did not flower in Kemit for four thousand years and then die on the vine in the rest of Africa. The kingdom of Cush (Meroe) continued Nile Valley civilization for 330 years after Kemit disappeared from the stage of world history as a sovereign state (30 BC). Indeed, dynastic stability in Cush exceeded almost all other kingdoms in Africa and outside it. The Cushitic dynasty founded by Kashta around 800 BC endured without letup for nearly

16 Ibid., passim.

17 Diop CA, **The Cultural Unity of Black Africa**, Chicago: Third World Press, (1963), 1978.

12 centuries; there was no dynasty in Kemit that could boast such longevity. However, following the collapse of Meroitic Cush, Axum flourished on the Horn of Africa and Axumite kings later became the kings of Abysinnia and then Ethiopia. Until the deposition of Haile Selassie in 1974, the kings of Ethiopia traced their line back—with one 300-year interruption—to Solomon 2,900 years earlier, claiming a dynastic lineage of 2,600 years. After Cush, civilization in Africa continued: (1) Nubian Christian principalities created urban cultures in the northern Sudan until the 15th century, (2) the great empire period of West African history flowered for 13 centuries, (3) the Swahili city states on the East African coast maintained a far-flung luxury trade with Arabia, Persia, India, and China, and (4) the builders of Great Zimbabwe constructed marvelous structures of cut stone that stand today as mute witnesses to ancient grandeur. Civilization prospered in many parts of Africa until the 17th century AD.

The West African imperial age—200 AD to 1591 AD—was unique in African history for the size and complexity of the empires. Ghana, Mali, and Songhay succeeded one another in more or less chronological sequence, each state emerging as an empire larger than the one it replaced. Mali, some 2,000 miles from west to east, was nearly twice the size of western Europe and Songhay was larger even than Mali. The wealth of these empires was so vast that an Arab proverb said, 'For a cure for poverty, take a trip to the Sudan.' Gold was so plentiful in ancient Ghana that the king hoarded all nuggets to keep the price of gold from plummeting. Moreover, unlike other great empires, the wealth was fairly well-distributed through the ranks of society. Famine and pandemic diseases were, compared to other parts of the world, uncommon. It was said of both Mali and Songhay that a solitary traveler could cross the entire span of the empire without fear of molestation. A stranger who lost his goods or valuables in any of the major cities would have it sent to him intact or held until his return. In the 16th century, Gao, the capital city of Songhay, and its sister city Tombouctou, each boasted a population of more than 140,000 persons. Even earlier in the 14th century, the Malian City of Djenne's metropolitan area consisted of *more than 7,600 villages* which, conservatively estimated, would have contained a population of three million (3,000,000) souls! By comparison, London's population at the time was 80,000, Venice's 130,000, and Paris's 200,000.[18] In these West African cities, book-learning flourished. It is said that after the conquest of Songhay in 1591, tons of books disappeared from the cities of the empire to find their way into private collections and into the libraries of the Maghrib, Egypt, and other parts of the Arab-Islamic world.[19]

The story of African civilization, with roots in the ancient Nile Valley, ends with the fall of Songhay in 1591. The African slavery holocaust, i.e., the *ma'afa*, already underway, accelerated to unimaginable proportions over the succeeding 250 years. Thus, the 400-year period since the fall of Songhay is not merely a 'Dark Age,' but veritably a historical 'black hole' for Africa. Professor Louise Diop-Maes, the noted historical demographer, wrote a book entitled **Afrique Noire Démographie, Sol et Histoire**,[20] in which she shows that in 1500, the population for the continent of Africa, conservatively estimated, was 700 million people. By 1900, it had plummeted to 95 million people. In those calamitous 400 years, Africa lost 85% of its population to the slave trade—European and Arabic—endemic internecine war, famine, and finally, European imperial conquest. For sheer scale, there is hardly anything like this catastrophe in all of human history except for the parallel conquest and decimation of the Indians of the Americas. Thus, the image of a 'bombed-out,' disease-ridden, poverty-stricken Africa of the last four centuries has colored the world's perception of all African history. It has been commonplace to assume, for example, that wherever Africans are found outside of Africa at any point in history, they are either slaves or descendants of slaves.

More troublesome, however, is the conflicted responses elicited from Africans contemplating earlier Africans kingdoms' complicity in the enslavement of African people. The truth is that the slave trade would have been impossible without that complicity. It does no good to insist that slavery within Africa was

18 See Diop-Maes LM, *Évolution de la population de l'Afrique noire du néolithique au milieu du 20e siècle*, **ANKH**, n° 2 - avril 1993 for a succinct but comprehensive examination of the population demographics of West African cities in the medieval period.

19 Since about 1990, it has come to light that as many as one million Western Sudanic manuscripts, all written in Arabic, were hidden away from conquerors seeking to expropriate them. Literally, they represent the 'missing pages' of Black history.

20 Diop-Maes, LM, **Afrique Noire Démographie, Sol et Histoire**, Paris: Presence Africaine, 1996

a benign affair compared to the chattel slavery instituted by Europeans. Even if true, slaves in Africa could be bought and sold. The comparatively desultory trade in slaves evident in the West African empires was, in the 16th century, aggressively penetrated by Europeans in search of plantation labor, eventually taken over, then turned entirely to their own purposes. Africa has not yet recovered from the disaster and the destructive edifice of modern racism, negatively impacting almost anyone with an identifiable trace of African blood, was founded on it.

Until recently, as a consequence of the slave trade and colonialism, with the rampant abuses perpetrated from them, it has been difficult even to detect any vestige of civilization in Africa. By the 19th century, it had become axiomatic that 'the Negro' was incapable of civilization and it was therefore impossible *a priori* for ancient Egypt, for example, to have been a 'Negro civilization.' Parenthetically, the conquerors and colonizers of Africa could then absolve themselves of the consequences of their continental robbery, rapine, and murder by insisting that it was the only way that civilization could be brought to the 'Dark Continent.' They were so successful in this auto-propaganda that they even persuaded their colonial dependents in Africa and the Diaspora of the truth of this assertion. There are still people of African descent, for example, who have been heard to say that the slave trade was a positive benefit to black people because it brought them the benefits of Christianity and civilization! But ancient Egypt was safely removed from Africa, despite its inconvenient location, and placed under the rubric of 'Near Eastern' civilization. This labeling abides even today; at the University of Chicago, a major epicenter of American Egyptology, the department of Egyptology is found in the *Oriental* Institute. Museums and libraries all over Europe and America routinely install their Egyptological materials in their Near Eastern wings. Typically, the large Egyptological scholarly fraternity holds onto Egypt with all the tenacity of a Gila monster with its teeth sunk into its prey, about which it is said that even if its head is severed from it body, the jaws of this thoroughly poisonous lizard never let go. Mixing metaphors, it can be truly said about modern Egyptologists that 'The Old Guard dies but never surrenders.'

It has been said that since all reality is based on perception, at any given moment what is real depends on a kind of collective interpretation. Or as

Voltaire once observed, 'all history is a collection of myths; it is merely a matter of which one you choose.' And yet all interpretations are not created equal. We could use the analogy of the medically critical patient brought into the Emergency Room. There exists a hierarchy of opinion (interpretation) in such a situation, from the anxious speculations of the relatives, to the more experienced opinion of the nurse, to the final decision-making at the hands of the physician. The doctor's opinion depends on the ability to ask the right questions, generate accurate data, and interpret the information received for a correct diagnosis and treatment plan. But even the doctor's 'informed' opinion may not be enough; other physician specialists may have to be brought in for their interpretation of the data to arrive at a more conclusive picture. Even here, there are times when the most experienced and knowledgeable physician, or group of physicians, is stumped. The point is simply this, arriving at a correct conclusion involves an interpretation, one chosen out of several possibilities. It is not enough to have the facts at one's fingertips; they must be ordered in such a way as to lead to the correct conclusion. Facts may be 'true' without necessarily leading to the truth. Historians of Africa—including Egyptologists—usually have an abundance of data at their disposal. Interpreting them properly is another matter and is usually conditioned by personal prejudice and the peculiar slant of the academic training the historian has received. At present, we are engaged in a re-interpretation based on a different perspective of the facts, one that puts Africa at the center of her own history.

If we seem to harp excessively on ancient Egyptian—or more properly speaking, Nile Valley—civilization it is because it is the crux of the whole matter. Eurocentric antiquarians recognize it for certain. As Cheikh Anta Diop said, Egypt and Cush, i.e., the Nile Valley, bear the same relationship to the later of history of Africa—Axum, Zimbabwe, Ghana, Mali, Songhay—as surely as Greece and Rome do to Renaissance Europe. To speak of the history of Africa for the last 2,000 years without reference to Nile Valley civilization is tantamount to trying to plant a tree by cutting off its roots.

Taking all that has been said above into consideration, the author feels constrained to 'balance the scales' a bit. If not evident already, it will be as the reader continues that the author is, like so many others, deeply admiring of Egyptian civilization. There is no point in pretending otherwise but it can, unrealized, lead imperceptibly to a romanticization of this ancient culture from which so much flowed. The ancient builders of Nile Valley civilization, supremely gifted though they were, were not free of ordinary human flaws and blemishes. Several pharaohs, for example, were victimized by palace conspiracies, slavery—derived largely from Western Asian captives—became more or less institutionalized in the country from the Middle Kingdom onward, and the priesthood of Amon became hopelessly corrupted by the vast and unprecedented wealth that flowed into its treasury during the New Kingdom. It is therefore essential to view the ancient Nile dwellers on the human scale. They may seem to have been divinely inspired in many ways but the human element—both admirable and discreditable—was ever-present and after the 20th Dynasty there was ever less to admire and ever more to deplore. It is therefore imperative to maintain a clear, full-dimensional perspective of a people who, then and now, have commanded the fascination of the world. No individual or group, once touched by exposure to ancient Egypt, could escape its palpable influence, an influence both divine and human at the same time.

In the next section, we will try to summarize the salient facets of the question concerning ancient Egypt's bio-genetic connection to Africa. Each topic could itself be a chapter—or a book—but the material introduced in *précis* here will be amplified as we proceed through the millenial story of Nile Valley civilization.

A. Definition of 'Negro.'

Two Views of Women from the Horn of Africa

Ethiopia

Somalia

By strict anthropological criteria, the racial designation 'Negro' pertains to a limited group of people living in West-Central Africa. Indeed, the 'Negro' in anthropological thinking was more of a caricature, featuring black skin, kinky hair, dolicocephalic skull, prognathous jaw, thick or everted lips, a broad, flat 'platyrrhinus' nose, and thin, 'weak' calves. Though it is possible to find such a type in different parts of Africa, there are significant phenotypic variations—determined by region, climate, and environment—of native African peoples. In fact, coloration can vary from reddish and yellowish-brown to deep black; such variation can occur within the same ethnic group or even clan. Hair texture is usually woolly but, here and there, can be curly or occasionally straight. Though the nose tends toward a flat, broad, and flaring shape, numerous African types have 'chiseled,' even 'aquiline,' nose shapes. While lips tend toward thickness—eversion in extreme cases—lips in other African morphological sub-varieties are more 'compressed.' Dolicocephaly, i.e., 'long-headedness' that can be extreme in parts of East Africa, is markedly diminished among various groups throughout the continent. Subnasal prognathism, or a 'jutting lower jaw,' is characteristic of human types throughout Africa but by no means invariable.

Whether describing the Negro 'caricature' or the numerous variations and deviations from the Negro type, all native African variations, including the 'classic' Negro, were found in ancient Egypt and portrayed on the monuments. The term 'Negro' has been out of favor for several decades but it is occasionally a useful descriptive because it instantly calls to mind a certain image of the African physical type. In the 1950s, Diop referred to ancient Egypt as a 'Negro civilization,'[21] which had the virtue of being categorical and unequivocal. Anthropology, ethnography, and ancient history were still profoundly burdened then by terms such as *Hamitic*, used to create invidious distinctions between African groups. Ethiopians, Somalis, Masai, etc., people who were considered 'handsome' in the European sense of it, were lumped under the rubric of *Hamite*, to dissociate them from the primitive, 'degraded' Negroes of the rest of Africa. People called *Hamitic* were often tall, regal-looking, with 'regular' features, and frequently brown or copper colored rather than black skin. In fact, many went so far as to say that these Hamites were really Caucasian-Africans, an off-shoot of the Aryan rather than the Negro type:

> The Hamites—who are 'Europeans', i.e., belong to the same great branch as the whites—are commonly divided into two great branches, Eastern and Northern.[22]

Moreover, wherever civilization was to be found in Africa, it was invariably the creation of the Hamite, i.e., the Caucasian-African, and/or the Semite from western Asia. Thus ancient Egypt was seen to have emerged from some combination of the Asiatic Semite and the Hamite from northeastern Africa, who was really, by this terminology, a 'white black.'

---

21 Diop CA, **Nations Negres et Culture**, Paris: Présence Africaine, 2 volumes, (1954), 1979.

22 See Seligman CG, **Races of Africa**, New York: Oxford University Press, (1930); 1979 for a discourse favoring this point of view.

"Hamite" from Ethiopia (Danakil)

Like the word 'Negro,' *Hamite* is no longer used in scholarly circles but Diop, in 1954 with publication of **Nations Negres et Cultures** (*Negro Nations and Cultures*), was throwing down the gauntlet: Egypt was a black African civilization, peopled during its prehistory mostly from sub-Saharan Africa. Diop was saying that it was impossible to circumvent this truth by trying to winnow away the Negro from the more 'favored' Hamite in the history of ancient Egypt. It might be noted parenthetically—a point to which we will return—that throughout the Old Testament there are numerous references to Egypt as the 'Kingdom of Ham,' but in ancient usage, *Ham* denoted black African people as a whole, without all the disingenuous nuances that modern ethnography has tried to associate with the term.

"Red" Egyptians—New Kingdom

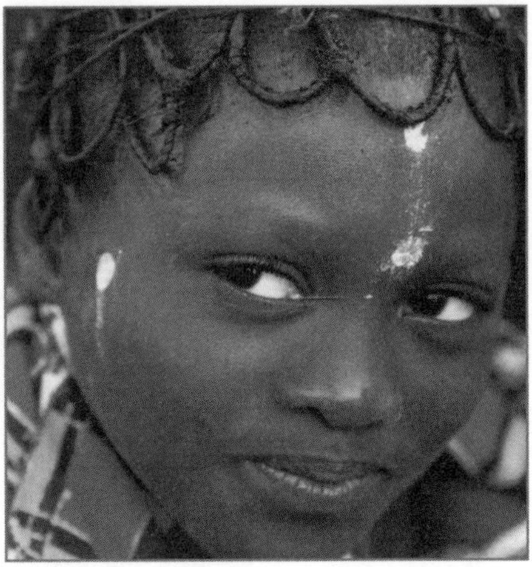

"Red" Krobo Girl from Eastern Ghana

Egypt during pre- and proto-dynastic times was probably peopled from four parts of Africa: (1) the Great Lakes of East Africa, (2) the Sudan, (3) the Sahara, and (4) the Horn of Africa. Though Asiatics, i.e., 'Syrio-Palestinians', had infiltrated into the Delta from early times, Egypt south of the Delta, i.e., Upper Egypt, was *always* ethnically African till the end of its history. Indeed, many of these Syrio-Palestinians moving into the Delta were themselves black and/or 'mulatto,' flowing back and forth into Africa from about 10,000 BC. The aboriginal Syrio-Palestines were people now referred to as 'Natufians,' incontestably black Africans who had settled in western Asia 12,000 years ago. In any event, the Panel of Races, in the tomb of Rameses III (c. 1,180 BC), incontrovertibly shows Egyptians representing themselves as black, phenotypically identical to the Cushite-Sudanese also shown in the Panel.

Egyptian Coastal Libyan Cushite Western Asiatic

Close-up of Egyptians in the Tomb of Rameses III

B. The Evidence of Egypt's African Origin.

Language: The Egyptian name for Egypt itself was *Kemit* meaning 'the Black Land' or 'the Black country.' Virtually to a man, Egyptologists have insisted that this reference to 'the Black Land' referred to the black topsoil deposited on either side of the Nile by the annual flood rather than to the people who inhabited this country. This point could be argued endlessly without resolution were it not for the Egyptians reference to themselves as *Kemmiu* or *Kemtjw*, i.e., 'the Blacks.' Thus one may take it that the term *Kemit* referred both to the black soil of the country and to the people. Additionally, the Egyptian word for 'south' was *khenti* also meaning 'first,' 'chief,' 'beginning,' 'origin;' thus the south, e.g., inner Africa, was the 'land of beginnings,' that is to say, the land where the Egyptians themselves originated from. Horus, the mythical and divine archetype of the living pharaoh, was said to have come from the south with his followers, known as the 'blacksmiths,' and colonized prehistoric Egypt.[23]

The Old Testament: The genealogy of Noah in the *Book of Exodus* makes Egypt (*Misr*) the son of Ham and brother to Ethiopia (*Cush*). The name *Ham* or *Cham* (Heb.) must derive from *Kam* (*Kem*) meaning 'black' in Egyptian, making *Ham* the eponymous ancestor of all Black people. As noted above, *Ham* is the root of the modern ethnic term *Hamite* to denote a certain African type. In any case, the ancient Hebrew writers, who were eyewitnesses to the fact, are

23 The Egyptian word for 'left' (*iabt*) is also their word for 'east'; the Egyptian word for 'right' (*imen*) is their word for 'west'. The east can be 'left' and the west 'right' only if facing or oriented to the south.

describing the ancient Egyptians as black African in race and as the greatest kingdom in Africa. They routinely referred to Egypt as 'the Land of Ham.'[24]

Classical Writers: Aeschylus (500 BC) in *Suppliants* has Danaos (one of the dramatic characters) say of an Egyptian sailing ship, 'I can see the crew with their black limbs and white tunics…' Herodotus (450 BC): in his **Histories**, states, 'It is in fact manifest that the Colchians are Egyptian by race… I had conjectured as much myself from two pointers, firstly because they have black-skins and woolly hair…' Herodotus was an eyewitness, having visited Egypt and spent seven months traveling through the country. His is one of the clearest and most categorical statements about the race of the Egyptians that has survived from antiquity.

Aristotle (340 BC) vouchsafes an uncomplimentary opinion about Egyptians, to wit: 'Those who are too black are cowards, like for instance the Egyptians and Ethiopians…' Uncomplimentary or not, he is giving evidence on the race and phenotype of the Egyptians. Again and again, writers of antiquity lump the Egyptians and Ethiopians together, being unable in many instances to distinguish between the two best-known African peoples. A further example of this tendency comes from Plautus (254 BC) who, in **Poenulus**, uses the word *ater*, meaning 'black' or 'dark'—commonly describing Ethiopians—as an adjective for Egyptians. Diodorus, in his **Library of History** (c. 40 BC), states that the Ethiopians asserted that the Egyptians were one of their colonies. Diodorus, who also traveled to Egypt (60–57 BC), did not question this assertion because, to him, the matter was self-evident. Again, this widespread tendency to lump the two peoples together is shown again by Horace (60 BC) who, in **Carmina**, calls Egyptians 'Ethiopian.' Lucian (125 AD), in **Navigations**, has his dramatic character Lycinus say of an Egyptian boy: 'This boy is not merely black; he has thick lips and his legs are too thin…' Sidonius (456 AD), in **Carmina**, describes the soldiers filling Cleopatra's ships as 'pitch black.'

We can see that as late as the second century, Graeco-Roman writers were calling Egyptians 'black' and lumping them with the Ethiopians. By this time—from 660 BC to 30 BC—there had been four non-African invasions of Egypt—Assyrian, Persian, Macedonian, and Roman—and yet the bulk

---

24 *Psalm 78, Verse 51; Psalm 105, Verse 23 and 27; Psalm 106, Verse 22*

of the population had remained untouched by non-African racial admixture. The native population of Egypt continued to be and look black African. The phenotypic shift in Egypt away from the black African type would not become evident until after the Arab invasions of the 7th century when great waves of in-migration from Central Asia and Eastern Europe would transform the ethnic landscape of Egypt in the ensuing millenium. Even so, Egyptians, to this day, have never lost completely the stamp of their anterior African origins, as a visit to the country will prove to even the most casual observer, especially as one travels south.

Melanin Dosage Test: this simple was devised by C.A. Diop[25] to determine the melanin concentration of Egyptian mummy skin, requiring only a square centimeter of skin from the mummy to determine its melanin content. Diop found that the melanin concentration in the skin of four 19th Dynasty pharaonic mummies was comparable to the concentration in his own skin. The Senegalese are among the darkest sub-Saharan African people and Diop was a native Senegalese. However, his findings provoked a reaction: after testing his four samples, he was never allowed to obtain any more mummy skin again. Considering that hundreds of mummies have been probed, eviscerated, x-rayed, and subjected to innumerable tests, there can be but one explanation for the refusal of the Egyptian authorities to grant Diop, a qualified investigator, any more small samples of mummy skin: the incontestable blackness of the ancient Egyptians cannot be allowed to gain academic (or public) currency.

C. Customs and cultural ideas of African origin.

Matrilyny: the Egyptian crown descended through female line, providing one of the motivations for royal incest, i.e. marrying the Chief Royal Wife to a brother or half-brother. In this manner, a dynastic clan could keep power in the family. Flinders Petrie speaks of 'king-bearing' mothers in Egypt who were the ancestral founders of their royal lineages[26] and further remarks that none of the kings in the early dynasties, though often portrayed in reliefs with

25 Diop CA, *Pigmentation des anciens Égyptiens - Test par la mélanine*, in **Bulletin de l'IFAN**, Tome XXXV, serie B, n°, Dakar, 1973.

26 Petrie WMF, **A History of Egypt**, Vol. 1, London: Methuen & Co., 1903, p. 29.

their mothers, appeared to be sons of the previous kings.[27] Furthermore, the Egyptian common people took their mothers' names. In the pre-dynastic period, the female graves tended to be wealthier and more prominent than male ones and the oldest deities of the pantheon were female, e.g., Ta-Urt. Prior to the in-roads made by Christianity and Islam, most African societies were matrilineal, even matrifocal. In Egypt's sister empire, Cush, the Queen Mother, the *Kendake*, was usually the second most-powerful person in the kingdom and in fact played the decisive role in choosing the Cushite pharaoh. By late antiquity, the Kendakes of Meroe, known as the *Candaces* by Romans, were able in several instances to rule entirely on their own account.[28] Even today, the institution of the Queen Mother is found among the Ashanti of Ghana and in Swaziland. Matrilineality in Egypt was one of its generic African customs; it was not brought into Egypt from outside Africa.

Totemism: in Africa, as elsewhere in antiquity, animals and other natural objects could represent the powers or forces of the cosmos. Ancient Egyptian culture was steeped in this mentality. For example, the Golden Hawk, because of its color and ability to soar high, evoked the Sun and as such, was the representative image of Horus and Ra. The Hippopotamus Cow symbolized the Earth floating in the Heavenly Waters just as hippopotami were seen to float in the lakes and rivers of Africa. The female Hippopotamus goddess in Egypt was named *Ta-Urt* which meant literally 'great earth.' The Scarab Beetle was an image of Self-creation and Evolution because just before the Nile flood, the scarab would create a near-perfect sphere of dung into which it would deposit its eggs, bury it, and three months later, when the flood had receded, scarab beetles would fly up out the 'primal ooze' of the Nile mud left behind by the flood. The scarab, indeed, was one of the most powerful images in Egyptian iconography.

Nearly all the Egyptian deities were identified with animal types and each sacred animal had temples and cities dedicated to it and the deity each represented. Egypt was divided first into 24, then 42, nomes or administrative

27 Ibid., p. 34.

28 See Budge EAW, **A History of Ethiopia**, Vol. 1, London: Methuen & Company, Ltd., 1928, p. 112; see also Leclant J, *Cushites and Meroites: Iconography of the African Rulers of the Ancient Upper Nile*, in **The Image of the Black in Western Art**, Vol. 1, 1976, pp. 120–26.

units, each with a guardian animal genius or totem. Early pharaohs such as Narmer had totem names such as 'Scorpion.'

Dance: dancing was a form of ceremonial worship and early pharaohs were seen dancing before the god. Pygmies—more properly called *Twa*—whom the Egyptians called *Deng*, were esteemed as those who could best perform the 'dance of the god.' Several pharaohs, including the great 18th-dynasty empire-builder Thutmosis III, were depicted dancing before the god, usually Osiris. Indeed, certain pharaohs took as a praise name 'the dancing Deng.' On two documented occasions during the Old Kingdom, representatives of the Twa were brought from deep in inner Africa to the court of the pharaohs as honored guests.

The soul and spiritual life: if ancient Egyptian spiritual beliefs are compared with the rest of Africa, the identity is categorical. To wit:

Egypt	Africa (beyond Egypt)
a. Ka - The Double	a. Energy Body/Double
b. Sahu - The Glorified Body	b. Dream Soul
c. Khaibit - The Shadow	c. Shade or Bush-Soul
d. Ba - The Soul proper	d. Life-Soul
e. Ib - The Heart	e. Body-Soul
f. Akhu - The Imperishable Spirit	f. Spirit Soul
g. Ren - The Name	g. Name

Like the Egyptians, sub-Saharan African peoples believe in a single Causative Power from whom emanate the various deities who represent the Actions of that Causative Power in the universe. Among the ancient Egyptians, these deities were called *neters*, among the Dogon *nommo,* the Dahomeyans *vodũ*, and the Yoruba *orishas*. These seemingly varied pantheons are so close in conception and activity that they are virtually interchangeable, differentiated primarily by language and ethnicity.

Ancestor Veneration: In Egypt, as everywhere in traditional Africa, ancestor veneration was deep and pervasive. Osiris, in fact, was considered the Divine Ancestor, and so strong is the evidence for the paramount importance of the ancestors, that Henri Frankfort was made to say concerning ancient

Egypt, '…the worship of the ancestors is as old as the monarchy.'[29] Diodorus Siculus, who visited Egypt in 60 BC, confirms this assertion:

> It is a most sacred duty in the eyes of the Egyptians, that they should be seen to honour their parents or ancestors all the more after they have passed to their eternal home.[30]

Likewise, the extreme veneration—amounting to worship—paid to ancestors throughout Africa is so pervasively documented as to require no further discussion.

Amulets: these protective emblems were worn by Egyptians of every class throughout their history. In the same fashion, *gris-gris* and *ju-jus* are worn for protective purposes by Africans of every class yet today.

Circumcision: a custom found early in Egypt and seen throughout Africa since the dawn of history was undoubtedly transmitted from there to neighboring peoples like the Israelites and Arabs. Herodotus himself (c. 450 B.C.) mentions the practice among the Ethiopians, the Colchians, as well as the Egyptians.

Serpent veneration: the Great Cosmic Serpent was prominently featured in Egyptian mythology and cosmology. The serpent *Sata*, to name but one of the many Serpent-forms present in Egyptian iconography, was one who died and was re-born daily. *Kematef*, the 'Uniter of Attributes,' was a cosmic Serpent who was the active force of creation. In fact, serpent-types—benevolent and malevolent—are the most ubiquitous figures in Egyptian mythic iconography, especially in the funerary rituals. Most traditional African religions have a sacred serpent, usually a python. Among the Fon and Ewe, the Great Cosmic Serpent named *Dă* and his wife *Dă Hlossu*, are pythons who appear as rainbows and are the active Creator of the Universe on behalf of Mawu, the Supreme Being. The Fon originate from the *homey*, i.e., 'the belly,' of *Dă*, hence *Dahomey*, the name of the West African kingdom which was the forerunner of modern day Benin.

29 Frankfort H, **Kingship of the Gods**, Chicago: University of Chicago Press, (1948)1978, p. 89.

30 **Diodorus Siculus: Library of History**, translated by CH Oldfather, Cambridge: Harvard University Press, (1933)2004, p. 317.

The counterpart of *Dă* among the Yoruba is the rainbow serpent *Oshumare*. Ethiopian annals prior to conversion to Christianity in the 4th Century AD, tell of the land being ruled by a Serpent Deity in the centuries before Christ.

Divine Kingship: pharaoh represented the most developed form of the Divine King but the institution of the Divine King is still a fixture in the traditional cultures of South, East, and West Africa. The Akan, Yoruba, Banyoro, Shilluk, and Swazi all have Divine Kings.

Linguistic Kinship: research has now shown that the Egyptian language belongs to the northeast African family of languages. Numerous contemporary African languages, i.e., Wolof, Akan, Yoruba, and Fulani (Peul) etc., bear a marked resemblance to ancient Egyptian. Several Peul family names, e.g., *Ba, Ka*, and *Dia* seem to have survived unchanged from the ancient Egyptian language to modern-day Peul.

A handful of Egyptologists over the last century have been forced by the clear evidence of such unambiguous cultural and linguistic similarities to recognize the African provenance of ancient Egypt. E.A.Wallis Budge, initially a firm believer in the Asiatic (Syrio-Palestinian) origin of Egyptian peoples, eventually changed his mind on the subject after his studies of early 20th century Sudanese peoples and cultures. It became obvious to him that innumerable Egyptian customs, beliefs, and life-ways could only be understood by reference to Africa, particularly the Sudan. In his large tomes, **Osiris: The Religion of the Resurrection** and **From Fetish to God in Ancient Egypt**[31], Budge set forth in extensive detail the vast range of Egyptian customs and practices that were clearly African in origin. He seems to have been alone in undertaking the study of late-19th century Sudanese peoples to illuminate the genesis of ancient Egyptian culture. In the coming chapters, the present author will bring forth additional evidence to amplify these themes delineating the emergence of Nile Valley civilization out of Africa and its continuing connection to it down to the modern era.

In this preface, we have tried to set the stage for an extended exploration of Egyptian civilization, one that will encompass a time line of nearly 11,000

31 **Budge** EAW, **Osiris: The Religion of the Resurrection**, New Hyde Park: University Press, (1911), 1961 and **From Fetish to God in Ancient Egypt**, London: Oxford University Press, 1934.

years, pushing back the conventional historical perspective of ancient Africa by 8,000 years. Of necessity, some space had to be devoted here to inaugurating the process of establishing the proper context of Egypt's place in the African historical continuum. This historical 're-contextualization' of Egypt in Africa must and will continue in the succeeding chapters, because, as C.A. Diop rightly intuited, Egypt is the key to that historical continuum of the entirety of African civilization with its proper appreciation and understanding. To remove Egypt from Africa, as European scholars have attempted to do, figuratively cuts Africa off at the knees, historically speaking, maiming and crippling Africa by doing so. No matter how academically polite and purportedly 'objective' this Eurocentric history-writing professes to be, it is really a savage attack, a killing blow, aimed at the mind, psyche and spirit of African people. There is no other way to look at it. But Africa can never relinquish Egypt and Egypt—in its timelessness—would never let go of Africa, out of whose womb it was born.

CHAPTER 1:

From South to North: The March of Civilization in the Nile Valley

> From Gizeh and Turah for 350 miles to Naqadeh there is no difference in the protodynastic work; and the same is true of the earlier prehistoric times for more than 300 miles from Gerzeh to Naqadeh. Moreover 200 miles farther south in Nubia the styles of this age are perfectly continuous, although mixed with other types which belong to Nubia. Thus for over 500 miles the prehistoric civilization seems to have been so well organized and unified that the same tastes, ideas, patterns and materials prevailed throughout. This shows that there were not isolated and warring tribes, which prevented intercourse and trade, but rather a peaceful, if not a united, rule over all Egypt and Nubia. —W.M. Flinders Petrie, **Prehistoric Egypt**, p. 3.

The truth of the matter is that we are having to radically re-adjust our entire conception of African historical chronology and, not coincidentally, the historical chronology of the world at large. As we have shown in an earlier work, there are far too many incongruities and unexplained facts bearing on this question to accept any longer the received chronology of academic historians. In fact, we may be in the middle of the latest of several *cycles* of civilization, this one having its beginnings nearly 13,000 years ago.[1] What can be said about the civilization of ancient Egypt with certainty is that it did *not*

1 See Chapter 2 for a full discussion of this chronology.

spring up fully-formed and operational on African soil without antecedents. As has already been alluded to, it has been profoundly embarrassing to academic Egyptology that Egypt, the parent civilization for most societies west of the Indus Valley, was conceived, born, raised, and brought to maturity in Africa. Therefore, there has been a pronounced tendency to think of Egypt as having been an anomaly whose existence in Africa was an inconvenient accident.

The contemporary chronology that places the beginning of the First Dynasty at 3,100 BC and that of the predynastic period at 4,500 BC is, *prima facie*, absurd. Egyptian dynastic history begins probably around 4,268 BC,[2] however, Egyptian civilization's earliest origins go back much further. The term 'predynastic,' coined by Petrie to describe the pre-unification cultures he was finding in the last decade of 19th century in the upper Nile Valley, accurately describes the socio-political structures characterizing those cultures. Many since Petrie's time seem to equate the term with 'pre-civilized.' It is a false notion and though we don't know nearly enough about those pre-unification societies, there is enough evidence to suggest that labeling them as 'pre-civilized' or even 'pre-historic,' if only by implication, is an erroneous interpretation of the historical reality.

It is worthwhile to examine with some care the available evidence tracing the development of Nile Valley civilization up to dynastic times (circa 4,268 BC). We will see that such an examination orients us southward, beyond the Nile Valley, where the true antecedents of Egyptian civilization are to be found. It is, of course, impossible to do the subject justice; there are simply too many gaps in the archaeological record. These gaps don't mean that the evidence is absent, but Africa south of the Nile Valley is territory largely untouched by the spadework of archaeology. Whole histories lay waiting to be unearthed by archaeological excavation. It is of fundamental importance to tie Egypt 'umbilically' to her southern cradle-land. It is southward that Egyptians always looked for their roots, their beginnings. In the dawn dynasties, the pharaohs repeatedly sent expeditions up the Nile toward the river's sources in Ethiopia and Africa's Great Lakes region. For the duration of her history Egypt kept alive that umbilical connection to inner Africa.

2 See Schwaller de Lubicz RA, **The Temple of Man**, translated by Deborah and Robert Lawlor, Rochester (Vt.): Inner Traditions, (1957), 1998, p. 495 for a 4,300 BC date for the launch of the 1st Dynasty.

Ishango and Katanga: Cradlelands of African Culture[3]

In the late 1980s and early 1990s, a married team of archaeologists from George Washington University, Alison Brooks and John Yellen, worked for a number of years in northeastern Zaire, along the shores of Lake Edward in the neighboring districts of Katanda and Ishango.[4] The artifacts they uncovered and tested by the most refined radiocarbon techniques available produced results that, in effect, forced the jettisoning of the conventional chronology of paleolithic East African culture. From the prehistoric rubble of Katanda where the team was working, Yellen, in 1988, extracted a finely-wrought, fossilized bone harpoon point.[5] This was the first of several such finds:

> ...two more whole points and fragments of five others turned up, all of them elaborately barbed and polished. A few feet away, the scientists uncovered pieces of an equally well-crafted dagger-like tool. In design and workmanship the harpoons were not unlike those at the very end of the Upper Paleolithic, some 14,000 years ago. But there was one important difference. Brooks and Yellen believe the deposits...were at least *five times that old* (emphasis added).[6]

Their conviction that a relatively advanced culture existed in east-central Africa 70,000 years ago underscored earlier work by Brooks on the related Ishango site. Ishango, just four miles from Katanda, was first excavated by the Belgian, Jean de Heinzelin in the 1950s, where he found a harpoon-rich 'aquatic civilization.'[7] His original date for the Ishango site was 8,500 B.P., but Brooks, re-dating the site more than 25 years later with more sensitive radiocarbon instruments, found, instead, that the site dates back to 25,000

3 This section has been imported more or less intact from the author's earlier work **The Star of Deep Beginnings**, Decatur: Khenti Publications, 1998, pp 1-24.

4 See Shreeve J, *The Dating Game*, **Discover**, September 1992, pp. 76-83.

5 Ibid., p. 78.

6 Ibid.

7 See De Heinzelin J, 'Ishango,' **Scientific American** (106), June 1962, pp. 105-16.

B.P., making it three times older than the original estimate![8] Furthermore, the stratigraphy of the Katandan deposits is much deeper than that of the adjacent Ishango site, and the Brooks-Yellen team thinks that the artifacts there are more nearly 70,000 years old. These dates are perplexing to archaeologists because they mean that the Katanda cultures had already reached a level of technical development not achieved outside Africa until 54,000 years later.

Storms of controversy persist around the locus of modern human origins. Several researchers continue to look for sites outside Africa for evidence of modern human beginnings,[9] but continually, the most compelling evidence fixing the geographic region of the emergence of modern humans continues to trickle in from the lacustrine regions of east-central Africa.[10] Even where Africa's role as the biological womb of humanity is conceded, many still assume that complex culture evolved elsewhere.[11] However, this recent work by Brooks and Yellen more firmly embeds the cultural cradle of humanity in Africa. Indeed, Brooks's re-dating of the Ishango site puts the famous Ishango Bone in an entirely new perspective.

When De Heinzelin first excavated the Ishango site with its cache of bony harpoon heads, he came across a bone tool displaying groups of peculiar horizontal markings on it. A close examination convinced him that these markings represented an arithmetic system revealing a familiarity with prime numbers, decimals, and addition by duplication.[12] The Harvard archaeologist, Alexander Marshack, could not accept evidence of 'mesolithic' mathematics in central Africa, but he did become convinced that the marks on the bone represented notations marking the lunar cycle.[13] Very likely, there is truth in both explanations and, therefore, the evidence of the Ishango Bone reveals

8 Shreeve, op. cit., p. 82.

9 Kittles R, **Mitochondrial DNA and Human Origins: Assessing the Debate**, Spring 1993, Unpublished.

10 Recently, fossil evidence from Chad in north-central Africa reveals the presence of early pre-human hominids going back 6.8 million years. See Brunet M, Guy F, et al, *A new hominid from the Upper Miocene of Chad, Central Africa*, **Nature**, Vol 418, 11 July 2002, pp. 145-151.

11 Shreeve, op. cit., p. 80.

12 De Heinzelin, op. cit., p. 111.

13 See Marshack A, **The Roots of Civilization**, Mt. Kisco: Moyer Bell Limited, 1991, pp. 21-32.

an intellectual sophistication that no one would have accorded mesolithic populations living in east-central Africa some 9,000 years ago. Brooks' recent radiocarbon datings have fermented the brew even more: since Ishango dates back 25,000 years, these people were not mesolithic but *paleolithic*. De Heinzelin had noted that the Ishango artifacts seemed archaic by comparison to other mesolithic populations, and Brooks' datings cleared up the mystery. But proto-mathematics and lunar calendars in Africa in the Upper Paleolithic period? With a tantalizing possibility that such scientific skills in that region might be older yet? The conventional model of cultural evolution may have to be reevaluated.

De Heinzelin's study of the harpoon heads and the Ishango Bone convinced him of something else: the culture revealed by these artifacts was carried virtually intact northward into the Nile Valley region of Africa. Thus, De Heinzelin tells us,

> From central Africa the [harpoon] style seems to have spread northward. At Khartoum near the upper Nile there is a site that was occupied considerably later than Ishango. The harpoon points found there show a
>
> diversity of styles...[other harpoons] have the notches that seem to have been invented first at Ishango. Near Khartoum, at Es Shaheinab, is a Neolithic site that contains harpoon points bearing the imprint of Ishango ancestry; from here the Ishango technique moved westward along the southern border of the Sahara.[14]

De Heinzelin goes on to say,

> The technology also seems to have followed a secondary branch northward from Khartoum along the Nile Valley to Nagada in Egypt. This site has both bone and copper harpoons. Made in the Neolithic period before the Egyptian dynasties began, many of them are notched at the head. Others show the influence of the Near Eastern Natufian

14 De Heinzelin, op. cit., p. 109.

technique and the Fayum technique which is closely related to it.[15]

It would seem, if De Heinzelin is correct, that a well-defined culture, like humanity itself, flowed out of the lacustrine African womb into the rest of the continent. The Nile River seems to have functioned 'umbilically' to link the northern tier of the continent to its East African 'placenta-land,' the land the ancient Egyptians called *Ta-Kenset*, literally 'placenta-land.' The reference to the Natufian harpoon technique in the quote by De Heinzelin is of interest because the Natufian culture of Syrio-Palestine can be dated back 12,000 years; the human fossil remains associated with this culture denote a clear Africoid type.[16] The similarities of Nile Valley and Natufian harpoon manufacture probably indicate a broader cultural kinship, and if the source of these harpoon styles is the Lake Edward horizon of east-central Africa, it is not implausible to assume that the Ishango/Katandan culture radiated beyond Africa directly into Western Asia.

The peopling of the Nile Valley (and Western Asia) from the Africa's Great Lakes region must have occurred in waves. The population wave from the Great Lakes directly ancestral to the historical Nile Valley peoples probably began to settle north of the second cataract no later than 15,000 years ago. This settlement did not pre-empt later migrations, of course, but most of these probably came in from the west—that is from the Sahara—beginning about 10,000 years ago.[17] There is archaeological evidence of a pottery-making, cattle-rearing Neolithic people inhabiting the lands west of the Nile as far back as 8,000 BC. Another line of migration apparently trickled in intermittently from the horn of Africa along the Blue Nile between 10,000 and 6,000 years ago. The dynastic Egyptians' never-ending fascination with *Punt*—their name for the Horn of Africa—and clear attestations from them regarding their kinship to the people of Punt compel us to look in that direction for an ancestral lineage of the peoples who created pharaonic culture. There seems to have been a touch

15 Ibid.

16 See Diop CA, *Processus de Semitisation*, **Parenté Génétique de l'Égyptien Pharaonique et des Langues Négro-Africaines**, Dakar: Nouvelle Editions Africaines, 1977, pp. xxix-xxvii.

17 See Wendorf F, Close AE, and Schild R, *Prehistoric Settlements in the Nubian Desert*, **American Scientist** (73), March-April 1985, pp. 132-41, for a discussion of

of religious awe associated with Punt since it was also referred to as *Ta-Neter*, i.e., 'Land of the God,' just as inner Africa was called *Ta-Iakhu* or 'Land of the Spirits.'

One last word regarding the Ishango Bone: De Heinzelin thinks that the Bone demonstrates a knowledge of addition by the method of duplication. This is of surpassing interest because the very same method of addition is utilized in the Rhind Mathematical Papyrus from Egypt, dating back nearly 4,000 years ago.[18] It is the oldest mathematical treatise on record. Is it possible that this mathematical procedure reached the Nile Valley directly from the lacustrine horizons of East Africa?

The Cultural Horizons of the Nile Valley During the Pre-Dynastic Epoch

The founder of pre-dynastic Nile Valley archaeology, William Flinders Petrie, excavated at Nagada and Ballas in Upper Egypt in 1894, exhuming the first artifactual evidence of the cultures antedating historical pharaonic society. Petrie eventually excavated more than 1,200 pre-dynastic graves. Other pre-dynasticists, such as Quibbell, De Morgan, Brunton, and Caton-Thompson, refined and extended his research considerably during the next 40 years, but Petrie established the basic principles of pre-dynastic archaeology and worked out a dating method that is still used.[19]

At Nagada and Ballas, Petrie found an almost invariant burial scheme: (1) the body contracted into the fetal position, (2) the head positioned toward the south, (3) the face pointed westward, and (4) personal possessions buried with the deceased. On the strength of this artifactual evidence alone, it seems clear that many of the ideas featured in later pharaonic religion existed in prototype among these predynastic people at Naqada. The fetal position evokes the idea of rebirth; the southward orientation of the body indicates the south as *khenti*, 'the land of beginnings,' and *Ta-iakhu*, 'the land of the spirits,' where the souls of ancestors dwell; the face pointing westward points toward *Amenta*, 'the

18 See Gillings R, **Mathematics in the Time of the Pharaohs**, New York: Dover Publications, Inc., 1982.

19 See Flinders Petrie WM, **Prehistoric Egypt**, London: Quaritch, 1920, pp. 3-6.

hidden land'—*Amenta* being the western region where the soul of the departed journeys after it quits the body. Finally, dynastic Egypt was notorious for the amount of worldly goods interred with the deceased. Taken together, all these customs are well-known dynastic funerary concepts, thus the elaborate funerary cult of dynastic times seems to have evolved directly from pre-dynastic practices.

Petrie found thousands of vases and pots of varying styles in these Nagada graves. After six years of continuous work, Petrie, in 1900, managed to group all the pottery into nine classes and, more impressively, assign a correct temporal sequence to each class. This method of classification became famous as Petrie's Sequence Dating—a method still in use. Sequence Dating allows the determination of the temporal relationship among different groups of pre-dynastic vases—and therefore of the cultures that produced them—but not the absolute dates of their manufacture. Petrie created Sequence Dates (SD) from 20 to 79, with 30 representing the earliest pre-dynastic pottery styles in his sample and their associated culture(s), and 79 representing the 1st Dynasty. He very sensibly reserved SDs under 30 for pottery sequences and cultures yet to be discovered. Petrie assigned a tentative date for his earliest pottery sequences, e.g. SD 30, of 8,000 BC. This chronology was, within his lifetime, down-dated considerably to 5,500–4,500 BC. Petrie, to the end, never accepted such low dates.[20] The low dates, nonetheless, have held sway up to now, though recent research has been compelling a re-consideration. The names given by Petrie to the two pre-dynastic cultural sequences delineable by his pottery classes were 'Amratian' and 'Gerzean.' Modern pre-dynasticists often use the terms Nagada I and Nagada II to refer respectively to Petrie's Amratian and Gerzean. These and other pre-dynastic cultural horizons extended into the Sudan. As more and more pre-dynastic material was recovered in Egypt and Nubia, it became clear, to Petrie at least, that there was a uniformity of culture that spanned Egypt and Nubia. It was Petrie's conviction that there was 'a peaceful, if not a united, rule all over Egypt and Nubia' during the entire pre-dynastic period.[21] More recent research has tended to confirm that assessment. In fact, there is evidence that this pre-dynastic cultural unity encompassed all of the lands hugging the river from the confluence of the White and Blue Niles at Khartoum to the apex

20 See Jones WD, **Venus and Sothis**, Chicago: Nelson-Hall, 1982, p. 80.

21 Flinders Petrie, op. cit., p. 3.

of the Delta, a distance of 1,500 miles.[22] That parts of this Nile Valley, or Nilotic, culture-complex can be traced to Africa's Great Lakes region has already been touched upon. Petrie's assessment, however, carries with it a strong implication that the Nile Valley had developed an organized state, or states, at a time far antedating the dynastic period, a point that will be amplified in the next chapter.

Though pre-dynasticists such as DeMorgan and Quibell found and excavated additional graves at Nagada and Ballas, no older cultures were unearthed until the excavations of Brunton and Caton-Thompson in 1928 at Badari, 100 miles north of Nagada. The artifacts discovered were clearly pre-dynastic and eventually determined to be more archaic than those recovered from Nagada and Ballas. These cultures became known respectively as 'Tasian' and 'Badarian' and were assigned SDs between 20–29. Though at first they seemed to be distinct horizons, the Tasian being older and more primitive, they were eventually linked together as the same culture in different phases, e.g., the 'Tasian-Badarian' sequence. Under Petrie's schema, this cultural sequence would be at least 12,000 years old (10,000 BC), but modern dating, though not consistent, takes it back maximally to 5500 BC and minimally to 4,000 BC[23]. The Badarians were culturally a thriving people, most renowned for their hand-made pottery. Their vases were fashioned with a durability, finish, and thinness that were never to be surpassed. They were also notable for well-turned ivory utensils and the use of copper. Theirs is the longest pre-dynastic sequence in the Nile Valley.

The Amratians succeeded the Badarians and their pottery was characterized by distinctive red bodies with black tops and also a style with white, crossed lines. It is in the Amratian sequence that stone vases appear for the first time. In an advance over the Badarians, the Amratians not only worked extensively and more variously in copper but also in gold. Faience and blue glazing of quartz appears with them.

The Gerzeans, the last distinct cultural sequence preceding the dynasties, reveal themselves as a people whose cultural attainments placed them, at the

22 See De Heinzelin, op. cit., p. 109 and Wendorf, Close, and Schild, op. cit., passim.

23 See Hoffman MA, **Egypt Before the Pharaohs**, London: Ark Paperbacks, 1980, p. 142, for evidence of the higher Badarian date of 5500 BC; also, Hassan FA, *The Predynastic of Egypt*, **Journal of World Prehistory** (2)2, June 1988, pp. 138-41, for dating results of the Badarian period at 4000 BC.

very least, at the stage of *proto*-civilization. Their pottery shows unique features: buff coloration with red zigzag lines and spirals, designs of many-oared boats, and representations of flamingoes and sometimes of people. Stone vases are more varied in shape and fashioned from more diverse materials. Copper use is general, as is gold, and small quantities of silver—probably imported from Western Asia—appear. Ornamental iron beads are present and glass-making appears for the first time in the Nile Valley.

Given the received 1st Dynasty date of 3,100 BC, the extremely low dating of 4,000 BC for the entire pre-dynastic era recently advanced creates a crowding problem.[24] If accepted, we are then required to assume that three successive, well-defined cultural horizons took root and then vanished in the Nile Valley in the space of 900 years. When, as will be noted below, evidence surfaces that pushes the dynastic period back to 3,500 BC and earlier, the crowding becomes even more severe, leaving only 500 years for the entire pre-dynastic era.

A word should be said about the pre-dynastic horizons discovered in Lower Egypt. The first was found near Merimde, just west of the Delta, and dated to 4,880 BC[25]. The Merimdens were a mixed farming and hunting people, roughly contemporaneous with, but culturally distinct from, the Badarians to the south. The difference seems so pronounced that the Merimdens have seemed 'un-Egyptian' to some. They were of small stature and rounder of head than the dolicocephalic Badarians, but more significant was their very different burial practices. The Merimdens buried their dead inside their settlements instead of in separate graveyards and included no personal belongings or food offerings with the deceased. As will be discussed below, a high proportion of mother-child burials among the Merimdens seems to reflect a 'matristic' or matrilineal cultural emphasis, but this element seems to have originated from a place very different from where the Badarians came from. Since their manner of house-building and their agriculture shares similarities with Neolithic Near Eastern societies, many have looked toward Palestine for the original home of these people. But there exists an older horizon in the Nile Valley that furnishes clues to the provenance of the Merimdens. About 150 miles south of Merimde, as the crow flies, lies the Fayum depression. In antiquity, it served as a water

24 Hassan, ibid.
25 Hoffman, op. cit., p. 169.

reservoir in the dry season for dynastic Egyptians, but it is also significant for two related pre-dynastic cultures discovered there. In archaeological terms, these horizons are called 'Fayum A' and 'Fayum B,' confusing because Fayum B is actually older, dated to 6,300 BC. The Fayum horizons seemed to have distinct affinities with Neolithic Saharan cultures, known to have been in existence as early as 8,100 BC[26]. The Fayum, Merimde, and Near Eastern horizons all seemed to share certain traits and may all have been extensions of the Saharan cultural complex. As noted, the Lower Egyptian pre-dynastic horizons at Fayum and Merimde appear markedly different from the Upper Egyptian/Nubian ones. In fact, they are not strictly considered pre-dynastic but rather late Neolithic horizons existing at a lower cultural stage than the Badarian or Nagadan sequences. Lower Egyptian pottery is very crude by Badarian standards and neither Fayum nor Merimde, unlike the Badarians and Nagadans, knew of metal. Thus, the civilizing impulse leading to dynastic pharaonic culture emerged in and from the south. It might be said that classical Nile Valley civilization evolved primarily in the region between Assiut (Badari) and the 2nd cataract (Ta-Seti).

Despite clear and unequivocal indicators, the geo-ethnic provenance of the creators of Nile Valley civilization continues to be a contentious issue. Though we have already devoted some space to a discussion of the matter in the **Introduction**, a few additional points are relevant. As we have seen, Petrie was of the opinion that there was a kind of cultural unity linking the pre-dynastic horizons of Egypt and Nubia. Sir Alan Gardiner shared this opinion:

> However striking the change from the one stage to the other may appear, the continuity of the evolution as a whole must be affirmed with all emphasis...there was an affinity between Libyans, Egyptians, and Nubians which confirms our description of the earliest culture of the Nile Valley as *essentially African* (emphasis added).[27]

Others echo this assessment. The noted pre-dynasticist Fekri A. Hassan asserts:

26 Wendorf, Close, Schild, op. cit., p. 132.

27 Gardiner A, **Egypt of the Pharaohs**, New York: Oxford University Press, 1978, p. 135.

> The earliest Neolithic levels in the Nile Valley...shared a common Saharan-Nilotic base, as well as some Near Eastern affinities...These regional cultural differences are not associated with biological differences. Investigations of crania from Badarian settlements indicated that they were similar to those from Nagada, Abydos, El-Amrah, and Hu.[28]

Petrie himself observed that the numerous female figurines found at Nagada—associated with the early Amratian and Gerzean sequences beginning SD 34—showed the steatopygy typical of the southern African Khoisan type.[29] While it is doubtful that these early Nile Valley dwellers were pure Khoisan, it seems evident that their place of origin is to be sought in Africa's southerly regions. Moreover, skull studies of the Badarians after their discovery by Brunton and Caton-Thompson have almost unanimously identified them as southern in origin.[30]

Recently, an excellent review of the data on the 'skull metrics' of Nile Valley/North African populations by S.O.Y. Keita has shed additional light on these questions.[31] Keita notes that previous studies of the Badarian and Nagada I (Amratian) series of skulls when compared to those disinterred from Kerma in the northern Sudan, show nearly identical phenotypes.[32] Keita conducted his own multi-variate analyses of 10 skull series from North Africa (west of Egypt), the Nile Valley, East Africa and West Africa to ascertain phenotypic clusterings on a broader continental scale. The Nile Valley series included 72 pre-dynastic skulls, 22 from Badari and 50 from Nagada. Keita duly noted the interpretive problems occasioned by the small sample size but still found, consistent with earlier data, that both the Badarian and Nagadan skull series clustered phenotypically around those of Kerma (Cush), East Africa (Kenya), and West-Central Africa (Gabon).[33] This phenotypic clustering extended to dynastic Abydos, the mythical home of Osiris:

28 Hassan, op. cit., p. 159.

29 Flinders Petrie, op. cit., p. 8.

30 See Gardiner, op. cit., p. 392.

31 Keita SOY, *Studies of Ancient Crania from Northern Africa*, **American Journal of Physical Anthropology** (83), 1990, pp. 35-48.

32 Ibid., pp. 36-8.

33 Ibid., pp. 38-46.

> The Nagada and Kerma [Nubia] series are so similar that they are barely distinguishable in the territorial maps; they subsume the first dynasty series from Abydos.[34]

In a follow-up article, Keita discussed the 1st Dynasty Abydos series more fully, finding that 57% of the skulls in that series could be assigned a southern origin.[35] But throughout his writings, Keita expressed a caveat also articulated by the late C.A. Diop, to wit: a 'monotypic' classification cannot be used to determine absolutely the pre-dominant ethnicity of the dwellers of the Nile Valley.[36] In this case, the monotype of the oft-caricatured 'Negro,' that is, the type possessing an elongated cranium, jutting jaw, crispy hair, flaring nostrils, everted lips, bandy legs, and black skin, cannot be considered fully representative of native Africans. As Keita suggests, native African populations are phenotypically 'polytypic,' that is, there exists in tropical Africa a variety of phenotypes that deviate significantly from the caricature. As noted in the **Introduction**, casual perusal of almost any indigenous African group can convince even an untrained observer of the truth of this assertion. Dolicocephalic skulls and sub-nasal prognathism, as seen in many pre-dynastic Nile series, do establish a southern African origin, but a deviation from or absence of this distinct phenotype in certain Nile Valley skull series do not necessarily 'de-Africanize' them.

Another feature of the pre-dynastic graves, from the Badarian epoch down through the Gerzean, pointing to a southern origin is the unmistakable 'matrifocal' ethos. A number of pre-dynasticists have noted the superior wealth of women's graves and the feminine gender of the greater number of pre-dynastic figurines.[37] Fekri Hassan gives us the clearest exposition of the implications of the feminine 'bias' of these artifacts:

> Ritual and supernatural beliefs associated with agricultural life must have emerged with the beginnings of the Neolithic. A study of figurines and mortuary goods from the Nagada

34 Ibid., p. 40.

35 Keita SOY, *Further Analysis of Crania from Ancient Northern Africa: An Analysis of Crania from First Dynasty Egyptian Tombs, Using Multiple Discriminant Functions*, **American Journal of Physical Anthropology** (87), 1992, p. 250.

36 See above-mentioned articles by Keita.

37 Cf. Hoffman, op. cit., p. 328; also, Hassan, op. cit., p. 170.

> region indicates that such beliefs and rituals were closely related to women. Lineage was probably matrilineal as indicated by the exclusive internment of women and children at Merimda. This may have been because women were associated with grinding grain and making bread and gruel as well as brewing bccr and, perhaps, initially planting grain.[38]

Thus, even the Lower Egyptian horizons, like the one at Merimde, evince a definite matristic character. As is well-attested, this matrifocality/matrilineality—at least in social and domestic relations—continued in Egypt to the end of dynastic history. Matrilineality, in fact, was the almost invariable rule of succession governing the pharaonocracy. The custom undoubtedly derived from African antecedents.[39] Since a linkage between the Merimden and Saharan horizons is evident, it can be inferred that the custom was more or less general throughout Neolithic Africa.

Early in this essay, evidence was brought forward linking the Ishango/ Katandan horizons with those in the Nile Valley, Sahara, and Syrio-Palestine. In fact, the Natufians of 10,000 years ago in Palestine shared phenotypic affinities closer to the Badarians than they did the Merimdens, whose culture is suppose to have been more closely related to those of the Near East. It has been customary to separate the Near East from Africa ethno-culturally, though in the light of increasing Neolithic evidence, it is more nearly correct to consider the lands between Khartoum in the south and the Tigris-Euphrates in the north as constituting one broad horizon in the period between 10,000 and 5,000 BC. This horizon was composed substantially of 'Nilo-Saharan' ethno-cultural elements. Regional differences and variations were certainly evident in this larger cultural complex, but on-going techno-commercial relations linked the various groups of this horizon.

It can be said that what is known as the Near East—or 'Middle East' as it is more commonly called—is more properly thought of as Africa's 'Northeast Extension' because geologically and geographically, that is what

38 Hassan, ibid., p. 169.

39 Cf. Finch CS, **Echoes of the Old Dark Land: Themes from the African Eden**, Decatur: Khenti, Inc., pp. 57-87. See also *Introduction* to this work.

it is.[40] It was the main corridor of human migration out of Africa into the rest of the world beginning 100,000 years ago and it makes sense to find that the earliest definable Near Eastern Neolithic populations—the Natufians—are indisputably Africoid. There seems to be no good reason not to assume that prior to 5,000 BC, this 'Northeast Extension' participated in the various cultural horizons of Africa. Thus when we look at the Neolithic Near East, we are looking culturally at a 'province' of Neolithic Africa.

Radiocarbon Dating of Nile Valley Horizons: Old Arguments, New Finds

As has already been intimated, the absolute chronology of the Nile Valley is a hotly contested subject. Despite his status as the founding father of pre-dynastic Nile Valley studies, Petrie's chronology very early underwent criticism and revision, resulting in considerable down-dating of his original estimates of pre-dynastic time. Recent work by Fekri Hassan, based on extensive radiocarbon datings of pre-dynastic sites, has pulled the Badarian epoch down to 4,400–4,000 BC. Even these dates are not consistent with thermoluminescent tests giving a Badarian date of 5,500 BC. Nonetheless, Hassan, a respected authority, published no fewer than six radiocarbon studies of pre-dynastic sites between 1980 and 1988. High resolution radiocarbon instruments have brought much greater precision to dating techniques, but anomalies still persist, judging from other work.

One such anomaly has arisen from recent radiocarbon datings of organic materials extracted from the Great Pyramid and numerous other pyramids, temples, and tombs in the Giza\Sakkara area by Herbert Haas and his colleagues.[41] Sixteen organic samples were extracted from the Great Pyramid, 13 of which were of charcoal. After instruments in the two testing laboratories were calibrated, results were obtained on the 16 samples that gave a range of ages the researchers found startling. The oldest radiocarbon date on the Great

40 The term 'Middle East' was invented by the American admiral and naval historian Albert Thayer Mahan in 1902. Though now a commonplace, the term cannot be said to have any precise or valid meaning pertaining to the region it purports to describe.

41 Haas H, Devine J, Wehnke R, Lehner M, et al, *Radiocarbon Chronology and the Historical Calendar in Egypt*, **Chronologies in the Near East**, Evin J and Hours F, editors, BAR International Series, 1987, pp. 585-606.

Pyramid came from a charcoal fragment from the 198th course, giving a date of 3,809 BC. The youngest date came from a mortar of limestone from the second course giving a date of 2,853 BC. Averaging all the dates on the 16 samples together, Haas and his team determined that, by radiocarbon testing, the pyramid was minimally 389 years older than the given 'historical date,' that is, it was built around 2,978 BC. In fact, all 10 of the monuments/temples evaluated were older than the received 'historical' dates by an average age of 374 years. If, in round numbers, it can be said that these Old Kingdom monuments are about 400 years older than previously believed, then the beginning of the 1st Dynasty goes back minimally to 3,500 BC. It is hard to reconcile these monumental radiocarbon data of Haas's with Hassan's radio-carbon readings giving a date for the beginning of the predynastic era of 4,000 BC. Even a somewhat remoter allowable date of 4,400 BC (Hassan) for the Badarian period hardly seems plausible. The thermo-luminescent date of 5,500 BC given by Hoffman for the Badarian period at least has the virtue of creating more chronological space for the pre-dynastic era.

Ta-Seti and the Beginning of Egyptian History

Complicating matters is the seldom-referred-to work by Bruce Williams concerning the Ta-Seti kingdom discovered at Qustul.[42] The site was excavated for the first time by Keith Seele in 1962 who, even then, thought that the size and wealth of the tombs marked them as royal.[43] Systematic analysis of the artifacts, however, did not take place until 15 years later by Bruce Williams at the Oriental Institute, adding a hitherto unknown chapter to Nile Valley history. In one sense, however, the Qustul artifacts confirmed what Egyptian annals had already attested: there were whole dynasties that immediately preceded the 1st Dynasty under Mēnēs.

Qustul lies in Nubia, more than 100 miles south of Aswan and the 1st cataract, and is now under the waters of Lake Nasser. Qustul was a well-known site for what is known as A-group Nubian culture, contemporaneous

42 Williams B, *The Lost Pharaohs of Nubia*, **Archaeology** (33)5, September/October 1980.
43 Ibid., p. 14.

with and related to the Gerzean pre-dynastic complex of Upper Egypt. The archaeological context of the tombs found in a burial spot known as 'Cemetary L' showed clearly that they were older than the 1st Dynasty. When the tombs were opened, a startling variety of goods and materials were present, including five different kinds of pottery, expensive, finely-crafted jewelry, copper weapons, gold bracelets, and incense burners. All or parts of 1,000 separate ceramic vases and 100 stone vessels were recovered. As Williams said,

> The range of these and other fragments from the plundered cemetery began to indicate a wealth and complexity that could only be called royal.[44]

The place and date of this find contravened all accepted models for the appearance of pharaonic civilization in the Nile Valley. Since Williams's original article in 1980, a kind of disbelieving intransigence on the part of Egyptologists has marginalized the Qustul finds:

> Tombs of this size, wealth, and date in Egypt would have been immediately recognized as royal. Their extraordinarily varied contents would have been taken as evidence of a complex culture exposed to wide outside connections. But because the discovery was made in Nubia at a time and a place when kingship was thought impossible, further proof of royalty is necessary.[45]

Most Egyptologists seem to find it difficult to divest themselves of the traditional assessment of Nubia as a 'second-rate' Egypt.

Hieroglyphic signs on a seal from another related find at Siali, also located in Nubia just above Aswan, furnished a name for the kingdom to which these royal tombs belonged: *Ta-Seti*, 'Land of the Bow.' Inscribed scenes from the seal and from an incense burner show Ta-Seti kings engaged in military campaigns in Upper Egypt and Libya. Moreover, some of the vases in the tomb were of Syrio-Palestinian manufacture. These pieces of evidence give a picture

44 Ibid.
45 Ibid., p. 16.

of a powerful regional kingdom conducting far-flung commercial, diplomatic, and military activities as distant as 1,000 miles away, even beyond Africa itself.

A sequence of tombs affiliated with 12 pharaohs comprise Cemetery L at Qustul. This complex of royal tombs led Bruce Williams to believe that the ruling dynasty of Ta-Seti stretched back 300 years prior to the 1st Dynasty. What Williams didn't categorically say, but what logically follows from the evidence, is that Ta-Seti represents the beginning of pharaonic civilization and is truly a founding or precursor dynasty, segueing directly into the unification dynasties inaugurated by Aha-Mēnēs. The line of pre-dynastic pharaohs mentioned in certain annals must be that of Ta-Seti, and therefore, Ta-Seti belongs in the scheme of 'proto-dynasties' that governed early Nile Valley history, almost assuredly as the southern one of the 'twin kingdoms' of *Taui*—or the 'Two Lands'—the name of Egypt prior to 4,268 BC. Bruce Williams himself implies something of the sort in the original article on the subject:

> Apparently, the demise of Qustul coincides with the campaign of Aha in Nubia, the first king of the Egyptian First Dynasty, who recorded the smiting of Ta-Seti.[46]

Ta-Seti was therefore brought down by its successor dynasty, that of Aha-Mēnēs, the one that unified Egypt and inaugurated the formal dynastic era. Ta-Seti can be said to represent the transition between the late pre-dynastic Gerzean cultural sequence and the formal dynastic period.

The temporal relationship of Ta-Seti to the 1st Dynasty is ascertained by the same contextual analysis that gave rise to Petrie's sequence dating. Thus, we have no absolute chronology for Ta-Seti; its dating is relative to that of the 1st Dynasty. Evidence has been adduced above that pushes the 1st Dynasty back to 3,500 BC. Thus, if Ta-Seti is known to have appeared 300 years before the 1st Dynasty, its date of origin goes back minimally to 3,800 BC. These additional chronological facts compress the pre-dynastic era too severely to entertain a Badarian date of 4,400 BC. Hassan's pre-dynastic chronology is simply untenable.

46 Ibid., p. 21.

Sphinx in Profile—Closeup

Full-Body View of the Sphinx

In spite of the contradictory mass of facts introduced so far, more recent evidence yet threatens to categorically deconstruct all of the carefully contrived schemes of Nile Valley chronology. This evidence comes from a wholly unexpected source that has sat literally in front of the very eyes of travelers, writers, and scholars for as long as there has been an Egypt; that is to say, the enigmatic and legendary Sphinx. One is reminded of the remonstrance of Sherlock Holmes to Watson: 'You see but you do not observe.' However, an independent Egyptologist named John Anthony West, acting on a clue from the writings of R.A. Schwaller de Lubicz, did see and observe. What is more, from what he saw and observed, West drew the obvious conclusion.

The late R.A. Schwaller de Lubicz, the aforementioned mentor of John Anthony West, was a decidedly heterodox metaphysician, mathematician, and antiquities scholar who boldly challenged some of the most cherished principles of Egyptology. Predictably, the academic Egyptologists have reacted to the ideas of Schwaller de Lubicz and his school with derision. Among other things, this school holds that Egyptian civilization is millenia older than the textbook Egyptologists claim. In support of this supposition, Egyptologists themselves unearthed at Giza the so-called 4th Dynasty 'Inventory Stele,' which indicates that Pharaoh Khufu, builder of the Great Pyramid, saw the Sphinx, meaning that it had to be older even than the Giza Pyramids themselves.[47] West—following lines of evidence suggested by Schwaller de Lubicz—found startling confirmation for this conviction in and around the Sphinx.[48] The evidence for a higher antiquity of Nile Valley civilization has been 'hiding in plain sight,' as it were. The Sphinx reposes in an enclosure or quarry just below and to the east of the plateau of Giza, the site of the three great pyramids of Egypt. Even a casual visitor to the Sphinx cannot fail to notice the deep and numerous fissures on the wall of the ditch surrounding it and similar patterns of wear on its body. What could have caused such wear? To answer this question, West enlisted the aid of a team of geologists led by Robert M. Schoch of Boston University who had this to say about the erosive patterns present on the Sphinx and the surrounding enclosure wall:

> Geologists date landforms (including huge sculptured statues) by analyzing weathering features and correlating them with the region's climatic history. In the case of the Sphinx, the sides of its body and the walls of its enclosure clearly exhibit a rolling, undulating vertical profile on the horizontal rock layers, which in turn are cut by vertical crevices. *These are textbook examples of rain-induced weathering* (my emphasis).[49]

The question that Schoch had to pose once he got a good look at the Sphinx and its surrounding ditch was how could the Sphinx and its enclosure walls sustain such deep, rain-induced weathering when Old Kingdom tombs immediately to the south of them and cut from the same limestone rock showed only wind-weathering? The deep, vertical fissuring caused by coursing water could not be found on any other monument, temple, or statue in the vicinity of the Sphinx. The only reasonable conclusion—the one West had arrived at

---

47 Vid. Hancock G and Bauval R, **The Message of the Sphinx**, New York: Crown Publishers, Inc., 1996, p. 12.

48 The story of West's efforts to have his theory confirmed appears in the February 1993 issue of **Conde Nast Traveler**, in a cleverly written and illustrated article entitled *Civilization Rethought*, pp. 100-5; 168-77.

49 Schoch RM, *One Geologist's Review*, **Conde Nast Traveler**, February 1993, p. 103. See also Schoch, R.M.and McNally, R.A., **Voices of the Rocks**, New York: Harmony Books, (1999), 2000.

20 years previously—is that the Sphinx was built in an entirely different epoch than those other well-known Old Kingdom structures.

Rain-induced vertical fissures of Sphinx quarry

Successive layers of repair Sphinx repair

Northeast Africa has not always been subjected to desert like conditions. From 10,000 BC to 3,000 BC, the Nile Valley experienced the 'Nabtian Pluvial,' a period of relatively heavy rainfall, before succumbing to an extremely arid climate with very sparse precipitation.[50] It is only during this pluvial period that sufficient rain could have fallen on the quarry where the Sphinx sits to have caused the deep fissuring present on the surrounding quarry walls and on its body. Since this pluvial period effectively ceased by 3,000 BC, the Sphinx must have been built prior to that time, well before the conventional date of 2,500 BC usually given for its construction. Schoch and his colleague Thomas Dobecki, a seismologist from Houston, accumulated data from their study that helped them arrive at a more definite age range for the Sphinx. They found that their seismic readings showed sub-surface water penetration in the bedrock of the Sphinx to six to eight feet deep in the front half of the Sphinx and four feet deep in the rear.[51] This differential could only be explained by presuming that the Sphinx had been carved in stages; the head and forepart first and the hind-quarters last. It is known from the work of Lehner and Gauri that the Sphinx had

50 Cited in Schoch RM, *Redating the Great Sphinx of Giza*, **KMT** (3)2, Summer 1992, p. 55.
51 Ibid., pp. 56-7

been renovated and repaired at least three times in history, and West and Schoch convincingly argue that the first repair occurred during the Old Kingdom.[52] The masonry and construction technique evident on the rump of the Sphinx undoubtedly derive from Old Kingdom building methods. An inscription on the rump, datable to the Old Kingdom, confirms this assessment.[53] There is every reason to believe that these Old Kingdom repairs and the carving of the hinderpart of the Sphinx, were undertaken by Khafre (a.k.a. Cephren), which accounts for the tradition linking Khafre with the Sphinx. If this first repair—along with the sculpting of the hinderpart—occurred during Khafre's reign, conventionally given as 2,500 BC, Schoch points out that it has taken 4,500 years—from Khafre's time until now—for water to penetrate to a depth of four feet into the bed-rock of the Sphinx's rear.[54]

Concerning the bedrock under the forepart of the Sphinx, it is known that the pace of water penetration slows the deeper it seeps into the bedrock. Allowing for the slowing of water penetration to the profounder depths of six to eight feet, Schoch has proposed dates between 5,000 and 7,000 BC for the initial construction of the Sphinx.[55] He considers these estimates conservative.[56] It must be borne in mind that the bed-rock upon which the Sphinx sits was freed from over-lying rock by human hands. Thus any water penetration measured from the surface of this bedrock must date from the time of human construction, not before. According to Schoch, the original Sphinx was built so that the head and forepart jutted outward from the limestone cliff. The rump did not exist, the effect not dissimilar to the one created by the presidential busts at Mount Rushmore. The rump was sculpted later, and in the process, a rectangular ditch was completed around the body as the lime-stone was removed from the quarry.

Expectedly, conventional academicians dismiss this work out of hand. There have been numerous knee-jerk academic rejections unsupported by any counter-evidence, but a few have endeavored to mount serious critiques of the

52 Cited by West, op. cit., pp. 170-1.
53 Schoch, 'Redating the Great Sphinx…', op. cit., p. 57.
54 Cited in by West, op. cit., p. 176.
55 Schoch, 'Redating the Great Sphinx…,' op. cit., p. 57.
56 Ibid., p. 58.

work of the West-Schoch team.[57] One line of argument contends, correctly, that there have been recurring, though infrequent, rainfalls in the Nile Valley since the end of the Nabtian pluvial period 5,000 years ago. These downpours, uncommon though they are, would, by this counter-argument, be sufficient to account for the water erosion on the Sphinx. Cited as an example of the effect of these intermittent downpours in Egypt is a mud-brick wall recently washed away by rain.[58] This argument is easily met. Mud-brick is the most ubiquitous building agent in Egypt precisely because rainfall is so infrequent. If rain was more frequent in Egypt than it is, it would be impossible to use mud-brick because it so readily dissipates when exposed to water. Thus, the washing away of a mud-brick structure by one of the occasional downpours that occur in Egypt cannot be compared to the deep and persistent fissuring in the limestone from which the Sphinx was constructed, caused by frequently recurring rainstorms at a remoter period.

Another argument brought forth to confute the West-Schoch demonstration involves discussion of the deterioration of the limestone due to condensation of moisture and precipitation of salt.[59] Again, this line of reasoning fails to account for the deep vertical fissuring evident in the enclosure walls and on the body of the Sphinx. Nor does it explain the differential water penetration into different parts of the Sphinx's bed-rock. Furthermore, why isn't the same pattern of water wear exhibited on any of the other Old Kingdom structures near the Sphinx built from the same formation of limestone?

Finally, the weathering patterns on the limestone body of the Sphinx are attributed to 50 million years of deterioration of the native limestone by the effects of the underground water table and accounts for the need—in the time of Khafre—for the sculptor to encase the body of the Sphinx in granite blocks.[60] Zahi Hawass, the author of this theory, insists that other unweathered limestone edifices on Giza were not constructed from stone quarried from the immediate vicinity but from nearby areas at a higher elevation. This assertion flies in the

57 Zahi Hawass, Mark Lehner, James Harrell, and K. Lal Gauri represent the chief critics of the West-Schoch thesis.

58 See *On the other hand…*, **Conde Nast Traveller**, February 1993, p. 105, for a synopsis of the counter-arguments put forward against the conclusions of the West-Schoch team.

59 Ibid.

60 Ibid.

face of Schoch's evidence which shows that the Sphinx and its neighboring Old Kingdom structures were constructed from blocks from the same limestone formation. Moreover, if the limestone in the quarry where the Sphinx was built had deteriorated so badly from the effects of the water table, why use it at all? Why not use the undamaged limestone so widely available from nearby formations? Moreover, the water table explanation still does not account for the deep external fissures on the walls of the ditch and on the Sphinx's body.

Taken as a whole, the objections to this elegantly simple geological study seem facile and obtuse. They do not falsify the thesis. What is unusual about this particular debate, though, is that its issues are intelligible to the lay public:

> It's not often that a scientific breakthrough is easily understood by nonscientists, still rarer that it makes good spectator sport. The quest to unriddle the Sphinx is an exception. Most of the evidence involves no microscopes, telescopes, or particle accelerators. All that's needed is a naked eye and the ability to follow an argument. And most of the action takes place not in the lab, but in Egypt, in public view.[61]

The Sphinx is one of the architectural and artistic wonders of the world. Sculpting such a marvelous piece of statuary could only have been realized in a civilization equal to the task. There was nothing 'prehistoric' or 'primitive' about the Sphinx or the culture that created it. The Sphinx thus seems to represent *prima facie* evidence of the existence of a full-fledged, flourishing Nile Valley civilization no later than *7,000 years ago*! Quite possibly it is as old as *9,000 years*![62] If the evidence holds up, the entire edifice of antiquarian scholarship will be faced with the prospect of revising all historical chronology and reinterpreting the emergence of civilization. Everything would have to be re-thought: the pre-dynastic sequences, the chronology of unification, the date of Ta-Seti and other ancient facts too numerous to mention. Much of the terminology, such as 'paleolithic' and 'neolithic,' would have to be re-defined or discarded. No wonder no self-respecting academician wants to touch it. West put it this way,

61 West, op. cit., p. 177.

62 Or, as we will see in the next chapter, 12,500 years.

> The theory, if correct, upsets the entire apple-cart of ancient history, and I could hardly expect enthusiasm from people who make a living selling apples.[63]

There is another facet of the debate over the Sphinx that merits careful attention: its racial representation. Robert Schoch is utterly convinced that the extant head and face of the Sphinx represents a re-carving of its original head and face. Whatever the case, it is the head and face of a black African. An untrained observer looking at the Sphinx up close can surely see it, but expert testimony was brought forward to substantiate the evidence of the eyes. As part of their systematic re-evaluation of the Sphinx, West and Schoch in 1991 brought to Egypt a forensic specialist from the New York City Police Department by name of Frank Domingo.[64] Domingo's entire career had been devoted to re-creating realistic heads and faces of criminal perpetrators and victims in New York City, usually just from descriptive evidence. By definition, he had to be expert in recognizing ethnic types to develop accurate portraits. He was brought to Egypt to apply his experience and skills to the head and face of the Sphinx by comparison to that of a statue of the pharaoh Khā-f-rā (Chephren) whose likeness, according to conventional Egyptologists, is represented by the face of the Sphinx.[65] Domingo came to two categorical conclusions: (1) the face of the Sphinx and that of the statue of Chephren were entirely different and (2) the face of the Sphinx could only be that of a black African.[66] For Schoch, it was additional evidence for the greater antiquity of the Sphinx: it could only have been carved at a time when black Africans—and black Africans alone—inhabited Egypt.

The work of the West-Schoch team was conducted in 1990–1991. In 1999, Schoch's book **Voices of the Rocks** was published, which not only brought his

63 Ibid., p. 170.

64 Schoch and McNally, **Voices of the Rocks**, op. cit., p. 45.

65 Mark Lehner has been the most vociferous proponent of this point of view, through the use of computer modeling. Schoch's comment: 'When Lehner made the face look the way he thought it should look, then it looked the way he thought it should look'. Schoch, RM and McNally RA, **Voyages of the Pyramid Builders**, New York: Tarcher/Penguin, 2003, p. 281.

66 Ibid.

geological work with the Sphinx up to date but also explored the evidence for the role of 'catastrophism' in the history of the planet and human civilization. More important for his geological studies, Schoch was able to point to several other similar studies by qualified geologists that completely validated the case for an older age for the Sphinx based on the rain-weathering patterns upon it and the walls of the enclosure in which it sits. The geological evidence is virtually conclusive: the Sphinx was built earlier than conventional Egyptologists assert, and the civilization that built must, *ipso facto*, also be considerably older.

In the appendix of a yet more recent book, **Voyages of the Pyramid Builders**, Schoch brings forth evidence that the structures and edifices associated with the Sphinx—the Sphinx Temple, the Valley Temple, the Great Causeway, and even the mortuary temple near the pyramid of Cephren—were all built at the same time the Sphinx was, so that an entire complex of monumental stone buildings are also, by his reckoning, at least 7,000 years old.[67]

Epilogue

Where do all these developments leave us? In spite of 100 years of consistent work, pre-dynastic Egyptian archaeology remains a hodge-podge of often contradictory facts and interpretations. What we can say is that the received chronology of the Nile Valley, to which academic Egyptology tenaciously clings, is hopelessly obsolete. But then it never did make much sense. As Robert Schoch observes,

> The arguments used to support the 2,500 BC dating of the Sphinx and attribute it to Khafre are ad hoc ideas invented to protect an established chronology.

67 Schoch and McNally, **Voyages of the Pyramid Builders**, op. cit. pp. 278-98, passim. Apart from the ***Appendix*** of this book, an informative updating of the arguments for re-dating the Sphinx further back in antiquity, this book's main thesis has to be viewed with a deep vein of scepticism, if not outright repudiation. In it, the authors advance the theory that civilization and pyramid-building was brought to the rest of the world, Egypt included, from a now submerged land in the seas off Southeast Asia given the name 'Sundaland'. Let the reader make of that what the reader will.

> Unwittingly, [Egyptologists] are caught in the trap of defending their own dogma rather than examining the evidence with the dispassion it deserves.[68]

New evidence is gradually bringing into focus a northeast African civilization existing farther back in antiquity than had ever been imagined. It may be plausibly presumed that this high culture evolved out of a confluence of migrations and influences coming down the Nile from the Great Lakes merging with those moving eastward out of the Sahara. But the Saharan horizon itself is ultimately traceable to the East African Great Lakes, exemplified by the Ishango-Katandan complex. That region must be considered the cradle-land of all African culture, especially that derivable from the Nilo-Saharan complex.

John Anthony West is convinced that there were one or more Nile Valley civilizations preceding that of dynastic Egypt by thousands of years. It is entirely consistent with Manetho's account of Egyptian history, recorded more than 2,200 years ago.[69] Fragments of evidence show that cultures of greater technical sophistication than previously assumed might have existed in paleolithic Africa between 50–12,000 years ago.[70] We also know that fewer than 10% of the known archeological sites on the continent have even been surveyed, let alone excavated.[71] Archaeologically, Africa is still largely *terra incognita*. When the mammoth task of systematically exploring the archaeology of old Africa is at last undertaken, West's suppositions concerning 'neolithic' and 'paleolithic' African civilizations may come to seem less and less farfetched.

---

68 Schoch and McNally, **Voices of the Rocks**, op. cit., p. 50.

69 See Waddell WG, translator, **Manetho**, Cambridge: Harvard University Press, 1980, for a compilation of and commentary on the fragments of Manetho's history that record king lists going back to 5,500 BC and legendary dynasties going back to almost 37,000 BC

70 See Finch CS, **Africa and the Birth of Science and Technology** (pamphlet), Decatur: Khenti, Inc., 1993, pp. 2-5.

71 At last report, there are supposed to be one million mounds in the northern Sudan that have never been touched by the spade! The Meroitic city of Naga is said to be so large that it may take 70 years to excavate.

Horizon: An archaeological cultural complex.

Lacustrine: Of or pertaining to lakes.

Mesolithic: A word meaning 'Middle Stone Age,' not strictly applicable to Africa since it refers primarily to a European cultural stage between the Paleolithic and Neolithic. The time span of the European Mesolithic extends from about 7,000 to 2,700 BC.

Neolithic: Means 'New Stone Age' and generally refers to a cultural stage in Africa and the Near East existing between 8,000 BC (or earlier) and 4,500 BC. Neolithic cultures were characterized by small farming villages and pottery, though little or no utilization of metals. Europe entered the Neolithic period later than Africa or the Near East.

Paleolithic: This term refers to the 'Old Stone Age,' encompassing the period between 2.5 million years ago and 10,000 BC The Paleolithic was divided into the three sub-periods, 'Lower,' 'Middle,' and 'Upper.' The Upper Paleolithic was the final phase of the Paleolithic, beginning about 40,000 BC and ending 10,000 BC. Paleolithic peoples were pre-agricultural hunters and gatherers.

Pluvial: Extended era of moderate to heavy rainfall.

Radiocarbon Dating: Method of determining the age of non-living organic materials by measuring the amount of decay of carbon isotopes in the sample.

CHAPTER 2:

Nile Valley Chronology and the Double Great Year

> ...they [the Egyptians] saw their cosmic environment (the sky, the Milky Way, the sun and the stars, the moon and the planets, and all their cycles) as being bound together in perfect duality with their earthly environment (their land and the Nile, their living king and his ancestors, and the cycles of the seasons and epochs).
> —Hancock and Bauval, **The Message of the Sphinx**, p. 132.

> ...history is the blueprint of the future; whatever happened then is likely to occur again.
> —Robert M. Schoch, **Voices of the Rocks**, p. 4

A major factor bearing on the complexities of early Nile Valley chronology is that of the calendar. Since the author has treated this question at length elsewhere, we can dispense with an extended discussion of all the different facets of this matter.[1] We can say, however, that from the point of view of historically-attested dynastic history, the earliest identifiable calendar date we have is 4,241 BC from Egypt's famed Sothic calendar, the one still in use today. The existence of such a sophisticated calendar, a seamless calendric inter-digitation of the movements of the sun and Sirius (the 'Dog Star'), presupposes

---

1 Finch, CS, **Echoes of the Old Dark Land: Themes from the African Eden**, Decatur: Khenti Publications, Inc., 1991, pp. 115-27.

an equally sophisticated culture creating it. The civilization of dynastic Kemit cannot have begun any later than this date of 4,241 BC.

Having said that, it is yet pertinent to return to the engrossing subject of the precessional Great Year(s), though the author has explored this topic in some depth in two earlier books. It is to be admitted that, when treating the subject of the Great Year, one is operating outside the normal and accepted boundaries of academic history-writing. Only a handful of present-day Egyptologists or antiquarians acknowledge that the ancient Egyptians knew anything about the precession, let alone that their history may have been tied to it. Still, that 'handful' represents a quantum increase over the state of matter a generation ago, so it can be said that progress has not been entirely lacking.

It is pertinent to quote R.T. Rundle Clark on the matter of the significance of the pole in the cosmic life of ancient Egypt:

> No other ancient people was so deeply affected by the eternal circuit of the stars around a point in the northern sky. Here must be the node of the universe, the center of regulation, able to be located but invisible—for in antiquity the Pole star was not in its present position. The celestial pole is 'that place' or 'great city.' Sometimes the pole is regarded as a tree with the circumpolar stars—as souls—perching on its branches; at others, it is a tower or pole with guide-ropes.[2]

Clark, at least, seems to tacitly recognize—without coming right out and saying it—the critical role of the polar precession in the cultural history of the Nile Valley. The Egyptian sense of Destiny—personal, national, and cosmic—was indissolubly linked to the Precession and the idea of the Great Year. To review: the earth experiences three motions—a rotation around its axis, a revolution around the sun, and a gyration of its pole around the pole of the ecliptic. This latter motion, caused by the 23½° tilt of the earth's pole from vertical due to the gravitational pull of the sun and the moon, results in a gyration of the magnetic

2 Rundle Clark RT, **Myth and Symbol in Ancient Egypt**, London: Thames & Hudson, (1959), 1978, p.58

pole backwards around the vertical pole—the 'pole of the ecliptic'—that takes 25,900 years to complete.[3] This motion is the precession and there are two ways to track it: (1) mark the succession of constellations in the band of the zodiac that rise heliacally (before the sun) at the spring equinox or (2) follow the movement of the circumpolar constellations that transit to (and through) the magnetic pole. The ancient Egyptians's description of the polar axis of the earth is revealed by Budge who says,

> There was a northern support called *UPT-TA*... like a tent pole. The moon and sun moved under the plate but the stars were hung in it like a lamp and the stars were called 'lamps.'[4]

Now *upt-ta* translates literally as 'top of the earth' so is the Egyptian term for the pole. The stars that were hung on the plate 'like a lamp' were the circumpolar stars. The Egyptian name for the circumpolar stars was *akhemu seku*, 'the never-setting stars,' or the 'imperishable stars.'

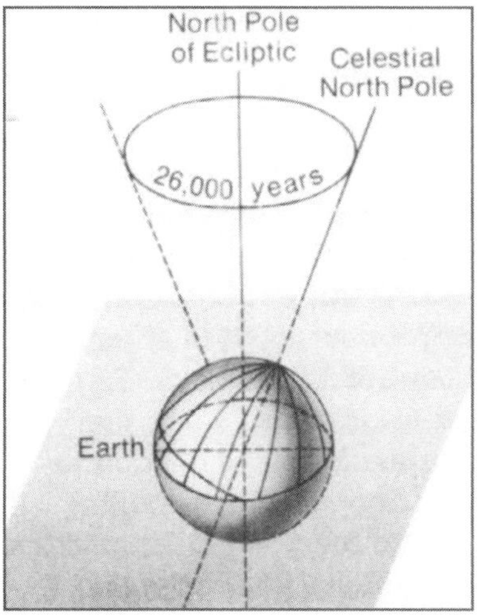

The Precession of the Earth's Axis

The Zodiac of Denderah with Two Precessions

3 The full precession period varies from 25,858 years to 25,920 years.

4 **Budge** EAW, **From Fetish to God in Ancient Egypt**, London: Oxford University Press, 1934, p. 239.

In the so-called **Old Chronicle** of Manetho, dating from about 200 AD (440 years after Manetho wrote his celebrated **History of Egypt**) and representing a redacted and corrupted version of the original ***Epitome*** of Manetho's **History**, there is recorded a 'super time-cycle' (or 'Super Great Year') of 36,525 years that encompasses ancient Egypt's 'legendary' plus her dynastic history. The **Old Chronicle** writer points out that this super-cycle of 36,525 years contains exactly 25 Sothic Years, each Sothic Year of 1,460 years of 365.25 days being equal to 1,461 calendar years of 365 days.[5] Thus 36,525 = 1,461 × 25. What is noteworthy about this figure of 36,525 years is that when it is added to the year 331 BC, when Manetho's **History** ends, it takes this 'super period' back to ***36,856 BC***. As will be shown below, the beginning of this current cycle of the zodiacal Great Year began 10,909 BC, meaning that the previous zodiacal Great Year began ***36,809 BC*** (10,909 + 25,900 = 36,809). Thus, these two datings fall within 47 years of one another. Such a close correspondence cannot possibly be coincidental, and as the author has said in an earlier work[6], it means that the **Old Chronicle**, attributed to Manetho, was making a reference to the precessional Great Year. In fact, Syncellus, the 9th century Christian writer reporting this information, makes a more categorical statement in this regard a few pages afterward:

> If this total [36,525 years] is broken up, or divided, 25 times into periods of 1461 years, it reveals the periodic return of the Zodiac which is commonly referred to in Egyptian and Greek books, that is its revolution from one point back to that same point again, namely the first minute of the first degree of the equinoctal sign of the Zodiac, the Ram as it is called by them, according to the account given in *The General Discourses of Hermes* and in the *Cyranides*.[7]

---

5 365.25 × 1,460 = 533,265 (days)
365.00 × 1,461 = 533,265 (days)

6 Vid., Finch, op. cit., p. 123.

7 Waddell WG, translator, **Manetho**, Cambridge: Harvard University Press (1940)1980, p. 231.

What deserves special notice from this quotation is that the writers of late antiquity *knew* that the ancient Egyptians had discovered, tracked, and tied their historical chronology to the precessional Great Year.

The zodiacal constellations number 12 and each of these constellations rises heliacally at the spring or vernal equinox for 2,158 years before yielding to the constellation in front of it (the precessional motion is retrograde). The 'yielding' is caused by the gradual, ever-later rising of the established vernal heliacal constellation—due to the precessional motion—until it can no longer be seen because it is visually blotted out by the dawning sunlight. The constellation that will follow it then begins to rise heliacally, that is, just early enough before sunrise not to be visually blocked out by the morning light. This equinoctal rising period of 2,158 years constitutes an 'Age' in the zodiacal precession, meaning that there are 12 Ages in the Zodiacal Great Year. On the other hand, the circumpolar constellations number seven (7), and each of these constellations inhabits the magnetic north pole for 3,703 years before yielding to the next constellation moving toward the pole. This 3,703-year period constitutes an Age in the Polar Great Year, and there are seven such Ages. It should be noted that the two Great Years are the product of the same phenomenon, both lasting 25,900 years. This phenomenon must have been known for a very long time, considering the way the ancient Egyptians interwove it into their history, as will be seen below. In fact, since it may have been discovered no later than 40,000 years ago (if not earlier), knowledge of the precessional phenomenon in ancient Africa would pre-date the existence of historical Egypt itself.[8] No self-respecting Africanist, Egyptologist, or Antiquities scholar is prepared to admit any such thing. Still, it is becoming harder to avoid the presumption that, at the very least, the Great Year calendar was in place and active no later than about 11,000 BC. The work of West and Schoch on the re-dating the Sphinx, discussed earlier, points ineluctably in that direction.

Below, are tables of the two precessional Great Years:

8 Cf., Finch, op. cit., p. 125.

POLAR CONSTELLATION-SIGNS DEFINING EACH AGE (3,703 YEARS)	PRESENT NAMES OF CONSTELLATIONS	DATES (APPROX.) FOR BEGINNING OF THE AGES (-) = BC (+) = AD
Shu, the Kneeler (incl. the star **Vega**) that later became *Hercules, the Kneeler*	**Hercules**	(-) 12,762
Ploughman, the Vinegrower—the earliest figure of Osiris (incl. parts of **Ursa Major**)	**Boötes**	(-) 9,059
Ta-Urt, Hippopotamus Goddess that became the Celestial Serpent later	**Draco** (Celestial Serpent)	(-) 5,356
Wep-wat, Divine Jackal in Egypt but 'Little Bear' in Greece	**Ursa Minor** (Little Bear)	**(-) 1,653***
Kaf, Ape of Thoth that became the Cosmic Ethiopian King afterward	**Cepheus** (Ethiopian King)	**(+) 2,050***
Nekhebit, Vulture Goddess in Egypt who became the Celestial Swan later	**Cygnus** (Swan)	(+) 5,753
Apesh, the Ancient Tortoise that furnished the shell to string the Lyre	**Lyra** (Lyre)	(+) 9,456

(* The Dates in **bold** indicate the beginning and the end of the current Polar Age.)

ZODIACAL CONSTELLATION-SIGNS DEFINING EACH AGE (2,158 YEARS)	PRESENT NAMES OF CONSTELLATIONS	DATES (APPROX.) FOR BEGINNING OF THE AGES (-) = BC (+) = AD
Atum, the Lion-Power/Cosmic Man	**Leo**	(-) 10,909
Khepera, the Scarab Beetle	**Cancer**	(-) 8,751
Set/Horus (or Shu/Tefnut), the Twins	**Gemini**	(-) 6,593
Ptah-Apis (Osiris), the Bull	**Taurus**	(-) 4,435
Amon, the Ram	**Aries**	(-) 2,277
Ant & Abtu, the Two Fishes of the Boat of Ra	**Pisces**	**(-) 119***
Hathor-Nut, Great Mother of the Waters	**Aquarius (Aquaria?)**	**(+) 2,039***
Menu, the Divine Goat	**Capricorn**	(+) 4,197
Shu (or Set), the Divine Archer	**Sagittarius**	(+) 6,355

ZODIACAL CONSTELLATION-SIGNS DEFINING EACH AGE (2,158 YEARS)	*PRESENT NAMES OF CONSTELLATIONS*	*DATES (APPROX.) FOR BEGINNING OF THE AGES (-) = BC (+) = AD*
Serqet, the Scorpion Goddess	**Scorpio**	(+) 8,513
Ma'at, the Scales	**Libra**	(+) 10,671
Isis, Virgin Mother (of Horus)	**Virgo**	(+) 12,829

(* The Dates in **bold** indicate the beginning and the end of the current Zodiacal Age.)

As Gerald Massey insisted, one can only grasp the meaning of astronomical mythology in ancient terms by reference to the Types, i.e., those natural images—turned into symbols—that were projected into the heavens by ancient African man and preserved intact in Egypt down to the Christian era. Thus each constellation-sign, as a Type, was endowed with a name, story, symbolic essence, and spiritual energy that embodied the ebb and flow of the cosmic forces that impacted man's fate, individually and collectively. To the ancients, there is a Plan, and that Plan can be read in the Book of Heaven, once the keys are accessible. In the Hermetic dictum, 'As above, so below,' resides one of those keys; it means that history is written first in the heavens before being enacted on earth. So says Thoth-Hermes to his disciple Asclepios in the Hermetic texts of the early Christian era:

> Do you not know, Asclepios, that Egypt is an image of heaven? Or, to speak more exactly, in Egypt all the operations of the powers which rule and work in heaven have been transferred down to earth below?[9]

Such ideas are maximally absurd to the modern historian but it is the way the ancients lived and thought. The antiquarian scholar of today—apart from his endless, obsessive gathering of often pointless minutiae—is therefore utterly unequipped to understand the history of ancient peoples, let alone their mind

9 Cited in Hancock G and Bauval R, **The Message of the Sphinx**, New York: Crown Publishers, 1996, p. 78; cf. also Mead GRS, **Thrice Greatest Hermes**, Vol. 2, London: John M. Watkins, (1906), 1949, p. 351.

and spirit, precisely because he refuses to admit that there is any connection between heavenly events and earthly ones.

Before going further, a word should be said about these Types depicted in the two Precessions, because these Types are the *neters*, or 'gods,' of Egypt. About these gods, Budge has the following comments:

> The original homes of many of the gods were in countries to the south of Egypt, and the funerary ceremonies which were performed in Upper Egypt under the Middle and New Kingdoms prove that their place of origin was in the south. From the south came all the great animal gods, and the... religious views of the peoples of the south, that is the regions which we now call Lower and Upper Nubia and the Egyptian Sûdûn, influenced greatly the inhabitants of Upper Egypt and the Delta.[10]

Everything in the life of dynastic Egyptians, including their religious beliefs, proclaims their southern origin. It must be admitted, therefore, that their astro-mythology, not to mention their astronomy, also had its roots in the lands south of Egypt. When Diodorus wrote that Egypt was a colony of Ethiopia (the lands south of Egypt), he was only reporting that which could not be disputed. Certainly no Egyptian ever tried to.

At any given time, the world is functioning under the influence of two Ages, one polar and the other equinoctal (zodiacal). Because of the difference in the number of constellation-signs that act as markers for each Age—7 for the Polar Great Year and 12 for the Zodiacal Great Year—the successive Ages of the two precessions never cycle in at the same time, though in this century, Aquarius (or *Aquaria*, feminine form of Aquarius) and Cepheus are cycling in within 11 years of one another (see the two Precessional Tables above).[11] This 'co-cycling' between 2,039 and 2,050 AD is about as close as it gets, portending immense shifts in the affairs of the world that are already being felt.

10 Ibid., p. 249.

11 The constellation of Cepheus does not actually supply a pole star until 3,000 A.D., but it does not affect the rule of Cepheus over the pole or the inauguration of a polar Age under his cosmic influence.

In earlier books, the present author reported that the current cycle of the Precessional Great Year began in the Age of Leo 10,858 BC. However, recent work by astrophysicist Thomas G. Brophy seems to pinpoint the start of the Age slightly earlier, i.e., 10,909 BC[12]. Brophy works from the evidence provided by the Nabta Playa Stone Circle, first discovered and described by Fred Wendorf and his team in southern Egypt west of Lake Nasser. The Wendorf team knew early on that the Nabta Circle was an astronomical observatory, but Brophy brought his considerably greater technical and scientific expertise to the study of this monument and uncovered astrophysical information encoded in the Circle that beggars the imagination. It is beyond the scope of this chapter to detail all of Brophy's amazing insights, but one of them concerns the Galactic Center of our galaxy, the Milky Way.[13] It should first be said that Wendorf's team concerned itself almost exclusively with the overlying Circle structure which was erected atop what Brophy refers to as the 'bedrock sculpture' that contains far more complex astronomical data than the Calendar Circle on the surface:

> Astonishing as it may be, the bedrock sculpture underneath 'Complex Structure A' at Nabta Playa appears to be an accurate depiction of our Milky Way Galaxy, as it was oriented astronomically at a specific time: vernal equinox heliacal rising of the Galactic Center in 17,770 BC[14]

The Galactic Center is in fact the Black Hole around which the Milky Way turns and the ancients apparently tracked the Center's movement in the heavens. The other structure excavated by the Wendorf team at the Nabta Playa site was 'Complex Structure B' also lying atop a sub-surface sculpture and

> ...the available drawings of the sculpture appears consistent with the Milky Way Galaxy plane as it was on

12 Cf. Brophy TG, **The Origin Map**, New York: Writers Club Press, 2002.

13 Cf. also Jenkins JM, **Galactic Alignment**, Rochester (VT): Bear & Company, 2002 for an extended discussion of ancient astronomical alignments and the Galactic Center. The Galactic Center is found between the southern constellations of Scorpio and Sagittarius and may represent, at least in part, a compensation for the lack of South Pole stellar markers in the cosmogonies of antiquity.

14 Brophy, op. cit., p. 54.

> vernal equinox sunrise on the date of the northern culmination of the Galactic Center, 10,909 BC[15]

Furthermore, Brophy insists that the Giza pyramids, among other things, *also mark the location of the Galactic Center at its northern astronomical culmination circa 10,909 BC*. Given these facts, Brophy contends that this date—10,909 BC—must mark the beginning of the Age of Leo and therefore the beginning of the current Precessional Cycle of the (Zodiacal) Great Year. There are compelling reasons for accepting this determination, not the least of which is that it gives a virtually exact date for the onset of the current Great Year, a date astronomically determined. We know that the ancients of the Nile Valley created and tracked several calendars, including that of the Precessional Calendar of the Great Year, and without exception, their marking and tracking points were all determined by precise and measurable astronomical phenomena (never by human events as is the case with the Christian and Moslem calendars). Recent work strongly suggests that the Galactic Center—situated 26,000 light-years away—actually emits energies that dynamically impact earth and all its living creatures, dictated by the precessional alignments.[16] These verifiable energies—mediated through earth's changing axial alignments to the Galactic Center—would go a long way to explain why different Ages embody distinct shifts in human cultural history, not to mention geo-environmental history. Brophy's intricate study of the Stone Circle (or stone map) may have uncovered another possible (and earlier) Precessional connection. The alignments in question concern the constellation Orion about which Brophy says,

> …the Shoulders [of Orion] angle reached angular maximum when their sky position was at the autumnal equinox in 16,500 BC, matching the stone map.
>
> Thus around 16,500 BC the diagram was equally ergonomically designed for use by a sky watcher, and its meaning was mirror image of its 5,000 BC meaning.[17]

15 Ibid., p. 55

16 Jenkins, op. cit., pp. 238-48.

17 Ibid., p. 15.

Now if the north polar precession is tracked backwards, it will be found that the North Pole was inhabited by Apesh/Lyra beginning 16,463 BC. In his book (page 10), Brophy makes clear that this congruence of the Shoulders of Orion and the stone diagram would have persisted for a span of time after 16,500 BC, easily encompassing this 16,463 BC polar date for Apesh/Lyra. Orion is a southern constellation and Apesh/Lyra a north polar one; nonetheless, it can be readily envisioned that the Polar Precession and that involving Orion were linked by the ancients through the Stone Circle. This supposition becomes stronger when it is realized that the re-alignment of the stone map with the Shoulders of Orion re-occurs in the era around 5,000 BC. The Polar Age of Ta-Urt/Draco begins 5,356 BC, again showing a close concordance between the stone map and the Polar precessional calendar. Thus we can say that the Age of Leo (zodiacal) begins 10,909 BC and the Age of Shu/Hercules (polar) begins 12,760 BC.

Leo is represented in Egypt by the Sphinx that, according to recent studies, was constructed with a precise orientation to the constellation of Leo as it rose heliacally around 10,500 BC[18]. At that time, in the Polar Great Year, Shu had been the ruler at the pole since 12,760 BC and Shu—representing the Airspace between earth and heaven as well as the light-rays of the sun—was a Lion figure, who with his twin sister Tefnut the Lioness, came forth from Atum, also a Lion. In the much later Greek planisphere, Shu would be replaced by Hercules who, as is well-known, dressed himself in the skin of the Nemean Lion which he slew on the first of his 12 Labors, probably alluding to the Lion sign as marking the beginning of the precessional Great Year. Furthermore, in the Heavens, the constellation Hercules was first known as the 'the Kneeler;' Shu was the very earliest 'Kneeler,' depicted as such as he lifted the sky up from the earth. Greek historians and mythographers such as Diodorus Siculus report that there were several Herculeses, the oldest one being Egyptian. This Egyptian Hercules lived more than 10,000 years prior to the time Diodorus

18 See Hancock G and Bauval R, **The Message of the Sphinx**, New York: Crown Publishers, Inc., 1996 for a thorough discussion of the age of the Sphinx as related to its stellar orientation. This date is much earlier than that of 7,000 B.C. proposed by Robert Schoch for the age of the Sphinx.

was writing (50–35 BC), wore a lion skin, and carried a club.[19] The ancient Egyptian Shu lived on through the archaic Egyptian Hercules, then, of course, the later Greek Hercules.

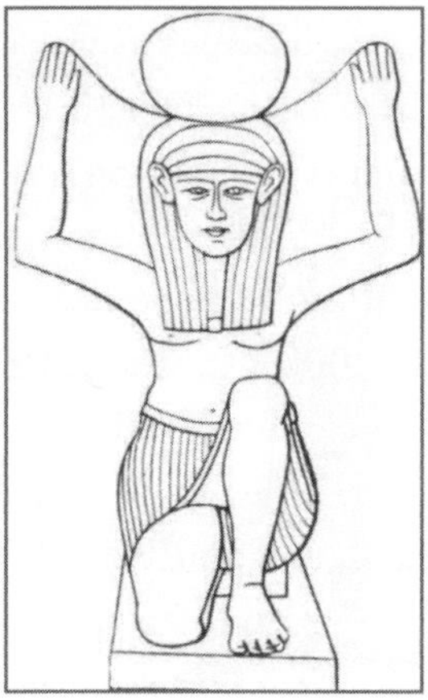

Shu—Kneeler and Upholder

Hercules the Kneeler

Shu is also Atlas, since both (and Hercules) are depicted raising and holding up heaven to separate it from earth. Thus the 'raising of the firmament'—one of the formative acts of Biblical Creation—takes place under the influence of the Circumpolar Lion—Shu in his Atlas mode. According to William Tyler Olcott, ancient astrologers, in fact, declared that the world was created when the sun was in the Lion-sign.[20] This occasion would be known by the ancient Nile Dwellers as *Sep Tepi*, the First Time; this First Time would be recurring, at intervals of 25,900 years. As the author has shown in an earlier work—following the lead of Gerald Massey—all the Types of *Genesis* are present in ancient Egyptian cosmo-mythology. It is also instructive to note that a little north of Heliopolis in Egypt is a place named *Tell al'Yahudia*, 'the Mound of the Jew', that in remote times was the site of the temple of Shu, the Lion-headed. Thus, the 'Lion of Judea' was in fact Shu in his earliest manifestation. E.A. Wallis Budge pointed out that Shu is the vapor or wind that existed over

19 Cf., **Diodorus Siculus: Library of History**, translated by CH Oldfather, Cambridge: Harvard University Press, (1933)2004, p. 77.

20 Olcott WT, **Star Lore: Myths, Legends, and Facts**, Mineola: Dover Publications, Inc., (1911), 2004, p. 235.

the Primal Abyss at the moment of creation and thus is the 'spirit' or 'wind' that moved over the waters of the Abyss as described in *Genesis*.[21]

Following the raising of the firmament by Shu, the Zodiacal Lion (Leo) Atum metamorphoses first into the Primal Serpent[22] then, later, the Primordial Adam, the Father of Humanity which, as we know, are two of the main figures in *Genesis*. It is well-established that the Sphinx, oriented to Leo as it rose heliacally 10,500 BC, was a form of Atum.[23] Strikingly, the Sphinx possesses a human head on a lion's body. Though the lion was one of Atum's most important symbols, most of the time Atum was represented as a man; he was in fact the Cosmic Man (*Adam Kadmon* of the **Kabbala**). R.T. Rundle Clark says, concerning Atum, 'The basic arrangement of the universe is...a combination of Atum as Primary Spirit, Life and the World Order.'[24] The Sphinx combines both representations of Atum as Celestial Lion and Cosmic Man and the sculpting of the Sphinx coincides with a new cosmic genesis for man, as the world's Great Year begins anew: *Sep Tepi*. For a period of 1,852 years after the advent of the Age of Leo, the world—certainly as it was conceived by the ancient Nile dwellers—was under the cosmic influence of the two Lion-signs, one sitting at the north pole as Shu and the other rising heliacally at the vernal equinox as Atum. This Leonine duality is depicted in ancient Egyptian chronology as the Double Lion or *Akeru*.

In 9,057 BC the Ploughman/Vine-Grower—most of which is today embodied in the constellation Boötes—moved to the polar position. The Ploughman/Vine-Grower was the earliest manifestation of the *neter*—'deity' or 'power'—now known as *Osiris*. In the succeeding millenia, the ritual scope and influence of Osiris would be magnified to such a degree that in the dynastic era (4,268 to 30 BC), he would assume the attributes of and be identified with every important masculine deity. However, in his earliest manifestation, Osiris was the god or *power* of growing things, especially as pertained to agriculture, and some say he was the reproductive power of all living things, plant, animal, and human. Since agriculture was most likely discovered as early as 18,000 BC (likely earlier)

21 **Budge**, op. cit., p. 143

22 In truth, Atum may have been the Serpent before he became the Lion.

23 Hancock and Bauval, op. cit., p. 155. Some think the Sphinx's face is female so might also have been a humanized form of Tefnut or Sekhmet.

24 Rundle Clark, op. cit., p. 47.

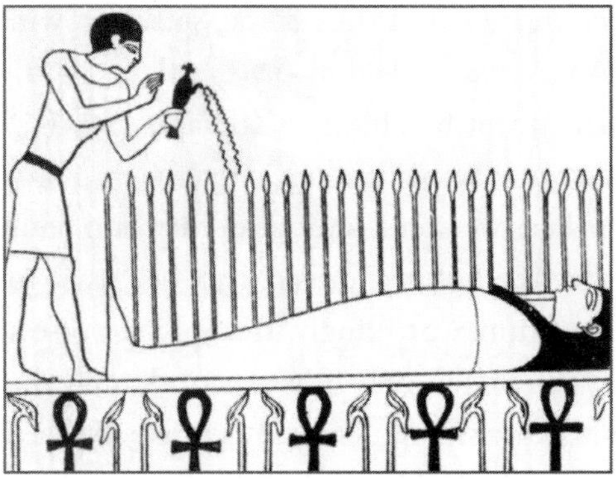

Wheat Growing from the Body of Osiris

Green Osiris, Deity of All Growing Things

by women—who presided over it through most of historical antiquity—the Osirian figure that would have taken possession of the pole just before 9,000 BC probably represents that stage of agriculture markedly affected by the introduction of the plough. The invention and utilization of the plough undoubtedly would have expanded crop production considerably and increased masculine importance in the indispensable enterprise of farming. A somewhat oblique confirmation of this assertion comes from Diodorus Siculus writing about 40 BC who says concerning Dionysus, the Greek figure identified with Osiris:

> He [Dionysus] is represented by them as the first man to have yoked oxen to the plough, human beings before that time having prepared the ground by hand.[25]

The Greeks customarily called Osiris 'Dionysus,' so the above quotation is entirely pertinent to the proposed celestial connection between the Ploughman (Boötes) and Osiris. The Ploughman is also the Vine-Grower and therefore the earliest Wine-Maker. The first fermented beverage—beer—was discovered and brewed by women (presided over by Hathor), but wine in ancient Kemit was always associated with Osiris, who on that account, was identified with Dionysus by the later Greeks. Osiris would eventually be envisioned as the Egyptian king who brought the blessings of agriculture and

25 Oldfather CH, **Diodorus of Sicily**, Vol. II, Cambridge: Harvard University Press, (1935)1979, p. 293.

wine-making to Egypt and from there spread them to the rest of the world. Wine would always thus be associated with the 'blood of Osiris' in a way entirely familiar to Christians in the sacramental transubstantiation of the blood of Christ.

With the advent of the Zodiacal Age of Khepera (or Cancer) 8,751 BC, 300 years after that of the Polar Ploughman, a new ritual and vitalist synergy would have emerged. Khepera was imaged as the scarab beetle whose natural habits in the lands along the Nile are powerfully suggestive. For one thing, Khepera can be seen as the harbinger of the flood since the scarab, just before the first waters of the annual flood begin to arrive in late June, rolls dung and mud into a perfectly spherical ball into which it has deposited its eggs. It then digs a hole into which it places this ball which is subsequently covered over by the Nile

Khepera Rolling the Dung Sphere

Khepera-Apur, "the Flyer"

flood. Three months later, when the flood has subsided, the incubating larvae inside the buried dung ball have matured enough to fly up out of the mud to begin life. The symbolic resonance with the Ploughman is evident: the scarab has dug a hole and planted its 'seed-ball' from which new life eventually emerges, out of the waters so to speak. Khepera was also called *Apur*, 'the Flier,' and became emblematic of that which created itself out of the Cosmic *Primum Materium*. As E.A.W. Budge explains, 'When *Neber-Djer* ('Lord of the Universe') took the form of Khepri, nothing existed except a vast mass of watery matter…

an abyss of slime.'[26] This liquid 'slime' or 'primal ooze' was *Nun* ('inertness'). Thus the life activities of the scarab beetle becomes the re-enactment on earth of this cosmological creation event. Moreover, the name *khepera* means variously (1) 'to make,' (2) 'to mold,' and/or (3) 'to become' or 'evolve.' Since the divine Scarab is the Flier out of the spherical ball of its incubation, it is also the image of the sun emerging from the primal darkness. R.T. Rundle Clark says, '...Khoprer is God as he appears in visible form, whether at the beginning or every day...'[27] Khepera the Scarab would also serve as the living image of the origin and evolution of *Kemit* (Egypt) itself which, as Herodotus noted, was the Gift of the River (and the mud of the River). Thus Khepera was the imperishable symbol of Ever-Becoming or Evolution—cosmic, terrestrial, and human.

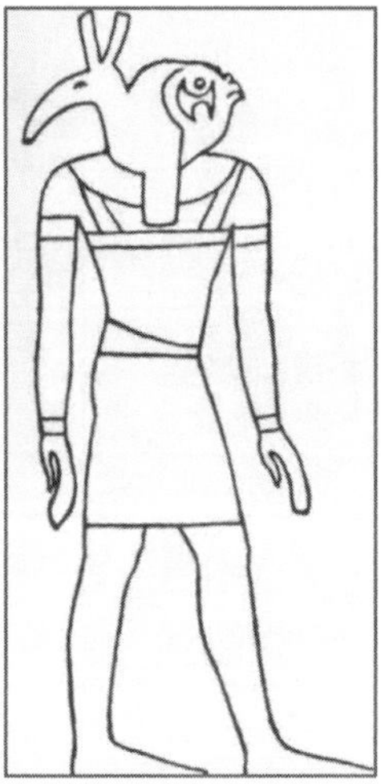

Twin Gods—Horus and Set

Around 6,593 BC, the constellation of the Twins—Set/Horus (or Shu/Tefnut)—begins to rise heliacally at the vernal equinox, inaugurating the Age of Gemini. In this Age, Egypt as *Taui*, 'the Two Lands,' comes into being. It is a known fact that Upper and Lower Egypt were separate kingdoms up to the time of unification circa 4,268 BC under Mēnēs. They were, in fact, the Twin Kingdoms with Upper Egypt in the south ruled by Set and Lower Egypt

26 **Budge**, op. cit., p. 141.
27 Rundle Clark, op. cit., p. 41

in the north ruled by Horus. In this Age, Horus and Set were complementary Twins, not antagonists as they would become in dynastic times. In the early dynastic period, several of the pharaohs bore both a 'Set name' and a 'Horus name' and it must be assumed that the pharoahs in each of the Twin Kingdoms beforehand had also done so. Even after unification, Egypt was often referred to as 'the Two Lands,' and the pharaohs typically wore the double crown—the red crown of Lower Egypt combined with the white crown of Upper Egypt. It isn't clear why in after ages a mortal antagonism grew up between Set and Horus or why Set became increasingly seen as a malevolent power. However, through dynastic times, Set's hostility and enmity toward Osiris and Horus is implacable and unalterable. It does seem that the initial conflict involved Set and Osiris—the latter gradually becoming the central, if not paramount, figure in the pantheon—and Horus got drawn into it, as it were, by his evolving role as the son of Osiris and therefore as Osiris reborn. As Rundle Clark puts it, 'The living king was Horus, *the son and heir of Osiris*.'[28] The **Pyramid Texts** simply recite, in praise, 'O Horus who is Osiris, the King…'[29] Osiris and Horus thus became one. Because of the greater prestige of the South, after the close of the Age of the Twins, Set and Horus switched places, thereby installing Horus as the Ruler of the South.

At the North Pole the Ploughman-Vine Grower, the early form of Osiris, rules until 5,354 BC, thus sharing cosmic rulership with the zodiacal Twins for more than 12 centuries. Without any clear indication of the cosmic, religious, and perhaps political dynamics of the situation, one can only speculate about whether it was in this period that Osiris the Ploughman formed the connection to Horus that would play itself out later in the Osirian drama that emerges fully-formed by dynastic times (circa 4,268 BC). Why such a thing happened to the detriment of Set is obscure. It is pertinent to note, however, that the southern pre-unification dynasty (4,600 BC–4,268 BC) discovered at Qustul pertained to the kingdom of *Ta-Seti*, whose name could mean 'Land of the Bow' or, just as readily, 'Set's Land.' Even after Ta-Seti was conquered and incorporated into the unified kingdom of historic Egypt, the southernmost

28 Ibid., p. 107

29 Faulkner RO, **The Ancient Egyptian Pyramid Texts**, Oak Park: Bolchazy-Carducci Publishers, 1969, p.316.

nome of Egypt—its first nome—was given the name *Ta-Seti*. Also, in dynastic times, Ta-Seti was the name for what later became known as Nubia. As we have

Set, Patron Deity of the Bow

noted already, Ta-Seti might have been the Southern Kingdom during the era (Gemini) of 'The Two Lands.' The thing is obscure in many ways, but Set never really loses his strategic place in the pantheon, though nominally superseded by Osiris and Horus.

Around 5,354 BC, the Ploughman/Vine-Grower moves off the pole and *Ta-Urt*, the Cosmic Hippo, takes over the pole. Ta-Urt, who became *Draco ('Dragon' or 'Serpent')* of later planispheres, is unique because she is so sizable

Ta-Urt at the Center of the Denderah Planisphere

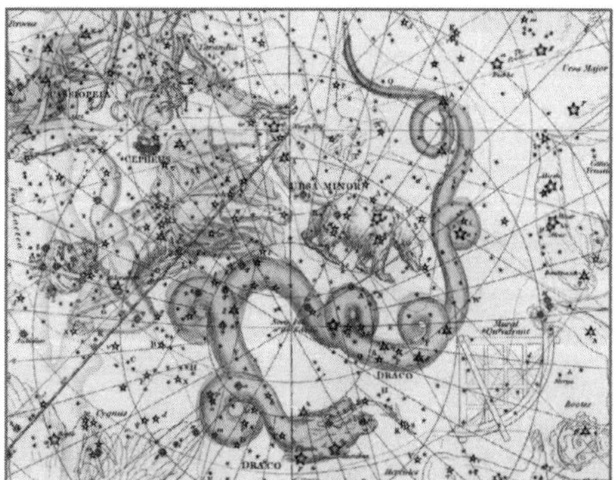

Draco and the Constellations of the Northern Heaven

and strategically placed as a constellation that the ecliptic runs through her while at specific periods in the polar precession, the magnetic pole is also situated in her. Draco too is so configured as to be the locus of the ecliptic pole and, in turn, the magnetic pole. Ta-Urt's strategic place in the northern polar heaven is indicated by one of her names: *Ment Uret*, 'the Great Mooring Post,' i.e., the ecliptic around which the circumpolar stars revolved.[30] Ta-Urt, the hippopotamus goddess of ancient Egypt, was probably the oldest deity in the pantheon. She had a number of other names: *Apit*, *Rerit*, and *Deb* and several other goddesses exhibited a hippo form. As Apit, Ta-Urt's holiest sanctuary was *Apit-Isut*, in what later became Amon's temple complex at Karnak. One could say that Ta-Urt loomed over the whole polar Great Year as the Determiner (or Mother) of Cosmic Time, since the ecliptic pole—around which the magnetic pole gyrated in a 25,900-year spin—passed through her. And, as indicated above, she also had a circumpolar location, around herself as it were.

In one of his forms, Set was the male hippopotamus and the son of Ta-Urt, participating in her stellar character. In fact it is said, concerning Set and his 'children,'

> 'The Children of Seth' were the inventors of that peculiar sort of wisdom which is concerned with the heavenly bodies and their order...[31]

The time comes when Ta-Urt falls away from the pole (1,653 BC) and when she does, so does Set. With this event, the cosmo-religious character of the hippopotamus shifts because this animal, at least in its Sethian aspect, becomes a type of the enemy of Horus who has emerged as the Cosmic Hero deity. This relationship is clear and unmistakable on the walls the Temple of Edfu, dedicated to Horus, in which Horus is depicted spearing the hippopotamus who threatens the cosmic order. However, this 'reversal of fortune' seems to have no affect on Ta-Urt herself who maintains pride of place in the pantheon.

30 **Budge**, op. cit., p. 243.
31 Temple RKG, **The Sirius Mystery**, New York: St. Martin's Press, 1976, p.103.

Horus Spearing the Hippo

It would be interesting to ascertain when Draco was substituted for Ta-Urt in the polar planisphere which may have happened outside of Egypt. Or Draco may have always been considered a 'co-type' of Ta-Urt even in Egypt itself. Certainly serpent symbolism plays a prominent, even ubiquitous, role in Egyptian cosmology from its remotest beginnings and the Cosmic Serpent *Kametef*, i.e., 'he who completed his time', participates in the formative creation of the universe itself. Serpent symbolism had to be as old as—perhaps older than—the figuration of the hippopotamus in the primordial Egyptian world-view and there were numerous serpent figures—benevolent and malevolent—in Egyptian mythology. It is said in the **Pyramid Texts**:

> I am the outflow of the Primeval Flood, he who emerged from the waters.
> I am the 'Provider of Attributes' *serpent with its many coils*,
> I am the Scribe of the Divine Book
> which says what has been and effects what is yet to be.[32]

Rundle Clark also tells us,

> When all differences have disappeared he [Atum] and
> Osiris, the transcendent and emergent forms of deity,

32 Cited in Rundle Clark, op. cit., p. 50.

> will be reunited in the universal primordial form of life, the original Serpent, the form in which divinity existed before the coming of gods or men.[33]

Atum himself was Serpent probably before he was Lion and in the Egyptian flood-story, two neters remain—Atum and Osiris—as serpents, as we see in the above quotation. Thus, after Rundle Clark, the serpent, as Atum, is 'an image of God at the beginning and at the end of time, Atum will become a serpent once more.'[34] It is not hard to believe that Draco the Serpent would have been a Determiner of Time and a cosmic polar type among the Egyptians, however prominently the Hippopotamus was featured in their polar planisphere.

In fact, the pervasive mythic symbolism of the Serpent-and-Tree undoubtedly stems from the figure of Draco coiled around the Pole, the Tree being always a type of the Pole. As seen above, Draco falls away from the Pole in 1,653 BC, and this event is captured in *Genesis* when the Serpent is pushed out of the Tree and condemned by God to crawl on the ground. There are, to be sure, Egyptian prototypes: Atum, the Egyptian Adam, is a serpent, and a form of the Mother Serpent in Egypt is *Hefa*, who becomes Havvah or Eve in *Genesis*. Thus the Fall of Adam and Eve is coterminous with the Fall of the Serpent, astro-mythically determined by the precessional shift at the pole. Related to this Fall in Egyptian mythology, the Serpent *Apep* becomes the image of the Destroyer. Several of the hated Hyksos pharaohs—who still rule Egypt around 1,653 BC—took the name *Apepa*. The Hyksos had been known as Set-worshippers, and in this period, Set and Apep conjoin mythically in the Egyptian mind as the Adversarial Power.

Around 4,435 BC, the Twins cease to rise heliacally at the spring equinox as the Bull-constellation moves into the vacated heliacal position at the spring equinox, thus inaugurating the Age of Taurus. This Age marks the beginning of documented Egyptian history with the unification of the Two Lands into a single kingdom known variously as *Kemit* ('the Black Land') and *Ta-Meri* ('the Beloved Land'). The neter *Ptah*, allied with the Bull *Apis*, astro-mythically comes to the fore and the symbolic ethos of the Bull dominates for the next 2,158 years.

33 Ibid., p. 141.
34 Ibid., p. 52.

Osiris Incarnate in the Apis Bull

The Constellation Taurus

Egyptian annals record that Mēnēs, the uniter of Egypt, c. 4,268 BC, is the one who installed the Bull cult in Egypt. Mēnēs moves the capital of Egypt to *Men-nefer* or *Memphis*, the city sacred to Ptah and the Apis bull. Within 600 years after unification, the classic era of pyramid-building in Egypt commences, by which time the ancient architects had completely mastered building with stone on a massive scale. Nothing like it was seen before or since; the pyramids of Egypt are the still the most magnificent edifices ever erected by human hands. Other sacred locales in Egypt also establish the primacy of Bull: in Heliopolis, the sacred capital of the sun-god Atum (later of Rā), Atum is represented in bull-form as *Mnevis*; in *Waset* (later Thebes), the bull neter is *Mentu*.

Osiris comes into his own in this period. Ptah, the Universal Architect, is the paramount neter ('god') of the Age, but Orisis becomes the dominant force in Egyptian religious life, a role he does not relinquish for 4,200 years. Osiris assumes the attributes of the very old underworld form of Ptah by name of *Sokar*, the deity who presided over the Land of Dead. From that time on, the Osirian role in achieving immortality for the soul makes him the one neter whose pre-eminence never wavers. Though Osiris assumes all the attributes of Sokar, he goes beyond Sokar's status as God of the Dead and Lord of the Underworld to become the embodiment of a *personal* hope for resurrection and immortality. The Way of Liberation—from death and 'the psychic hindrances of life'—is accomplished through Osiris. Osiris also assumes a bull-form and eventually becomes fused with the Apis Bull. The potency and power of the bull accounts for the impact and influence of his symbolism. Even after the Era of the Bull (Taurus) fades in the course of the Precession, bull symbolism continues to exercise its influence down to the end of Egyptian history.

Osiris does not relinquish his older attributes, however; he remains the god of agriculture, vine-growing, and wine-making. Mystically, because of his connection to grain, he becomes 'the bread of life;' wine becomes symbolically his 'blood.' Indeed, these disparate images and symbols are interwoven: Osiris, who dies (killed by Set), is resurrected in the new grain (or plants) of spring; the fermentation of grape juice into wine—the 'spiritous' beverage—images the transubstantiation of Osiris who triumphs over and transcends death. Thus, all people can hope for resurrection and immortality through Osiris.

The Ram of Amon

The Constellation Aries

Around 2,277 BC, the Bull constellation-sign of the Taurus Age is replaced by the Ram constellation-sign, launching the Age of Aries. Thus lamb, ram, and shepherd symbolism come to overshadow history for the next 21 centuries. In Egypt, the Ram-god Amon comes to the forefront of the pantheon, merging with the sun-god Rā as Amon-Rā. *Waset*—known later as *Thebes*—becomes the capital city of Egypt and Amon's temple at Karnak eventually becomes the country's 'Vatican.' Some think that the name *Thebes* was derived from *Ta-Apit*, 'Land of Apit,' the place-name stemming from the earliest divine ruler of the city. It is also pertinent to recall that prior to the rise of Amon, the other paramount deity (with Apit) of Waset was *Mentu*, a bull-headed deity, thus showing the effects of the change from Bull to Ram *in situ* as it were. When the Arian (or

Amonian) Age begins, the north polar Age of Ta-Urt (Draco) is still in force and the original temple, Ipet Asut, had been dedicated to Ta-Urt as Apit. In fact, even after Amon appropriates the sacred city and its temple, Apit continues to have a noticeable presence there; the Amonian priesthood continues to exhibit a careful deference to Apit. As a matter of unalterable custom, the Egyptians never expel or suppress an earlier deity even as the Ages shift; they always reconfigure and find an honored place for the earlier neter in the pantheon.

The other Ram deity of note is Khnum—always shown as the flat-horned ram—who rules over the 1st cataract region of southern Egypt. He is said to control the flood and is depicted as fashioning human beings out of clay on a potter's wheel. Clearly, there is a synergy between him and Amon.

This era of Aries marks the advent of a people who would eventually exert an influence on world history all out of proportion to their actual numbers: the Children of Israel. Their remote ancestor Abraham emigrates from Chaldea sometime after 1,900 BC and from the first, the history of these people is decisively impacted by lamb, ram, and shepherd symbolism as Abraham's son Isaac is saved from sacrifice by a ram caught in a thicket. A connection to Egypt is evident early, as Abraham migrates there and in fact takes an Egyptian consort, Hagar, who gives birth to his first son, Ishmael. Only after leaving Egypt, do certain events transpire—including the covenant by circumcision—that change the course of the history of Abraham and his descendants. Probably around 1,660 BC or so, Jacob-Israel, a descendant of Abraham, re-migrates to Egypt with 70 of his clan at a time when Egypt was ruled by the Hyksos. The Hyksos, though originally from Egypt's eastern desert, were probably ethnically and culturally allied to Canaanites such as Jacob and his clan, allowing the latter to settle in northern Egypt without difficulty. Four hundred thirty (430) years later, the descendants of Jacob-Israel are saved by 'the blood of the lamb' (*Exodus*) and depart Egypt under the leadership of a dissident Egyptian priest *Osar-siph*, later called *Moses*. Especially after the critical episode at Sinai where the Decalogue—clearly modeled on the Egyptian *42 Declarations of Innocence* in the **Book of the Coming Forth By Day**—is given to Moses by a newly-Hebrewized Egyptian lunar deity *Yah*, the Children of Israel follow a path that eventually alters the course of history.[35]

35 Cf. Finch, op. cit., pp. 129-78 for a fuller discussion.

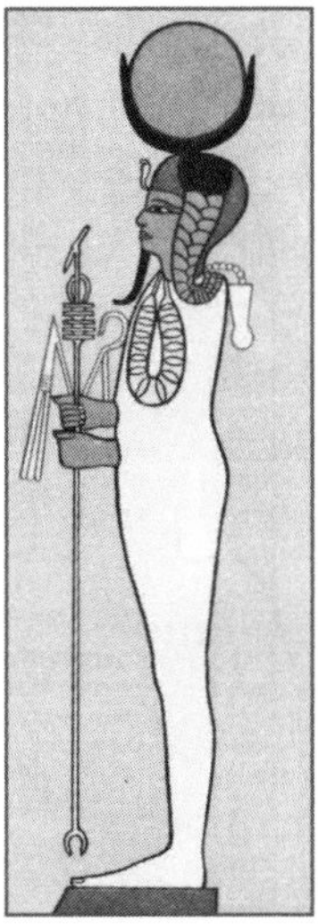

Egyptian Lunar Deity—Yah

The Jackal Wepawat—Opener of the Way

It is while the Children of Israel are sojourning in Egypt that the Polar Age shifts from Ta-Urt/Draco to the Jackal *Wep-Wat* ('Opener of the Way') or *Anubis* circa 1,653–1,651 BC. Their religio-mythic history will be given to them by Moses/Osar-siph (after 1,230 BC) and this astro-mythical shift will provide the core material for the Genesis story of 'the Fall.'

A word should be said about the so-called 'Intermediate Periods' of Egyptian history. The idea of an 'Intermediate Period' is, in truth, a scholarly artifice, one invented by 20th century Egyptologists. None of the ancient historical writers about Egypt—including Manetho—ever refer to an Intermediate Period or anything that can be construed as one. Neither do the Egyptologists of the late 19th and early 20th centuries. In fact, Nicolas Grimal, writing in 1988, says it is a term 'which is arguably almost meaningless.'[36] But modern Egyptologists have, for the sake of conceptual convenience, demarcated two—some say three—such Intermediate Periods, each delimiting, one from the other, the successive 'kingdoms' of Egyptian history: the Middle Kingdom from the Old Kingdom, and the New Kingdom from the Middle Kingdom. Even in New Kingdom

36 Grimal N, **A History of Ancient Egypt**, translated by Ian Shaw, Cambridge (USA): Blackwell, 1988; 1992, p. 137.

times, and continuing down to the present, each of these Intermediate Periods has carried an obscure and mysterious air because each seems to represent a complete collapse of political, moral, and religious authority in Egypt, leading to more or less extended epochs of anarchy. Nevertheless, Grimal informs us,

> It is...clear that the Egyptians themselves did not consider the First Intermediate Period a major disruption in the flow of their history.[37]

He goes on to say concerning the Second Intermediate Period,

> Like the First Intermediate Period [the Second Intermediate Period] is not truly a historical phase in itself but simply a convenient label for a chronological gap.[38]

Since precious little historical information survives from those eras, conventional Egyptologists can only imagine the socio-political forces that defined these periods and are completely at a loss to explain them. But the modern insistence of discontinuity that these periods supposedly represent undoubtedly requires significant re-evaluation. It is probably more fruitful to think of them as Grimal does as 'chronological gaps.'

The first of these chronological gaps (First Intermediate Period), begins about 2,806 BC and brings the 6th Dynasty to a close. The end of this dynasty is customarily thought of as representing the termination of the Old Kingdom, though this notion may reflect the somewhat artificial constraints imposed by scholarly convention. It is more likely to be true that the Old Kingdom lasted at least until the end of the 8th Dynasty. Flinders Petrie thinks that the 7th and 8th dynasties *in toto* lasted 216 years[39] so that the Old Kingdom, though on its last legs, might not have come to an end until 2,590 BC. The chronological information gap does not allow much more to be said about the events of these terminal dynasties of the Old Kingdom. From that point, the 9th and 10th

37 Ibid.

38 Ibid., p. 182.

39 Petrie WMF, **A History of Egypt**, Vol. 1, London: Methuen & Co., 1903, p. 110.

Dynasties carry the history forward until about 2,320 BC at which time the 11th Dynasty commences, continuing until 2,261 BC with the inauguration of the 12th Dynasty and the rise of the so-named Middle Kingdom with its capital at Thebes (e.g. *Waset*).[40] The second chronological gap (Second Intermediate Period), begins with end of the 12th Dynasty about 2,032 BC, though the Middle Kingdom probably continues at least to the end of the 13th Dynasty whose end date is uncertain. The end of the 12th to the beginning of the 18th Dynasty, around 1,580 BC, encompasses a period of 452 years, the latter date marking the advent of the New Kingdom. The 15th and 16th Dynasties mark the era of Hyksos domination of Egypt that only partially abates during the Theban 17th Dynasty. It is impossible—given this chronological gap and the inaccurate information conveyed by Manetho's transmitters—to assign reliable dates for any dynasty during these 452 years. The 'Intermediate Periods' of the Egyptologists frustrate their attempts to reconstruct, let alone understand, the history and dynastic chronology of Egypt because of the extended information 'black-out.'

However, using the admittedly imprecise chronology that the surviving annals permit, there are two very interesting correlations that reveal themselves. We can note that the termination of the first chronological gap (First Intermediate Period) occurs around 2,320 BC and a little over 43 years later, 2,277 BC, the Age of Aries (the Ram) commences. About this time, a pharaoh named *Amenemes* ('born of Amen') comes to the throne, and from this time forward, Amen or Amon, whose sacred symbol is the Ram, rises to the pinnacle of the Egyptian pantheon which he rules for the next 21 centuries. The second chronological gap (Second Intermediate Period) is terminated sometime between 1,600 BC and 1,580 BC. Just before that, the point of the polar precessional shift that replaces Ta-Urt with Wep-Wat takes place sometime between 1,653 BC and 1,651 BC. Ta-Urt is also Draco, one of whose Egyptian forms would have been the Serpent *Apep*.

40 If the 'Intermediate Periods' represent scholarly artifices, so do the concepts of Old, Middle, and New 'Kingdoms.' The Egyptians never thought of their history in that way.

Apep, "the Dragon of Darkness", destroyed by Set in the prow of the boat of Rā

One of the last Hyksos kings to rule in Egypt was named *Apepa*, after the Celestial Serpent, and his reign would have ended close to the time that Ta-Urt/Draco (Apep) was 'falling' from the pole, to be superseded by the Jackal, Wep-Wat. This period would also have encompassed the 17th Dynasty, the transitional dynasty between Hyksos rule and the advent of the New Kingdom (with the rise of the 18th Dynasty). The 17th Dynasty probably arose in Thebes about 1,731 BC.

Once it is understood how closely and ineluctably Egyptian history was tied to such celestial cycles, it is evident that the timing of the noted shifts was unlikely a matter of coincidence. The chronological gaps or Intermediate Periods could represent nothing except periods of terrestrial adjustments to the celestial shifts, certainly in Egypt—and if looked at closely—beyond Egypt as well. During these gaps, the ground was prepared for the approaching Age; the society had to be 're-wired' for the new dispensation. The disruption and discontinuity of the established social and political order may have been more apparent than real, but in any case, were not fatal to Egyptian civilization. In this way, Egypt exhibited a tremendous internal resilience, allowing the country to rebound with renewed vigor from seeming national catastrophes. Having said that, exact datings for these events can only be considered provisional, no matter who is proposing them. There are simply too many gaps in the chronological records for it to be otherwise.

Since it is being suggested that the alteration or re-direction of terrestrial events in Egypt's history are tied to celestial shifts, we can also think of these so-called Intermediate Periods, at least in part, as 'Inter-Age Transitions.' An Inter-Age

Transition is a period of tremendous flux and fluidity in all domains of life, and in fact, represents a historical paradigm shift. Typically, the transition occupies a time span between 100 and 200 years at the end of which a new order has emerged. This pattern is clearly evident in Egyptian history from the beginning of the dynastic period circa 4,268 BC. An Inter-Age Transition (Gemini to Taurus), from about 4,600 BC to 4,435 BC, had determined the course of events that eventually converted the earlier Two Lands of the Geminian era into the unified kingdom of the Taurean Age. Subsequently, the transformation of the Old Kingdom into the Middle Kingdom and the Middle Kingdom into the New Kingdom are also distinguished by Inter-Age Transitions, as seen above: Taurus to Aries on the one hand; Ta-Urt (Draco) to Wep-Wat (Ursa Minor) on the other.

In 1,653 BC, the polar Age of the Jackal, Wep-wat—a form of Anubis—begins. In Greek times, this constellation will be given the name *Ursa Minor* ('Little Bear') while, however, retaining its 'canine' attributes with its secondary name *Cynosuris*, i.e., 'Tail of the Dog.' Moreover, the Greek sun deity, *Apollo*, is often figured as a wolf, in which guise he was called the *Lycian* ('wolfish') Apollo. However that may be, things change. Anubis the Jackal, assumes a central role in the funerary ritual as the embalmer of Osiris and therefore as the embalmer *par excellence.* In fact, though originally the son of Set and Nephthys, he is turned into a son of Osiris and Nephthys, the sister of Osiris and Isis. In truth, he had been the Lord of Abydos *before* that locale became sacred to Osiris. As the first Lord of Abydos, Anubis was *Khenti Amentiu*, 'Chief of the Westerners,' i.e., Lord of the spirits of the dead. Moreover, Anubis/Wep-Wat is the guide of the souls of the deceased as the 'Opener of the Way.' The Jackal, heretofore, had possessed a Sethian aspect—that it never entirely relinquishes, especially since Anubis had earlier been considered the son of Set—but now, as Anubis, it joins the ranks of the Osirian dispensation as an indispensable member. The embalment of Osiris, where he is washed, anointed, wrapped in linen bandages, and set upright in the mode of resurrection, turns him into the *Krs(t).* Much later (300 BC), the word *krst* will enter the Greek language as *kristos*, 'the anointed,' which in Roman times becomes *christ.* Thus, Anubis is the one who 'christifies' Osiris, anticipating by 16 centuries the role of Joseph of Arimaetha who, taking the body of Jesus down from the cross, washed, anointed, and wrapped it in linen bandages, turning him into *Krs(t)* or *Christ.*

Anubis anointing the body of Osiris under
the direction of Isis.

Evidence that the impact of these celestial Ages affected peoples and societies beyond Egypt is particularly evident in the figure of Anubis/Wep-Wat. Mention has already been made of the so-called 'Wolfish Apollo' of Greek religious mythology, and it must be pointed out that Apollo is the slayer of *Python*, the Serpent Deity of Delphos, thus a type of Draco. Apollo as the Wolf—co-type of the Jackal—replaces Draco the Serpent. Roman legendary history portrays the founders of Rome, Romulus and Remus, as suckled by a she-wolf. In Norse mythology, *Fenrir* the Wolf is chained to the pole and *Ragnarok*, the 'Twilight of the Gods,' that is to say, the end of a World-Age, will take place when Fenrir breaks his chain and falls away from the pole (2,050 AD). The Dogon say that the earth's axis (or pole) is 'turning under the movement of the Fox's paws', and the Dogon divination system depends on the footprints of the pale fox that has walked across the sand divination table because the fox is the 'master of speech.' Since he is sacred to Elegba among the Fon—also considered a master of sacred speech—this aspect of the dog or jackal abides among them as well. Among the southwestern Indians, the coyote is the symbol of chaos and disorder—a role he also plays among the Dogon and indicative of the inherently Sethian character of the dog, jackal, fox, coyote, or wolf, all co-types of one another.

Wep-wat/Anubis and Amon the Ram co-ruled celestially for more than 15 centuries (up to 119 BC). The two conjoined in the figure of the dog as shepherd; indeed the mythical Hermes the Shepherd was dog-headed, called

Hermes Kuon by name.[41] Moreover, in human affairs, dogs were trained to herd sheep, becoming indispensable assistants to man in this regard as shepherd-dogs. In addition, the pole-star is sometimes referred to as 'the eye of heaven,' making Wep-wat/Anubis a type of 'Watcher.' Thus the dog as a 'guardian' or 'watch-dog' resonated with heavenly elements. These are just some of the ways in which the dog became thought of as 'man's best friend.'

In 119 BC, the Egyptian Double-Fish Sign of *Ant* and *Abtu* moved into the heliacal position at the vernal equinox, initiating the Age of Pisces. By this time, Egypt was coming to the end of its effective history; in ninety years it would be turned into merely a province of Rome and permanently cease to exist as a sovereign kingdom. And yet, even its final throes, currents flowed out of Egypt that would continue to affect the course of history. In the 3rd century BC, the Hebrew holy book, the Torah, was, for the first time, translated into Greek, the lingua franca of the Mediterranean world, in Egypt (Alexandria) by 70 learned Hebrew scholars. This seemingly innocuous occurrence would eventually have profound consequences for the world and for the first time, the sacred scripture of the rather obscure Canaanite kingdom of Judea (Israel) came to wider notice. The Septuagint ('the 70'), as it came to be called, would become the 'enabling document'—as the Bible—for a new religion that would sweep the world.

In an earlier book,[42] the present author summarized the biographical story of the Essene sage Yahushua Ben Pandera who, though born Jewish, lived most of his life in Egypt in a community of Essenes known as *Therapeutae*, so called because of their wide reputation as healers. Clearly, the sacred thought of these Therapeuts was monumentally informed by the vast and ancient wisdom of Egypt, though they seemed to have adopted much of that wisdom as had been handed down through the Pythagoreans. This Yahushua—*Jesu* in Greek—was born probably 120 BC, and through training received in the community of Egypt-based Therapeuts, would become a great healer, sage, and teacher. He began an itinerant teaching and healing ministry in Palestine, probably around 73 BC, but in 70 BC was arrested, tried, and hanged by Jewish authorities for

41 See Hall M, **Secret Teachings of All Ages**

42 Cf. Finch, op. cit., pp. 208-10; also Mead GRS, **Did Jesus Live 100 BC?**, London: Theosophical Society, 1903; 1949.

practicing 'magic.' A century-and-a-half later, sacred stories about his life and teachings began to circulate, eventually referred to as the *Gospels*, i.e., 'the glad tidings' or 'good news.' It is not without interest that the Jewish Rabbis who compiled the Mishna and Talmud beginning about 200 AD, referred to this Yahushua (Jesus) as '*the Egyptian sorcerer*'.[43]

The Double Fish of Pisces
Anet and ***Abtu*** among Egyptians

Though there came to be at least a dozen known Gospels (some say as many as 80), only four were canonized (from *kanon* meaning 'rule' or 'standard') at the Council of Nicaea in 325 AD. But throughout these scriptures, fish symbolism abounds. Jesus, for example, as he approaches his future disciples says to them 'Come, I will make you fishers of men.' When he feeds the crowds after the Sermon on the Mount, he multiplies two fishes and five loaves. When the Pharisees demand of him a sign, he replies, 'The only sign I will give…is the sign of Jonah,' the fish-man. What is more, before they were called *Christiani*, the followers of Christ referred to themselves as *Pisiculi*, 'Little Fishes.' Only by studying the ancient Egyptian astro-mythical typology embodied in the Great Year is it possible to make sense of the life, work, and symbolic essence of the man Yahushua who, after crucifixion, death, and resurrection, became *imitatio Osirii*, the *Krst* or the *Christ*. That the Gospel of Jesus was the re-manifestation of Osiris cannot possibly be doubted once the vast saviour mythology of ancient Egypt is examined, particularly since Egypt is the first country, as a whole, to convert to

43 Mead, ibid., pp. 122-263, passim.

Christianity. Moreover, the infrastructure of historic Christianity was, step-by-step, elaborated in Egypt for more than 200 years and Alexandria was the first capital of Christendom before Rome. It must also be pointed out that Yahushua Ben Pandera, the historic Jesus, was born 120 BC; just a single year separates the birth of this Piscean avatar and the advent of the Piscean Age in 119 BC.

Following the reasoning elaborated above, there would have been an Inter-Age Transition in and around the shift into the Piscean Age. The dynamics of this Inter-Age Transition unfolded largely outside Egypt. It involved Rome, which, however, would eventually annex Egypt and become, in time, the sacred center of burgeoning Christianity. This Inter-Age Transition would have begun with the outbreak of the first of the three Punic Wars—the culminating life-and-death struggle between Rome and Carthage—in 264 BC and ended with the destruction of Carthage in 146 BC. Carthage was the westernmost outpost of the Phoenician world, located near the present coastal city of Tunis in Tunisia, North Africa, and as such, closely connected to ancient Egypt as its parent Phoenician cities had been 1,000 years earlier. With respect to Rome, Carthage represented the last major outpost of the 'old world'. With Carthage destroyed, Rome now stood alone as the paramount power in the Mediterranean, free to pursue her obsessive empire-building for another 300 years. However, relatively soon after the fall of Carthage, Rome herself underwent a period of upheaval—sometimes referred to as the 'times of revolutions'—beginning 133 BC and ending 27 BC. In that fateful period, Rome, because of increasing Republican decadence and the intractable unrest of its plebeian classes, eventually succumbed to the ambitions of the first Caesars, Julius and Augustus, that turned Rome into an *imperium* ruled by an emperor. Egypt, despite the clever manipulations of the remarkable Cleopatra, was at last conquered for good and incorporated into the Roman empire by Augustus in 30 BC. The old Roman republic thus enters its death throes and expires, interred forever when Augustus Caesar is formally crowned emperor in 27 BC. From that date, the Roman Republic is no more; the old order has passed away to make way for the new. It is not without interest that the later Egyptians came to know Rome as *Remu*, a name associated with *Remi*, the Divine Fish, making Remu 'the Fish-City.' The Aries-Pisces Inter-Age Transition would have lasted 145 years, from 264 BC to 119 BC. Looked at another way, it can be seen as a process that began with the Roman revolutionary turmoils beginning 133 BC and ending 106 years later with the crowning of Augustus as emperor (27 BC). The final *dénouement* that culminates in the establishment of imperial Rome at the turn-of-the-Age comes 92 years after onset of the Age of Pisces.

Christendom, that would in time conquer most of the world, turned its back on Egypt, its vast knowledge, and above all its astronomical mythology. Though coming into being through Egypt and achieving global dominance in the Piscean Age, the Christian world paid no attention to its role in the Piscean dispensation and still does not. Informed and enlightened men like the Renaissance polymath Giordano Bruno were burned at the stake (1600) by the Papacy for, among other things, professing an admiration for and belief in the wide wisdom of ancient Egypt. However, the deep and venerable astro-mythic system of ancient Egypt, especially as related to the Piscean Age, did not die or disappear; it was preserved in what might seem to be an unlikely place—southeastern Mali among the Dogon.

The Dogon of Mali are among the most unusual, and fascinating, people of Africa. They live along the Bandiagara Cliffs of southeastern Mali, eking out an agricultural existence in the harsh scrub-land at the base of the Cliffs. They report that they originally came from the northeast, beginning their migrations into the Western Sudan 1,460 years ago (circa 545 AD). Some writers locate their original home in what is now Libya.[44] However, there are so many close similarities—amounting to clear identities—in their thought to that of ancient Egypt, it is impossible to look elsewhere other than the Nile Valley for their remoter origins. In fact, the present author proposes that they undertook their migration out of the Nile Valley on the occasion of the closing of the last functioning Egyptian temple, the Temple of Isis on the island of Philae, by the Roman Emperor Justinian in 540 AD. Undoubtedly, after the forcible closing of this temple, there were persecutions and proscriptions launched against the people of the region still loyal to Isis and the remaining relic of Egyptian religion. It is surmised that this closing and its attendant persecutions impelled the last great migration out of the Nile Valley, westward to what is now Mali toward the middle of the 6th century AD.

44 See Temple R, **The Sirius Mystery,** New York: St. Martin's Press, Inc., 1976, pp. 158-9.

In the Dogon system, *Amma* is the Creator who, like Amon-Ra, caused creation to be set in motion when he 'opened his eyes.' The connection between the Dogon *Amma* and the Egyptian *Amon* is further enhanced by noting that *amma* (Dg.) means 'to hold firmly' or 'to keep in place' while *amon* (Eg.) means 'to make firm' or 'establish permanently.' Moreover, there are four paired Primordial *Nommos*, eight in all, who correspond to the four paired Primal Neters of Egypt (8 in all), from which all that exists comes. One of these Nommos, *Ogo* the Fox, is the agent of all disorder (and also the turner of the earth's axis). Ogo is, therefore, the counterpart to the Egyptian Jackal who is Set/Anubis (in earlier times, Anubis was the son of Set). Moreover, we can see that Anubis was an aspect of Set from E.A.W. Budge who tells us that Set '... was incarnate in the so-called 'Set animal', a kind of hunting dog which became extinct in Egypt before the close of the dynastic period.'[45] As we have indicated earlier, dog, jackal, wolf, fox, and coyote are all co-types. Having said that, with the exception of Ogo the Fox, all other nommos are Fish-Beings. One of these, *Nommo Anagonno*, the Twin of Ogo, personifies the seeds and growing plants and will be sacrificed—killed by Ogo as Osiris was killed by Set—then resurrected to bring back order into *Amma's* creation. Beyond a shadow of a doubt, this Nommo Anagonno is none other than Osiris himself. Nommo Anagonno, the Fish-Being, is also the Image of Man and was separated from his penis at his sacrifice which was swallowed by a fish; similarly, Osiris at the time of his death and dismemberment was separated from his penis which was swallowed by a fish. But the Dogon mythic imagery is yet more striking: Nommo Anagonno is the sacrificed victim who will be resurrected; he is tied to the *kilena* tree standing up, fins outstretched, then attached to two branches extending at right angles from the tree. Nommo Angagonno is thus the Dogon Crucified Savior. As if that weren't enough, the Dogon say that the sacrificed Nommo, in order to 'reorganize the world' must suffer greatly in the course of being crucified.[46]

There is more that can be adduced to correlate the Dogon world-system to that of Egypt, but the above examples show clearly that not only do the Dogon

45 **Budge**, op. cit., p.207.

46 Griaule M and Dieterlen G, **Pale Fox**, translated by Stephen B. Infantino. Chino: The Continuum Foundation, 1986.

have an unmodified Osirian figure in their system, *but also a Christ-figure*, exactly like the one crucified in the Gospels.[47] They show in an irrefutable way that, astro-mythically, Jesus the Christ could only have been the re-manifested Osiris. Whoever and whatever else the man Yahushua Ben Pandera—whom later followers worshiped as *Jesus the Christ*—may have been, his story was/is locked inextricably into the cosmic astromythology of the ancient Nile Valley. What is more, Ogo, veritably the 'Master of Speech' and the 'Opener of the Way,' is none other than Wep-Wat/Anubis who (still) rules the pole. Unlike in Christianity, one finds in the Dogon world-system a more-or-less seamless inter-digitation of the current Polar astromythic archetype with the Zodiacal one; the Jackal and the Fish, cosmically speaking, conjoin in the Dogon system in a way undetectable in the world-dominating Christian system. Thus, if one really wants to study and understand the ethos of Piscean Age and that of the (polar) Jackal Age, it is to the Dogon system, as detailed in Marcel Griaule's and Germaine Dieterlen's **The Pale Fox**,[48] that one must refer. Official Christianity simply threw away (or buried) the keys to understanding its true mission, in heaven and on earth. Robert Temple, in **The Sirius Mystery**, reflecting on the impurity represented by Ogo, the Dogon Cosmic Fox, offers an interesting observation on Christianity that resonates with this assessment:

> The perversions of Christianity have always seemed to me to incorporate a perversion of the notion of 'sin' and the means by which 'sin' can be exploited as a means of temporal blackmail over other human beings. To rid ourselves of some impurity may be closer to what is needed…[49]

In this chapter we have attempted to outline the supra-historical dynamics of Nile Valley—indeed world—history linked to and dictated by definitive and measurable cosmic events. It is simply impossible to understand the subject otherwise. Nonetheless, the conventional historian of antiquity will refuse to

47 Cf. Temple, op. cit., p. 32 for another author who recognizes the explicit Christ parallels in the Dogon world-system.

48 Griaule M. and Dieterlen G, op. cit.

49 Temple, op. cit., p. 32.

consider the matter in this light. Such persons, therefore, remain fundamentally clueless concerning who the people of the ancient Nile Valley were and what they accomplished. Thus, they possess mountains of facts yet seem incapable of deriving any real knowledge from those facts. Because facts may be true without on that account leading to the truth, they are in mortal danger of making themselves irrelevant.

Chapter 3:

Historical Survey—The Old Kingdom (The Memphite Dynasties)

I. Prologue: The Scheme of Dynastic Chronology

The reader may well feel—perhaps with some justification—that the present author is unduly preoccupied with matters of ancient Egyptian chronology and its astro-mythic ethos. In the previous chapter, considerable space was devoted to the controversial and disavowed topic of the relation of the Precessional Great Years to remote Nile Valley history. In this Prologue, the dynastic or historical chronology of ancient Egypt—beginning with the Unification under Mēnēs—will be examined because the manner in which this chronology has been distorted constitutes one of the most serious travesties of Nile Valley historiography. Academic Egyptology lopped off nearly 1,200 years from the historical chronology of ancient Egypt without a shred of justification, akin to the effect created if historians of China had arbitrarily elected to commence the history of that multi-millenial civilization at the birth of Christ instead of 12 centuries earlier when it really began. In our present state of knowledge, an iron-clad, irrefutable chronology is not possible, but enough is known to make the 'received' short chronology (SC) of academic Egyptology, commencing dynastic history at around 3,200/3,100 BC, completely untenable.

Up until 1905, most Egyptologists—taking their cues from the available fragments of Manetho's **History**—favored what is now known as the long chronology (LC) with dynastic launch dates from the time of Mēnēs varying from 4,300 BC to 5,800 BC. Manetho, whose Egyptian name seems to have been *Maā-en-Tehuti* ('gift of Thoth'), was a native Egyptian priest of Rā who flourished during the reign of Ptolemy II of the Macedonian Dynasty. At Ptolemy's request, he compiled in Greek a complete history of the country from its beginnings, **The History of Egypt**, about 241 BC. Manetho was born in Sebennytus, in the eastern Delta, and may have learned Greek at an early age. Manetho is remarkable for being completely fluent in reading, writing, and speaking Greek at a time when the vast majority of Egyptians—whether priest or peasant—held themselves aloof from the Graeco-Macedonian rulers of Egypt. Though little is known of Manetho's life, he seems to have risen to the position of high priest in the Temple of Rā at Heliopolis and was therefore learned in the ancient lore of Egypt. He would serve as an invaluable link between the Ptolemies and their Egyptian subjects, and his other great achievement—at least from the point of view of the Ptolemies—was to render indispensable service consolidating the position of the composite deity *Serapis* into the religious life of the country. Serapis, whose worship had been organized even before Manetho was born, was a deity combining the attributes of Osiris, Apis, and Hades (Pluto), consciously designed to appeal to the religious sensibilities of both Greek and Egyptian. Aided by Manetho, Ptolemy II seemed to have more or less successfully achieved this aim.

Relatively soon after the appearance of Manetho's **History**, an ***Epitome,*** or summary of the book, was produced and it is this ***Epitome***, rather than the **History** itself, that would survive and provide the basis for the later summaries of Manetho's work appearing in Christian times. The most important of what remains of Manetho's **History** is to be found in the works of three authors, Josephus (circa 75 AD), the Libyan Julius Africanus (circa 217 AD), and Eusebius (circa 326 AD). The complete dynastic chronology of the ***Epitome*** was preserved mainly in the writings of Africanus and Eusebius and the consensus is that Africanus is the one who most accurately preserved the original ***Epitome*** of Manetho's **History.**[1] Nonetheless, it is clear that corruptions and deviations crept into the surviving extracts, especially since the authors of the Christian era were primarily interested in harmonizing Manetho's chronology with that

1 Cf. **Manetho**, translated by W.G. Waddell, Cambridge: Harvard University Press, (1940), 1980, pp. xvi-xvii.

of the Bible. Not only that, but the List of Africanus and that of Eusebius diverged considerably in the stated number of kings and the lengths of their reigns. Moreover, though Manetho used Greek equivalents of Egyptian names for the kings in the dynastic list, many of these names were hopelessly garbled by the later transmitters of the ***Epitome***. Taken together, these corruptions compelled a 20th century writer to say,

> ...it is extremely difficult to reach certainty in regard to what is authentic Manetho and what is spurious or corrupt.[2]

Nonetheless, Wallis Budge had this to say concerning Manetho,

> We have no right to blame Manetho for the mistakes which his editors and copyists made, and in considering his list the wonder is that the version of Julius Africanus agrees as closely as it does with the monumental evidence. The discrepancies in the numbers are due chiefly to the misreading by the scribes of the Greek letters which stood for figures...[3]

In spite of these caveats, Manetho has, from nearly 23 centuries back, imposed his scheme of Egyptian dynastic chronology on all modern Egyptological dynastic chronology. It has been said that he was the one who actually invented the word *dynasty.* His basic structure—organizing Egyptian dynastic history into 30 dynasties (some add the last nine-year Persian dynasty to the list to give 31)—is the scaffold upon which is constructed all current Egyptian historiography. Most of his named pharaohs have been identified from other sources as have many of their regnal years. All agree that Manetho had at his disposal all the available annals of ancient Egypt—a people known everywhere for their diligence in recording the events of their history—and therefore was uniquely qualified to compose an authentic history of Egypt for a non-Egyptian readership. The problem comes when Manetho's stated lengths

2 Waddell, op. cit., p. xvii.

3 **Budge** EAW, **A History of Egypt**, volume 1, Oosterhout N.B. The Netherlands: Anthropological Publications, (1902)1968, p. 146.

of reigns and dynasties, as given by Africanus, are compiled and added up: Manetho's chronology, from the 1st Dynasty of Mēnēs to the end of the Persian Dynasty of Darius (332 BC), gives a total length of Egyptian history of 5,500 years. Since 1905, Egyptologists have rejected this time span categorically.

Several 19th century Egyptologists—most notably William Flinders Petrie—accepted the Manethonian chronology unrevised, pushing back the beginnings of dynastic Egyptian history to 5,800 BC. Others, like Heinrich Brugsch and E.A. Wallis Budge, modified this date down to 4,400 BC. There were probably good reasons for down-dating the 1st Dynasty launch date to this extent, given the definite corruptions that had crept into the extant sources from the original ***Epitome*** of Manetho's **History**, and other considerations that had to do with the role of the Sothic or Sirian Period of 1,460 years in the determination of Egyptian historical and dynastic dates. There is a known Sothic date in Egyptian history of 4,241 BC—which Breasted accepts as the date for the introduction of the calendar[4]—that many Egyptologists have attempted to argue out of Egyptian chronology, though not convincingly. The Sothic date previous to 4,241 BC–5,701 BC—is close to the date of 5,800 BC imposed by Manetho's chronology. It is to be wondered if in the later versions of the ***Epitome*** of his **History** that perhaps one additional, unwarranted period of 1,460 years was interpolated into the basic chronology in some as yet indefinable manner.

After 1905, Eduard Meyer first, and James Henry Breasted afterward, inaugurated the process of further down-dating the advent of the 1st Dynasty. Though unable to discard Manetho, they turned to the monuments and five ancient Egyptian king lists, only two of which were of any importance for reconstructing the ancient chronology: (1) the Turin Papyrus, aka the Turin Canon, and (2) the Palermo Stone. Also, they relied heavily on seemingly known and definite Sothic dates indicated in Egyptian annals. Meyer and Breasted felt justified in conflating numerous reigns mentioned by Manetho (and corroborated by the documentary and monumental sources) because there were time spans—most particularly during the Intermediate Periods (Chronological Gaps)—when very little historical information survived and it

4 Cf. Breasted JH, **A History of Egypt**, New York: Charles Scribner's Sons, (1909)1937, p. 21.

was evident that more than one king must have ruled at the same time. Many of the reigns in these Periods were ephemeral and short-lived and in any case, next to no records were transmitted to posterity from those eras of upheaval. Not even Manetho had good data from those strange and troubling times: there are spans of centuries when the ***Epitome*** (Africanus) gives the total number of reigning kings but without their names. In fact, Manetho lists 561 kings for the entire dynastic period but only gives the names of 200, meaning that 361 regnal names were unknown to him, at least by the testimony of the ***Epitome*** that comes down to us from Africanus. That means, if Africanus is accurate on this point, that the names of 64% of the historical kings of Egypt were not even known. Whether this situation represented the true state of Manetho's knowledge or was the outcome of faulty copying cannot be determined. Whatever the case, Meyer, after a detailed study of the available evidence, felt entitled to propose a revised date of 3,400 BC for the 1st Dynasty and, later, Breasted accepted that date, included it in his **A History of Egypt**, and therefore gave credibility to it. Though Meyer's exhaustive work on establishing the chronology of Egyptian history was hailed and essentially followed, the archaeological writer Wilbur Devereaux Jones was moved to observe:

> This writer has never read a satisfactory explanation of exactly how Meyer's system worked. Meyer's own descriptions of it were brief.[5]

If one substituted the word 'arbitrary' for 'brief' in the above quotation, it might come closer to the mark. Notwithstanding, later Egyptologists, basing their calculations on Meyer's system and following Breasted's lead, would continue the process of down-dating, first to 3,200 BC then to 3,100 BC, the date that today is routinely given for the commencement of Egyptian dynastic history, as if it were a rock-solid, unarguable launch date for that history. It is clear, after examining Manetho's chronology preserved by Africanus that some serious amending of the surviving chronology was in order. There were too many unknown and unnamed kings on the list and it seems certain that there were a significant number of concurrent reigns. Thus, the length of many reigns

5 Jones WD, **Venus and Sothis**, Chicago: Nelson Hall, 1982, p.78.

cannot be considered additive for the purposes of determining accurately the span of Egyptian dynastic history. The issue, then, is not the down-dating of Manetho's chronology from 5,800 BC *per se*, it is the extremes to which Meyer and Breasted went shaving off 2,400 years, when 1,500–1,600 years would have been far more accurately allowable.

The Turin Canon and the Palermo Stone have only limited utility in reconstructing dynastic chronology because the extant artifacts are but partial remnants of the originals. Had they been intact, they would have in all likelihood provided the definitive and irrefutable documentation of Egyptian dynastic history from the 1st Dynasty to the 19th. As it was, more than half of each chronology—one inscribed on papyrus and the other on stone—was missing. Even so conventional and conventionally respected an Egyptologist as Sir Alan Gardiner was constrained to write:

> We clutch at a straw…when we assume that the Turin Canon is to be implicitly trusted.[6]

The Turin Papyrus had been obtained early in the 19th century by the King of Sardinia who donated it to the Turin Museum in 1818 but failed to have it properly packed. When it arrived at its destination, it had disintegrated into hundreds of bits of papyrus. The attempt eight years later to reconstruct the original from these fragments was botched, and though the Turin Papyrus has supplied valuable information to chronologists—it provides names of pharaohs that are entirely missing from Manetho's ***Epitome***, for example—it has never been able to serve as the definitive source document for dynastic questions, as the above quote from Gardiner makes clear. Walter Emery echoes this assessment when he writes, 'Valuable as it is, the Turin Papyrus is a tragedy, for more than half its value has been lost by careless treatment.'[7] However, taking into account the Turin Canon's king-names through the 19th Dynasty, Samuel Birch calculated that there were 330 kings who ruled Egypt during the dynastic span of her unified history, the same total of Egyptian kings given by

---

6 Gardiner A, **Egypt of the Pharaohs**, New York: Oxford University Press, (1961)1978, p. 42.
7 Emery WB, **Archaic Egypt**, New York: Penguin Books, (1961)1984, p. 22.

Herodotus. It is generally assumed that 330 is close to the actual number of legitimate pharaohs who ruled Egypt.

Concerning the Palermo Stone, Emery says,

> ...the so-called Palermo Stone which...represents another tragedy for archaeological research. Only five small fragments of a great stone slab...are in our hands and no record remains which will give a clue to where these pieces were found.[8]

The Palermo Stone, when intact, probably provided the name of every king from the 1st Dynasty to the 5th, along with the length and the chief events of his reign. Like the similarly mangled Turin Papyrus, the Palermo Stone has served as an invaluable aid but also an exasperating enigma for the reconstruction of the earliest eras of Egyptian history. Intact, its historical authority would have been unimpeachable because it is the only chronological artifact ever found that was produced so early in Egyptian history and therefore so close to its dynastic beginnings. As it is, the Palermo Stone, like the Turin Canon, can only function as an adjunct in the study of the ancient chronology.

After Meyer and Breasted proposed their changes in the dynastic chronology, Egyptologists almost universally accepted them without argument, except to shave off a few more centuries. Petrie was one, however, who never 'fell in line' with his colleagues vis-à-vis the short chronology though by the end of his life (d. 1941), he had revised his proposed First Dynasty date down to 4,326 BC, more in line with that of Brugsch and Budge (4,400 BC). Among other things, Petrie, on the basis of his chronology, seems to have taken issue with what he considered the excessive conflation of reigns and regnal years employed by Breasted's chronology out of the admittedly shadowy Intermediate Periods. All that being said, it is undeniable that the Sothic Cycle is essential for arriving closer to a more accurate estimate of dynastic chronology, and no authority trying to reconstruct the truest possible picture of Egyptian chronology can dispense with it. In this connection, E. A. Wallis Budge was alone in his willingness to cite the authority of astronomer Norman Lockyer, author

8 Emery, ibid.

of **Dawn of Astronomy**, when he asserted that the rising of Sirius (Sothis) occurred on the 27th of Epiphi in 3,192 BC in the reign of Pharaoh Pepi-Meri-Rā, one of the kings of the Sixth Dynasty.[9] Now the Sixth Dynasty was an Old Kingdom dynasty and the length given by Manetho (Africanus) for the duration of the Old Kingdom—1,291 years—is fairly well-corroborated by the known king lists and monuments. Thus adding 1,291 years to 3,192 BC gives a date of 4,483 BC for the beginning of the Old Kingdom. If we take the more conservative modern estimate for the duration of the Old Kingdom of 1,000 years, that still takes us back to 4,192 BC. The actual commencement of the Sothic Cycle of that era would have begun approximately 50 years earlier in 4,241 BC. However, if the true length of Old Kingdom is somewhere between Manetho's figure of 1,291 years and the modern estimate of 1,000 years for say a length of 1,145 years, then we could legitimately anchor the unification date and the launch of the 1st Dynasty at around 4,337 BC. In a later section of this work (see section on Khufu), we will discuss reasons why the actual 1st Dynasty onset date is probably closer to 4,263 B.C., 22 years before the onset of the new Sothic Cycle in 4,241 B.C. But it can be said that the combination of evidence adduced from Lockyer, who studied and accurately determined the astronomical orientations of all the major temples in Egypt, and the Sothic or Sirian Cycle are thus indispensable aids in arriving at a more definite chronology, one that pushes the beginning of Egyptian dynastic history back into the late 5th millenium BC.

The chronology favored by Brugsh, Budge, and Petrie is called the Long Chronology (LC); that of Meyer, Breasted, and nearly all other 20th century Egyptologists, the Short Chronology (SC). The LC's 1st dynasty launch date is said to have occurred sometime between 4,400 and 4,300 BC; the SC's dynastic launch date is pinpointed to sometime between 3,400 and 3,200/3,100 BC. The present author favors a Long Chronology date of 4,263 BC, the reasons for which will be detailed in the later discussion of the orientation of the Great Pyramid. This LC date is situated 177 years after the advent of the Age of Taurus in 4,435 BC and precedes the Sothic Calendar date of 4,241 BC by just 17 years. Though orthodox Egyptologists stoutly resist it, ancient

9 Cf. **Budge**, op. cit., pp. 148-9

Egyptian history followed celestial cycles. Until that truth is accepted, most of the important elements of that history will remain terminally obscure to conventional historians. Having said that, let us admit that any scheme of ancient Egyptian chronology will always be controversial and obscure until a definitive, intact ancient king list, in papyrus or stone, is discovered that puts to rest all speculation. Otherwise, as Budge said, no exact date can be assigned to any Egyptian king prior to the 26th Dynasty (664 or 660 BC), though by the beginning of the 18th Dynasty (c. 1,580 BC), a maximum of 50 years of error is tenable.[10]

II. **Old Kingdom I** (4,263 BC–3,698 BC): **The Archaic Period, Dynasties 1–2**

Herodotus spoke truly when he said that Egypt is 'the gift of the river.'[11] The annual flood, caused by the rains in the Ethiopian highlands that wash into the Blue Nile, bring tons of mud and silt down the Nile, that is to say northward, depositing them on the banks of Egypt and continually building up the Delta[12]. The narrow, 500-mile strip of Egypt from the First Cataract (Syene/Aswan) to Memphis, fans out into the Delta for another 100 miles to the Mediterranean coast. For many millenia the Delta has been a green, well-watered, fertile fan of land that made Egypt the breadbasket of the ancient world. But the green, habitable stretch of Upper Egypt, south of the Delta and running 500 miles north to the Delta from Syene, never spanning more than 12 miles wide, is also watered by the annual flood making it as fertile a property as can be found anywhere in the world. Without the Nile and its flood there would have been no Egypt. For good reason, the Nile was deified by the people who depended so completely on it and called by them *Hapy*, also the name of the sacred bull that embodied the fertility of the Nile. In god-form, Hapy is often shown tying

10 **Budge**, op. cit., p. 161.

11 Herodotus, **The Histories**, New York: Penguin Books, (1954), 1972, p. 131.

12 Or it did until the Aswan High Dam was built. Since 1974, the annual mud and silt from the flood backs up behind the dam and for the first time in its history, Egypt depends on chemical fertilizers for its agricultural production. Moreover, the Mediterranean Sea now is steadily encroaching on Egypt's northern coast.

together the symbols of Upper and Lower Egypt, the lotus and papyrus, indicative of his unifying mission and power in the *Two Lands*. It is the Greek mythographer and poet Hesiod who, about 750 BC, first uses the word *Neilos* as the name for the river, coming down to us as *Nile*. The Nile was the source

Two images of the Nile God Hapy unifying Upper (lotus) and Lower Egypt (papyrus)

of all sustenance for Egyptians but also an indispensable highway, enabling them to consolidate national unity and, not inconsequentially, travel southward into inner Africa and northward to the Mediterranean and Western Asia for the purposes of trade, diplomacy, and, at various times, conquest.

At the beginning of the dynastic period of Egyptian history, we find separate 'twin' kingdoms of consolidated petty chiefdoms—one in the Delta (Lower Egypt) and the other in the stretch of country from Memphis to the 1st cataract[13] known as Upper Egypt—in place just prior to the beginning of the Old Kingdom. Following the chronology of the Precession, the twin kingdoms, i.e., *Taui*, the 'Two Lands,' would have come into existence sometime between 6500–6000 BC, i.e., at the celestial beginning of the 'Age of the Twins' (Gemini). Walter Emery, commenting on the political condition of Egypt in the early Unification period, asserts:

13 By the convention of modern scholars, looking from north southward, the northernmost cataract is called the 'first' cataract. In truth, since the Nile flows from south to north and the ancient Egyptians considered the south direction to be 'up' or 'first', what is now called the first cataract is actually the sixth cataract; what is now called the 'sixth' cataract is actually the first.

> ...it was a dual monarchy and, so soon after the unification, the individuality of two states of the North and South was more marked than in later times. In fact there appear to have been two separate administrations united only under the throne.[14]

Though national unity was fully consolidated in later times, Egyptians called their country the Two Lands down to the end of its sovereign history.

At all times, the western Delta felt the influence of the *Lebu* (Libyans); after the beginning of dynastic history, the Eastern Delta was susceptible to incursions from Western Asia. Lower Egypt's symbols were the bee, the red crown, and the papyrus reed; its pre-dynastic capital was *Buto* whose patron goddess took the form of a cobra. The patron deity of the whole realm of Lower Egypt was *Horus*, who, nonetheless, was said to have come from the south with followers called the *Mesniu* or 'blacksmiths.' After the beginning of the dynastic period, Horus came to be seen as the ruler of the South or Upper Egypt. Upper Egypt, whose southern quarter took the name *Ta-Seti* from the older Nubian kingdom of the same name, was always considered the true heartland of Egypt, always more distinctively Egyptian than Lower Egypt. Alan Gardiner observed,

> Throughout the best part of Egyptian history the Delta is silent.[15]

Moreover, the northern Nubian kingdom of Ta-Seti that pre-existed the dynastic period may have been the southern one of the Twin Kingdoms that constituted the 'Two Lands,' a name retained after the era of unification that created the Kingdom of *Kemit*, 'the Black Land.' Several Old Kingdom pharaohs, though ruling both Lands, kept only the title 'King of Upper Egypt.' Upper Egypt's symbols were the lily or lotus and the white crown. That of Lower Egypt were the papyrus and the red crown. The pre-dynastic capital of Upper Egypt was *Nekheb* whose patron goddess took the form of a vulture. The patron deity of the whole realm of pre-dynastic Upper Egypt was *Set* but in

14 Emery, op. cit., p. 105.

15 Gardiner A, **Egypt of the Pharaohs**, London: Oxford University Press, 1961, p. 103.

dynastic times, he was gradually supplanted by Horus. Set and Horus switched places: Set became the ruler of Lower Egypt and Horus of Upper Egypt. Set's prestige had declined and Horus's had risen, hence the switch.

Red Crown (Lower Egypt) left
White Crown (Upper Egypt) right

A. Unification of the Two Lands

By the long chronology, unification took place 4,263 BC; by the short chronology 3,100 BC. Though virtually all contemporary Egyptologists favor the short chronology, as has been argued earlier in this work, the conventional 3,100 BC date for the beginning of the dynastic era is far too low. Seven names of pre-dynastic kings survive and all these were from Lower Egypt; we do not know the names of the Ta-Seti pharaohs or any of the other known kings who ruled prior to the 1st Dynasty. For the purposes of this narrative, the author will only discuss, dynasty by dynasty, those pharaohs and national personages that were of some historical consequence. Where there are two pharaonic names listed, the second one in italics will be the Greek form of the name as given by Manetho. Below, is a list of pharaohs from the first two dynasties who initially ruled from *Thinis*:

Dynasty I (4,307–4,047 BC)	**Dynasty II** (4,047–3,745 BC)
Narmer	Hetepsekemwy
Aha-Mena	Reneb
Djer	Nutjeren
Wadjit	Weneg
Den	Sened
Anedjib	Peribsen
Semerkhet	Sekhemib
Ka`a	Khasekhem
	Khasekhemwy

Narmer [*Mēnēs*?] (4,308–4,268 BC: Period of 'Proto-Unification')

Proto-Dynastic Narmer Palette

Nar-mer, 'the Scorpion,' made the greatest strides toward unification prior to *Aha-Mena* or *Mēnēs*. In fact, some think that Narmer and Mēnēs are the same person and that Aha followed as the second king of the dynasty.[16] Petrie introduces the name of another king prior to Mēnēs by the name of *Sma* who is said to have ruled for 17 years between Narmer and Mēnēs but his name is not

16 The term *per-āa* or *pharaoh*, meaning 'great house,' as the title for Egypt's king did not come into common usage until sometime after the early dynasties.

on any of the king lists and is not known to Manetho. He is only known from inscriptions on a number of recovered vases. For this reason, most authorities pose Narmer as the ruler during the last period of proto-unification leading up to the accession of Mēnēs. Greater centralization of the Two Lands had been in progress for some centuries prior to formal political unification, and Mēnēs is the pharaoh to whom tradition and the records accord the achievement of finally unifying the Two Lands into one kingdom. Narmer reigned for 50 years.

Aha-Mena or *Mēnēs* (4,268–4206 BC: Actual Unification)

Aha-Mena—Unifier of Ancient Egypt

Mēnēs did more than just usher in a 4,000-year period of unparalleled national unity and sovereignty for Egypt; with him is inaugurated the classic model of Egyptian divine kingship, one rooted deeply in the African cultural matrix and whose fundamental legitimacy is never challenged in 40 centuries of dynastic history. In his classic study of Egyptian kingship,[17] Henri Frankfort cogently evokes the role of the king as a balancer of opposites:

> That form was the dual monarchy, the kingship of Upper and the kingship of Lower Egypt united in the single person of the ruler. This extraordinary

17 Frankfort H, **Kingship and the Gods**, Chicago: University of Chicago Press, (1948)1978.

> conception expressed in political form the deeply rooted Egyptian tendency to understand the world in dualistic terms as a series of pairs of contrasts balanced in unchanging equilibrium.[18]

Thus for the Egyptian, 'a totality comprises opposites.' Especially in the early Old Kingdom, we find the opposite Powers of Horus and Set embodied in the person of the single ruler:

> This embodiment of the two gods [Horus and Set] in the person of Pharaoh is another instance of the peculiar dualism that expresses a totality as an equilibrium of opposites. In later times, when the titulary of the king had become standardized, it is no longer found…[19]

But the king also becomes the embodiment of Osiris, the dying god-king resurrected to become Judge and Lord of the Dead who thus expresses the transcendence of the life energy. The living pharaoh therefore assumes the powers and potency of his kingly forebears, and through the earthly lenses of the newly-realized kingship, Horus and Osiris, fuse. Horus becomes the living Osiris, and Osiris the Horus resurrected and renewed. This new divine scheme of royalty will mean, as mentioned in earlier pages, that the complementary twinship of Horus and Set will fade from view—though never fully disappear—to be supplanted by the Father-Son partnership of Osiris and Horus.

Horus Rising from Osiris at the Command of Atum

18 Ibid., p.19.
19 Ibid., p. 21.

The pharaoh is the focal point for both sets of dynamics. Henri Frankfort insisted that the antecedents of the Egyptian divine kingship could only be sought in Africa; all of the elements, characteristics, and values that infused the mental and cultural construct of 'pharaoh-as-god' are essentially African in character. Thus, contemporary societies of the Baganda, Nuer, Shilluk, and Dinka—to name but a few—preserve divine kingship features that fully illuminate the role and function of this office in ancient Egypt. Moreover, Frankfort categorically rejects the idea that these examples of divine kingship flowed outward into Africa from Egypt; rather, they derive from a common cultural and religious African foundation that is traceable back before the advent of dynastic Egypt. Franfort simply says 'It seems that Pharaonic civilization arose upon this Northeast African Hamitic substratum.'[20]

Though the pharaoh, as divine king, is theoretically the absolute ruler of his land and people—ancient Egyptians used to refer to themselves as 'pharaoh's cattle'[21]—he, like everyone, is subject to the rule of *ma'āt*, i.e., the ideal of harmonious balance and justice in all actions. Pharaoh must live according to ma'āt and strive at all times to uphold it throughout the Two Lands. In fact,

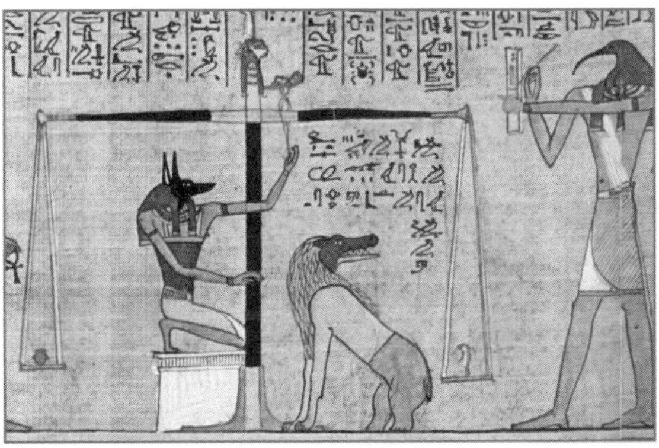

Ma-āt on Center of Balance Beam during the Weighing of the Heart

Goddess Ma-āt wearing the Feather of Truth

20 Ibid., p. 16.

21 In the same way Christians might call themselves 'the Lord's sheep.'

Ma'āt was a goddess, and in this connection had to be worshiped. That the pharaohs of Egypt adhered with remarkable consistency to this ideal may be indicated in the singular fact that in all of its 4,000-year history, there was never a popular uprising against the king. In the context of palace politics, there were regicides, usurpations, intrigues, and internecine wars from time to time—even these, though real, seemed fewer compared to the histories of other nations[22]—but not a single popular revolution against the established order *per se*. In the latter periods of Egyptian history, there are records of famine-induced peasant riots and revolts by disgruntled soldiers, but none of these disorders ever threatened the person of pharaoh himself or pharaonic government. The Egyptians of old could not/would not contemplate an Egypt without pharaoh.

Each pharaoh possessed three names, a circumstance that often created confusion among the later historians of Egypt. The first and most prominent was the 'Horus name,' always identifiable by the figure of a hawk sitting atop the rectangular frame known as the *serekh*[23] containing the name. In two instances in the 2nd Dynasty, there were two serekhs side-by-side, one containing the Horus name and the other the Set name. The second name category was the *nebti*, i.e., the 'Two Ladies', name. The nebti were the vulture goddess Nekhebit of Upper Egypt and the cobra goddess of Wadjet of Lower Egypt which, when linked together over the king's nebti name, signified the unity of the Two Lands. Another name indicating the unity of the Two Lands was the *nesu-bit* name, the third of the pharaonic names, which was represented by the pairing of the sedge plant, representing Upper Egypt, with the wasp, representing Lower Egypt, over the name. The confusion has come from the custom of using mainly the Horus names on the monuments but then, beginning with the New Kingdom, the nebti and nesu-bit names on the king lists. Manetho seems to have Grecianized either the nebti or the nesu-bit names for his chronological list and it isn't always clear which king is which by comparison to the lists in the native language.

---

22 Compare, for example, the imperial histories of Assyria, Persia, and Rome.

23 In Egyptian hieroglyphs, a **serekh** is a rectangular enclosure representing the gated façade of a palace surmounted by (usually) the Horus falcon, indicating that the text enclosed is a royal name. The serekh was the earliest convention used to set apart the royal name in Egypt, predating the later and better known cartouche by four dynasties and five to seven hundred years. ---*Wikipedia*

The original capital of Mēnēs and his immediate successors was Thinis in Upper Egypt, but during the reign of Mēnēs, the shift of the royal capital to Memphis, the City of Ptah and Apis (the Bull), had begun. As we have seen, the dynastic period began early in the era dominated by the Celestial Bull (Taurus) which began to rise heliacally[24] at the vernal equinox 4,435 BC. Mēnēs' immediate predecessors may have made inroads into northern Nubia and been connected to the line of Ta-Seti. Mēnēs assumed the title *Horus*, making him (and all subsequent pharaohs) the human avatar of the divine son of Isis and Osiris. Despite this identification with Horus, at least two pharaohs of the early Old Kingdom retained their *Set* names with their Horus names, emblematic of the equality and twinship of Horus and Set in force during the preceding Age of the Twins (Gemini). Mēnēs combined the crowns of Upper and Lower Egypt, white and red, into one and also combined the two symbolic figures, the vulture of Upper Egypt and the cobra of Lower Egypt, into the double symbol of royalty.

Vulture—Upper Egypt—and Cobra
Lower Egypt on the Crown of Pharaoh

Mēnēs was viewed with unflagging reverence by all Egyptians for the 43 millenia that followed dynastic unification. Both Herodotus (5th century BC) and Manetho (3rd century BC) report that he caused the course of the Nile to be altered in order for the city of Memphis to be built. He apparently conducted military campaigns into Nubia, at the time still known as Ta-Seti. These campaigns might be considered 'mopping up' exercises against the pre-

24 The word 'heliacally' means "before the sun".

unification Nubian kingdom of Ta-Seti whose reach had extended northward into what became 'corporate' Egypt as far as Edfu. Thus we find that the well-documented Egyptian preoccupation with Nubia was active from the beginning of its formal history and never abated. It is worth pointing out again that the land that is today referred to as Nubia was not known by that name until Roman times, the name clearly deriving from the Egyptian word *nub* meaning 'gold'. However that may be, nearly one-fifth of Egyptian national territory was considered to be Nubia. Thus the relationship between Egypt and Nubia finds an analogy in modern times in the relationship between Germany and Austria or England and Wales. Especially in the south, Egypt was as much Nubian as Egyptian, and in much later times, peoples like the Greeks and Romans frequently made no distinction between them. Mēnēs is said to have reigned 62 years and was always considered by posterity to be one of the greatest rulers that Egypt ever had.

The older Egyptologists liked to insist that Mēnēs and his immediate forbears were members of a 'New Race'—Walter Emery even used the term 'Master Race'—that conquered the indigenous people of Egypt and Nubia and ushered in pharaonic civilization. Yet they found it impossible to ascertain with any certainty from where this supposed New Race originated. A few, like the Aryanist Heinrich Brugsch, assumed that they were Asiatics but could adduce little substantive evidence to support this assertion. In the annals, the 'New Race' unifiers were referred to as the 'Followers of Horus,' and because Horus was the patron deity of the Delta in the north, that is, Lower Egypt, it emboldened Brugsch and others to assign an Asiatic origin to them. The Ta-Seti finds studied, analyzed, and described by Bruce Williams in 1980—and remarked on above[25]—show instead that the antecedents of pharaonic civilization are to be found instead in the Nubian south. The Ta-Seti pharaohs, judging from the artifacts recovered from Qustul, were also Followers of Horus. Though Horus may have been the divine patron of Lower Egypt in the north during the era of the Two Lands, his origins, too, must be sought in the south.

All of the major deities of the Egyptian pantheon were well-entrenched by the time of unification. Their names and/or symbols are all in evidence from

25 See Chapter 1.

the very beginning, meaning that their worship could really be traceable to the pre-dynastic era. The connection of the pharaohs to Horus from the earliest times has been mentioned. Moreover, Mēnēs' queen was *Nit-hotep* ('Neith is at peace') by name, showing that this goddess of weaving from Sais in the Delta, was already well-established by the time of unification. It is also noteworthy that all of the Old Kingdom pharaohs beginning with Mēnēs were buried at Abydos in Upper Egypt. Abydos was originally the sacred site of *Khenti-amenti*, a jackal god, a form of *Anubis*, whose name means 'chief of the westerners,' i.e., 'chief of the dead.' Later, Anubis/Khenti-amenti ceded his place at Abydos to Osiris but became well-ensconced within the Osirian dispensation. Abydos became the holy city of Osiris and even after the mortal remains of Egyptian pharaohs ceased to be buried there, every one of them had a cenotaph[26] installed at Abydos. Horus, who in short order would assume his primary role as the son and heir of Osiris, was incarnated on earth as the living pharaoh; Osiris became the embodiment of the pharaoh resurrected after death. To the end of their history, Egyptians venerated to the point of worship their dead kings who were considered to affect events on earth long after they departed life. Living kings consulted the spirits of their deceased predecessors in policy matters as readily as they did the gods. They went further: they tapped into the imperishable energetic power of these deceased (and resurrected) kings whenever the country was in peril. In the first two dynasties, most of the kings' tombs were surrounded in orderly fashion by the graves of household family members, retainers, and servants. Walter Emery assumed that these persons were sacrificed at the time of the kings' death to accompany and serve them in the next world. Though there is some equivocal evidence that suggests that the practice of human sacrifice was not unknown in Egypt, at least until the end of the Middle Kingdom, it was never practiced on a large scale. In any case, persons sacrificed to accompany the king would have been buried with him, not in their own graves. Members of the king's household desired to be near him in death but they were not sacrificed upon his death on that account. Such evidence of possible human sacrifice as exists applies to scenes involving war captives.

26 A cenotaph is a memorial plaque or stele installed for a deceased person whose remains are buried elsewhere.

Djer/Zer or *Athōthis* (4206 BC–4149 BC)

The second king of the First Dynasty is named *Zer* or *Djer*, called *Athothis* by Manetho, and is as interesting a figure as his father and predecessor, Mēnēs. He was a physician and an author of a textbook of anatomy according to Manetho, and later Egyptians considered him the earthly avatar of Osiris himself. Thus, his tomb became the object of pilgrimage by the pious. Zer's successor, *Meri-Nit* ('beloved of Neith'), has caused some controversy among Egyptologists because it appears that this ruler was actually a queen. Emery says of her:

> ...alone among the royal ladies of the dynasty Meryet-nit is the only one to have great monuments both at Abydos and Sakkara adjacent to the kings suggest[ing] that she was more than a consort, but may have been a reigning monarch.[27]

She would therefore be the first woman known to history to have ruled Egypt as a sovereign monarch and the first identifiable female monarch known anywhere. She was one of the several 'Neith-queens' so prominent in the Old Kingdom, testifying to the importance of Neith in the religious observances of that period.

Den or *Usaphais* (4,095 BC–4,075 BC)

The next important pharoah was *Den* the 5th pharaoh of the 1st Dynasty. On an ebony tablet that has been recovered, this king is depicted as dancing before the god Osiris in an act of worship. His reign is significant for a number of important cultural developments, including the composing of some of the early portions of the so called **Book of the Dead**, more correctly called, the **Book of the Coming Forth by Day**, a compilation of the all-important Osirian funerary ritual. Also, certain medical textbooks in their original form, e.g., **The Ebers Papyrus**, are also said to date from this period. Den's reign was also noted for a certain 'precocious' architectural development; his tomb boasted a 78-foot stairwell

27 Emery, op. cit., p. 66.

paved with granite, a stone which did not come into widespread building use for another three centuries. The outstanding non-royal personage of the time was the chancellor or vizier Hemaka, whose name is engraved on numerous seals. The reign of Den is also notable for a successful military campaign into Western Asia, reportedly bringing back a cohort of female prisoners who were added to his harem.[28] His prime minister *Hemaka's* rich funerary remains marked him as a man of importance. Den's tomb at Abydos shows evidence of the first known architectural construction built in stone. There is a discrepancy in the reported length of Den's reign. Manetho records the reign as having lasted 20 years but Grimal insists that it endured for fifty years, a divergence not easily explained.[29] Petrie says there were two Dens, one sur-named *Merneit* and the other *Setui*.[30] To Grimal, *Merneit* was actually the name of Den's wife and so the two Dens can be assumed to be the same person. When the two apparently separate Den-reigns are fused together, a longer period of 43 years is obtained, still not quite as long as the 50 years ascribed by Grimal but more than the 20 or so years seen in the Manetho List (Africanus).

In Den's reign, Egyptian military power is established further afield as is seen with four fortresses in the frontier regions. Scientific and intellectual activities of a sophisticated order are evident from the Berlin and Ebers Medical Papyri whose originals are traced to the period under Den's kingship. Additionally, chapters of the **Book of the Coming Forth By Day** seem to derive from the period. Clearly, Den was one of Egypt's most able early pharaohs.

Second Dynasty (4,005 BC–3,703 BC)

Bezau or *Boethos* (4,005 BC–3,967 BC)

After Den, three more pharaohs ruled to the end of the 1st Dynasty. There seems to have been a weakening of the kingly line among the last three First Dynasty pharaohs since Manetho reports a definite increase in corruption at the highest

28 Grimal N, **A History of Ancient Egypt**, translated by Ian Shaw, Cambridge (USA): Blackwell, 1988; 1992, p. 52.

29 Ibid., p. 53.

30 Petrie, op. cit., pp. 19-20.

levels of government which may have led to a certain political instability. Be that as it may, a more vigorous king ascended the throne, *Hetepsekhemui* or *Bezau* by name, inaugurating the Second Dynasty. Though Manetho begins the Second Dynasty with this pharaoh, this lineage does not seem too distinct from that of the First Dynasty. Bezau reigned 38 years but his reign is marked by an earthquake at Bubastis in the Delta that caused widespread death and destruction.

Raneb or *Kaiechos* (3,967 BC–3,928 BC)

Bezau was succeeded by *Raneb*, also called *Raneb-Kakau*, who reigned 39 years and who is credited by Manetho with introducing the worship of the Apis Bull at Memphis (sacred to Ptah) and the Mnevis Bull at Heliopolis (sacred to Ra). However, evidence for Apis worship at Memphis is already evident in the time of Mēnēs so perhaps this pharaoh merely established the supremacy of the Bull avatar throughout the land.

Baneteren or *Binothris* (3,928 BC–3,881 BC)

Succeeding Raneb was *Baneteren*, who is said to have reigned 47 years, having instituted the practice of passing the throne down through the female line and for enabling women themselves to occupy the throne. Flinders Petrie says that these customs represented a 'reversion to the prehistoric system,'[31] and in any case, the first of these practices survived down to the end of Egyptian history. However, there are only four women known to have ruled Egypt in their own right in that same 4300-year period, five if the Ptolemaic Cleopatra is included. A definite bias toward male pharaohs had become well-entrenched.

Perabsen or *Tlas* (3,881 BC–3,864 BC)

Perabsen, also *Sekhem-ab*, ascends the throne as the fourth king of the Second Dynasty and his is the first documented serekh that displays both the Horus

---

31 Petrie WMF, **A History of Egypt**, Vol. 1, London: Methuen & Co., 1903, p. 25.

and Set names. In fact, the name by which he is known, *Perabsen*, is his Set name. In this reign, there is concrete evidence of an expanding administration and bureaucracy shown by the proliferation of official titles and offices along with the divine iconograpy.

Khasekhemui or *Kheneres* (3,733 BC–3,703 BC)

After Perabsen, the next ruler of note is the last king of the Second Dynasty, *Khasekhemui* by name. Like Perabsen, he too boasts a double serekh with a Horus and a Set name. Khasekhemui was referred to in the following manner, 'the crown (glory) of the two deities [Horus and Set]', and also 'the two deities are at peace'. He seems to have expended great effort reconciling what had become the conflicting claims of these once-compatible divine partners, and those of Upper and Lower Egypt, as if he wished to uphold the bilateral harmony embodied in the previous Twin Age (Gemini). It would be the last time that Set would be so exalted by a native Egyptian ruler until the 19th Dynasty, with a brief pro-Set interlude in the 13th Dynasty. The ascendancy of Set during the later period of Hyksos rule is a separate case since the Hyksos were not native Egyptian rulers. Set was never expelled from the pantheon—a prominent place was found for him in the front of the Boat of Ra, for example—and his devotees maintained his worship in Egypt and Cush for the next three thousand years. But in the end, Set became the Great Adversary among the Divine Powers of Egypt.

Double Horus-Set Serekh
Khasekhemui, 2nd Dynasty

II. Old Kingdom II: 3rd Dynasty–6th Dynasty—Age of the Pyramid Builders

A. 3rd Dynasty (3,703 BC–3,489 BC)

Third Dynasty Pharaohs
Nebka
Djoser
Turis (*Man.*)
Mesokhris (*Man.*)
Soufis (*Man.*)
Djoser-teta
Sezes
Neferkara
Seneferu

Nebka or *Necherofës* (3,703 BC–3,675 BC)

This dynasty boasted at least two outstanding rulers, but of the rest, though identified by name from Manetho's ('*Man.*' above) or the other king lists, little is known about them. The first king of the 3rd Dynasty is Nebka. Egypt by this time had established its dominion over certain tribes of Libyans in the Western Desert. Some of these revolted in Nebka's time but this rebellion was apparently put down. It is not always clear ethnically who the Libyans were, at least at this stage of Egyptian history, because many of them were indistinguishable from the people the later Greek writers called *Ethiopians*, i.e., 'sunburnt people.' The name *Libya* was a name that could be applied confusedly by the Greeks to North Africa or all of Africa. In the New Kingdom, a definite fair-skinned type of coastal Libyan was distinguishable, but the interior of Libya was always inhabited by tribes who were, in effect, Ethiopians in the manner the Greeks used the term.

Djoser or *Torsorthros* (3,675 BC–3,646 BC)

Pharaoh Djoser of the 3rd Dynasty

The second ruler of the 3rd Dynasty was one of Egypt's greatest kings, the justly famous and revered Djoser. Though stone-built tombs were already known, he commissioned the building of what has been considered the first great edifice in stone ever erected by human hands, the Stepped Pyramid of

Stepped Pyramid of Djoser with Forecourt and Temple Columns

Sakkara. This building consisting of six stepped, progessively smaller squared concourses rising upward to a height of 204 feet, with the rectangular base encompassing an area of 14,000 square yards and the entire structure encased in smooth white limestone, was not a true pyramid. It was a magnificent structure all the same, especially when the entrance temple at the south end of the grand, spacious forecourt and the massive wall that surrounded the entire complex are considered. These parts of the whole complex were constructed according to architectural principles and building techniques that, from the point of view of aesthetic impact and engineering skill, have never been surpassed. Though the Great Pyramid (3,440 BC) holds pride of place as Egypt's most fabulous architectural and engineering accomplishment, the methods of quarrying, squaring, smooth planing, and setting in place massive blocks of stone with exacting precision and fineness had already been mastered at the time of the building of the Stepped Pyramid complex. As the author has said in another context:

> The entrance temple is simply an amazing structure whose rectilinear design shows a cleanness of line with a refinement and grace of conception that became the hallmark of Old Kingdom architecture. The aesthetic perfection elicited by the elegant simplicity of Old Kingdom architecture, first realized at Sakkara, was never again achieved in Egypt...[32]

Moreover, the erection of beautifully fluted columns in the hallway of the entrance temple anticipate by 3,000 years the use of the so-called 'Doric column' by the Greek builders of the Parthenon.

The man through whose genius this architectural marvel was realized was the fabled Imhotep, Djoser's vizier, chief astronomer, architect, physician, and purveyor of wise sayings. Imhotep, the undoubted designer and builder of the Stepped Pyramid, actually won greater renown as a physician.[33] Within 100 years after the reign of Djoser, Imhotep was venerated; 31 centuries later, he was deified as a god of medicine. So great was his reputation many centuries after he flourished, that the Greeks identified him with their own god of medicine Asclepios. Sir William Osler aptly calls Imhotep 'the first figure of a physician to stand out clearly from the mists of antiquity.' This author has called him the first universal genius of whom we have any knowledge.

32 Finch CS, **The Star of Deep Beginnings**, Decatur: Khenti Publications, 1998, p. 106.

33 See Hurry JB, **Imhotep**, London: Oxford University Press, passim.

Imhotep: Architect, Physician, Polymath

Having said all this about Imhotep, following Egyptian usage, the one who is accorded due credit for the Step Pyramid is pharaoh himself, Djoser. Only under his patronage in a nation prosperous and well-organized enough to undertake such an enterprise, could the Step Pyramid have been conceived, let alone constructed. Manetho says too that Djoser himself was a famous physician. This attribution could be true but most historians think that Manetho is conflating Imhotep with his pharaoh.

Seneferu or *Sifouris* (3,515 BC–3,489 BC)

The last pharaoh of this dynasty is Seneferu who, like Djoser, ranks among Egypt's greatest. He was one of the most dynamic and energetic rulers ever to sit on a throne anywhere. Under him, the true pyramid-building age begins. Two major pyramids are attributed him—the 'Bent' Pyramid and the 'Red' Pyramid—and some say that the Meidum Pyramid was also commissioned by Seneferu. The Meidum Pyramid was at first a seven-terraced then an eight-terraced structure akin to the Step Pyramid at Sakkara whose terraces were filled in with a white limestone casing, giving it the outward appearance of a true pyramid. At a later time, some of casing stones were either removed or extruded on their own, causing the entire facing to collapse, leaving the stepped core intact. It was the one and only 'failure' among the major pyramids. The Bent Pyramid is so-called because half-way up, the slope of the pyramid changes to a sharper angle, giving the visual effect of two separate pyramids being seamlessly joined together in one structure. The Red Pyramid is usually thought of as the first true Pyramid and was called 'Red' on account of the coloring of the limestone used in its construction. Never before or afterward was massive building in stone on such a scale attempted in the course of a single reign (26 years). Taken together, the total tonnage of just the Bent and Red Pyramids was nine million, two-and-half tons more than that of the Great Pyramid. It meant that all the technical skill, knowledge, and logistical organization for massive building in stone had been mastered in Egypt on the eve of the storied 4th Dynasty.

Great builder though he was, Seneferu exhibited an exuberant energy in other domains of royal activity as well. In the 13th and 14th years of his reign, Seneferu built a substantial navy that included two great ships of the line 172 feet long plus 60 smaller ships. As we shall see later, even at this early date, there is every reason to believe that the Egyptians were not only sailing the Nile but also the oceans—the Mediterranean Sea, the Red Sea, and the Indian Ocean. Seneferu also showed certain initiative as a military campaigner, having launched a successful incursion into the Sinai Peninsula. Also, a military campaign into Nubia (Ta-Seti) is recorded which netted 7,000 captives and 200,000 cattle. In Egypt, as in the rest of East Africa, cattle were a form of wealth, and Henri Frankfort remarks that 'cattle played an altogether extraordinary role in the consciousness of the ancient Egyptians.'[34] On the same subject, he goes on to say '…some modern Africans, related to the ancient Nilotes, display a similar attitude toward cattle…'[35] Though in Canaan cattle herds also were highly valued as the Old Testament reveals, almost nowhere outside of Africa—including Egypt—is the reverence and attachment to cattle so highly developed and so woven into the socio-cultural fabric of life. The possible exception to this assessment is India where a similar reverence for cattle still abides.

34 Frankfort, op. cit., p. 163.
35 Ibid.

Egyptians and Cattle

Seneferu stands as an elite ruler in a country with a history of outstanding kings. Like all of Egypt's major pharaohs, divine honors—complete with temples and offerings—were paid to him until the end of Egypt's history. He begins the epoch which, with the kings of the 4th Dynasty, may be considered the zenith of the Old Kingdom, whose glory remains undiminished even at the time of this writing more than 5,000 years later.

B. 4th Dynasty (3,489 BC–3,212 BC)

4th Dynasty Pharaohs

Shaaru
Khufu
Kha-f-ra
Men-kau-ra
Ra-ded-f
Shepses-ka-f
Sebek-ka-ra
Thamfthis

Petrie called the 4th Dynasty of Egypt 'one of the grandest periods of human activity.'[36] That seems an understatement. The 4th Dynasty is utterly unique in the annals of recorded history, representing the absolute pinnacle of the Pyramid Age. The wonders thus created still stir the human imagination and make all superlatives seem insufficient. Many are those who think that even with all the marvels Egypt would produce in the ensuing millenia, no era of achievement would ever quite match that of the 4th Dynasty. In fact, one looks in vain anywhere else in the world for a comparable era of sheer accomplishment.

Khufu or *Cheops* (3,460 BC–3,397 BC)

For a long time, Khufu, the second pharaoh of the 4th Dynasty, was considered the son of Seneferu, so that this latter king was thought to belong to the beginning of the 4th Dynasty instead of the end of the 3rd. However, a rock inscription linking Khufu to *Shaaru* was discovered, and the name *Shaaru* was seen to be a good fit for Manetho's *Soris* who is placed at the beginning of his 4th Dynasty king list. Manetho's Soris, i.e., Shaaru, was said to have reigned 29 years.

Khufu's enduring fame as the second king of the 4th Dynasty rests entirely on his link to the Great Pyramid. The Greeks called him *Cheops*, the name by which he is most frequently identified. He seems to have been a devotee of *Khnum*, the principal deity of the 1st Cataract (and allied to Ptah), because his full name was *Khnum-Khufu*. Compared to the Great Pyramid, no other man-made structure in history has called forth as much awe, inspection, study, and speculation as does the first, largest, and most splendidly-built of the three pyramids at Giza: a 200-feet high plateau 10 miles west of Cairo and 10 miles north of Memphis. Whole books have been written on the Great Pyramid, engendering heated controversies that swirl around this edifice to the present day. In fact, 'pyramidology'— though disavowed by academic Egyptologists— has become a whole sub-genre of literature on ancient Egypt.

36 Petrie, op. cit., p. 36.

The Great Pyramid at Giza

The author has dealt at length with the Great Pyramid in an earlier publication,[37] and with all the volumes available on the topic, it is not necessary to go into great depth and detail here. However, a few salient facts can be noted. Few doubt the report of Herodotus that rotating levees of 100,000 men were drafted to work on the Great Pyramid for three months at a time, nine months a year. Herodotus informs us that the Great Causeway, over which the massive limestone and granite blocks were conveyed on a system of rollers (wheels were apparently never used in the construction project), took 10 years to build and the Pyramid itself, 20 years. Egyptologists, almost without exception, insist that the Great Pyramid was the tomb for Khufu's mortal remains, and yet there is nothing about it that gives any credence to that supposition. There is not a single inscription or illustrated scene of any kind—funerary or otherwise—anywhere in or on the Pyramid. There are none of the ordinary accoutrements associated with ancient Egyptian burial practices. In fact the interior of the Pyramid is remarkably bare and always has been. There is a granite coffer sitting in the so-called 'King's Chamber' which is too wide to have been brought in through the chamber entrance, so must have been sculpted while the chamber itself was being built. Nothing about the granite coffer suggests that any mummy was ever laid in it. Apart from this coffer, there is nothing else to be found anywhere in the inner Pyramidal chambers. The Great Pyramid could never have been used as a tomb for mortal remains, and to insist that it was testifies to the power of belief over objective fact.

37 Finch, op. cit., pp. 110-32.

The Great Pyramid, when intact, rose to a height of 480 feet 10 inches, composed of 210 courses of masonry. It was built with 2.3–2.7 million blocks of stone, weighing from one to seven tons (average 2½ tons), though certain granite stones used to construct the King's Chamber weigh 60 tons. The Pyramid, when complete, would have weighed 6½ million tons (13 billion pounds) and yet in its construction, there is not the slightest 'twist' from straightness in the orientation of its faces. Like all the ancient pyramids, the Great Pyramid was covered with an external casing of fine, polished white limestone blocks so evenly and closely fit together that the joints of the still extant casing stones will hardly admit a strand of hair between them. The intact faces rise at an unvarying angle of slope of 51°51' which could only have been achieved by a mastery of applied trigonometry. The average measure for each side of the square base of the pyramid is 755 feet 9.45 inches, with an average error, one side to another, of 2.3 inches, or 1/4,000 of the mean length of the sides.[38] This minute accuracy caused Petrie to say that here was precision that only an optician could obtain, but on a scale of acres compared to millimeters.[39] The base of the Pyramid covers an area of more than 13 acres.

Certain mathematical and scientific features were incorporated into the design and construction of the Pyramid. For example, the Descending Passage on the Pyramid's north face is perfectly straight and is inclined at an angle of 26°17'. It was used to orient the Pyramid's faces accurately to the four cardinal points because the Descending Passage was perfectly aligned to *αDraconis*, the north pole star at its nightly culmination in 3,440 BC.[40] When so aligned, the light from *αDraconis* would have beamed down the Passage to be mirrored in the reflecting pool at the bottom of the shaft. This date, 3,440 BC, is the best date possible for the early phase of construction of the Great Pyramid; it would take another 15 years to complete it. If, as the weight of scholarly opinion has it,

38 The greatest error from the mean length of the sides of the base (775 feet 9.45 inches) is 4.35 inches; the smallest is 0.25 inches. The two sides with the greatest variance–north and south–are 7.9 inches different from one another.

39 Petrie WMF, **The Pyramids and Temples of Giza**, London: Histories and Mysteries of Man, Ltd., 1990, p.

40 Vid. Tompkins P, **Secrets of the Great Pyramid**, New York: Harper & Row Publishers, 1971 for a comprehensive study of all the facts surrounding the history of the Great Pyramid.

Khufu is the pharaonic builder of the Great Pyramid, 3,440 BC also fixes a date in his reign. Oddly, no one—not even those who have called attention to this alignment of the Pyramid's Descending Passage to *αDraconis*—has thought to use this fact as a way to more accurately and definitely fix the chronology of Khufu's reign, not to mention that of the 4th Dynasty and the Old Kingdom as a whole. If the Great Pyramid, by the evidence of this polar alignment, was being built in and around 3,440 BC, it completely refutes the short chronology that doesn't admit a commencement of Egyptian dynastic history before 3,200 BC.

This author proposes to use the pole star alignment date of 3,440 BC as a means of arriving at a chronology closer to the true one of dynastic Egypt. The date is precise and astronomically verifiable. With the regnal dates supplied by Manetho, we can see that from the beginning of the reign of Mēnēs in 1st Dynasty to the end of the reign of Khufu in the 4th Dynasty, a period of 871 years elapsed. It was in the reign of Khufu that the Great Pyramid was oriented and built so that reign encompasses the orientation date of 3,440 B.C. Most authorities accept the Pyramidal building time of 30 years—10 years for the Great Causeway plus 20 years for the Pyramid itself—reported by Herodotus but no one knows at what point in the reign of Khufu the actual construction activities commenced. If the orientation of the Pyramid via the Descending Passage was accomplished in 3,440 BC, that would make it 20 years after the beginning of the reign of Khufu, 3,460 BC by the chronology cited above. The orienting of the Pyramid with construction of the Descending Passage probably commenced between Year 5 of the building process and with 10 years added for the building of the Great Causeway, it took a total of 15 years from the start of the Causeway to completing the construction of the Descending Passage. The entire project, therefore, would have begun in Year 5 of Khufu's reign, e.g., 3,455 BC and the completion of the Great Pyramid would have been accomplished by 3,425 BC.

Khufu's reign lasted 63 years, and though it is not certain, it is not unreasonable to assume that he ascended the throne by age of 20. Conceivably, the planning and construction of the Pyramid, though it was erected during his reign, were not initiated by Khufu as such, and it had a purpose and function totally unrelated to his or anyone else's funerary rites. Since the Great Causeway by the report of Herodotus took 10 years to build, it would mean that actual pyramidal construction probably began when Khufu was about 35, making Khufu 40 years of age by the time the Pyramid's orientation to α-Draconis in 3,440 BC was achieved and foundational concourses laid. Khufu's reign lasted 63 years. If he ascended the throne at age 20—at the time the Great Pyramid was oriented—at age 40, we might assume he would have had another 43 years to live. By Manetho's Chronology, there were 871 years between the beginning of the 1st Dynasty under Mēnēs and the end of Khufu's reign. That means there were 828 years from the beginning of the 1st Dynasty to the orientation of the Great Pyramid which dates the beginning of the 1st Dynasty to 4,268 BC. This date is the one the author uses to anchor the Dynastic chronology.

The Great Pyramid also possesses other unusual technical and mathematical features. The height of the Pyramid is equal to the length of a radius of a circle whose circumference is equal to the perimeter of the Pyramid's square base. The perimeter of the Pyramidal base = 3023.25 feet. By the formula $2\pi R$ for finding the circumference of a circle, where $\pi=3\ 1/7$, one gets $2 \times 3\ 1/7 \times 480'10''$ (height of the Pyramid) = 3022.38 feet, a difference of about 10.4 inches (less than 3/100%) from the measured base perimeter.[41] Thus the geometric π constant of 3 1/7 was built into the dimensions of the Great Pyramid more than 54 centuries ago. Moreover, the famous 3-4-5 triangle, usually referred to as 'Pythagorean', is found in the meridian triangle of the Pyramid as well as in the dimensions of the King's Chamber.[42]

When Napoleon conquered Egypt in 1798, he commissioned his surveyors to measure Egypt. They found something very interesting: if they projected a line due north through the Great Pyramid, where it crossed Egypt's Mediterranean coast, it divided the Delta into two equal parts that could then be measured by triangulation. Moreover, from the work of Charles Piazzi Smyth, we find that the Great Pyramid sits on the one latitudinal line that passes through more of the earth's east-west land surface than any other latitude; at the same time, it sits on the one meridian (longitudinal) line that passes through more of the earth's north-south land surface than any other meridian. From

41 Vid. Pochan A, **The Mysteries of the Great Pyramids**, New York: Avon Books, 1971 pp. 8-10; also Clarke S and Engelbach R, **Ancient Egyptian Construction and Architecture**, New York: Dover Publications, Inc., (1930)1990, pp. 65-66, for the Pyramidal dimensions.

42 Vid. Tompkins, op. cit., p. 101 and p.379.

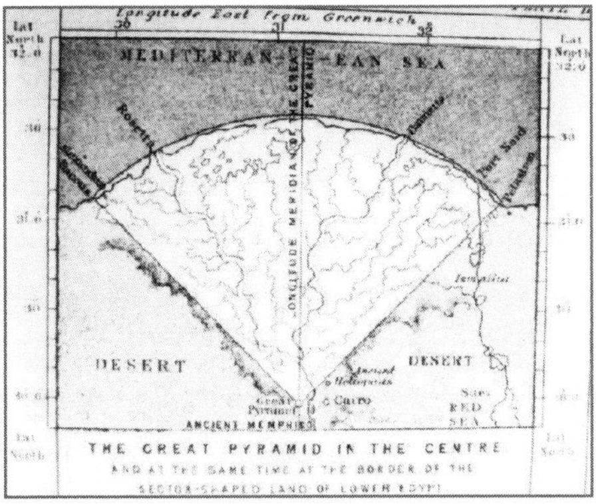

Longitude through the Great Pyramid
Bisecting the Delta into Two Equal Halves

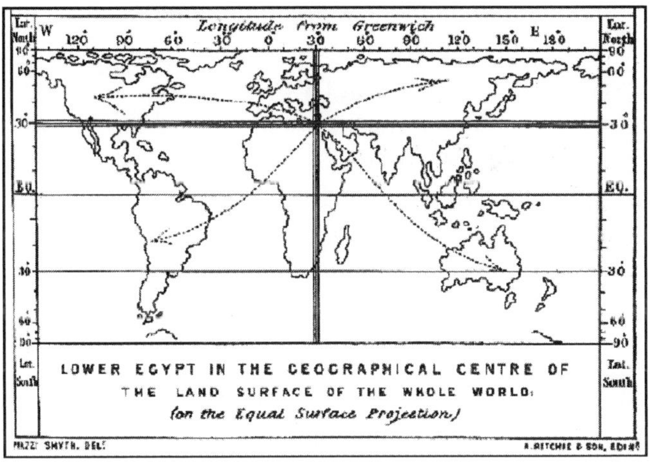

Latitude and Longitude of Great Pyramid go through more of Earth's land surface than any other.

the point of view of the earth's land masses, the Great Pyramid sits at the center of the earth's surface. The sages of ancient Egypt obviously knew it, and they knew that the Great Pyramid locates the earth's only true Prime Meridian. Thus the Great Pyramid was a major geodetic marker, a major landmark for measuring not only Egypt but the earth. The pyramid-builders knew the earth, its shape, and its dimensions.[43]

43 Vid. Piazzi Smyth, **The Great Pyramid**, New York: Bell Publishing Company, 1880/1978, p. 225.

It was mentioned earlier that Khufu's renown rests entirely on his sponsorship of the Great Pyramid. If its construction was completed in his lifetime, then it would have consumed nearly half his reign of 63 years. The Great Pyramid was not, however, merely a stupendous engineering *tour de force*, nor, as many have simple-mindedly presumed, was it an oversized monument to the outsized ego of pharaoh. As the above discussion makes clear, its construction had vast ramifications for the country and indeed the world, many of which have not been touched on in this brief synopsis. The uncanny Egyptian skill in organizing hundreds of thousands of persons in the implementation of major national tasks was brought to the highest possible level in this massive project. The Great Pyramid left a permanent legacy for Egypt and the world.

Kha-f-rā or *Cephren* (3,387 BC–3,321 BC)

Khufu's successor was *Kha-f-rā*, called *Cephren* by Herodotus, who built the second of the fabled pyramids at Giza. Khafra's pyramid sits at a higher elevation than the Great Pyramid so seems larger to the naked eye seen from a distance. However, it is smaller than the Great Pyramid—about three-quarters of its size—and did not attain the extraordinary engineering standard of the larger pyramid. Khafra's pyramid rises to a height of 450 feet (481 feet for the Great Pyramid) and the sides of its base measure 700 feet (755 for the Great Pyramid). It is nonetheless a magnificent edifice and suffers only by comparison to Khufu's Pyramid. The causeway from Khafra's pyramid connects it with the so-called Valley Temple in which the marvelous Old Kingdom stone-building methods are shown to maximum effect. This temple—built of alabaster and granite, sits in front of, and slightly to the southeast of the Sphinx—after the Great Pyramid, is undoubtedly Egypt's most famous monument. What was true of Khufu's pyramid was also true of Khafra's, and, for that matter, Menkaura's pyramid that followed: there are no funerary inscriptions of any kind in the internal chambers and corridors of these pyramids. Referring to this total absence of such funerary inscriptions and lavishly painted scenes of the pharaoh's life in the three major Pyramids of Giza, Graham Hancock observed:

> This was exceptional. No other proven burial place of any Egyptian monarch had ever been found undecorated.[44]

Much of Khafra's fame derives from his putative linkage to the Sphinx that, until recently, was said to be a statue of him. As we have seen in earlier chapters, the Sphinx—a huge statue of a recumbent human-headed lion sculpted out of living rock—sits just east of and below the Giza Plateau. The entire body, from rump to paw, is 150 feet long; the head sits 70 feet above the monument's base. In antiquity, its face was painted red, though at present, all color has been worn away by the unrelenting, sand-filled wind. Owing to the work of West and Schoch, re-dating the age of the Sphinx on the basis of the visible evidence of water erosion on its body and the walls of the surrounding quarry, the Sphinx has been the center of a roiling controversy. These investigators now date the carving of the Sphinx to at least 7,000 BC, and more radical work by Graham Hancock concerning the Sphinx's alignment to the constellation Leo at its vernal heliacal rising pushes that date back to 10,500 BC. On the basis of these re-datings and the work of the forensic artist Frank Domingo comparing the face of Khafra to that of the Sphinx, the idea that Khafra was the model for the Sphinx is no longer tenable. It is evident that Khafra commissioned the refurbishing and repair of the Sphinx, but on this account, in later millennia the sculpting of the entire monument was attributed to him. The Sphinx was said to be the personification of *Heru-khuti* or *Harmachis* (Gr), i.e., 'Horus of the Horizons,' a form of the Sun god in his rising. This identification of the Sphinx, if authentic, is late; originally, the Sphinx represented Atum. The Sphinx was buried, cleared, and re-buried by drifting sand several times during the dynastic period. After the Roman occupation (30 BC), the Sphinx was once again covered over with sand up to its neck and remained that way until its latest clearing in the 20th century.

There is another 'anomaly' concerning whom the Sphinx might represent. The Greeks sometimes referred to the Sphinx as *Rhodopis*, meaning 'rosy cheeked', because of the reddish color of its face,[45] and in this way they assumed that the Sphinx was female, a notion reproduced in the myth of Oedipus. It

44 Hancock G, **Fingerprints of the Gods**, New York: Three Rivers Press, 1995, p.301.

45 Cf., **Diodorus: Library of History** (Oldfather), op. cit., note 1, p. 222.

has always been supposed that the Greeks were wrong on this point, especially since there seem to be Egyptian attestations linking the Sphinx to Atum or Harmakhu. However, standing in front of the Sphinx itself and framing only its face with one's two hands, the observer is struck by how feminine the face does in fact look. No matter how many times the Sphinx has been viewed before, it's as if one is seeing this remarkable figure for the first time. From then on it seems indeed to be a mythically monumental woman at which one is looking.

The Sphinx controversy aside, there are a number of surviving statues of Khafra that are marvelous artistic pieces. The delicacy, control, refinement, and mastery evident in these sculptures have never been surpassed. Just as architecture and engineering reached an acme of achievement in Egypt in the 4th Dynasty, so did the sculptor's art. Khafra reigned 66 years.

Men-kau-rā or Mycerinos (3,321 BC–3,258 BC)

The fourth pharaoh of the dynasty was *Men-kau-rā*—called *Mycerinos* by Herodotus—and under him, the third and last of the three pyramids of Giza was built. This was by far the smallest of these pyramids, with a height just over 210 feet and a base side of 350 feet, making it less than half the size of the Great Pyramid. It is the only one of the three pyramids of Giza in which a coffin containing a mummy was actually found, seemingly clear evidence that it was in fact utilized as a tomb. However, there are doubts about the identification of the mummy as Menkaura and at least one Egyptologist thought it represents a later interment.[46] One of Menkaura's sons was the famous *Hardeduf*, a sage and learned man whom later generations mentioned in the same breath with Imhotep. Several chapters of the **Book of the Coming Forth by Day** are ascribed to Hardeduf. Menkaura reigned 63 years.

Like the pyramids they built, the three aforementioned kings, Khufu, Khafrā, and Menkaurā are linked together in any perspective of the 4th Dynasty. They all enjoyed long, prosperous reigns filled with unprecedented accomplishment. Their efforts brought the Pyramid Age to the summit of

46 Petrie, op. cit., p. 58.

human achievement whose imprint remains indelible 54 centuries later. A total of nine pyramids survive at Giza as mute witnesses to the grandeur of the Age. The six smaller pyramids were all dedicated to the wives and daughters of the pyramid-builders. But there is more to their seemingly obsessive pyramid-building than previously realized by even the most ardent 'pyramidologist.' Evidence has come to light in the last 20 years to show that the three pyramids at Giza are so situated as to accurately represent on earth the configuration of the three stars that comprise *Orion's Belt*.[47] It means, among other things, that the three Giza pyramids considered together were built according to a specific ground plan, developed before the first cornerstone was laid. Their sizes and placements on the Plateau were not random or idiosyncratic but arranged carefully and precisely to reflect a heavenly arrangement in the constellation of Orion, once again demonstrating that the ancient Nile Dwellers consciously created an Egypt that was a mirror image of the visible Cosmos.

Shepses-ka-f or Bikheris (3,233 BC–3,211 BC)

The next king of any interest in the 4th Dynasty is *Shepses-ka-f*, the sixth pharaoh of the dynasty, and him chiefly for an autobiographical account left by one of his retainers, *Ptah-shepses*. Though not of the royal family, this man was raised and educated among the royal children of Pharaoh Shepses-ka-f. From that point on, he rose steadily in the administrative ranks, winning pharaoh's confidence to such a degree that he was even given a royal princess as a wife. Ptahshepses held many offices which he evidently discharged with exemplary skill and integrity. He seems to have been close to the king in a very personal way. Though Ptahshepses may have been a scion of a noble family, he might also have been a commoner whose uncommon abilities were recognized at an early age and given maximum scope to develop and employ in the service of pharaoh and the state. In the coming dynasties, other commoners would follow in the footsteps of Ptahshepses, becoming 'new men' ennobled by their loyalty and unstinting service to pharaoh. This class of 'new men,' exemplified by Ptahshepses, shows that common birth was not only no bar to rising in the ranks through merit but

47 Cf. Bauval, Robert and Gilbert, Adrian. **The Orion Mystery**. London: Heineman, 1994.

also to marrying into the royal family itself. In the kingdoms and empires of West Africa 48 centuries later, this practice of raising commoners—even slaves—to high positions in the realm, of creating 'new men,' was well-followed, an effective buffer against the pretensions of an otherwise restless and contentious nobility.

C. 5th Dynasty (3,202 BC–2,984 BC)

5th Dynasty Pharaohs

User-ka-f
Sahu-ra
Nefer-ar-ka-ra
Shepses-ka-ra
Nefer-f-ra
Ra-en-user
Men-kau-her
Ded-ka-ra
Unas

The 5th Dynasty appears to have originated in the South at Elephantine near the 1st Cataract, according to Manetho,[48] meaning that its antecedents had to have been Nubian. With this dynasty, a new religious force comes to the forefront of the Egyptian religious pantheon, *Rā* the sun-god—specifically the sun in its full power at high noon—and it will mean that, among other things, Heliopolis (e.g. *Annu*), the sacred city of Rā, will grow in importance to eventually hold pride of place as the center of Egyptian religious learning. Rā is fused with the pre-extant patron deity of Annu, Atum, and is also woven into the Osirian cycle since Horus—and with Horus, pharaoh himself—is now titled 'Son of Rā.' In this schema, Horus is the rising or morning Sun, Rā the Sun at its full strength at noon, and Osiris the setting or twilight Sun. In this latter aspect, Osiris merges with Atum who is also styled the 'evening Sun.' The Sun is pictured as riding the heavens in a barque, the 'barque of Rā,' and—in his Osirian form—through the netherworld at night before being re-born each morning as Horus. Set is not left out of this new dispensation: he is given a place in the prow of the barque of Rā

48 Manetho, op. cit., p. 51.

Rā—Paramount Solar Deity of Egypt

Primordial Solar Deity of Annu (Heliopolis)

where his task is to spear the Dragon of Darkness, *Apep*, who constantly threatens the Light as it makes it way through the Underworld. In fact, the apparent amity between Rā and Set contrasts starkly with the mortal enmity between Set on the one hand and Horus/Osiris on the other.

The kings of the 5th Dynasty, though able to push Rā to the pinnacle of the pantheon, do not abandon Memphis as Egypt's capital. Annu or Heliopolis ('Sun city'), in any case, is no more than 20 miles distant from Memphis. Bull symbolism, indicative of the Taurean celestial Age, still abided; in Heliopolis, the Bull is *Mnevis*, the counterpart to Apis in Memphis. In typical Egyptian fashion, a workable accommodation was apparently reached between the Temple of Ptah in Memphis and the new royal Rā-worshipers whose religious center would become Heliopolis. The royal capital remained at Memphis, and the vizier or prime minister to pharaoh would be drawn as a hereditary official from a family dedicated to the service of Ptah, according to Breasted. Each incumbent prime minister for the next five reigns, for example, bears the name *Ptah-hotep* ('Ptah is at peace')[49]. The development of hereditary offices both in the central government and among the chiefs of the nomes, the 'nomarchs',

49 Vid. Breasted JH, **A History of Egypt**, New York: Charles Scribner's Sons, (1909)1937, p. 126.

gathers momentum from the 5th Dynasty on and becomes entrenched in Egyptian political life to the end of the Middle Kingdom.

User-ka-f or *Userkherēs* (3,195 BC–3,167 BC)

Though originally from the South, the first king of the new dynasty was a priest of Rā—probably the high priest—at Heliopolis. The accession of a priest to the throne was unprecedented, and wouldn't be seen again until the advent of the 21st Dynasty some 2,000 years later (1,100 BC), when the high priests of Amon ascended the throne of Egypt. A curious bit of folklore—containing a nugget of historicity—is recounted in the Westcar Papyrus in which Pharaoh Khufu is informed by an ancient sage that after his next three successors, a different line of pharaohs would ascend to the throne whose first three representatives would be sons of a wife of a priest of Rā. These three kings would be the offspring of the god Rā himself. This 'enabling myth' of divine descent served two purposes: (1) to raise Rā to divine ascendancy in Egypt and (2) to solidify the claims of the 5th Dynasty pharaohs to the throne of Egypt. The first king of the 5th Dynasty was *User-ka-f*, by name and as the high priest of Rā, consolidated sufficient power and authority to become pharaoh and start a new dynasty. From this time on, every one of the pharaohs added a Rā name to the Horus name; every pharaoh henceforth was to be considered the 'son of Rā.' Userkaf had his own pyramid built at Abusir, but neither his pyramid nor those of the kings of the ensuing dynasty were built to the scale or level of technical perfection of the Pyramids of Giza. The reign of his successors *Sahu-rā* and *Nefer-ar-ka-rā* complete the trio of 5th Dynasty kings whose ascension to the throne had been part of the prophecy recorded in the Westcar Papyrus.

Rā-en User or *Rhathūrēs* (3,107 BC–3,063 BC)

The next important pharaoh of this dynasty is the sixth ruler of the dynasty, *Rā-en-user*, who reigned 44 years and was known as an active and dynamic ruler. Like his predecessors, he erected a pyramid at Abusir and carried out military campaigns in the Sinai, that peninsula becoming Egyptian national territory thanks to the operations of the 5th Dynasty kings—for Sinai was rich in copper, an indispensable metal for the Egyptians of this era. In his reign, another commoner by name of *Thi* rose high in the ranks of pharaoh's service. He too became a close personal friend of pharaoh, marrying one of pharaoh's female relatives, and holding a succession of important civil offices. He may not have actually been prime minister, but he was apparently entrusted with a number of essential duties that probably made him, in effect, the second most powerful official in the land.

Ded-ka-rā or ***Thankerēs*** (3,054 BC–3,010 BC)

The pharaoh *Ded-ka-rā*, also known as *Issi*, is the eighth pharaoh of this dynasty who also ruled 44 years. One of the most notable events of this reign is the effort expended to bring back a *Deng*, i.e., a 'pygmy' (*Twa)*, from inner Africa. This long-distance congress with the Deng apparently began as far back as the 1st Dynasty since the mummies of two Twa have been found. There must have been a touch of religious awe associated with this keen interest in the Deng—evident in all dynasties of the Old Kingdom—because the Ptah was often depicted as a Deng! It was said that only the Deng knew how to dance the 'dance of the god.'

The first known Egyptian voyage to *Punt*, occurs in this dynasty. Punt has been located in or around the Horn of Africa and will play a prominent role from then on in Egyptian foreign trade relations. Apart from other African luxury goods, Punt—and the Arabian coast opposite—is the source of myrrh, important as an aromatic incense and an ingredient in medicaments used to treat infections. Medicinally, myrrh inhibits the growth of bacteria.[50]

The famous **Proverbs of Ptah-hotep** date from this reign. This Ptah-hotep was the latest of the line of ministerial Ptah-hoteps that date from the beginning of the dynasty. He served as tutor to the king and his eventual prime minister. The existing papyrus of these Proverbs dates from the 12th Dynasty but is clearly a copy of an Old Kingdom original. Wallis Budge says concerning **Proverbs**,

50 Cf. Majno G, **The Healing Hand**, Cambridge: Harvard University Press, (1975) 1982, pp. 215-8.

> These 'Precepts' show that the Egyptians in the Vth Dynasty possessed moral ideas of a very high character, and that their conceptions of truth, justice, duty, humanity, and of a man's duty towards his neighbor, were not inferior to the counsels on the the same subjects which are to be found in the Books of Proverbs and Ecclesiasticus.[51]

Unas or *Onnos* (3,010 BC–2,977 BC)

The last king of the 5th Dynasty is *Unas* who is the only king in the dynasty who does not have a Rā name. Unas is the first known pharaoh to have built a temple to Hathor at Memphis, and his pyramid is to be found just south of Djoser's step pyramid at Sakkara. The pyramid itself, compared to those that preceded it, would be of marginal interest were it not for the fact that the interior is covered with inscriptions of a religious, spiritual, and funerary nature that are unique in Egyptian annals. These inscriptions constitute the famous **Pyramid Texts**, and from the point of view of recording Old Kingdom religious beliefs they are irreplacable. It is said that they are the conceptual product of the priests of Rā at Heliopolis and reflect the paramount religious ideas of the time involving the future life of the king mediated through Horus and Osiris. Nearly all of the major Egyptian deities are mentioned in the Texts, and it is clear that other scriptural texts then and later—such as the **Book of the Coming Forth by Day**—are but paraphrases of them. Having said that, it is also clear that many of the ideas expressed in the Pyramid Texts are very old, older than the dynastic period itself. To the student of Egyptian religion, therefore, they are perhaps the only available source of information on Egyptian religious consciousness as it was evolving from early pre-dynastic times. The Pyramid Texts, in fact, take the reader back into the primeval inner African wellspring of Egyptian thought.

---

51 **Budge** EAW, **A History of Egypt**, volume 1, Oosterhout N.B. The Netherlands: Anthropological Publications, (1902)1968, p. 80.

D. 6th Dynasty (2,977 BC–2,779 BC)

6th Dynasty Pharaohs

Teti
User-ka-ra
Merira (Pepi I)
Mer-en-ra
Nefer-ka-ra (Pepi II)
Mer-en-ra
Neter-ka-ra
Net-aqerti

This dynasty, the last of the Old Kingdom, starts out imbued with more dynamism than the previous one. There is more widespread monument-building than at any time since the 4th Dynasty and more vigorous prosecution of military, diplomatic, and trade initiatives beyond Egypt, particularly southward. It was probably the most adventuresome of the Old Kingdom dynasties.

Teti or *Orthoēs* (2,977 BC–2,947 BC)

The first king of the 6th Dynasty is Teti who possesses the dubious distinction of being history's first known victim of regicide. According to Manetho, after 30 years of rule, he was apparently done away with by his palace guard, though the motivation for the plot has not come to light. Teti's pyramidal interior, like that of Unas, is covered with religious inscriptions. One brief excerpt is of 'Christian' interest: "O ye gods, the water of Teta is as wine, even as [is that of] Rā".[52] Here seems to be an allusion to transubstantiation, 3,000 years before the first books of the New Testament were written.

52 **Budge**, op. cit., p.91.

Meri-rā/Pepi I or *Fios* (2,947 BC–2,894 BC)

The next important pharaoh was the 3rd of the dynasty, *Meri-rā*, better known as *Pepi I*, who is usually thought of as the most able of the 6th Dynasty kings. He erected more monuments than any other Old Kingdom pharaoh—in fact, more than any other pharaoh until the 12th Dynasty. Like his predecessors, he found it necessary to pacify restive tribes in the Sinai to enable the active exploitation of the turquoise and copper deposits there. In Syene (Aswan) in the south, he opened many granite quarries so that he could have a ready supply of the stone for his numerous building projects. Stone sculpture and metalwork attained a very high standard during Pepi's reign, and, according to Budge, left a permanent legacy of excellence for Egyptian crafts in the centuries to come. Bronze especially was now being worked with the customary Egyptian skill and delicacy.

As has already been seen, the tombs of exceptional non-royal servants of the Old Kingdom pharaohs are often inscribed with their autobiographical exploits, and Pepi's reign follows this pattern. The personage in this case was Uni who, in the course of his career, performed the services of quarry master, judge, palace overseer, and general in the service of pharaoh. As palace overseer, he was charged with the delicate and dangerous task of investigating charges of conspiracy among the pharaonic consorts, and Uni seems to have seen this thankless task through to a satisfactory conclusion. It was not the first, nor would it be the last, time that political trouble for pharaoh was brewed in the royal women's quarters.

Uni was also given the charge of subduing a confederation of tribesmen stirring up trouble in the Eastern Desert, the Ā*amu Heru-shā*, possible ancestors of the later *Hyksos*, who would achieve lasting infamy in Egyptian annals. Uni apparently believed in waging war with overwhelming force because he recruited and drafted thousands of soldiers from every part of the realm. He drew massive numbers of soldiers from no fewer than seven Nubian nations to fill his army: the *Irerthet*, the *Yam*, the *Imam*, the *Wawat*, the *Medjay*, the *Kaau*, and the *Thamehu*, oasis-dwellers in the Western Desert. The Medjay from Northern Nubia from then on entered the Egyptian military and security forces in such numbers that the word *medjay* came to mean 'soldier' and/or 'policeman.' Egypt's army would be, until the end of the New Kingdom, a Nubian army. The campaign was singularly successful. The Āamu and their allies were driven out of the Sinai and pursued deep into Canaanite (Palestinian) territory. Uni led five more campaigns of pacification against the troublesome Āamu and with his unrivaled success, was eventually rewarded with the governorship of the Ta-Seti nome, Egypt's southernmost province and considered one of the most important postings in the nation.

The Yam People of the Old Kingdom

Modern Descendants of the Medjay

Meri-en-rā/Mehti-em-sa-f or ***Methusūlûs*** (2,894 BC–2,887 BC)

Pepi's successor was *Mer-en-rā* and like several previous kings, much of what is known about the events and activities of his reign is actually derived from the tomb-inscribed autobiography of an outstanding royal servant. Uni's successor as governor of Ta-seti was *Harkhuf* who was, like Uni, of Nubian extraction himself[53] and also faithfully recorded his exploits under pharaoh Merenra. He began early in life, in the company of his father, to take part in expeditions of trade, diplomacy, and exploration southward into Nubia and beyond. As was true throughout Egyptian history, Nubio-Cush in the 6th Dynasty was the primary focus of Egyptian interest, attention, and activity in lands beyond its own immediate borders. Harkhuf's story reads like an adventure novel or like the story of the 19th century explorations of Speke and Burton for the source of the Nile. His first trip with his father to the Sudanic Land of Yam took

53 Gardiner, op. cit., p. 99.

seven months to complete and the expedition returned to pharaoh laden with all manner of luxury goods and products of the southern lands craved by the Egyptians. Egyptian pharaohs made it a priority to keep trade routes to the south open and protected because from those lands came goods the Egyptians valued most: gold, ebony, ostrich feathers, myrrh, panther skins, other rare woods, ivory, and spices, not to mention multitudes of livestock.

On his second expedition southward, Harkhuf and his company traveled eight months, visiting certain Sudani countries for the first time, these being *Irerthet* and *Sethu*. Again, he returned home laden with valuable merchandise and important ritual necessities. Harkhuf, who survived the pharaoh Merenra—who apparently reigned just seven years—made at least one more long-distance expedition to the south during the reign of Merenra's successor, Pepi II. On this occasion, he joined the king of Yam in a military campaign against the Themehu, oasis dwellers in the western Sudanic desert, and after helping his allies bring that war to a successful conclusion, continued his journey. This time, Harkhuf may have reached the southern Sudan or northern Uganda. The remote reaches of inner Africa were called *Ta-iakhu*, 'Land of the Spirits,' by the ancient Egyptians and it is here that Harkhuf duplicated the feat of *Bar-ur-dedu* in the time of Issi who won lasting fame for having brought back to the Egyptian court a Deng (pygmy) from the southern regions. Harkhuf was able to do the same and the excitement and sense of anticipation felt by pharaoh's court at the prospect of meeting the Deng emissary from deep in Africa is recorded on Harkhuf's tomb. Pharaoh writes Harkhuf summoning him to court:

> Come north to the Residence at once. Hurry and bring with thee this Deng…My Majesty desires to see this Deng more than all the tribute of the Mine-Land and Punt.[54]

His successful completion of the mission to bring the Deng to pharaoh was apparently the capstone of Harkhuf's adventurous and illustrious career.

From this time forward, Egyptian relations with the Sudanese countries to the south will intensify, alternating between military hostility on the one hand

54 Ibid., p. 59.

and peaceful co-existence, and even amalgamation, on the other. Pharaoh *Menere* is depicted in a remarkable relief traveling to the southern lands to receive the homage of allied Nubian princes in person, the first pharaoh to do so. It is eloquent testimony to the overriding importance of a peaceful Nubia. It is around this time that the actual name 'Cush,' i.e., *Kesh*, appears for the first time in Egyptian annals. This name for the country of the northern third of Sudan will become standard in the Middle Kingdom. Much later, Cush will come to be called *Ethiopia*, 'land of the sun-burnt people,' by the Greeks.

Nefer-ka-rā/Pepi II or *Fiōps* (2,887 BC–2,792 BC)

Nefer-ka-rā, better known as Pepi II, is the fifth king of the 6th Dynasty. He ascended the throne when he was six years old and ruled for 95 years, the longest reign in world history. Becoming king as a young child, Pepi's mother was regent throughout his minority, at least until he was 20. His reign was notable for the fact that a woman, *Nebt*, held high political office. She may have been someone put in place under the tutelage of Pepi's mother. Apart from its sheer longevity, the other noteworthy feature of the reign has been noted above—Harkhuf's expedition to the deep south that resulted in the bringing back of an envoy from among the Deng. After Pepi's reign, a definite decline is seen in the fortunes of state. Some, in fact, attribute this reversal of Egypt's fortunes to the extreme length of Pepi II's rule which, as he became enfeebled, enfeebled the state.

Net-aqerti or *Nitōcris* (2,791 BC–2,779 BC)

The last ruler of the 6th Dynasty is *Net-aqer-ti*, better known as *Nitocris*. Nitocris was a female pharaoh, the second of the four who would rule Egypt as pharaoh, and like her predecessor Meri-Nit, she was a devotee of the goddess Neith. Manetho calls her the 'noblest and loveliest woman' of her time.[55] A tradition reported by Herodotus claims that Nitocris came to power after her

55 Manetho, op. cit., p. 55.

brother—the previous, short-lived pharaoh (less than a year)—was murdered in a palace conspiracy. According to this story, Nitocris found a means to revenge herself on the conspirators and assume the throne.[56] In circumstances like these, it is not always easy to know how much Herodotus can be relied on. Half the time he recites correct or partially-correct traditions that can be verified from other sources. The other half of the time it is clear that he merely regurgitates aprocryphal stories he picked up during his travels in Egypt that have no basis in fact. Herodotus claims that Egyptians priests themselves recited this story, and Egyptologists, on the whole, don't question the historicity of the tradition. Egyptologists assert that with her, the 6th Dynasty and the Old Kingdom end, but it is an arbitrary conclusion since it is evident that the Old Kingdom, though diminished, continues through the 8th dynasty. Nitocris is significant as the second woman to become pharaoh and her reign does mark the termination of the 6th Dynasty.

E. Material Culture of the Old Kingdom

In the Old Kingdom, a high level of craftsmanship and art in stone working, metal working, painting, and sculpture is very evident which is a product of a long evolution of artistic development in the pre-dynastic era. In fact, in sculpture, architecture, and metal-working, the artists and artisans of the Old Kingdom have never been excelled. Tomb-building becomes more elaborate first for royalty and then for nobility and the upper echelons of society. Simple pits give way to rectangular, brick-lined structures partitioned into many chambers. These early tombs are now known as 'mastabas' and were filled with abundant material goods for the occupant including food, wine, ornaments, furniture, and pottery. Beginning with Djoser, the mastabas were replaced by pyramidal tombs, though there is no real reason to believe that the three Pyramids of Giza—particularly the Great Pyramid—were employed for the purpose of pharaonic burial. But even beyond pyramid-building, the distinctive architecture of Egypt reached its most highly developed form in the Old Kingdom as evidenced by the temples from the era, with a level of stone-

56 Herodotus, op. cit., p. 166.

building technique and engineering ingenuity that still defies anyone's ability to account for it at such a remote period.

What was called by the Greeks 'hieroglyphic' writing, i.e., *medu neteru*, 'the divine writing,' is already well-developed. The *medu neteru* were present in Ta-Seti, the pre-unification pharaonic kingdom of Nubia (c.4,600 BC–4,268 BC), but underwent major development from the time of Mēnēs on. Hieratic writing, a cursive form of hieroglyphics, is also well-elaborated, adapted to rapid transcription of administrative and other documents. Medicine, as evidenced by the Edwin Smith Papyrus, attained a high degree of sophistication. The extant scroll dates from 16th century BC but is known to be a copy of an Old Kingdom original, 2,500 years earlier.

F. Civil administration and Political Organization

The Old Kingdom of Egypt from the outset was a highly-organized, well-ordered state exhibiting a real genius for administration and governance. Neither pharaoh nor the royal family lived in idleness: they were trained from childhood in the duties, tasks, and responsibilities of rulership and administration. Sons and other male members of the royal family served as superintendants of quarries, scribes for pharaoh, and if very talented—vizier and/or chief architect. Women, particularly the royal mothers and great royal wives, had important roles to play ritually, symbolically, and administratively in the royal domains. Two royal women became pharaohs and others attained high rank in government. Every aspect of the kingdom—agriculture, trade, crafts, religion, the funerary cult—was organized down to the last detail. Minute records were kept of all economic and administrative transactions. An almost obsessive concern for exactitude is seen throughout all facets of life; weights and measures, for example were rigorously maintained for correct accounting of all goods and services. Almost at a moment's notice, thousands of laborers of all descriptions could be summoned for any great national task. Trade with foreign lands, already evident in pre-dynastic times, was very brisk during the Old Kingdom. As time when on, the bureaucracy expanded and provided tremendous scope for advancement for the very talented non-royal individual. Several men in the Old Kingdom, undoubtedly commoners by birth, had inscribed on the walls of their tombs their autobiographies detailing the extraordinary high offices they attained in the service of pharaoh. Especially later in the dynasty, the pharaohs found it prudent and politic to cultivate a class of 'new men,' i.e., men who were born outside of noble lineages, to serve them in the most important governmental duties and, not coincidentally, function as a bulwark against a noble class that was steadily trying to increase its power and privileges. However, eventually these new men, raised high by pharaoh, contrived to have their offices and titles made hereditary, meaning that they, in effect, joined the ranks of the aristocracy.

As a kind of side bar to this discussion about the Old Kingdom material culture, there are two singular facts worth noting: (1) the wheel was not employed in the massive building projects for which the era was known and (2) neither then nor in the ensuing 4,000 years did the Egyptians utilize a currency in their economic transactions. For movement of huge stone building blocks, rollers were employed with extraordinary efficiency. It is not known why the wheel, though known, was not used as a tool in the Old Kingdom. The later Incas of the Andes, also masters of megalithic stone construction, similarly did not use the wheel except on children's toys. In the matter of economic exchange, the Egyptians perfected methods of in-kind payment and trade. It is thought by some that the Egyptian reliance on the unit fraction system—the method of only allowing fractions, with the exception of ⅔, to be expressed with 1 as the numerator—was, at least in part, motivated by their economic system:

> The Egyptians' concern for the accurate dealing with fractions almost certainly originated from practical problems, such as the division of food supplies, and other things, either equally or in some specific ratio, among families, troops, members of working gangs, large crews, etc., in a country which had no metallic currency or money, and in which payments were made in kind.[57]

57 Gillings R, **Mathematics in the Time of the Pharaohs**, New York: Dover Publications, 1982, p. 105.

G. Important Deities in the Religious Pantheon

Ptah is the pre-eminent deity of the Old Kingdom whose name means 'opener.' He is the Egyptian Divine Architect, the patron of craftsmen and builders, and is often pictured standing on the cubit. In his underworld form he is Sokar, most of whose attributes are eventually assumed by Osiris. His consort is Sekhmet, the lion-headed goddess who represents the fiery heat of the sun and is also the bringer of disease. Yet she is the patronness of physicians because she can also ward off disease. The third member of the Memphis triad is *Nefer-Tem*,

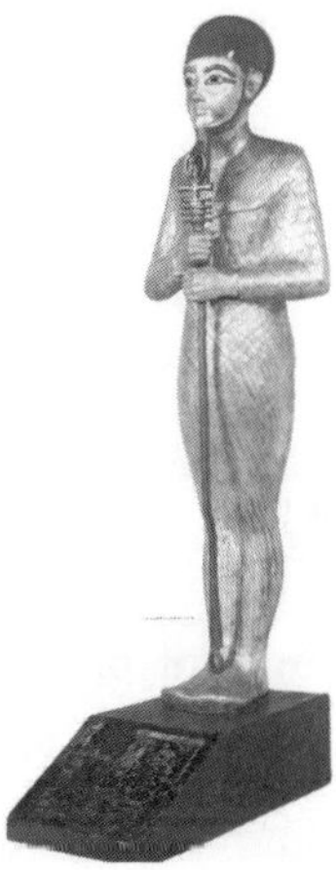

Ptah, Standing on the Cubit

Sekhmet the Lioness—Wife of Ptah

i.e., the child *Tem* (or Atum) who is depicted rising out of the bulb of the water lotus flower. Other major members of the pantheon include Atum (later fused with Rā), Ta-Urt, Nut, Nun, Geb, Shu, Tefnut, Set, Thoth, Anubis, Isis, Osiris, Horus, and Hathor. Each nome (or administrative unit) of Egypt had its divine patron, but the above-named deities were worshiped throughout the entire country.

The sun-cult of Rā makes its appearance in the 3rd dynasty, becomes prominent in the 5th dynasty, and is propelled to the forefront of the state religion for the remainder of Egyptian history. Rā becomes fused with Atum at Annu (Heliopolis), and Khepera, an old deity with links to Ptah, becomes a member of the triad at Heliopolis. He is the golden scarab and the image of the sun rising out of the primeval darkness. *Khepera* derives from the

Egyptian word meaning 'becoming' or 'evolution.' Despite the multiplicity of deities—2,000 major and minor gods throughout the country—the Egyptians from the first describe the Creator as *Uā* or 'One.' The Egyptian word usually translated as 'god' is *neter* which some have translated instead as 'principle' or 'power.' The formal religious ideas and doctrines of Egypt are well-elaborated by the time of Mēnēs, as the Pyramid Texts show. The **Book of the Coming Forth by Day**, which will eventually become the paramount religious and funerary scripture of Egypt, is already taking shape in the Old Kingdom.

VIII. Old Kingdom Epilogue

The pharaohs of the Old Kingdom, though ruling the Two Lands, still considered themselves primarily kings of the South. In civil, social, economic, political, and religious matters, the pharaonocracy is paramount in Old Kingdom life, though this state of affairs begins to change after the 4th Dynasty. The 5th Dynasty is inaugurated by a family of priests of Rā and certain high offices start to become hereditary, thus giving more leverage to the nobility. This process of aristocratic empowerment becomes even more marked in the 6th Dynasty which witnesses the steady rise of noble and hereditary families. Pepi I, an early 6th Dynasty pharaoh, is still strong enough to control the rising aristocracy, but after his reign, the nobility is able to carve out ever-greater prerogatives for themselves. Contacts and relations with Nubia, or *Cush*, are evident from the beginning of the Old Kingdom, and by the time of the 6th Dynasty, figure very prominently in the affairs of Egypt. Numerous trading and diplomatic expeditions are launched southward to Punt and the lands beyond. The Nubian *Medjay* enter the army of pharaoh in such numbers that their tribal name becomes the name of the army and constabulary itself. The pharaohs did not neglect trade relations with their northern neighbors but found it necessary to wage war from time to time to repel the threat of tribesmen from Canaan and the Eastern Desert.

After the reign of Pepi II, the longest in history, a noticeable decline sets in and the position of pharaoh becomes weakened. This process is highlighted by events surrounding the accession of Nitocris, the eighth ruler of the dynasty, who seems to have succeeded her murdered brother on the throne only to turn the tables on the conspirators. After her reign of 12 years, the 6th Dynasty closes, though the Old Kingdom continues, much weakened, through two additional dynasties.

Chapter 4:

The First Chronological Gap (2,779 BC–2,278 BC)[1] First Inter-Age Transition (2,466 BC–2,277 BC)

I. 7th and 8th Dynasties—A Time of Shadows (2,779 BC–2,563 BC)

The author follows the admittedly complex reasoning of Petrie in endeavoring to arrive—amost impossibly—at a time span for the First Chronological Gap.[2] All investigators seeking to find order in the chronological chaos of the First Chronological Gap are compelled to extract information from both Eusebius's Manetho and the Abydos King List, both sources of which are too corrupt or damaged to give clear indicators. Thus for Petrie, Dynasties 7 through 10 occupy a historical time span of 501 years, ending 2,278 BC, marking the advent of the 11th Dynasty, the first glimmer of light out of the chronological darkness of the First Chronological Gap. There is reason to believe, along with Petrie, that there was an extended period of overlap between the 10th and 11th Dynasties so that the 43 years assigned by Manetho to the 11th Dynasty would represent only the latest period of that dynasty (2,278 BC–2,235 BC) when it ruled Egypt supreme and alone. Before then, the two dynasties ran in parallel from different parts of the country. The Inter-Age Transition, on the

1 In Chapter 3, the author has substituted the terms 'chronological gap' and 'Inter-Age Transition' for the standard concept of 'Intermediate Period.' However, 'chronological gap' and 'Inter-Age Transition' are not synonymous or interchangeable.

2 Petrie, op. cit., pp. 108-11

other hand, would have encompassed the period between 2,464 BC and 2,277 BC, a time span of 187 years. In terms of dynastic chronology, it would mean that the Inter-Age Transition commenced in the overlap period of the 10th and 11th Dynasties and was completed at the beginning of the 11th Dynasty. It also means that the beginning of the Age of the Ram ('Aries') and that of the 11th Dynasty—the forerunner of the Middle Kingdom—began at the same time (2,278/2,277 BC).

In all of these four 'Gap' dynasties, Manetho mentions only one king, *Achthoês*, of the 9th Dynasty, and by the report of this author (after Eusebius) left a reputation for extreme cruelty. What names are available for the 7th and 8th Dynasties are reclaimed from the fragmentary king lists and monuments. Sixteen royal names are all that can be gleaned from the Abydos King List for these two dynasties; two identifiable from the 7th Dynasty and 14 from the 8th. All of these kings rule at Memphis, reinforcing the supposition that what is generally called the Old Kingdom continued at least until the end of the 8th Dynasty. Breasted was of the opinion that these ephemeral 7th and 8th Dynasty pharaohs were part of an aristocratic oligarchy that sprung up to take control of Memphis and the country during this period of collapse. He says this about them:

> He [Manetho] follows them with an Eighth Dynasty of Memphite kings, who are but the lingering shadow of ancient Memphite power. Their names as preserved in the Abydos list show that they regarded the Sixth Dynasty as their ancestors…[3]

This passage indicates that the derelict Old Kingdom continued through the 8th Dynasty.

Using Petrie's reconstruction for the duration of each of these Gap Dynasties, the 7th Dynasty would have run from 2,779 BC to 2,709 BC (70 years) and the 8th Dynasty from 2,709 BC to 2,563 BC (146 years).[4] From the existing records, nothing more can be said about the events of Dynasties 7 and

3 Breasted, op. cit., p, 147.

4 Petrie WMF, **A History of Egypt**, Vol. 1, London: Methuen & Co., 1903, p. 110. The author's dates differ from Petrie's but he follows Petrie's scheme for the time length of each of these dynasties during the First Chronological Gap.

8 or the activities of the reigning kings. To date, no monuments or documents have been unearthed to shed any further light on this shadowy period. Indeed, the First Chronological Gap, roughly coeval with the 7th and 8th Dynasties, was apparently no less shadowy to Manetho as it is to us. Thus, we can only speculate about the political forces at work that precipitated a decline in the strength and effectiveness of the established order to such a degree as to have caused such a catastrophic information black-out for the period.

II. 9th and 10th Dynasties—The Beginnings of Recovery/ A Tale of Two Cities (2,563 BC–2,278 BC)

The 9th and 10th Dynasties seem to represent a partial recovery of the political circumstances of the kingdom, though now the center of power has shifted southward from Memphis to Heracleopolis (*Hensu*), the City of Horus, closely allied with Lycopolis (*Saut*), the City of Wep-wat or Anubis (the Jackal). In fact, so close is this association between the nomarchs of Heracleopolis and those of Lycopolis that though the pharaohs of this tenuous period are from Heracleopolis, it is as if the two cities rule the country jointly. The situation could almost be seen as a throw-back to the pre-unification epoch of the Two Lands when Horus and Set ruled jointly. In this vein, it is worth pointing out again that in earlier times, Anubis/Wep-wat was closely entwined with Set and never entirely lost this Sethian character even after being folded into the Osirian system.

The 9th Dynasty based at Heracleopolis begins around 2,563 BC and lasts until about 2,463 BC (100 years). Achthoês, aka *Khati* and the only king identified by Manetho for the entire period of the First Chronological Gap, is the first pharaoh of this dynasty. From Manetho, he gets a bad report: he is described as a brutal and vengeful tyrant who is eventually seized with madness, meeting his end between the jaws of a Nile crocodile. Consistent with the paucity of records from the era, the successor to this king is not known. Moreover, it has been impossible to ascertain with which pharaohs the 9th Dynasty ended and the 10th Dynasty began. This latter dynasty would have covered the period from 2,463 BC to 2,278 BC (185 years). What is clear is the close alliance with the princes of Saut (Lycopolis), who preserved a more detailed record of the activities of their lives than did the Heracleopolitan pharaohs. In particular, three of the princes of Saut—Kheti I, Tefaba, and Kheti II—left tomb records of their reigns and their military services on behalf of their pharaonic allies at Heracleopolis. Kheti I records that he caused a canal to be built from the Nile that provided his nome with water during the dry season and increased the abundance of crops for his realm. Tefaba suppressed the reigning lawlessness in the surrounding regions. That there was an intimate association between the princes of Saut and the pharaohs at Heracleopolis is demonstrated by the report on the nomarchs' tombs that they had been raised in the household of the pharaohs as part of the family.

But the nomarchs of Saut provided their most valuable service to the pharaohs at Heracleopolis in the defense of their patrons against the recurring incursions from the far south, a region increasingly dominated by Thebes (Waset). Theban nomarchs, originally minor princes situated in a relative backwater of the realm, had steadily grown in power after the decline and collapse of the Old Kingdom. By the time of the 10th Dynasty, they had become strong enough to establish their own dynasty with royal pretensions, i.e., the 11th Dynasty (circa 2,278 BC) which, as Petrie surmised, functioned as a parallel dynasty in the far south of the country. The Thebans began to assert their power militarily, at times coming into open conflict with the regime at Heracleopolis. It was the Saut princes who took the lead against the rebellious southern nomes led by Thebes on the field of battle, perhaps keeping the pharaohs of Heracleopolis on the throne rather longer than otherwise might have been the case.

In the 10th Dynasty, the names of six kings have survived. The back-and-forth struggle with Thebes reaches its climax in the latter phases of this dynasty ending with the ultimate triumph of Thebes. However, before that happens, the able nomarch Tefaba of Saut, wields a strong hand in maintaining some semblance of order on behalf of the Heracleopolitans. He seems to have made much of the country safe from brigandage. When an army from the southernmost nome of Elephantine is sent northward against Heracleopolis, it is met by Tefaba and utterly defeated. Tefaba apparently followed up this success with a southward campaign of pacification that secured, at least for the time being, the position of his pharaonic patron. His son, Kheti II serving under pharaoh Ka-mery-rā, continued the exploits of his father by putting down a revolt from within the nome of Heracleopolis itself and re-installing Ka-mery-rā on the throne. Again, the scanty records, coming preponderantly from the tombs of nomarchs of Saut, indicate that Egypt was, in effect, under a co-rulership. Nominally, the dynasts of Heracleopolis were pharaohs but their reliance on their allies—and likely relatives—at Saut was so complete that these latter were effectively the 'chief executives' under the titular rulership of pharaoh.

The period just discussed comprises the First Chronological Gap, ending with the rise of the 11th Dynasty, followed by the Inter-Age Transition from the Bull-Age of Taurus to the Ram-Age of Aries. The Gap dynasties, i.e., the 7th and 8th, reveal the unmistakable decline and collapse of the Memphite dynasties that comprised what is now called the Old Kingdom. There is nearly nothing that survives from that period to give an account of what happened; it is a gaping lacuna in the historical record of ancient Egypt. With the rise of the 9th and 10th Dynasties at the Horus-city of Heracleopolis, a measure of order and stability is restored with the unstinting and able support of the nomarchs of the Jackal-city of Saut. Without the nomarchs of Saut, the Heracleopolitan hold on the throne of Egypt would not have lasted as long as it did. Nonetheless, pressure began to build from the far south under the emerging Theban dynasts, leading to armed confrontation in the latter phases of the 10th dynasty. Three of the Saut nomarchs were able to stave off these incursions from the south. The Taurus-Aries Inter-Age Transition would have begun during the 10th and 11th dynasty overlap period around 2,466 BC and would have been completed on or around 2,277 BC near the beginning of the 11th Dynasty (Manetho). The 12th Dynasty begins 42 years later around 2,235 BC whose first pharaoh is *Amenembat* or *Amenemes*, the first ruler in Egyptian history to incorporate the name *Amen (Amon)* into his name. The god Amen or Amon is the Ram-deity and his time has arrived. Thebes or *Waset* (Eg.), his sacred city, becomes the capital of Egypt for the next 2,100 years and Amen rises to the summit of the pantheon, fused with Rā as Amon-Rā.

III. The 11th Dynasty—Thebes Ascending (2,278 BC–2,235 BC)

The 11th Dynasty, which more or less ran parallel to the 10th Dynasty centered at Heracleopolis, emerges more or less supreme and unchallenged around 2,278 BC. However, a succession of rulers reigned at Thebes for 184 years prior to the ascendance of the dynasty in 2,278 BC. It was clearly the bridge dynasty in the prolonged period of national political ferment that culminated in the rise of Thebes to the acme of power and, by the end of the 11th Dynasty, its patron deity Amon to the summit of the pantheon. Thebes, it could be said, was the instrument of transition from the Bull-Age of Ptah-Apis (Taurus) to the Ram Age of Amon (Aries). Indeed, three of the important pharaohs of the 11th Dynasty were named *Mentuhotep*, 'Mentu is at peace,' and Mentu was the reigning Bull-deity at Thebes. The very first pharaoh to reign after the close of the 11th Dynasty is *Amenemhat I*, as seen above, so that the 11th Dynasty ensures the closure of one age, Taurus, and paves the way for the commencement of the next, Aries.

There were 10 rulers associated with the 11th Dynasty, the first of whom, *Repa-ha-antefa*, was not styled a pharaoh, but rather a hereditary prince of Thebes who is the forerunner of the 11th Dynasty pharaohs. This Repa-ha-antefa is not ordinarily considered a member of the 11th Dynasty because he was under vassalage to the 10th Dynasty pharaohs, but the 11th may be said to start with him because he is the earliest identifiable ancestor of the subsequent pharaohs. Six of the dynasts carried the name *Antef* either as *Antefãa* (4) or *Antef* (2) and three the name *Mentuhotep*. The 11th Dynasty kings were unmistakably Nubian in provenance as were their successors in the 12th Dynasty. Herodotus reported that there were 18 Ethiopian pharaohs that sat on Egypt's throne, an undetermined number of whom must have reigned in the 11th and 12th Dynasties.

Though most of the 11th Dynasty kings were named Antef, it is the three Mentuhoteps who are the most identifiable and dynamic pharaohs of the 11th. Mentuhotep I is the second king of the dynasty and is the one who begins to re-assert Egyptian hegemony in the lands south, east, and west of the country. Mentuhotep II, the 5th pharaoh of the dynasty, is revealed by an inscription describing the rock cutting activities for his sarcophagus in the quarries of Hammamat. Petrie has an interesting comment to make concerning a Sirian festival commemorated in this reign:

> …in his [Mentuhotep II's] second year a *Sed* festival of Sirius' rising took place; another instance which shows that these festivals were at fixed astronomical dates, and not dependent of the years of the reign.[5]

Later, the Sed festival—a ritual of pharaonic rejuvenation—was celebrated routinely on the 30th anniversary of a pharaoh's reign, should he live so long. In pre-dynastic times, it is likely that any ruler that had lived that long would have been ritually put to death or committed suicide because of the imminent danger posed to the country on account of his failing physical powers. The Sed festival came to function as a ceremonial renewal of the king, thereby forestalling the practice of ritual regicide. Mentuhotep II's mother's name was *Yam*, which is also a name for a Sudanese country well known to the Egyptians. A noted statue of Mentuhotep II pictures him in a white linen gown, seated in the Osirian pose (arms crossed), wearing the red crown of Lower Egypt and of coal-black skin. As alluded to earlier he might well have been one of the 18 Ethiopian pharaohs mentioned by Herodotus.

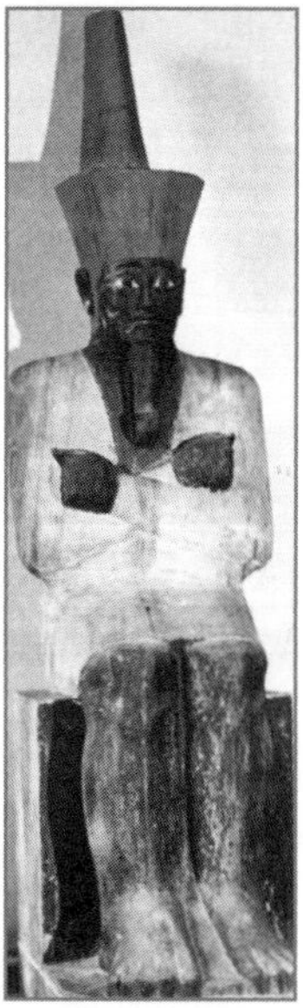

Mentuhotep II—
11th Dynasty

5 Petrie, ibid., p. 131.

A comment by Walter Fairservis is illuminating in this regard:

> It is of interest that among the wives of the Theban king Mentuhotep II there were several with Negro blood and some with body tattooing, indicative of the closeness of Africa to the southern nomes.[6]

Mentuhotep's vizier is Amenemhat by name and it may be conjectured that this personage was an ancestor to the later pharaonic Amenemhats so prominent in the 12th Dynasty. The kings of the 11th Dynasty were, as might be expected, preoccupied with consolidating their position in the face of still fractious provincial nobles whose loyalties could shift like wind-blown desert sand. The fifth Antef of this dynasty is remembered for a decree that degraded one of these treasonous nobles and his entire family, depriving him and his descendants of all titles, lands, and emoluments. Such a man could be replaced, and was. The third (and last) Mentuhotep was undoubtedly the most outstanding ruler of the 11th. He is said to have reigned 46 years and erected numerous monuments all over Egypt. Before the end of the second decade of Mentuhotep III's rule, the Heracleopolitan pharaohs, who had steadily declined in power, were no more, and the Theban kings thenceforth ruled unchallenged. Petrie, in fact, cites later 18th Dynasty testimony that confirms Mentuhotep III's status as 'the restorer of the kingdom.'[7]

The last king of the 11th Dynasty is Antef VI, the son of Mentuhotep III. Antef's proudest accomplishment, typical of all the pharaohs who managed it, was the sponsorship of a successful expedition to Punt, usually said to be where present-day Somalia is located. Punt was sacred land to the Egyptians and the source of one the ancient population streams that flowed into Egypt before the dynastic era. Moreover, Punt was the source of the ritual and commercial goods most highly prized by the Egyptians: myrrh, frankincense, ivory, and ostrich feathers.

Petrie sees in the history of this dynasty evidence of unbroken political and cultural empowerment. The first, or 'ancestral' Antef, is but a princely vassal of the Heracleopolitan pharaoh, though afterward, the early kings of the dynasty style themselves pharaonically as *sa rā*, i.e., 'son of Rā'. However,

6 Fairservis WA, **The Ancient Kingdoms of the Nile**, New York: Thomas Y. Crowell Company, 1962, p. 93.

7 Ibid., p. 140.

their real authority is limited to the southern-most provinces. But the steady improvement in the fortunes of this Theban ruling family is seen in the fine tombs and mummy cases constructed for the second and third Antefs. By the time of Mentuhotep II, the pharaoh is sending crews to Hammamat to quarry for stone for his sarcophagus and is boasting of victories over 13 rebellious Nubian tribes. The fifth Antef is, in his reign, putting up obelisks and claiming conquests over Nubians and Asiastics, meaning that he was campaigning beyond Egypt's borders both south and north. With the accession of Mentuhotep III, the final triumph of the Thebans is inevitable, and he is strong enough to erect temples, commission monuments, and encourage art. He is very likely the first 'real' pharaoh of the dynasty in that midway through his reign, he has become the sole sovereign of Egypt. Antef VI is secure enough to sponsor an expedition to Punt, always an epochal event for any pharaoh, and with his death, the dynasty comes to a close 2,235 BC. The 11th Dynasty at Thebes brought Egypt back to the threshold of greatness, and it is a united, stable, prosperous, thriving country that is passed on to the 12th Dynasty, inaugurating the Middle Kingdom.

Chapter 5:

The Middle Kingdom—The Triumph of Thebes (2,235 BC–1,743 BC?)

Yet again when looking at the next phase of Egyptian history, we are faced with intractable problems of chronology. To repeat, there really was no Middle Kingdom *per se* in Egyptian history, but it is for the historian, a conceptually useful construct by which to clarify the dynamics and permutations of that history. When the terms *Old Kingdom*, *Middle Kingdom*, and *New Kingdom* are employed, they help the reader understand that these are the high points of Egyptian history, the succession of 'golden ages' within the 4,200-year span of dynastic history. Likewise, no one can say that there was a concrete period that was the 'Dark Ages' in European history, but the term—invented in the 18th century—helped the modern student grasp some of the social, political, and cultural dynamics that dominated the 500-year era in Europe between 500 and 1,000 AD.

There are reasonably good dates for the duration of the 12th Dynasty—2,235 BC–2,022 BC—which inaugurates the Middle Kingdom. After that, the historical time sequences are a veritable blur until the launching of the 18th Dynasty—and the New Kingdom—around 1,570 BC. The present author differs from contemporary historians of Egypt who define the Middle Kingdom only by the 12th Dynasty or, in the case of Gardiner, by the 11th and 12th Dynasties. The Middle Kingdom would have continued right up to the end of the 14th Dynasty, i.e., until the advent of Hyksos rule and the 15th Dynasty, estimated to have begun around 1,743 BC. The 2nd Chronological Gap would have begun after the 12th Dynasty and continued until the 15th Dynasty when Egypt, at least the northern half of it, came under the domination of the Hyksos about whom more will be said later. The polar Inter-Age Transition (1,651 BC), highlighted by the 'fall' of Draco and the 'rise' of the Jackal Wep-wat at the North Pole, took place during the Hyksos era.

I. The 12th Dynasty—The Rise of Egyptian Classicism (2,235 BC–2,022 BC)

With the 12th Dynasty, Egypt recovers all her former glory and power. Indeed, some see it as the age of Egypt's greatest cultural efflorescence. Under the increasingly dynamic tutelage of the last pharaohs of the 11th Dynasty, Thebes is already supreme as the capital of the kingdom, and now the Theban Mentu, a form of the Divine Bull, gives way to Amon who becomes the pre-eminent deity of the city and the country, fused with Rā as Amon-Rā. Amon is the Ram-deity and Thebes becomes the Ram-city in the morning of the Ram-age, Aries (begins 2,277 BC). He was an ancient deity who, with the onset of the Middle Kingdom, becomes fused with an equally ancient neter of fertility, the ithyphallic Min, who brought the occasional storm of thunder, lightning, and rain to the Eastern Desert. This incarnation of Amon-Min, the representational power of fertility, thunder, and lighting whose zoomorphic form is the ram, shows him to be an ancient prototype of the Yoruba *orisha* Shango (and the Germanic-Norse deity Thor).

Amenemhet I or ***Amenemēs*** (2,235 BC–2,205 BC)

The first king of this fabled dynasty is Amenemhet I, the first pharaoh to name himself after the god *Amen.*[1] He may have been another of the 18 Ethiopian pharaohs about whom Herodotus reports. In the *Prophecies of Neferti*, it is said concerning the first king of the 12th Dynasty:

1 This author uses the two spellings, Amon and Amen, interchangeably.

> A king shall come from the South, Ameny, the justified by name, the son of a woman from Ta-Seti, child of Upper Egypt. He will take the White Crown, he shall wear the Red Crown...Rejoice, O people of his time...[2]

This Ameny is none other than Amenemhet I and *Ta-Seti* was the contemporary name of Egyptian Nubia. His mother as 'a woman of Ta-Seti' is a Nubian woman, *Nefert* by name. The father of Ameny was the southern priest *Sesotris*,

Amenemhet I—Founder of the 12th Dynasty

several of whose pharaonic descendants took his name in the ensuing 12th Dynasty. Completing the work of his 11th Dynasty predecessors, Amenemhet proves himself to be one of the most able and energetic sovereigns ever to rule Egypt. The proof of his vigorous administration is evident from one end of the country to the other as temples, busts, statues, and monuments of the highest artistic quality are found in abundance. He re-established ancient landmarks, carried out water works, and in every way enabled Egypt to regain the magnificent prosperity she had enjoyed in the Old Kingdom. Moreover, Amenemhet establishes the Temple of Amon at Karnak which will be enlarged and expanded by successive pharaohs for the next 2,000 years, becoming the most famous and largest cult center in Egypt, indeed the world. Nubia, ever restless, is once again pacified as are several Asiatic tribes.

2 Lichteim M, **Ancient Egyptian Literature**, Vol. 1, Los Angeles: University of California Press, (1973)1975, p. 143.

The unflagging importance of a peaceful Nubia is indicated by the building of a series of eight river bank fortresses, the most prominent ones at Semna, the southernmost fortress at the second cataract, and at Buhen, the northernmost of these fortresses, that, until submerged by the waters rising behind the Aswan High Dam (1971), served as some of the most sophisticated examples of military architecture ever achieved.[3] Some say the impetus to build these fortresses began with Amenemhet I, others say they were begun in the reign of his son Sesostris I and completed in the reign of Sesostris III. Whatever the case, they were built in the most strategically advantageous places, on elevations right near the Second Cataract overseeing, on the one hand, the narrow channel through which the Nile was forced at the cataract thereby controlling all boat traffic and, on the other hand, the overland trade routes whose terminus was situated at the same location. At Semna, two fortresses were built—one on the eastern side of the river, and the other on the western side. Three miles to the north another fort, built on an island in the middle of the river, amplified the command exerted by the Egyptian garrisons over the entire Second Cataract region. It was able to monitor river and ground traffic moving north and south, in addition to the land based caravan traffic that moved east and west.

The fortresses were not merely military installations but also customs stations, imposing excise tariffs on the considerable flow of goods moving up and down the river. As in any custom station, the baggage of travelers and merchants was searched for contraband or untaxed goods. The bulk of the luxury goods and religious appurtenances in Egypt came from far to the south and the presence of so many fortifications along a stretch of the Nile that offered maximum control of commerce testifies to the indispensable importance of the inner African trade and the paramount need to protect it. As described by Fairservis, the interiors of the forts were geometrically divided by a straight central main street intersected by side streets at right angles, thus creating blocks for the buildings for administration, garrison offices, and habitation for the soldiers and officials.

---

3 See Fairservis WS, **The Ancient Kingdoms of the Nile**, New York: Thomas Y. Crowell Company, 192, pp. 96-102 for a concise description of these Middle Kingdom river fortresses.

The fortresses were constructed of mud brick, the outer walls being 20 feet thick. Stout wooden beams were inserted at intervals into the walls to strengthen them, reinforced further by buttresses supporting the walls externally. A wide path ran between the habitations inside the fortresses and the outer wall, facilitating rapid movement to the defensive towers built into the walls or to the tops of the ramparts accessible by stairways.

Considering the fortress of Buhen, we find that it extended nearly 500 feet along the West bank of the Nile. It covered more 137,000 square feet and enclosed within its walls a small town laid out in a grid system, able to sustain a population of well over 3,000 people. Its fortifications included a moat 10 feet deep, drawbridges, battlements, loopholes, and a catapult. On the town side of the dry moat was a brick rampart fortified at intervals by circular towers with loopholes along both ramparts and around the outer perimeter of the towers. It was constructed in such a way as to permit the firing of arrows at any attacking force investing the fortress from below. Furthermore, Fairservis tells us,

> The loopholes in the bastion rampart were ingeniously arranged so that a single archer or slinger had a choice of three slots by standing at one aperture. This reduced the number of blind spots where an assaulting enemy might take cover.[4]

The entrance gate at Buhen stood between two massive walls crossing the outer parapet, dry moat, first defensive rampart, inner alley, and finally forming a perpendicular joint with the stout city wall. The narrow entrance passage was served by a drawbridge passing over the dry moat and which moved on rollers. The great entrance portal was closed by double doors and the main wall was protected by square bastions with high towers at the corners.

The methods and designs incorporated into the fortresses were not improved upon ever after, representing the very acme of military architecture. Only the introduction of gunpowder—specifically cannon—made such fortifications obsolete. The ingenuity and resources committed to building, garrisoning, and provisioning these massive fortifications lead ineluctably to the conclusion that the warlike Cushitic kingdoms, especially the one at Kerma, must have

4 Ibid., p. 100

presented a formidable threat to Egypt's dominance of the Nile up to the Second Cataract. That this threat was real is shown in later centuries when Kerma actually took these fortifications by storm and controlled them for several centuries, obviously during a period of comparative Egyptian military weakness. During the heyday of the 12th Dynasty, these fortresses were, for all practical purposes, inviolate. Egypt's geopolitical priorities always focused on Nubia and Cush first. Her economy depended on commerce with a pacified Nubio-Cush as did her indispensable sacerdotal requirements.

Beginning a practice that was to continue through the New Kingdom, Amenemhat associated his son and heir with him in a co-regency toward the end of his reign. This practice had the salutary effect of avoiding an interregnum upon the death of an old king, thus preserving political stability in the country. But despite his power and authority as pharaoh, Amenemhat had to confront one of the recurring threats against those who sat on the throne of Egypt: a treasonous conspiracy, probably hatched in the women's quarters. It nearly cost the pharaoh his life[5] and, on the evidence of a document left behind entitled *The Admonitions of Amenemhat*, left him an embittered and cynical man toward the end of his reign. Indeed, the creation of the co-regency with his son and heir, *Senwosret I*, aka *Sesostris I*, may have been impelled by the near escape from regicide. Amenemhet reigned 30 years, the last 10 years as co-regent with his son Sesostris I.

Senwoseret I or *Sesostris I* (2,205 BC–2,171 BC)

The line of 12th Dynasty of pharaohs was a vigorous line and the reign of Sesostris I was characterized by this vigor. He had inherited a rejuvenated, supremely powerful Egypt from his father and worked assiduously to maintain it. He took it upon himself to re-vitalize the temple of Rā and his sacred city Heliopolis (Annu), both of which had fallen on hard times during the previous centuries of upheaval. Two famous obelisks, one still standing, were erected at Heliopolis at the order of Sesostris. He built a temple and set up monuments dedicated to Osiris at Abydos under the direction of his chief architect

5 Some authorities insist that Amenemhat did in fact succumb to the assassination attempt.

Mentuhotep, who ranked so high in the regime that it may be reasonably supposed that he was a direct descendant of the 11th Dynasty pharaonic Mentuhoteps. Sesostris continued the work started by his father at Karnak and was the first pharaoh to begin the development of the Fayum basin, a large, well-watered oasis about 30 miles west of the Nile in middle Egypt that would

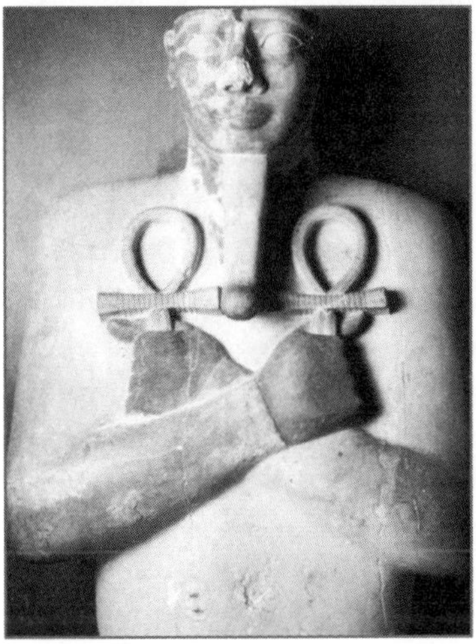

Sesostris I

become an important center of agricultural production. The securing of Nubia continues as one of the highest priorities of the 12th Dynasty pharaohs and Sesostris led a major expedition southward, establishing an Egyptian presence as far as the 3rd Cataract. Some attribute the building of the fortress at Buhen to him, companion to the one built by his father slightly up-river and on the opposite bank at Semna.

It is with the 12th Dynasty that the kingdom of Cush begins to figure prominently in Egyptian annals. The name *Cush* (Eg. *Kesh*), a kingdom situated between the 3rd and 4th Cataracts, is first encountered in the 6th Dynasty (circa 2,900 BC). The oldest archaeologically attested Cushite kingdom was based at Kerma (circa 2,400 BC), near the 4th Cataract, and with the advent of the 12th Dynasty, Egypt and Cush engage in back-and-forth military hostilities—interspersed with periods of peaceful diplomacy and trade—that continue for the next 500 years. At issue is the region now called Nubia, stretching from the 1st Cataract in the north to the 3rd Cataract in the south. The control of Nubia is the essential lynchpin of Egypt's policies directed at peoples and countries beyond her immediate borders. Cush, during this period, is clearly Egypt's most formidable rival, requiring, as has been seen, the construction and garrisoning of the large fortresses on the Nile at the 2nd Cataract. When the 12th Dynasty begins to decline, Cush becomes strong enough to push northward and extend its control all the way up to the 1st Cataract, including the occupation of the fortresses at Semna and Buhen. Wallis Budge, taking his cues from the contemporary reports that mention bodies of 400 Egyptian soldiers 'campaigning' in Nubia, makes this point concerning the 12th Dynasty incursions southward:

> ...it is clear that Egyptians never attempted in the XIIth Dynasty to occupy the country of Kash [Cush]...as far south as the Fourth Cataract, and the companies of soldiers which were sent...on such expeditions were only intended to form a guard to protect whatsoever they might succeed in squeezing out of the Nubians as they were bringing their spoil down the river. Comparatively small bodies of men, such as those which Ameni took... would be no match for any stubborn resistance the Nubians might make...it is clear that his expeditions were nothing but armed caravans, which made their way south from time to time for purely trading purposes.[6]

Western Asia in this dynasty begins to occupy increasing pharaonic attention. There had always been trade relations with Syrio-Palestine and from Old Kingdom times, the most active pharaohs made sure to secure the Sinai Peninsula, an important source of copper. Now, Sesostris extends his activities as far north as Ugarit near the border of Anatolia (modern Turkey). The surviving accounts from Manetho claim that Sesostris reigned for 46 years, but Petrie puts the length of reign at 44 years. This includes 10 years as co-regent with his father prior to ruling alone, and then another two years as co-regent with his son and successor, Amenemhat II.

6 **Budge** EAW, **A History of Egypt**, volume II, Oosterhout N.B. The Netherlands: Anthropological Publications, (1902)1968, p. 19.

Amenemhet II or *Amenemēs II* (2,171 BC–2,136 BC)

Amenemhet II

Amenemhet II, the son of Sesostris I, is elevated to co-regent with his father and accedes to the throne after two years, inheriting an Egypt at the peak of her power and prosperity. There exists now a kind of *pax Aegyptica* in the region because for the next 50 years, there is hardly any military activity. Huge statues more than 22 feet high, weighing 60 tons are erected. Gold and turquoise mines are exploited to the fullest and trade is intensified with Syrio-Palestine, the Aegean, and Mesopotamia. In this peaceful atmosphere, Egypt extends her hegemony in all directions. Statuettes of royal family members and officials are found throughout western Asia and a pharaonic cult center is even established in Anatolia. Relations with the Minoan I kingdoms of Crete are invigorated and Egyptian cultural influences find their way into the Minoan civilizations that will eventually give rise to Mycenae on mainland Greece. Moreover, Grimal says,

> Egypt exerted particularly strong influence over Byblos [Phoenicia], where the chiefs gave themselves Egyptian titles, wrote hieroglyphics and used artefacts originally made on the banks of the Nile.[7]

7 Grimal N, **A History of Ancient Egypt**, translated by Ian Shaw, Cambridge (USA): Blackwell, 1988; 1992, p. 166.

This formative Egyptian cultural impact on the mercantile city states of Phoenicia never abates, so much so that it is possible to think of the Phoenicians as an Egypto-Canaanitic people. The close political, cultural, and religious linkages between Egypt and Phoenicia were exceeded only by those that existed between Egypt and Nubia. Amenemhet II reigned 35 years, capping off a successful reign by sponsoring a voyage to Punt. Despite the peace and prosperity of his reign, he was assassinated in another palace conspiracy, if Manetho is to be believed.

Senwoseret II or *Sestostris II* (2,136 BC–2,112 BC)

Sesostris II

Amenemhet II's successor is Sesostris II who served as co-regent with his father for the last three years of Amenemhet's life. The name *Sesostris* is one that developed a legendary character in the time of classical Greece because of the reports of Herodotus, Manetho, and others that an Egyptian king by that name, unquestionably Sesostris II, campaigned and conquered as far north as Thrace, meaning that Sesostris had conquered all of Western Asia, a good portion of Anatolia, and southeastern Europe. No other Egyptian king, including the redoubtable Thutmosis III of the 18th Dynasty, ever extended his conquests so far. Egyptologists reject these reports as fabulous because there have never been any contemporary inscriptions discovered in Egypt itself attesting to military action this far afield in the 12th Dynasty. Herodotus—who also maintains that Sesostris's military exploits carried him to Arabia and into the Indian Ocean—had this to say about Sesostris's conquests in Europe:

> ...his [Sesostris's] victorious progress through Asia continued, until he entered Europe and defeated the Scythians and Thracians; this, I think, was the furthest point the Egyptian army reached for the memorial columns are to be seen in this part of the country but not beyond.[8]

This report may be yet another instance where the testimony of the classical writers might be more reliable than that of modern Egyptologists. In addition to the above testimonial, Herodotus also reports that two rock-carved images of Sesostris—each more than 7½ feet tall—could still be seen in Ionia (southwestern Turkey).[9] Moreover, Manetho, the Egyptian priest-scribe with access to the ancient records of Egypt, corroborates Herodotus 200 years later. In fact, it was the contention of Herodotus that the Colchians—famous in the story of Jason and the Argonauts as guardians of the Golden Fleece—must have descended from remnants of Sesostris's army because they were black skinned, woolly-haired, and practiced circumcision.[10] The Colchians lived on the northern shores of what is now the Black Sea[11] in the Caucasus region of Russia, showing just how far Sesostris and his army ranged. One modern authority accepts the classical traditions concerning the far-reaching European conquests of Sesostris: Martin Bernal, author of **Black Athena: The Afroasiatic Roots of Classical Civilization**. He writes:

> Herodotus and later Greek writers wrote at some length and in considerable detail about his [Sesostris'] conquests, achieved in campaigns that took him and his army across Asia, Scythia—the South Russian Steppe—to the Caucasus. Writers after Alexander the Great's conquests, which had reached India, argued that Sesostris had gone equally far.[12]

8 Herodotus, **The Histories**, New York: Penguin Books, (1954), 1972, p. 167.

9 Ibid., p. 168.

10 See note 6 in the Introduction to this work. The fabled Colchian royal women, Medea and Circe (**Odyssey**)–both reputed to be sorceresses–were black African women.

11 It might legitimately be wondered if the name *Black Sea* was derived from the presence of the ancient black Colchian civilization on its shores.

12 Bernal M, **Black Athena: The Afroasiatic Roots of Classical Civilization, Volume II**, New Brunswick: Rutgers University Press (1991) p. 25.

For Bernal, Sesostris and his army would have been one of the earliest culture-bearers from northeast Africa to the lands bordering the northern Mediterranean and Aegean and he devotes all of Chapter V of his book to documenting this premise. However, the military expeditions of the three Sesostrises became confused in the minds of later historians and Bernal notes this confusion. In fact to his mind, the Sesostris of legend is Sesostris I when there might be as much or more reason to believe that it was Sesostris II. Since Bernal also devotes a chapter to the presence of Sesostris II in Asia Minor and the Black Sea (Colchis), he is evidently of the opinion that both Sesostris I and II carried out military campaigns and conquests in the same regions, which would account for the confusion surrounding the matter leading to the later conflation of the two conquering pharaohs into one Sesostris.

Concerning the above-mentioned military presence of Sesostris's army on the shores of the Indian Ocean, Budge tells us,

> ...in the first year of the king's [Sesostris's] reign
> his monuments were stablished in Ta-Neter, i.e.,
> the country which lay on each side of the Red Sea
> and extended to the south as far as Somaliland.[13]

Though the empire of Sesostris II does not seem to have lasted much beyond his reign, if these attestations concerning the geographic range of his conquests are true, then he was not only Egypt's first but also her greatest conqueror, one on whom Alexander the Great might have later modeled himself. In fact, Diodorus—over-enthusiastically in the minds of most—asserts that the much earlier conquests of Sesostris equaled and even exceeded that of Alexander.[14] Be that as it may, Sesostris is the only ruler in antiquity whom the Greeks compared to Alexander as an empire-builder and therefore his legendary cachet equaled that of the fabled Macedonian.

Sesostris was not merely a great soldier but also an energetic administrator. He plunged into the further development of the Fayum Basin, begun by his grandfather, the first Sesostris. He commissioned the construction

13 **Budge**, op. cit., p. 26.

14 Vid. **Diodorus I**, translated by Oldfather CH, 55. 1-7, Cambridge: Harvard University Press, 1933 (2004), p. 193.

of extensive waterworks and irrigation projects designed to maximize the agricultural potential of the Basin that continued through the two reigns that followed his. He decided to build his pyramid at Kahun, not too far from Fayum, and this pyramid was completely unique in that it incorporated solid rock into its base and lower structure. The mid-portion of this pyramid was constructed of stone and its upper portion completed with dried brick. The entire assemblage, as the case with all pyramids, was finished with fine white limestone. Nearby, an entire workers village was established—the earliest 'planned community' developed in Egypt—that, however, was soon abandoned to lapse into ruin after the completion of the pyramid. Petrie allots 24 years for the length of this reign, differing from Manetho who gives it a length of 48 years.

Senwoseret III or *Sesostris III* (2,112 BC–2,074 BC)

Sesostris III

The third Sesostris, following well-used tradition, served as co-regent with his father for some years before ascending the throne. Though perhaps somewhat overshadowed by the legendary greatness of his father, he was nonetheless another capable ruler in a dynasty consisting of routinely able rulers. Like his predecessors, he was an active builder, especially in the Delta. In the south, he re-dredged a canal 34 feet wide and 24 feet deep around the 1st Cataract, first excavated in the 6th Dynasty, in preparation for an all-out invasion of Cush. The ever-restless Cushitic nations were pushing north of the 3rd Cataract toward what Egypt considered the southern boundary of her imperial domain at the 2nd Cataract. Sesostris led a formidable army southward, re-pacifying the tribes as he went, finally re-confirming Egypt's boundaries at the 2nd Cataract. The fortresses built in the time of Amenemhet I and Sesostris I at Semna and Buhen were reinforced, and a chain of smaller forts were constructed between Semna and Buhen. It is not without interest, however, that inside Semna itself, Sesostris found it prudent to build a temple to Dedun, a Nubian god. During his reign, Sesostris III found it necessary to campaign southward three (some say four) times to confirm Egypt's power and rule in the region. As already noted, Cush was by far the primary pre-occupation of the 12th Dynasty pharaohs and virtually every one sent armies southward to secure the region and the all-important trade routes. Petrie makes an interesting comment about Sesostris III worth quoting:

> In after ages this king [Sesostris III] was revered as the *founder of Ethiopia* (italics added), and the later kings of the XVIIIth dynasty specially adored him in their temples...[15]

Who it was that revered Sesostris III as the 'founder of Ethiopia' is not said but, again, it does reveal the deep and abiding link between the Middle Kingdom and the lands to the south, impelling numerous military campaigns in that region to secure Egypt's hegemony there. The pharaohs did not ignore Syrio-Palestine or even lands further afield in the north, as the military escapades of Sesostris I and II reveal, but Cush was always uppermost in the minds of these pharaohs when engaged with peoples beyond Egypt's borders. Sesostris III reigned for 38 years.

15 Petrie, op. cit., p. 181.

Amenemhet III or *Amenemēs III* (2,074 BC–2,030 BC)

Amenemhet III

Certain historians consider Amenemhet III the greatest of the 12th Dynasty pharaohs, a line in which virtually every king was endowed with extraordinary qualities of rulership. By the time of his accession, all of Egypt's external enemies, north and south, had been so completely subdued that the third Amenemhet undertook no real military campaigns. He inherited a country at its peak in all domains and proceeded to usher in one of Egypt's finest eras. In this manner he is completely like the later Amenhotep III of the 18th Dynasty who also presided over an Egypt whose magnificence in all domains of society and culture bordered on the fabulous. In a line of vigorous builders, Amenemhet III outdid all his forbears. And more than they, he turned his attention to massive irrigation and land reclamation projects, especially in the Fayum region, an area whose development had become the special enterprise of the 12th Dynasty pharaohs. Before the end of his reign, Amenemhet's engineers, by means of a vast embankment 20 miles long, had reclaimed 20,000 acres of land (40 square miles) from the lake of Fayum—later called Lake Meru or Moeris by the Greeks—which added vast tracts of cultivable land to Egypt's agricultural system. Though cultivable land was thus reclaimed, the lake itself was actually made far larger by artificial means becoming, as will be seen below, the largest man-made water reservoir in the ancient world. Egypt had always been a farm-rich country but from this point on, it became the breadbasket of the entire ancient world. This fact is memorialized in the Book of Genesis in the story of Joseph and his brothers. Petrie gives a good description of Amenemhet's efforts:

> The great work of Amenemhet was not only the reclaiming of all this land, but also the regulation of the flow of the Nile in and out of the lake. Down to the time of Herodotos [450 BC] this annual flow continued, and the lake served to hold part of the surplus of the high Nile, and to let that flow out again during the low Nile.[16]

If these massive and sophisticated water works were still functioning in the time of Herodotus, it means that they had been in operation for 22 centuries. Later in the time of the Ptolemies—circa 330 BC—this system ceased to function because of the Ptolemaic policy of settling veterans on reclaimed land.

Under Amenemhet III, mining operations were carried out on an immense scale, especially at the turquoise and copper mines of Sinai. The feverish building activities meant that quarries of limestone and granite were systematically exploited. Much of this cut stone must have been used to build the famous Labyrinth, a building in the Fayum that eventually encompassed 800,000 square feet. The Labyrinth, consecrated to the crocodile god, Sebek, the patron deity of the Fayum, was visited by several Greek writers, including Herodotus, Diodorus, Strabo, and Pliny, and for one and all the edifice beggared their powers of description. They considered it an even greater marvel than the Great Pyramid, one of the seven wonders of the world:

> ...[the Egyptian kings] constructed a labyrinth, a little above Lake Moeris...I have seen this building, and it is beyond my power to describe; it must have cost more in labour and money than all the walls and public works of the Greeks put together...The pyramids, too, are astonishing structures...but the labyrinth surpasses them.[17]

16 Petrie WMF, **A History of Egypt**, Vol. 1, London: Methuen & Co., 1903, p. 191-2.

17 Herodotus, ibid., p. 188.

Herodotus actually toured the inside of the Labyrinth and found it to be a two-storey building with a continuous wall surrounding it, containing 12 covered courts and 3,000 rooms, half of them underground and the other half directly above them. He was not allowed to descend to the lower tier of the Labyrinth that contained, according to his guides, the tombs of 12th Dynasty kings and the sacred crocodiles, figures of the god Sebek. However, Herodotus did tour the upper level of rooms and says concerning them:

> ...it is hard to believe that [the upper rooms] are the work of men; the baffling and intricate passages from room to room and from court to court were an endless wonder to me, as we passed from a courtyard into rooms, from rooms into galleries, from galleries into more rooms, and thence into yet more courtyards.[18]

The entire Labyrinth was built of stone—probably limestone and granite—and its walls were covered with beautifully incised figures and inscriptions. None of the other known Labyrinths, including the one in Crete—famous in the story of Theseus and the Minotaur—bore comparison to the original in Egypt and, in fact, must have been modeled on Amenemhet's Labyrinth. The artificial expansion of Lake Moeris, the reclamation of 20,000 acres of arable land, and the construction of the marvelous Labyrinth account for Amenemhet's enduring reputation for greatness.

With all his extraordinary building and land-reclamation activity, Amenemhet III did not neglect to perform the duty that guaranteed his fame and prestige for Egyptian posterity: he sent two expeditions to Punt. A recently-discovered temporary naval installation in six caves on the Red Sea has revealed a stele erected by Amenemhet detailing the two expeditions to Punt.[19] The ships themselves were built at a Nile shipyard, carried 94 miles across the Eastern Desert to the Red Sea, then reassembled for the voyage to Punt. As always, the expedition returned to this base laden with gold, frankincense, myrrh, ivory, skins, and exotic animals.

Amenemhet's reign lasted 44 years.

18 Ibid., p. 189.

19 Vid., Ward C, *World's most ancient ship timbers found in Egypt*, **USA TODAY,** 3/7/2006.

Amenemhet IV or *Amenemēs IV* (2,030 BC–2,021 BC)

Amenemhet IV

Up to the accession of this pharaoh, the first six 12th Dynasty rulers might, with some justification, be considered the most remarkable line of kings ever to reign in Egypt. Each sovereign was an outstanding ruler in his own right and at least four—the first and third Amenemhets and first and second Sesostrises—must be considered among the greatest kings to sit on any throne anywhere. However, with Amenemhet IV, there is a noticeable, almost abrupt, decline in the fortunes of the 12th Dynasty. His reign only lasts nine years and monuments dating from this reign are few and unremarkable. He did continue the policy of his forefathers of developing the Fayum basin and at least two temples there are attributed to him.

Sebek-neferu or *Skemiophris* (2,021 BC–2,017 BC)

Sebek-neferu—Pharaoh-Queen
Last Ruler of the 12th Dynasty

Sebek-neferu ('the beauties of Sebek'), the sister of Amenemhet IV, succeeds him as the third woman pharaoh to sit on Egypt's throne. Some suggest that she was his wife as well and like Nitocris before her she ends as the last pharaoh of the dynasty. Her rule lasts a little less than four years but at least one pyramid seems to have been commissioned by her which may have begun even before her accession. Again, her primary historical interest rests in (1) her position as only the third of four woman pharaohs known to rule Egypt, (2) her obvious connection to Sebek, the crocodile-god of the Fayum so revered by the 12th Dynasty pharaohs, and (3) the manner in which the 12th Dynasty comes to a close with her. It is noticeable that the first two women pharaohs were named after Neith and this last pharaoh of the 12th Dynasty was named after the son of Neith – Sebek. The explanation for this evident connection to Neith among these three women pharaohs must be speculative. After Sebek-Neferu's reign, the Middle Kingdom continues through the 14th Dynasty but another chronological gap sets in that enshrouds Dynasties 13 to 17.

The World of the Middle Kingdom

It is generally conceded that Egypt may have reached its greatest cultural heights during the Middle Kingdom. Certainly the quality, quantity, and diversity of its literature attained a level of accomplishment never equaled afterward. In fact, the most perfect form of the Egyptian language is said to be that which was achieved during the Middle Kingdom; Middle Kingdom literature in after times became the classic literature of Egypt. Scientific texts, proverbial literature, popular novels, plays, and poetry all flourished as never before in this era. More than 100 manuscripts from the Middle Kingdom have been found. Below are listed the categories and titles of the most important surviving literary works from the Age:

Instructions (actually political tracts in the form of maxims)

Maxims of Ptahhotep
Instructions of Kagemni
Maxims of Djedefhor
Instructions of Amenemes I
The Loyalist Instruction
Instructions to the Vizier
Admonitions of Merikare
The Kemyt
The Satire of Trades
The Prophecy of Neferti
Instructions of a Man to his Son
Admonitions of Ipuwer (some conclude that this tract was composed after the Middle Kingdom)

Proverbial Sayings and Lamentations

Song of the Harper (11th Dynasty)
Dispute of a Man with his Ba
Collections of the Sayings of Khakheperreseneb

Fictional Stories

The Eloquent Peasant
Sinuhe
Tale of the Shipwrecked Mariner

Mythic Epics

Destruction of Humanity
Tale of Isis and Ra
Tale of Horus and Set
Drama of the Coronation (Revived in the 25th Dynasty as *The Memphite Drama of Creation*)

Scientific Texts

The Kahun Gynecological Papyrus
The Rhind Mathematic Papyrus

It has been oft-noted that the Middle Kingdom, in sharp contrast to the Old Kingdom, spawned a category of writing that might be called a 'pessimistic' literature. This pessimism is seen in works such as *Dispute of a Man with his Ba, The Prophecy of Neferti*, *The Admonitions of Ipuwer*, and even the fictional tale *The Eloquent Peasant*. Indeed, *Song of the Harper*, an 11th Dynasty composition, can be included in this category of literature because it appears just as Egypt is beginning to emerge from the nightmarish times of the 1st Chronological Gap, i.e., at the dawn of the Middle Kingdom. James Henry Breasted in fact sees in the works attributed to Neferti and Ipuwer evidence of the prophetic and messianic ethos that would later become the driving leitmotiv of the Old Testament:

> Just as the literatures of modern Europe have grown up saturated with our ancient inheritance from Greece and Rome, so it was in Palestine inevitable that the Hebrews should be profoundly influenced in their thinking and their writing by the literature of the great nation which had held Palestine as its cultural and political province longer than Rome held Gaul.[20]

20 Breasted JH, **The Dawn of Conscience**, New York: Charles Scribner's Sons, 1933, p. 383.

In the compositions of Neferti and Ipuwer, a long litany of the evils and terrors of political and social anarchy is mitigated by the prediction of the appearance of a savior-king who would be a 'shepherd to his people'. In *The Prophecy of Neferti*, this 'shepherd' would be none other than Amenemhet I, the founder of the 12th Dynasty. In the *Dispute of a Man with his Ba*, a litany of complaints of a man suffering from the vicissitudes of life clearly prefigures the lamentations of Job and Jeremiah. Beyond a doubt, the cause of this moral hand-wringing was the traumatic after-effects of the shadowy events of the 1st Chronological Gap. By the end of the 11th Dynasty, the worst was over and with the advent of the 12th, Egyptian civilization and political power had regained its previous ascendancy. Still, the complacent confidence in an Egypt expected to permanently endure undistracted and undisturbed was definitely shaken. The country could never again take for granted its place in the world; the forces of division, desecration, and disintegration from then on would be thought of as hovering never far from the visible horizon.

It is probably no coincidence that from the 12th Dynasty on, Egyptian imperialistic fervor gradually intensifies, coming to a head in the New Kingdom. Beginning with the accession of Amenemhet I, Egyptian government is stabilized, re-ordered, and strengthened in a manner not seen since the height of the Old Kingdom. Each of the pharaohs down to the end of the dynasty is extremely powerful and accomplished, able to ensure an uncommon level of internal peace, prosperity, and development. Nonetheless, the limitless power of pharaoh, in spite of the vigor of the reigning monarchs, is now something of a *pro forma* facade. That is to say, the position and privileges of the hereditary nomarchs and others of the higher landed nobility, acquired during the extended period of political disarray, could not be abrogated. Though the Middle Kingdom was one of Egypt's most magnificent periods, it was also her feudal era, with hereditary nomarchs and landowners retaining a certain degree of autonomy. As Breasted remarks, they owed pharaoh their loyalty and service, but they were not his officials or employed by him.[21] This state of affairs is shown to best effect in the tombs of many of these nobles, many of them representing royal tombs in miniature, so to speak. Thus, what was good

21 Breasted JH, **A History of Egypt**, New York: Charles Scribner's Sons, (1909)1937, p. 158-9.

for pharaoh in the afterlife was, on a smaller scale, good for anyone wealthy and important enough to imitate the royal prerogatives. These nomarchs, many of whom could trace their families and inheritance back to the Old Kingdom, controlled all the machinery of government in their nomes, including police powers and the court system. Moreover, the nomarch collected taxes and functioned as the high priest of his own sacerdotal college. In the Old Kingdom, no official, no matter how well-favored, would have presumed so much. However, in the Oryx nome, scenes on some of the walls of the tombs of several nomarchs actually depict tribute-bearers from Asia and Libya bringing gifts and one nomarch was able to send his own army on expeditions into Nubia and the Libyan Desert. Clearly, some of these nomarchs looked upon themselves as mini-pharaohs and ran their domains accordingly. That such liberties were tolerated, even by the seemingly all-powerful 12th Dynasty kings, testifies to the continuing power of the hereditary noble class acquired during the 'Gap' dynasties. It is probable, therefore, that the 12th Dynasty custom of associating the pharaonic heir-apparent to the living king as co-regent was motivated by a need to (1) pre-empt palace conspiracies and (2) preserve pharaonic power against the simmering pretensions of the landed nobility.

The Middle Kingdom sees an expansion of governmental administration, especially as concerns raising revenue, and the emergence of a middle class of officialdom. Breasted makes the point that the quasi-autonomy of the nomarchs has the effect of cutting into the traditional revenue sources of the crown so other means of filling the treasury had to be exploited. The fiscal needs of these pharaohs to finance their ambitious projects may explain (1) the almost obsessive attention paid by the 12th Dynasty kings to the agricultural development of the Fayum (Lake Moeris), (2) the extensive exploitation of turquoise, copper, and gold mines, and (3) the repeated military campaigns into Nubia, ensuring pharaonic control of that country—and its luxury goods—up to the 2nd Cataract. Expeditions to Punt served the same purpose. With the increased inflow of such revenue, the pharaonic treasury—called *het hedj*, or 'the White House'—expanded apace. With the intensified interest in the further reaches of Nubia and Punt, extensive river- and sea-going fleets were built, largely under the supervision of the chief treasurer. A vast army of scribes and functionaries evolves to meet these administrative demands and new, previously unknown directorates, offices, and secretariats are created within this expanding bureaucracy. Within this new officialdom are included the engineers, skilled artisans, and technicians necessary to exploit the ever-expanding sources of wealth. For the first time, a real middle class develops in Egypt.

Now, more than ever before, pharaoh must depend on the class of 'new men' that had first come into being in the Old Kingdom. These are talented commoners recruited into official service—often in boyhood—who serve entirely at the pleasure of pharaoh and whose personal loyalty to him and his enterprises is absolute. This practice is yet another means by which the royal house constrains the pretensions of the landed nobility. Among other things, these officials maintain the tax records and the on-going population census of Egypt. There is a comprehensive registration list that bears the name of every family head nation-wide along with names of every member of his household. This census list is up-dated every 10–15 years. A special category of these 'new men' were the military officers because for the first time, Egypt possesses a standing army with a trained and carefully organized soldiery. Such an army makes possible Egypt's military adventures in Nubia, Palestine, Asia Minor, and Europe (if the Greek commentators' reports are correct). This army, again, gave pharaoh a certain amount of necessary leverage not only abroad but also at home.

The Medjay—The Egyptian Army

Nonetheless, the nomarchs were obliged to supply military contingents to pharaoh in wartime.

A certain caste-like structure, already nascently evident in the Old Kingdom, becomes more deeply entrenched in Egyptian society. By this system, a son follows his father into his profession generation after generation, so that almost all professions become hereditary, from peasant to priest, farmer to functionary. These castes are occupational but clearly that of the scribe—a subset of the priestly caste—is the most desirable and prestigious among the common run of people. There are thousands of such scribes producing hundreds of thousands of papyrus manuscripts for all sorts of economic, official, religious, judicial, and technical purposes. Nonetheless, the vast body of the populace is illiterate. However, it is not unknown for a son of a peasant revealing unusual ability to be taken out of his mud-laden surroundings and co-opted into the scribal caste to serve pharaoh and the state. The system, therefore, is not inflexible; a certain amount of structural fluidity allows upward mobility for the unusually talented. Egypt's caste system has none of the racial and religious rigidity inherent in the Hindu caste system. Egyptian caste membership implied no *a priori* presumption of moral or spiritual worth or lack of same; there were no Untouchables in Egypt. A similar system of occupational castes can be found in the Western Sudan—Senegal, Guinea, and Mali—even today.

As is to be expected in a dynasty that constitutes one of Egypt's golden ages, temples, monuments, statues, and tombs were constructed and erected all over the country, without letup. All of the kings revert back to pyramid-building for their tombs and several of them exhibit unusual features. However, unlike in the Old Kingdom, the core masonry of these pyramids are of brick, though the outer casing is made of the traditional white limestone. The inside chambers of these pyramids are more remarkable than their outer structures, the architects having contrived to create extremely clever systems of passageways, portals, false doors and rooms with the sole aim of confusing tomb robbers. Indeed, the inner arrangements of the 12th Dynasty pyramids were, in effect, cunning mazes. But this era was to represent the 'last gasp' of Egyptian pyramid-building; there would be no further pyramids built in Egypt after the end of the 12th Dynasty.

As already seen, the rise of the 12th Dynasty parallels the ascendance of Amon to the pinnacle of the pantheon, an ascendancy firmly secured by the fusion with Rā as Amon-Rā. This deity now represents the Supreme Being in his visible (Light and Sun) and invisible manifestations (Dark and Hidden when traveling through the Underworld). Breasted calls this newly-fused deity Amon-Rā a manifestation of a 'pantheistic solar monotheism' which in the New Kingdom will seguè into the exclusive solar monotheism of Aton under Akhenaton.[22] There are reasons to believe that Amon, like a number of other important Egyptian deities, was originally Nubian or Cushitic and in later

Amon—Supreme Neter of Thebes,
Paramount Neter of Egypt's Pantheon

Amon Amon-Min Amon-Rā

centuries his most important cult centers will be located in Cush. The other deity who flourishes is Osiris. Osiris is already an important deity at the beginning of the Old Kingdom but by Middle Kingdom times, his sway over the general populace of Egypt is uncontestable. Amon-Rā reigns as the supreme ruler of the state pantheon but Osiris is beloved and venerated by the people as a whole. In fact, Osiris is the only deity whose central importance persists unmodified through the entire 40 centuries of Egyptian history. His sacred city, Abydos, becomes the holiest shrine in the land, a pilgrimage destination for the truly pious. All the pharaohs erected cenotaphs at Abydos. The Egyptians who could made arrangements to be buried there, testifying to the enormous pull of Osiris on everyone in Egypt from peasant to potentate. The Osirian drama—involving as divine *dramatis personae* Osiris himself, Isis, Set, and Horus—developed an elaborate presentation and was enacted yearly at Abydos. Osiris's unquestioned spiritual authority derives from his position as the

22 Ibid., p. 171.

guarantor of resurrection and immortality for the faithful, inherent in his role as Lord of the Underworld and Judge of the Dead. There are well-defined ethical and moral components in the Osirian dispensation and these are emphasized with ever-greater clarity and insistence. This ethical emphasis is seen to good effect in *The 42 Declarations of Innocence*, a crucial chapter in **The Book of the Coming Forth by Day**, which dates back to early unification times but has turned into a wholly Osirian document and spiritual manifesto. **The Book of the Coming Forth by Day** is now the central religious document in the culture, providing, as has been said, 'a road map for the soul.'

Osiris Kem Wer
"Great Black One"

Isis the Divine
Virgin Mother

Horus, the Divine Son
and Rising Sun

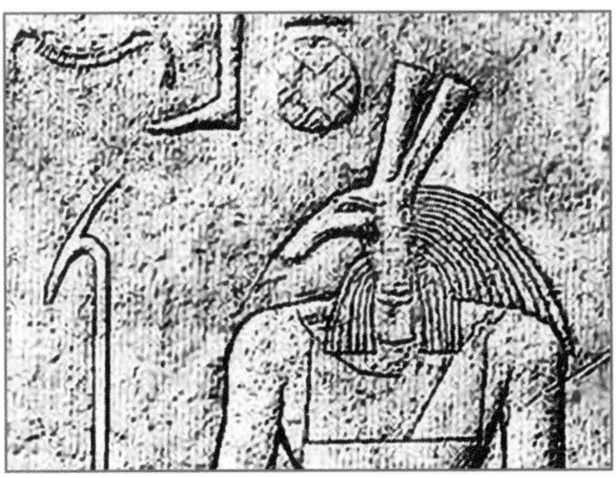

Set—The Great Adversary

By now, Set's main role is that of the Great Adversary, though he yet retains his place in the pantheon. The pharaohs of this and later times do not hesitate to call on Set's prowess in battle when embarking on military campaigns. Isis as the sister-wife of Osiris and mother of Horus emerges as the paramount goddess in Egypt, with virtually as much prestige and power as Osiris. This prestige and power only increases as the centuries wear on, and it is her cult that is propelled out of Egypt to establish itself everywhere in the Mediterranean world in late antiquity. Horus, who is both Rā and Osiris re-born, shares in the power and prestige of the Osirian dispensation. All pharaohs are considered the human avatars of Horus. In their earlier manifestations, Horus and Set were complementary Twins; now they are implacable enemies, though uncle and nephew. Some see in the murderous rivalry of Set-Horus the prefigurement of the Hamlet story.[23]

In after-ages, the Egyptians viewed the Middle Kingdom—most particularly the 12th Dynasty—as their classical Age. Later pharaohs strove to emulate the achievements of the epic rulers of this period and, indeed, the era continuously evoked a persistent nostalgia in the centuries to follow. Not even the herculean accomplishments of the Old Kingdom left such an indelible impression on the consciousness of Egypt from the New Kingdom on, at least not until the time of the 25th Dynasty.

23 See de Santillana G and von Dechend H, **Hamlet's Mill**, Boston: David R. Godine, 1977, passim.

Chapter 6:

The Second Chronological Gap (2,017 BC–1,738 BC) and Second Inter-Age Transition (1,770 BC–1,651 BC)

With the close of the 12th Dynasty, Egyptian history reverts to a phase of information black-out that encompasses Dynasties 13 through 17, what Flinders Petrie calls 'the second of the two great periods of obscurity in Egyptian history'. The same problems and conundrums that bedevil historians concerning the 1st Chronological Gap are met with again in this era. It is also clear that the Middle Kingdom does not come to an end with the close of the 12th Dynasty. Neither the government nor the society itself undergo any tremendous upheaval until the end of the 14th Dynasty, which makes the dearth of records in this part of the 2nd Gap period all the more puzzling. But the most traumatic event in Egyptian history gets underway at the end of the 14th Dynasty as Egypt is taken over by the Hyksos—or 'Shepherd Kings'—who inaugurate the 15th and 16th Dynasties and are not completely expelled from Egypt until the end of the 17th. The era of domination by the Hyksos must be seen as the 'continental divide' of Egyptian history. Egyptian history ever after flows in a different direction, though the great 18th Dynasty restores to Egypt all she has lost and, in fact, creates the first true Egyptian empire. The 18th Dynasty, as will be seen, joins the 4th and the 12th Dynasties as Egypt's greatest epochs and a not inconsiderable body of opinion considers it the most magnificent of all of Egypt's historical epochs.

The Hyksos rule more or less coincides with the Inter-Age Transition that marks the shift of the north magnetic pole from Ta-Urt/Draco to Wep-wat/Ursa Minor, inaugurating another 3,703-year polar age (begins 1,651 BC). This polar precessional transit is meaningless to modern historians who, with one or two exceptions, ignore its historical relevance to Egypt or simply know nothing about it. All reference to the precession is absent from the standard histories of Egypt. With the 'accession' of the triple Jackal neter Anubis-Wepwat-Sab at the pole, the role of the jackal figure is greatly magnified in the religious symbolism and ritual of ancient Egypt, becoming an extremely important element in the Osirian funerary ceremonies. Anubis in the ritual enactments related to Osiris, in his role as the guide, embalmer, and resurrector assumes a role secondary only to that of Osiris himself. Henceforth, Anubis is frequently depicted as the help-mate and 'right-hand man' of Isis. In some ways, he seems to assimilate to himself, or at least share, some of the ritual functions of Horus. All-in-all, the Anubis-Wepwat-Sab figure becomes a prominent feature of Egyptian religion and is transferred to Greek mythology as the three-headed dog Cerebrus, guarding the entrance to the Underworld.

I. The 13th and 14th Dynasties (2,017 BC–1,738 BC)

Though these dynasties are properly Middle Kingdom dynasties, we find that the 2nd Chronological Gap begins with them and so should be considered under the rubric of the 'Chronological Gap' (or Petrie's 'period of obscurity'). As with the 7th and 8th Dynasties in the twilight of the Old Kingdom, next to nothing is known about the 13th and 14th Dynasties apart from the names of numerous kings about whom little can be said from the fragmentary state of the Turin Papyrus and other monumental sources. Though Manetho is used as a guide by the early 20th century Egyptologists for the chronology of this period, it is difficult to credit the length of time—637 years—accorded to these two dynasties from the versions of his *Epitome*. Furthermore, it is difficult to accept Manetho's duration for the Hyksos era of 511 or 518 years, depending on the version of his *Epitome.* It would mean 1,150 years elapsed between the end of the 12th and the beginning of the 18th Dynasties, representing an impossible chronology based on everything else known and taking into account the severe corruptions that crept into the *Epitome* from the pens of the later redactors and copyists.

There are at least 55 13th Dynasty kings named from the monuments, it being largely a Theban dynasty, but none of them ruled very long. Still, there is little evidence of political collapse or military upheaval. However, this dynasty presided over an ever-weakening central government and probably lasted no more than 155 years. Certain monuments and stele of these kings survive and there is evidence that several of the kings may have been Nubian. One—Rā-Nehsi—was incontestably so on the strength of his name *Nehsi,* which means 'Nubian.' Morever, several others are depicted adoring the Nubian goddesses *Anqet* and *Sati,* the divine consorts of *Khnum* at the 1st Cataract in

Khnum—Guardian of the First Cataract

Sati and Anquet: Goddesses of the Nile Cataract and Flood, Consorts of Khnum

Nubia. Recalling that the Egyptian priests told Herodotus that 18 Ethiopians sat on Egypt's throne, it is reasonable to surmise that a few of these may have reigned during the 13th Dynasty. Rā-Nehsi is also of interest because he was apparently a Set-worshiper which testifies to a well-known but unheralded connection between Set and Rā. The other singular fact concerning the 13th

Dynasty kings is that many of them bore the name of the crocodile god Sebek in their own royal names, showing that they continued the 12th Dynasty practice of venerating Sebek. It is thought, in fact, that the earliest of the 13th Dynasty kings were related by marriage to the family of Amenemhet III meaning there was no sharp break between the Dynasties 12 and 13. But Budge's assessment of the 13th Dynasty kings, whom he says cannot be considered kings in the same way the Amenemhets and Sesostrises of the previous dynasty were kings, must be substantially correct:

> It is hard not to come to the conclusion that the kings of the XIIIth Dynasty, whatever their number may have been, little by little lost their hold upon the country, and that, once having done so, Egypt was rent from one end to the other by internal dissensions.[1]

This reversal of fortune for Egypt was exacerbated by a series of low floods and the onset of near-famine conditions in the country. Given the role the Nile and its floods played in the national life of Egypt in all domains, these low-water events could not have been interpreted as anything other than omens of evil times to come.

With the steady decline of Egypt's political power, her traditional enemies, tentatively at first but more actively as time went on, begin to make bolder incursions into what had previously been Egyptian imperial territory. Nowhere is this pattern more evident than with Egypt's southern rival Cush, centered at Kerma, which began to push its way northward. By the time of the Hyksos era, Cush had seized control of the 2nd cataract, occupied the two fortresses at Semna and Buhen, and encroached on Egyptian territory as far north as the 1st Cataract, Egypt's southern national boundary. From the north, Canaanitic tribes had begun to infiltrate across the Sinai and into the eastern Delta regions. To the extent the Old Testament story of Abraham can be considered true history, his sojourn in Egypt would have undoubtedly transpired in the late 13th or early 14th Dynasty. Though originating in Chaldea, Abraham wandered through Canaan and thence into Egypt, after which the whole

1 **Budge** EAW, **A History of Egypt**, volume II, Oosterhout N.B. The Netherlands: Anthropological Publications, (1902)1968, p. 83.

character and direction of his life and that of his clan changed. He was born sometime between 2,000 BC and 1,900 BC.

The 14th Dynasty, according to Manetho, lasted 184 years though it is difficult to believe that it lasted longer than 125 years. Again, the names of a number of 14th Dynasty kings have been preserved on the monuments but very little can be said about them. For Petrie, this dynasty represented the period in which Egypt was being 'harried' and raided by eastern desert peoples in what amounted to a 'softening up' campaign that would culminate in the final conquest of Egypt by the Hyksos. The 14th was clearly the dynasty of decline and collapse of Egyptian power, representing the true termination of the Middle Kingdom. None of the reigns lasted longer than three years, and it is not unlikely that at any given time, more than one ruler was calling himself pharaoh, if in name only. Thus of the numerous kings attributed to this dynasty, not many had any real claim to being so and the country slid inevitably into anarchy. All the Hyksos really had to do was walk in and take over the country, and that is in fact what they did.

II. The 15th and 16th Dynasties: The Epoch of Hyksos Rule (1,738 BC–1,630 BC)

The era of Hyksos domination of Egypt utterly traumatized the Egyptian national consciousness and left an indelible scar on its history, but this era has always been extremely mysterious. The etymology of the name *Hyksos*, from the Egyptian *Hikau khasut*,[2] is variously rendered as 'shepherd kings' or 'captive shepherds,' though the first meaning is to be preferred. They are assumed to be 'Asiatics' or Canaanites but there is little certainty about it. The term 'Hyksos', as Alan Gardiner points, out must refer to the rulers themselves rather than the people they led and no one can say for certain to what race they belonged or their national origin. The most striking aspect of their conquest of Egypt is how easy it seems to have been. Manetho, quoted by the 1st century Jewish apologist in the essay *Against Apion*, says

> There was a king of ours, whose name was Timaus.

2 Aldred C, **Akenaten: King of Egypt**, London: Thames & Hudson, Ltd., 1988, p. 117.

> Under him it came to pass, I know not how, that God was averse to us, and there came, after a surprising manner, men of ignoble birth *out of eastern parts,* and had boldness enough to make an expedition into our country, and with ease subdued it by force, yet *without our hazarding a battle with them* (emphasis added)[3]

It is noteworthy that Manetho calls them men who came out of 'eastern parts,' which might just as readily have been Egypt's eastern deserts as Canaan. So while the Hyksos might have had some affinity to Canaanitic peoples, it is by no means certain, as noted above, that they themselves were 'Asiatic'. In fact, given the way they infiltrated and eventually took over Egypt, it is more plausible to assume that they were tribes of Egypt's eastern desert who if not Egyptian nationals themselves had, under their chieftains and 'kings', lived as 'dependents' under an Egyptian 'protectorate' for many centuries. Though he gives conflicting testimony regarding the origin of the Hyksos, Cyril Aldred nonetheless writes:

> A painting in the tomb of the nomarch Khnumhotep at Beni Hasan, dating to c. 1890 BC, shows a trading party of…men, women, and children, in their leather buskins and long coats of many colors being received by Khnumhotep *in his capacity as governor of the Eastern Desert* (emphasis added). The Egyptians referred to the tribal chiefs of these nomads as *Hikau Khasut…* a term which Manetho rendered as *Hyksos* or 'Shepherd kings'.[4]

During the 12th Dynasty, these eastern chieftains would have supplied auxiliary troops to pharaoh's army, especially that of the imperialistic Sesostrises. It is not unlikely that this troop levy would have continued through the succeeding dynasties, placing these 'shepherd kings' in an advantageous position to monitor Egypt's political decline and, at the strategic moment, take advantage of it to seize power themselves. Moreover, a definable Asiatic population had settled more or less permanently in the Delta, providing an eventual locus of support for the incursions of the Hyksos. The Egyptian government would have been

3 In *Against Apion*, **Josephus: The Complete Works**, translated by W.P. Whiston, Grand Rapids: Kregel Publications, (1867)1981, pp. 610-1.

4 Aldred, ibid.

so weak and ineffectual by this time that the 'coup' was simplicity itself; the Hyksos met no effective opposition.

Hyksos—1700 BC

Parenthetically, it can be noted that this scenario would play itself out repeatedly through subsequent history of Egypt and indeed the world when dominant, hegemonic civilizations found themselves caught in a downward spiral of irresistible decline. Pastoral 'barbarians' would then step in and take over, usually without much effective resistance. But the essential point to establish here is that the Hyksos, a loose confederation of northeast African shepherd peoples, if not actually Egyptian, would have already been at least partially Egyptianized. However, if Manetho is correct, the invaders truly were barbarians, burning cities, demolishing temples, slaughtering inhabitants, and reducing many to bondage. Later, however, they settled down to become pharaohs completely in the Egyptian manner. In fact, apart from the initial savagery of their conquest, the Hyksos change nothing in the civilization.

There are a group of statues reputed to be from the Hyksos period revealing faces that Petrie describes as showing 'high cheek-bones, flat cheeks...a massive nose, firm projecting lips, and thick hair...'[5] Such a description would seem to deviate very little from the well-known African type that characterizes other Egyptian pharaohs, making it difficult to think of the Hyksos as 'Semitic' as so many want to do. The other factor bearing on this question is that at no time

5 Petrie WMF, **A History of Egypt**, Vol. 1, London: Methuen & Co., 1903, p. 237.

is it possible to pinpoint a Hyksos kingdom or empire in Western Asia, before, during, or after their rule of Egypt. A few scarabs found in Palestine with the names of Hyksos pharaohs only testifies to their political reach into the region during their ascendancy in Egypt. If, however, they were nomadic peoples from Egypt's eastern desert as seems probable, the utter lack of material evidence of their existence as a formal kingdom makes complete sense.

The other striking aspect of Hyksos rule is the elevation of the god Set to supremacy. Set was *par excellence* the paramount deity of the desert and desert peoples. That Canaanitic peoples during the Hyksos dynasties could more or less freely migrate into the Delta—including the clan of Jacob-Israel that was ancestral to the Hebrews of history—was facilitated by the prominence of the god Sutekh, the Canaanitic Set, among them. The worship of the goddess *Anath*, a war-goddess and a consort of Set, is also established at this time and becomes a permanent, if minor, fixture in the pantheon, assimilated to the goddess *Nit* (Neith) of the Western Delta. Toward the end of the 17th Dynasty, according to one tradition, the final war between the Thebans and the Hyksos that ended in the complete expulsion of the Hyksos was precipitated by the insistence on the part of the Hyksos pharaoh Apepa that the Thebans acknowledge the supremacy of Set. This act would have had the effect of setting aside Amon, a circumstance no Theban was prepared to endure. In the early decades of the 18th Dynasty that launched the New Kingdom, Set was anathemized as never before, with numerous of his statues hacked to pieces. This fury against Set is attributed by some to his association with the hated Hyksos whom the Egyptians—at least among the priesthood and royalty—called *iati*, meaning 'unclean' or 'accursed.' With the advent of the 19th Dynasty, however, Set recovers much of his former prominence if only because the pharaohs found that they needed his power in the prosecution of their wars.

With the accession of the Hyksos to power, the Delta becomes more fully populated by Canaanitic peoples than ever before and though these immigrants in time become fully Egyptian in culture and outlook, the imprint of Canaan or Palestine on the Delta would be permanent. Much of this population movement from Palestine into the Egyptian Delta was propelled by geo-political events farther east, as the first Babylonian empire took root and began to expand. Babylonia, in turn, started to feel political and military pressures from the Kassites and Assyrians and the combination of these forces impelled certain of the rootless, nomadic peoples of Canaan to seek a haven in an Egypt now more or less open to them in the Delta. Again, the sojourn of the Children of Israel in Egypt can be appreciated in this light. Cyril Aldred sees the story of Joseph, which would have taken place against the background of Hyksos rule, as an example of the introduction of slaves into Egypt on a significant scale.[6] There was comparatively little evidence of slavery in the ordinary sense of it in Egypt before the Hyksos period but afterward a steady stream of slaves do appear to have been brought into Egypt, largely from Western Asia, at least down to the end of the New Kingdom. Nicolas Grimal sees evidence that there was a greater degree of integration of the Hyksos people into the body politic of Egypt than the later recriminatory texts of the New Kingdom would suggest.[7] The Hyksos became in all things Egyptian and the Hyksos kings especially worked diligently to immerse and present themselves in the tradition and style of Egypt's long line of pharaohs. In every day affairs, life went on much as before: temples were built, statues were erected, trade and diplomacy carried on, literature published, and scientific endeavors pursued. The extant copy of the renowned Rhind Mathematic Papyrus, though originally produced during the Middle Kingdom, was re-published in the reign of Apepa I. And for awhile the Hyksos were able to rule through loyal Egyptian vassals even in Upper Egypt. Moreover, Egyptian women were espoused to Hyksos officials and Hyksos women to highly-placed Theban nomarchs in the south. Thus, there was a far greater degree of mutual accommodation between the Egyptians and the Hyksos than the New Kingdom annals would have posterity believe. This relative stability between the two peoples would not abide for long, however.

The Hyksos established their capital at Avaris on the eastern-most of the seven Delta channels of the Nile near Tanis. Avaris was an older Egyptian town appropriated, re-built, and expanded by the first Hyksos pharaoh *Salatis*. It would remain the Hyksos stronghold until the end of their rule of Egypt. It is conventionally thought that one of the reasons that the Hyksos overwhelmed Egypt so easily at first is that they had at their disposal horses and chariots.

6 Aldred, op. cit., p. 117.

7 Vid. Grimal N, **A History of Ancient Egypt**, translated by Ian Shaw, Cambridge (USA): Blackwell, 1988; 1992, p. 186.

Thus it is them who are given credit for introducing the horse (and war chariot) into the Nile Valley. In more ways than one this introduction would represent a revolution in the course of Egyptian history. In fact, Cyril Aldred insists that the major innovations in Egyptian armament and tactics—the composite bow, the spear-thrower, the heavy falchion, and bronze armor—were all outgrowths of the extended war against the Hyksos.[8] The Egyptians learned from, adopted, and perfected the lessons fighting the Hyksos had to impart. By the end of the 17th Dynasty, the Theban kings in the south would have mastered these new military elements and in the 18th Dynasty the chariot corps would become the shock troops of a near-invincible Egyptian army and therefore the military 'engine' of Egypt's burgeoning imperial ambitions.

Petrie is of the opinion that six of the Hyksos pharaohs ruled Egypt from top to bottom, and these were probably the Hyksos that inaugurated the 15th Dynasty. Without attempting the near impossible task of accurately dating their reigns they can be listed in order of succession as follows:

Salatis
Bnōn
Apakhnas
Apōthis
Sēthos
Asēth

Later Egyptologists would go so far as to say that there really were just six Hyksos pharaohs at all, ruling Egypt over a period of 108 years. The first of these was *Salatis*, the Hyksos pharaoh who established the Hyksos capital at Avaris. There were three kings named *Apepa*, the most important being *Apepa I*, one of the kings who would have mastered all Egypt. It has been stated that Joseph and the clan of Jacob-Israel would have entered Egypt during the reign of Apepa I.[9] Several other kings had Sethian names, testifying to the ascendancy of Set during the Hyksos period. Petrie lists the 16th Dynasty Hyksos kings as follows:

8 Aldred, op. cit., p. 119.
9 See Budge, op. cit., Vol. II, p. 153.

Apepa I or *Apophis I*
Rā-hotep
Apepa II or *Apophis II*
Dudu-mes (Apepa III?)
Rā-se-beq-ka

It has already been pointed out that *Apepa* is derivable from *Apep*, the Egyptian cosmic serpent/dragon that came to have a Sethian aspect. The three pharaonic Apepas, therefore, reigned at the end of the polar Age of Draco, the Cosmic Serpent (or Dragon). Thus, by 1,651 BC, Draco would have been superseded by *Wepwat* (Anubis) thus inaugurating the north polar Jackal Age. In Greek times, the Jackal became the Little Bear (*Ursa Minor*), though retaining the name *Cynosuris*, 'tail of the Dog'.

Flinders Petrie has an interesting comment to make concerning a 'calendar reform' by one of the major Hyksos pharaohs:

> As the last of the great Hyksos kings, Aseth (or Assis) is stated by Syncellus in his extracts to have revised the calendar, it is the more likely that some such era was established then. This statement is not…satisfactory, as he is said to have added the 5 days to the year of 360 days, which are known to have been in use long before his time; but it may well be that *some other reformation has been thus misstated.*[10]

It is to be wondered that if in fact a calendar 'reformation' did take place in the Hyksos era, might it have been the adjustment of the (polar) precessional calendar of the Great Year that brought the Jackal Age forward at this time, superseding the preceding Age of Draco? By the time of Syncellus early in the 9th century AD, knowledge of the precessional cycle would have been lost or, at the very least, its meaning and relation to ancient history no longer understood, so an assumption was made by this Christian redactor that the calendar being reformed in Hyksos times had to have been the ordinary solar calendar. But Petrie, as the above quote makes clear, does not rule out some kind of calendric

10 Petrie, op. cit., p. 244.

or chronological correction during the Hyksos era and the precessional Inter-Age Transition was well in progress at the time that Aseth would have reigned. That Aseth would have taken the lead in authorizing such a calendric adjustment is one indication among several that the Hyksos pharaohs were not quite so foreign or alien to Egyptian civilization as later history has painted them.

The cultural, historical, and religious development of more than one-third of the world's population—encompassing Jews, Christians, and Muslims—has been decisively impacted by events depicted in the Hebrew Torah, the Christian Old Testament. The sojourn in Egypt of the clan of Jacob/Israel and its descendants, culminating in the Exodus story, is central to the subsequent development of the religious consciousness of the aforementioned peoples. How much of it is actual history and how much of it is mythic fable has always incited controversy. That there was an exodus of a people in the 19th Dynasty who had broken away from the established religion of Egypt is generally agreed, but exactly whom these people were has never been satisfactorily settled historically, however insistent the claims of 'divine revelation' on the matter vouchsafed by religious enthusiasts. A people depicted as war captives in Theban inscriptions dating back to 1,480 BC called the *Apiru* by the Egyptians are assumed to be Hebrews. They were first employed as wine-makers and later as stone-movers. But in the Exodus, it was a 'mixed multitude' that departed Egypt behind Moses so that the Hebrews of history can hardly be descended from the Apiru and the Apiru alone.

Though the story of the Exodus will be taken up in a later chapter, its roots ramify back into the Hyksos era because it is then that the ancestors of the reputed Children of Israel might have entered and settled in Egypt, presumably under the pressure of famine and/or political instability in Canaan. This in-migration into the Delta region of Egypt by Jacob-Israel's clan, under the presumed auspices of their kinsman Joseph, could have taken place as early as 1,722 BC or as late as 1,660 BC. That this episode, if at all historical, took place during the Hyksos era is given further credence in *Genesis* (41:43) where Joseph is given a chariot as a mark of pharaoh's favor, a conveyance not introduced into Egypt until Hyksos times. What is not readily acknowledged, except by Gerald Massey,[11] is that these Canaanitic Children of Israel would,

11 Vid. Massey G, *Egyptian Origin of the Jews Traced from the Monuments*, in **Book of Beginnings**, Vol. II, London: Williams and Norgate, pp. 363-442.

in the end, have become completely Egyptianized if they remained in Egypt 430 years as the *Book of Exodus* declares. Thus, as the priest Apion asserts (after Josephus), it was a band of Egyptians who went out into the desert across Sinai in the episode that later became memorialized as the Exodus.

Egypt's decline during this Gap period provided room for Cush's rise. In fact, Cush would ascend to a position of political pre-eminence it would not see again until the 8th century BC. Sometime during the 14th Dynasty, king *Nedja* came to the throne of Cush (based at Kerma) apparently with the active aid and support of Egyptian officials.[12] These circumstances are all the more unusual because Nedja took over the 2nd Cataract fortresses at Buhen and Semna and ruled as far north as Elephantine, that is, the southern portions of Egyptian national territory. The Cushite kings of this period assumed all the trappings of the pharaohs and clearly there was a not inconsiderable number of Egyptians in their service. Notwithstanding, Cush, allied with the Hyksos, remained in control of its royal domains from Kerma to Elephantine until the end of the 17th Dynasty (1,573 BC). Clearly, the political situation up and down the Nile Valley was extremely fluid and political allegiances were not very clear-cut. Again, it makes the contemporary investigator question the relentless demonization of the Hyksos carried out by the later dynasties, especially the 18th. Nicolas Grimal also points out that the Nubian tribes from which the Egyptians recruited their soldiers also supplied soldiers to the Cushite kings.[13] Cush, at this time, was a power equal to Thebes and to the Hyksos regime further north.

III. **The 17th Dynasty: End of the Hyksos Rule/Beginning of the Reconquest** (1,630 BC—1,573 BC)

With the advent of the 17th Dynasty, Hyksos power was clearly on the wane. The country was divided into two spheres of influence: the north controlled by the Hyksos and the south by an emerging dynasty of energetic Thebans. In this way, the contemporary situation replicated the political circumstances in Egypt

12 Vid. Grimal, op. cit., p. 188.
13 Ibid.

at the time of the 11th Dynasty, the dawn of the Middle Kingdom. The 17th Dynasty kings at Thebes seem to have arisen from a branch of the 13th Dynasy pharaohs and the first king of the 17th was *Rahotep* by name. Though the records differ, there were probably no more than 10 pharaohs in this dynasty and for the first 75 years or so, the Thebans controlled the area stretching from Elephantine (1st Cataract) to Abydos, the southern third of the country. Their economic circumstances were quite marginal but they managed, on a limited scale, to revive and maintain the civilization of the Middle Kingdom. Though building stone pyramids had been discontinued, the tombs of these kings were constructed as mud brick pyramids. While little new literature was produced, the copying and preservation of ancient texts was revived.

In the north, the Hyksos aspect of the 17th dynasty was first represented by *Yaqeb-Har* who reigned 18 years. His seals are found as far south as Kerma (Cush) and even in Upper Egypt so while he did not control Upper Egypt, the Theban kings paid tribute to him and at least the facade of the vassalage of Thebes to Avaris was upheld. Again, early in the dynasty, a *modus vivendi* with the Hyksos was achieved. The name *Yaqeb-Har* shows that the name *Jacob* was known in Egypt and may have had, as the author has argued, an Egyptian derivation.[14] Yaqeb-Har was succeeded by Khian, a name well-known in Egypt whose seals and stone vessels with his name turned up in Crete, Palestine, and Mesopotamia. Under his reign, an active foreign commerce and diplomatic missions were maintained in Western Asia and the Mediterranean.

Khian was succeeded by Apepa III or Apophis III, the most dynamic and famous of all the Hyksos pharaohs. Apophis is said to have ruled 40 years but by the time of his reign, Egypt was effectively divided into two separate kingdoms, the Hyksos ruling in the north and the Thebans in the south. Be that as it may, for most of the reign, the Hyksos and the Thebans were at peace and there is even some suggestion that Apophis married a Theban princess.[15] Apophis upheld the fiction that he was ruler of the entire country since he was not above referring to himself as 'King of Upper and Lower Egypt.' However, by the end of his reign, a new and militant set of Theban rulers ascended the throne and military hostilities

14 See Finch CS, **Echoes of the Old Dark Land: Themes from the African Eden**, Decatur: Khenti Publications, Inc., 1991, pp. 153-4.

15 Vid. Grimal, op. cit., p. 189.

broke out once again. Rahotep was succeeded at Thebes by a succession of kings three of whom were named *Antef* or *Inyotef.* The reigns of the first two Antefs did not even cover four years but that of Sobekemsaf II who followed was rather more substantial. During his 16-year rule, prosperity returned to Thebes and the king added to the ever-expanding temple of Amon at Karnak. Three more ephemeral rulers followed Sobekemsaf at Thebes—Djehuti, Mentuhotep VII (a name not seen since the 11th Dynasty), and Nebiryau I. But, as a harbinger of things to come, a more dynamic and active king ascends the throne at Thebes, the third Antef. He was evidently the most active Theban builder since the 12th Dynasty and it seems he may have carried out military forays in Cush as well as to the north, though undoubtedly away from the Hyksos sphere of influence. Antef III's reign is contemporaneous with that of the second Apophis and relations remained peaceful at least to the end of Antef's life. Later tradition suggests that the line that leads to the 18th Dynasty can be traced back to Antef's queen.

Seqenen-Rā Ta'o I (1630 BC–1605 BC)

The stalemate between the Hyksos in the north and Thebans in the south could not endure indefinitely; sooner or later, hostilities were bound to break out. With the accession of a Theban king named *Ta'o I*, all pretense at peaceful co-existence ceased and the great campaign of retaking Egypt and driving out the Hyksos began. The next three Theban reigns were characterized by this single-minded determination. Petrie was of the opinion that these new dynasts were actually of Cushite or 'Ethiopian' extraction whose forbears had escaped south to escape Hyksos domination.[16] Though most Egyptologists never say so, the 17th and 18th Dynasties were, in effect, 'Ethiopian' Dynasties. But what is remarkable about the *reconquista* that was launched is that it seems to have been inspired and prosecuted as much by a succession of remarkable royal women as it was the kings themselves, i.e., three 'Isabellas' to a like number of 'Ferdinands' who won Egypt back to native rule.[17] In fact, similar to the case

16 Petrie, op. cit., Vol. II, p. 4.

17 Ferdinand and Isabella were the rulers of Spain who launched and financed the voyage of Columbus to the New World in 1492.

of Ferdinand and Isabella, the figures of these redoubtable Theban royal wives seem to stand out in sharper historical relief than their husbands. The first of these extraordinary queens, the wife of Ta'o, was *Tetisheri* who would live to see the launching of the 18th Dynasty, and became in effect its 'grandmother'.

Seqenen-Rā Ta'o II (1,605 BC–1,581 BC)

Ta'o I died after a reign of 25 years, probably a victim of skirmishes with the Hyksos, and was succeeded by his son *Seqenenra Ta'o II.* His wife was the fabled *Ahhotep* who, because Seqenenra II was also killed during the conflict, was obliged to carry on in his place. The last straw, apparently, was the command by Apophis in the north for the Thebans to promulgate the exclusive worship of Set among them, a *casus belli* if there ever was one.

Queen Ahhotep—17th Dynasty

Ahhotep I—Mother of Kamose

One can only guess why Apophis chose to provoke Thebes in this manner; but possibly he was alarmed by its growing militancy under Ta'o I, and was determined to nip the insurgency in the bud. Under Seqenenra, Ahhotep, and their successors, it was now or never for Thebes, and the consequent path chosen could lead only to unconditional defeat or victory. It would be a veritable fight to the finish. The fate of Seqenenra II is known by his still surviving mummy which shows several fatal head wounds obviously obtained in battle. Before his death, Seqenenra managed to take the fight as far north as Cusae.

Kamose (1,581 BC–1,573 BC)

Two of Seqenenra II's sons by Ahhotep would carry on the fight with Hyksos to the bitter end, though, as already noted, Ahhotep had to serve as regent for a number of years until the first, *Kamose*, was old and fit enough to assume the throne. Kamose was indeed the man for the job of carrying the fight to the Hyksos and, for that matter, to the unreliable Cushite king to the south who still ruled as far north as the 1st Cataract and maintained an alliance with the Hyksos. Kamose took his Medjay and marched north to Beni Hassan, deep into territory normally controlled by the Hyksos where he fought and defeated an Egyptian provincial lord loyal to the Hyksos. More strategically, he systematically gained control of the Nile, with his river squadrons advancing first into Middle Egypt but then closing in on the regions around Avaris itself. Kamose was not strong enough for an all-out military confrontation with Apophis. Having made significant incursions into Hyksos territory, he gained control of river-borne commerce, and cut off the Hyksos from their Cushite allies. Then Kamose returned to Thebes. There he began forays against the Cushites in the south designed to loosen their hold on the territory around the 1st Cataract. Just as important, he began to consolidate the gains made by strengthening his position at home and the now-expanded Theban kingdom itself.

Ahmose (1,573 BC–1,548 BC)

Ahmose-Nefertari, Founding Ancestress of the 18th Dynasty

Pharaoh Ahmose - Founder of the 18th Dynasty, Husband of Ahmose-Nefertari

With the death of Kamose, his younger brother Ahmose, also a son of Seqenenra II and Ahhotep, ascended the throne and would complete the expulsion of the Hyksos. Strictly speaking, Ahmose is the founder of the 18th Dynasty—and the New Kingdom—but since final Hyksos expulsion is only completed in his reign, it is pertinent to discuss him here. His adversary is also Apepa or Apophis and by this time the Hyksos can only claim control of Avaris and its immediate surroundings. However that may be, Apophis and his successor Apophis III cling tenaciously to these drastically reduced lands in the north. Ahmose ruled for 25 years and in Year 11 of his reign, he resumed the military assault on the Hyksos. Ahmose campaigned northward over a period of several years taking Memphis and other cities still loyal to the Hyksos, finally taking Avaris itself. The re-conquest of Egypt was now complete, but Ahmose did not stop there. There was still a Hyksos enclave at Sharuhen in southwestern Palestine and Ahmose stormed it with his army. The Hyksos remnants scatter into Palestine and disappear permanently from history. Ahmose's capture of Sharuhen is the opening salvo of a conquering impetus that fires the imperial ambitions of the 18th Dynasty, eventually leading to the conquest of all of Western

Asia, even into Anatolia. The capture of Sharuhen occurs in Year 16 of the reign; in Year 22 (1,551 BC), Ahmose pursues the initiative gained from his Palestinian victory by campaigning deep into Syria and beyond, almost to the Euphrates.

Having routed the Hyksos, Ahmose turns his attentions south and in two hard-fought campaigns, pushes the Cushites back to Kerma, south of the 2nd Cataract. As in the north, Ahmose's military success would stimulate an unparalleled southward conquering impulse among successive 18th Dynasty kings. Eventually, Cush would be conquered almost as far south as the 4th Cataract and as a consequence would experience a thoroughgoing Egyptianizing process that would make it a reservoir of traditional Egyptian culture and religion even when Egypt itself was being changed and modified by foreign influences. It was during his reign that the first of 25 officials, each entitled 'the Royal Son of Cush', was appointed to govern the Nubian domains on behalf of pharaoh. In time, the Royal Son of Cush would become the most powerful official in the empire, save pharaoh himself. The position was so important and prestigious that it was reserved for a member of the royal household. Indeed, some of these officials might actually have been chosen from among the numerous sons of the reigning pharaoah.

Ahmose's posterior reputation is as Egypt's liberator, but despite his exalted status in the Egyptian historical imagination, he seems to have been eclipsed by that of his wife *Ahmose-Nefertari*, the third of the three remarkable women—Tetisheri, Ahhotep, and Ahmose-Nefertari—who, with their husbands and/or sons, spear-headed the re-conquest. But Ahmose-Nefertari seems to have stood out in a country with a long history of extraordinary queens. This is known because there are more surviving examples of her name etched in monuments all over the country than any other individual in Egyptian history, with the possible exception of Rameses II. It is not unlikely that she reigned with her husband at equal or near-equal status; that she was, in effect, co-ruler of Egypt. Whatever the case, she inspired an almost goddess-like devotion among the Egyptians of after-centuries. Not co-incidentally, she was anointed the first-ever *Divine Wife of Amon*, a title that made her, in effect, the 'co-pontiff' of the Temple of Amon and its cultus, along with the Chief Prophet of Amon. A coterie of Amon-serving priestesses sprung up under the Divine Wife, a system that would endure to the end of the 25th (Ethiopian) Dynasty.

Chapter 7:

The New Kingdom
(1,573 BC–1,083 BC)

As already indicated, the New Kingdom was launched by Ahmose I and his wife Ahmose-Nefertari. Despite the real accomplishment of Ahmose, he seems to have been overshadowed by Ahmose-Nefertari in the memory of posterity. For one thing, he pre-deceased her, and she had to serve as regent for Amenhotep I, the crown prince of Egypt. Moreover, she was the first to hold the priestess title 'Divine Wife of Amon' and, like the previous two queens of the 17th Dynasty, was posthumously honored in Thebes with her own cult, an object of veneration for centuries afterward. Her name is invoked in 50 private tombs, 80 monuments, and numerous other inscriptions the length and breadth of the country. She was in every sense the founding mother of the New Kingdom and no figure in Egyptian history was ever more beloved.

With the advent of the New Kingdom, Egypt embarks on a new course that will permanently alter her history. For one thing, a new militancy emerges that carries all before it, eclipsing even the militaristic impulses of the latter Middle Kingdom pharaohs. It will become Egypt's imperial age wherein she achieves a level of power, glory, and international influence never seen before or afterward. As a result, Egypt will become increasingly preoccupied and enmeshed in the geopolitical events of Western Asia, which she perforce dominates for more than 500 years. This entanglement with the kingdoms and peoples of the southern Mediterranean and Western Asia will last until the end of her effective history, and it is from that direction that her enemies will eventually prevail over her for good. The New Kingdom will be a period where the priests of Amon will reign supreme on the religious front and whose increasing power will eventually clash with that of pharaoh, upsetting the balance of power that had long undergirded the stability of the state. It will be an era of unprecented monument-building, fueled by the vast wealth flowing into Egypt's coffers from the burgeoning empire. As one commentator puts it:

> The colossal temples of the New Kingdom were probably meant to impress not only Egyptians, but the whole civilized world. The number of these monumental structures, both in Egypt and in Nubia, far exceeds the total of surviving monuments from all other ages.[1]

The New Kingdom represents the apogee of Egyptian civilization and during this period, Egypt exerts a cultural and religious influence on the rest of the world the residuum of which can be felt even to the present day.

I. The 18th Dynasty—Imperial Egypt (1,573 BC–1,308 BC)

There are three dynasties that uncontestably represent the pinnacles of Egyptian civilization: the 4th, the 12th, and the 18th. In the 18th, there were 15 pharaohs who sat on the throne of Egypt and at least one commentator has vouchsafed the opinion that it was the greatest line of rulers ever to sit on the throne of any country, anywhere, anytime. While some might debate that assertion, the 18th dynasty shines to this day as one of the most glorious epochs in history, a veritable Golden Age of Nile Valley civilization. In this period, Amon—'the Hidden One' whose zootype was the ram—was in his ascendancy; though as a way of maintaining the special place of Rā, Amon was fused with Rā as Amon-Rā. Karnak, the sacred home of Amon, had become the Vatican of Egypt, and for the next 15 centuries, the rulers of Egypt—including the later Persians, Greeks, and Romans—never failed to expand and add to the temple complex at Karnak. In fact, to the Greeks, Amon was Zeus and Amon's wife, Mut, was Hera. So close was this and other identifications in the Greek mind that Herodotus (450 BC) would state categorically that all the gods of Greece came to her from Egypt.[2]

1 Adams WY, **Nubia**, Princeton: Princeton University Press, 1977, p. 218.

2 Herodotus, **The Histories**, New York: Penguin Books, (1954), 1972, pp. 145-52, passim.

Though the names and reigns of all the 18th Dynasty rulers are well-established, as with all Egyptian history through its first 3,000 years, the chronology is by no means certain. But enough data has come to light to provide a much clearer picture compared to the murkiness evident in the Second Chronological Gap. Beginning with the 18th Dynasty, there is not such a wide discrepancy of dates between the Egyptological long and short chronologies as is true for the earlier eras.

Ahmose or *Amasis* and Ahmose-Nefertari (1,573 BC–1,548 BC)

Summarizing what has already been remarked about Ahmose, he is the first pharaoh of the 18th Dynasty and considered the 'Great Liberator' of Egypt from the Hyksos yoke. Within five years of his accession, he had driven the Hyksos completely and permanently out of Egypt, pursuing them into Palestine, capturing their stronghold at Shahuren, then making additional forays as far as Phoenicia. Upon returning to Egypt, Ahmose campaigns south of Aswan, pushing the Cushites back to Kerma. Remaining pockets in Egypt sympathetic to the previous regime had to be further pacified. Significant among these would have been a population, more or less Egyptian, that shared Hyksos religious beliefs as worshipers of Set, contributing to the residual turbulence caused by the regime change. They were either suppressed or forced to follow their previous overlords into Palestine. As has been alluded to above, the expulsion of the Hyksos and their co-religionists from Egypt in all likelihood provided one of the historical sources for the later Exodus story. Certainly the Jewish historian Josephus, writing in the 1st century AD, thought so.[3] It is worth quoting E.A. Wallis Budge at length on the matter:

> An examination of the facts derived from the Egyptian monuments shows that a vast number of people, probably Semites, were expelled from the Delta at the close of the XVIIth Dynasty, and that the process of the expulsion went on vigorously under the reigns of the first three or four kings of the XVIIIth Dynasty; thus there must have been on sev-

3 **Josephus: The Complete Works**, translated by W.P. Whiston, Grand Rapids: Kregel Publications, (1867)1981, p.

eral occasions an exodus of Semites, or at least of Canaanites, from Egypt. Of this great series of forced emigrations traditions no doubt remained among the Canaanitish tribes of Palestine and, when the Hebrews had occupied the country, were very possibly, in the process of time, incorporated by Hebrew annalists in their account of the emigration of their own ancestors from Egypt.[4]

But having completed the expulsion of the Hyksos, the pacification of the country, and the first forays into Cush, the remainder of the reign of Ahmose was dedicated to economic, political, and religious recovery. Trade with southern, northern, and even Aegean regions was re-inaugurated; Minoan (Crete) jewelry, for example, has been found. As has been noted above, the Great Royal Wife Ahmose-Nefertari becomes the paramount symbol of a resurrected Egypt and is adored as a goddess from then on. Ahmose reigned for 25 years.

Amenhotep I or *Amenōphis I* (1,548 BC–1,517 BC)

The first Amenhotep's reign seems, in retrospect, to represent a gathering of forces. The only military campaign recorded is a brief foray into Cush to pacify some fractious tribes. However, it is clear that the national renewal was proceeding apace. The economy was reviving, trade expanding, and building

Amenhotep I

Amenhotep I with his mother Ahmose Nefertari (left)

4 Budge, op. cit., p.118.

projects launched. Art shows a high level of skill and vigor. It is said that the clepsydre, or water clock, was invented during this reign (https://en.wikipedia.org/wiki/Water_clock). Also, the extant copy of the Ebers Medical Papyrus—a copy of a much older document—dates to this time.

The principle of pharaonic inheritance through the female line is shown clearly in this succession of 18th Dynasty pharaohs. Ahmose-Nefertari, the Great Royal Wife of Ahmose, was the daughter of a Great Royal Wife, and her daughter, Ahotep II, became Great Royal Wife to Amenhotep I. Thus the ancient African matrilineal system is evident in this custom of royal succession; it meant that the pharaoh did not have to be completely of royal descent and only ascended the throne by virtue of his marriage to the Great Royal Wife presumptive. This practice also drove the custom of royal incest since the man selected to be pharaoh was inevitably the half-brother, sometimes the full brother, of the Great Royal Wife presumptive as a way of keeping the succession in the family.[5] There was no automatic primogeniture among Egyptian royalty so typical of the royal dynasties of later civilizations. The son of an otherwise obscure wife of pharaoh might ascend to throne if he showed outstanding ability. Though brother-sister marriage was virtually absent in the non-royal classes, at least until Ptolemaic times (after 300 BC), it thrived in literature and poetry as a kind of romantic ideal insofar as lovers, though unrelated, routinely referred to each other as 'brother' or 'sister.' This same feeling is encountered in the *Song of Songs*, i.e., *The Song of Solomon*, where the bride and bridegroom frequently speak to one another as 'brother' and 'sister'. All this being said, it was the daughter of the Great Royal Wife Ahotep II, the queen of Amenhotep I, who would pass on the inheritance of the royal line through her daughter *Ahmose*, Great Royal Wife of *Tehuti-mes* or Thutmosis I. Amenhotep I reigned 31 years.

5 It is of interest that royal sister-brother marriages were the rule among the Incas and Hawaiians.

Tehuti-mes I or Thutmosis *I* (1,517 BC–1,492 BC)

Thutmosis I

Thutmosis I exemplifies the dynamics of the foregoing discussion. He was a son of Amenhotep I by a minor wife who was able to claim the throne by virtue of his marriage to the Great Royal Wife Presumptive Ahmose. Though the principle of co-regency had been well-established since the time of the Middle Kingdom, Thutmosis does not appear to have served in a co-regency with his father, possibly because he was not the first choice to inherit. His older half-brother Amenemhat who, presumably would have been elevated to the co-regency with Amenhotep, died young. The daughter of Thutmosis I and the Great Royal Wife Ahmose was the fabled Hatshepsut who would later turn the dynastic succession on its ear and precipitate a dynastic crisis. If anything, this state of affairs was brought on by Thutmosis I himself who, before he died, took the radical step of naming Hatshepsut his successor, though some insist that Hatshepsut effected this outcome on her own initiative. We will examine this state of affairs more thoroughly below.

Thutmosis I began to more actively campaign abroad in what must clearly be construed as empire-building. His military thrusts took him deep into Nubia, on a pacification mission, then northward as far as Nahrain, well into Syria, right to the edge of the Euphrates River. In fact, it appears as though he was consolidating military gains that might have first been obtained by his father Amenhotep I. Typically, he inaugurated building projects, almost all of them in Upper Egypt, even rebuilding a temple of Set at Nubt. Again and again, in the 18th and 19th dynasties, one finds unexpected evidence of a continuing reverence for Set perhaps because in their battles, the pharaohs depended on the might and ferocity of Set for victory. During his reign, it is evident that there is complete internal peace, security, and order in Egypt.

Tehuti-mes II or Thutmosis *II* (1,492 BC–1,479 BC)

Thutmosis II was the son of Thutmosis I by a secondary wife *Mut-nefert.* His reign was but 13 years long and he is chiefly known as being the husband of his phenomenal half-sister *Hatshepsut* and the father of her daughter. He was 17 and she was 24 when they married, she being Great Royal Wife-presumptive. His chief activities consisted of punitive raids against restive pastoral tribes in the south and in Western Asia. Apart from Hatshepsut, one of his wives was *Aset* the mother of Thutmosis III and the titanic clashes between the two compelling, indomitable personalities of Hatshepsut and Thutmosis III. The titanic clashes for control of Egypt following the demise of Thutmosis II would reverberate down through Egyptian history.

Hatshepsut (1,479 BC–1,459 BC)

Dynastic Egypt's 4,000-year history is filled with unusual and extraordinary rulers but Hatshepsut stands alone. She was one of four female pharaohs, but only she among them ruled Egypt for 20 years during a period of remarkable peace, prosperity, and power. The other three female pharaohs of Egypt had short, ephemeral reigns during periods of transition. As a female pharaoh, the manner in which Hatshepsut rose to, and retained, supreme political power for two decades, is without parallel in Egyptian history. This truism is thrown into sharper relief when it is realized that in maintaining her position, she was able to resist for many years the rising and ultimately irresistible claims of her nephew Thutmosis III, an overpowering personality who could easily vie for the title of Egypt's greatest pharaoh. And as will be seen, being balked of the throne in this manner propelled Thutmosis into a permanent rage against the

Hatshepsut "The Great"

legacy and memory of Hatshepsut; he spared no effort during his reign—ultimately unsuccessful—to erase her memory from history. But too much had been accomplished by Hatshepsut during her reign: unrivaled political peace and stability; vigorous, highly artistic monument and temple building; promotion and expansion of profitable foreign trade and diplomacy—all these achievements made it impossible to relegate her permanently to the dustbin of history. She could rightfully be called "Hatshepsut the Great".

Tempermentally, Egyptians always seemed to prefer and extol the past over the present and the most dynamic of New Kingdom pharaohs always sought to re-create the splendors of that past. Hatshepsut was no exception and for her as well as for other pharaohs of her lineage, the 12th Dynasty provided the ideal cultural, political, artistic, and ritual model to emulate. In so many ways, Egypt of the 18th Dynasty was a very different place from Egypt of the 12th and yet Hatshepsut and the other pharaohs of the 18th Dynasty constantly measured themselves against those of the 12th. The art, architecture, and religious observances of the latter period were consciously seen as re-manifestations of those of the former. It was therefore no accident that Hatshepsut's famous temple at Deir el-Bahari was constructed on the site of the earlier temple of Mentu-Hotep II who, though strictly speaking an 11th Dynasty pharaoh, was one of the progenitors of the 12th Dynasty and participated in its prestige. Having said that, the marvelous multi-terraced structure of Hatshepsut's temple was an utterly unique creation, representing a real departure from standard architectural forms.

Hatshepsut's Temple at Deir el-Bahari

Hatshepsut was the daughter of Thutmosis I by his Chief Royal Wife Ahmose; she was destined from birth to be the Queen Consort of the heir to the pharaonic throne. Typically, she was married to her half-brother Thutmosis II, the son of her father by a secondary wife, Mutnofret. Joyce Tyldesley, who wrote a biography of Hatshepsut,[6] rejects the notion that Hatshepsut—a notably powerful personality from an early age—worked to undermine the authority of her less-than-robust husband. Surviving royal scenes and inscriptions suggest that Hatshepsut played no other role than that of a dutiful queen, working alongside her husband in a subsidiary role and bearing him one daughter, Neferure by name. Nonetheless, Thutmosis II was only 30 when he died and his young son, Thutmosis III, by another consort, Aset, was not old enough to ascend the throne. Hatshepsut therefore assumed the position and title of regent, the normal procedure in the case of the designated heir to the throne not being old enough to reign. However, what happened in the ensuing years was without parallel in Egyptian history, before or after.

6 Tyldesley J, **Hatchepsut: The Female Pharaoh**, London: Viking Press, 1996

Initially, Hatshepsut served as regent in the traditional manner. However, over a period of seven years, her powers steadily expanded so that by the end of that time, she had become pharaoh. As seen earlier, there was no absolute bar to a woman ascending the throne, and in the course of Egyptian history, four women managed to do so. But by the 18th Dynasty, the custom and prejudice in favor of male rulers was so strong and ingrained that Hatshepsut's accession would have sent shock waves through the upper echelons of government. It is a testament to her extraordinary personal qualities that she was able to do so. Fully sensitive to this preference for male rulers during her reign, Hatshepsut often had herself depicted wearing a false beard, as if to proclaim that she was *king* rather than queen. Her other stratagem was to ally herself fully and totally to Amon, the reigning Supreme Being of the Egyptian pantheon, in fact inscribing the myth on her temple that made her a begotten daughter of Amon rather than Thutmosis I. Hatshepsut spared no effort or expense to solidify her legitimacy by recourse to her relationship with Amon, and inscriptions abound that pronounce her to be Amon's chosen and prophesied representative on earth.

Had Hatshepsut been merely a power-hungry usurper, the most cunning of stratagems would have been useless against centuries of near-inviolate tradition. But Hatshepsut's reign was a golden age within a New Kingdom golden age. In fact, it was a blessed and peaceful respite from the incessant war-making and empire-building carried on by most of the other New Kingdom pharaohs. The land was uncommonly prosperous, trade flourished, monument and temple building reached new heights—in every way, the 'Two Lands' benefitted from a kind of 20-year *pax Hatshepsuta*. At least two high officials from her father's reign continued to serve her, the most outstanding of these being Ineni, vizier and chief architect. But the one who did more than any other to make the era of Hatshepsut a glorious undertaking was the man, born a commoner, by name of Senenmut.

Every great pharaoh had as his 'right hand' a man of equal or near-equal greatness to carry out the royal designs, and Hatshepsut was singularly fortunate to have recruited and elevated such a man. Senenmut was one of the most outstandingly talented men in the history of a country known for burnishing the careers of talented men. Senenmut's position, influence, and authority were unmatched and he saw to it that all the great projects of Hatshepsut's reign were successfully undertaken with maximum efficiency and effect. It was said of Senenmut,

> ...his was the organizational brain behind Hatchepsut's impressive public building program, and to him has gone the credit of designing *Djeser-Djeseru* [temple at Deir el-Bahari], one of the most original and enduring monuments of the ancient world.[7]

Senenmut was Hatshepsut's vizier, Overseer of Royal Works, Steward of the Estates of Amon, and personal tutor to her daughter Neferure. He was also without a doubt her morganatic husband and possibly the actual father of Neferure, given the numerous statues showing him holding Neferure with the

Senenmut - Holding Neferure, His Pupil

gentle affection of a father. Born in a village 15 miles south of Thebes to a solid, well-educated family of scribes, he might well have been of direct Nubian ancestry and in any case, his life is the classic example of that of a talented 'new man', raised to the greatest heights by the favor of pharaoh. Since he was a commoner by birth, he could only have been a morganatic husband but it is evident that he was more than a mere paramour. The assumption that he was in a consortial relationship with Hatshepsut is strengthened by the total absence

7 Tyldesley, ibid., p. 177.

of a wife in any pictures of or inscriptions about him. Joyce Tyldesley concurs with this assessment of Senenmut's relationship to Hatshepsut:

> An intimate relationship with the queen would account for the rapid rise in Senenmut's fortunes and would explain why Senenmut chose to defy tradition and remain unmarried. It is certainly tempting to see Senenmut's unprecedented privileges, such as burial within the confines of *Djeser-Djeseru* and the linking of their two names within Tomb 353, as Hatshepsut's tacit acknowlegement of Senenmut's role as her *morganatic partner, if not her consort.*[8] (italics added)

There are three landmark events in the reign of Hatshepsut: (1) the erecting of twin obelisks made of pink granite within the confines of Karnak Temple, (2) the sailing expedition to the fabled Land of Punt on the Horn of Africa, and (3) the construction of the temple of recessed terraces dedicated to Hathor at Deir el-Bahari. Senenmut was responsible for the successful completion of two of those monumental tasks, the creation and erection of the obelisks in the Temple of Amon at Karnak and—the *magnus opus* of the reign—the construction of the magnificent Temple of Hathor at Deir el-Bahari. Nothing like it was ever seen in Egypt before or after. Mentu-hotep II had his mortuary temple constructed on the same spot in the earlier 11th Dynasty but by Hatshepsut's time, it had fallen into almost complete ruin. Deir el-Bahari was situated on the West Bank and the temple was aligned directly to Karnak Temple on the East Bank. This Temple of Hathor was cut out of the western cliff in such a way as to create a series of recessed terraces. There are no free-standing structures anywhere in or connected to the temple; everything about it was carved out of living rock *in situ*. It was an architectural *tour de force*, showcasing as nothing else could Senenmut's enduring genius. It remains today one of the finest architectural creations in the world. In ancient Egypt, all created monuments and temples were attributed to the reigning pharaoh instead of the actual builder or artist and so it is with the Temple at Deir el-Bahari. Though he was the architect, even today we do not think of the Temple as Senenmut's temple but as Hatshepsut's temple. Of course without her there would have been no Senenmut raised up to Chief Architect and no commission to design

8 Ibid., p. 192.

and build the temple. It really was Hatshepsut's temple dedicated, as she was, to the goddess of the sun, Hathor.

In every reign in ancient Egypt where a voyage to Punt is recorded, it is invariably accounted one of the grandest accomplishments of the individual reign. It is hard to know why such an expedition conferred so much prestige on the sponsoring pharaoh apart from the fact that there was always a sacred and mysterious aura associated with Punt and it was a land full of the highly treasured spices and luxury goods the Egyptians craved. Hapsetsut, too, sponsored a highly successful voyage to Punt of a fleet of Egyptian ships captained by Nehesi. By his very name, he was Nubian by birth. Not only did Nehesi's fleet come back loaded with luxury goods of every description, but also the Queen of Punt and a large entourage came back with them on what was a major diplomatic mission from Punt to Egypt. It was quite remarkable really: two northeast

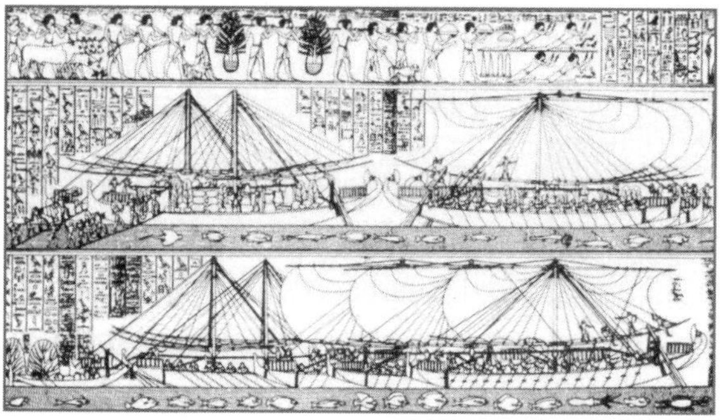

Hatshepsut's Fleet and the Voyage to Punt

Queen of Punt in Egypt

African queens engaging in mutually profitable trade and coming together in person to forge ever-stronger commercial and political ties. The expedition to Punt and the visit of the Queen of Punt to Hatshepsut's court are carefully and beautifully carved and inscribed on the walls of the Temple at Deir el-Bahari.

Hatshepsut, considered herself a daughter of Amon and was completely devoted to serving and worshipping him. But Hatshepsut had an equally strong affinity to Hathor as did many queens throughout the 18th Dynasty. Hathor, whose name meant 'mansion of Horus', was linked to Nut, Sekhmet, and, of course, Isis, especially in her character as the mother of Horus. In her solar aspect, she was daughter of Rā and wife of Horus. She was the mistress of love, beauty, music, merry-making, and motherhood. She was 'Lady of the Sycamore' and is most often represented as a cow or cow-eared. Her celestial emblem was the moon. Deir el-Bahari was a site sacred to Hathor. Moreover, one of the reasons why Egyptians over the centuries were consumed by an interest in Punt

Hathor the Cow-Eared at Denderah

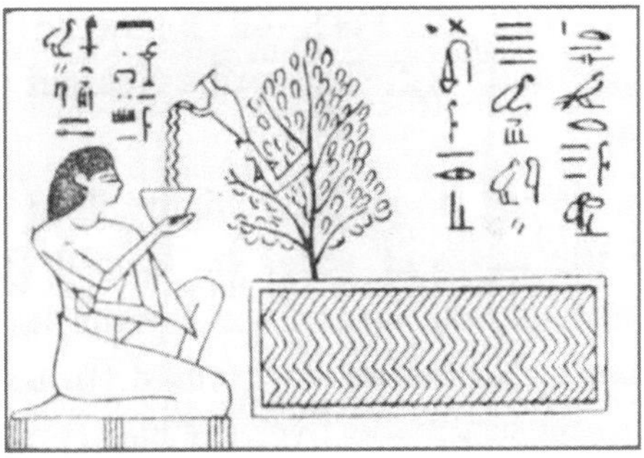

Hathor as Sycamore Pouring Water to the Thirsty Soul in Amenta

was that Hathor was called 'Mistress of Punt;' she was thought to have originated there. As one of Egypt's most perennially popular goddesses, her birthplace would be considered a place of national pilgrimage. Hatshepsut certainly subscribed to this notion.

As Hatshepsut's consort, favorite, prime minister, and chief architect, Senenmut had his hand in nearly every aspect of pharaonic administration. Though he became an extremely rich man on account of his position, there is little suggestion that he was anything but an outstandingly able administrator. In addition to the myriad of duties, he was entrusted with the education of Hatshepsut's daughter by Thutmosis II, Neferure. Neferure occupied an unusually prominent place in Hatshepsut's court and would have been the Great Royal Wife presumptive for the future pharaoh, i.e., Thutmosis III. Though disputed, it seems likely that she did in fact wed Thutmosis eventually, though was probably thrust into the background in favor of Meritre-Hatshepsut, a younger sister or Hatshepsut's adopted daughter by Thutmosis III when he ascended the throne. During his reign, no mention is ever made of Neferure, though Meritre-Hatshepsut is featured as the mother of Thutmosis III's successor, Amenhotep II. The dynastic marriage to Neferure may have been personally uncongenial to Thutmosis III, given his aversion to Hatshepsut, but would have been mandatory if he expected to inherit the throne. All that being said, many statues of Senenmut and Neferure together, as teacher and pupil, have survived. A multi-talented genius, Senenmut rose to the heights under the patronage of Hatshepsut.

For more than 20 years, Hatshepsut, as pharaoh, held supreme power in Egypt. However, for at least the last five years of her reign, she found herself increasingly under siege. She had started out as regent for her nephew Thutmosis III but shortly became pharaoh. All of his life, Thutmosis III and his partisans considered her a usurper. However, there were definite precedents in Egyptian history for a female pharaoh and, strictly speaking, there were no legal barriers to Hatshepsut's accession to the throne. But the custom of male pharaohs had become so embedded that her accession could seem like a usurpation by some. What intensified the tension is that Thutmosis was one of the most powerful and dynamic personalities in all the history of Egypt. He would go on to become Egypt's greatest empire-builder, a military genius who, in 17 years of campaigning, never lost a battle. It is easy to see how a man like that would chafe under the domination of anyone, let alone an aunt who, by his lights, had no right to the throne. It is a measure of the extraordinary capacity of Hatshepsut that she could maintain herself on the throne for two decades against the ever-rising and insistent challenge of Thutmosis. In the end, however, Thutmosis won out.

It is not known what happened to Hatshepsut—or Senenmut for that matter—but she disappears from history. She probably did not die a natural death; possibly she was given the option of suicide—the manner of her demise will probably never be known for certain. Conceivably she was sent into an exile sufficiently remote from Thebes as to make her permanently disappear. Killing a Great Royal Wife, no matter how viciously hated, was not something to be undertaken lightly, if at all, even by an overpowering personality such as Thutmosis III. After her passing, Thutmosis ruled for 33 years and during that time did his utmost to erase her memory from the public record. Despite his own magnificent accomplishments on behalf of Egypt, he never seems to have released the anger, resentment, and hatred he felt toward his predecessor and the fire of retribution was directed toward her legacy. In the end, of course, he and his successors failed to eradicate Hatshepsut from history; she had seen to it that her achievements were inscribed indelibly on the monumental records of Egypt.

A good deal of space as been devoted to Hatshepsut and her reign and for good reason: Hatshepsut has to be assessed as one of the most astounding of Egypt's pharaohs and one of the most redoubtable women in history. There never was an era like hers in all the history of Egypt. Under her, Egypt thrived and prospered; foreign adventures were almost completely avoided. The arts, trade, and monumental building flourished—the Temple at Deir el-Bahari remains to this day one of the finest architectural structures ever created. She should have been venerated with as much fervor as was shown to Egypt's greatest personages, but her successors pretended that her reign never happened. However, in the fullness time, her full due was recognized and proclaimed—if not in Egypt, then certainly beyond it, long after the Egypt of these times ceased to exist.

Thutmosis III (1,479 BC–1,446 BC)

Of the 330 pharaohs that sat on Egypt's throne, an elite minimum of 30 of them can be said to have been outstanding rulers—truly great and exceptionally accomplished sovereigns. Thutmosis III, by any measure, is among these and might well be one of the three or four greatest pharaohs in Egyptian history and therefore one of the greatest men in history. As indicated above, that Hatshepsut was able to stymie the ambitions of such a man for two decades testifies to her own transcendent greatness and power. If there is a shadow over his greatness it rests in the savage retribution exacted against his predecessor.

Thutmosis III reigned for 33 years after the passing of Hatshepsut,[9] 21 of them spent in almost incessant military campaigning in Western Asia and Nubia during which time he never lost a battle. He was already the commander-in-chief of the army during the latter phases of Hatshepsut's reign and so was well-trained and well-experienced in military matters as to make the most of his latent genius once he ascended the throne. The first challenge he faced was a revolt among a coalition of Western Asiatic princes allying themselves to the Prince of Qadesh and supported by the King of Mitanni. In fact Mitanni, a

9 Thutmosis always reckoned his reign as beginning with period of Hatshepsut's rule – refusing to recognize her as a legitimate pharaoh – therefore giving himself a regnal length of 54 years.

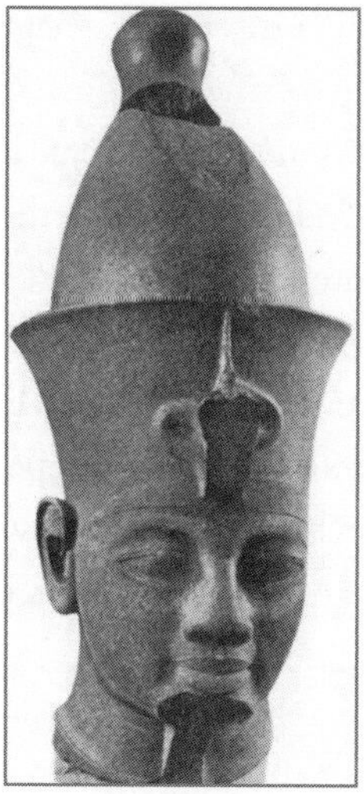

Thutmosis III
Egypt's Greatest Conqueror

Thutmosis the Empire-Builder
in Osirified Pose Holding Ankhs

powerful kingdom situated in the northern reaches between the Tigris and Euphrates, would contest Egypt for the next 100 years for control of the lands of what is now northern Syria, called *Naharin* in ancient times. In 21 years of military action, Thutmosis engaged in 17 separate campaigns to secure the empire being carved out for Egypt by the rulers of the 18th Dynasty. For the first time in its history, Egypt's geo-political fortunes became enmeshed with those of Syrio-Palestine and—further afield—the Fertile Crescent. They would remain so for the next 11 centuries.

The Syrio-Palestinian country of *Retjenu*, previously under Egyptian domination, had fallen away and into the orbit of the king of Qadesh, the paramount ruler of northern Syria. In throwing off Egyptian suzerainty, Qadesh was actively aided and abetted by Mitanni which, at all costs, wanted an independent and pliant buffer state between it and Egypt. Mitanni was the power in the Fertile Crescent; Assyria, further south, had not yet risen to such a position. Thutmosis, upon his accession, immediately made plans to reclaim this territory, confronting a coalition of states from northern Palestine headed by the king of Qadesh. To meet the advancing armies of Thutmosis, the king of Qadesh and his allies occupied a fortress on the Mount of Megiddo, in what is now northern Israel, a highly strategic venue controlling the main route to

Lebanon and the Euphrates Rivers from the south. The events leading up to, and including, the actual battle were recorded in detail by a military scribe in Thutmosis's army *Tjaneni*, giving to posterity the earliest comprehensive account of a military campaign in ancient times.[10] Tjaneni's record is inscribed on the walls of the Hall of Annals in the Temple of Amon at Karnak.

Megiddo would be the first major battle for Thutmosis as general and the first one fought by the Egyptian army in 20 years. Victory was by no means a foregone conclusion but early on, Thutmosis demonstrated his tactical daring and shrewd use of military intelligence. There were three approaches to Megiddo, the northern and southern roads being easy to traverse and the third, the *Aruna* path, ran through a narrow and difficult pass. Neither Thutmosis's generals nor the enemy commanders expected any invasion through the Aruna road, since any army foolhardy enough to attempt it could be ambushed and slaughtered. Indeed, the Qadesh king arrayed his forces in defensive positions covering the northern and southern roads. But Thutmosis, informed of the positions of the enemy troops, ignored the advice of his own generals and ordered the army to march to and through Aruna. It took five days to reach the entrance to Aruna, and very early in morning, the Egyptian army commenced to file through the pass. It took 12 hours for the entire army to march through and when it came out, it was on the plain less than a mile from the city of Megiddo. Too late, the Qadesh coalition forces recognized their peril and hastily tried to regroup to defend the city. It was to no avail. Though outnumbered, Thutmosis's legions held the tactical advantage and when the attack was launched, it was a rout. The only thing that kept the city itself from being taken on the day of the battle was the Egyptian soldiers who stopped to loot the vacated camp of the enemy instead of pressing the attack. It meant that Thutmosis now had to lay siege to the city. Thutmosis sternly rebuked his troops for the break-down in discipline but wasting no further time, proceeded to invest the city. Megiddo capitulated in seven months. The number of captives and the wealth of the booty was staggering; it was the first of many such victories. Scores of Asiatic princelings came to proffer submission to the victor; neither Thutmosis nor any of the succeeding pharaohs exacted harsh measures against the defeated,

10 For a concise and informative account of the Battle of Megiddo, see *The Battle of Megiddo*, a Feature Story by Troy Fox, on **Touregypt.net**.

a stark contrast to the gratuitous cruelty for which the later Assyrians became infamous. However, the family of the king of Qadesh, who had fled the city, was taken hostage.

Though Thutmosis had to continue fighting for another 20 years, Megiddo was still a decisive battle. It meant that Egypt now controlled all of Canaan from which Thutmosis could deploy his armies against Qadesh and Mitanni free of worries of attack from the rear. It meant that Qadesh—and more crucially Mitanni—would be on the defensive and in fact, Thutmosis was able to conquer Qadesh eight years later. Thutmosis, a man of matchless energy and resource, also had the Egyptian navy enlarged and strengthened so that his future campaigns could be supported from the sea and the Phoenician coastal towns could be kept under control. It also meant that, in the 18th Dynasty at least, the Eastern Mediterranean would become an Egyptian lake.

It would not be the last time Megiddo would be associated with decisive battles: (1) the pharaoh Necho in 609 BC defeated and killed the Hebrew King Josiah at Megiddo, (2) Megiddo served as a staging ground for the Roman army in 69 AD preparing for its assault on Jerusalem which fell in 70 AD, and (3) in World War I, the British general Edmund Allenby (1918), using the same tactics as Thutmosis III by routing his army through Aruna, surprised and defeated the Turkish army at Megiddo, thus bringing to an end Ottoman imperial control of Palestine. Because of the mount there, the place was called *Har-Megiddo* ('hill of Megiddo') in Hebrew and—no doubt owing to the decisive battles fought there in 1478 BC and 609 BC—gave its name to *Armageddon*, the final, cataclysmic battle to be fought between the Forces of Light and the Forces of Darkness mentioned in ***Revelations 16:16***. Still, it is interesting that the example of Thutmosis III tactically instructed a modern British general 3,400 years later.

Thutmosis continued his offensive northward. He penetrated as far north as southern Lebanon, capturing important cities as he went. The king of Qadesh still eluded him but to pre-empt any further thrusts southward by his enemy, Thutmosis had fortresses built on a strategic road running north. He re-organized these newly conquered territories by replacing the dynasts who had fought against him with more pliable regimes. The Egyptian manner of empire-building was not nearly so heavy-handed as later imperial states would be; conquered territories were allowed to continue very much as before with their own rulers as long as tribute was paid, fealty to Egypt was sustained, and levees of troops were contributed to pharaoh in times of war. However, Thutmosis expanded the practice of ensuring the loyalty of these vassal rulers by remanding their oldest sons to the Egyptian court where they were educated and trained, Egyptianizing them to make them well-disposed vassals who would one day rule their home countries.

Thutmosis had accomplished the conquest, pacification, and re-organization of Canaan all in a scant six months, a testament to his peerless military and administrative genius. Breasted, comparing his to a similar campaign by Napoleon nearly 33 centuries later, is favorably struck by the greater dispatch with which Thutmosis carried out his campaign compared to the far more famous Napoleon.[11] In fact, Thutmosis has been called the 'Napoleon of Antiquity', though his career was rather more successful. Like all the pharoahs of the Dynasty, Thutmosis was extremely devoted to Amon, to whom he attributed all his victories. Amon and his priesthood, in consequence, received a vast bounty of riches, livestock, and lands. Moreover, Amon's temple at Karnak was expanded as never before. The Amonian priesthood would soon achieve a level of power and wealth never before seen by any priestly college in Egypt. Inevitably, this immense concentration of wealth and power in a priestly oligarchy would have untoward consequences for the Egyptian state, exemplifying the well-known adage 'power corrupts, absolute power corrupts absolutely'.

For the next three years, Thutmosis contented himself with making triumphal tours of already conquered domains as a way of ensuring their compliance and submission. Assyria, farther to the east, was still an up-and-coming state—not to be a threat to Egypt for another 800 years—and sent tributary gifts to the conquering monarch while on the triumphal tour. But in these years of relative quiescence, Thutmosis was preparing himself, his army, and his kingdom for the grand enterprise of empire. He developed a three-pronged strategy: (1) subdue the northern Phoenician coastal cities to protect his flank, (2) defeat Qadesh once and for all, and (3) strike at Mitanni and the region dominated by Mitanni,

11 Breasted JH, **A History of Egypt**, New York: Charles Scribner's Sons, (1909)1937, p. 294.

Naharin by name. The manner in which Thutmosis implemented this grand three-part operation is characterized by Breasted as follows:

> No modern strategist could have conceived a series of operations better suited to the conditions, nor have gone about putting them into execution with more indomitable energy than Thutmose now displayed.[12]

As noted earlier, he had his fleet expanded and up-graded, and with this fleet launched his first attack on northern Phoenicia. Breasted thinks that the Phoenician city of Tyre reached an accommodation with Thutmosis in the midst of this campaign because it is known that Tyre maintained a privileged position vis-a-vis Egypt for the next 500 years. In any event, from this era onward all Phoenicia becomes part of the Egyptian hegemony, heavily Egyptianized culturally and religiously. But as he intended, Thutmosis obtained a secure foothold on the northern coasts, giving him an indispensable base of operations for future military forays.

Phoenician Queen (?) with Egyptian Cartouche

Phoenician—Another View

12 Ibid., p. 298.

Thutmosis, in the sixth year of his reign, was now ready to launch a push to Qadesh from the coast, confident that his flank was secure. He now controlled the most direct road to Qadesh, a city which, however, was formidably fortified and surrounded on all sides by the Orontes River tributaries. A long siege ensued and during that siege, one of the previously conquered coastal cities, Arvad, chose to revolt. After finally completing the investment and subjugation of Qadesh, Thutmosis turned back toward Egypt and on his way, re-subdued the rebellious city. It can be inferred that the city was treated with much less leniency on this occasion compared to the first. The revolt of Arvad demonstrated to Thutmosis that he needed to tighten his control of the Canaanite coast so he spent most of his seventh year re-pacifying recalcitrant cities and sailing from port to port to overawe any potential rebels. He also used this occasion to stockpile supplies and materials in these ports in preparation for his next big push against Mitanni.

Thutmosis, after returning to Egypt, spent an additional year expanding, strengthening, training, and logistically preparing his army. From the point of view of expanding the empire and neutralizing Mitanni completely, Thutmosis could be said to have had 'the bit in his teeth'. When ready, he led his army by the sea route to the coastal city of Simyra in northern Canaan and after landing there, marched his army for the second time *en route* to Qadesh, fighting as he went, reducing and capturing cities. For the first time, he crossed the Orontes River putting him in the land of Naharin. His first major battle was at Aleppo and as always, his army proved victorious. Naharin was Mitanni territory so now there was constant campaigning, taking Egyptian troops deep into the valley of the Euphrates River, finally crossing it into Mitanni proper for the first time. However, given the lateness of the year, Thutmosis elected not to push forward any further beyond the eastern bank of the Euphrates and in fact re-crossed the river to begin the march home. One or two other strategic, unvanquished cities were conquered without much difficulty thus securing Thutmosis's conquests in Naharin.

Thutmosis's string of invincible military successes were reverberating throughout the known world. Babylon, though not an object of Thutmosis's imperial designs, deemed it prudent to send him rich gifts as a token of goodwill; more importantly, envoys from the Hittite kingdom of *Kheta* met him on the

Canaan coast on his return march, bringing him massive, highly valued silver rings. Because of its scarcity in Africa, silver was more valuable than gold in Egypt, particularly because it was used to make an alloy called *nub-hedj*, 'white gold' called 'electrum' by the later Greeks, that was used for the creation of certain important sacred objects. The Hittite kingdom dominated Asia Minor (Turkey) and was a formidable power in its own right. Thutmosis made sure that the coastal cities were still under control and laid upon them the obligation to supply his military warehouses with foodstuffs and other materials required for Thutmosis's incessant northern campaigns. Thus, Thumosis controlled a string of harbors on the coast of Canaan that could be reached by sea in a few days from Egypt and provide staging arenas for his military offensives. By now, his naval power was being felt all over the eastern Mediterranean and Aegean.

By the time he returned to Thebes, Thutmosis found that other enterprises that had been launched in his absences had been successfully carried out. The all-important expedition to Punt—always viewed as the crowning achievement of any reign—had returned laden with the typical rich African luxury and trading goods. Moreover, the oasis region west of Egypt now fell under Egyptian control and would remain so through the rest of Egyptian history. The main oasis, the Great Oasis, became famous for the production of particularly fine brands of wine.

Thutmosis's years of unrelenting—and successful—warfare in the north brought to fruition three important strategic aims: (1) the complete subjugation of the petty kingdoms of Canaan and Syria begun by Thutmosis I two generations earlier; (2) the extension of Egypt's imperial boundaries across the Euphrates as a deterrent to the countervailing imperial ambitions of Mitanni; (3) the establishment of a loose tributary vassalage of kingdoms further afield such as Assyria and the sea nations of the eastern Mediterranean as far north as the Aegean. Especially by adding territory beyond the Euphrates to the empire, Thutmosis accomplished what no other Egyptian pharaoh ever had or would again. There was a classical tradition reported by Herodotus that the 12th Dynasty pharaoh Sesostris II had commanded military expeditions that ranged as far north as the Black Sea, but if so, these remote territories were never integrated into an Egyptian empire. Sesostris is said to have left memorial stelae of his campaigns in Asia Minor and points north, but no attempt was made to claim these lands for Egypt. For this reason, Thutmosis claims pride of place as Egypt's greatest empire-builder. Fittingly, he spared no expense back home commissioning commemorative monuments, including numerous obelisks, marking his victories, detailing the territories won and the rich booty acquired.

Egypt had never seen such a spectacle as now greeted the eyes of an astonished populace. Strange-looking peoples (to Egyptian eyes) from Palestine, Syria, the Aegean Islands, and the northern Euphrates now paraded down the streets of Thebes laden with exotic animals, spices, bronze implements and weapons. The finest horses graced pharaoh's stables and his warehouses could barely contain all the gold and silver—worked and unworked—that flowed into Egypt from the north. Every imaginable luxury item in quantity was now proffered to Thutmosis by delegates from the numerous vassal states. As noted earlier, large quantities of this tribute were dedicated to Amon, to be controlled and managed by his ever-burgeoning priesthood. Thutmosis was unstinting in the gratitude he showed Amon, and Amon's temples and priesthood profited immensely as a result. The truth is Egypt, never a poor country, had never been so rich and, not surprisingly, it fostered a resplendence and opulence in the royal house, among nobility, and in the temples never seen again. In the end, it also was the driving force behind a decadence that inevitably set in as the New Kingdom wore on.

The Canaanitic peoples—or 'Asiatics' as the Egyptians called them—who now come into Egypt in numbers not seen since Hyksos times were captives or hostages put to work on temple estates, building projects, and royal domains. Many found work as skilled craftsmen. Especially in the north, they become a more-or-less permanent presence in Egypt and, over time, mingle with the descendants of those Canaanites—including the putative 'Children of Israel'—who remained in Egypt after the Hyksos expulsion. It didn't take long for them to become in all things Egyptianized; in Lower Egypt and the Delta, these Canaanitic peoples formed the greater part of the 'mixed multitude' mentioned in the Book of Exodus.

Thutmosis comes across as a restless spirit of unflagging energy, never slowing down from his interminable tasks of expanding, consolidating, and managing his empire. After his first series of conquests, he is found touring the entire country of Egypt, personally inspecting the officials of the land and stamping out any vestige of corruption wherever he finds it. He commissioned the construction or renovation of scores of edifices and monuments along the 1,000 mile extent of the Egyptian kingdom from the Delta to the third cataract. Though preoccupied in the early part of his reign by his military adventures in Western Asia, when Thutmosis had imposed a measure of peace, he turned his relentless energies to Nubian affairs. Despite the increased importance of Western Asia in Egyptian geopolitical concerns, it does not eclipse Nubia in this regard. Consistent with age-old pharaonic policy, Thutmosis devotes maximum attention and energy to the development of a stable and prosperous Nubia. In fact, from this time forward for 500 years Nubio-Cush is fully integrated into Egyptian national territory as never before. But it is not merely government and war that preoccupy Thutmosis; he is a multi-faceted genius who took an interest in botany and drew exquisite sketches of designs for sacred gold and electrum vessels to be put to use in his temples.

Restless genius that he is, Thutmosis continues his activities in the Asiatic empire he has conquered. Every year, in late spring, he embarks north with his army to inspect the cities of his coastal domains to ensure that they are well-provisioned for future offensives. At every stop, regional Syrian princes attend the king whose 'executive officer' Intef reviews and ensures the proper and prompt payment of tribute and taxes. Like any successful empire-builder, Thutmosis commanded the services of men of outstanding talent in their own right. One of his top generals, Thutiy, devised a ruse for the capture of the Phoenician city of Joppa that reverberates legendarily down to our own day. He and a handful of picked men hide themselves in grain baskets which are carried into the city unbeknownst to the inhabitants by a caravan of donkeys. They are then able to open the gates from within to the army lying in wait. This episode, an apparently true occurrence, survives almost verbatim in the story of *Ali Baba and the 40 Thieves* from **Arabian Nights**, still told and re-told to the present day.

In spite of his vast accomplishments, Thutmosis cannot rest on his laurels, and it will yet be years before his work of empire-building can be said to be finished. He launches his ninth campaign against the Syrian kingdom of Zahi and its allies, the Asiatic domains not yet reconciled to vassalage to Egypt. His

10th campaign ensues the following year against the ever-rebellious Naharin but by now, Thutmosis has organized his supply lines and routes of march so effectively that his army appears back on Naharin soil almost before the revolt can gather steam. Again, Thutmosis's army carried the day on the plains of Araina and was able to plunder the rich booty left behind by the routed army of Naharin.

Campaigns 11–14 have the character of pacification and mopping up operations, focusing mainly on the southern portions of Syrio-Palestine. His unmatched success and military might brought much in the way of further tribute from countries outside his imperial borders—Cyprus, the Hittities, and Assyria all again send rich gifts and diplomatic protestations of friendship and fealty. Clearly none of them wanted to attract the wrong kind of attention from Thutmosis.

The kings of Naharin and northern Canaan were not quite through. Instigated by Qadesh, Thutmosis's unreconciled enemy, a new coalition was formed to attempt one last great overthrow of Egyptian domination. Since Thutmosis was no longer young by now, it was probably assumed that he could not muster the same energy and enterprise that had guaranteed his unbroken string of victories up to that time. They were wrong. Thutmosis, rapidly mobilizing and moving his army northward, nonetheless switched strategies. Instead of attacking Qadesh and Naharin from the south as he customarily had, he outflanked them by hitting them from the north. He landed and moved against two important cities of the opposing alliance, Erkatu on the coast and, more strategically, Tunip, one of the strongest and most active members of the coalition. He captured both towns in due course, then marched southward, laying waste to all that stood before him. Only Qadesh stood against him, completely isolated.

Thutmosis laid siege to Qadesh, the city fighting desperately in a last-ditch battle to retain its independence. The king tried a desperate strategem to disrupt the invading army: a mare in estrus was released among the Egyptian war-chariots in an effort to stir up the stallions sufficiently to cause havoc among the chariot corps, thereby giving the Qadesh soldiers an opportunity to exploit an opening and mount a successful counter-attack. The ploy might have met with success but the quick-thinking general Amenemhab leaped down from his chariot sword drawn, ran to the mare, and disemboweled her on the spot. The siege ranks now re-formed and the assault commenced. Amenemheb, always one of Thutmosis's most daring and energetic generals, was placed at the head of the assault troops who did in fact breach the walls, allowing the Egyptian army to pour through. The outcome from that point was never in doubt.

The final defeat of Qadesh would prove to be Thutmosis's final battle and the culmination of 17 brilliantly-executed offensive campaigns in Western Asia over a period of 19 years. Thutmosis was now too aged to pursue any more military adventures, but in any case, his empire had been completely secured and pacified. The imperial vassals from the third cataract in Nubia to the borders of the Hittite kingdom in Asia Minor were completely overawed and cowed; for more than 100 years afterward, there was little trouble for Egypt in Western Asia. It is thought by historians that Qadesh in particular had maintained itself as a Hyksos outpost after their expulsion from Egypt, and if so, the final defeat of Qadesh means that the Hyksos permanently disappear from history. With Western Asia under complete control, Thutmosis returned his attention to Nubio-Cush with an extensive building program, intensified administrative re-organization, and pacification campaigns by designated generals against fractious tribes. By the end of his reign, Thutmosis had pushed Egyptian power south beyond the third cataract almost to the fourth cataract, which meant that Napata, the capital of Cush now became incorporated into Egyptian territory. Thutmosis had created the greatest empire Egypt had ever known or would know, without losing a single battle.

After the last battle with Qadesh, Thutmosis III lived another 12 years. James Henry Breasted leaves us with one of the most eloquently and accurately concise assessments of Thutmosis III's life, career, and character:

> His [Thutmosis's] reign marks an epoch not only in Egypt but in the whole east as we know it in his age. Never before in history had a single brain wielded the resources of so great a nation and wrought them into such centralized, permanent and at the same time mobile efficiency, that for years they could be brought to bear with incessant impact upon another continent...The genius which rose from an obscure priestly office to accomplish this for the first time in history reminds us of an Alexander or a Napoleon. He

built the first real empire, and is thus the first character possessed of universal aspects, the first world-hero.[13]

There are perhaps only a half-dozen men in the last 35 centuries who revealed and exhibited in their lives the kind of genius that combined outstanding military leadership with remarkable administrative and organizational ability at the same level as Thutmosis III. Alexander and Napoleon, Hannibal, Julius Caesar, Genghis Khan, and Askia Muhammad come to mind. But Thutmosis III was the first, the prototype, as Breasted informs us above, and it is hard not to believe that Alexander—who set up his imperial capital not in Greece but in Egypt—knowing of Thutmosis's exploits, consciously modeled himself after this 'first world-hero', as later conquerors would model themselves after him. Thutmosis left such a lasting impression on the world around him that in after-centuries, his name was placed on amulets as a word of power.

Amenhotep II or *Amenophis II* (1,446 BC–1,421 BC)

Amenhotep II

Amenhotep II inherited the throne bequeathed to him by his father and, in physical resources at least, he seemed a match for his father. He was renowned for his great strength and battle prowess, a veritable pharaonic Hercules, and

13 Ibid., p. 320.

indeed when, inevitably, rebellion broke out in Western Asia on the death of Thutmosis III, Amenhotep was equal to task of putting it down. The traditional enemies, Naharin aided and abetted by Mitanni, revolted against the Egyptian yoke. Amenhotep lost no time mustering his army and marching northward. In his initial skirmishes in northern Lebanon, he demonstrated a real zest for personal combat, joining the battles much as his father Thutmosis III had, personally capturing 18 enemy soldiers at Shemesh-Edom. Amenhotep's army crossed the Orontes, the Naharin frontier, winning battle after battle, pushing on and defeating the revolting cities of Niy and Ikathi. He was able to carry his campaign across the Euphrates and into Mitanni, the true instigator of rebellion against Egypt.

There is some discrepancy about the number of campaigns required for Amenhotep II to re-pacify the restless vassals of Egypt's northern empire. Breasted thinks it was a single campaign; more recently, Grimal reports on three campaigns carried out by Amenhotep to secure the peace in his northern domains.[14] However this may be, Amenhotep demonstrated in his victories a cruel streak not evident in his father Thutmosis III in all of his 19 years at war: Amenhotep is reported to have had seven of the rebellious kings executed and their bodies hung from the walls of Thebes (Waset) and Napata in Nubia as a warning to other potentially disaffected dynasts. Whatever the case, under Amenhotep II, Egypt was able to establish control of the northern Sudan all the way to the 4th cataract, just south of Napata, the farthest south the Egyptian empire was ever able to penetrate. Nubio-Cush would remain peaceful and become more Egyptianized for the next 500 years. It is noteworthy that on several stelae erected in Nubia, Amenhotep II is pictured worshiping Nubian deities right along with Egyptian ones.[15] This practice was to be repeated by pharaohs till the end of the New Kingdom.

Egyptian texts in the time of Amenhotep II (c. 1,430 BC) mention a people called the *Apiru*, who will be encountered again in the Amarna Letters

---

14 Vid. ibid., pp. 324-5 and Grimal N, **A History of Ancient Egypt**, translated by Ian Shaw, Cambridge (USA): Blackwell, 1988; 1992, pp. 218-9.

15 'At Kalabsheh…is a scene of the king offering to Min and to the Nubian god Merutru-hor-ra.' Petrie Flinders WM, **A History of Egypt**, Vol. 2, London: Methuen & Co., 1896, p.159.

during the reign of Akhenaton some 70 years later (c. 1,360 BC), and yet one more time on a stele erected by Seti I in 1,300 BC where he describes the defeat of the Apiru. In the record of prisoners captured by Amenhotep II's armies, 3,600 Apiru are listed among the captives. The manner in which these Apiru are described make clear that they are nothing more than freebooters, 'gypsies', outlaw bands, or 'ancient Cossacks' as one writer has described them, a loose association of nomads and stateless persons, pillaging up and down Canaan as opportunities presented. Up until recently, there has been a distinct tendency to equate them with the Hebrews of history (*Apiru = Hebrew*). Against this assumption are the records of them going back to Sumerian writings around 2,100 BC, pre-dating the birth of Abraham. Moreover, it is nearly impossible to assign a specific ethnicity to them. What has made the Apiru attractive candidates for the modern historian seeking corroboration of Hebrew history is (1) Apiru captives apparently were, from time to time, brought into Egypt to work as serfs and (2) the Apiru wars against settled peoples in Canaan accords well with Hebrew history as described in Exodus and Deuteronomy. Moreover, it is not unlikely that a coterie of Apiru captives might well have been among the mixed-multitude that was led out of Egypt under Osar-siph. The point is, the Apiru were not originally Hebrews but, in the years after the Exodus (c. 1,230 BC), the Apiru name may have been applied to the descendants of the expatriates departing Egypt with Osar-siph and in that way become equated with the ancient Hebrews.

Amenhotep II, though prodigious in strength and military valor, does not, in the end, measure up to his father. He had not the wide and protean interests of his father and his main accomplishment seems to have been to have preserved the imperial edifice his father had erected. Moreover, there was a streak of sadism that revealed itself in Amenhotep II that Thutmosis III never demonstrated, invincible and implacable conqueror though he may have been. Still, Amenhotep did manage to extend Egypt's imperial border north and south; under him, Egypt's empire reached its greatest extent.

Amenhotep II, through his tomb oddly enough, served another purpose of great value to later archaeologists. His tomb was never found or looted by grave robbers, and when finally discovered and opened in 1898 by the French archaeologist Loret, an astonishing cache of royal mummies had been stashed there. There were six such mummies, including those of Thutmosis III, Mereneptah, and Rameses III, all placed there by the 21st Dynasty High Priest Pinudjem to keep them away from the depredations of ever more active tomb robbers.

Tehuti-mes IV or *Thutmosis IV* (1,421 BC–1,412 BC)

Thutmosis IV in Ivory

Amenhotep II was succeeded by Thutmosis IV, whose elevation to the throne was occasioned by the premature death of an elder brother who was the heir apparent. Thutmosis IV's unexpected accession had been prophesied to him in a remarkable dream that was vouchsafed to him as he took a midday nap in the shadow of the sphinx after a hunting expedition in and around the plateau of Giza. In the dream, the solar deity *Harmachis-Khepri-Rā-Atum*, of whom the Sphinx was said to be a concrete symbol, came to Thutmosis and promised him the throne of Egypt if he would clear the sand away and make the necessary repairs on the body of the statue. In ancient times as later, the Sphinx was repeatedly buried by the wind-blown sands coming off the Sahara and was subject to several sand-clearing and renovation projects, visible even today. In the event, Thutmosis IV was subsequently crowned king and duly fulfilled his promise by clearing the sand away from the Sphinx and probably embarking on the necessary repair projects. This entire episode was described on a 14-foot stele commissioned by Thutmosis IV and installed between the forepaws of the Sphinx. The lower third of the stele was severely eroded so the complete story as told by Thutmosis was not available, but enough survived to grasp the import of the inscription. The name of the 4th Dynasty pharaoh Kha-f-Rā (Cephren), builder of the third of the great pyramids of Giza, was found in the damaged part of the stele and it has led Egyptologists to assume that this pharaoh was the actual builder of the Sphinx, all the more so since it sits directly in front of and below the pyramid of Kha-f-Rā one-quarter mile distant. However, Flinders Petrie reminds us,

> And though the name of Khafra occurs in this inscription, yet, owing to the unfortunately broken state of it, there is nothing to show whether the Sphinx was attributed to Khafra…or in what way Khafra is involved.[16]

As discussed earlier, Khafra was the pharaoh in the Old Kingdom who had commissioned the repair of the Sphinx, hence the appearance of his name on Thutmosis IV's stele in the 18th Dynasty, but the evidence simply does not support the assumption that he was the actual builder of the Sphinx or that the Sphinx head is a sculptured portrait of him as many have asserted.

In foreign affairs, the formerly implacable enemy of Egypt, Mitanni, switched allegiance completely, allying itself with Egypt for the first time as a bulwark against the more dire threat posed by the expanding Hittite empire from Anatolia. Mitanni and Egypt, in the new spirit of *entente* ("cooperation"), apparently made territorial concessions to one another, sealing the bargain with a marriage between Thumosis IV and a royal daughter of Mitanni. Thutmosis made what was probably an obligatory and symbolic military incursion into Naharin, but the political animosities with Mitanni were definitely on the wane and the effort served little more than to create a record of military activity in the northern domains by pharaoh as proof of his military bona fides. A friendly concordat with Babylonia was also signed during this early period of Thutmosis's reign.

16 Petrie Flinders, ibid., p. 167.

Nubio-Cush remained securely in Egyptian hands at the beginning of Thutmosis IV's reign. That didn't stop restive outside tribes from infiltrating the Egyptian-held arenas and causing trouble. Consequently, Thutmosis was compelled to send an army of pacification southward to quell the disturbances. They must not have caused serious disruption because trade went on undiminished and, like all the pharaohs of the New Kingdom, temple-building in the region continued without letup. As will be seen over and again, the potentates of the New Kingdom undertook nearly as much building in Nubia as they did within corporate Egypt itself. Thutmosis IV's regime is also noteworthy for the amount of temple building and renovation conducted in and around Memphis, as shown by the clearing of the Sphinx and the renovations to its adjoining temple.

Thumosis IV died prematurely after nine years of rule and was succeeded by his son Amenhotep III.

Amenhotep III or *Amenophis III* (1,412 BC–1,373 BC)

With Amenhotep III, Egypt attains the apogee of its power and glory. Veritably, the 39 years of his rule represent the high noon of the New Kingdom and,

Amenhotep III aka
Amenhotep the Magnificent

Amenhotep III—Pharaonic
Egypt at its Apogee

indeed, of Egyptian civilization. He was the son of Thutmosis IV by a secondary consort named *Mutemwa* ('Mother of the one') and, typically in Egyptian dynastic succession, was named heir, and therefore consort-designate of the Great Royal Wife, by virtue of discernible native talent. It is worth repeating that primogeniture was not the rule in Egyptian royal succession and the annals are full of otherwise obscure royal sons elevated to the throne. It has to be believed that the higher echelons of the priesthood, possibly a priestly 'Council of Cardinals' with representatives from all the major temples, had a hand in the ultimate selection of the pharaoh and they would have been largely motivated by evidence of superior character, intelligence, and ability in the available pool of royal sons. It is a singular fact that Egypt probably produced more incontestably outstanding rulers over its 4,000 year dynastic history than any other civilization.

Amenhotep III ascended the throne when he was 12 and his mother, Mutemwa, served as regent until he attained his majority. He was married to Tiye, who would ultimately show herself as equal in every way to Amenhotep and eventually become the *de facto* co-ruler of Egypt. What is strange is that Tiye was not of royal lineage; her parents, Yuya (father) and Tuyu (mother), were high-born and prominent aristocrats who would play a prominent role in government and produce a later pharaoh in the person of their son Ay, Tiye's brother. Tiye became the wife of record and in every way the partner of Amenhotep III but unless she represents a break with a tradition that went back to the foundation of the Egyptian state itself more than 25 centuries earlier, the apparent absence of a Great Royal Wife married to Amenhotep III must be explained. The pharaoh always obtained legitimacy on the throne by his marriage to the Great Royal Wife, an office and title passed down from mother to daughter who was often a half-sister to the new pharaoh. It has to be wondered if Amenhotep III truly broke with such an inflexible tradition, hoary with age, or whether there was another marriage to a legitimate Great Royal Wife presumptive who died early. If so, it opened up unlimited prospects for Tiye and her family. Tiye was just the woman to make the most of the opportunity and had a hand in the historic shift occasioned by the following reign of her son about which more will be said. The other, and more probable, explanation for the extraordinary elevation of Tiye to queenship is that she represented a collateral branch of a female line that might have had ancestral ties to the succession of Great Royal Wives that began at the onset of the dynasty with Ahmose-Nefertari. She might therefore have ascended to the position of Great Royal Wife because no direct lineal female descendant had survived to adulthood.

One indication, among many, of Tiye's prominence and power during the reign of Amenhotep III is shown in the statuary of the time. For the first time since the Old Kingdom, king and queen were, on occasion, represented monumentally as equal in stature. That is to say the queen, when represented sitting with the king, was sculptured to correct proportion in relation to the

Amenhotep III and Queen Tiye
of Equal Stature and Importance

king instead of being rendered in smaller, knee-high form as had become the custom since the end of the Old Kingdom. This reversion to ancient artistic practice would not survive the 18th Dynasty. As has been noted, Tiye's family thrived and prospered during this period. Amenhotep III's father-in-law, Yuya, served as commanding officer of the Chariot corps and as Master of the Stud Farms and he successfully engineered the installation of his son Inen to the posts of Second Prophet of Amon and Chief of Seers at Karnak Temple. His other son Ay, the future pharaoh, eventually inherited Yuya's own office as Master of the Stud Farms.

Tiye was another of those remarkable Egyptian queens whose personality left an indelible imprint on the reigns of both her husband and son. She outlived her husband, surviving well into the reign of her son Amenhotep IV. Another testimony to her influence and importance is indicated in the building of a temple to her in her lifetime in Nubia, between the second and third cataracts. However, the most telling legacy of her 'co-reign' with Amenhotep III can be seen in the domain of foreign affairs. In the latter half of her husband's reign and in the early part of her son's, foreign potentates actually addressed diplomatic correspondence to her, almost as if she were 'Secretary of State'. It might reasonably be surmised that it was in fact the true nature of the role she played in the latter stages of the regime.

Perhaps not surprisingly, Tiye exercised a decisive influence on the character and personality of her son Amenhotep IV, known to history as Akhenaton. It was Tiye who undoubtedly introduced him to the veneration of Aton—which became an exclusive worship—and in this way, she can be thought of as the 'midwife' of the 'Atonian heresy', upon which Akhenaton's notoriety rests. More will be said about this aspect of Tiye's impact on the destiny of Egypt in the discussion of Akhenaton's reign.

Amenhotep's reign was particularly noteworthy for its stability, matchless prosperity, and wide activities in foreign affairs. He was obliged to embark on one campaign at the end of his fourth year, again to pacify the always restless Cushitic tribes in the south making incursions into Egyptian-controlled territory. As always, Nubian levies made up a large part of the army and Amenhotep, over a period of several months, campaigned as far south as the 4th cataract. In Napata, always plentiful gold was collected for use in the various temples of Thebes. By now the full Egyptianization of Nubio-Cush, as far south as the 4th Cataract, was nearly complete. Cush would remain an Egyptian protectorate until 900 BC. One consequence of this development is that Napata became an important center of Amon-worship that in time would eclipse that of Thebes. So important did Amon-worship in Napata become that numerous Egyptians, including priests, made pilgrimages there, many of them settling in and around Napatan Cush permanently.

Egyptian hegemony extended far to the north, east, and southeast as well. Amenhotep III's name and cartouche could be found in Yemen, Babylon,

Anatolia, Crete, Cyprus, and Mycenae. Crete especially fell under the sway of Egyptian influences as the amazing Minoan frescoes attest and Crete was the earliest staging ground for the infiltration of Egyptian cultural ideas into the Greek mainland, at that time under the dominion of the pre-Doric civilization of Mycenae. But the most significant development in foreign affairs was the steady rise of the Hittite empire of Anatolia. Mitanni was the one that felt the increasing political and military pressure created by Hittite expansionism, the prime reason for the rapprochement between Mitanni and Egypt, evident as far back as the reign of Thutmosis IV. Characteristically, Amenhotep took as a wife a princess royal of Mitanni to cement the continuing alliance. A series of usurpations and counter-usurpations in Mitanni led to the rise of a new regime there whose new king duly betrothed his daughter to the Egyptian emperor. Babylon followed suit; two princesses royal of Babylon found their way into the harem of Amenhotep III. It was a time when mere political and diplomatic prudence dictated fostering cordial relations with the region's reigning super-power. The ebb and flow of these multifarious international activities were captured in correspondence, written in cuneiform, between these aforementioned states and the Egyptian court. This correspondence was written on clay tablets, a group of 379 of which were discovered in 1887 near the ruins of the royal palace of Amarna, Akhenaton's capital. Parts of this correspondence were directed, as noted above, to Queen Tiye directly. A number of the letters were in fact demands for gold and lots of it. Egypt was thought of as a land where gold was as 'plentiful as dust' and pharaonic allies missed no opportunity to demand more of it. In the end, Hatti (Hittite empire) would supplant Mitanni as the dominant empire in Western Asia whose borders eventually extended to Lebanon. But this Hittite ascendancy in and around Anatolia would not achieve fruition until the following reign, that of Amenhotep IV (Ahkenaton).

As has already been commented upon, the reign of Amenhotep III was one of unmatched splendor in ancient Egypt. A frenzy of building all over Egyptian domains ensued, especially in Nubia, continuing the interesting New Kingdom policy of building as assiduously in Nubia as in Egypt itself. The New Kingdom pharaohs' dominant internal policy in this light could be seen as one of binding Nubio-Cush ever more closely to the kingdom. It must be repeated, therefore, that Nubio-Cush was not thought of as 'foreign' territory *per se*, in the manner of Egypt's Western Asiatic domains, any more than Scotland or Wales are thought of as foreign territories in the United Kingdom. In Lower Egypt, Amenhotep III built or refurbished temples in the Delta cities of Athribis and Bubastis, sacred to Horus and Bast respectively, as well as at Heliopolis, the sacred city of Rā, and Sakkara, sacred to Ptah. In addition, Amenhotep built edifices at Abydos in honor of Osiris and Hermopolis in honor of Thoth.

However, his most lasting accomplishment in temple-building is the Temple dedicated to Amon-Rā, Mut, and Khonsu at Luxor. This temple is especially noteworthy for a side chapel (now locked off by the authorities) that contains an extraordinary account of Amenhotep III's birth. Thutmosis IV died early and by the time Amenhotep III was rendering an account of his birth, a divine parent had stepped in, so to speak, in the person of Amon-Rā himself. As a divine king the idea of having a divine parent was not considered outlandish. There are four panels in the divine birthing *mise en scène* at Luxor depicting the following events (see figure following):

1. Thoth, the Divine Messenger, announces to the royal mother, Mut-em-wa ('Mother of the one'), the impending conception and birth of the Divine Child who as Amon-hotep, Son of Amon-Ra, will grow up to reign as the Divine King over Egypt;

2. In the second panel, the pregnant royal mother stands before Hathor, the mistress of childbirth, and Nef, the embodiment of the Divine Breath (Spirit), both holding the ankh, the symbol of Life, to the mouth of Mut-em-wa;

3. In the third scene, Mut-em-wa sits on the birthing chair while in the same panel, tended by nurses, is the new-born royal infant, represented as the Child Horus, holding his finger to his mouth;

4. In the final panel, the heavenly hosts of the Egyptian pantheon gather around the newborn Divine Child to render him homage; in front of him stand three divine personages offering gifts.

At Luxor—Annunciation, Conception, Birth, And Adoration Of The Divine Child Involving Mut-Em-Wa, "Mother Of The One"

Here, in the early 14th century BC, was represented on a wall in Luxor Temple the Annunciation, the Conception, the Birth, and the Adoration of the Divine Child and it is hard to see this remarkable pageant of a Divine Birth as anything but a prefigurement of the Gospel Nativity as represented in the first two chapters of Matthew. It was not the first such Divine Nativity depicted in Egypt; Hathor had a similar *mise en scène* carved onto the walls of her temple at Deir el-Bahari, but Amenhotep III's version resonates rather more closely to the familiar Gospel Nativity. No other pharaoh built as much as Amenhotep III except for Rameses II in the 19th Dynasty.

A noticeable change is revealed in artistic technique in the reign of Amenhotep III, brought to fuller realization in the reign of Amenhotep IV. Freer modes of expression and an enhanced naturalism show themselves in Egyptian sculpture and painting. One such technique was the 'clinging drapery' style of rendering clothing on statuary which more realistically depicted the folding of apparel worn around the subject's body. Again, this was rendered to its best effect in the following reign.

This shift in artistic taste was not the only foreshadowing of things to come in the so-called 'Amarna Period'. Already, Aton—a solar deity represented symbolically by the sun's flaming disc—has achieved an ever-growing presence in court religious ceremonial. Tiye is usually the one given credit for this development but she evidently was supported in this innovation by her husband. As a result of the spectacular success of the previous 18th dynasty pharaohs in the creation of the Egyptian empire, prodigious amounts of wealth flowed into the coffers of the Amonian priesthood since the victorious pharaohs were convinced that their steadily expanding glory was attributable to the good offices of Amon and his priests. With this flood of wealth came greater concentration of material power in the hands of the priesthood of Amon, so much so that it began to infringe on the age-old political prerogatives of pharaoh. Up to then, a delicate balance of power between priest and pharaoh had been rigorously maintained, but a triumphant Amonian priesthood began to tip this balance more definitively toward itself. Even Amenhotep III, the most politically powerful ruler in the world, was feeling the effects of this gradual encroachment. His wife Tiye, supported by her husband, sought to counterbalance this tense state of affairs by bringing onto the royal religious stage Aton and the ceremonial worship surrounding him. All of these developments would come to a head in the pivotal, history-changing reign of Amenhotep IV, known to the world as Akhenaton. As was customary in the 18th Dynasty, Amenhotep IV was associated with his father as co-ruler in the 37th year of the latter's reign. Amenhotep III died two years later.

The world in which Egypt now finds itself is radically different than anything she has known before. Egyptian garrisons, manned largely by Nubian soldiers, are firmly ensconced all over Egyptian-controlled territories in Canaan, Lebanon, Syria, and along the Tigris-Euphrates. There is in fact a *pax Egyptiana* over the entire eastern Mediterranean and Western Asia, fostering security and trans-national trade as never before. Egyptian merchant ships roam as far north as the Aegean and even into the Black Sea as well as down the Red Sea into the Indian Ocean. River trade from inner Africa remains as remunerative as ever; overland caravans from Mesopotamia and points farther east beat a steady path to the borders of Egypt. Foreigners from Crete, Cyprus, Mycenae, Rhodes, Babylonia, and Phoenicia, as merchants, diplomats, and merchant sailors, are now common sights on the streets of major Egyptian cities. Copper from Cyprus and silver from Anatolia pour into Egypt in never-before-seen abundance. At the beginning of the 18th Dynasty, silver, because of its rarity was more valuable than gold; by the end of the dynasty, gold surpassed silver in value and never again relinquished its paramount place among precious metals. Egyptian customs officials regulated this influx of foreigners, goods, and raw materials but the permanent population of peoples from Western Asia steadily increased, most of whom were absorbed gradually into the native population by intermarriage.

Never had Egypt experienced such opulence and material splendor. The rich abundance now flowing into the Nile Valley along with unmistakable foreign influences began to foster a more elaborate culture and complex of customs that are entirely new. Clothing becomes more varied and ornate compared to earlier epochs; the well-dressed Egyptian of the 18th dynasty now walked the streets garbed in a long, plaited skirt, a tunic with flowing sleeves, any variety of wigs fashioned from human hair, and fine sandals. This finery represented a marked change from the unadorned kilt customarily worn from waist to knee as the common everyday dress of an earlier Egypt. With this pervasive wealth percolating throughout society, men of means built for themselves expensive mansions and villas, complete with pleasure gardens and artificial lakes, on a scale and in number that was without precedent in previous Egyptian society.

The splendor of reign has been commented on several times already and as a way of cataloguing some of this splendor for the modern reader, James Henry Breasted gives a description of Amenhotep's adornments added to Karnak Temple:

> [Amenhotep] raised a massive pylon before the temple of Karnak, adorned with unsurpassed richness; steles of lapis-lazuli were set up on either side and besides great quantities of gold and silver, nearly twelve hundred pounds of malachite were employed in inlay work... The king also built a temple to Mut, the goddess of Thebes...on the south of Karnak, and excavated a lake beside it. He then laid out a beautiful garden in the interval of over a mile and a half, which separates Karnak from the Luxor temple and connected the great temples by avenues of rams carved in stone, each bearing a statue of the Pharaoh between the forepaws. The general effect must have been imposing in the extreme; the brilliant hues of the polychrome architecture, with columns and gates overwrought in gold and floors inlaid with silver...all this must have produced an impression both of gorgeous detail and overwhelming grandeur...[17]

Thebes was becoming the capital of the 'known world' and Breasted refers to it as the 'first monumental city of antiquity'. As pharaoh, Amenhotep III would not neglect his own mortuary temple which he duly constructed on the west

17 Breasted, ibid., pp. 344-5.

bank of the Nile. Almost none of it survives to the present day, apart from the of the remains two gigantic, 70-foot colossi of himself, but it was the largest and most sumptuous temple built during his reign. The two colossal statues of Amenhotep III were famous down to the end of antiquity—called by the Greeks 'the colossi of Memnon'—as much for their size as for the 'voice' that issued from within the massive statues every morning at dawn. In all of the sacred buildings erected by Amenhotep III, one finds exquisite gold and silver inlaying of walls and floors, with superbly-rendered frescoes displaying a superb artistic delicacy along with brilliantly realized color schemes. A new naturalism creeps into Egyptian art that is fully consummated in the reign of Akhenaton. In short, the arts, crafts, sculpture, and architecture achieve a stunning virtuosity. However, despite the manifest changes and shifts in taste in the culture of the New Kingdom there remained a nostalgia, an almost ineradicable longing, for the past. It was a time of enthusiastic antiquarian research and Amenhotep III commissioned the chief scribes to consult the ancient scrolls so that certain rituals and ceremonies could be revived according to ancient practice. This revival included recitation of prayers, chants, and incantations in a lingual form of Egyptian that hadn't been spoken in perhaps 2,000 years. Few Egyptians, pharaoh included, would have understood the words and phrases being uttered, almost as if the reciters were 'speaking in tongues'—a kind of *xenoglossia* or 'strange language'—a phenomenon frequently encountered in the religious devotions of modern fundamentalist sects.

Looking back from the perspective of 3,500 years later there is discernable and hard-to-define unease about this matchless material brilliance and luxury, as if it were in some way overdone, certainly by comparison to earlier cultural conceptions in Egypt. Through the Middle Kingdom, Egyptian cultural expression was marked by a harmonious, elegant simplicity remarkably rendered in even the most massive structures like the pyramids. Simplicity seems to have been more or less abandoned in the New Kingdom in favor of a highly developed sophistication that just missed being over-refined, almost decadent. Flinders Petrie notes that many well-to-do persons lived in greater luxury than the royalty of past ages. Still, there is no gainsaying the extraordinary heights attained during the 18th Dynasty in nearly every sphere of human endeavor. It is recognized by most as being Egypt's most spectacular age.

The impact of Egyptian culture was felt everywhere in the region. Egyptian artistic, architectural, and craft techniques were disseminated far and wide throughout the eastern and northern Mediterranean. Egyptian religion, ritual, and symbols made substantial inroads in Crete and Mycenae (Greece); Herodotus more than 900 years later would say that all the Greek gods came originally from Egypt. No peoples benefitted more from the Egyptian connection than the Phoenicians in their maritime cities, and on a near-daily basis, Phoenician ships laden with goods from all over the Mediterranean docked in Egyptian ports. After 1,200 BC, the Phoenicians became the *de facto* merchant marine for Egypt. The impact of Egypt on the cultural development of Mediterranean nations and peoples reverberated for the next 15 centuries, informing the evolution of, among others, the sacerdotal systems of Judaism and Christianity.

Like all the great pharaohs before him, Amenhotep III was blessed with the services of an outstanding public servant, one whose genius and talent led him to be compared to the legendary Imhotep (3rd Dynasty): Amenhotep, son of Hapu. Like Imhotep before him, he excelled in every field of endeavor he undertook as prime minister, architect, philosopher, and—of paramount importance to Egyptians—one completely learned in the Books of Thoth, which included magic.

Amenhotep, Son of Hapu
Great 18th Dynasty Polymath

Indeed, so great was his reputation that Amenhotep son Hapu was considered to be the reincarnation of Imhotep and in fact was deified in Ptolemaic times (after 320 BC) in the same manner as Imhotep. Like so many before him, going back to the Old Kingdom, Amenhotep son of Hapu was born in humble circumstances but his extraordinary, polymathic genius enabled him to rise to the pinnacle of pharaoh's service and favor. In what was a dazzling era in Egyptian history, Amenhotep son Hapu could be seen as the country's leading light, the highest ornament of Egyptian civilization of the time. He was an adept of the highest order.

Many new developments took place in the reign of Amenhotep III, including one that was occasioned by his death. Amenhotep III was the first pharaoh to have his tomb carved out of the sandstone cliffs on the west bank of the Nile in the so-called Valley of the Kings and for the next 1,000 years, nearly all the succeeding pharaohs followed suit. The particular location of these pharaonic burial sites on the western side of river is heralded by a striking pyramidal rock structure that surmounts and overlooks the entire valley. There

Pyramidal Structure over Valley of the Kings

Vulva Form at Entrance to Valley of the Queens

can hardly be any doubt that situating the kings' burial ground right at this spot was intended, just as the entrance of the Valley of the Queens, the burial place of the royal women from Amenhotep III's time onward, is proclaimed by a rock form at its entrance looking exactly like a female vulva. The ancient Egyptians almost never did anything haphazardly, randomly, or coincidentally; in life and death, they knew the effect they wanted to achieve and almost invariably succeeded in obtaining the exact result desired.

Another new departure inaugurated under Amenhotep III was the entombment of the Apis Bull—sacred in turn to the Nile god Hapi, Ptah, and Osiris in the Ptolemaic era—at Sakkara, the necropolis of Sokar, just outside Memphis. Each Apis bull was kept alive 30 years after which he was sacrificed in favor of the new bull which was selected on the basis of highly specific markings, as if the new bull were the re-incarnation of the recently deceased one. This practice lasted 14 centuries, to the end of sovereign Egyptian history (30 BC). The Macedonian Ptolemaic pharaohs introduced a new deity during their dynasty they called *Serapis*, a fusion of Osirs and Hapi or Apis.

Amenhotep IV/Akhenaton (1,375 BC–1,357 BC)

Amenhotep IV ascended the throne in the 37th year of his father's reign in or around 1,375 BC. He reigned as co-regent with his father for two years until, upon his father's demise, he became the sole ruler of Egypt (1,373 BC). In a nation whose history knew many conspicuous and unusual pharaonic personalities, Amenhotep IV, known more familiarly as Akhenaton, was certainly the most singular individual ever to sit on Egypt's throne. Though there were winds of change in play in the previous reign of Amenhotep III,

Amenhotep IV/Akhenaton

Akhenaton propelled these changes to such a wholesale level of intensity that he truly can be said to have inaugurated a religious revolution—perhaps better thought of as a reformation—that set Egyptian culture and civilization on a radical new course. Akhenaton's radical, exclusive monotheism was something never before seen in Egyptian history or, truly speaking, in the history of the world up to that time. In the end, such a course was too radical and too far 'outside of its time' to last beyond his reign; in the extreme reaction afterward, there was a concerted attempt to erase him from history.

In the context of the times, Akhenaton was clearly an odd personality, one, however, who possessed an unbending will. But for all his determination and intensity, he never attempted to impose his new religion by violent coercion, apart from his systematic endeavor late in his reign, ultimately unsuccessful, to chisel Amon out of the Egyptian iconographic record. In spite of that, there is no record of anyone being exiled, imprisoned, or executed in the name of Akhenaton's Atonist revolution. As will be seen, Akhenaton preferred peace to war, apparently relying on the psycho-spiritual sway of Aton himself—combined with his own pharaonic 'leverage'—to establish Aton's worship on a permanent basis. On one level, Akhenaton was implacable in his opposition to Amon and his priesthood but on another, he was not prepared to spread the new religion at the point of a sword. As is well known, later monotheistic enthusiasts were not so scrupulous or restrained.

Though it will be examined again in succeeding chapters, much speculation has arisen about the impact of Akhenaton on the formation of Hebrew religion. There is evidence enough to show that he is the world's first documented monotheist; the pre-Mosaic patriarchs, if it is assumed that they were truly historical personalities, never entirely shed the thinking and worship patterns of their polytheistic origins. Indeed, neither did the post-Mosaic Children of Israel up until the time of the Captivity (circa 586 BC). If as seems likely, the historical Moses was an Egyptian priest[18] who, more than 100 years after Akhenaton, apostasized from the established Egyptian religion and led a band of dissenters out of Egypt and into Canaan, it is no great stretch to presume that he had been influenced posthumously by the life, work, and example of Akhenaton. It would suggest, moreover, that the monotheistic seed planted by Akhenaton during his 18-year reign, did not entirely wither and die after his passing but bore belated fruit in the formative events that led to the emergence historically of the Hebrews and their monotheistic religion centered around Yahweh.

18 Vid. Finch CS, **Echoes of the Old Dark Land: Themes from the African Eden**, Decatur: Khenti Publications, Inc., 1991, pp. 140-43 for this discussion.

The expansion of the now-overweening power of the Temple of Amon and its priesthood has been commented on. The tension created as this augmented priestly power began to encroach on that of pharaoh was a sub-surface current running through a reign that otherwise represented the acme of Egyptian imperial majesty and cultural efflorescence. The introduction of Aton, an ancient god symbolized by the sun disc and situated at Heliopolis as part of the solar complex of deities centered on Rā, into court religious ceremonial was clearly aimed at counteracting the pervasive and overbearing presence of Amon. Even the early 18th Dynasty fusion of Amon with Rā as Amon-Rā did nothing to mitigate the

Aton's Rays Shining Down on Akhenaton and Nefertiti

intensifying rivalry between priest and pharaoh in the time of Amenhotep III. As noted, Queen Tiye seems to have been at the forefront of this new development that plucked Aton out of obscurity and bestowed upon him a prestige and importance that Aton had never before known. It appears to have been Queen Tiye who imbued her son, Amenhotep IV, with both an aversion to the pretensions of the Amonians and a fanatical espousal of Aton. Perhaps even she could not have anticipated where this 'evangelization' on behalf of Aton would lead.

The early part of Amenhotep IV's reign began normally enough, probably because he was under certain constraints as the co-ruler of Egypt with his father. However much Amenhotep III might have chafed under and resented the intrusive, even invasive, influence of the priesthood of Amon and no matter how much he might have silently supported his wife's advancement of the cause of Aton within the royal house, he was not prepared to provoke an open break with Amon. But his tacit assent to her activities was occasioned by the situation in Egypt that enabled one of the high priests of Amon to be treasurer of the realm and another to be the vizier. Moreover, the reigning Chief Prophet of Amon was also the 'grand master' of the religious body that included all the priests in the realm. The priests of Amon had been instrumental in the accession of pharaohs since the beginning of the dynasty; clearly too much power was concentrated in their sacerdotal hands, to the detriment of the royal house. In the person of the newly ascended pharaoh, Amenhotep IV, this priesthood confronted an adversary whose determination and will had not been foreseen and who would battle them until the end of his life.

Tiye is the outstanding and dominant female figure in the reigns of both her husband, Amenhotep III, and her son Amenhotep IV/Akhenaton. However, it is Akhenaton's lovely wife, Nefertiti, who has captured the modern imagination. There has been a lot of confusion about her antecedents. For a long time, it was said that she was a foreign princess who had captured the heart of Amenhotep IV but was then wed to him for political reasons. It was

The "Real" Nefertiti

Nefertiti in Profile

said that she was Mitanni by birth though some have claimed that she was 'Persian'. It has now become indisputably clear that she was a native Egyptian woman who, like her mother-in-law Tiye, had ancestral connections to the royal house. In fact, since Tiye did not have any daughters that survived to adulthood, Nefertiti assumed the role of Great Royal Wife in the same way Tiye had, that is, by virtue of a collateral blood connection to the line of Great Royal Wives. She must have been related, therefore, to both Tiye and Akhenaton. All of these suppositions are given strong support by Cyril Aldred:

> There seems to be little doubt…that she [Nefertiti] was descended from Ahmose-Nefertari, the virtual female ancestress of the dynasty whose cult as a Theban divinity had been greatly expanded by one of her descendants, Queen Tiye. Nefertiti was doubtless of the same family as Tiye, who was perhaps her aunt.[19]

She was to bear Akhenaton six daughters, the second of whom died early in life, and throughout the first decade or so of his reign Nefertiti was frequently portrayed with him—and her daughters—in various sculpted tableaus on the walls of the temples and monuments in the newly-built city of Akhetaton, 'the horizon of Aton'.

Nefertiti's ancient 'glamour' in the eyes moderns is entirely due to a bust of her now sitting in the Berlin Museum, found in the ruins of a sculptor's studio,

Bust of Nefertiti in the Berlin Museum

19 Aldred, op. cit., p. 261.

depicting her with Europeanoid facial features and light skin. However, other representations of her in bas reliefs all over Akhetaton show a woman with typical Africanoid Egyptian features. It is not easy to reconcile the two seemingly conflicting images, and recently Swiss art historian Henri Stierlin, after 25 years of careful investigation into the matter, has declared the famous Berlin bust a forgery, commissioned by Ludwig Borchardt in 1912 and carried out by Gerardt Marks. And when it is recognized that all of her daughters—as well herself—are depicted with the facial features and cranial structures of people whose ancestors would have originated in East Africa, what can be said for certain is that Nefertiti was Egyptian—and therefore African—by birth and ancestry. The now infamous bust need no longer cause confusion about Nefertiti's antecedents but as a fraud, it is the Egyptological equivalent to the Piltdown Man.

Amenhotep IV, like pharaonic heirs apparent before him, rose to the throne first in a two-year co-regency with his father. Cyril Aldred thinks the co-regency might have lasted as long as 12 years, but this appears to be a minority view. According to Aldred, he would have had his own coterie of 'officials-in-waiting' from which to draw members of his cabinet at the time of his sole accession:

> On his crowning as co-regent, the new pharaoh would appoint his own men to office and these would usually be the young companions and followers who had been brought up with him as a kind of shadow court.[20]

These officials-to-be were usually sons of the senior officials of the previous regime who inherited the offices and duties of their fathers, so that 'It is evident that whole families of officials existed side by side with the dynasties of kings whom they served...'[21] Under these circumstances, the panel of officials serving the old pharaoh would retire immediately upon his death to make way for their successors. Thus the co-regency of the pharaonic tandem of father and son was matched by a 'co-regency' among the royal officials and their filial successors. In the first six years of his reign, Amenhotep IV ruled from Thebes and though he actively promulgated the worship of Aton, he made no overt moves against Amon or his priests. Aton was promoted as the deity embodying the principle

20 Aldred C, **Akenaten: King of Egypt**, London: Thames & Hudson, Ltd., 1988, p. 172.
21 Ibid.

of light and beneficence whose rays, when represented in relief, ended in hands carrying the ankh, the symbol of life. Though Aton was the unseen self-created Creator, his visible emblem was the sun-disc whose life-enabling light bathed the entire earth bringing blessings to all living things. From the beginning, Akhenaton worshiped him and him alone, and encouraged all who would to do the same. During this period, Akhenaton made perfunctory obeisances to Amon simply because it was expected of him and he was not quite ready for a clean break. However, this superficial deference to Amon did not prevent Akhenaton from initiating a visible—and provocative—manifestation of his true sentiments by commanding the construction of a Temple of Aton, called the *Gempaaton*, on the very grounds of Karnak Temple, heretofore sacred to Amon. That Amenhotep IV was still paying at least nominal homage to some of the traditional neters of Egypt is revealed in the colossal figures of the king stationed on the outside of Gempaaton where he appears in an Osirified pose, with crossed arms holding crook and flail, in the guise of Shu and Atum. Doubtless, the young, iconoclastic pharaoh was a bit more comfortable posing as Shu and Atum, both part of the divine solar complex at Annu (Heliopolis), the original home of Aton. One of the notable innovations in constructing this temple, later replicated in the royal edifices built at Akhetaton, was the insertion of the 'Window of Appearance' where the pharaoh, his wife, and his children would appear in public view on regular occasions. Already, this custom, one of many radical breaks with tradition yet to come, embodied the motto—the rubric—that governed the entire reign: *ankh em maāt*, or 'living in truth'.

Gempaaton was one of four temples Amenhotep IV had built on the premises of Karnak; two others included *Rud-menu* ('powerful shrine') and *Teni-menu* ('exalted shrine'). They are noteworthy for scenes of massive quantities of food both as offerings to Aton and as victuals for the temple servants as well as the public at large on important feast days. The idea that an important role of the king was to provide liberal quantities of food to the populace would be seen again in the kingdom of Ghana (c. 1,000 AD) where the king was said to set a table every evening sufficient to feed 10,000 of his subjects.[22] One is even permitted to wonder if this kingly largesse is echoed

22 See deGraft-Johnson JC, **African Glory**, Baltimore: Black Classic Press, 1954, 1986, p. 82, citing the 11th century Arab traveler and writer El Edrisi.

in the New Testament scene of the Sermon on the Mount where Christ ('the King') multiplies the loaves and the fishes to feed the multitude. The fourth noteworthy temple erected in Karnak at the behest of Amenhotep IV was the 'Mansion of the Ben-ben' (obelisk) constructed exclusively for the ceremonials to be conducted by Queen Nefertiti. Within 15 years of Akhenaton's death, every one of these temples was demolished.

Amenhotep IV continued to follow hallowed tradition by building in Nubia between the third and fourth cataracts, an entire city in fact, also named *Gempaaton*. Other cities in Egypt were favored with Atonian temples in the early years of the reign, none of which remain standing today.

In the 6th year of his reign, Amenhotep IV was no longer content to pretend continued piety toward the age-old neters of established Egyptian religion and especially not any fealty toward Amon. This year marks his particular 'crossing the Rubicon'; he was forcing an open and permanent breach with Amon and he never looked back. He now proclaimed the single and exclusive worship of Aton, who could and would not be represented in any anthromorphic or zoomorphic form. Amenhotep IV changed his name to the one by which henceforth he would always be known, *Akhenaton*, 'the spirit of Aton'.

To throw off the yoke of the Amonian priesthood entirely, he undertook to move himself, his family, his court, and the entire governmental administration to a brand new city, to be built on the eastern bank of the Nile within a semi-circle of cliffs. It was to be the first 'planned' city ever built in Egypt and given the name *Akhetaton*, 'the horizon of Aton'. Historians profess to be entirely mystified as to why this particular spot was chosen for the new city; the only information ever vouchsafed by Akhenaton himself in his inscriptions was that Aton himself had chosen the spot and that it did not belong to nor was it claimed by any other deity or person in Egypt. However, the late Livio C. Stecchini, an international scholarly expert on ancient measures, was of the decided opinion that the choice of the site of Akhetaton was dictated by Akhenaton's determination to reset the geodetic center of Egypt to re-establish the original pre-dynastic geodetic system of Egypt:

> The new capital for the god Aten, who was raised to the status

> of the one true god, was set at latitude 27° 45' north, at the middle point between the northernmost point Behdet and the southern limit of Egypt at latitude 24° 00' north.[23]

Work began in the 5th year of his reign and it was then that Akhenaton oversaw the raising of 14 boundary stelae that defined the geographic limits of his new capital, the arising sacred center of Aton. In his 6th regnal year, he had moved himself, family, and court temporarily to Akhetaton, even though it was not finished, for the formal dedication and consecration of the boundary stelae, with everyone domiciled in temporary shelters as work proceeded at a feverish pace. Full and permanent occupation of the new city would have to wait two additional years.

On the north side of the new city, a massive temple—possibly built with the aim of rivaling Karnak in size—the House of Aten, was constructed. It contained within it three subsidiary temples, the 'House of Rejoicing', the *Gem-aten* ('Aten is found'), and another 'Mansion of the Ben-ben' similar to the one already built at Karnak. Aldred succinctly describes the great edifice as follows:

> This, then, was the Great House of the Aten in Akhetaten, the sanctum and arcanum of the king's deity, and the centre of the Aten cult, the ultimate destination not only of the king and his family, but also of all worshippers living and dead who would be joined together there forever.[24]

In the central part of the city was constructed the 'Island Distinguished in Jubilees' which served as the administrative hub of the city, region, and country. In this quarter was situated the king's Great Palace, residences of high officials, courts, warehouses, scribal offices, ateliers, record storage facilities, and a 'House of Life' (*per ankh*) which served as university and professional training ground for priests with specialized duties such as medicine. Foreign dignitaries and merchants now flocked to Akhetaten and were scarcely seen in Thebes or

23 See Stecchini LC, *Notes on the Relation of Ancient Measures to the Great Pyramid*, Appendix to **Secrets of the Great Pyramid**, by Peter Tompkins, New York: Harper and Row Publishers, 1971, p. 338.

24 Aldred, op. cit., p. 275.

Memphis, the usual destinations for foreigners traveling to Egypt. The entire focus of the empire had shifted to a spot situated exactly halfway between the northern boundary of corporate Egypt at Behdet on the Mediterranean and the southern boundary at Syene (Aswan) at the first cataract of the Nile.

The high point of Akhenaton's reign comes in the 12th year of his reign when delegates from all parts of the empire, south and north, journeyed to Akhetaton to pay homage to pharaoh accompanied by the typically dazzling array of gifts and tributes. Representatives from the Hittite empire, Naharin, Cyprus, Syria, Palestine, Cush, Libya, and Punt were all present. Receiving them in state were Akhenaton, Nefertiti, and their six daughters. The gifts of a quality, quantity, and variety as would befit an emperor were recorded in relief on the temple walls. Slaves, both from Western Asia and Africa, were part of the tribute presented to pharaoh. Slaves had become a common feature of Egyptian life since the end of the Middle Kingdom and are routinely represented yoke-bound on the monuments. Egypt always employed war captives in the country for certain kinds of heavy labor but now slaves in the usual sense become more ubiquitous. This seeming affirmation of the power, control, and mastery over the Egyptian domains of pharaoh was already an illusion soon to be shattered.

The one crucial arena that did not capture the interest of Akhenaton was that of foreign affairs, and his neglect of the empire was to cost Egypt dearly. For that, he was permanently vilified by Egyptian posterity. Egypt's ally was Mitanni who, with its vassals, now became embroiled in a war with the Hittites. Any of the earlier pharaohs of the dynasty would have rushed immediately to aid of a valued ally at the head of the army. Akhenaton chose to do nothing. The outcome was inevitable; though the war dragged on for a time, the Hittites conquered Mitanni in the end, executed her king, and incorporated Mitanni territories into the empire. When it became clear that Akhenaton had no taste for war, predatory vassals in Western Asia began to encroach on their neighbors' lands and, in effect, declare their independence from Egypt. Pleas of faithful vassals to the court at Akhetaton were ignored, as if Akhenaton's single-minded preoccupation with Aton and the spread of his worship made him oblivious to the demands of ruling a far-flung empire. Cyril Aldred gives a picture of the debilitating effect the shift in policy on what had heretofore been the most competent and best-trained army in the region:

> The army, which had been trained in the profession of arms by fighting in the field under the leadership of valiant pharaohs, had now become an instrument of centralized domestic policy, more concerned with laboring in the quarries and vast builing projects than combating in foreign theatres of war.[25]

Needless to say, Akhenaton never took the field at the head of an army.

Domestically, Akhenaton, in the last years of his reign was assailed by mounting tragedy. His second daughter and his mother both died. For reasons that are wholly obscure, Nefertiti either retired or was exiled from public life in favor of a secondary consort named Kiya and his oldest surviving daughter, Meritaten. Some authorities think that Nefertiti simply died at this time also, but there is no firm evidence for the manner of her public disappearance, leaving modern historians free to speculate. Akhenaton's devoted female family members, on whom he had depended on for major support during his struggle against the Temple of Amon, were passing away, one by one. Moreover, his inattention to the details of governing the realm meant that local officials and tax collectors could oppress the populace with illegal extortions and exactions. Food production and the economy generally were visibly declining, yet Akhenaton seemed unaware of the troubles afflicting the nation as he continued to worship Aton in splendid isolation. In his last two years, he turned on Amon in a fury of imprecation and destruction, expending great effort to tear down Amon's monuments wherever he could and effacing Amon's name from monumental inscriptions. He had become a fanatic for Aton and he took it out on Aton's most imposing rival—Amon.

In assessing the 'Atonian heresy', there are those who think that this effort of religious 'purification' was largely motivated by an intense desire to return to the most ancient Egyptian beliefs, centered on a deity whose antecedents went back to pre-dynastic times.[26] Gerald Massey informs us,

> The monarch [Amenhotep III] introduced afresh the Aten disk

25 Ibid., p. 282.

26 Gerald Massey maintained that Aten actually preceded and metamorphosed into Atum before the advent of the dynastic era. See Massey G, **Book of Beginnings**, Vol. II, London: Williams & Norgate, 1881, p. 324.

> of the sun, designated the Aten-Nefer, or youthful solar god. This, when rightly understood, was no new thing in Egypt.[27]

Indeed, in this view, Aten or Aton gives his name to the Semitic *Adon*, meaning 'lord', from which the name *Adonis*, consort of Aphrodite is derived. Thus, the heresy actually had its beginnings in the reign of Akhenaton's father—a period of unmatched national glory and power. If it is true that there was a yearning to return to a simpler, purer form of ancient worship through Aton, it had been magnified by the unfettered augmentation of the power of Amon's priesthood since the beginning of the dynasty with its proliferation of symbols, ceremonies, rites, and tithes inundating the country from the Amonian sanctuary at Karnak.

Aton's was considered by its primary devotee, Akhenaton, to be a religion of light and peace, a god alone and unaided by other gods, creating all living things and bringing to his creatures the gift of life and salvation. Akhenaton was uncompromising in his claim for the exclusive primacy of Aton, reaching the point where he would not allow the name of any other god to be mentioned or image to be displayed. In this attitude, he was no different from the Old Testament prophets who relentlessly excoriated the Children of Israel for their apostasy against Yahweh, their sole, exclusive deity. The Children of Israel were constantly being lured to the worship of numerous local Canaanitic gods and the fearful anathemas of the prophets could never bring them back permanently to orthodoxy until the Babylonian captivity, the trauma of which finally turned the Jews unswervingly to Yahweh as the sole abiding power of national regeneration. Akhenaton had the style and fervor of those later Hebrew prophets, one reason among others, that it can readily be believed that his life and legacy were re-manifested and re-configured not in Egypt but among the mixed multitudes that departed Egypt with Moses. Before the end of the 18th year of his reign, Akhenaton died under highly mysterious circumstances. It is not hard to believe that he was quietly done away with by men, strategically placed, who could no longer countenance his apostasy or the way in which the affairs of the nation and empire were being mismanaged. The Atonian legacy he created did not survive him by even a dozen years.

27 Ibid., p. 405.

Akhenaton's reign was an utterly unique episode in the history of Egypt. The launching of the Atonian religion generated a new mantra—*ankh em maāt* or 'living in truth'—and an unexampled, though short-lived, cultural revolution ensued. It was immediately noticeable in the arts; for the first time a complete naturalism was allowed full expression in the busts, statues, and reliefs in Akhetaton and throughout the nation. Akhenaton permitted the unthinkable: he, his wife, and his daughters were represented frequently in intimate household scenes with their faces and figures carved in a realistic portraiture that was shocking to the traditional Egyptian taste. Pharaoh and family had never been portrayed in such a manner and never would be again. Pharaoh and family partook of divinity and to show them in a common human guise of intimate familiarity was not merely unimaginable but virtual blasphemy. Not only that, but Akhenaton and his family often showed themselves at the Window of Appearance at the palace and Great Temple Aton completely in the nude, an extreme and literal application of the injunction to 'live in truth'. When they weren't displaying themselves in their total nakedness, they would appear in the sheerest of diaphanous gowns that showed them, for all practical purposes, naked. It must be said that nudity or semi-nudity was not in itself shocking to the Egyptian sensibility since, in a hot climate, the populace of all classes wore as little clothing as necessary. Youth up to the age of adolescence, and even older, routinely walked around *en déshabillé* (unclothed). But for pharaoh and the royal family to routinely parade themselves publicly in such a manner was to be considered beyond the pale. The very worship of Aton was often carried on in such a state of undress which, however, may be related to the traditional African belief that the strongest petitions to the religious Powers should be made completely naked. It is hard to know what aspect of this behavior was shocking, the nudity itself or its very public presentation by the pharaoh. Given what we know of Egyptian traditional mores, ideas, and customs it has to be presumed it was the latter. Pharaoh and the royal family were governed by a very different set of rules than ordinary people.

The other radical aspect of this new cultural attitude was the manner in which Akhenaton not merely permitted but apparently required that he and his family be represented in the plastic arts. Never before or after was any pharaoh sculpted with such anatomical realism. There were canons to be followed when artistically representing pharaoh though it must be said that the master sculptors of ancient Egypt were often able to capture the personality of individual pharaohs when carving the royal faces while staying within the confines of the canon. Having said that, Akhenaton's cultural revolution unleashed a wind of artistic naturalism that breathed fresh life into ancient art forms. Akhenaton himself was shown to have a narrow face, a slender nasal bridge with flaring nostrils, full lips, and big, bulbous thighs that were almost feminine in aspect. So strange-looking to the eye did he appear by comparison to earlier pharaonic portraits that there have been concerted attempts to prove that he was afflicted with Frölich's Syndrome, a condition usually brought on by a pituitary tumor causing the patient to develop a body with abnormal fat deposits in the breast, abdomen, pubis, thighs, and buttocks but with spindly legs. There is clearly an anatomic feminization of afflicted males. Certainly Akhenaton's body habitus as shown by numerous statues and reliefs conforms to this description. However, the genitalia of such persons never develop beyond the infantile stage at puberty and they are therefore unable to bear children. Akhenaton sired six daughters; whatever the cause for his abnormal body type, Frölich's Syndrome must be ruled out.

The other 'odd' anatomical element in the busts and reliefs of Akhenaton's family is that his daughters show an extreme long-headedness, what anatomists refer to as 'hyperdolicocephaly'. Some authors wish to attribute these 'abnormal' skulls of his daughters to hydrocephaly, an abnormal accumulation of cerebrospinal fluid within the crania of a young child that causes his head to grow abnormally large. The problem with attributing hydrocephalus to the skulls of Akhenaton's daughters is that (1) it afflicts less than one-percent of all newborns and (2) without the insertion of a cranial shunt, infants will inevitably die. Even if one of Akhenaton's daughters was born with hydrocephalus, none of the other five would have been; nor would any of them have survived into puberty as they all clearly did. The hyperdolicocephaly characteristic of Akhenaton's daughters represents a skull type found predominantly in East Africa, among the Tutsi as well as other ethnic groups. The authorities discussing the unusual anatomic features of Akhenaton and his daughters have never addressed this aspect of the matter. Akhenaton's facial features and the hyperdolicephaly of his six daughters are simply attributable to an East African ancestry; one need not look for exotic medical conditions to explain what the busts and reliefs show us about Akhenaton and his family.

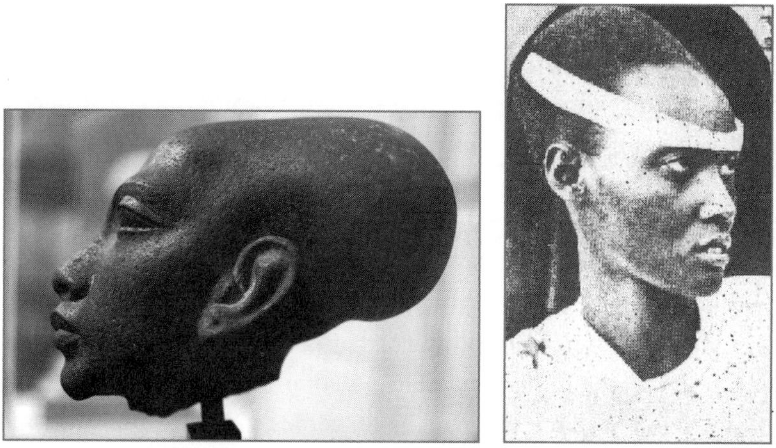

Ancient Egyptian (Akhenaton's daughter) and Watutsi:
Two African Princesses with Dolicocephaly

Akhenaton's reign and the inauguration of the 'Atonian Reformation"—some would say 'heresy'—represent an utterly singular episode in the history of Egypt. Clearly the era had the effect of a two-edged sword: a new dynamism and naturalism in art and culture was ignited, a religion that promoted peace was promulgated, and an attempt to reform and purify the existing state religion was initiated. These are contrasted with a neglect of imperial responsibilities coupled with an inattention to the administration of the daily domestic affairs of the nation. Akhenaton, in the modern view, will always be seen to have had a mixed record—admired by some, condemned by others. His name and reputation in Egypt were seen in a decidedly more unambiguous light: ever after, he was never referred to by name but by the epithet 'the criminal' and he was struck from the king lists of Egypt. In truth, though there was some imperial recovery under the kings of the 19th dynasty, Egypt never again attained the summit of unmatched power, dominion, and glory characteristic of the era of Amenhotep III. As has already been inferred and will be explored further in a later chapter, Akhenaton's permanent legacy may have been transmitted to world history through a different people altogether: the Children of Israel.

The Aftermath of Akhenaton's Reign and the End of the 18th Dynasty (1,357 BC–1,312 BC)

Smenkhare (1,357 BC–1,354 BC)

The passing of Akhenaton inaugurated a period of ever weaker kingships. His immediate successor was his half-brother—some say full brother—Smenkhare who ascended the throne at age 17 upon marrying the Great Royal Wife presumptive, Meritaten, the oldest surviving daughter of Akhenaton and Nefertiti. It is not too much to infer that a 'counter-reformation' set in rapidly with Akhenaten's demise but it did not result, as yet, in the precipitous

Smenkhare and Meritaten

overthrow of Aton. It is significant that, however much the orthodox party detested Akhenaton, they did not abandon the near-inflexible custom of passing on the royal inheritance through a royal daughter who was directly descended from the line of Great Royal Wives, though the previous reign was gradually repudiated. Whatever the case, Meritaten died a year after Smenkhare's ascension, whereupon he married her sister Ankhesenpaaten to sustain his claim to the throne through the female line. The names of both his queens—suffixed by the name *aton*—shows that Aton was not yet overthrown. But Smenkhare died three years after his own accession, leaving little imprint on the gathering events.

Tutankhaten/Tutankhamen (1,354 BC–1,345 BC)

Smenkhare was followed to the thrown by his younger brother, Tutankhaten, who was a mere lad of eight when his rule began. Very shortly after the beginning of his reign, he assumed the name Tutankhamun, the name by which he is known to history down to the present day. Moreover, his wife's name was also changed from *Ankhesenpaaten* to *Ankhesenamun*. It is in fact under Tutankhamun that the inexorable shift back toward the paramountcy of Amon begins to show itself most clearly. He was, after all, but a boy when he began to reign and therefore subject decisively to the influence of adult

Tutankhamon's Funerary Mask

Tutankhamon and Wife Ankhensenamon

counselors who knew that, for the sake of national unity if nothing else, royal policy had to be swung back toward Amon. Still, there was no wholesale repudiation of either Akhenaton or Aton. That would come later.

Tutankhamon reigned only nine years and therefore did not even see his 18th birthday. Under the guiding hand of men like Ay, father to Nefertiti and grand vizier to all the kings from the reign of Akhenaton, a program of temple restoration and rehabilitation of the destroyed icons was undertaken in earnest. In fact, it is the high officials appointed by Akhenaton who besides Ay included Minnakht and Horemheb, both army generals, Maya, the royal treasurer,

Pentu, the chief physician, and Huy, the Royal Son of Cush, that gradually but steadily worked to restore the old regime. No one knows what Tutankhamon thought of this turn of events but he had no choice but to comply, nor did he live long enough to establish an independent course of action even if he had been so inclined. Still, these high officials were able men and wasted no time launching the long, drawn-out campaign to restore Egypt's imperial fortunes. Central Palestine was reinforced, remaining firmly in Egyptian hands. However, further north in Syria, other vassals had fallen under the domination of the Hittites. Qadesh was briefly captured but subsequently reclaimed by the Hittites. In fact Qadesh, as the key to northern Canaan, would be contested back and forth between Hittite and Egypt for the next century. A few desultory forays were also conducted in Nubia and Cush. It was evident that Egypt's attempt to reclaim its Asiatic empire beyond central Canaan was going to be a long, expensive, exhausting affair.

To the contemporary popular mind, Tutankhamon is the most famous of the Egyptian pharaohs, though historically one of the least significant. This fame rests entirely, of course, on the discovery of his tomb in Valley of the Kings on the western bank of the Nile opposite Thebes (modern Luxor) by Howard Carter in 1922, untouched and containing everything that had been placed within from the time of his burial nearly 33 centuries earlier. No other Egyptian royal tomb to date has ever been found unopened and intact; tomb robbers absconded with the interred riches even within decades of the ancient burials. The cache of treasure discovered in Tutankhamun's tomb was staggering and it remains the greatest of all archaeological discoveries, making world-wide headlines in 1922. King Tut, as he is called, became a household name and even now the magnificent treasures of his tomb excite popular awe and admiration. His exquisitely modeled funeral mask, of pure gold, represents the finest example of the goldsmith's and sculptor's art anywhere. What it really showed, though, was that if such riches could be buried with a rather minor and inconsequential pharaoh, what mind-boggling wealth would have been buried with kings such as Thutmosis III or Amenhotep III or Rameses II? As if all this archaeological splendor wasn't enough, the deathly warning above the tomb to anyone presumptuous enough to violate it—especially since a number of deaths among the excavation team including the sponsor Lord Carnavon followed unexpectedly soon after the tomb opening—has provided grist for the macabre delight of movie-goers and other popular purveyors of the 'Curse of King Tut'.

Tutankhamon died before reaching his 18th birthday; Aldred suggests that he might have actually died from a battle wound.[28] Others note the head wound without attributing it to battle. Be that as it may, it is a singular fact that most of Akhenaton's line—direct and collateral—died young. Only one daughter appears to have lived long enough to see Vizier Ay, Nefetiti's father, rise to the throne. Royal incest was a custom that seems to have gone back to the beginning of the dynastic period, motivated by two factors: (1) the re-enactment of the mythical brother-sister marriage between Osiris and Isis and (2) keeping the throne in the family in the face of the unchanging custom of passing the throne down through the royal females. However, our modern knowledge of genetics makes it clear that after a number of generations of marriage of royal sisters to brothers and half-brothers, a decided genetic decline would inevitably set in. One may be permitted to think that when this degeneration progressed too far, dynasties were—perhaps more or less deliberately—changed to infuse fresh blood and vigor into the pharaonic institution. One sign of lineage degeneration might well have been an evident tendency for royal descendants to die prematurely. Though Akhenaton's reformation, with its indifference to foreign affairs and the needs of empire, was a major force in the decline of the 18th Dynasty, it has to be wondered if the aforementioned 'lineage degeneration' also played a major role in this decline, as it had in earlier dynasties and would in the future.

Ay (1,345 BC–1,340 BC)

The pharaonic inheritor to Tutankhamun reveals just how decrepit the 18th dynasty line had become. The only one left to step in was none other than the ubiquitous, long-lived Ay who was father-in-law to Akhenaton and grandfather to Ankhensenamun. Nothing daunted, he duly married his granddaughter and ascended the throne, though the record is silent as to whether this marriage was

28 Aldred, op. cit., p. 297.

ever consummated. Like his predecessors, Ay's reign was short-lived, lasting no more than five years. As Aldred remarks, 'The rehabilitation of Amun and the steady abandonment of the more extreme aspects of the Aten religion were quietly pursued'.[29] He had already served Akhenaton and his successors faithfully and well and was shrewd enough to bow to the inevitable restoration of Amon. He also commissioned some building projects at Karnak, consistent with the policy of the Theban pharaohs since the 17th Dynasty. But he was far too aged to inject any real vigor into the reign. He was clearly a 'caretaker' pharaoh who lived long enough to hand the royal sceptre to someone with the requisite energy and ability: General Horemheb.

Horemheb (1,340 BC–1,312 BC)

Horemheb was not of royal birth and therefore not related to any of the royal family. Nonetheless, in time-honored fashion, he secured his position on the throne by marrying one of the royal women related to Ay and, more importantly, Nefertiti: *Mutnodjme*, a sister of Nefertiti. Horemheb, however, did not start a new dynasty and is considered, in fact, to represent the last pharaoh of the 18th Dynasty. After Akhenaton, there were three pharaohs in 17 years, clearly representing the 'agonal rhythm' of a dying dynasty, the most storied one in the history of Egypt. But Horemheb was definitely the man to begin the reversal of Egypt's fortunes. His first acts were to stamp out the widespread corruption that had sprouted under the weakened central authority of his predecessors. Extortionate tax collectors and an increasingly rapacious soldiery—all unchecked by previous kings or their officials—had wrought havoc in the civil administration, the peace, and the security of the country. Horemheb undertook to change all that, issuing edicts proscribing the exploitative and predatory practices of government officials. To enforce these edicts, Horemheb toured the country incessantly, investigating and monitoring the governance of the country at large. The civil bureaucracy was reformed and tightened; the army was re-organized with military discipline re-established. Like all other important pharaohs before him, Horemheb inaugurates an

29 Ibid., p. 300.

ambitious building program, mostly in and around Thebes. Typically, he made sure to leave his mark on Karnak Temple.

Horemheb reigned 28 years and in his 15th regnal year, Queen Mutnodjme died. With this last representative of the family associated with Akhenaton gone, Horemheb threw off all restraint and spent the rest of his reign removing every vestige of Akhenaton and his religion. Not even the monuments of Tutankhamun and Ay, who had already begun the process of 're-Amonization', were spared the fury of the Akhenaton-haters, as if anyone connected to him by blood was tainted by his apostastic guilt. Thus, by the time the 19th Dynasty supervened, the Atonian reformation and its sponsor, had been expunged from Egyptian history.

II. The 19th Dynasty—The Afternoon of Empire (1,312 BC–1,195 BC)

The 19th dynasty represents, in effect, a monumental attempt at reviving the empire that was ultimately unsuccessful. It did produce two of Egypt's greatest pharaohs in Seti I and Rameses II though some of Rameses's greatness and grandeur seems, in retrospect, to be the product of his own vainglorious bombast. Egypt had passed beyond the summit of its power and glory, though the efforts of the 19th dynasty pharaohs restored enough of its former prominence to make it the reigning power in the region for some centuries to come. Still there was no arresting the long thousand-year decline, though under Seti I and Rameses II, the Egyptian people could still preserve the perception that all was as it had been, that Egypt still reigned supreme. Collective self-delusion in the face of decline is the common lot of empires whose heyday has passed and the history of Egypt after the 19th Dynasty presents a classic study of the phenomenon.

Rā-messu I or *Rameses I* (1,312 BC–1,310 BC)

Rameses I

Rameses I, not of royal blood, was the successor to Horemheb and the founder of a new dynasty, the 19th. He was in fact both a military and governmental official under Horemheb and apparently so close to him that he was 'adopted' by the pharaoh and made his heir. Grimal states that Rameses's wife, *Satre*—mother of the future pharaoh Seti I—was the daughter of a fellow officer.[30] Either he is mistaken or Rameses married another wife, an unknown female member of the royal family descended from the Great Royal Wives of the 18th Dynasty. It was simply not possible for any man to ascend the throne unless married to a royal woman descended from the line of Great Royal Wives whose roots ramified back into the Middle Kingdom, if not beyond. The older Egyptologists such as Petrie assert that Satre was indeed one of these royal women who was married to Rameses I 20 years before his accession.[31] Some have speculated that Rameses might have been related to Horemheb given the closeness of their relationship but this has never been proven. In the event, both he and his son Seti were products of the last years of the 18th Dynasty under Pharaoh Horemheb and the dynastic shift did not portend any abrupt changes or a chaotic interregnum. Budge gives a striking description of the mummy of Rameses I:

30 Grimal, op. cit., p.245.

31 Petrie Flinders WM, **A History of Egypt**, Vol. 3, London: Methuen & Co., 1896, p. 6.

> Near the fragments of the coffin was the unswathed mummy of a man of large and powerful build, with short hair and a black skin; this mummy is believed by M. Maspero to have been that of Rameses I.[32]

Parenthetically, one finds that Budge, nearly alone among Egyptologists, is willing here and there to highlight the inner African—one could say Nubian—antecedents of the dynastic Egyptians. But Rameses I is already of advanced age when he ascends the throne and his reign is brief, lasting no more than two years. He therefore left no lasting monumental legacies, though he began the building of the Hypostyle Hall at the Temple of Amon at Karnak which would eventually be completed by his successors.

One other notable feature of Rameses I's accession is the prominence given to Rā and his sacred city of Annu (Heliopolis), as evidenced by the king taking the name Rā-messu—'born of Rā' or 'begotten of Rā'—and by the shift of the pharaoh's residence northward. Though neither Rameses nor his successors failed to honor fully the national god Amon, as shown by their massive works at Karnak, it seems evident that this movement of the king's residence away from Thebes and the prominence given to Rā and Heliopolis was a way of counteracting and modifying the overbearing influence of Amon's priesthood which had precipitated the Amarnian crisis—the 'heresy' of Akhenaton—in the latter decades of the 18th Dynasty. No pharaoh afterward until the 25th Dynasty would choose to reside at Thebes though the city's national prominence continued.

Seti I or *Sethos I* (1,310 BC–1,290 BC)

This second king of the 19th Dynasty is generally regarded as one of those supremely able pharaohs who at recurring and strategic intervals were enthroned in Egypt ensuring her millennial greatness. He was one of Egypt's elite rulers. Moreover, his evident personal qualities leave a much more favorable impression of the man than do those of his far more famous and flamboyant son, Rameses II,

32 **Budge** EAW, **A History of Egypt**, Volume III, Oosterhout N.B. The Netherlands: Anthropological Publications, (1902)1968, p. 4.

whose life and reign seemed touched by a megalomania not associated with even the most vigorous empire-builders of the 18th Dynasty. Flinders Petrie says of him,

> The character of Sety is one of the best in the history. His zeal for upholding the power of Egypt is worthy of the previous dynasty; and his pious regard for his predecessors exceeds that of any other king.[33]

As mentioned above, Seti I was, in effect, a man of the 18th Dynasty, born nearly 40 years before the end of Horemheb's reign and through him it is almost as if the spirit of the 18th Dynasty was attempting to re-assert itself throughout the Egyptian state. The striking thing about Seti is the manner in which the assumption of this name amounted to a partial—if temporary—rehabilitation of the *neter* Set. Seti is associated with his father as his vizier and heir-apparent from the beginning of the reign of Rameses I. This association reflected the continuing fear of every dynasty of a chaotic interregnum occasioned by the death of a pharaoh, hence the continuation of the long-standing practice of installing the heir-apparent as the co-pharaoh as soon as he was old enough to begin to assume administrative duties. The recent upheavals occasioned by the Amarna Reformation and its aftermath confirmed the urgency of having the crown prince in place prior to the death of the reigning pharaoh, and so it was with Seti and his father. In the event, he made a seamless transition onto the throne of Egypt, with the full pharaonic title, without incident upon the death of his father. He was married to Queen Tuya, mother of Rameses II, who, according to Budge, "was probably related or connected with the royal house of the Amen-hetep kings, and who therefore had, in the eyes of the Egyptians, a claim to the throne; Seti himself was not of royal descent, and could only assert a right to the throne through his wife."[34] This was all the more reason why at the outset of his reign, the newly-crowned king of a brand-new dynasty, Seti went to great pains to establish the legitimacy of his line. He and his son Rameses II are depicted venerating the cartouches of 67 previous pharaohs, beginning with Mēnēs, a list that was amplified and embellished with more

33 Petrie, op. cit., p. 10.
34 **Budge**, op.cit., pp. 19-20.

names in succeeding reigns. Not surprisingly, neither the name of Hatshepsut nor Akhenaton appears on any of these 19th Dynasty lists, the official attitude of the court being one of anathema toward these two unconventional rulers. Seti clearly had no intention of calling his own line into question by going against the prevailing sentiment.

Continuing a policy instituted by his father, Seti did much to strengthen the position of the northern cities and *neters* such as Memphis (Ptah) and Heliopolis (Rā). He also renovated the sanctuary of Set at Avaris, a clear departure from the policy of the previous dynasty. However, Seti was no revolutionary and made sure that proper respect and tribute still flowed to Amon at Karnak at Thebes, still the national cult center of Egypt, veritably its 'Vatican'. He undertook the construction of the great hypostyle hall at Karnak—one of its most striking features to the contemporary eye—that was completed by Rameses II. In the end, there were 134 columns 68 feet high 78 erected by Seti. For sheer size and massivity, these columns are quite unlike anything erected before or since. He also sponsored extensive building projects at Gebel Barkal in Cush, both Karnak and Gebel Barkal being major centers of Amon worship.

Karnak's Hypostyle Hall

However, his most lasting monumental achievement was his mortuary temple built of white limestone at Abydos, the sacred center of Osiris. Some of the finest art work in Egypt or anywhere was achieved with breathtaking skill and finesse at Abydos. If Seti was not known for anything else, his name would be indelibly cast in history as a consequence of the realization of the masterful artistry of the Osirian-themed mortuary temple at Abydos. Within the temple seven chapels were lined up along the west wall dedicated

Seti I at Abydos Holding Ma-āt

respectively to Horus, Isis, Osiris, Amon, Harmachis (a form of Horus), Ptah, and Seti himself. Nearby, the temple dedicated solely to Osiris, called the *Osireion*, where he was said to have been buried, was rebuilt by Seti since it had fallen into ruin and disrepair. Abydos was one of the holiest religious sites in Egypt, receiving crowds of pilgrims daily seeking to pay homage to Osiris, the *neter* of resurrection and immortality, as a way of ensuring their own. Again, it is somewhat incongruous that he would have taken such pains to honor Set on the one hand yet build such a fabulous mortuary temple under the tutelage of Osiris on the other, the two *neters* famously being mortal enemies. Be that as it may, from the beginning of pharaonic history, the pharaoh was seen to incarnate Horus while living but becoming Osiris after death. Osiris, therefore, was the pharaoh immortalized. Nicolas Grimal has this to say about the Osireion:

> The tomb was clearly intended to commemorate the funerary rites of Osiris, in which his body—swollen with fluids—was re-

> stored to life in the water by Isis. This rebirth through fermentation was still remembered in the form of the 'Osiris bed': a receptacle in the shape of the body of Osiris, in which cereal grains were sown. But the tomb chamber of the Osireion…was also a model of the universe; it represented the primeval mound emerging from chaos on which the first creator breathed life into the universe.[35]

The idea that the body of Osiris was 'the bread of life' clearly prefigures the exact same imagery as applied to Yahushua the Christ 13 centuries later.[36]

Hathor with Seti
Hands Intertwined

This careful attention and monumental effort lavished at Abydos, both on his mortuary temple and the Osirieion, clearly reflects Seti's determination not only to legitimize his dynasty but ensure its continuation. The mortuary temple was not completed in Seti's lifetime but his son Rameses II, pious toward his father as all pharaohs, finished the work early in the subsequent reign. In fact, when Rameses first visited Abydos, he found the temple complex in a deplorable state, due largely to the embezzlement of funds by those entrusted to maintain

35 Grimal, op. cit., p. 250.
36 Vid. Finch C, op. cit., p. 181.

the temple. Rameses set all of this mismanagement to right and, in addition, did much to restore and maintain the tombs of the Old Kingdom pharaohs buried at Abydos.

Seti was determined to re-establish the empire which had slowly disintegrated since the end of the 18th Dynasty. Some initial forays had been made by Horemheb and Rameses I, but the bulk of Egypt's former Asian territories remained out of reach. It was to be a protracted struggle, continued without surcease by Rameses II and Seti made a valiant start. Within a year of his succession, he launched a campaign north- and eastward, since the turbulent tribes of the eastern desert and Canaan chose to test his mettle immediately by revolting. Very quickly he engaged hostile bedouins, called Shasu, to gain control of a series of wells that lined the route through the Sinai and into Canaan. Seti proceeded rapidly into Canaan, dividing his forces and sending one army to take control of the cities Beth Shan and Reheb, that were under attack by the allied cities of Hamath and Pella assisted by bands of Apiru, of whom mention has been made in connection with the 'proto-Hebrews'.[37] Seti's second army marched north toward Hamath and Yenoam, taking the Phoenician cities of Acre and Tyre and entering Lebanon. After achieving their objectives, the victorious armies in the north returned southward, capturing Pella in the process. Once again, local chieftains and dynasts—seeing with their own eyes a pharaoh marching at the head of his army for the first time in 50 years—tendered their allegiance and tribute again began flowing to pharaoh from Syrian tributary states.

Seti led two more campaigns into Asia and one into Libya, all of them successful. On the second Asian campaign, he was able to regain control of Qadesh and pacify the country of Amurru (Amorites), re-establishing Egypt's hegemony over Syria. His third campaign was waged against the Libyans, belligerant western tribesmen who constantly stirred up trouble. His fourth, and last, major military thrust was carried out against the Hittites, e.g., the kingdom of *Hatti* of Anatolia, who had encroached deep into areas traditionally under Egyptian suzerainty. It was the first, though not to be the last, direct confrontation between Egypt and Hatti. The Hittites were no pushovers,

37 Cf. above, page 195.

having established a powerful and dynamic kingdom in Anatolia, and on this occasion, after re-establishing and reconfirming his overlordship over areas south of Qadesh, Seti reached a truce with Muwatallis, king of Hatti, which, in the long run, solved nothing but gave each side breathing space to marshal its forces for a future renewal of hostilities. Seti must have inflicted some damage on the Hittite foe because on his return to Egypt, Hittite captives were driven before him. However that may have been, Seti claimed overlordship of all lands from northern Syria and Cyprus southward to the third cataract in Nubio-Cush and even to Punt on the horn of Africa. Thousands of captives from Syria, Palestine, and Libya—in addition to a mountain of gold and silver booty—were brought back to Egypt by Seti. With these glittering military successes, a renewed sense of empire was restored.

On the home front, development activities were renewed as turquoise mines were re-opened in the Sinai. Gold mining in the eastern desert and in Nubia at Wadi Allaqi was re-implemented with renewed energy. Great building projects were commenced all over Egyptian territory, some of which—the mortuary temple at Abydos being the most conspicuous example—exemplified the highest and finest traditions of Egyptian art and architecture. The vigor of Seti's building projects is evident from Asia to Cush. Much of this building effort was one of restoration, especially those monuments, dedicated to Amon, that had been disfigured by the Atonians under Akhenaton. Seti's artisans exhibited great care and exactitude in restoring defaced inscriptions so that the previous destruction was barely noticeable. Payment of the thousands of workers employed in the service of the state was recorded by Seti which were, as always, in kind but the epitome of kingly generosity for all that:

> At Silsileh…every one of the thousand workmen employed there received daily nearly four pounds of bread, two bundles of vegetables, and a roast of meat; while twice a month each man was given a clean linen garment.[38]

One other note of importance mentioned by Petrie is the celebratory welcome received by Seti from high government officials and nobles along a canal that

38 Breasted, op. cit., p. 414.

seems to have joined the Mediterranean—some say the Nile—to the Red Sea.[39] Though a canal was probably built as early as the Middle Kingdom—with re-dredgings later on—it all indicates that there was a 'Suez Canal' built by Egyptians 35 or more centuries before Ferdinand de Lesseps accomplished the feat in 1868.

Seti's attested reign of 15 years—some authorities say 20 years—seems short compared to the 67-year reign of his successor, Rameses II, but impressive accomplishments in everything he undertook can be credited to him. Seti was at least 60 years of age at death—lending credence to the assertion of a 20-year reign—and appears to have suffered cruelly from severe arthritis, given the condition of his hands as seen on his mummy. He made major strides in re-establishing Egypt as a world power though he fell short—as Rameses II would—in reclaiming all of the Asian empire carved out by the kings of the 18th Dynasty. Under him, Egypt experienced a definite revival and he laid a firm foundation for the storied, vainglorious epoch of his heir, Rameses II. He must be accounted among the greatest of Egypt's pharaohs.

One final word concerning Seti and the advent of the 19th Dynasty. Sir Alan Gardiner voiced the opinion that,

> After the recovery from the religious revolution Egypt was a changed world. It is not easy to define the exact nature of the change...yet it is impossible not to notice the marked deterioration of the art, literature, and indeed the general culture of the people.[40]

In the main, Gardiner's assessment is accurate but not as applied to Egypt under Seti I. His may be considered the last great epoch of Egyptian art and architecture. Though his son and successor would outstrip all other pharaohs in the sheer number of temples and monuments raised, none of them, with the possible exception of the temples at Abu Simbel, can be considered to be on a par with the finest artistic and architectural renderings of his father Seti. In this respect, the reign of Seti I, though in and of the 19th Dynasty, can almost

39 Petrie, op. cit., pp. 13-4.

40 Gardiner A, **Egypt of the Pharaohs**, London: Oxford University Press, 1961, p. 247.

be thought of truly as the coda to the great cultural enterprises of the 18th Dynasty, generally regarded as Egypt's grandest era.

Rameses II (1,290 BC–1,223 BC)

We come at last to the storied reign of Rameses II, which, at 67 years, was the second longest reign in Egyptian history and, for that matter, in world history. Only the 94-year reign of Pepi II exceeded that of Rameses. There is no question that Rameses left a conspicuous impression on history that has been sustained to the present. His exploits are the stuff of legend and he cast a shadow so

Rameses II—"The Great"

immense that in the ensuing 20th Dynasty, 10 additional kings carried the name Rameses. It is a not an uncommon Egyptological opinion to proclaim him the greatest of all Egyptian pharaohs; Egyptologists seem dazzled, apparently, as much by his personal brilliance as any of his contemporaries.[41]

41 See Grimal, op. cit., p. 250, for such an exalted opinion of Rameses.

His military campaigns were recounted in epic fashion and he out-built every pharaoh who preceded him, in fact erecting more monuments and temples than all the preceding pharaohs combined.[42] His epoch seemed to underscore the renewed status of Egypt as an impregnable empire. And yet closer examination seems to dampen the flames of sun-like brilliance that is customarily attached to his name. For one thing, he does not measure up to Thutmosis III in military genius; he who, in 17 campaigns in Asia, never lost a single battle and carried the imperial frontiers of Egypt as far north as present-day Turkey. Even Sesostris II might justifiably be thought of as the greater general. Moreover, though Rameses outstripped all other pharaohs in the sheer number of building projects, it is impossible to think of the edifices attributed to him as being in any way comparable to the fabulous pyramids of the third and fourth dynasties. Impressive Rameses-inspired monuments certainly exist—especially in Nubia at Abu Simbel—but they do not really rise up to the artistic standard of his own father at Abydos[43] or even of Hatshepsut and Senmut at Deir el-Bahari.

But where Rameses excelled was as a master self-promoter; no pharaoh ever matched him in this regard. Every pharaoh did his utmost to solidify his place in the annals of pharaonic achievement with fabulous building projects, inscriptions innumerable trumpeting his great works, sumptuous monuments designed to withstand the ravages of time, but not even the pharaohs most adept at such auto-propaganda could compete with Rameses on these terms. He not only built vast numbers of monuments on his own but co-opted those of his predecessors without qualm or scruple. One can't visit any region of Egypt without encountering his handiwork. Rameses is everywhere, testament to his (1) megalomania and (2) his unmatched genius for self-promotion.

It is perhaps tempting in light of the comments above to simply dismiss Rameses as nothing more than a pharaonic posturer and poseur extraordinaire, but such an assessment would be entirely too facile. There were real and lasting accomplishments during the reign and, for the most part, he was able to back up his boastful self-assertions by bringing back to Egypt an era of wealth,

42 Adams WY, op. cit., p. 222.

43 'As a whole, the art of sculpture and architecture was in its decline; scarcely anything can be shown [of Rameses] equal to the works of Sety'. Petrie, op. cit., p. 72.

power, and international influence not seen since the time of Amenhotep III. Both his enemies and his allies were awestruck by him and clearly there was a personal majesty and power that simply couldn't be faked. In the 18th century Louis XV liked to say 'I am the state' ("L'état, c'est moi"). In him it was bluster, in Rameses II it was the simple, irrevocable fact. A 'clinical' evaluation might categorize him as an exaggerated personality such as had never before been seen on any throne and he might be thought of as the first pharaoh around whom an international cult of personality coalesced. Pharaohs, by definition were larger than life, but during and after his reign, Rameses seemed larger than the world. He still seems so to not a few.

Before an examination of the reign, it might be pertinent to deal with Rameses in his putative Biblical connection because there are serious authorities who identify him as the pharaoh of the Exodus. To investigate the matter, it is pertinent to return to the ancient period of in-migration into the Delta region of Egypt by Jacob-Israel's clan during the Hyksos domination, under the presumed auspices of their kinsman Joseph, which could have taken place as early as 1,722 BC or as late as 1,660 BC. There are strong cases to be made for either date. The earlier date (1,722 BC) recommends itself because Hyksos power in Egypt was secure and, at that moment, unchallengeable. If the sojourn of the Children Israel in Egypt of 430 years given in the Old Testament is provisionally accepted, an entrance date of 1,722 BC would place the exodus event at 1,292 BC, during the reign of Rameses II.

However, there are several arguments against this earlier Exodous date. For one thing, there are no records in the reign of Rameses II that report anything remotely resembling such an event or its aftermath. Moreover, Rameses II was such a powerful king—who carried out major campaigns in and ultimately dominated Canaan—that it is impossible to accept the idea that a band of dissenters led by a renegade priest, Moses-Osarsiph, could have rebelled, departed Egypt, and migrated into Canaan with impunity during his reign. Thirdly, during the reign of Mereneptah—the son and successor of Rameses—around 1,220 BC, there is preserved an inscription at Thebes that reads,

> 'Israel is wasted, his seed is not.'

It is the earliest reference to Israel on record. It has made many historians believe that the Exodus would have taken place in the time of Mereneptah, close to 1,230 BC, putting the entrance of Jacob-Israel and his clan into Egypt at or around 1,660 BC. Though we can believe that an out-migration, e.g. the Exodus, did take place before the end of the 13th century BC, it seems to have been an event of minimal consequence to the Egyptians, hardly worthy of royal notice. It has therefore assumed a magnitude all out of proportion to its actual contemporary significance simply because of the way the Hebrew Torah became so deeply imbedded in the world-dominating religions of Christianity and Islam. Though the Book of Exodus is touted by believers—Jewish, Christian, and Muslim—as true and factual history, it is curious that the name of the pharaoh who figures so prominently in the story is never mentioned. In the event, the 30-year period after the death of Rameses II in or around 1,223 BC was an unsettled one in Egypt, with at least four lesser rulers sitting on the throne in relatively quick succession. It is in such a confused era that an out-migration of religious dissenters and general malcontents would have most likely taken place with little more than token opposition. We can return to this subject when looking at the reign of Mereneptah.

What can be said with certainty is that natives from Western Asia—Canaan, Syria, and Phoenicia—moved into Egypt in massive numbers during the 19th Dynasty, especially during the reign of Rameses II. Concerning this phenomenon, Breasted writes:

> The country swarmed with Semitic and other Asiatic slaves, while Phoenician and other alien merchants were so numerous that there was a foreign quarter in Memphis, with its temples of Baal and Astarte... The dialects of Palestine and vicinity...lent many a Semitic word to the current language of the day...[44]

The history of Egypt had already been, and would continue to be, profoundly altered by its preoccupation with the geopolitics of Western Asia from which it would never be extricated.

44 Breasted, op.cit., 448.

Rameses's military adventures began very quickly after his accession circa 1,290 BC. He had been trained in warfare at an early age and by the time of his accession his thirst for military glory was at peak intensity.[45] In the second year of his reign, he was obliged to do battle with Sherden pirates, a sea people who had, 100 years previously, settled on the Libyan coast west of Egypt. These he conquered in short order in a sea battle and incorporated a whole battalion of them into his own army, a policy that would continue for the next 60 years. But serious campaigning was launched in Year 4, with Rameses leading his armies into Canaan and Syria, advancing through Phoenicia and then eastward into Amurru, the land of the Amorites. The Amorites were a ubiquitous Canaanitic and Mesopotamian people who had established powerful kingdoms in Western Asia in the centuries between 1600–1200 BC and, at the time of Rameses, were allies of Hatti, Egypt's most formidable rival. A branch of the Amorites, the Jebusites, were the apparent founders of Jerusalem and occupied the city right up until David conquered it early in the 10th century BC. In the event, Rameses defeated the Amorites who tendered their submission to him. As Petrie observes, these renewed military initiatives by the Egyptians in Western Asia, roused Hatti and its allies to action, leading to the explosive events of the following year.[46]

The epic, semi-legendary military event of Rameses's career took place in the 5th year of his reign, circa 1,285 BC. Though Seti I had begun to build at the site of Pi-Ramesse during the previous reign, Rameses II turned it into the site of his new capital. Pi-Ramesse was situated in the northeastern Delta on the ancient site of Avaris, the old capital of the Hyksos that had been captured and razed in the wars that had led to the expulsion of the Hyksos more than 300 years previously. There were three apparent motivations for this move: (1) in continuing his father's quest to recover Egypt's Asian empire in its entirety, it was essential from a strategic point of view to establish his royal capital—as opposed to the religious capital at Thebes—close to the Sinai land bridge to Canaan, the gateway to Syria; (2) the 19th Dynasty pharaohs were clearly intent on rehabilitating the position and importance of Set[47] and the old Avaris had been sacred to him; (3) like most

45 '...we are right in thinking that he was trained with the soldiers and accustomed to military command when he was 10 or 12 years of age.' **Budge**, op. cit., p. 23.

46 Petrie, op. Cit., p. 47.

47 **Budge** mentions that Rameses had written about himself "...one in valour like his father Set...", ibid.

of the kings after Akhenaton, subtle royal policy was aimed at emancipating the throne from the oppressive grip of the Amonian priesthood, entrenched at Thebes in Upper Egypt. Every pharaoh after Akhenaton repudiated and reviled him, while making every effort to curry favor with the all-powerful coterie of Amonian priests. At the same time, they did whatever they legitimately could to put distance between themselves and Thebes. Rameses, who could brook no restraints on his authority and ambitious plans, was no exception. All that being said, Rameses now set out to complete his father's work to reestablish the Asiatic domain of the empire along its ancient boundaries. As mentioned, the placement of a new capital at Pi-Ramesse had become a strategic necessity. It became the most important, vibrant, populous, and beautiful city in Egypt, if not the world. A magnificent temple—built to himself, of course—was overshadowed by a 90-foot statue of Rameses (nearly one-fifth the height of the Great Pyramid). There were 10 additional Ramessid kings after Rameses II, all of whom inhabited, maintained, and embellished the capital at Pi-Ramesse,

Once again, Rameses, at the head of his army marched north through Canaan and Phoenicia, with the goal of recapturing Qadesh in northern Syria, a strategically important city that had once been in Egyptian hands but was now a vassal city-state of Hatti. Hatti, whose capital city was *Hattusa*, had established, as seen earlier, a powerful northern empire, centered on the central plateau of Anatolia, that entered the stage of world history in the mid-1700s BC and reached the pinnacle of its power and territorial extent in the mid-1300s BC, not coincidentally about the time of the Amarna period in Egypt whose pharaoh, Akhenaton, allowed much of the Asian portion of the empire to slip away so monomaniacally obsessed was he with the promulgation of the worship of the single god Aton. Despite the herculean efforts of both Seti I and Rameses II, the Hittites, whose main strike force was a phalanx of skilled charioteers, would prove themselves nearly a match for the might of Egypt during the 19th Dynasty.

The Battle of Qadesh is the best known, best-documented, and most celebrated battle in the annals of Egyptian history. There are 13 known versions of the battle recorded on monuments, stelae, and papyri all over Egypt, including an epic poem by the scribe Pen-ta-urt.[48] Rameses seems to have considered it his

48 Ibid., p. 38.

greatest military triumph. All this for a battle that, for all practical purposes, ended in a draw. Perhaps because of the momentous attention paid to the battle by Rameses himself it came to assume epic proportions in after times, in and out of Egypt. The Egyptian army was formed of four divisions of about 4,500 soldiers each and given the names of the major deities representing the regions of the country from which the divisions were drawn: Amon (Thebaid), Ptah (Memphis), Rā (Heliopolis), and Sutekh/Set (Tanis). In addition, Sherden, Libyan, and Nubian auxiliaries had been conscripted in significant numbers. The four divisions crossed the Sinai peninsula without hindrance or difficulty aided, in large part, by the series of nine wells previously dug by the armies of Seti. It was 400 miles to Qadesh and with rapid marching, Rameses's army reached it in under a month.

As Rameses approached Qadesh preparing for battle, his relative inexperience as a general began to reveal itself. He allowed his divisions to get strung out at the fording of the River Orontes, the river on which Qadesh, the capital of Amurru or Amorites, was situated. In fact, the Army of Set (or Sutekh), bringing up the rear, was so far behind the advance units that it never even saw action in coming battle.[49] But even before that happened, two Shasu spies in the pay of Hatti were captured and after being beaten, gave out information on the location of the Hittite army. The whole scenario was in fact a clever ploy by the Hittite king Muwatallis to spread disinformation among the Egyptians. It is evident that the spies were instructed by their Hittite masters not to give up information too easily, hence their willingness to suffer a beating before giving out information under 'duress'. In the event it worked, because Rameses started forward with the Army of Amen with the other three armies strung out behind him as he crossed the Orontes. The entire Hittite army, led by their king Muwatallis lay hidden behind the fortress of Qadesh, unseen by the Egyptians. Rameses's overconfidence actually allowed him to cross the river and make camp just northwest of the city awaiting the arrival of the other three armies. The army of Rā, having crossed the river behind the Army of Amen, marched in desultory, straggling fashion toward the camp of Rameses, leaving the two rearmost armies behind to cross at their leisure. It was at this

49 Breasted, op.cit., p. 428.

precise moment that Hittite army of charioteers charged in force against the Army of Rā and, catching it completely unawares, breaking the line in two, and routing the army in total disorder, half of it fleeing northward to where Rameses was encamped. An incomprehensible military disaster loomed for the Egyptians but it was here that Rameses showed the mettle that later would give such awestruck luster to his name. After encountering the advance guard of the fleeing remnants of the Army of Rā, Rameses immediately gathered what forces he could and at the head of this highly outnumbered corps of charioteers counterattacked with mad ferocity. The only apt description is that Rameses went beserk because his headlong dash carried him alone into the midst of the enemy troops. As the story is told, Rameses calls upon his father Amon to come to his aid as he finds himself surrounded on all sides by enemy charioteers:

> I found Amun came when I called to him,
> He gave me his hand and I rejoiced.
> He called from behind as if nearby:
> 'Forward, I am with you, I, your father,
> My hand is with you, I prevail over a
> hundred thousand men, I am lord of
> victory, lover of valour.[50]

It has been said of Viking beserkers that, when possessed by the 'demons of battle' in a trance-like fury, they were impossible to kill. So it was with Rameses. All of the war gods of Egypt—Amon, Montu, Set—seemed to infuse Rameses with their power and six times he charged the enemy lines with his chariot-driver, wreaking destruction all around him with his battle axe and bow, striking ever more fear and awe in the Hittite enemy. Eventually, reinforcements reached Rameses but by then, the tide had been turned—single-handedly by Rameses it would appear. The Hittites withdrew from the field and the next day sued for peace. Though Rameses ever afterward would refer to the battle as a victory, it had none of the effects of victory. As Nicholas Grimal observes, what Rameses had done was rescue his army; the Hittites lost nothing in the way of territory or geopolitical power and indeed, an even-handed truce was the outcome of

50 Lichteim M, **Ancient Egyptian Literature**, Vol. II, Berkeley: University of California Presss, p. 66.

this battle. What made this a victorious battle for Rameses is the manner in which he seems to have turned the tide of defeat and repulsed the Hittites by a stupendous feat of individual valour and combat prowess, aided decisively by the gods of Egypt. It was thus not a victory for the Egyptian army but a victory for Rameses personally. It is undoubtedly for that reason that he caused the Battle of Qadesh to be celebrated and recorded over and over during the long course of his reign. And, though his impetuosity set the stage for a near-defeat—catastrophic in its implications—Rameses did manage, virtually alone, to save himself, his army, and Egypt. Had the unthinkable happened—the crushing of Rameses's army—the way was open and clear for Hatti and its allies to sweep southward into Egypt unopposed. In the aftermath, the rest of his army felt the full weight of his fury for having quailed before the enemy. Rameses left the field without a mark on him. Two fascinating aspects of the battle that gave it a quasi-mythic quality are revealed in the aid that Rameses received as he charged by his favorite dog and a tame lion, tame, that is, in his presence. Ever after, he remembered and rewarded his charioteer, his two chariot horses, the fierce dog, and the lion, memorializing them in accounts and illustrations of the battle. But this battle of Qadesh embodied the very meaning of a 'pyrrhic victory', that is, a win that confers no advantage to the victor.

Rameses was not finished in Asia by any means, but the short term setback to his plan for total reconquest had the Hittites under Muwatallis, after the Battle Qadesh, deposing the prince of Amurru and installing a puppet responsive to Hittite interests. This move had the effect of creating a buffer zone between Hatti and Egyptian territory in Asia, at least temporarily, demonstrating like nothing else the limits of Rameses's 'victory' at Qadesh. This turn of events should have been cause for great rejoicing among the Hittites but they were very shortly confronted with an even greater menace than Rameses: Assyria. Assyria was fast revealing itself to be the rising power in Mesopotamia and Western Asia generally. Assyria had already subdued Mitanni, Egypt's old enemy, in the northern lands between the Tigris and Euphrates. Mitanni had been a Hittite ally (one of the queens of Hatti was Mitannian) so her defeat was a blow to Hittite interests in Mesopotamia. But Rameses too had to face a threat on Egypt's western front—the Libyans who were constantly raiding and harrying Egyptian territory from their bases in the Western Desert. The Libyans, at this time, did not constitute a threat of the magnitude of an aggressive, rapacious Assyrian kingdom bent on conquest but they caused sufficient trouble to induce Rameses to build and garrison a series of forts just beyond the westernmost delta tributary of the Nile. Thus, both Hatti and Egypt were, at least for the moment, too occupied with other threats to renew hostilities with one another.

After settling his military affairs with the troublesome Libyans, Rameses once more turned his attention to Western Asia in the seventh year of his reign, two years after the Battle of Qadesh. In its attempts to establish a hegemony over Western Asia, Hatti had provided cover for the independent initiatives of 'break-away' states in Syria—Moab, Edom-Seir, and the ever-turbulent Shasu. This campaign shows a marked growth in Rameses as a tactician and strategic planner. He divided his army in two and, initiating a classic envelopment led one army west and northward, reducing Jerusalem and Jericho, while the other wing of his army under the able command of his son *Amon-hirk-khepeshef*, swept eastward toward the Dead Sea, overrunning the Shasu bedouin and capturing Edom-Seir. The two armies then re-linked in the country of Moab and marched northward toward Damascus, capturing several major towns and regaining control of the whole region between Jerusalem and southern Syria.

Campaigns to consolidate and extend the advantage already gained in Western Asia were renewed in the eighth and ninth years of Rameses's reign and met with unstinting success, aided no doubt by the troubles besetting the Hittite kingdom from within and without. With the death of the formidable Muwatallis, a dynastic crisis erupted in the kingdom that took some time to resolve while still being preoccupied with matters in Mesopotamia where Babylon and Assyria were at war. The outcome was of serious moment to the Hittites and they did everything they could to form an alliance with Babylon to meet the dire threat posed by Assyria. In this geopolitical atmosphere, Rameses launched new forays into Western Asia, re-taking yet again the Phoenician cities of Acre, Byblos, Tyre, and Sidon, advancing northward into Amurru, recapturing Qadesh—decisively this time—and marching toward the northern borders of the Amorites, not far from Hatti itself. Though Rameses's reconquest of Western Asia did not go so far as reclaiming the ancient imperial borders established in Asia by Thutmosis III 200 years earlier, his campaigns in Year 9 enabled him to recover more of Asia than had been Egyptian hands for 120 years, nor would it ever reach that extent again. Thus, he went far to redeem the near-fiasco at Qadesh four years before, showing himself, finally, to have matured into a brilliant and able military commander. Thus his boastful assertions concerning his military prowess on monuments and stelae that blanketed Egyptian territory all over the empire did rest on a foundation of truth.

Rameses's last incursion into Western Asia took place in Year 18 of his reign. Rameses found himself unintentionally embroiled in the internal politics of Hatti when a rebellious pretender to the Hittite throne, Urhi-Teshub, sought asylum in the Egyptian court against his uncle Hattusilis III, the reigning monarch of Hatti. Hattusilis demanded the extradition of the would-be usurper and the tension threatened to ignite another war between Egypt and Hatti. The status quo was destabilized enough to provoke renewed rebellions in Edom and Moab, requiring Rameses to lead his armies north once more to subdue the local princelings seeking to shake off Egyptian rule. And yet, the long-term outcome of this flare-up of restrained hostilities actually resulted in a permanent peace between Rameses and Hattusilis. Three years after the last military incursion into Canaan and Syria by Rameses, the two sparring kings signed a peace treaty that included, among other things, a provision for extradition of political dissidents—an obvious outcome of the Urhi-Teshub affair—as well as pledges not to encroach on each other's territory and a mutual protection pact. High level diplomatic correspondence ensued between the two countries and, indeed, there were no further wars between Hatti and Egypt for the rest of Rameses's reign. In fact, two Hittite royal daughters were given to Rameses in marriage to seal the new alliance, the first of whom married Rameses in Damascus. A remarkable incident is preserved where a Hittite princess fell violently ill, apparently by 'demonic' possession, and Rameses sent the god Khonsu to Hatti, with his priests, upon request to heal the girl of her madness.[51] The healing exorcism was evidently so successful that the Hittite king wanted to keep the god in Hatti. In the end, however, Khonsu and his priests returned to Egypt. Rameses would never again enter Western Asia on a war footing. In the ensuing decades, a Hittite crown prince and king actually paid Rameses state visits.

51 There is some confusion on this point since the records indicate that the two daughters were those of the Chief of Bekhten, but some think that Bekhten was just a region of the Hittite kingdom. See Petrie, op.cit., pp. 69-70 and Breasted, op.cit., p.440..

Rameses, after 20 years of active enmity with Hatti, finally decided to accept the status quo in Western Asia, with a partially restored Asian empire for Egypt.

In the south, the empire remained remarkably secure though a revolt of a Sudanese people known as the *Irem* erupted in Year 20 of Rameses's reign and was severely crushed. Annals of the time report Rameses bringing back 7,000 prisoners from Irem. There were no further disturbances from that quarter for another 24 years when the ruling viceroy—called 'the Royal Son of Cush'—was obliged to put down an uprising of the southern Libyans, Libyans north and south always representing a truculent element requiring periodic pacification raids against them. All of Nubia and Cush down to the fifth cataract had become an integral part of Egyptian national territory, essential because of the vital, millennia-old trade in African luxury items and materials necessary for ritual observances plus the seemingly inexhaustible supply of Nubian gold. Numerous temples were built and renovated by Rameses in Nubio-Cush that were as well-maintained and supplied as any of Rameses's temples north of the first cataract. In fact his most awe-inspiring monument, the temple at Abu Simbel with the four magnificent giant statues dedicated to himself was built in Nubia along the west bank of the Nile. That Nubia under Rameses was not viewed or treated as some imperial backwater is evidenced by his active building projects there.

Rameses's Temple at Abu Simbel

Perhaps more than his military campaigns, Rameses's outsized image and reputation for posterity rest largely on the astonishing array of temples and monuments he caused to be built, from Syria in the north to the 5th cataract in Cush in the south. From the beginning of Egyptian history to the end, no pharaoh could rival Rameses for the sheer volume of monumental construction accomplished during the 67 years of his reign; there wasn't a year in it where building projects commissioned by him weren't being undertaken somewhere. Having said that, he was a shameless usurper of the temples and monuments of nearly all his predecessors, his name ingeniously carved into almost every temple complex of any importance as if he were the builder. On the one hand, he seemed piously scrupulous about honoring his ancestors while on the other hand utterly unscrupulous about co-opting their monuments, even razing some of them to extract the stones for his own building projects. Early in his reign, he engineered the final demolition of Akhenaton's surviving buildings and monuments at Akhetaten (el Amarna), re-using the stone to enlarge Hermopolis Magna on the opposite bank of the Nile, a city sacred to Djehuti (Thoth), god of learning and wisdom. One may be permitted to wonder if at least some of the pharaohs after Akhenaton harbored such unyielding rancor towards him as their iconoclastic destruction of his sacred monuments would seem to indicate. One and all—each in his own way—endeavored to put themselves beyond the tangible reach of the priesthood of Amon, the most powerful in the country[52], following a precedent set by Akhenaton himself. But it wouldn't have done the kings of the 19th Dynasty any good, Rameses included, to have antagonized the Amonians, especially since their legitimate claim to the throne was a bit tenuous. So each played his part in the remorseless endeavor of erasing Akhenaton from history, ultimately without success. As Breasted observes, '… there was gradually arising the sacerdotal state described by Diodorus, upon which the Egyptian priests of Greeks times looked back as upon a golden age'.[53]

Another notable temple complex was the Ramesseum, built as a mortuary temple on the West Bank alongside that of Seti I. Rameses filial piety towards his father seemed genuine and he spared no effort to burnish and proclaim

52 It is pertinent to remember that the high priest of Amon was the sacerdotal head of all the priesthoods of the country, veritably Egypt's 'pope'.

53 Breasted, op.cit., p. 457.

the name and fame of Seti I whose accomplishments, as seen earlier, were of an exceptionally high order. In fact Seti's adjacent temple served as the basic model for the Ramesseum. There is a way in which this temple seemed to emulate that of Seti's temple in Abydos in that it was constructed as an homage to Osiris. Numerous statues of Rameses in the guise of Osiris lined the eastern and western walls of the second peristyle court. Moreover, a smaller temple dedicated to Osiris stood just south of the Ramesseum. However that may be, the Theban triad of Amon, Mut, and Khonsu were not neglected since a temple-within-a-temple was dedicated to them and Seti on the south side of sanctuary. The temple's axis—like so many others—was oriented west-to-east so that at certain times of the year, the rays of the rising sun shone with almost laser-like precision on the statue of Rā set in the holy of holies. It is worth quoting Nicholas Grimal on the subject because the design of the temple followed a template used in the construction of numerous other temples:

> The approach consisted of a gradual movement from light to shadow, reaching total darkness in the holy of holies, where the god dwelt. At the same time the ground slowly rose, achieving its highest point under the naos, which was thus located on the primeval mound emerging from Nun, the lake of chaos.[54]

All such temples consisted of a courtyard, a double colonnade, and a pylon entrance. The court usually led to a hypostyle hall in which the central row of columns were raised higher than the peripheral rows, creating window-like apertures at the top that let in just enough of the sun rays to create a half-light illumination that deepened the numinous atmosphere inside the temple. Crowds of worshipers were allowed into the outside courtyard but never permitted inside the roofed section of the temple that was composed of the hypostyle hall and the sanctuary. Only priests of a certain rank could enter these environs to carry out religious ceremonies. But in the holy of holies, as the domicile of the deity itself, only the pharaoh or chief priest could enter there for the necessary offerings and rituals.

54 Grimal, op. cit., p. 265.

Rameses, like all the pharaohs of the New Kingdom, made sure to leave his mark both on Luxor and Karnak Temples. Luxor, like all the important temple sites in Egypt, had been the home of older temples but the major temple that now stands was first built by Amenhotep III, 150 years before Rameses, who linked it with Karnak Temple by an avenue 1½ miles long lined on both sides

Entrance to Luxor Temple Flanked
by Two Statues of Rameses

by ram-headed sphinxes (criosphinxes) emblematic of Amon. It was called 'the southern harem of Amon' and every year, Amon, Mut, and Khonsu made a stately procession to Luxor from Karnak along the avenue of criosphinxes. The temple built by Amenhotep III stopped at the processional colonnade of 14 magnificent columns, seven on each side. Rameses extended the temple by adding a peristyle forecourt and a new pylon, flanked by two obelisks and six colossal statues of himself, three on each side of the entryway of the pylon. The new terminus of the avenue of criosphinxes was now the pylon portal, dominated by the statues of Rameses and his obelisks. If Rameses was not exactly trying to upstage Amenhotep III, he was at least setting himself as

Amenhotep's equal by the manner and magnitude of his additions to Luxor Temple.

Rameses's additions—peristyle court and pylon—had the effect of changing the axis of Luxor Temple so that when a modern visitor enters the temple he is walking in one direction but as soon as he reaches the colonnade of Amenhotep III, he perforce must change direction to continue through the temple. Nicholas Grimal attributes this change of axis to a change in the position of the heliacal rising of the star Sirius at the onset of summer, heralding the Nile flood.[55] Luxor, like all Egyptian and Nubian temples, was oriented to a specific heavenly body, in this case Sirius the Dog Star, the brightest star in the heavens seen from earth. It bears repeating that the Egyptian calendar was based on this once-a-year heliacal rising of Sirius, giving a year of 365¼ days, and was also the means by which the civil calendar of 365 days was rectified every 1,460 years. What Grimal does not say is that this change in the axis of the temple in order to follow the change in the position of Sirius rising at the summer solstice is one more piece of evidence among many that the Egyptian architects and astronomers were precisely acquainted with the precession.[56]

The hypostyle hall at Karnak Temple has already been mentioned, begun by Seti I and completed by Rameses. Typically, the hall, with its 134 columns of 68 feet or more, dominates the temple and excites the most comment by visitors and historians. Seti erected 78 of the columns and Rameses 56. It must have presented an awesome spectacle when intact and complete. In the half-light that illuminated it by day, one proceeding through it might feel swallowed up by the effect created by these massively high columns. Despite their size and majesty, the preponderance of authoritative opinion thinks that as architectural and artistic representations, they are inferior to other monumental columns in other temples. Nonetheless, Rameses exhibited a distinct tendency to commission huge statues and monumental constructions and Karnak's hypostyle hall is typical for the 19th Dynasty. In fairness, his father Seti had set the pattern for column size at Karnak but it fit in perfectly with Rameses's own

55 Ibid., p. 267.

56 See Lockyer N, **The Dawn of Astronomy**, Cambridge: The M.I.T. Press, (1894), 1964, pp. 120-32, for a discussion on the connection between the precession and Egyptian temple-building.

predilection for achieving majesty with sheer size. Rameses, even more than his father Seti, wanted to leave a legacy that would rival, if not exceed, that of the 18th Dynasty and nowhere is it better appreciated than when contemplating his various monuments.

We cannot leave the subject of Rameses's monuments without returning once again to Abu Simbel. Nothing that Rameses ever built exerts the awe-inspiring impact of Abu Simbel on the beholder with its four colossal statues of Rameses himself, two on each side of the entrance. It was one of six rock-cut Nubian temples and is generally considered to be the 'crown jewel' of all of Rameses's building projects. Indeed, some of the best and most prolific of Rameses's *de novo* temple building was accomplished in Nubia and Cush.[57] In fact, there is a Ramessid temple that was built as far south as the 4th Cataract at Napata, a center of Amon-worship of ever-growing importance and the eventual capital of independent Cush. The temple at Abu Simbel was yet another dedicated to the deification of Rameses in association with Amon- Rā, Ptah, and Rā-Horakhty. A smaller temple to south of it was dedicated to his paramount queen *Nefertari* ('indwelling beauty') and Hathor, only the second temple in Egyptian history to be dedicated to a queen[58]. Though comparatively little is known about her, she undoubtedly was a descendant in the line of Chief Royal Wives through whom the throne descended and was legitimized. The entire complex,—the two temples and the four Ramessid colossi—were hewn out of living rock, 175 miles south of Aswan and, before the building of the Aswan High Dam, reposed at the level of the Nile. As is well known, an international effort in the late 1960s removed both temples and all statues upward onto the plateau above the Nile and the flood plain created by the completion of the dam. Every year, when the sun rose at the winter solstice, a shaft of sunlight would shine directly into and through the central corridor of the temple to light up the sanctuary. It still does today, but because of the relocation of temple, it occurs one day later than it did in Rameses's time. But it is the four colossal statues of a seated Rameses that continues to fascinate, not only for their epic size but also for the genius of the sculptor in creating an indelible image of the stern majesty of Rameses. The statues are each 65

57 Petrie, op.cit., p. 78.

58 The first was a temple built by Akhenaten and dedicated to Nefertiti.

feet high making them taller than the massive presidential busts at Mount Rushmore by 6½ feet.[59] Rameses, on his temple at Abu Simbel, lavished more time, care, effort, and artistic attention than anything he ever built anywhere else. It is the one complex of Rameses's edifices that does not suffer by artistic comparison to Egypt's finest architectural constructions.

Rameses died after 67 years of rule. No pharaoh had ruled that long for more than 2,000 years (Pepi II of the 6th Dynasty—94 years). On account of Rameses—continuing the work of Seti I who preceded him—Egypt was once again the dominant power in the region even without having regained all of its erstwhile Asian empire. It was as wealthy as it had ever been and its influence spread in every direction beyond its borders, largely because of Rameses's incandescent personality. However, as will be seen, his death provoked something of a succession crisis. Though he sired more than 160 children, including 111 sons, he outlived three of his designated successors and the generation following his demise was one of relative dynastic instability. Be that as it may, Rameses's obsessive pursuit of personal fame seems to have accomplished the effect intended. He was in the immediate period after his death, and continuing down to the present day, the most famous of Egyptian pharaohs both at home and abroad. Having said that, it is again essential to put him in proper context: he did not possess the military genius of Thutmosis III nor, on the strength of aesthetic quality and engineering prowess, did he outdo the architectural accomplishments of the 4th Dynasty pyramid-builders or even of Hatshepsut, Amenhotep III, or Seti I. Moreover, as Breasted observed,

> With the Asiatic campaigns of Rameses II the military aggressiveness of Egypt which had been awakened under Ahmose I in the expulsion of the Hyksos was completely exhausted. Nor did it ever revive.[60]

Still, Rameses left his mark everywhere in Egypt and in the minds of many in centuries to come he came to epitomize Egypt itself.

---

59 Breasted correctly observes that the monumental Ramessid statues such as the ones at Pi-Ramesse, the Ramesseum, and Abu Simbel represent the largest monolithic statues ever sculpted and erected anywhere. Breasted, op.cit., p.445.

60 Breasted, op.cit., p. 441

Mereneptah (1,223 BC–1,213 BC)

Mereneptah: Pharaoh of the Exodus

Being the 'follow-up act' to a great man—especially one who was a legend in his own time—is never an enviable position to be in; one can seldom live up to the expectation. Mereneptah, Rameses II's successor, was his 13th son whose mother was his consort *Isisnofret* ('beauty of Isis'). Rameses was nearly 90 at the time of his death and so Mereneptah himself would have been if not elderly then in late middle age on his accession. There were three heir-presumptives prior to Mereneptah, including the justly famous *Khaemwaset*, elder brother of Mereneptah by the same mother, all of whom predeceased Rameses. Khaemwaset ('he rises serene') won fame for his learning, sagacity, and spiritual power evincing a keen interest in archaeology. He excavated and restored a number of Memphite monuments, consistent with his noted piety toward Ptah, of whom he became the Chief Priest. In the event, Khaemwaset died before he could assume the throne, clearing the way for Mereneptah. Nonetheless, Petrie refers to him as Rameses's 'most important son' and with ample justification. His name was mentioned with great reverence for another 1,000 years or more, down into Greco-Roman times.[61]

Mereneptah ('beloved of Ptah') ascended the throne in or around 1,223 BC, reigning for a little less than 10 years, though he had been associated

61 Gardiner, op.cit., p.267.

with Rameses as co-ruler perhaps as early as 1,234 BC, 11 years prior to his accession[62]. He maintained himself at the capital Pi-Ramesse established by his father Rameses but, as his name indicates, he was a devotee of Ptah and did much to restore and refurbish Memphis, the sacred city of Ptah. He built a palace for himself in the city, renovated a major temple, and built his mortuary temple there. He also built or restored temples dedicated respectively to Rā, Djehuti, and Hathor. Following conventional pharaonic practice, he usurped the Osireion at Abydos and Mentuhotep II's temple dedicated to Hathor at Denderah. Most of his building efforts, however, were directed toward refurbishment and renovation with comparatively few new edifices erected in his name. Though his capital was in Pi-Ramesse and Memphis was his theological center, at his death he was buried in the Valley of Kings in the manner of all previous 18th and 19th Dynasty pharaohs.

Abroad, the cordial relations with Hatti were sustained and Mereneptah even sent grain to the Hittites during a period of famine. The forts established by Rameses II in Western Asia remained garrisoned and there was no diminution in the Asian territories of Egypt. However, there was an uprising of the vassal states of Ashkelon and Gezer that Mereneptah was obliged to suppress and it was during this campaign that the earliest record of the name of Israel is found on Mereneptah's victory stele. Some restive tribes in Cush, goaded apparently by the southern Libyans, also required the military intervention of Mereneptah's forces.

The Libyans north and south—called *Lebu* by the Egyptians and also *Tehennu*—were becoming ever-more active players in the geopolitics of northeast Africa. In fact, the Libyans had made such substantive inroads into the western delta that, as Breasted put it, the whole region was 'tinctured with Libyan blood'. Moreover, a line of fortresses in the northwestern delta had been erected to deal more effectively with this rising threat.[63] But in addition to the Lebu and Tehennu, the northeast littoral of Africa west of the Delta had become home to the Sherden, a northern Mediterranean people pushed south by invading Indo-Europeans from Central Asia. The Sherden, allied with other tribes from the northern Mediterranean, were called 'the Sea Peoples' by the

62 Budge, op. cit., p. 97.
63 See Gardiner, op. cit., p. 270.

Egyptians and not surprisingly, lost no time making incursion into Egyptian territory.[64] They raided and plundered the western Delta and eventually made their way to the frontier town of Per-irt and further into the country of the Tehennu, the western neighbors of Egypt. The Libyan invasion, from the west, was apparently timed to seize the harvest, generally commencing around May 2nd in the Delta. Success in war for an Egyptian pharaoh commonly depended on divine aid and in this Mereneptah was no exception. His patron deity Ptah came to him in a dream with clear battle instructions, handing him a sword and admonishing him to abandon all fear. Mereneptah's army, after a rapid march, confronted the enemy at Per-irt, the western limit of the Delta. The Egyptians attacked the Libyans in force and, after a six-hour battle, routed them completely. Most of the damage was done by a continuous, withering rain of arrows from Mereneptah's archers that set the stage for the final devastating charge with regular troops.[65] Māreiui, the Libyan king, fled for his life, leaving his entire army, his wife, and all his children at the mercy of the victorious Egyptians. Six brothers and sons of Māreiui died that day and more than 9,000 prisoners were taken. It was a crushing defeat for the Libyans and their allies the Sea People, and, as Petrie observes, Mereneptah through his skillful tactics and strategy revealed himself as a true general. Once again, Egypt was saved from foreign conquest, but, as will be seen in the 20th Dynasty, the matter with the Sea Peoples was by no means finished. Though not as vigorously commemorated as Rameses's victories had been, this was a decisive victory for Mereneptah and Egypt, preserving the peace on the western front for another two decades.[66] There are two engraved 'battle reports', one engraved on the wall of the Temple at Karnak, including the Victory stele with a 'hymn of triumph' containing the passage describing the conquest of Israel, which suggests that some part of this military riposte took Egyptian armies into Canaan. It is to be noted that Mereneptah rebuilt and repaired a number of frontier forts, doubly motivated, no doubt, by the Libyan war.

64 These northern Mediterranean peoples included contingents ancestral to the Sardinians, Sicilians, Etruscans, and archaic peoples of the Greek Aegean. It is the first significant invasion attempt of Africa by Europeans and their first appearance on the stage of recorded history.

65 Petrie, op.cit., p. 109.

66 See Budge, ibid., pp.100-2 for an extended discussion of the Libyan war.

There have already been several references in this book to the people that history has come to know as the Children of Israel—or the Hebrews—and their interface with Egyptian history. Their own story, as captured in the Torah or the Old Testament (Christian), has become the foundation of the sacred history of three world religions—Judaism, Christianity, and Islam—now claiming the allegiance of nearly three billion people. Most of what we know about their remote history comes from their own account of their origins, migrations, travails, and, of course, their covenant with Yahweh. What they managed to do with history-changing success is take a purely tribal deity and turn him, eventually, into an exclusive, universal one. Several points can be made about the Children of Israel and the Exodus story:

- Though their story is purported to be true and actual history, it is as much (or more) filled with mythic and semi-mythic material as factual history;
- Their history, their culture, and their religion are all enabled and informed by the transformative experience of living in Egypt for 430 years;
- In the Old Testament version of the Exodus, never once is the pharaoh named who is reputed to have oppressed the Children of Israel so cruelly, a curious omission for an event so assiduously treated as factual history. They are said to have been forced to build the cities of 'Pithom and Raamses', and though 'Raamses' here is not employed as a personal name, it is closest mention there is of any word that might have indicated an actual pharaoh.[67]
- When they leave Egypt, they are thoroughly Egyptianized and even the deity introduced to them at Mount Sinai, *Yahweh*, has a prototype among the Egyptian neters called *Yah*, a lunar form of the god Osiris.[68]

67 Exodus I,11.

68 See Finch, op. cit., pp. 129-78, passim, for a full discussion of the Nile Valley sources of the Old Testament. It is to be noted that Yahweh is called 'Yah' 25 times in the Old Testament.

Concerning the third item above, the putative conscription of Hebrew workers for the building of the city of Raamses, might well be a reference to Pi-Ramesse, built on the ancient site of Avaris, originally sacred to Set, first by Seti I and more extensively by Rameses II who made it his capital. Work was continued in the construction and beautifying of Pi-Ramesse by the successor of Rameses II, Mereneptah. It might therefore legitimately be supposed that the events recorded in Exodus refer both to the end of the reign of Rameses and the beginning of the reign of Mereneptah, more specifically during the period of co-regency when Mereneptah was taking over the effective reins of government from the aged and infirm Rameses. In fact, in Exodus itself it is recorded that the king who conscripted the Children of Israel for the building of Pithom and Raamses died but that the oppression was carried on by the succeeding pharaoh.[69] It is evident that there were two pharaohs on the throne during the historical appearance of Moses on the scene leading to the out-migration of the multitudes depicted in Exodus. The first must have been Rameses in the last years of his reign; the second Mereneptah, the enthroned co-regent ruler at the time of the Exodus. Thus it is said by one early 20th century Egyptologist:

> ...there seems to be no doubt that period of greatest oppression described in the Book of Exodus fell in the reign of Rameses II, and that the works wherein the Israelites toiled were in connexion with rebuilding of the city of Tanis (Pi-Ramesse) and the founding of the frontier fortress of Pa-Temu, or Pithom[70].

Egyptologists one and all make at least passing references to the Exodus story, mostly to argue whether it took place under Rameses or Merèneptah. However, in so doing, they make the presumption that—minus the 10 plagues and the drowning of pharaoh's army in the Red Sea—the main outlines of Exodus are indeed veritable history. But few of them, apart from E.A. Wallis Budge, seem to have taken into any account the Exodus version of Apion. Apion was an Egyptian priest-historian in the 3rd century BC who, along with

69 Exodus II, 23-5.

70 Budge, op. cit., p. 126.

Manetho, wrote an account of the out-migration of the people who would become the Hebrews of history from the Egyptian point of view. We have only a short summary of Apion's writings in the essay by the first century Roman Jewish author Josephus entitled *Contra Apion* (*Against Apion*), written to refute Apion and Manetho in favor of the standard Jewish interpretation of the Exodus events.[71]

The Josephian version given by Apion and Manetho, both of whom had full access to the historical records of ancient Egypt going back to the Old Kingdom, does confirm an exodus. Its numbers, however, did not exceed 80,000 persons and these migrants were considered 'leprous' malcontents by the Egyptians themselves. As Budge observes, whether these persons were actually lepers or whether the term used by the Egyptians to mean 'lepers' in reference to them was merely a term of abuse cannot be determined with certainty.[72] They were organized and led by an apostate Egyptian priest of Rā named *Osarsiph* ('son of Osiris')—very plausibly a posthumous disciple of Akhenaton—who changed his name to 'Moses', gave the 'mixed multitude' of migrants their first laws, encouraged them to rebel against and renounce the gods of Egypt, and taught them the worship of the deity that would guide their destiny, *Yah* or *Yahweh* ('Yah increases'). There were two exodes or expulsions out of the Delta: one at the end of the 17th Dynasty in 1,570 BC or before which consisted of the Hyksos and their loyalists, numbering maybe 250,000 persons and another toward the end of the 19th Dynasty, around 1,230 BC, numbering 80,000 persons. Clearly the two expulsions/out-migrations, 350 years apart, became conflated in the accounts of later Hebrew chroniclers between the 10th and the 6th centuries BC.

The mention of Israel on the stele attributed to Mereneptah, discovered by Flinders Petrie, is dated to either 1,230 BC or 1,220 BC. The earlier date is the one usually accepted for the Exodus, taking place during the co-regency of Mereneptah with Rameses II. The latter date for the erection of the stele would have occurred at a time when Mereneptah reigned as pharaoh alone

71 Whiston WP, translator, **Josephus: The Complete Works**, *Against Apion*, Grand Rapids: Kregel Publications, (1867), 1981, pp. 610-2. It must be noted that Josephus's account, reported from the history by Apion (and Manetho) is heavily redacted and historically garbled. Still, certain elements in it that may be historically plausible are discernible.

72 Budge, op. cit., p. 116.

and reflected a post-Exodus punitive campaign against the Children of Israel. As already indicated, it is this first historical mention of Israel that lends credence to the supposition that the exodus of the Children of Israel occurred while Mereneptah sat on the throne probably as co-regent but nonetheless the effective ruler of Egypt. He would have dated the beginning of his reign with his accession to co-regency with his father Rameses II. In the event, Mereneptah seems to have struck a blow against these erstwhile Delta dwellers who had abandoned Egypt during the Libyan war. If indeed there was a 40-year period of wandering by the Children of Israel, this strike by Mereneptah against the people of the Exodus would have occurred in the early part of that wandering. Whether this blow represented a belated punishment for the trouble they had caused Egypt or whether, like the Apiru before them, they had taken to raiding and brigandage that demanded a severe Egyptian military response can only be a matter for conjecture. It is assumed that some component of these Egyptian expatriates wandering in the deserts of Canaan were indeed Apiru who had worked as brick-makers and stone-cutters in Egypt during the 19th Dynasty[73] and that 'Apiru' eventually became the word 'Hebrew'. But apart from the single line about Israel—*'Israel is wasted, his seed is not'*—there are no surviving contemporary 19th Dynasty records of any events remotely resembling the Exodus story. Apion and Manetho writing about it 1,000 years later provide really the only valid evidence available that gives the Exodus any claim to factual historical truth instead of merely serving as a founding national myth. The Exodus must be considered in the same light as the Iliad—mythologized versions of actual historical events, the departure from Egypt on the one hand and the conquest of Troy on the other.

73 'So they [the Egyptians] treated their Israelite slaves with ruthless severity, and made life bitter for them with cruel servitude, setting them to work on clay and brick-making...', Exodus I,14.

End of the 19th Dynasty

Amenmesse (1,213 BC–1,210 BC)

An unsettled phase of Egyptian history ensued after the death of Mereneptah contributing severely to successional instability that eventually leads to the termination of the 19th Dynasty. In fact, there are differences of opinion on the exact order of succession of the next three pharaohs that abide even to the present day. In the event, none of them reigned very long. Following Grimal, a grandson of Rameses II through his daughter Takhat, *Amenmesse* ('born of Amen'), followed Mereneptah to the throne but only ruled for three years before his demise. For reasons unknown, he was later cast in the role of usurper leading to the destruction of his tomb by his successor. Popular unrest began to stir for the first time since the reign of Akhenaton due in no small part to inadequate and inconsistent disbursement of the in-kind wages due to various guilds of workers.

Seti II or *Sethos II* (1,213 BC–1,207 BC)

Seti II ascended the throne at age 56 after Amenmesse's demise and since he was the designated heir of Mereneptah, he was considered the legitimate claimant instead of his cousin Amenmesse. For that reason, his reign is said to have begun at the same time as Amenmesse was said to have usurped the throne. His reign lasted six years but left no lasting historical impression. His building projects, such as they were, were limited to additions to existing temples rather than any *de novo* building projects. The famous story, *Tale of the Two Brothers* that some have seen as the prototype of the story of Joseph running afoul of the amorous attentions of Potiphar's wife, seems to have been re-written—or possibly re-copied—in this reign.

Rameses Siptah (1,207 BC–1,201 BC)

In the twilight years of the 19th Dynasty, things went from bad to worse. Seti II died after just six years of rule and the only viable heir remaining was *Rameses Siptah* ('son of Ptah'), the oldest son of Seti II's third queen, who himself was still a child when he ascended the throne and therefore had to be a supervised by a regent, in this case Queen *Twosre,* Seti II's second wife[74] whose own son had died before he could ascend the throne. She was therefore the stepmother of Rameses Siptah and it is not at all clear why she could step into the role of regent at the expense of the heir's natural mother. Clearly it was a successful power play on the part of Twosre who must have exercised an unusual amount of influence at court. Even as regent, Twosre had to enlist the collaboration of a powerful ally and she turned to *Bay* (aka '*Yarsu*'), the Syrian chancellor, which meant that these two co-ruled Egypt during Rameses Siptah's minority. Indeed, the connection seems redolent in miniature of Hatshepsut's reign with Senenmut serving as her right hand man and her morganatic husband. Later records paint the whole arrangement as a corrupt bargain with Twosre and Bay as partners in court and the boudoir. Given a free hand by Twosre, Bay rifled the treasury at will and during the regency, misrule, robbery, and crime generally afflicted the country:

> The land of Egypt was in the hands of chiefs and of rulers of towns; one slew his neighbor great and small. Other times having come after it, with empty years, Yarsu [Bay], a certain Syrian was with them as chief. He set the whole land tributary before him together; he united his companions and plundered their possessions. They made the gods like men, and no offerings were presented in the temples.[75]

Clearly things had changed in Egypt: not since the time of the Hyksos more than 400 years earlier had a foreigner—an Asiatic (Syrian)—risen so high in

74 Petrie calls her the daughter of Seti II instead of his wife. Petrie, op.cit., p.122.

75 Breasted JH, **Ancient Records of Egypt - Part Four** (*Papyrus Harris),* London: Histories & Mysteries of Man LTD., (1905), 1988, pp. 198-99.

government, high enough to exercise control over the administrative apparatus during a period of weak central control.

Rameses Siptah soon changed his name to Mereneptah Siptah—'beloved of Ptah; son of Ptah'—indicating his total allegiance to Ptah of Memphis. He lived only three more years and when he died, Twosre became, in effect, the sole ruler, e.g., pharaoh, of Egypt until her death two years later.[76] Her reign was not totally bereft of pharaonic accomplishment in that there is evidence of monument-building commissioned by her at Heliopolis, Thebes, and the West Bank. With her death, the 19th Dynasty comes to a rather inglorious close.

III. The 20th Dynasty—The Long Decline Begins (1,201 BC–1,083 BC)

Setnakhte (1,201 BC–1,199 BC)

There are differences of opinion as to whether *Setnakhte* ('strength of Set') properly belongs to the end of the 19th Dynasty or is the first pharaoh of the 20th. There are valid reasons for either viewpoint but here we will follow the format of Grimal that places him as the first pharaoh of the 20th Dynasty. Otherwise, the entire dynasty consisted of 10 pharaohs all named Rameses, from the 3rd to the 12th, testifying to the immense prestige and legendary impact Rameses II exerted on the history of Egypt immediately after his time. Setnakhte was himself undoubtedly a descendant of Rameses II, assuming the throne after the death of Twosre, and was given credit by posterity for having reorganized and stabilized the kingdom. Again, his name reveals him to have been a devotee of Set like other 19th Dynasty pharaohs. A report of the restoration of order by Setnakhte was recorded by his son Rameses III and preserved in the Papyrus Harris:

> ...he [Setnakhte] set in order the entire land, which
> had been rebellious; he slew the rebels who were in
> the land of Egypt; he cleansed the great throne of Egypt...[77]

76 Twosre therefore represents the fourth—and last—of the royal women in Egyptian history to reign as pharaoh. Some, however, count Cleopatra VII as the 5th and last.

77 Breasted, op.cit., p. 199.

Setnakhte's rule only lasted two years before he died and there is a certain amount of skepticism on this account about Setnakhte's ability to have achieved such an outstanding result in such a short period of time. However it may have been, he was succeeded by Rameses III, his son by Queen *Tiyemerenaset* ('Tiye, beloved of Isis'), who had been made co-regent while Setnakhte was still living. Before moving on from the reign of Setnakhte it is worth calling attention to an opinion vouchsafed by Budge concerning the timing of the Exodus:

> The Exodus of the Israelites from Egypt is far more likely to have taken place in the period which followed the rule of Seti II than under Mereneptah, because the condition of the country, with its lack of a central government and with uprisings on every side, was far more favorable to the flight of the children of Israel immediately after the death of Seti II, than earlier.[78]

There is something to be said for this point of view, though the weight of opinion and the scanty historical evidence favor a timetable between the end of the reign of Rameses II and that of Mereneptah.

78 Budge, op. cit., p. 148.

Rameses III (1,199 BC–1,167 BC)

Rameses III—Conqueror of the Sea Peoples

With Rameses III we come to the very last of the great Egyptian pharaohs, the one responsible for preserving national sovereignty that lasted another 500 years. If, as some historians insist, he is actually the first pharaoh of the 20th Dynasty, he would represent not only the third pharaoh named Rameses but also the first of an unbroken line of 10 dynasts named Rameses that finishes 100 years later at the death of Rameses XII. It would be the only dynasty in Egyptian history with all its rulers carrying the same name, so by some, is aptly referred to as the Ramessid Dynasty. However that may be, Rameses III ranks among the most able and accomplished New Kingdom rulers. Accordingly, he went out of his way to model himself and his reign as closely as possible on that of his glorious predecessor, Rameses II:

> From the very outset Ramesses III's role-model was Ramesses II. His successors also modelled themselves on the earlier Ramesses, but it was Ramesses III who went to the greatest lengths, from the choice of his titulature to the construction of a mortuary temple copying the plan of the Ramesseum.[79]

79 Grimal, op. cit., p. 271.

In time-honored fashion, Rameses III reigned as co-regent with his father before his own accession upon the death of the latter. Concerning his reign, Petrie makes the point that most of what is known of the events therein comes from the inscriptions carved on his mortuary temple at Medinet Habu about which more will be said.[80]

Though Mereneptah had defeated the Libyans toward the end of the 19th Dynasty, they had taken the opportunity afforded by the presence of relatively ineffectual rulers on the throne of Egypt to revive their incursions into and attacks on the Western Delta. Between the fifth and eleventh years of his reign, Rameses III was twice obliged to take the field against the coalition of Libyans arrayed against Egypt and on both occasions soundly defeated them. The pharaohs had adopted a policy of transferring defeated populations into Egypt, incorporating the men into the army as auxiliaries, and enabling their families to settle as colonists in the Delta, eventually becoming more or less Egyptianized. This policy was also followed with the Libyans—though they were dealt with perhaps more harshly by being made galley slaves—and would eventually set the stage for the emergence of a Libyan dynasty that came to power during a later period of national turmoil and political weakness.

But a much greater threat to the Egyptian nation presented itself during Year 8 of Rameses's reign in between the two Libyan wars—the invasion of the Sea Peoples. As noted earlier in this work, these were an alliance of maritime

Egyptian ship on the Red Sea, about 1250 B.C. [From Torr's "Ancient Ships."]
Mr. Langton Cole calls attention to the rope *truss* in this illustration, stiffening the beam of the ship. No other such use of the truss is known until the days of Modern engineering.

19th Dynasty Egyptian Warship with Stabilizing Center Truss

80 Petrie, op. cit., p. 147.

peoples from the northern Mediterranean based mainly in Crete and Rhodes but with allies from the Greek coast as well. This band of maritime allies had begun a campaign of conquest down the coast of Western Asia and with the Canaanitic Philistines attacked Egypt first by land in the western Delta then by water through the Nile tributaries of the eastern Delta. Rameses defeated them utterly and decisively, achieving a brilliant dual victory on both land and sea. The naval battle in the eastern Delta presented a more dire set of circumstances and must be counted as Egypt's greatest naval victory. There is a persistent belief that the Egyptians had never attempted to create ships suitable for anything but riverine navigation, though a closer examination dispels that assumption.[81] One thinks that Rameses and his strategic command must have had ample warning of the impending invasion because there were refinements and improvements in shipbuilding that made the Egyptian ships more sea-worthy and effective against an enemy that was already well-versed in the ways of naval warfare:

> The [Egyptian] hulls are longer and lower, sterns are more elevated to give the helmsman a better view, hogging trusses are no longer needed because the interior structure of the ships have been considerably strengthened, and sails are no longer attached to the lower yard but remain "loose footed'. This latter feature allowed for better control of the sail from the deck and selective shortening of the sail for greater maneuverability.[82]

The invading forces were utterly demolished and, according to Cheikh Anta Diop, many of their remnants fled westward across northern Africa to become the founding ancestors of the present-day Berbers. In this way is the presence of these white-skinned peoples in northern Africa explained.[83] After this victory, there would be no further invasions of Egypt attempted for the next five centuries. This achievement alone would rank Rameses III among Egypt's most capable and effective rulers. Parenthetically, in the following generations,

81 See Vinson S, **Egyptian Boats and Ships**, Buckinghamshire, U.K.: Shire Publications, 1994, passim.

82 Finch CS, **The Star of Deep Beginnings**, Decatur: Khenti Publications, Inc., 1998, pp. 210-11.

83 Diop CA, **Civilization or Barbarism**, translated by Y-LM Ngemi, Brooklyn: Lawrence Hill Books, 1991, p. 34.

Egypt would permanently cede much of its maritime enterprise to its coastal Canaanitic allies the semi-Egyptianized Phoenicians who would, in effect, become Egypt's merchant marine.

Rameses III's most notable architectural legacy is at Medinet Habu, about a half-mile south of the Rameseum and completed in the 12th year of his reign, following all his major battles. It was already a sacred site before the time of Rameses III, called the 'mound of the west' in relation to the Luxor Temple on the eastern side of the Nile. Temple complexes at the site had been built first by Amenhotep I then enlarged by Hatshepsut and Thutmosis III. With the addition of the mortuary temple of Rameses III, Medinet Habu had evolved into a miniature sacred city. It is obviously modeled on the Rameseum and had its own enclosing walls. As in the temples of Rameses II, the walls of Rameses III's temple are decorated with battle scenes from his most famous victories over the Libyans (twice) and the Sea Peoples, the latter being depicted with especial care and detail since it was one of the most decisive battles in Egyptian history. Typically, the spoils of war were shown dedicated to Amon who was always seen to be the one ultimately responsible for Egyptian military success. Also in imitation of his legendary forbear, Rameses III had the names of all his sons inscribed on the west portico in the second court.

No Egyptian pharaoh could count himself among the great rulers in the illustrious Egyptian pantheon of rulers who didn't undertake great monumental building projects, and Rameses III adhered vigorously to this pattern. He could not hope to duplicate the sheer volume of monumental building of Rameses II—no one could or did—but Rameses III managed to build on a fairly wide scale. Every New Kingdom pharaoh added to the massive complex at Karnak and Rameses III built a temple there to Khonsu, the divine son Amon and Mut. He also left monuments at Luxor while adding important edifices at 11 other sites in Egypt along with temples in Nubia and Syria. His tomb was decorated with a number of striking frescoes, including the remarkable 'Panel of Races' that show the four major ethnic groups—with their natural coloration—with whom the Egyptians were in common contact: (from left to right) black Egyptians (*Remetou*); reddish-brown Libyans (*Temehou*); black Nubians (*Nehesu*); dark-red Western Asiatics or Canaanites (*Amu*). This revealing panel is usually seen as graphically rendered by the early Prussian Egyptologist, Karl Richard Lepsius, in *Denkmäler aus Aegyten aus Aethiopien* ('Monuments of Egypt and Ethiopia') from work done in 1844. However, Lepsius, though depicting the Egyptian and Nubian figures correctly in black as the panel depicts them, has colored the Libyan and the Asiatic as light-skinned Caucasoids (Refer to page 20 of this work). If one actually goes to the tomb of Rameses III (as the author has) and looks at the panel directly, the realization dawns that Lepsius has altered the color of these two figures because on the tomb mural, both the Libyan and the Asiatic are colored dark reddish-brown. Not even Cheikh Anta Diop, who was one the first to publish a photo of Lepsius's Panel of Races[84], realized the deception perpetrated by Lepsius. Eleven centuries before Christ, neither the Libyans nor the Western Asiatics could have been Caucasians in the present sense of the term, though one wouldn't know that by looking only at the Lepsius reproduction of the tomb-based Panel.

Despite his outstanding accomplishments, especially as the defender of Egyptian national sovereignty, his reign was marred by internal disturbances. Rameses apparently lost confidence in his vizier Athribis who was dismissed as the king was obliged to personally supervise the distribution of rations to the temples. The problem would re-surface toward the end of his reign of 33 years when economic stringency meant that wages to the royal workers at Deir el-Medina lapsed for two months, provoking the first known labor strike in history. The royal artisans laid down their tools and refused to work. This event is all the more remarkable because uprisings from the lower echelons of society against pharaoh and established government had been all but non-existent throughout Egyptian history up to that time. Pharaonic regimes and dynasties came and went, sometimes amid conflict and violence, but never, till the very end of Egyptian history, was the pharaonic institution itself ever called into question or threatened. Having said that, Grimal is of the opinion that the royal treasury during the reign of Rameses III found itself in severe financial straits because so much of the national wealth and property had been concentrated in the hands of the Amonian priesthood.

84 Diop CA, **L'Antiquité Africaine Par L'Image,** Dakar: Institut Fondamental d'Afrique Noire, 1976, p. 33.

But it was a palace conspiracy late in the reign that more directly threatened the legacy of Rameses III and his regime. From time to time, secondary wives and concubines of the pharaohs had attempted to interfere with the order of succession in favor of their own sons, and it appeared to have occurred again toward the end of Rameses III's reign. Grimal thinks that Rameses was not married to a Great Royal Wife while on the throne which seems highly unlikely. Descent from Ahmose-Nefertari, the Great Royal Wife who was the founding ancestress of the 18th Dynasty and the New Kingdom, even in a collateral line, was the *sine qua non* for a Great Royal Wife, and no pharaoh could claim legitimacy unless married to her. It might have been that the Great Royal Wife was no longer living at the end of his reign which may have opened the succession up to intrigue and conspiracy. The plot was hatched by Rameses's second wife, *Tiye*, who was determined to secure the throne for her son *Pentaweret*. Tiye was able to enlist the support of several of her co-wives, one of whom even sent a message to her son in Cush, commander of Egypt's troops there, to return home to aid in the coup attempt. Another of Rameses's generals was also implicated. The plan was to launch the coup during the annual festival at Medinet Habu with the aid of sorcery and magical figurines. However, the usurpation ended in complete failure. In all, 28 conspirators were hauled before a tribunal of 12 selected civil and military officials and found guilty. Seventeen of them were executed forthwith and the would-be pharaoh, Pentaweret, was forced to commit suicide. It turned out to be a very convoluted matter, however, because five of the judges were themselves implicated in collusion with the women involved; one's guilt was so pronounced that he too was obliged to commit suicide, three others had their faces mutilated, and but one was let go with a reprimand. Most of this affair, including all of the court proceedings, took place right at, and shortly after, the death of Rameses III because the court documents show that Rameses IV was on the throne during the arrest and trial of the conspirators.

Recent evidence seems to strongly suggest that, though the usurpation itself failed, Rameses III was in fact murdered. As reported in the **British Medical Journal** in 2011, his unwrapped mummy showed a deep gash in Rameses's throat and a CT scan confirmed that the cut extended all the way down to the cervical spine, a wound impossible to survive. It was the ignominious end to a reign whose early years had covered Rameses III in substantial glory, especially on the military front. Nonetheless, economic uncertainty, the labor strike, and the palace conspiracy as his life was nearing its end represented clear signs that, despite Rameses III's most valiant efforts, Egypt, though safe from foreign invasion for another five centuries, was in slow but inexorable decline.

Rameses IV (1,167 BC–1,161 BC)

Rameses IV was but 14 years old when he succeeded his father on the throne of Egypt. With the chronological uncertainties attending the history of Egypt, we cannot be sure, since he was apparently co-regent with Rameses III for four years, whether the date of his accession is marked from the commencement of his co-regency or from his time as independent ruler. His tender age at accession reinforces the supposition that his reign is actually marked from the beginning of his co-regency. As indicated above, the trial of the would-be usurpers who would have deprived him of the throne took place soon after his accession. He was certainly a pious pharaoh, scrupulously endowing the temples. Pious or not, he was afflicted with the family tendency toward grandiosity and hubris. He petitioned Osiris to grant him a reign as long and glorious as that of Rameses II since he had shown his fidelity and generosity to him:

> Thou [Osiris] art he in whom is might, and that which thou doest is that which shall come to pass. Give me the reward of the great deeds which I have done for thee, even life, prosperity and health, long existence, and a [prolonged] reign…And thou shalt give to me every land and every country——that I may present their tribute to thy ka and to thy name.[85]

Rameses IV did his utmost to emulate Rameses II as a builder, making his presence felt at Abydos, Heliopolis, and of course, Karnak as well as numerous other temples in Upper Egypt. He sent a large expedition of more than 8,000 men to the stone quarries of Wadi Hammamat but the severity

85 Breasted JH, **Ancient Records of Egypt - Part 4**, London: Histories and Mysteries of Man Ltd., 1988, p. 22.

of the enterprise was such that 900 men died. His aims for this expedition, ultimately so costly in human lives, seem to have been (1) to pacify desert tribes harassing the region and (2) to build a road to facilitate the movement of caravans through it.[86] Despite his plea to Osiris, he died at age 21 patently unable to follow in the footsteps of Rameses II. Breasted had this to say concerning the precipitate decline of the Ramessid line and the pharaonic state from Rameses IV onward:

> The sources of that virile political life that had sprung up with the expulsion of the Hyksos were now exhausted. The vigorous grasp of affairs which had once enabled the Pharaoh to manipulate with ease the difficult problems of the dominant oriental (*sic*) state had now given way to an excessive devotion to religious works and superstitious belief in their effectiveness, which were rapidly absorbing every function of the state.[87]

Rameses V (1,161 BC–1,157 BC)

This Rameses succeeded his father to the throne but did not rule longer than four years. During his reign some minor building projects were undertaken in the Valley of the Kings—his mortuary temple—Heliopolis, and Buhen. One document, the Turin Papyrus 1887, describes financial embezzlements on the part of the priesthood situated at Elephantine (Aswan) an indicator of the manner in which, in the face of weakening government, corruption permeated the ranks of priestly officialdom.

Rameses VI (1,157 BC–1,149 BC)

The Ramessid epoch shows progressive decline and deterioration in Egypt's national fortunes. The sixth Rameses seems to have actually been one of the younger sons of Rameses III unlike his predecessors. Grimal insists that to the

86 **Budge**, op. cit., p. 187.

87 Breasted JH, **A History of Egypt**, op. cit., p. 506.

end of the Ramessid period, there was near open conflict between two lines of contending pharaonic heirs after the death of Rameses III.[88]

The royal decadence showed itself ever increasingly in the shrinking empire; Rameses VI was the last pharaoh able to erect any monument to himself in Sinai. Into the widening power vacuum, the chief priests of Amon asserted themselves ever more forcibly. The overweening power of the priests of Amon has already been commented on, slowly increasing from the beginning of the New Kingdom. Pharaohs from the time of Amenhotep III onward took steps to counteract this burgeoning usurpation of pharaonic prerogatives by the priests, most radically during the reign of Akhenaton with the Atonian 'heresy'. But with the accession of a line of weak rulers after Rameses III, exacerbated by Egypt's inability to maintain its empire, the locus of national political power shifted more and more to the Amonian priesthood. The daughter of Rameses the VI, Ast (Isis), was the female 'pope' of Amon as the Divine Wife of Amon, whose pedigree went back to the fabled Ahmose-Nefertari 450 years earlier. The peculiar circumstances of the time found her married to the Chief Priest of Amon, probably Amenhotep at the time, when rightfully, as the Chief Royal Wife-presumptive, she should have been the wife of the reigning pharaoh.[89] This marriage to Amenhotep, the Chief Priest, would, in succeeding years, bolster the claims of his heirs to full kingship given the time-honored custom of marriage to the Great Royal wife as a pre-requisite for sitting on the throne.

An oasis in this dreary litany of the decline of a great nation comes from the inscriptions attributed to Penno, who is called 'the deputy of *Wawat*' a gold-producing district in Nubia.[90] He also seems to have carried the more conventional and prestigious title, 'Royal Son of Cush'. Here was a peaceful and prosperous outpost, seemingly oblivious to the turmoil wracking the central government. It was clear that by this time that many Egyptians were migrating south to Nubia, establishing themselves there permanently.[91] This steady Egyptian migration into Nubia and even further south into the heartland of

88 Grimal, op. cit., p. 288. This contending for the Ramessid throne seems to have been carried out by a line of sons of Rameses III on the one hand and their nephews on the other.

89 Petrie Flinders WM, **A History of Egypt**, Vol. 3, London: Methuen & Co., 1896, pp. 174-5.

90 See Breasted, **Ancient Records of Egypt – Part 4** (*Tomb of Penno*), op. cit., pp. 231—35.

91 Breasted, **A History of Egypt**, op. cit., p. 508.

Napatan Cush would continue well into the 26th Dynasty and may account for the shift of dominance of the Temple of Amon from Egypt to Cush by the onset of the 25th Dynasty. By Ramessid times, Nubio-Cush had become a more stable, more prosperous land than Egypt itself.

Rameses VII (1,149 BC–1,141 BC)

The seventh Rameses was a ruler of no consequence whatever, the only thing of note happening during his reign is a noticeable rise in prices. He is said to have reigned eight years but it might not have been nearly that long. Petrie thinks the reign lasted only one year.

Rameses VIII (1,141 BC–1,138 BC)

This Rameses was one of the very last sons of Rameses III and died on the throne after a three-year reign. Petrie puts this reign at one year also.

Rameses IX (1,138 BC–1,120 BC)

Less than 30 years separate the death of Rameses III from the accession of Rameses IX, making him the sixth king in less than a generation to ascend to the throne of Egypt. With this Rameses, a modicum of royal vigor returned to Egypt and his reign lasted 18 years. Like earlier Ramessids, he undertook to build and refurbish Heliopolis (Annu), the sacred city of Rā, again, part of the ongoing attempt to establish a counter-balance to the Amonian priesthood in Thebes. Even so, he was careful to pay due homage to Amon, decorating the north wall of Karnak near the seventh pylon. The chief priest of Amon at this time was one *Ramesesnakht* ('strength of Rameses') who was able to assign all the powerful subordinate posts in the Temple of Amon to his sons, an example of the way in which power was being consolidated among priestly families of Amon that would eventually jeopardize the power of pharaoh outright. In fact, his son Amonhotep would succeed him as Chief Priest, and though it was not unheard of for son to succeed father in this office, it was clear that this particular priestly family was bent on creating a dynasty of high priests parallel, it could be said, to the pharaonic line.

But the worse incident in his reign was a series of thefts involving the royal tombs in the Valley of the Kings. Such a thing was not merely a heinous criminal act in the eyes of the Egyptians but wanton sacrilege. Making it worse was the realization that the perpetrators were workers and officials from nearby temples. In the end, 17 of the gang were rounded up and brought to trial of which a transcript remains. Most of these, when convicted, suffered death by impaling. It was yet another indicator, among many, of the steady, irreversible decline of societal discipline and religious piety. From then on tomb robbing became the bane of Egyptian authorities and in order to protect royal mummies, many of them were removed from their place of burial into more secure quarters. These moves must have served the purpose because in the 19th century more than 300 mummies of kings, queens, high nobles, and royal officials were found at four different re-burial sites.

Rameses X (1,120 BC–1,111 BC)

This ruler was another of the ephemeral Ramessid kings; it is not known whether he ruled for three or nine years. Grimal has this to say about the fallen state of the pharaonic empire about this time, even in Nubia:

> He [Rameses X] is the last Egyptian king whose rule over Nubia is attested, at least at Aniba. Nubia was then the only territory outside Egypt which was still subject to Egyptian domination; Egypt's influence in Syria-Palestine had been negligible for some time.[92]

Rameses XI (1,111 BC–1,082 BC)

Rameses XI ruled the longest of any of the Ramessid successors to Rameses III—29 years. Despite its comparative longevity, the reign was one continual litany

92 Ibid., p. 291.

of royal failure. Tomb robberies began again in earnest, insecurity prevailed throughout the land, and famine gripped Upper Egypt. By now, most of the actual governance, including providing police security for the populace, fell to the Chief Priests of Amon. The fiction of pharaonic supremacy was observed less and less, with the contemporary Chief Priest Amenhotep depicting himself at Karnak on the same scale as the pharaoh, something that had never been done in the previous 3,000 years in Egypt. This Amenhotep had managed to gain control of the royal treasury and, more critically, the collection of taxes with which to fill the royal treasury. Like the Catholic Pope of a later age, Amenhotep maintained his own troop of soldiers. It cannot be emphasized too often how radical a departure these developments were from the custom and practice in Egypt for 30 centuries and how devastating they were to the power, prestige, and authority of the pharaonic kingship. However in this instance, the naked usurpation of royal prerogative proved premature; Amenhotep, the priestly offender, was summarily arrested and sent into exile.[93] Civil unrest broke out very shortly thereafter though it isn't clear that the two events were connected. The Royal Son of Cush, the Viceroy of Cush and himself a Nubian by name of Panehsy, had to intervene to restore order—foreshadowing the events leading to the advent of the 25th Dynasty—entering Thebes and taking his troops as far north as Hardaj.

By now, the accession of the Chief Priest at Karnak had become an event as momentous as crowning of a new pharaoh. Succeeding the disgraced Amenhotep was a Chief Priest Ramesesnakht, the second one by that name. He does not seem to have held the position long because a stronger, more dynamic Chief Priest ascended to the office by name of *Herihor.* Though previously the duty and prerogative of pharaoh, Herihor himself now commissioned new construction at Karnak at the Temple of Khonsu, a moon deity and the son of Amon. Herihor was secure and powerful enough to assume certain quasi-royal titles and though he refrained at first from stepping in fully as pharaoh, the plain fact was that he was the true ruler of at least Upper Egypt. He even had himself styled 'commander-in-chief of the armies of the South and North', another tradition-shattering precedent never before encountered in the whole history of

93 Grimal, op. cit., p. 291.

Egypt. In fact, a kind of triumvirate appeared to rule the country: Rameses XI, who died in 1069 BC, his Chief Vizir *Nes-su-ba-neb-tet* ('his soul belongs to the lord of the tet' [Osiris]) or Smendes (Gr.), who ruled the northern part of the country (Lower Egypt) from the royal seat of the Ramessids at Pi-ramesse, and Herihor in Thebes. More than any Amonian Chief Priest before him, Herihor turned himself into both pope and potentate, creating a theocracy in which Upper Egypt was ruled by the Amonian priesthood of which he was the Supreme Pontiff. One consequence of this state of affairs is that, after 500 years as an integral part of Egyptian national territory, Nubio-Cush established its independence from Egypt and would largely remain independent until the conquest of the northern Sudan by Muhammad Ali in 1820. Corporate Egypt assumed the boundaries that defined its territory between the Mediterranean and Aswan (1st Cataract).

This poorly defined and historically unprecedented triumvirate did not survive the demise of Rameses XI, Egypt reverting to a political condition not seen since late pre-dynastic times where the country was divided into two kingdoms—Upper and Lower Egypt—each ruled from different capitals. In the north, Smendes, possibly a descendant of Rameses II, founded a new dynasty, abandoning Pi-Ramesse and moving the new dynastic capital to Tanis. The Amonian priesthood, headed by their Pontiff, ruled Upper Egypt from Karnak.[94] The Amonian priesthood had triumphed over pharaonic power by usurping it but with grave long-term consequences for the future sovereignty of Egypt. The cost to the vitality of the state of an excessive intrusion of religious affairs and functionaries into government operations is highlighted by Breasted:

> ...the state was rapidly moving toward a condition in which its chief function should be religious and sacerdotal, and the assumption of royal power by the High Priest of Amon but a very natural and easy transition.[95]

94 Though Nubio-Cush had achieved *de facto* independence by this time, Herihor still called himself 'Viceroy of Cush'. This independence was probably not challenged as long as gold continued to flow north from Nubian mines.

95 Breasted, op. cit., p. 507.

Rameses XII (1,082 BC–1,055 BC)

The last of the Ramessid pharaohs, Rameses XII, could not have been more than a figurehead since, by this time, Egypt was once again divided into two kingdoms, ruled on the one hand by a dynasty created by *Smendes* in the north at Tanis and on the other hand by the Amonian Chief Priest *cum* Pharaoh Herihor in the south at Thebes, e.g., at Karnak. The complete deterioration of Egyptian influence abroad is indicated by the misadventures of the envoy *Wenamon* sent to the Phoenician city-state of Byblos to obtain the cedar necessary to construct the bark of Amon. The report is filled with a succession of disasters and near-disasters for Wenamon who was treated with sovereign contempt by nearly every petty princeling he encountered, not the least of which was the Phoenician prince Zakar-Baal to whom this embassy was sent. When Wenamon, after much delay, finally obtains an interview with Zakar-Baal, it is baldly pointed out to him out how far Egypt has fallen since the days of the 19th Dynasty. Wenamon, therefore, possessed no real leverage in these negotiations especially since the gold and silver specie that was to pay for the cedar had been taken from him by one the vassals of Zakar-Baal, the Chief of Dor of the Thekel people. Though Wenamon is able to recoup much of this theft by confiscating silver from other Thekel he encountered, he still lacks the customary amount of remuneration expected of such an embassy to Phoenicia. In the end, Zakar-Baal relents and after many months, the cedar is ready for export. It is not the end of Wenamon's difficulties, however, since he must escape a Thekel fleet sent after him to recover the previously confiscated silver bullion, only to fall victim to contrary winds that blow his vessels to Cyprus. He barely escapes assassination in Cyprus but somehow manages to find his way home to tell this harrowing tale. Such treatment of Egyptian envoys of even 100 years earlier would have been unthinkable, but now no one fears Egyptian military might any longer and Egypt's vassals in Western Asia have gone their independent way.[96] In the event, with the demise of Rameses XII, the 20th Dynasty, and therefore the New Kingdom, comes to an inglorious close.

96 See Breasted, **Ancient Records of Egypt – Part 4** (*Report of Wenamon*), op. cit./, pp. 274-91 for a transcript of Wenamon's report.

It should be noted that there is confusion among historians of Egypt concerning which events befalling the Ramessids happened in which reign. For example, most of the events attributed to the reign of Rameses XI by Grimal are assigned to that of Rameses XII by Breasted and Budge and for Budge, it is this Rameses who reigned for 27 years instead of Rameses XI. The present author has chosen to follow the lead of Grimal on most of these matters whose information may be more recent and conceivably more accurate. Nonetheless, it seems evident that certain occurrences attributed to the reign of Rameses XII by the older authors can be accepted while keeping in mind the discrepancies present in the various histories written in the 20th century.

The World of the New Kingdom

The New Kingdom era of more than 500 years must be considered the most remarkable and complex era of all ancient Egyptian history. Though the pharaohs of the 18th Dynasty consciously sought to re-create the ethos and grandeur of the Middle Kingdom, the course of Egyptian cultural and political evolution as the New Kingdom history progressed, while evoking its own grandeur, could hardly have been more different from that of the Middle Kingdom. It represented the apotheosis of Egyptian cultural and political supremacy on the one hand but, on the other, the engine of Egypt's permanent decline. Thus the New Kingdom must be considered the watershed of Egyptian history.

A pattern emerged that foreshadowed the fate of all subsequent empires: the will to conquer that would increase the size of Egypt's national territory by nearly three-fold, makes it the supreme power in Africa and the eastern Mediterranean, and brings unimaginable wealth into its coffers, ultimately waned and weakened, leaving in its wake a devitalized government and body politic finally leading to the break-up of Egypt into two independent kingdoms, a circumstance not seen since pre-dynastic times 3,000 years earlier. In the pantheon of neters, though Amon had achieved ascendancy after 2300 BC with the steady, inexorable rise of Thebes and blossoming of the Middle Kingdom, in the New Kingdom, the conquering impetus of the 18th and 19th Dynasty pharaohs brought wealth into the Temple Amon on a scale never before imagined. Sacerdotal power for the entire country became increasingly concentrated in the hands of the priesthood of Amon but more ominously, that priesthood's political power, enabled by the vast wealth accruing to it, steadily grew apace, eclipsing that of pharaoh by the end of the 20th Dynasty thereby impelling the termination of the New Kingdom. Throughout the New Kingdom, the Chief Priest of Amon was the country's 'Pope', eventually taking power as pharaoh as well, totally without historical precedent in Egypt, with one incongruous exception in Old Kingdom.

The imperial enterprise of the New Kingdom not only brought fabulous wealth into Egypt but also the mass introduction of non-African foreigners and foreign ways. Many of these were war captives from the country's Asiatic wars who were brought into Egypt as laborers, artisans, and military conscripts, but a large number of merchants and traderss also found their way into the country, often settling permanently. These foreigners tended to concentrate in Lower Egypt, especially in the nomes and cities of the Delta. They brought their strange dress and personal adornment along with their even stranger tongues. They also carried their gods into Egypt without any noticeable opposition from the Egyptians who themselves recognized and propitiated some 2,000 deities. In fact, some of the more important of the foreign divine importations eased their way into the Egyptian pantheon whose worship was often fused with a local deity. For the first time, significant numbers of foreign words were incorporated into the Egyptian language and among the upper classes, there developed a taste for luxury items, wearing apparel, ceramics, jewelry, and even hair styles from these lands which had an exotic flavor to Egyptians of the aristocracy. Slavery became established in Egypt on a scale larger than ever before. There is scant evidence of slavery prior to the Middle Kingdom but by New Kingdom times, the use of slave labor, especially in the mines and on the large plantations of selected officials, became fairly well entrenched. Egypt never developed or depended on slavery to the extent of the later Romans, but the imperial wars brought into the country thousands of captives who could be employed in various revenue-producing enterprises. There does not seem to have been much reliance on an established slave trade *per se*.

The scale and scope of building in the New Kingdom dwarfed every other era in Egyptian history. No king, even during the decadent period of the later

Ramessids, failed to build on some scale. During the acme of the New Kingdom, the 18th and 19th Dynasties, Egypt and Nubia were fairly covered with temples and monuments. A king's posterior reputation rested as much on his exploits as a builder as it did his military victories, perhaps even more so. Apart from the pyramids, the most magnificent and enduring edifices in all Egypt were constructed during the New Kingdom and there is no place on earth where monumental building was carried out on such a scale over such an extended period of time. Egyptian monuments fairly dwarf the architectural constructions of other lands in size, extent, and number, especially when one considers that they are nearly all built with stone—limestone, sandstone, and granite. The two places that invite comparison are the Meso-American pyramids and the Great Wall of China. But the Mexican pyramids, while magnificent, simply do not match the sheer number and mass of stone building constructed in Egypt over a period of 4,000 years. The Great Wall of China, one of the Wonders of the World with nearly 4,000 miles of construction, is only partly built of stone.

The temple complex at Karnak, dedicated to Amon-Rā with smaller satellite temples dedicated to Mentu, Mut, and Khonsu, along with 10 pylons, chapels, and a large man-made lake fed by the Nile in ancient times, is the largest temple complex in the world. Its construction started in 1700 BC and continued with additions and supplementations into the Roman period. Thirty pharaohs contributed to the expansion and development of Karnak, including every pharaoh in the New Kingdom. The Hypostyle Hall contains 134 columns, 122 of which are 38 feet tall and 12 of which—forming the central corridor—are nearly 69 feet tall with diameters of nearly 10 feet. It has been estimated that at its height, 10,000 priests, scribes, and functionaries (some estimate 80,000) worked at Karnak. As has been already mentioned, it was Egypt's Vatican and, after the New Kingdom, the administrative center for Upper Egypt for 130 years.

Other monumental masterpieces from the New Kingdom abound throughout Upper Egypt and Nubia. Hatshepsut's terraced temple at Deir el-Bahari—cut out of living rock without a single free-standing column or pillar—is perhaps the most unique structure of its kind in the world. Amenhotep III's Temple of Luxor, linked in ancient times to Karnak by an avenue of criosphinxes, is much smaller than Karnak in scope but possessing undeniable grandeur in any case. Rameses II's Nubian temple at Abu Simbel is fronted by four massive statues of Rameses himself attached to the face of the cliff and each of greater size than the famous presidential busts at Mount Rushmore. The temple dedicated to Osiris at Abydos by Seti I exhibits some of the finest mural art not only in Egypt but the world. There are whole temples that were covered over by the sands of time that have yet to be discovered. There are numerous areas where a modern visitor can walk without realizing that he is walking over a temple, tomb, a village, or a city. There never was a monumental civilization to equal Egypt, especially during the New Kingdom; whole careers have been dedicated to studying but one of these temples.[97]

Nubio-Cush was wholly incorporated into Egypt from the beginning of the New Kingdom; under Thutmosis III, Egypt's southern territories stretched southward to the 4th Cataract, encompassing the Cushitic capital at Napata. It bears repeating—since conventional historians have so studiously ignored or denied the fact—that dynastic Egypt was a civilization that unfolded from south to north; Cushite informants told Diodorus in the 1st Century BC that Egypt was a colony of Cush. Nubia comprised the northern quarter of Cush and the relation of Nubio-Cush to Egypt remained of capital importance down to the end of Egyptian history. The cultural, religious, ethnic, and historical ties were such as to make Kemit and Cush one great geo-cultural complex, entirely analogous to that of Austria and Germany or Scotland and England. The seemingly inexhaustible gold supply coming from Nubia—as well as the other African luxury items—explains much of this Egyptian pre-occupation with Nubia but does not tell the whole story. Major deities—including Amon himself and Hathor—were thought to have originated to the south of the 1st Cataract. The Viceroy of Cush, called 'the Royal Son of Cush', was one of the most prestigious jobs in the entire administration; it was so prestigious that the post was held by a number of the pharaonic sons. Herihor, the Chief Priest of Amon at the end of the 20th Dynasty, took as one of his titles the Royal Son of Cush. However this may have been, Nubio-Cush became thoroughly Egyptianized during the New Kingdom and the vast extent of temple-building in Egypt was matched by that in Nubia, especially by Rameses II. His most striking temple of the scores he erected is undoubtedly the one at Abu Simbel,

97 See Schwaller de Lubicz, RA, **Temple of Man**, translated by Deborah and Robert Lawlor, Rochester: Inner Traditions, 1957/1998.

one of 10 major temples he had constructed in Nubia. As the New Kingdom wore on, Nubio-Cush became a calmer, more stable, and more prosperous region than the rest of Egypt, attracting ever greater numbers of Egyptian immigrants from all walks of life. After the end of the 20th Dynasty, Napata, the capital of Cush, became progressively a more important center of Amon-worship than Thebes.

We have already remarked that despite the New Kingdom's spectacular success as an empire, it was, at crucial times, fraught with profound internal turmoil. The epic struggle between the woman-pharaoh Hatshepsut and her redoubtable nephew Thutmosis III reverberated for decades after the end of Hatshepsut's reign. But nothing rattled the status quo and the existing order like the 'Amarna Heresy' under Akhenaton who attempted at a single stroke to undo 3,000 years of religious tradition by introducing and vigorously promulgating the worship of a single, exclusive deity for the first time in history. This attempted reformation was motivated by two factors: (1) a messianic religious ardor for his monotheistic god of choice—Aton—and (2) an equally messianic determination to free Egypt and the crown from the grip of Amon as fostered by an overly-powerful priesthood. The efforts of an unshakably determined Akhenaton shook the priesthood of Amon to its foundations and when at last Akhenaton died—probably not of natural causes—no effort was spared to erase his name and works from history. He was never called by name ever after; when it was necessary to refer to him at all it was by the epithet 'the criminal'. His enemies thought they had rid the world of him forever, not realizing that seeds were planted during his attempted reformation that would sprout unexpectedly in the emergence 100 years later of a new people and a new religion whose deity was also one and exclusive—Yahweh. And it was an apostate priest of Rā—no doubt posthumously influenced by Akhenaton—who led these people, who became known as the Children of Israel, out of Egypt and bestowed upon them their god Yahweh, himself an offshoot of the Egyptian moon deity Yah. It would, in time, change the course of history in a way no priestly partisan of Amon could ever have anticipated. But in the short term, Amon's priesthood triumphed, eventually ascending to the throne of the pharaohs for the first time in the 3,000-year history of Egypt. After that, Egypt could never be the same.

The Abode of Truth: Artisans of the Sacred[98]

It is instructive as a coda to this chapter on the New Kingdom to do a short study of the workmen's village at Deir El-Medina that sheds light on the manner in which sacred craftsmanship informed the entire history of the New Kingdom. The subject is given fact-based fictional treatment in the **Stone of Light** series (2000), a set of historical novels by the French Egyptologist and writer Christian Jacq that nevertheless sheds instructive light on this unique settlement. This workmen's village—whose resident artists and artisans were dedicated exclusively to the construction and decoration of the tombs and mortuary temples of the pharaohs—is traceable back to the 11th Dynasy (c. 2,300 BC), though it was not established formally until the reign of Thutmosis I (c. 1,540 BC), eventually taking the name *Set-Maāt*, 'the Abode of Truth'. From the time of its formal inception, it was an isolated, relatively self-contained community that, at its height, was comprised largely of 120 workmen and their families, abutting the western cliffs at the bottom of a valley within easy access of the Valley of Kings on the one hand and the Valley of the Queens on the other. A 20th Dynasty census records that 1,200 persons actually lived in the village and shows that smaller groups of Nubians, Libyans, and Syrians lived side-by-side with the numerically dominant Egyptians, all, however, involved one way or another in the life and function of the community. Because of several thousand inscribed artifacts found there, more is known about the life and function of the community than almost anywhere else in Egypt, traceable over a period of more than 300 years. Predictably, there is no record of activity during the reign of Akhenaton but Set-Maāt resumed its function under Horemheb at the close of the 18th Dynasty, enlarged and arranged according to a more definite urban plan. The peak of its activity was in the 19th and 20th Dynasties, especially during the early Ramessid period. However, Set-Maāt was buffeted by the same contrary economic and political winds blowing through the rest of the country at the end of the 19th Dynasty, then again after the death of Rameses III when corruption interrupted wages and supplies to the community, leading to the first labor strike in Egyptian

98 This discussion is largely drawn from Nicholas Grimal's treatment of the subject in his **History of Ancient Egypt**, pp. 277-87.

history. Set-Maāt declined as Egypt declined over the course of the later 20th Dynasty. However, evidence of habitation and work at the site was still evident as late as the 25th Dynasty (c. 700 BC). It declined again in 26th Dynasty but then revived sufficiently for its work to continue down to the end of the Ptolemaic era (30 BC).

Because of the sacred character of the work of these royally-subscribed artisans, their village was a walled enclosure, forbidden to all but those who worked there, brought in supplies, or guarded it. The New Kingdom pharaohs went to great expense to create extravagant tombs for themselves and therefore the artisans and artists employed at Set-Maāt were the finest in Egypt. Their near-total isolation was dictated by the pharaonic obsession for secrecy concerning the location and contents of their tombs. When large-scale tomb robbing began to occur with ever-greater frequency in the 20th Dynasty, it is a singular fact that not a single one of the artisans of Set-Maāt was ever implicated in the grave-robbing during the huge scandal and trial during the reign of Rameses IX. Even this evidence of the integrity of the inhabitants had degenerated by the time the priest-kings ascended to the throne of the pharaohs at the beginning of the 21st Dynasty. But during the best years of Set-Maāt, these artisans were not just high-grade craftsmen and impeccable artists, they were priests of a kind—initiates in effect—selected for their matchless talent and imbued with sacred knowledge, often taking years to ascend to the master's level. In this they were the forerunners of the medieval masons' guilds of Europe who created the Gothic cathedrals and, beyond them, the so-called 'occult masonry' of the modern Freemasons. Their work was intended to last, if not for eternity, then far into the indefinite future. One only has to tour the tombs in the Valley of the Kings to witness the degree of success achieved toward this end. The vibrant colors of the funerary scenes have hardly faded after more than 30 centuries. Here, as everywhere else in Egypt, there existed no *l'art pour l'art* ('art for art's sake'); art functioned as an essential vehicle for the ineffable communion between the human soul and the Divine. The Valley of Kings and Queens, though commissioned by the pharaohs, is entirely the work of these sacred craftsmen.

The schematic organization of the village was modeled originally on that of a boat—perhaps an implied reference to the solar bark—divided along its north-south axis, creating a 'starboard' (right) sector and a' port' (left) sector, each with its specific team that worked in alternating shifts. There were two gates of entry and exit, a southern gate and a northern gate, both locked and guarded at night. When the village was enlarged, the southern gate was closed off and a new sector with its own gate was built to the west, possibly a reference to the mortuary function of the village since the west was always the direction of the land of the dead. With this western addition, streets were built east-to-west to provide access to the new sector.

The houses all opened to covered-over alley-ways and were single storeys with a roof terrace. Each house was, from the ground up, built of undressed stone to nearly 5 feet in height with the remainder of the house walls constructed of mud-baked brick. The exterior of the houses were all white-washed and the front doors painted red with the names of the occupants of the house inscribed on each door. The roofs were of sun-dried mud held in place by a wooden framework, mud being the best medium for maintaining a cool interior during the heat of the day. There were two fore-rooms, a foyer, and a larger reception whose ceiling was set higher than the other rooms in the house letting in sunlight through clerestory windows, a feature seen on a much grander scale in the Hypostyle Hall at Karnak. Clerestory windows serve the function of letting in air and indirect sunlight. From the reception room, a stairwell descended into the basement which, among other things, was used for storage. The private living rooms of the house were situated behind the reception room and beyond them was the kitchen which also had a stairwell providing access to its own cellar. The roof-top terrace was accessed from the kitchen and the family customarily repaired to the terrace in the evening for the cooling northern breezes that always spring up in Egypt when the sun goes down.

There was no water to be had anywhere in the vicinity of the Set-Maāt. Consequently, a steady caravan of donkeys carried in jars of water from springs near the Ramesseum and Medinet Habu during the day. The transport of such supplies was always conducted under the watchful eyes of the Medjay, the Nubians who had served Egypt as policemen and soldiers for 3,000 years. The guardian divinity of the community was the cobra goddess *Meretseger* ('lover of silence') but Hathor was evidently the most revered deity in the Abode of

Truth, judging from the size and prominence of her temple. Chapels for eight other deities[99] were also present there; services and worship ceremonies to them were carried out in rotation.

Guardian Cobra Divinity Meretseger

As Nicholas Grimal has said, Set Maāt functioned as a microcosm of Egyptian society. Each team of workmen consisted of 60 men, commanded by a master architect, living and working for 10 days in rotation at the mortuary sites under construction. The teams each consisted of draughtsmen, painters, wood-carvers, sculptors, stucco-workers, plasterers, masons, quarriers, miners, and their apprentices. An official scribe served as liaison to the government and ombudsman keeping a daily log of the work accomplished, materials used, wages paid, absenteeism, and workplace incidents or accidents. The water supplied by the donkey caravans has already been noted but all foods and other living materials also had to be brought in daily. As always in Egypt, wages were paid in-kind; the interruption of the supply of these tangible and essential goods and services provoked, as has been mentioned, a strike at Set-Maāt at the end of the reign of Rameses III which had to be rectified quickly so that the work could continue. As among the priestly castes of the New Kingdom, the occupations at Set-Maāt became hereditary having the effect of creating *de facto* dynasties among the workmen and their descendants. The Abode of Truth was insular and inward-looking by its very nature but the community

99 These were Amon, Mut, Min, Ptah, Sebek, Heru-em-khuti, Ta-Urt, and Renenut.

experienced its share of tensions characteristic of a small, closed-off society with clear evidence of thievery, adultery, crimes of revenge, and even a case of murder. Nonetheless, there is no gainsaying the entrenched role of Set-Maāt in the all-important rites and ceremonies surrounding pharaonic death during the entire span of the New Kingdom. Its work seems to have continued on and off in Egypt down to the time of the Caesars.

Chapter 8:

The Era of Priests and Libyans—The Decline Continues (1090–750 BC)

> It will be noted that Egypt's fall…was not really due to foreign invasion but to internal collapse.
> —Walter Fairservis, **The Ancient Kingdoms of the Nile**

It is hard to know how to characterize this era; many contemporary Egyptologists want to call it the '3rd Intermediate Period'. Considering that the category 'Intermediate Period' is a wholly artificial one to begin with where the history of Egypt is concerned, it hardly seems a satisfactory or edifying label. The period fails to bear comparison to the previous eras called 'Intermediate' for the following reasons:

- There is no real information black-out as was true for the 1st and 2nd Intermediate Periods, i.e., no real 'chronological gap';
- There is no correspondence to the Inter-Age Transitions that characterized the two earlier Intermediate Periods.

Having said all that, the era is one of blinding confusion to the modern historian trying to sort out who ruled what, when, and for how long. More than any other period since the Hyksos era much of the chronology is guesswork, undoubtedly the reason for considering it an 'Intermediate Period'.

Egyptological dates for the beginning of the Dynasty, accession dates, and lengths of reign vary considerably depending on which author is being read. But there are names of rulers that have come down attached to each reign as well as specific events within the reigns that can be attested. A period of turmoil and confusion it was, but it stops short of being the kind of chronological gap that would qualify it for inclusion as an Intermediate Period which, as has already been noted repeatedly, is a scholarly artifice in any case. The author mostly follows Petrie's scheme of chronology and kingly succession if for no other reason than it is the clearest one to follow compared to those of other Egyptologists.

I. The 21st Dynasty—Thebes

With this Dynasty, there are two lines of kings because the country has split in two, one whose capital is situated at Tanis in the Delta and the other at the traditional seat in Upper Egypt at Thebes. At Thebes, it is the era of Egyptian priest-kings where the *de facto* rule of the Chief Priests of Amon evident at the end of the 20th Dynasty becomes institutionalized by their installation on the throne.

Herihor, 'Face of Horus' (1,090 BC–1,074 BC)

We have already seen that Herihor was the Chief Priest of Amon before the final collapse of the 20th Dynasty and already in charge of the reins of government—the treasury, tax collection, and the military, the latter commanded by his son Pianki. Rameses XII was purely a titular pharaoh and when he died, the way to Herihor's accession to the throne was open and unobstructed. Herihor himself appears to have been a scion of the royal family, a grandson of Rameses IV, which he undoubtedly used to justify his assumption of royal power both in name and actuality:

> [Herihor]...would be of royal descent and thus have a legitimate right to the titles 'Heir over both lands, great companion

> in the whole land" and the "Hereditary prince" which he uses during the reign of Rameses XII. After that he appears as enjoying full sovereign rights and titles as completely as any other king of Egypt.[1]

The evaporation of Egyptian power in Western Asia has already been discussed vis-à-vis the report of Wenamon detailing his misadventures in Lebanon and Cyprus as envoy sent to obtain cedar logs for building the solar bark.[2] He was sent on this mission by Herihor though it is not clear whether this humiliating episode occurred during the life of Rameses XII who was still nominally pharaoh or during Herihor's actual reign immediately following that of Rameses XII. In the event, neither of the two kings' rule or even influence—Smendes in the north or Herihor in the south—extended beyond Egypt's Mediterranean borders.

Breasted tells us that Herihor, both Chief Priest and Pharaoh, ruled through a series of divine oracles. That is to say, when a matter of state had to be implemented or a dispute resolved, it was always submitted to the Oracle of Amon for a final ruling. Egypt had indeed become a theocratic state, the presumption being that Amon ruled the country directly through his earthly 'vicar' Herihor, making his decrees known via the oracle. Priest and Pharaoh had merged as like no other time in Egyptian history.

Herihor was well into his sixth decade by the time he ascended the throne. His queen *Nezemt* seemed to have occupied a relatively equal position with him or, at least, was represented as such iconographically. There is no clear indication that she was descended from the line of Great Royal Wives originating with Ahmose-Nefertari though it would seem that some connection must have been present since Herihor would have needed all the elements of legitimate succession he could muster to achieve the precedent-breaking feat of moving from Chief Priest to Pharaoh. His immediate successor, Piankh, was his son by Nezemt, though he sired a total of 37 sons and daughters by collateral wives. As pharaoh, he ruled 16 years.

1 Petrie WF, **A History of Egypt: From the XIXth to the XXXth Dynasties**, London: Methuen & Co., 1905, p.196.

2 See [pp. 310-11] above

Piankh (1,074 BC)

Piankh during his official career served as the Royal Son of Cush and the 'Commander of the Archers' (probably the Medjay). Though he succeeded his father as High Priest, most authorities insist that he could not have ruled very long or independently. It is assumed, therefore, that for a brief span of time, the entire country was under the rule of Smendes at Tanis (about which more will be said). Piankh seems to have passed away very quickly after becoming Chief Priest and it is doubtful that he ever held pharaonic powers in the manner of his father Herihor.

Pinezem I 'Happiness' (1,074 BC–1,062 BC)

Pinezem was the son of Piankh by the Great Royal Wife *Hent-taui* ('repose of the two lands'), who was also the mother of his sister-wife since she is referred to as the Great Royal Wife, Mother of the Great Royal Wife. Hent-taui's parentage is of interest because her father was *Nebseny* who was not only a royal physician but the publisher of a version of the **Book of the Coming Forth by Day** that survives to the present day. Pinezem was 18 at the time of his accession, the reason usually given for the large role played by his mother Hent-taui early in his reign. Pinezem did not initially regain the royal prerogatives that Herihor had exercised but he did rule Upper Egypt from Thebes. Pinezem actually exhibited some of the old energy of the New Kingdom pharaohs, continuing the construction of Khonsu's temple at Karnak, restoring other dilapidated temples, and initiating the process of moving many of the royal mummies from their burial places to a tomb, that of Seti I, where they could be properly protected.

As Breasted observed, Pinezem revealed his political acumen by marrying *Maāt-ka-rā* ('the truth of the ka of Rā'), daughter of the pharaoh *Pesibkenno* I at Tanis. This marriage was a master-stroke of diplomacy for two reasons: (1) the new queen was a female descendant of the Ramessids and would have brought greater legitimacy to the aspiring priestly pharaoh at Thebes and (2) the marriage served the purpose of re-uniting the whole country under Pinezem's rule after the death of Maāt-ka-rā's father, Pesibkenno I. It also shows, as other indicators do, that despite the division of the country, the kings in the two capitals functioned more or less amicably in a kind of *entente cordiale* ('cordial agreement'). It could be speculated that the priest-kings of Thebes never felt secure enough to press their pharaonic claims too aggressively. Be that as it may, Pinezem appointed his first then his second son as High Priest of Amon at Thebes, the office clearly serving as the crucial stepping stone to the throne, but each of these sons died in his turn before Pinezem. His third son, *Menkheperrā* ('abiding firmly in Kheper-Rā'), not only became High Priest in the 25th year of Pinezem's reign but managed to live long enough to be crowned pharaoh. Pinezem reigned for 40 years though he did so from Tanis rather than Thebes, part of the on-going confusion for this dynasty about who ruled and where.

Men-Kheper-Rā 'Kheper-Rā abides' (1,062 BC–1,013 BC)

This pharaoh, succeeding to the throne from his position as High Priest of Amon, apparently had a reign longer even than that of his father, i.e., of 48/49 years. But the reign, like so many in this dynasty, is very clouded to the eyes of posterity. Men-Kheper-Rā was evidently the pharaoh in Thebes but his sister—possibly even sister-wife—whose name was *Astemkheb* ('Isis of the waters') also claimed royal honors on behalf of her father Pinezem in whose name she ruled posthumously. Eventually, however, the two rulerships were joined together more or less voluntarily. In spite of its length, there is not much to show for this reign. Oddly, Men-Kheper-Rā seemed to have ruled from somewhere other than Thebes since a long inscription describes his travels to that city to consult the oracle and stabilize the southern domains of the kingdom. It is assumed by some that if Men-Kheper-Rā was not ruling from Thebes then he must have been in Tanis, but like so much in the period, the matter is very obscure as is his relationship with Astemkheb. There is continued evidence of progressive decline and unrest; there was no more tribute coming in from foreign victories, nor was international trade promoted on a scale large enough to sustain the prosperity Egyptians had come to take for granted. The Temple of Amon, moreover, had siphoned off so much of the economic production of the land that the common people started to suffer as never before. Thus tomb robbery and general lawlessness increased to such an extent that tens of thousands of malcontents and trouble-makers were deported to the Great Oasis in the South. Eventually, however, the authorities saw fit to repatriate them back to Egypt, based on consultation with the Oracle of Amon. Otherwise the misguided policy was sure to have precipitated open revolt such as Egypt had never seen.

Pinezem II (1,013 BC–994 BC)

Another of the undistinguished pharaohs of this line whose rule lasted about 19 years. The inscriptions from this reign are noteworthy for the phenomenon noted earlier by which royal decrees were accomplished by oracle, in consultation with Amon.

Pasebkhanu (994 BC–940 BC)

He was the last in the line of Amonian priest-kings, confusing because there was also an older, earlier Pasebhkhanu at Tanis (see below). There is nearly nothing of interest to say about him apart from the fact that he held office for 54 years.

II. 21st Dynasty—Tanis

It has already been noted that in the 21st Dynasty, Egypt had once again become 'the Two Lands', creating much dynastic confusion. There seemed to be two lines of pharaohs, one at Tanis and the other at Thebes, but from time to time, the rule of the country was united under a single king, only to fall back into its divided state in succeeding reigns.

Nesi-ba-dadu or *Smendes* (1,105 BC–1,079 BC)

This king, known more familiarly as Smendes, was considered by Manetho the first king of the 21st Dynasty. It was he who established the pharaonic court at Tanis in the Delta, not far from Piramesse, at the close of the reign of Rameses XII and the advent of the succession of Herihor. Nesi-ba-dadu had governed the north as viceroy but when it became evident that the High Priest of Amon was intent on usurping pharaonic authority, Nesi-ba-dadu, having none of it, took matters and the entire northern part of the country into his own hands. Though the capital of this line of kings was established nominally at Tanis, Nesi-ba-dadu seemed to have governed primarily from Memphis, the ancient seat of Ptah. This appropriation of Memphis as a royal seat could support the kingly fiction that he was indeed pharaoh of all Egypt. Fiction or not, he had enough reach to send 3,000 men to Thebes to repair and reinforce the Temple of Amon at Karnak, experiencing increasing water damage from the Nile. It cannot be too oft stated that the situation in Egypt was in a state of flux; there were two governments, at opposite ends of the country, and their activities overlapped and perhaps worked at cross-purposes but without precipitating a civil war. Again, the Amonian Priest-Pharaohs, throughout the 21st Dynasty, were obliged to tread lightly given the precarious foundation of their rule. The kings at Tanis saw fit to tread equally lightly. Once again, none of it did anything to bolster Egypt's influence abroad. Nesu-ba-dadu's queen was *Thentamen* ('throne of Amen'), daughter of Rameses XII, which in itself conferred legitimacy on Nesu-ba-dadu's assumption of royal authority. Nesu-ba-dadu ruled for 26 years, though Budge gives him 29 years.

Pasebkhanu I 'Dweller in the planet Mercury or *Pausennes I* (1,079 BC–1,038 BC)

This son and successor of Nesu-ba-dadu is noted mainly for the temple and large wall he constructed at Tanis. The wall, built entirely of brick, was nearly 7/10ths of a mile long, 80 feet thick, and 30 feet high. It seems to have been a military fortification but since Tanis did not appear to be under military threat from north or south, the reason for its construction is unknown. In this period, it is possible to discern the development of a fledgling Canaanitic country called Israel, ruled by the early Judges. It is Pasebkhanu's daughter that marries Pinezem I leading, eventually, to a brief re-union of Egypt after Pasebkhanu's death following a reign of 41 years.

Amen-em-apt ('Amen in Apt') or *Amenemope* (1,038 BC–1,029 BC)

The tangled web of this dynasty has resisted all attempts of Egyptologists to arrive at a consistent picture that all can agree on. There is a royal non-entity, *Neferkheres* by name, to whom Manetho gives a reign of four years in between Pausennes and Amenemope. According to Breasted, this Amen-em-apt (Amenemope) became the true ruler of all Egypt, eclipsing Menkheperraā ruling from Thebes entirely while to Petrie, he was but another ephemeral Tanite king who left scant impression and, in any case, did not control the whole country. Also, the historians differ on which events occurred in which reign. The only thing that is agreed on is that there are few records to indicate what he may have accomplished if anything. He is said to have reigned 9 years according to Petrie.

Siamon 'Son of Amon' (1,029 BC–1,003 BC)

Siamon is noted for having once again transferred the mummies of deceased 19th Dynasty pharaohs out of the tomb of Seti I and into that of an obscure queen *Inhapi* because of the increasing breakdown in security in the royal necropolis in the Valley of the Kings. Siamon managed to build a temple of some magnificence at Tanis and to carve various inscriptions at Karnak, Heliopolis, and Memphis. At Memphis, a column erected by Siamon is notable for votive inscriptions to Astarte and Yah, indicative of the way in which northern deities had been insinuated into the pantheon. Siamon reigned for 26 years.

Pa-seb-khanu II or ***Pausennes II*** (988 BC–953 BC)

This king is the last one to rule at Tanis and the last of the entire 21st Dynasty, though there may have been an obscure ruler who sat on the throne for nine years prior to the accession of Pausennes II. Apart from his role as the last of the 21st Dynasty kings, Pap-seb-kanu's reign, in conjunction with that of his predecessor Siamon, is noteworthy to Biblical historians because the span of both reigns (1,010 BC–953 BC) encompasses all of the reign of David and most of the reign of Solomon in Israel (1003 BC–931 BC). In fact, it has been suggested that the emergence of the united kingdom of Israel under David was facilitated by the manifest political weakness of Egypt and the consequent evaporation of her hegemony in Canaan. Moreover, Budge cites an opinion vouchsafed by Wiedemann that it was a daughter of this king who was wedded to Solomon as mentioned in ***Kings***, chapter ix, verse 16.[3] Whatever the case, the rule of Egypt now passes, in the 22nd Dynasty, to the Libyans. Budge's epitaph for the Dynasty is as follows:

> Neither the Tanite kings nor the Theban priests did much for the country, and the little energy which both groups of rulers possessed seems to have been absorbed in repairing or beautifying the shrines of the gods whom they worshipped.[4]

III. The 22nd Dynasty—The Libyans, (953 BC to 751 BC)

Sheshonq I (953–931 BC)

By the end of the 21st Dynasty, certain chieftains of the Libyan Meshwesh had achieved ascendency by virtue of their prominence in the Egyptian army. Breasted makes the entirely valid point that in the latter half of the 21st Dynasty, 'from the west of the Delta was now the peaceful conquest of the Libyans, who accomplished by gradual immigration what they had failed to gain by hostile invasion'.[5] Though the Theban priest-kings of the 21st Dynasty had maintained

3 Cf. Budge, op. cit., Vol. VI, p. 10.
4 Ibid., p. 31.
5 Breasted, op. cit., p. 526.

a native militia in the south, the Tanite kings had turned increasingly to Libyans to fill the ranks of their armies, especially the Libyan Meshwesh. In Lower Egypt, therefore, the military garrisons increasingly came under the command of Libyans. The Libyans gradually extended their influence as far south as Heracleopolis, where a Tehennu Libyan by name of *Buyuwawa* had established himself so prominently early in the 21st Dynasty that one of his sons became a priest at the temple at Heraceleopolis and commander of the mercenary militia, both offices of which became hereditary. Most of what we know of the Libyan genealogy beginning with Buyawawa comes from a stele inscribed by *Heru-pa-sen*, probably a priest of Ptah (or Osiris), at the end of the dynasty.[6] Five

Sphinx of Sheshonq I

generations later, a descendant of Buyuwawa by name of Sheshonq had climbed to the rank of commander-in-chief under Pausennes II who was also his father-in-law. With the death of Pausennes II—and with marriage to his daughter *Karamat* who would become his queen—Sheshonq was the only figure powerful enough to assume rulership of the entire country and he became Sheshonq I, the first pharaoh of the Libyan Dynasty, the 22nd. It also worked to his advantage that Karamat had ties to Karnak—probably as a priestess—as is evidenced by one of her names which indicates that she was 'beloved of Mut'.

6 Budge, op. cit., Volume VI, pp. 62-3.

The Libyans had, for quite some time, been well ensconced at Bubastis, an ancient city that had existed since the beginning of the Old Kingdom in the Delta, and under Sheshonq I it became the capital of the new dynasty. Maintaining a policy established by the priest-kings of the 21st Dynasty at Thebes, he installed his son *Iuput* as Chief Priest of Amon, Commander-in-Chief, and paramount governor of Upper Egypt. This Iuput was evidentally a very able official and apart from his work renovating portions of Karnak, it was he who undertook to find a final resting place for the royal and priestly mummies of Dynasties 17 through 21 safe from the tomb-robbers whose depredations and descretions of the royal graves in search of treasure had been one of the most baneful and nefarious developments in Egypt of the 20th and 21st Dynasties. He found a suitably obscure tomb of a wife of one the high priests of Amon on the West Bank whereupon he had scores of mummies re-interred in it, filling the entrance with rock and rubble and sealing off the entire enclosure with a thick wall. It had the desired effect; the tomb with these royal mummies remained undiscovered until 1872.

A series of marriages of the daughters of Sheshonq, two important and powerful personages in the new regime, cemented the position of the new dynasty. Sheshonq reinforced this position further by installing yet another son, *Nimlot* (Nimrod), as military commander of Middle Egypt based at Heracleopolis, the established stronghold of his ancestors. Despite Sheshonq's strength and dynamism, his best efforts, in the end, would not be sufficient to re-organize the kingdom into the consummate empire it had once been. The Libyan chiefs, though supportive at the outset of the new dynasty, were always a potential source of power-seeking factionalism. Not only that, though Sheshonq ruled the entire country, the Theban ascendancy in Upper Egypt was not appreciably dimmed, and the high priests continued to exercise a certain amount of autonomy from their national stronghold at Karnak. With the benefit of hindsight, it becomes clear that the undivided national unity of Egypt was a thing of the past and there was no force strong enough—not even Sheshonq—to reverse that trend.

It is pertinent to consider again the people called the 'Libyans' because there were clearly two groups of them living west of Egypt who, over time, infiltrated the Western Delta. One of these groups was the *Tehennu* or *Temehu* who, though usually thought of as 'leucoderms' (white-skinned), are painted a deep reddish brown on the Panel of Races found in the tomb of Rameses III.[7] The other group was known as the *Lebu*, whose modern representatives can be found among the Lebu of Cap Vert on the coast of Senegal. These people are today black-skinned and there is no reason to doubt that they were black-skinned ('melanoderms')

Modern Lebu Women - Senegal

7 It bears repeating that the author has seen the Panel of Races with his own eyes in the Tomb of Rameses III, giving lie to the coloration rendered by Lepsius in **Denkmäler** that represents the Tehennu/Temehou as white-skinned.

also in antiquity. In the event, the name *Libya* was derived by the Greeks from the ancient Egyptian name *Lebu* for these western inhabitants, and at various times was used by the Greeks as a name for all Africa. The point to be grasped here is that, whether as Tehennu (Temehou) or Lebu, the Libyans of the 22nd Dynasty cannot be considered Caucasian, though that inference is always subtlely present in the modern histories of ancient Egypt.

Sheshonq lost no time re-establishing Egyptian power in Canaan, taking the field against the two formerly united kingdoms of Israel and Judea, defeating each in turn and reducing them to a state of vassalage. The united kingdom of Israel had enjoyed a brief period of power and prosperity under David and Solomon but an irreconcilable conflict among the 12 tribes after the death of Solomon caused a split into two kingdoms, Israel in the north created from 10 of the tribes and Judea in the south from the two remaining tribes (Judah and Benjamin). This schismatic factionalism had the effect of weakening both kingdoms making them susceptible to the military ambitions of powerful neighbors, beginning with Sheshonq. Sheshonq had, in fact, provided asylum to a rebellious official under Solomon by name of Jeroboam who had designs on the throne of Israel. Sheshonq even went so far as to wed one of his daughters to Jeroboam, very likely with an eye to the future following in the wake of Solomon who also had taken an Egyptian princess to wife.

When Solomon died in 931 BC, his son Rehoboam was anointed king. There was already considerable unrest in the north because of the perceived unfair burden of taxes and when Rehoboam refused to relieve these taxes, the 10 northern tribes revolted, setting up an independent kingdom which retained the name Israel in contrast to the southern kingdom which became known as Judea. Jeroboam was recalled from Egypt to become the first king of the newly-independent Israel. As noted above, the immediate effect of this secession was to provide an open road for Sheshonq who invaded Judea, conquering all the country including Jerusalem in 925 BC. Not stopping there, he continued into Israel, defeating and capturing his former client Jeroboam. The account of this conquest is recorded in the Old Testament in *1 Kings 14* and *2 Chronicles 12:3* where Sheshonq was said to have led a formidable army of 1,200 chariots and 60,000 cavalry against Judea and Israel composed primarily of Egyptian and Cushite regiments, *Lubim*, that is to say Lebu, troops, and *Sukkim*, normally thought to be

Tehennu. Not inauspiciously, Sheshonq halted his advance at Megiddo, the site of the storied battle won by Thutmosis III six centuries previously that guaranteed Egypt's imperial conquest in Western Asia. Sheshonq erected a stele at Megiddo proclaiming his suzereignty and, once again, Egypt could lay claim to an empire in Syria-Palestine, almost entirely at the expense of Judea and Israel. It had been 270 years since an Egyptian army had marched into Western Asia and Sheshonq took full advantage of his victories to bring back loads of plunder and tribute with which to re-stock the depleted royal coffers. Jerusalem was not spared and much of the fabled wealth accumulated by Solomon ended up in the hands of Sheshonq and his army. Moreover, at least through his reign, northern tribute continued to flow southward into Egypt as it had during the heyday of the 19th Dynasty pharaohs. The Old Testament accounts of Sheshonq's conquest of Judea and Israel are corroborated on the south tower of the second pylon of Karnak temple, where Sheshonq's victories over 133 cities and towns in Palestine are recounted.[8]

Sheshonq, who now had the financial means and the incentive to establish his pharaonic bona fides, conducted important building work at Karnak in addition to beautifying Bubastis. His son Iuput oversaw the construction of the forecourt in front of the second pylon at Karnak. Not only did military affairs and temple construction revive under Sheshonq I but so did trade as evidenced by the renewed commercial ties established with Byblos, a Phoenician city state with a long anterior relationship with Egypt. Phoenicians, by this time, were the most active mariners and sea merchants in the Mediterranean and had become the *de facto* merchant marine for Egyptian trade goods. Under Sheshonq, the Egyptian position on the international stage was measurably enhanced as at no time since the reign of Rameses III.

Osorkon I (931 BC–895 BC)

The reign of this pharaoh is another one clouded largely in obscurity, although there was active temple-building in the Libyan capital of Bubastis—sacred to the cat-goddess *Bast*—and Illahun where a fort was established. A noteworthy inscription found at Abydos at this period concerns the discovery by one

8 Budge, op. cit., p. 70.

Pashedbast, a descendant of Rameses II, of an ancient stele dedicated to Osiris. It is evident from the record that the descendants of Rameses II continued to hold an honored place in the officialdom of the country centuries after the death of their legendary ancestor:

> The enormous family of Rameses II had doubtless a very wide-spread posterity and seem to have largely filled the official berths of the country.[9]

Osorkon I

In 897 BC, Osorkon was supposed to have sent another large army against Judea and Israel, under the command of the Ethiopian Zerah (*2 Chronicles, 16:8*), the troops made up of both Cushite and Lebu conscripts. This time, according to Old Testament account, the Egyptian army was defeated and sent fleeing back to Egypt. However, this event is known only from the Old Testament accounts; no surviving monuments in Egypt attest to it as was the case for Sheshonq I's invasion of Palestine. In fact Budge states quite categorically '...there is no evidence that Osorkon I made any expedition into Judea'.[10] When the report in *2 Chronicles* asserts that an Egyptian host of 1 million men ('a thousand thousand') was led by the Ethiopian Zerah against

9 Petrie, op. cit., p. 242.
10 Budge, op. cit., pp.77-8.

Judea only to be soundly defeated by Judaean king Asa, the historical veracity of the account must be rejected. Apart from the absence of any independent corroboration of an invasion of Palestine by such a host, there was never an army of that size put into the field anywhere at this time in history. It is just another example among many in the Old Testament of a purely legendary event being recorded as factual history.

Osorkon was evidently the beneficiary of the country's continued prosperity and wealth as evidenced by the rich benefactions bestowed on a number of the more important temples. As per established custom, Osorkon installed one of his sons named Sheshonq—whose mother was the royal princess *Maāt-ka-Rā* ('the righteous truth of the ka of Rā')—as high priest of Amon at Karnak, and this Sheshonq, also as customary, had bestowed upon him royal honors which suggests he may have actually been elevated to co-regency with his father for a time, though he never succeeds to the throne on his own account. This position is reserved for another son, *Takerat*. The queen of Osorkon who gives birth to his successor Takerat I was *Thentsa* by name although some have identified her as *Ta-shed-khonsu* ('land of Khonsu's nurse'). Osorkon's original heir, the above-named Sheshonq, seems to have died before the end of his father's reign, leaving the way clear for Takerat to ascend the throne.

Breasted makes the point that the Libyans, as a result of their assumption of military command and ultimately the throne, became, over time completely Egyptianized. It is a fate duplicated everywhere when a semi-barbaric pastoral people seizes control of a more advanced civilization—they become totally assimilated to the culture over which they have achieved rulership, losing not only their own native identity but, ultimately, the force and dynamism that made them conquerors in the first place. By the end of Osorkon's reign, the Libyans as a whole were worshiping the gods of Egypt and the Libyan upper echelons were living entirely in the Egyptian manner. Osorkon did thereby celebrate the sed heb festival, commenorating his 30-year jubilee, a custom dating back to the Old Kingdom.

Takerat I (895 BC–877 BC)

Though there is a fairly extensive geneaology associated with this king, little is known about his reign. The Great Royal wife was *Mut-meri Karomama* who is the mother of the eventual heir Osorkon II.

Osorkon II (877 BC–852 BC)

This is yet another of the inconsequential reigns that characterize the 22nd Dynasty after Osorkon I. Nonetheless, the sculptor's art flourished to a significant degree as evidenced by some magnificent statuary found in Tanis datable to this reign. Not only that, but there seems to have been a military incursion into Syrio-Palestine but it is only vaguely reported and, in any case, exerted no lasting influence on the geopolitics of the region. Other notable monuments of the period include a red granite pylon raised at Bubastis to celebrate the Osorkon's *sed heb* festival—the festival of kingly rejuvenation. Inscriptions attributable the reign of Osorkon II were also found at Karnak and Luxor. Pharaohs always married multiple wives, but usually it was the Great Royal Wife that was most prominently showcased during the reign. However, Osorkon married two women who seemed to have commanded near equal status and attention, *Karama* and *Mehtienusekht*. Each of them was a mother of a pharaoh, Karama of Sheshonq II and Mehtienusekht of Takerat II.

Sheshonq II (852 BC)

This prince, though he became co-regent with his father Osorkon II, pre-deceased his father. So though he was technically a pharaoh, he suffered the singular fate of never succeeding to the throne on his own account.

Takerat II (852–832 BC)

Following the death of his half-brother in 844 BC, Takerat II became co-regent with his father Osorkon II, ascending the throne as sole ruler five years later in 839 BC. Though he reigned another 20 years, there is, again, not much to show for this reign in the historical record, apart from some of the ever-recurring border troubles, squabbling among the Libyan feudal lords of the Delta, and internecine conflict with the Thebans. Presumably, pacification was successful on all fronts but there is no way of knowing the how or what of it, though Takerat did go to live in Thebes for a short time, presumably to foster more congenial ties with the priests of Amon. This diplomatic effort, though well-meant—and fostered by his Theban wife—did not have the desired effect, so the king went back to his stronghold in Bubastis. Takerat II also appears to have sent 1,000 troops to a Western Asiatic coalition, which included the Israelite king Ahab, arrayed against the Assyrians, the rising power in region, but said coalition was soundly defeated by the Assyrian king Shalmaneser II on the Orontes in 854 BC. This was the first military encounter between Egyptians and Assyrians, and the latter, growing more aggressive and bellicose as time went on, would become Egypt's most daunting enemy in the 7th century BC (25th Dynasty). There is some dispute even here whether this confrontation with Assyrians happened in Takerat II's reign or that of Osorkon II. In the event, Assyria, though victorious was temporarily halted in its southern expansion and, according to Grimal, the Libyan pharaohs were committed to supporting the Palestinian kingdoms of Judea and Israel as buffers against Assyrian expansionism since it was evident even then that Assyria had cast its imperial eyes toward Egypt.[11]

Unusually, the name of the Great Royal Wife is unknown; however, that of one of the royal concubines is—*Kakat.* Conceivably, she eclipsed the queen both in the favor of pharaoh and in political importance. In the event, though her sons achieved high positions, none of them succeeded to the throne.

11 Grimal, op. cit., p. 326.

Sheshonq III (832 BC–787 BC)

This son of Takerat II became co-regent in the last six years of his father's life and enjoyed a rather long reign of 51 years if Petrie's regnal dates are to be believed. Such building as was accomplished during the reign took place chiefly at Tanis—a pylon and a temple. In doing so, however, he followed the the time-honored custom of usurping the monuments of earlier pharaohs, in this case those of Rameses II, even going so far as destroying the huge colossus of Rameses II at Tanis—the tallest statue in the world—and using the materials taken from it in his own building projects. Like all pharaohs from the beginning of the 18th Dynasty, he left his mark at Karnak, not in new buildings, pylons, columns, or monuments but in several datable inscriptions. As pharaoh, if one could not build at Karnak, one at least carved inscriptions there as a personal testament documenting the size and extent of the endowments. Even if Waset (Thebes) was no longer Egypt's political capital, Karnak remained Egypt's sacerdotal center and no pharaoh failed to pay due homage to Amon with gifts and endowments. However, Sheshonq was enmeshed in the political strife of the Theban region that involved his half-brother Osorkon, commander-in-chief at Heracleopolis, the traditional Libyan stronghold in Middle Egypt, who had made himself the nominal ruler of Upper Egypt. The priests of Karnak refused to cede their authority, and a low-level civil war ensued that may have lasted a decade before it was finally sorted out. It has been suggested, in fact, that Shesonq III may have at least partially owed his accession to the throne over the claims of Osorkon because of an *entente* he reached with the priests at Karnak. It is during his reign that, in 776 BC, the First Olympic Games were held in the lands of the northern Mediterranean, later called Greece.

Sheshonq III's Chief Royal Wife is *Thent-amen-apt* ('the dwelling place of Amon's throne'?) by name which is recorded in the Karnak inscriptions.

Pamay (787 BC–783 BC)

Pamay became co-regent in 774 BC, the same year that his father Sheshonq III died. Unlike his father, his reign was short, barely four years in duration. The so called *Serapeum*, dedicated to the Bull-god Apis—sacred to both Osiris and

Ptah—contains a number of stelae which provide genealogical information for the reigns of the 22nd Dynasty and nothing is known about Pamay except what is recorded genealogically on a stele in the Serapeum.

Sheshonq IV (783 BC–750 BC)

This last Sheshonq, also the last pharaoh of the 22nd Dynasty, would have begun a co-regency in the last year or two of his father Pamay's life. As with nearly all the pharaohs in the last 150 years of the 22nd Dynasty, he reigned while leaving a neglible impact on the historical record. By the end of his life, the Delta had broken up into a collection of petty princedoms without allegiance to any central government. Like the previous dynasties, the 22nd, based in Bubastis, ended in ignominy.

The Libyan Dynasty was launched by one, Sheshonq I, who had risen in the ranks of the Egyptian army to become commander-in-chief, capping a century-long trend that saw Libyans sedulously migrating into the Delta and taking an increasing number of positions in the army. When the last king of the 21st Dynasty, Pausennes II, died, no one in the country was in a stronger position than Sheshonq and no one could deny him the throne. His claim was strengthened by the fact of his marriage to the daughter of Pausennes and his dynasty was launched seemingly auspiciously. He was a vigorous and able ruler and recovered a significant portion of Egypt's Western Asiatic empire by conquering Judea and Israel after the death of Solomon and the dissolution of the united kingdom of Israel. His campaigns brought tribute, plunder, and a measure of restored international prestige back to Egypt. But it wasn't to last. His son Osorkon I was not nearly as competent a ruler as his father. There are no reliable records of any military campaign; the account in *2 Chronicles* of the defeat in Judea of Osorkon's army, numbering a 'thousand thousand men', cannot possibly have any basis in historical fact, especially since there is not a single surviving inscription in Egypt testifying to such a momentous military event. Even so, Osorkon was able to maintain some semblance of national and international integrity for Egypt which however steadily eroded in the reigns of his successors. Very little is known about the reigns of the kings who followed

Osorkon I. Hereditary Libyan princelings of the Delta asserted ever greater independence so that by the end of the dynasty, northern Egypt at least had been broken up into a multitude of feudal states. And ominously for the future of Egypt, Takerat II joined a war coalition of Canaanitic states allied against Assyria that was soundly defeated.

In the south, the priests of Amon continued to govern the Thebaid and Nubia, even during the periods when the Libyans ruled the whole country. There, at least, the centrifugal forces that impelled the breakup of Lower Egypt into a collection of petty states did not effect the same result. Amon's position and power in the pantheon remained undiminished; Karnak had no rival as the religious and sacerdotal capital of the nation. Even the Libyan dynasts, ensconced at Bubastis in the far north, continued to pay honor and homage to Amon and, whenever means permitted, add to the splendor of Karnak. What is apparent as time goes on, is the ever-closer ties developing between Thebes with its southern territories on the one hand and Nubio-Cush on the other. Napata, the capital of Cush far to the south, was gradually becoming an important center for Amon-worship in its own right. Cush, an independent and sovereign nation by the end of the reign of Sheshonq I, would steadily grow in power and influence, increasingly felt in Egypt itself. Egyptians by the thousands, including priests, had been migrating southward to Cush since the 20th Dynasty, and Cush had long since ceased to be thought of as 'foreign' territory.

When one looks at the tenuous position of the pharaohs of the 22nd Dynasty after Sheshonq and the dearth of historical information about them, one can appreciate why Egyptologists have fallen into the habit of calling this era the 'Third Intermediate Period'. But as the author has discussed earlier in this book, the whole notion of 'Intermediate Period' is completely artificial, invented by 20th-century Egyptologists to describe the chronological gap periods after the 8th Dynasty and the 14th. Though so much of the 22nd Dynasty is admittedly obscure, it does not qualify as a chronological gap and so the term 'Intermediate Period' applied to it is inadmissible. The term, in any case, has nothing whatever to do with the way in which the Egyptians viewed and recorded their own history; Manetho, for example, knows nothing of Intermediate Periods. Nonetheless, writers such as Robert Steven Bianchi insist on referring constantly and routinely to the 'Third Intermediate Period' as if it were an authentic historical era instead of a mere scholarly artifice as it truly is.[12]

There is a side-bar discussion that reflects some interesting light on the Libyans at this juncture of Egyptian history. It has been noted that they established their capital at Bubastis, the sacred city of Bast, and built monuments and temples to her there. Bast was the cat-goddess, clearly indicating the Libyan

Bast the Cat Goddess
Sacred to the Libyans

veneration of cats as her natural avatar. In fact, there seems to have developed an exaggerated love and reverence for cats by the Libyans that permeated Lower Egypt and was carried down into Roman times in Egypt, at least in the northern part of the country. Diodorus (writing between 60 and 50 BC) informs us that a person who killed a cat in Egypt, intentionally or accidentally, would be, if caught, summarily put to death, often by enraged crowds.[13] Diodorus actually witnessed such an event with his own eyes in Alexandria.

12 See Bianchi RS, **Daily Life of the Nubians**, Westport: Greenwood Press, 2004, pp.147-92 passim.

13 See Diodorus of Sicily's **Library of History**, Book I, Chapter 83, translated by C.H. Oldfather, Cambridge: Harvard University Press, 1933/2004.

There is another interesting—and evocative—element connecting ancient Egyptian history of the 22nd Dynasty to contemporary times alluded to in earlier pages of this book. It concerns the Lebu people of Senegal now living along the coast in the Cap Vert region that includes the capital city of Dakar. We have already mentioned that the Lebu of Senegal trace their origins back to Libya and have likewise mentioned that the name 'Lebu' was anciently turned into the name 'Libya' by the Greeks. Also in the ancient Egyptian language 'lebu' was the word for 'lion'. Moreover, it has been pointed out that the Lebu of Senegal seem to have a special affinity to the lion, as evidenced by the ritual game played by them called 'the Lion game' where actors dress up and act the part of male and female lions while chasing gathered spectators all over the place.[14]

But it is even more nuanced than that. The modern Lebu have a special affection for cats which roam around their compounds and are routinely fed by the inhabitants. We have noted the ancient Libyans' adoration of the Cat-Goddess, Bast, and the establishment of their capital in her sacred city of Bubastis. It is pertinent to note also that Bast was not uncommonly represented as lion-headed and identified with the Lion-Goddess, Sekhmet; she was therefore both Cat and Lion-Goddess. She was also sometimes referred to as the consort of Atum, one of the earliest lion-headed deities.[15] We have speculated that the extreme reverence paid to cats in the late phases of Egyptian civilization as observed by Diodorus is a holdover from the Libyan domination of Lower Egypt who would have idolized cats (and lionesses) right along with Bast, the Cat-Goddess. One of the forms of Rā was the male cat, but it was a lesser avatar since he was pre-eminently the Golden Falcon. The profound cat-worship of Egypt in its latter days seems to resonate more directly to the veneration of Bast brought to the forefront by the Libyans of the 22nd Dynasty. Moreover, the cat was always seen by the Egyptians as a kind of lion in miniature, so lion-veneration and cat-veneration were of a piece. Thus the ancient Lebu (Libyans) and the contemporary Lebu (Senegalese) were and are archetypically bound to the lion and cat.

14 The present author has twice witnessed the Lion Game among the Lebu in Senegal (1997).

15 See Budge, E.A. Wallis, **Gods of the Egyptians**, Volume 1, New York: Dover Publications, 1904/1969, pp. 446-8, for a fuller discussion of the representations of Bast.

Chapter 9:

The Twilight of Egypt

I. The 23rd and 24th Dynasties (750 B C–715 BC)

These last Libyan dynasties are so inconsequential, hardly lasting 35 years taken together, that little space is necessary to dispose of them. Indeed, they are really dynasties enfolded into the Ethiopian epoch of Egyptian history and seemed to have reigned as parallel dynasties to the 25th. Little can be said about the 23rd and 24th dynasties except that they set the stage for the 25th, or Ethiopian Dynasty, one of the last two dynasties of any importance prior to the Alexandrian conquest and the advent of the Ptolemies.

Pedubast (755 BC–730 BC)

Pedubast ('the gift of Bast') reigned at Thebes for about 25 years, though he originated in Bubastis. He seems to have assumed the mantle of kingship in Thebes before the end of the reign of Sheshonq IV at Tanis (750 BC) so that there was a 5-year dynastic overlap. Grimal says about these two 'quasi-dynasties' that they represented 'one of the most confused periods in Egyptian history, a period which historians have been unable to disentangle satisfactorily...'[1] The confused chronology reflects the unstable condition of Egypt at the time. The only noteworthy event recorded in his reign is an inspection carried out by the priests of Amon. A new high priest took office in year 19 of the reign. The first invasion from Napatan Cush, under the rulership of Piankhy, took place at the outset of this reign. By this time, the rule of Pedubast was so nominal that

1 Grimal, op. cit., pp. 331-2

the 'epic' of Piankhy's invasion was accomplished with absolutely no regard for Pedubast. He was pharaoh in name only. This incursion was meant to restore order and stability there as well as shore up the position of the priests of Amon at Karnak. After the successful conquest of Egypt, Piankhy returned to Napata but his invasion foreshadowed the complete Cushite conquest of Egypt and the advent of the 25th Dynasty.

Osorkon III (730 BC–721 BC)

As indicated by their names, the two kings of the 23rd Dynasty were really relicts of the Libyan dynasty. Two of the sons of this king successively became high priests of Amon at Thebes. This Osorkon wore the crown but was absolutely powerless to contend with the disintegration of Egypt north of Hermopolis into nearly 20 quarreling principalities. One of these princelings was Sheshonq V at Tanis whose rule stretched as far as the northern precincts of Heliopolis but not further. The western half of the Delta was ruled by Tefnakht at Sais, sacred city of Neith, one of whose titles was Paramount Chief of the Lebu. Other princelings ruling during this chaotic period included Takerat III at Thebes, associated with his sister Shepenoupet I, who became the Chief Wife of Amon at Karnak; Rudamon, brother of Takerat III, who succeeded him; Iuput, Rudamon's successor; Nimrod at Hermopolis. At this juncture, there were three petty rulers who were calling themselves 'pharaoh'. The Cushites dominated the southern half of the country from Thebes in any event even while the self-proclaimed pharaohs pretended to assert royal prerogatives over Thebes and Karnak. Egypt was ripe for further intervention from Napata.

II. 24th Dynasty

Bakenranf or *Bocchoris* (721 BC–715 BC)

The lone 24th Dynasty king was Bakenranf by name, called *Bocchoris* by Manetho, who reigned but six years as a king from his capital at Sais in the northwestern Delta; though in fact, the reigning power in Egypt by this time were the Cushite kings from Napata. He really seems but an artifact of history and is only included in the dynastic lists because Manetho apparently put him there. Petrie refers to his reign as 'a brief rebellion in the midst of three generations of the Ethiopian Dominion'.[2] Having said that, later Greek writers gave him an incongruous reputation for wisdom, legal acumen, and administrative prudence on the one hand coupled with avarice and venality on the other.[3] Moreover, he was reputed to have been bodily weak and small in stature. There is evidently little monumental or inscriptive evidence for these ruminations about Bocchoris though the fact that he only lived for six years after his coronation might indicate that the sickly constitution reported by later Greek writers was in fact true.

An incongruous development in the latter stages of the 22nd and throughout the short-lived 23rd Dynasties is the flourishing of art. Some of the finest sculptures ever produced in Egypt occur in this period. This creative artistic impulse would survive the upheavals of the following centuries and reach a peak with the 26th Dynasty based at Sais.

III. **The 25th Dynasty** (750 BC–653 BC)

The 25th Dynasty—the 'Ethiopian' Dynasty—is often thought of as unique in the history of ancient Egypt. The kingdom of Cush whose capital was at Napata nearly 700 miles south of Aswan near the 4th Cataract, had emerged as sovereign and independent no later than 850 BC and probably as early as 900 BC. Thenceforward, Cush had steadily grown more powerful and wielded ever greater influence in Upper Egypt. By the early 8th century BC, Napatan Cush had established its hegemony over the Thebaid, impelled in no small measure by the influx of priests of Amon from Karnak throughout the 22nd Dynasty. Napata had become a thriving, dynamic center of Amon-worship; the Temple of Amon at nearby Gebel Barkal reveals a sacerdotal stronghold parallel to that of Karnak itself. The priests of Amon and other emigrants from Upper Egypt found a congenial home in Cush. The Amonian theocracy at Napata exerted

2 Petrie, op. cit., p. 267.
3 Diodorus, op. cit., pp. 321-3.

even greater control over state and society than was true in Egypt inasmuch as the priests of Amon had the authority to depose Cushitic pharaohs as they saw fit.[4] Moreover, Breasted tells us, 'In Greek times the priests in Egypt were wont to depict the Ethiopian theocracy as the ideal state…'[5] All this being said, the evolving Cushitic hegemony in the Thebaid was welcomed by the priestly caste at Karnak to, among other things, counteract the Libyan dynasts at Bubastis and Heracleopolis.

The delineation of a completely artificial 'Third Intermediate Period' by Robert Bianchi, and others, has been noted. Bianchi has in fact placed the 25th Dynasty within the context of the Third Intermediate Period as if it too participated in the general weakness and instability that had beset the Egyptian state in the previous 300 years.[6] This characterization of the 25th Dynasty is utterly fallacious, especially since the dynasty represented a temporary sanctuary against the general decline that had engulfed the country. The pharaohs of the 25th Dynasty not only rescued Egypt from anarchy but created, prior to the end of the Assyrian wars, a kind of mini-Renaissance in Egypt, a welcome respite from the turmoil of the earlier centuries. There is nothing about a so-called Third Intermediate Period that in any way reflects on the 25th Dynasty.

It is well-known that Nubio-Cush had been thoroughly Egyptianized from the outset of the 18th Dynasty, so much so that it was not seen as foreign territory by the Egyptians. It bears repeating that Herodotus informs us that up to his time, 450 BC, 18 Ethiopians had sat on the throne of Egypt, a number of whom would have ruled during the Middle Kingdom.[7] Furthermore, Egypt itself emerged from the late pre-dynastic Nubian pharaonocracy known as *Ta-Seti* and it was a ruler 'who came out of the South, the son of a woman of Ta-seti', i.e., a Nubian woman, who restored peace and stability to Egypt, unifying it, and launching the 12th Dynasty. More than once, Egypt's fortunes

4 Breasted, op. cit., p. 539. This priestly control over pharaonic succession in Cush would change dramatically in later Meroitic times.

5 Ibid.

6 Bianchi RS, **Daily Life of the Nubians**, Westport: Greenwood Press, 2004, pp.147-92 passim.

7 See Herodotus, **The Histories: Book Two**, translated by Aubrey de Sélincourt, New York: Penguin Books, 1954/1972, p. 166.

were revived by interventions from the South. To return to the analogy of Great Britain, no one in the recent history of the United Kingdom found anything strange about prime ministers from Wales (Lloyd George) or Scotland (William Gladstone, Ramsay MacDonald) holding office; nor did Egyptians find it strange about kings from Cush doing so. The analogy can be carried further by the recognition that the current British Windsor dynasty was and is a German dynasty, Germans being the Teutonic cousins of the Anglo-Saxons of Britain. In the event, by the middle of the 8th century BC, Egypt had been thoroughly destabilized, tottering precariously close to anarchy. The priests of Amon, both in Napata and Thebes, clamored for intervention from the kings at Napata and in 750 BC, it was forthcoming.

Kashta ('the Cushite') is the first known king of Napatan Cush about whose reign anything is well documented in Egyptian records. Before him, a king name *Alara*, the seventh in a line of kings going back at least 100 years, acceded to the Cushite throne around 780 BC.[8] Alara is the older brother of Kashta who succeeds him about 760 BC, an example of the custom in Cushite royal succession for the throne to pass through a group of royal brothers before passing to the next generation. Under Kashta's rule, Cush won control of all Nile Valley lands up to Aswan, just north of the First Cataract. Kashta probably extended Cushite hegemony even farther north to Thebes. He was able to place his daughter, *Amenirdis,* in position as the Divine Wife of Amon at Karnak, making her, in effect, the female 'co-pope' of Karnak with the traditional male high priest. The reigning Divine Wife of Amon was Shepenoupet I, daughter of Osorkon III, who was induced to adopt Amenirdis as her daughter and successor. This installation would not have been possible without an incontestable hegemony over the entire Thebaid which must have meant that troops from Cush were stationed throughout the region. In this position, Amenirdis was the *de facto* ruler of all the lands of Upper Egypt from Thebes south. Two of Kashta's sons would succeed him to the throne of Cush, the first being *Piankhy.*

8 Grimal. op. cit., pp. 334-5.

Piankhy (748 BC–716 BC)

Piankhy ('ascending life'?) was one of the two truly outstanding sovereigns of the 25th Dynasty and, in truth, must be placed on the historical list of Egypt's elite rulers. Many chroniclers do not include him in the list of 25th Dynasty kings presumably because after re-unifying and re-stabilizing Egypt, he returned to Napata and ended his reign there. But it is impossible to think of him apart from the 25th Dynasty because he was the one who set it up and, for the purposes of this discussion, the 25th Dynasty begins with him.

Piankhi the Ethiopian – first pharoah of the 25th Dynasty

Piankhy, who married his cousin the daughter of Alara, ascended the throne in 747/748 BC. By 736 BC, Cushite power in Egypt was growing to such an extent as to compel Tefnakht, the Saitic pharaoh of Lower Egypt, to form a coalition of northern princelings to halt Cushite expansion. The consolidation of Cushitic power was effected by Piankhy through the expedient of having Osorkon III authorize the adoption of Piankhy's sister Amenirdas by Shenpenoupet, the Divine Wife of Amon, as her 'daughter' and successor because by this time, the Divine Wife of Amon had eclipsed even the Chief Priest of Amon in prestige and authority.[9] Tefnakht was even able to

9 Bianchi, op. cit., p. 151.

persuade the petty Middle Egyptian kings of Hermopolis and Herakleopolis to ally themselves with the coalition, though Budge reports that the dynast of Herakleopolis was coerced into the alliance after Tefnakht laid siege to his city. In 726 BC, led by Tefnakht, the coalition armies invaded the south intent on driving the Cushites out of Egypt. Notified of this military advance and implored by the Theban military high command to take action to protect the domains of Amon, Piankhy ordered his troops in Thebes, led by the generals *Puaarma* and *Lāmersekni*, to march north and engage the northern coalition at Herakleopolis, backed by reinforcements sent from Napata. The Cushite forces were able to block the advance of Tefnakht's army and force them to retreat northward to Hermopolis, to which the Cushites laid siege. In the process of capturing cities loyal to the coalition, breaking down gates with battering rams, one of Tefnakht's sons was slain. Piankhy, incensed that the northern army had escaped back toward their bases after their defeat, now joined his army in the field, after first celebrating the Opet festival at Karnak. The full story of Piankhy's conquest and unification of Egypt is recounted in his commemorative stele which has been called 'one of the masterpieces of ancient literature'.[10]

The war had been going on for five months and, in Middle Egypt, Hermopolis and its ruler Nimrod had managed to hold out against the Cushite generals. With Piankhy taking command the army now overwhelmed the defenses of Hermopolis, taking the city by a storm with the aid of siege towers. Nimrod's peace overtures to Piankhy went unheeded until at last the defeated ruler sent a delegation of his wives and daughters to meet with Piankhy's queen to entreat her to intervene with 'Horus the King' on behalf of Nimrod and Hermopolis and accept his submission. The queen, evidently possessing immense influence over her husband, apparently did successfully intervene on behalf of the royal women of Hermopolis since Piankhy proceeded to lift the siege and enter the city without further bloodshed. However, Nimrod was nearly undone yet again when Piankhy, a passionate lover of horses, inspected the stables only to find the horses in a deplorable state of neglect and starvation, thunderously reprimanding the hapless king by saying:

10 Adams, op. cit., p. 248.

> I swear as Rā loves me…it is more grievous in my heart that my horses have suffered hunger than any evil deed that thou hast done in the prosecution of thy desire.[11]

However, keeping his promise, Piankhy did not punish Nimrod but sent the tribute to the treasury of Amon at Karnak. He proceeded to make large sacrifices at the Temple of Eight Gods, in honor of Thoth (Djehuti), the patron deity of Hermopolis and to whom the number 8 was sacred.[12]

Very shortly thereafter, Piankhy received the unconditional surrender of the ruler of Herakleopolis *Pefnefdibast*, and continued his campairn of conquest northward until he had conquered all the lands as far north as Memphis, appropriating the accumulated wealth of each ruler for his treasury and that of Amon. All the cities that voluntarily surrendered to him were left unmolested though laid under tribute. However, Memphis remained allied to Tefnakht who thought the city was impregnable behind its high walls and able to withstand siege because it was well-provisioned with food and water, allowing him to depart northward to raise another army against Piankhy. Piankhy at first sent a peace mission to entreat the city, sacred to Ptah, to surrender without a battle to avoid unnecessary slaughter but to no avail.[13] Seeing that an investment of the city was inevitable, Piankhy devised a cunning stratagem that testifies to his outstanding military ability: since the Nile was at high tide, he did not directly storm the stout walls from land but commandeered all watercraft available to lash them together to form a pontoon bridge at the northern wall bordering the river which the defenders had neglected to defend adequately. Because of the high water, it was relatively easy for the besiegers to cross the makeshift bridge, climb over the walls, and take the city. Memphis was overwhelmed with the predicted slaughter and the entire region very quickly laid down arms. Then 15 dynasts of Lower Egypt, seeing the proverbial handwriting on the wall, came to offer submission and tribute. Capping this victorious campaign, Piankhy next went to Heliopolis in order to be consecrated and anointed pharaoh by the priests of Rā while performing ablutions, rites of purification, and sacred

11 Breasted JH, **Ancient Records of Egypt - Part 4**, London: Histories and Mysteries of Man Ltd., 1988, p. 429.

12 Budge, op. cit., p. 106.

13 Ibid., pp. 107-8.

offerings to the Heliopolitan triad of Rā, Atum, and Khepera. White oxen, milk, incense, and precious woods were among Piankhy's sacrificial offerings. He was scrupulous in every conquered city to pay homage to the local deities with lavish gifts and sacrifices.

In the end, the entire country and all reigning dynasts, including his most active adversary Tefnakht, capitulated to Piankhy. Tefnakht knew when he was beaten and, from a hideout deep in the Delta swamps, was able to negotiate more favorable terms for his surrender than would have been the case had he been defeated on the battlefield. On his part, Pianky had managed to unite the entire country without a single setback making him the most successful general in the Nile Valley since the time of Rameses III. It had been a hard-fought, bloody campaign, but when all of his erstwhile enemies came to offer obeisance to him he restored them to their former offices though with tighter controls. The entire story of Piankhy's campaign to re-unite and restore order in Egypt was recounted on the famous Victory Stele, copies of which were placed at Karnak, Memphis, and, of course, Gebel Barkal. What is evident from this long inscription is not only the scope of his success but that Piankhy was fighting under the banner of royal legitimacy, as the rightful ruler of Egypt and Cush under Amon. Cushite rulers at least from the time of Kashta had established their control over Egypt to such an extent that, in the uprising led by Tefnakht, the petty kings of the coalition of Lower and Middle Egypt were considered rebels and referred to as such. Piankhy was now hailed as 'King of Upper and Lower Egypt'. Rich tribute of every description poured into his camp which accompanied him on his triumphant return to Napata. Piankhy was indeed a conquering hero-king in the legendary tradition of Sesostris, Thutmosis III, and Rameses II, but he was not merely that. More so than any other such king, his humanity and magnanimity shine through his justly famous Victory Stele from which all accounts of his reign are drawn. His love of horses, his susceptibility to the gentle influence of his queen, and his willingness to forgive his enemies, allowing them to hold on to their high offices, are testaments to a man who conscientiously adhered to the tenets of Ma'āt, embodying the best and noblest aspects of the pharaonic kingship. His comparatively benign personality serves as a stark contrast to the exaggerated royal egotism of Rameses II.

Piankhy returned to Napata, leaving the governance of most of Egypt in the hands of his sister Amenirdis, the Divine Wife of Amon at Karnak. Though not pharaoh in the manner of Hatshepsut, Amenirdis is a remarkable example of a woman in the history of Egypt combining ecclesiastical with temporal authority. The subsequent history of Cush shows that female rulership was not uncongenial to its citizens in the same manner as it apparently was to Egypt from the middle of the 18th dynasy onward. Piankhy allowed a certain amount of autonomy to Tefnakht and a small coterie of northern kings who, though in reality vassals to the reigning monarch at Napata, did not disdain from giving themselves royal honors. Tefnakht managed to rule a kingdom carved out of Lower Egypt for another eight years and we have already seen that around 718 BC, Bocchoris, son of Tefnakht and ruler at Sais, established an ephemeral dynasty of one, called the 24th Dynasty by Manetho, that lasted but six years. In Napata, Piankhy enlarged and beautified the city; the Temple of Amon at Gebel Barkal was expanded with additional constructions including an enclosure wall around the sanctuary, a hypostyle hall, a second pylon, and a new peristyle court behind another pylon from which radiated an avenue of criosphinxes exactly like the ones on the avenue connecting Karnak and Luxor at Thebes. The temple at Gebel Barkal had been first been established by Thutmosis III and was subsequently englarged by Rameses II, the two most storied Egyptian pharaohs of the previous 800 years. Piankhy, determined to follow in their footsteps, added further to Amon's temple there, with his name and exploits indelibly inscribed on its walls. He clearly saw himself as the true inheritor of the legacies of both Thutmosis III and Rameses II and in fact adopted their throne names as his own.[14] His successors continued to build and enlarge both at Gebel Barkal and Karnak. Piankhy also revived the custom of pyramid-building which became the superstructures for the burial chambers of all subsequent Cushitic kings at the necropolis of el-Kurru. None of these pyramids matched the sheer size of those at Giza but, in the end, there were more pyramids built in Cush than in Egypt or anywhere else. Two of his favorite chargers were buried with him.

14 Bianchi, op. cit., p. 162.

E.A. Wallis Budge's assessment of Piankhy is unquestionably the most just and reliable of all the modern commentary concerning him:

> Piānkhi was not a barbarian invading Egypt for the mere sake of conquest and spoil, but a man who was seeking to guard his own interests and country, as he understood them; he worshipped the gods of Egypt, he spared their temples, and though when he struck he struck hard and swiftly, he was on the whole a merciful conqueror.[15]

Shabaka (716 BC–704 BC)

Shabaka—25th Dynasty

Shabaka was another son of Kashta and therefore brother to Piankhy from whom he inherited the crown. Though it is clear that Egypt was under the hegemony of Napatan Cush by virtue of its conquest by Piankhy who stabilized the country and restored order, the formal beginning of the 25th Dynasty is usually credited to Shabaka. He was actually the son of the aforementioned Kashta by his Great Royal Wife Shepenoupet and Shabaka inherited the throne through the custom in Cush of brother-to-brother succession before descending to the next generation. He is thought to have reigned 12 years. By

15 Ibid., p. 114.

his accession, it had become well-evident that trying to rule an empire that included Egypt was impossible from Napata, thus the decision by Shabaka to move his capital to Thebes. Like Piankhy before him, Shabaka had to re-assert his authority in the ever restive nomes of Lower Egypt where another Saitic nomarch by name of *Bakenrenef* seized control of Lower Egypt, establishing Memphis as his base of power. Shabaka drove the usurper out of Memphis and, to maintain effective authority over the entire country, left Thebes to establish his capital in Memphis. But another threat dictated this change of geopolitical venue: Assyria was the surging power in Western Asia, having conquered and destroyed the kingdom of Northern Israel or Samaria in 720 BC, four years before the accession of Shabaka. As is well known, Assyria would soon threaten Egypt of the 25th Dynasty. In **2 Kings** xvii.4, it is mentioned that Assyria had sent messengers to *So*, King of Egypt, and most think this So was Shabaka.

In the long-standing tradition of the kings of Egypt, Shabaka undertook projects of temple renovation and building at Memphis, Heliopolis, Denderah, Edfu, Bubastis, and, of course, Thebes. Indeed, for a period in the early part of his reign, Shabaka took up residence in Memphis. It is well-documented that the kings of the 25th Dynasty took special pains to resurrect interest in the feats and accomplishments of the Old Kingdom whose capital was Memphis.

Karakhamun—Son of Shabaka and High Priest of Amon

The justly famous ***Memphite Theology*** stele, known more commonly as the ***Shabaka Stone***, is a valuable synopsis of the religious thought of the Old Kingdom, carved during Shabaka's reign. Moreover, as of the summer of 2013, an excavation of the tomb of a 25th dynasty Cushite nobleman, *Karakhamun*, ongoing since 2008, is being conducted in South Asasif on the West Bank of Luxor, directed by Dr. Elena Pischikova and assisted by her collaborator-funder Mr. Anthony T. Browder. On the wall fronting recently-discovered steps into Karakhamun's burial chamber are extensive reproductions of the ***Pyramid Texts***, astro-religious writings dating from the 5th Dynasty and representing the oldest recorded religious thought in Egypt and indeed the world.[16] Moreover, Shabaka's throne name, *Neferkara*, is exactly that of Pepi II, the longest lived and longest-reigning pharaoh in history and the last pharaoh of the Sixth Dynasty. This preoccupation with the Old Kingdom evident among the 25th Dynasty Cushites contrasts noticeably with the dynasts of the New Kingdom who, as has been seen, took their inspiration from the exploits of the Middle Kingdom, the 12th Dynasty in particular, possibly because the conqueror-kings of that era resonated more closely to the militaristic ethos of the New Kingdom.

More of the cultural accomplishments of the 25th Dynasty is coming to light. The Shabaka Stone was not the only literary composition created during Shabaka's reign. Two other quasi-fictional literary papyri have been revealed, one entitled ***The Tale of King Neferkare and General Sasenet*** and the other ***The Tale of a King and the Ghost of Senefer***. The subject matter and title characters, again, hearken back to the Old Kingdom. The 25th Dynasty's fascination with the lore and history of the Old Kingdom seems to be similar to that of the modern Briton vis-à-vis the Arthurian saga.

It has been noted above that Amenirdas, sister to both Piankhy and Shabaka, was, during Shabaka's reign, the reigning Divine Wife of Amon, the 'Mother Superior' at Karnak, and governor of Upper Egypt. Though she entailed her position during the life of Piankhy, the accession of Shabaka seems to have done nothing to curtail her prerogatives. In fact, she carried out more temple renovations and constructions than did Shabaka judging by the

16 See Browder AT, **Finding Karakhamun**, Washington, D.C.: IKG, 2011 for an account of this excavation and its preliminary finds.

large numbers of monuments upon which her name is found. As was fitting, Karnak temple received her special care and attention but statues, repairs, and inscriptions commissioned by her have also been found in abundance at Rameses III's temple at Medinet Habu.

The interaction between Egypt and Assyria during the 25th Dynasty intensified during Shabaka's reign. Egyptian pharaohs after the 20th Dynasty were never completely reconciled to the loss of their empire in Western Asia and this included those of the 25th Dynasty but by this time, the dominant power in the region was unquestionably Assyria. Evidence of diplomatic correspondence between Shabaka and Sargon, emperor of Assyria, has surfaced and, for awhile, a détente seems to have existed between the two powers. However, when Assyria was drawn away from Canaan to cope with uprisings elsewhere in its empire, Shabaka did not lose the opportunity to re-establish a foothold in the lost Asiatic territories. In the end, this act would impel Assyria and the 25th Dynasty into a desperate conflict.[17]

Shabaka seems to have left a happy memory of his reign to posterity, at least by the testimony of the later Greek writers Herodotus and Diodorus. Shabaka, called *Sabacos* by Herodotus, was reported to have maintained a policy of not condemning a convicted criminal to death but instead sentencing him to labor raising earthenworks in his community upon which a rebuilt village could be elevated to a height above the flood crest. Moreover, Herodotus tells us that having been sent a horrific dream urging him to cut down the priests of Egypt, Sabacos instead chose to leave Egypt and return to Napata rather than commit such a sacrilegious crime. There is no independent verification of any of these stories about Shabaka but these anecdotes seem to preserve a benign reputation for justice and mercy in the Cushite monarch of Egypt.[18] Diodorus, echoing Herodotus, relates much the same tale and finishes by saying, '...Egypt was ruled by Sabaco, who was by birth an Ethiopian and yet in piety and uprightness far surpassed his predecessors.'[19] The well-documented magnanimity of Piankhy, Shabaka's brother and predecessor, makes it easy to believe the testimony of the

17 See Bianchi, op. cit., pp. 165-6.

18 Herodotus, **The Histories**, New York: Penguin Books, (1954), 1972, pp. 183-5.

19 **Diodorus Siculus: Library of History**, translated by CH Oldfather, Cambridge: Harvard University Press, (1933)2004, p. 225-6.

Greeks writers—whether or not accurate in the details—revealing an equally high caliber of moral character in the person of Shabaka. This assessment is given definite expression by a modern Egyptologist:

> ...there can be no doubt that his [Piankhy's] reign was publicly portrayed in conformity with ideal, religious paradigms of kingship. This impression, which posterity gains from a study of the reigns of other Nubian rulers, may well explain the unsullied reputation Nubia and its rulers enjoyed in the Classical tradition as exemplars of moral and ethical rectitude.[20]

Shabataka (704 BC–690 BC)

Shabataka was the most obscure of the 25th Dynasty pharaohs. He was the son of Shabaka and may have served as co-regent for a time toward the end of Shabaka's reign though it is by no means certain.

Pharaoh Shabataka

After the funerary rites for his father at El-Kurru in Napata, he returned to Memphis to rule. Events in Western Asia were once again taking center stage in the geopolitical dramas facing Egypt. Assyria was still embroiled in quelling

20 Bianchi, op. cit., p. 162.

uprisings, especially in Babylonia and most authorities think that Shabataka, like his father before, took advantage of Assyria's preoccupation with rebellion among its subject peoples to make further inroads into Syrio-Palestine. His reign seems to be but a prelude to the dramatic events of the following reign, that of Taharqa.

Taharqa (690 BC–664 BC)

From the point of view of historical data, Taharqa is the best known of the 25th Dynasty pharaohs and his reign is the best documented. In part, this high level of documentation derives from the Assyrian records of the time. Assyrians, mortal enemies of Taharqa, fought a series of wars against him that finally ended in Taharqa's defeat and retreat to Napata. These wars against Taharqa and Egypt are diligently recorded in Assyrian annals.

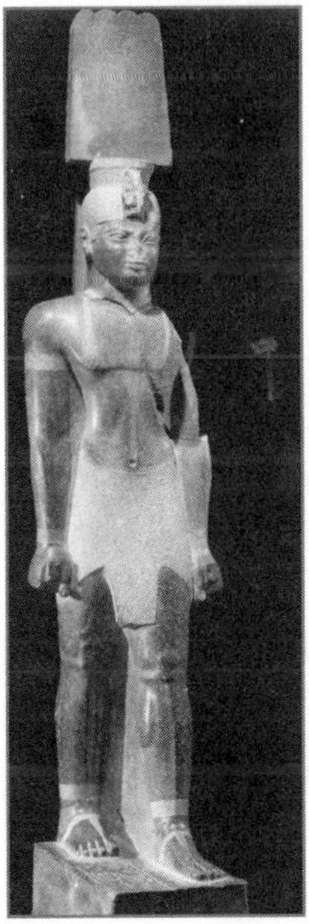

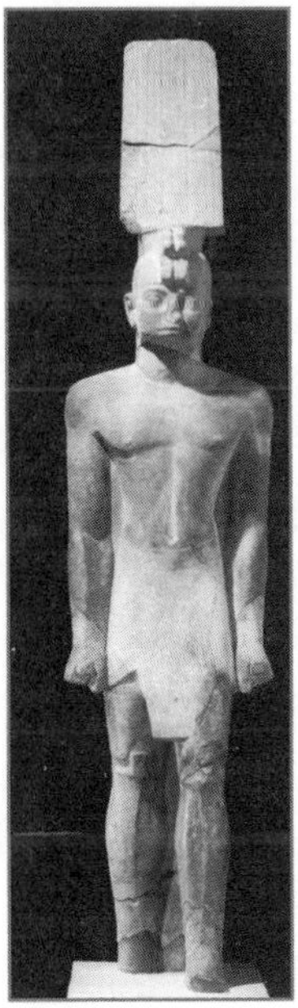

Taharqa—Greatest Pharaoh
of the 25th Dynasty
Two views

Sphinx of Taharqa

Taharqa seems in every respect to have been a brave and resourceful general but, in the end, his army was no match for the military might of Assyria, the dominant military power of the era. Nonetheless, Taharqa's reign, judging from the scale of monument and temple-building throughout Egypt and Napatan Cush, is generally seen as the most glorious of the 25th Dynasty, despite years of incessant war. He too is mentioned in the Old Testament records[21] and is the most recognizable of the 25th Dynasty pharaohs.

Though there is ambiguity in this matter, Taharqa seems to have been one of the younger sons of Piankhy and Abar, a junior queen-consort of Piankhy. As would be seen among other Cushitic kings in later reigns, Abar is prominently featured on Taharqa's coronation stele. When Taharqa was 20, the reigning pharaoh Shabataka summoned him to Memphis as his designated heir and five years later, Taharqa was crowned pharaoh himself. Evidently, Taharqa showed unusual ability from a young age and for that reason was tapped to ascend the throne. It isn't clear if Taharqa was a brother, cousin, or nephew of Shabataka but the rule of succession among Cushite pharaohs often saw the crown passing to surviving brothers, cousins, or nephews instead of lineal sons. It is even suggested that the heir to pharaoh from among the numerous royal Cushite male progeny was determined by divine oracle,[22] a method not unknown in earlier Egyptian dynasties.

For the first dozen years or so of his reign, Egypt was at peace, enabling Taharqa to focus on the monument-building so characteristic of the era. It was the most monument-building seen in Egypt since the time of Rameses II nearly six centuries earlier. Assyria was afflicted with various dynastic troubles and the strenuous demands of holding an empire together. The emperor Sargon, whose reign was more or less contemporaneous with that of Shabaka died in the course of one of Assyria's many battles and his son *Senneracherib* ascended the throne in 705 BC. At first, the new emperor was too preoccupied with consolidating his position on the throne to pay any attention to either Egypt or Palestine, but Hezekiah, king of Judea, a vassal state, revolted against Senneracherib in 701 BC. Senneracherib invested Judea at the head of his army and at first was successful in conquering numerous towns and villages. But when it came to attacking Jerusalem itself, a catastrophe overtook him in the

21 **2Kings** 19:9; **Isaiah** 37:9

22 Bianchi, op. cit., p. 168.

form of a plague. By this time, an Egyptian army led by Taharqa had come to the aid of Hezekiah, and Senneracherib's position had become so untenable in the face of the devastating plague and the advancing army of Taharqa that he had no choice but to retreat, never again approaching Egypt.

The episode is of interest on two accounts: (1) the Biblical identification of *Tirhaka* (Taharqa) as the Cushite king that came to the aid of Jerusalem and (2) it represented the first military encounter between Egypt and Assyria, one that eventually would have fateful consequences. The date of this Assyrian attack on Judea presents problems because if, as some authorities insist, the Assyrian invasion took place in 701 BC, it would have been 10–12 years before Taharqa ascended the throne of Egypt. Some try to get around this difficulty by positing that Taharqa was the general at the head of the Egyptian army while Shabataka still sat on the throne. If the date of 701 BC is maintained, that makes Taharqa far too young to have led an army against the Assyrians. And yet the Biblical account is quite clear in naming Taharqa as the military commander of the Egyptian army coming to defend Jerusalem, meaning the event would have taken place much closer to the year of his accession, 690 BC. As a side bar to this whole chain of events, nothing went right for Sennerachib afterward who was eventually assassinated in 681 BC because of the impiety he committed by destroying the sacred precincts of the gods of Babylon. It has been suggested that the assistance Taharqa rendered to Hezekiah against the Assyrians altered the course of history for Judea. The Assyrians had already conquered and totally dismantled the northern king of Israel in 720 BC, deporting much of the population. The remainder fled southward to Judea causing the population of the city of Jerusalem to expand five-fold. In after years, the remnants of Israel became known as Samaria and though following the same basic religion as the inhabitants of Judea, developed an antagonism with them based on the Judaic assumption that sacrifices to Yahweh could only be carried out at Jerusalem. In the event, Judea remained independent for another 90 years or so until the conquest by Babylon (586 BC) and the subsequent Babylonian captivity detailed in **Jeremiah**, **Chronicles**, and **Kings**. Unlike the catastrophe that befell the Northern Kingdom of Israel, the exiles, after the Persian conquest of Babylon, were allowed to return 50 years later to Judea and Jerusalem, re-build the Temple, and function once more as a nation-state, though as a client to

Persia. However, at least half of the Jewish population remained in Babylon permanently, creating a Jewish cultural, intellectual, and theological center whose influence would be felt for another 1,000 years. It might be inferred that this very different outcome for the Southern Kingdom (Judea) was a result of the Assyrian defeat in which Taharqa's army played an essential role.

For a brief span of years, Taharqa's geopolitical enterprises in Western Asia thrived at the expense of the Assyrians. Not only had he cemented a firm alliance with Hezekiah of Judea, but he also gave support to the Phoenician trading cities whose alliances with Egypt stretched back to early New Kingdom times. However, the successor to Sennerarchib, *Esarhaddon*, was determined to win back all the territory that had revolted against Assyria when Sennerachib's misfortunes overtook him, and that meant a systematic reduction of all the centers of resistance. Esarhaddon had to wage war on a coalition of Phoenicians and was only able to bring them back under Assyrian control when he overran Sidon, sacked it, and razed it to the ground. He now turned his attention to Egypt, the greatest threat to Assyria's imperial designs.

Esarhaddon attacked Egypt in force. In this campaign, Esarhaddon had at least the tacit support of a group of Delta nomarchs led by the ruling party at Sais. It is not clear that these Delta princes actually fought with the Assyrians but they evidently reached an *entente* with Esarhaddon that kept them out of the fighting, allowing the Assyrian king to concentrate his attention on defeating Taharqa. Esarhaddon's army marched inexorably toward Memphis, meeting and defeating Taharqa in three desperate battles. The Cushite king himself received five wounds in the course of these battles, none of them fatal, to the chagrin of the Assyrians.[23] Esarhaddon now invaded the city. Taharqa, knowing that conquest was imminent, was obliged to flee south, leaving a number of family members behind in the haste to escape. However, the inhabitants of Memphis mounted a desperate defense; the Assyrians were obliged to take the city house by house and street by street before the city finally fell. By Assyrian accounts, bodies of the Memphites piled up in the streets, a gruesome testament to the do-or-die effort to defend the sacred city. Taharqa's queens, children, and siblings were among the captives taken by Esarhaddon. Many Cushites and

23 Ibid., p. 171.

their Egyptian allies were deported to Ninevah, capital of Assyria; it is not known whether any members of the Cushite royal family were included among the deportees. When it came time to install new administrators and governors of Lower Egypt loyal to Assyria, Esarhaddon pragmatically drafted these men not from among the Assyrians, but from the ranks of the elites of Lower Egypt that had stayed out of the conflict, tacitly siding with the Assyrian king.

The disaster, devastating as it was to Taharqa, did not bring an end to the conflict. For one thing, Assyrian control was limited to Lower Egypt; Upper Egypt, especially Thebes, remained entirely independent and loyal to Taharqa. Secondly, Esarhaddon was compelled to return to Assyria to put down another of the endemic revolts that beset Assyria. When Esarhaddon departed, Taharqa wasted no time marching back to Memphis and wresting control of the city from the men installed by Esarhaddon. Having dealt with contentious matters back home, Esarhaddon once again took the field at the head of his army, resolved to settle the situation in Egypt once and for all in favor of Assyria. But as it happened, he took ill and died *en route*.

After a brief period of struggle and uncertainty, *Assurbanipal*, son of Esarhaddon won the throne, and within two years was ready once again to march into Egypt. The princes of Syrio-Palestine clearly understood that they were over-matched by the Assyrians and dutifully lined up with them to supply material support and auxiliaries. Once again, Assyrian and Egyptian forces met on the field of battle at Karbaniti, whose actual location remains obscure, and once again the Assyrian army was victorious. Once again the Assyrians invested and overwhelmed Memphis; once again, Taharqa was obliged to retreat to Thebes. And once again, the Assyrian king installed administrators and bureaucrats from the Delta nomes to govern the conquered provinces in Egypt. However, as Assurbanipal was marching toward Thebes to re-engage Taharqa, some of the very Lower Egyptian princes who had been placed administratively in charge of the new Assyrians dominions decided to rebel. It didn't take Assurbanipal long to reverse his march, capture the rebellious princes, and summarily execute them. However, one family managed to retain the confidence and good will of the Assyrian monarch, that of Necho of Sais and his son Psametticus. This ability to maintain a treacherous balancing act between Assubranipal on the one hand and Taharqa on the other put them and

Sais in an advantageous position when the war between the Assyrians and the Cushites finally wound down. The self-interest and opportunism of the Saitic nomarchs were such that they harbored few qualms about siding with a foreign invader against the legitimate government of their own country. They must have had some sense of the future political prospects that awaited them.

There is no clear-cut indication that Assurbanipal ever successfully pursued Taharqa as far as Thebes. He certainly never captured Taharqa who retired to Napata, too far away for the Assyrians to campaign so far from their northern bases. At least during Taharqa's lifetime they were never able to establish control over Upper Egypt. Taharqa died in 664 BC in Napata and was the first Cushite pharaoh buried at Nuri, northeast of Gebel Barkal. In keeping with the monumental splendor he inaugurated in both Egypt and Cush, a pyramidal tomb nearly 200 feet high was constructed as his final resting place, the largest pyramid ever constructed in Cush.

Tantamani or Tanutamon (664 BC–653 BC)

Tanutamon—Last Pharaoh of the 25th Dynasty

Tantamani, who may have been cousin to Taharaqa, succeeded him as pharaoh. He was evidently the governor of Upper Egypt when Taharqa died and thereafter was summoned to Napata to be crowned. He was obviously the designated heir when Taharqa was alive. His first regnal act was to undertake a religious piligrimage north first to the temple of Khnum on Elephantine Island at the First Cataract and from thence to Karnak to sacrifice to Amon. Clearly, Upper Egypt was still under the political sway of Cush since Tantamani was able to return to Karnak without opposition. The northern part of the country was still ruled by princelings loyal to Assyria, and Tantamani, determined to re-assert Cushite authority over the entire country, successfully stormed Memphis once again. It is essential to re-emphasize that the Cushite pharaohs of the 25th Dynasty were never regarded as foreign usurpers, especially not in Upper Egypt; they were clearly and unambiguously regarded as the defenders of Amon both in Napata and in Thebes. The Assyrians were seen as the foreign invaders, even by the dynasts of Lower Egypt, who were forced to come to an accommodation with them by military and political circumstances too powerful to resist and because it suited their own political ambitions within the country to do so.

Assurbanipal, though back in Ninevah and faced with the vexing problems of holding together a fractious empire, was determined not to lose Egypt to Cush. Yet again, the Assyrian emperor led his army back into Egypt, drove Tantamani back to Thebes, then marched on to Thebes where, for the first time, it was overwhelmed and sacked by a foreign army, forcing Tantamani to seek refuge in Napata, his own capital. The Assyrians, however, balked at chasing him to Napata, fully daunted by the dangerous prospect of carrying on a war in an unfamiliar environment far from home surrounded by drought-stricken desert. Tantamani died in Napata, unmolested any further by the Assyrians, and was buried at El-Kurru.

It should be noted that the Assyrian army was the most formidable fighting force of the era, besting nearly all enemies in battle during the imperial period of the 8th and 7th centuries BC. Consequently they managed to acquire an empire of imposing size. The armies of the late 25th dynasty, though courageously led, were no match for them, but then no army of the time was. However, the Assyrians were unable to incorporate Egypt into their own empire despite 20 years of war with the Cushite pharaohs. The best they could do was leave Egypt in the hands of the Saitic dynast Psametticus, while continuing to exercise a kind of remote control over Egypt, undoubtedly exacting periodic tribute as a way of proclaiming and upholding this control. Even this nominal suzerainty over Egypt didn't last long; Psametticus of Sais was able to proclaim himself pharaoh and rule an independent Egypt. Thus, the Assyrians managed, in the course of two decades of war, to defeat and drive out the Cushite pharaohs of the 25th Dynasty, but they never profited from their victory. All they did was pave the way for the rise of the Saitic pharaohs of the 26th Dynasty. Some 40 years later, the Assyrian empire itself collapsed, never to rise again.

Though the Cushites were obliged to retreat to Napata, never again to rule Egypt, remnants of their regime still retained power at Thebes for the time being. The Divine Wife of Amon, the Cushite Shepenoupet II, was still in office and Metemhet, the governor-general of Upper Egypt and 4th Prophet of Amon installed during the 25th Dynasty, continued to govern with power extending from Aswan in the south to Hermopolis in the north. As will be seen, the succeeding dynasty, the 26th under Psametticus I, found a way of reaching an accommodation with these individuals representing the last vestiges of the 25th Dynasty who were still too powerful to summarily dislodge.

The World of the 25th Dynasty

By any measure the 25th Dynasty was unique in the 4,000-year history of Egypt. If one takes the pre-dynastic Nubian pharaonic kingdom of Ta-Seti into consideration and the emergence of the glories of the 12th Dynasty by the unifying rise of Ameny or Amenemhept I, the emprise of Piankhy, who marched into Egypt from Napata to save it from anarchy and political disintegration, represents the third example of the manner in which political currents emerging from the south decisively impacted Egyptian history. Generations of misrule had brought Egypt to the brink of collapse and the strong hand of Piankhy saved Egypt from itself. Egyptians themselves rejoiced at the deliverance from anarchy, especially in Upper Egypt. The Cushite kings of the 25th Dynasty had another factor on their side that facilitated the acceptance of their rule: they were devout worshipers of Amon, working assiduously to uphold and strengthen his religion in Cush and Egypt. By this time, in fact, Napata had become a more important center of Amon-worship than Thebes, and quite a few members of the Amonian priesthood from Egypt had simply relocated to Napata. The kings of Cush had become the true 'Defenders of the Faith' of Amon.

Not coincidentally, once ensconced in Egypt, the 25th Dynasty pharaohs made important additions to the Temple of Amon at Karnak, especially Taharqa who added the Edifice of Tarhaqa to the forecourt between the First and Second Pylons which meant that the avenue of sphinxes were moved to the sides of the court, where they are still located. Even more impressive is the colonnade added to the Precinct of Montu, consisting of four rows of five columns. One of the building innovations introduced by the Cushites into Egypt was excavating foundations beneath the buildings under construction, a technique not used in Egypt until that time. Following the custom of their predecessors, the 25th Dynasty pharaohs built extensively throughout Egypt but equally so at Napata, the imperial capital of Cush, especially in the shadow of Gebel Barkal, the Holy Mountain. Gebel Barkal is a yardang, that is to say a natural formation that appears to have been shaped by human hands. In this case, the yardang takes the form of a rearing cobra, and so striking is the natural likeness, that it was inevitable that it would become a religious site. As early as the time of Thutmosis III in the 18th Dynasty, a temple was constructed there, but it was under aegis of the 25th Dynasty that Gebel Barkal and Napata, the city at its base, would come into such prominence. There was a temple built at the summit of the mountain, on each side of the gap that creates the cobra image—itself an extraordinary engineering feat—and a temple complex built at the foot of the mountain as well.

It has already been noted that while the New Kingdom pharaohs strove to extol and emulate the achievements of their Middle Kingdom predecessors, the pharaohs of the 25th Dynasty adopted a different perspective, working assiduously to revive the memory and highlight the glories of the Old Kingdom. They revived many Old Kingdom texts, the most famous being found on the Shabaka Stone that set forth in detail what has become known as the Memphite Theology. The Shabaka Stone is a stone slab measuring 66 cm in height and 137 cm in width and incised with the surviving hieroglyphs of a worm-ridden, decaying papyrus. This papyrus was found as pharaoh Shabaka was inspecting the temple of Ptah in Memphis. Shabaka, concerned about the loss of the information on the papyrus, had the rest of the text carved onto this stone and it became a fruitful source of insight into the culture and religious doctrines of the ancient Egyptians. The Memphite Theology embodied in the text places Ptah at the center of existence and as the creator god, remaining our best source of information on the Ptah-centered religion of the Old Kingdom. Two other surviving literary compositions of Cushite authorship come down from the 25th Dynasty: ***The Tale of King Neferkare and General Sasenet*** and ***The tale of a King and the Ghost of Senefer***, both set in the Memphis of the Old Kingdom. Again, for the kings and priest-scribes of the 25th Dynasty, Egypt's true classic period was the Old Kingdom, and that was the Egypt from which they drew inspiration.

This preoccupation with the Old Kingdom is brought into even sharper relief by the on-going excavation of the tomb of Karakhamun in South Assasif, on the west bank of Luxor. As seen, Karakhamun was a high-level 25th Dynasty Nubian nobleman and priest of Amun who flourished during the reign of Shabaka. The chief excavator is Dr. Elena Pischikova and collaborating with her is Mr. Anthony Browder who has not only provided hands-on assistance with the excavation but has been its primary fund-raiser. He has published a brief report on the progress of the excavation up to the summer of 2010.[24] The tomb is complex and extensive and there have been several notable discoveries. In fact, Browder refers to it as a "temple tomb". Early in the field work, Dr. Pischikova discovered an exquisitely carved relief of Karakamun himself in a style and posture that was clearly a throw-back to the Old Kingdom. Over the years, interest in the excavatory work at the tomb of Karakhamun has grown and Anthony Browder describes the investigations of a pair of Spanish collaborators:

> A pair of Spanish Egyptologists working with our team made another interesting discovery as they examined the hieroglyphic inscriptions carved on the wall in front of the steps leading down to the burial

24 Browder AT, **Finding Karakhamun: The Collaborative Rediscovery of a Lost Tomb**, Washington DC: IKG, 2011.

compartment. After careful analysis, they concluded that the writings on the wall were copies of passages from the Pyramid Texts that were discovered inside of a burial chamber beneath the pyramid of Unas, the 5th Dynasty king who was buried at Saqqara near the Step Pyramid of Zoser.[25]

Incorporated into the Pyramid Texts carved in Karakhamun's tomb is his very name, followed by the phrase *maa-kheru*, meaning 'true of voice', a phrase dating back to the Old Kingdom. It proclaims that the beatified soul of the deceased (Karakhamun) has been justified by Osiris who gives him his voice, allowing him now to join the company of the resurrected elect. The pharaohs of the 25th Dynasty, especially Shabaka, were fired by a zeal to reconstitute the values and spirit of the Old Kingdom, the era that had made Egypt the wonder of the world.

Another major innovation that occurred toward the end of the 25th Dynasty is the appearance of the Demotic script, the word 'demotic' meaning 'popular' in Greek. Up to the 25th Dynasty, only two scripts were utilized in ancient Egypt, the *medu neter*, e.g., the 'hieroglyphs' and the hieratic, a cursive form of the hieroglyphics. Demotic emerged as a script more suited to everyday business, though it came to be used for all writings in ancient Egypt, especially during the 26th Dynasty. In fact, one of the three inscriptions on the Rosetta Stone was written in Demotic. Though dates vary, it probably made its first appearance around 660 BC and its use continued down to the early 4th century AD, when it was supplanted by Coptic which came from it. Though first making its appearance at the end of the 25th Dynasty, no Egyptologist credits the Cushites for having developed the script. Still, given the birth of Demotic while Cush still ruled Egypt, it is hard to fathom under what other circumstances it could have been created.

Perhaps the most striking element in the 25th Dynasty is the prominence and importance of the Cushite royal women in the dynasty. Already we have touched on the significance of Egypt's Great Royal Wives, through whom the pharaonic kingship passed. We have also noted that four such women ruled as pharaoh over the course of Egyptian dynastic history, the most powerful

25 Ibid., p. 70.

being Hatshepsut whose reign of 20 years brought an amazing era of peace and prosperity to the kingdom. All that being said, it is clear that the force of custom and political preference meant that nearly all of the dynastic rulers of Egypt—with the exceptions noted—were male, in spite of an Old Kingdom attestation that women were as entitled to rule as men. Though there were no female pharaohs during the 25th Dynasty, it is still manifestly evident that the Cushite royal women wielded more political power than their northern sisters.[26] In fact, William Y. Adams says:

> On some occasions the succession seems to have passed not to the son of any previous king but to the son of one of the king's sisters.[27]

It shows the ancient custom of matrilineal succession had not disappeared in Cush. It can be noted parenthetically that, by Meroitic times in the 4th BC in Cush, a number of the royal women actually did ascend to the throne and rule on their own account. The quasi-autonomous power wielded by the Queen Mother of Cush, called the *kendake*, was already well-established by the time a fully-independent Cush, with its capital at Napata, had emerged by or before 800 BC. And the sister of the king of Cush was able to wield nearly supreme authority in Egypt during the 25th Dynasty. Beginning with Piankhy, the Divine Wife of Amon, an office first established in the 18th Dynasty, passed into the hands of a succession of Cushite women, all sisters of the reigning pharaoh. When Piankhy entered Egypt, the reigning Divine Wife of Amon was Shepenoupet I, daughter of pharaoh Osorkon III of the 22nd Dynasty, and Piankhy ensured the succession of his sister in that office by the simple expedient of having Shepenoupet I adopt his sister, Amenirdas I, as her daughter and heir.[28] Amenirdas was a daughter of Kashta and given the expanding power of the Divine Wife of Amon, Piankhy was determined that both royal and sacerdotal power were to be kept within the family. The office

26 The material in this section is largely drawn from Williams L and Finch C, *The Great Queens of Ethiopia*, in **Black Women in Antiquity**, edited by Ivan Van Sertima, New Brunswick: Journal of African Civilizations Ltd., 1988/1992, pp. 12-35.

27 Adams, op. cit., p. 260.

28 Some authorities make Shepenoupet I one of the wives of Kashta, father of Pianky, and therefore the natural mother of Amenirdas instead of her adoptive mother.

of Divine Wife of Amon was no mere ceremonial sinecure; she was in effect the 'female pope' of Amon, reigning from Karnak, and, in the case of Amenirdas, actually ruling over all Upper Egypt on behalf of her brother. Records of her reign as the Divine Wife Amon abound the length and breadth of Egypt along with numerous statues, statuettes, portraits, and items of personal property.

Amenirdas was succeeded by Shepenoupet II, who was either a natural daughter of Amenirdas or a niece adopted by the former as a daughter. But it is plainly evident that during the 25th Dynasty, the office was a quasi-royal one handed down through female relatives of the reigning Cushite pharaoh. As already stated, it was an office carrying great political as well as sacerdotal power, especially in Upper Egypt.

Shepenoupet—Divine Wife Amon

Either Shepenoupet II or a successor, also named Shepenoupet, was the reigning Divine Wife of Amon during the years of struggle with the Assyrians. Moreover, she was still in office at the advent of the 26th Dynasty under Psametticus I based in Sais. As a way of legitimizing his accession, Psametticus married Shepenoupet and made sure that she adopted his daughter who would then be in the line of succession for the position as Chief Wife of Amon. But Shepenoupet's authority was not usurped by Psametticus during her lifetime. She stands as the last of the royal dynasty of Cush and represents the bridge between the 25th and 26th Dynasties. Statuettes and portraits of her have also survived down to our own

Amenirdas—Divine Wife of Amon
Sister of Piankhy

era. To re-iterate, this series of events underscores a central fact about the 25th Dynasty: it was a legitimist dynasty, not a dynasty of invading usurpers as some commentators would have it.

Other royal women figured prominently in the history of the 25th Dynasty. Taharqa's mother was *Abar* and Taharqa informs us that he lived under her roof until he was 21. Soon after his 21st birthday, he was crowned pharaoh of Egypt and Cush and on his coronation stele he describes the voyage of his mother downstream from Napata to officiate at his coronation at Thebes. Unlike in Egypt, the office of pharaoh in Cush was elective, and it was usually the kendake or queen mother who cast the deciding vote for the successor out of the pool of eligible royal princes. Since Abar obviously decided in Taharqa's favor, it is clear why he held her in such reverence and why she was the chief officiant at his coronation. Two other royal queens whose names are known to us are *Amendukhat*, Chief Royal Wife of Taharqa, and *Qalhata*, mother of Tantamani, successor to Taharqa. Nearly nothing is known about these queens, apart from their names and royal connections, but it is safe to assume they played the same or similar role in the affairs of the kingdom as Abar and other royal mothers and wives.

The devotion of the dynasts of the 25th Dynasty to Amon is well-known but there was a similar rise in the devotion to Isis among the same dynasts, especially among the royal women.[29] It is for this reason that so many noble and royal women were buried at Abydos, the traditional sacred burial ground for the royal deceased. Abydos was sacred to Osiris but since Osiris was the brother-husband of Isis, it was sacred to Isis also. Whatever the case, Isis exerted a powerful influence on the royal women of the 25th Dynasty and through them the pharaohs as well.

IV. **The 26th Dynasty** (664 BC–525 BC)

Psametticus I (664 BC–610 BC)

The story of the ascent of the 26th Dynasty, based in Sais in Lower Egypt, has its genesis in the years of war between Assyria and the Cushitic 25th Dynasty. During the ebb and flow of military fortunes during that 20-year war, the Saitic dynasts had played the dangerous game of manipulating both sides. During one of the interludes, when the Assyrian king withdrew to Assyria to take care of pressing affairs at home leaving what he presumed to be Egyptian loyalists in charge of northern Egypt, the officials there lost no time revolting against Assyria once Taharqa renewed his assault on Assyria's Egyptian holdings. The Assyrian king Ashurbanipal immediately re-invaded, recaptured the northern cities, and proceeded to execute the ruling elites *en masse* in Sais, Mendes, and Pelusium. Those not executed were deported to the Assyrian capital of Nineveh. And yet somehow, Necho I of Sais, father of Psametticus, managed to avoid both execution and deportation. More than that, Ashurbanipal re-established Necho on the throne of Sais and made his son Psametticus ruler of the nearby nome of Athribis, bringing a large swath of northern Egypt under the control of the Saites. Ashurbanipal not only spared Necho and his son but gave them mastery over more territory than before. One can but speculate on his reasons for doing so. That Necho and Psametticus had both won complete favor with the Assyrians is attested in the Assyrian names bestowed upon them by which

29 Bianchi, op. cit., pp. 178-9.

they were henceforth known in the Assyrian annals.[30] Clearly they, somehow, had managed to convince their Assyrian overlords that they were men to be relied on.

As seen above, after yet another Assyrian withdrawal with hand-picked governors left in place in Egypt, the new Cushite pharaoh Tantamani again marched north to re-conquer the lands the Assyrians had won. It was during this Cushite re-conquest that Necho I was killed as Tantamani re-asserted, temporarily, his authority in the region.

Assyria, determined not to allow Cush to re-take Egypt, again marched south, routing Tantamani, laying waste to Thebes, and pushing him all the way back to Napata, permanently.

With the death of Necho I, his son Psametticus I was confirmed as the sole ruler of Sais, Athribis, Heliopolis, and the lands of the western Delta. Though Tanutamon was still making forays into Lower Egypt to reclaim Egypt for Cush, Psametticus still dated the onset of his reign from 664 BC, nine years

Psametticus I—Founder of 26th Dynasty

before the final defeat of Cush at the hands of Assyria. However, the kingdoms of the eastern Delta, Sebennytos and Busiris, were still independent of Psametticus's authority and Psametticus was too vigorous and ambitious a ruler

30 Budge, op. cit., p. 203.

to allow such autonomy so near his own domains for long. In the eighth year of his reign (645 BC), Psametticus was able to compel the submission of both Sebennytos and Busiris, making him the master of all Lower Egypt. By that time he was able to establish his complete independence from Assyria whose multiplying problems were systematically destabilizing its empire. It didn't take Psametticus long to assert his authority over all Egypt, from the Mediterranean to Aswan; in fact, Elephantine Island at Aswan henceforth became Egypt's southern boundary. His power was such that he was able to have his daughter Nitocris adopted by Shepenoupet II, thence to become her successor as the Divine Wife of Amon. Psametticus did not try to remove Shepenoupet while she was alive and some authorities report that, in fact, he married her.[31] Though he had benefited enormously from the Assyrian defeat of the Cushite pharaohs, Psametticus was careful to cement his legitimacy by upholding the position of Shepenoupet II during her lifetime—even marrying her as already mentioned—as well as reaching an accommodation with Mentemhet, 4th Prophet of Amon and governor of Upper Egypt. This policy toward the hold-over powers from the 25th Dynasty in Thebes is yet another indicator that must be stressed repeatedly (since so many don't) that the 25th Dynasty line of pharaohs was the legitimate line; they were not and were never seen as usurpers—not even by their Egyptian enemies in the north. In the event, in the aftermath of the Assyrio-Cushite war for control of Egypt, Psametticus became the re-unifier and ruler of Egypt. By staying aloof from the conflict between Assyria and Cush, Psametticus was now in a position to take full advantage of his opportunistic ambition.

However, even though Psametticus was able to establish his daughter Nitocris as the heir to the crucial office of Divine Wife of Amon, thereby cementing his hold over Upper Egypt, his work was by no means finished. There were still petty rulers in Lower Egypt not reconciled to his rule who were stirring up revolt against him. To strengthen their position, they formed alliances with the Libyan tribes, the traditional strategy of the princelings of the Delta seeking to establish independence from the central authority in Thebes. Psametticus was a man of no mean ability and, levying troops from all the nomes re-unified under his authority, marched westward against this Libyan-dominated coalition and

31 Ibid., p. 204.

handily defeated it, thus establishing incontestably a united rule over all Egypt. Garrisons were established on the western borders of the Delta, on the Pelusian branch of the Nile in the eastern Delta, and on Elephantine Island (Aswan), the new southern border between Egypt and Cush. But Psametticus's reign marked a new departure in an entirely different way: among his conscripts were cohorts of mercenaries from among Egypt's Mediterranean neighbors as far north as southern Europe. These included warriors from among mainland Greeks, Ionian Greeks, and Carians (southwestern Anatolia) in addition to Phoenicians, Syrians, and Israelites[32], all of whom had been driven out of their homelands by the Assyrian onslaught. But the inclusion of Greeks was especially significant for two reasons: (1) it was the first time that Greeks in any numbers had ever come into Egypt and (2) it marked the beginning of a trend in the 26th Dynasty for the pharaohs to recruit the largest contingents of their mercernaries from among the Greeks. We have already remarked that individual Greeks such as Orpheus and Homer were reputed to have visited Egypt in the 8th and 7th centuries BC but the number of Greeks and Carians that now started to flow into Egypt meant that the Saitic pharaohs were obliged to set aside Egyptian lands for them to settle on. This policy was totally unprecented up to that time. It also meant that the pharaohs of the 26th and succeeding dynasties would minimize that portion of their troops from among Egyptian and Nubian levies as had been the custom from the earliest dynasties. From then on, it was no longer a purely native army responsible for the defense and protection of Egypt.

There is a curious incident reported by Herodotus that, if related correctly, must have compromised Psametticus greatly. There were a number of garrisons of Egyptian soldiers that had not received pay or relief for three years. According to Herodotus, 240,000 men revolted against Psametticus and went off in a body to Cush to offer their services to the reigning king there.[33] No entreaty by Psametticus could induce the soldiers to alter their course of action and upon arriving in Cush, presumably in the capital city of Napata, they were given a fervent welcome by the king and incorporated into his army. If in fact such a thing happened, it might explain the policy adopted by Psametticus and all

32 A Jewish military colony was eventually established at Elephantine Island. Vid., Grimal, op. cit., p. 355.

33 Herodotus, op. cit., p. 140.

his successors in the 26th Dynasty to rely increasingly on foreign mercenaries, especially Greeks, to fill the ranks of the pharaonic army.

During the 54-year reign of Psametticus, Egypt opened up to foreigners as never before. Merchants from Grecian lands and elsewhere began to trade with Egypt on an ever larger scale. Grecian cities such as Miletus (Anatolia) and Samos (eastern Aegean) established thriving mercantile connections with Egypt, importing grain, papyrus, gold and other of Africa's exotic luxury goods while bringing in pottery, olive oil, and textiles. Because, compared to earlier epochs, Greeks were pouring into Egypt as mercenaries and merchants in continuing surges, a new class of Egyptian-Greek interpreters, spurred by the policy of Psametticus, sprang up serving as much as tour guides as intermediaries in business transactions. It would have been interpreters such as these who were employed by Herodotus nearly 200 years later as he traveled from one end of Egypt to the other gathering information about the history of the country. It may or may not have been apparent to Psametticus, but once in Egypt, the Greeks were in the country to stay.

Though Psametticus had grown to depend on the Greeks to staff his army and for the lucrative trade they brought in, he was not an unabashed Hellenophile. If anything, in the religious and cultural spheres, he promoted an intensification of Egyptian values and ideas. He continued the policy of previous regimes by fostering and promoting artistic themes and styles from the Old and Middle Kingdoms. He more effectively nationalized Egyptian religion by de-emphasizing the Asiatic cults that had crept into Egypt since the time of the late New Kingdom. Psametticus even went to the extreme of 'de-Egyptianizing' Set, turning him into the god of the Hyksos. Until the effective end of Egyptian history, Set would be increasingly demonized in the country. On the other hand, the cults of the sacred animals, notably those of the Apis Bull, the Ibis of Thoth, and the Cat of Bast, grew increasingly prominent. The cult of Apis outdid all others, especially in the mortuary domain. The death of an Apis bull was attended with as much ceremony as that of the pharaoh—all of the deceased Apises being buried in the famous Serapeum, each in his own granite sarcophagus, typically weighing 60 tons.

By this time, Thebes and the Temple of Amon had ceased to be of capital importance in Egyptian affairs—another reason that the main locus for the worship of Amon shifted south to Napata. Thebes's and Amon's influence could not be completely nullified, obviously, as seen in the steps taken by Psametticus to establish his daughter as the heir to Shepenoupet II, the Divine Wife Amon. Thebes was still the main center of cultural and religious life in Upper Egypt. But, continuing a trend seen distinctively in the 25th Dynasty, Memphis and its patron deity, Ptah, experienced a resurgence in the spiritual life of the country, once again becoming the nation's administrative center when Psametticus moved his capital there. What is more, the Demotic script, making its appearance toward the end of the 25th Dynasty, became the standard method of writing throughout the country, superseding hieratic almost entirely. This near-exclusive employment of the Demotic script for non-sacred writing continued in Egypt until the 5th century of Roman times, a period of 1,000 years.[34] Though Memphis was re-established as the political and religious center of Egypt, the home city of Psametticus, Sais, began to enjoy a new prominence. Psametticus maintained a residence there; it was the site of the royal necropolis for the dynasty. Sais was an ancient city sacred to Neith, a very ancient goddess. It held special appeal to Athenians from the seventh century BC onward because they identified their own patron goddess, Athena, with Neith. In fact, concerning Sais and other major northern Egyptian cities, Petrie tells us:

> The large number of splendid private monuments and statues show the riches of the bureaucracy, and the magnificence of the temples astounded the wandering Greek.[35]

Egypt prospered greatly during Saitic Dynasty, and the era ushered the last great efflorescence of Egyptian art and architecture. After its prolonged war with the 25th Dynasty, Assyria entered into an extended period of upheaval at the edges of its empire created by kingdoms determined to throw off the Assyrian yoke. Though the Assyrian king Ashurbanipal managed to maintain Assyrian ascendancy among the subject states in his empire during his life, eventually, with his death in 627 BC, Assyrian strength rapidly dissipated.

34 The inscription on the Rosetta Stone, the key to the eventual decipherment of the ancient Egyptian language, was written in hieroglyphics, hieratic, and demotic.

35 Petrie WF, **A History of Egypt: From the XIXth to the XXXth Dynasties**, London: Methuen & Co., 1905, p. 331.

This decline was punctuated by a series of savage civil wars among contenders for the Assyrian throne. Assyria's numerous enemies and restless vassal-states now began to take advantage of Assyria's obvious and increasing weakness, and in 605 BC Nineveh would be overrun by an alliance of Babylonians and Persian Medes. It was the death-blow to Assyria, and once conquered, it would never rise again. The steady decimation of Assyrian power played right into the hands of Psametticus, who had managed to extricate Egypt from Assyrian domination, and under his rule Egypt once again became the dominant power in the region, though it could not recover its Western Asiatic empire. Many of the northern cities of Egypt, especially Sais and Memphis, received rich benefactions from Psametticus but, according to Petrie, '...little was done in Upper Egypt, and Thebes was left entirely to the dominance of the Divine Wife of Amen', the *de facto* queen of Upper Egypt.[36]

One of the subject peoples that started tearing away at the carcass of the Assyrian empire were the nomadic warriors from the steppes known as the Scythians. After the death of Ashurbanipal, they had become bold enough to invade Asia Minor, penetrating as far as southern Palestine. Psametticus went out with his army to meet this emerging threat and defeated them at Ashdod, pushing them out of Palestine altogether, although Petrie asserts he turned them aside with gifts and bribes.[37] However, in a dramatic turn-about, Psametticus began to aid Assyria, sensing the changing balance of power had the potential of throwing the entire region into chaos in a manner potentially threatening to Egypt's interests. In the end, the forces banding together against Assyria—the Chaldeans, Persians, and Scythians—were too formidable and too determined to be thwarted. A series of repeated attacks sustained over a period of 15 years brought down Assyria for good.

When Psametticus died at the end of a long reign of 54 years, Egypt had revived from the devastations of the wars with Assyria, re-establishing much of its influence in Western Asia and experiencing a cultural flowering at home—in reality, a continuation of the renaissance inaugurated by the 25th Dynasty. There is an interesting comment about Psametticus vouchsafed by Budge worth quoting:

36 Ibid., p. 332.
37 Ibid., p. 331.

> An interesting black basalt "Intercolumnal Slab" in the British Museum shows us the king [Psametticus] making an offering to the gods… attempts were made many years ago to prove from the figure of the king cut upon it, which is undoubtedly intended to be a portrait, that Psamettichus I, was of Nubian or Ethiopian origin, but some think that it proves him to have been a Libyan.[38]

This comment by Budge is revealing from several standpoints. It shows that there was no racial distinction between the Saitic pharaohs of the 26th Dynasty and the Cushite pharaohs of the 25th. It also shows that the term 'Libyan' does not imply a non-African ethnicity as nearly all modern writers of ancient history presume. In fact when Herodotus, among others, refers to the entire continent of Africa, his name for it was 'Libya'. This passage is also of interest because of Ameres, the Ethiopian, reported to be the first king of the 26th Dynasty in the King List of Manetho as recounted in the version by Eusebius.[39] Conceivably, confusion might have risen with Eusebius, one of the later translators and transcribers of Manetho. In that translation, Tanutamon, the last king of the Cushitic or Ethiopian 25th Dynasty, was somehow conflated and combined with the 26th Dynasty. In Eusebius's version, Taharqa is listed as the last king of the 25th Dynasty without any mention of Tanutamon. Nonetheless, it is essential to insist that ties at several levels bound the 26th Dynasty to its predecessor Dynasty, the 25th, and one of those ties was ethno-racial. A quote from William Flinders Petrie further substantiates this premise:

> There is in the name Psamtek [Psametticus] a suggestion of Ethiopian influence; and it would be quite likely that at about 690, when Taharqa was at his strongest in Lower Egypt and across to Palestine, he may have tried to secure the young prince Nekau [Necho] by alliance with one of the Ethiopian princesses, who became the mother of Psamtek.[40]

Again, indelible ties linked the 26th to the 25th Dynasty.

---

38 Budge, op. cit., p. 209.

39 Waddell WG, translator, **Manetho**, Cambridge: Harvard University Press, 1980, pp. 171-73.

40 Petrie, op. cit., p. 320.

Psametticus I at death was succeeded by his son Necho II after a 54-year reign—the first 10 years overlapping with the reign of Tanutamon—the longest since that of Rameses II. His reign is considered one of Egypt's finest epochs.

Necho II (610 BC–594 BCBC)

In spite of previous enmity, Necho II's father Psametticus had reached an *entente cordiale* with Assyria, a policy continued by his son. Necho's army actually crossed the Euphrates in 609 BC to assist Assyria in its attempt to re-take Harran which had been captured by the Medes and Babylonians. This

Necho II

endeavor was unsuccessful, and the inexorable decline in Assyrian fortunes continued unabated. Though he was ostensibly coming to the assistance of the Assyrians, their inability to maintain their place in Syria-Palestine meant that Necho could now assert his power there. The kingdom of Judea felt the brunt of Necho's imperial ambitions, who took the battle to King Josiah of Judea at Megiddo, killing him and bringing Judea under his control. When Jehoahaz, Josiah's son succeeded his father, Necho, not approving this accession, removed Jehoahaz and set his brother Jehoiakim on the throne instead.[41] The king in his capital Jerusalem was required to pay tribute to Necho for the next four years, and Necho controlled Western Asia as far north as Syria.

41 See *II Kings 23: 29-35* for the Biblical version of these events.

But by 605 BC, the rising power and imperial ambitions of the Babylonians could not be denied. The Babylonian king's son, Nebuchadnezzar, invested the city of Carchemish, driving out the Egyptian garrison, soundly defeating them as they fled south near Hamath. It was in 605 BC that Nebuchadnezzar ascended the Babylonian throne after the death of his father, Nabopolassar. Having already driven Necho II back to his own lands, he turned the Phoenician cities of Tyre and Sidon, as well as Damascus and Jerusalem, into tribute-paying vassals. However, a Babylonian attack on Egypt's border was successfully repelled to the extent that Necho was able once again to seize control of Gaza.

In line with the policy of his father, Necho II continued to cultivate good relations with the Greek world, actively promoting the establishment of Greek colonies. It is probable that the much-remarked sojourn of Thales of Miletus (b. 624 BC – d. 546 BC)—mathematician and philosopher—to Egypt took place during the reign of Necho II. Thales is usually credited with being the first Greek philosopher and mathematician, and yet, though born in Miletus, a Greek city in Anatolia, both of Thales's parents were Phoenician, a heritage that, no doubt, facilitated his discourses with the Egyptian priests among whom he spent seven years. The close Phoenician connection to ancient Egypt had been in force for at least 900 years.

Most of the Greeks coming into Egypt were Ionians, originating in cities on the Anatolian coast or on islands just off that coast. Under Necho, these Ionians served not only as mercenaries but as shipbuilders and mariners for Necho's burgeoning navy. As a means of facilitating the ever-increasing Egyptian desire for commerce, Necho employed 12,000 workers (Herodotus reports 120,000) to dig a canal between the Pelusiac Nile branch of the eastern Delta and the Red Sea. It was just the latest of several Egyptian canals connecting the Nile to the Red Sea excavated several thousand years before the Suez Canal, but, according to Herodotus, Necho's work team never actually finished the canal.[42]

Given Necho II's consuming interest in the East African trade, it was no accident that he was the pharaoh who commissioned the first circumnavigation

42 Herodotus, op. cit., p. 193. The canal was, however, completed by the Persian emperor Darius I.

of Africa known to history. This voyage was reported by Herodotus[43] who says that an Egyptian fleet captained and manned mostly by Phoenicians sailed from Egypt's Red Sea port and from there into the Indian Ocean. Herodotus further reports that his informants told him that when the fleet rounded the southern end of the continent, the sun was seen crossing the sky to their right, exactly as would be expected for any ship sailing from east to west around the Cape of Good Hope. Oddly, Herodotus did not believe this report, but modern scholars are convinced that the voyage did take place solely on this piece of evidence. Herodotus was told that as the fleet made its way down the coast of East Africa, it would put into a suitable port every autumn and plant grain, harvesting it in the spring to re-provision itself before continuing the voyage. By the time the fleet returned to Egypt through Gibraltar and across the Mediterranean, it had been sailing for three years. It must be supposed that during all that time, numerous landfalls were made to collect specimens. The time spent cultivating grains for provisioning the voyage must have provided ample opportunity to conduct limited exploratory excursions into an African interior that no one from the countries bordering the Mediterranean had ever seen or even knew existed. Contact must have been made with indigenous peoples, but there is no record that any were brought back to Egypt on the return voyage home. The traditional date given for this east-to-west circumnavigation of Africa is 600 BC, 21 centuries before Vasco da Gama was able for the first time in European history to round the Cape of Good Hope from west-to-east and sail part-way up the east coast of Africa before embarking across the Indian Ocean to India, his primary destination. Categorically, it can be said that da Gama did not circumnavigate the entire continent in the manner of Necho's Phoenician mariners. Though da Gama's round-the-cape African voyage has been endlessly celebrated in the histories of Europe's 'Age of Discovery', by comparing the voyage of Necho's fleet to that of Vasco da Gama, the reader can judge which one was the greater navigational feat.

Necho II died in 594 BC, leaving behind three daughters and a single son to inherit the throne, Psametticus II.

43 Ibid., p. 283-4.

Psametticus II (594 BC–589 BC)

Psametticus II was married to Takhut, and his daughter by her—*Ankhnesneferibre*—following a tradition in place since the 25th Dynasty, was established as the heir to Nitocris, the reigning Divine Wife of Amon at the time of Psametticus's succession. Ankhnesneferibre did not succeed to the position until 584 BC, five years after the death of Psametticus II, but she held the office for another 59 years, that is, until the time of the Persian conquest in 525 BC.

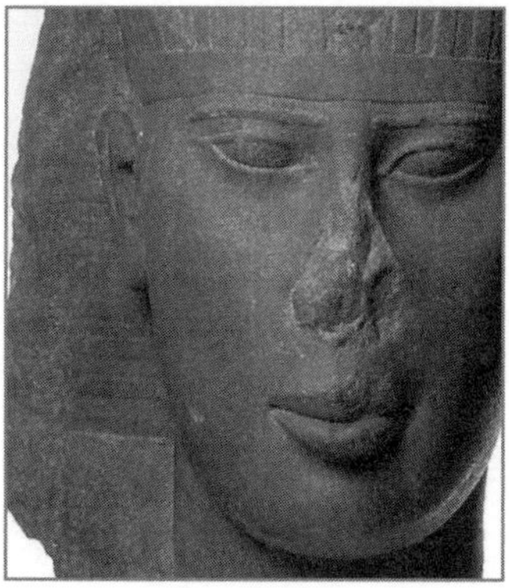

Psametticus II

It is during the reign of Psametticus II that the last military confrontation between Egypt and Cush, now ruled by *Anlamani* took place. It is not at all clear what the *casas belli* was, but the Egyptian army, stocked with the requisite number of Greek mercenaries, was sufficiently powerful to advance as far south as the third cataract, threatening Napata itself. However, Psametticus II attempted no permanent conquest and his army retreated back to the Egyptian lands north of Elephantine. Thereafter, a buffer zone 90 miles long, the *Dodekaschoinos*, extended southward from Aswan,[44] becoming especially important geopolitically during the conflict between Rome and Meroe in the time of Augustus. But this invasion had the profound effect of causing the Cushites to shift their capital southward from Napata to Meroe, the latter city flourishing brilliantly for the next 700 years. As if to punctuate his invasion of Cush, Psametticus undertook a campaign of destruction and defacement of the

44 The word *Dodeskaschoinos* means '12 *schoinoi*', a schoinoi measuring 7 ½ miles.

monuments of the 25th Dynasty. But he did the same thing with those of his father and predecessor Necho II, the motives for which are totally obscure.[45] After a reign of just under six years, Psametticus II died in 589 BC.

Apries (589 BC–570 BC)

Sphinx of Apries

Apries, son and successor to Psametticus II, upon his accession found himself immediately embroiled in conflicts in Western Asia. He was able to overmaster the Phoenician cities of Sidon and Tyre as well as Cyprus. Apries then found himself entangled in events unfolding in Canaan. Zedekiah, king of Judea since the time of Necho II, had, with urging from Egypt, launched a rebellion against Babylonia, now the reigning power in the Fertile Crescent and Western Asia. A triple alliance consisting of Judea, Phoenicia, and Egypt struggled to push Babylon out of Syria and Canaan. Nebuchadnezzar II, the Babylonian king, invested Jerusalem for two years while at the same time capturing the Phoenician city of Sidon. However, the other major Phoenician city, Tyre, held out against Nebuchadnezzar, supplied from the sea by Apries' navy, and would continue to do so for the next 15 years. In the end, the Babylonians were able to drive the Egyptian army supporting Judea back to Egypt, and Jerusalem fell to the Babylonians in 587 BC. Zedekiah was eventually captured at Jericho. He

45 Grimal, op. cit., p. 362.

was forced to watch the execution of his son after which his eyes were put out. He was then sent with the bulk of the Jewish population to Babylon, marking the beginning of what has subsequently become known as the Babylonian Captivity, though there were in fact three deportations of Jews to Babylon, 597 BC, 587 BC, and 582 BC.[46] The last deportation in 582 BC was occasioned by the assassination of the Babylonian governor of Jerusalem by partisans of the prophet Jeremiah. Jeremiah and these followers subsequently fled south to the Egyptian city of Tahpanhes. Nebuchadnezzar was determined to rid newly-conquered Jerusalem of all malcontents, hence the final deportation that sent Jews into the Captivity. The Captivity and Exile ended in 538 BC with the conquest of Babylon by the Persians who allowed the captive Jewish population to return to Judea and re-build the Temple. No more than half returned, and the remainder stayed in Babylon maintaining themselves as a distinct Jewish community in Babylon for another 16 centuries. From about 200 AD onward, the Babylonian Jews were the primary writers of the Talmud, and hence the purveyors of a Rabbinical Judaism that went beyond the Torah, making Babylon the center and wellspring of Jewish culture and religious evolution.

Apries' entire reign was beset with internal military strife, starting with a mutiny that broke out in the garrison at Elephantine by soldiers disgruntled by the poor showing of the Egyptian army against Nebuchadnezzar. On that occasion, his general, Nes-Heru, managed to suppress the revolt.[47] Later, in 570 BC, he sent a mercenary army to the aid of a Libyan ally *Adikran* of Cyrene who was beset by Dorian marauders from the Grecian mainland. Apries' army was soundly beaten, and on the ignominious retreat back to Egypt, a battle broke out between Apries' regular Egyptian troops and the Greek/Carian mercenaries, turning into a full-scale civil war. The Egyptians turned against Apries altogether, raising one of their generals, Amasis, to the status of pharaoh. Apries now had only his Greeks and Carians, 30,000 strong, to support him, eventually confronting Amasis outside Memphis. This cohort of mercenaries was defeated by the military corps with Amasis. Apries himself was killed. Amasis, however, paid due respect to his predecessor and had him

46 Jeremiah 39–43; 2 Kings; 2 Chronicles; Ezra.

47 Budge EAW, **A History of Egypt**, Volume IV, Oosterhout N.B.: Anthropological Publications, 1902/1968, p. 14.

buried with honor and ceremony in Sais. In fact, some reports have Apries surviving the battle and living for another three years in Sais, though he was eventually executed when he attempted to lead a contingent of Greeks in revolt against Amasis.[48] Nebuchadnezzar thought he saw an opportunity with such internal strife besetting Egypt and launched his own army southward. In this attempt, however, he failed since Amasis was able to turn him back.

As Budge relates, in spite of the military reverses that eventually cost him his kingdom and life, Apries' reign is remembered as one of great prosperity and even opulence for Egypt.[49] His name is found carved all over Egypt and he lavished no small attention to the maintenance and beautification of temples in Memphis (Ptah) and Heliopolis (Rā). Many monuments, art work, and bronze work are of an exceptionally high standard, so Apries' lack of success politically and militarily on the international front did not preclude prosperity and cultural achievements at home.

Amasis (570 BC–526 BC)

Pharaoh Amasis

Amasis, another Saite, was a man of humble origins, whose reputation to posterity was that of a *bon vivant*, a characteristic that made him seem 'un-pharaonic' to many Egyptians. He was married to the noblewoman *Thent-*

48 Petrie, op. cit., pp. 351-2.
49 Ibid., pp. 4-5.

kheta, who would be the mother of his successor, Psamettichus III. Another of his wives was Ānkh-*nes-nefer-ab-Rā*, important because she became the adopted daughter and designated heiress of Nitocris, the reigning Divine Wife of Amon. Marriage to Ānkh-nes-nefer-ab-Rā enabled Amasis to legitimize his claim to the throne.

Though Amasis was to continue the policy of good relations with the Greek maritime cities, he had to make some concession to the nationalistic fervor of his own people who detested the presence of Greek foreigners on Egyptian soil. He accommodated both imperatives by giving the Greeks the port city of Naucratis, southeast of present day Alexandria, limiting their settlements to that city and its environs. Herodotus has this to say about this policy of Amasis:

> Amasis favored the Greeks and granted them a number of privileges, of which the chief was the gift of Naucratis as a commercial headquarters for any who wished to settle in the country.[50]

Naucratis had, in fact, served as a city for Greek expatriates since the time of Psametticus I, but Amasis awarded the city certain commercial privileges, giving it the status of a trading post. This allowed the Greeks and other foreigners to build temples to their own gods. According to Herodotus, foreign goods could not be transshipped through any other Delta port. Given wide commercial latitude within Naucratis, Amasis was able to keep the Greek expatriates contained and controlled. Naucratis rapidly became the most important trading city in the Mediterranean while remaining in all respects, a Greek city on Egyptian soil.

It is thought that the policy of encouraging foreign trade and giving foreigners the opportunity to establish their own entrepots contributed greatly to the prosperity of the regime of Amasis, reaching the highest peak of the entire 26th Dynasty. Modern estimates of Egypt's population size at this time are 7.5 million, thought to be very populous for the era.[51] Despite the evident wealth of Amasis, he was constantly seeking sources of revenue to support his navy and his army of mercenaries upon which the security of his realm

50 Herodotus, op. cit., p. 200.
51 Grimal, op. cit., p. 364.

depended. It meant practically that the spigot of wealth that had customarily flowed into the temples during the New Kingdom had to be if not turned off then turned down—considerably. Temple revenues began to be restricted during the late Saite period, a trend that would become more pronounced in the later dynasties under the Persians and Ptolemies. It was just one more factor, among many, that progressively diminished the power and influence of the priesthood. While not deliberately neglecting the gods, it was evident that the drive to make money had taken possession of the royal house as never before. The hidden, unacknowledged god of the Saites was Mammon.

All things considered, posterity generally recorded a good opinion of the reign of Amasis, certainly with the Greeks among whom he was universally admired. He was able to establish a military overlordship over a number of cities of Cyprus, giving him access to a fleet that allowed him to trade all over the Mediterranean. He used his fleet to help allies against the growing might of Persia which had supplanted Assyria as the dominant empire in that part of the world. His new alliances included Croesus, King of Lydia, Polycrates of Samos, and even Nabonidus, King of the Babylonians. The alliance with Polycrates is also noteworthy for the history of Greek philosophy because one of Polycrates's subjects was none other than the 18-year old Pythagoras who had already shown incontrovertible evidence of genius. Thales, a relative of Pythagoras, advised him to travel to Egypt to study and it was Polycrates who gave him the necessary letter of introduction to Amasis.

Pythagoras was the first—and only—Greek to be allowed to ascend to the highest levels of temple initiation, having spent 22 years studying and learning in the Egyptian temple system. But it is worth pointing out that Pythagoras was only half Greek; his father (some say his mother) was Phoenician.[52] Pythagoras is an important historical figure from a number of standpoints but he is especially interesting because his late biographers, most notably Iamblichus (c. 300 AD), provided descriptions of his initiation, the only such records extant of higher initiation in the Egyptian priesthood. It is hard to gauge just how accurate these reports are; certainly some parts of the descriptions must be taken with the proverbial grain of salt. Nevertheless, when corroborated from

52 See Kenneth S. Guthrie, **The Pythagorean Sourcebook and Library** (Grand Rapids: Phanes Press, 1987), for biographical material on Pythagoras.

other material, it may be possible to arrive at some semblance of a picture of initiation in the inner temple. One thing for certain was that foreigners attempting to win admittance to the temple had a harder way to go than the native. The priests went out of their way to discourage Greeks, not the least of which was because their impatient and skeptical mentality simply made them

Pythagoras—Egyptian Temple Initiate
First and Greatest of Greek Philosophers

unfit for the deeper knowledge the temple had to impart. Greeks always wanted to ask questions, and there was little scope for such questioning attitudes in the temple. Pythagoras was given all manner of demeaning and meaningless tasks to perform as a way of discouraging him. His persistence, patience, humility and cheerful willingness to accept whatever trial was put before him eventually won the priests over, but then Pythagoras was perhaps the most unusual man of his time.

Born in 570 BC and raised on the isle of Samos, Pythagoras was the son of a wealthy merchant and a woman named *Parthenis* which probably accounts for traditions asserting that his was a 'virgin' birth: *parthenos* = 'virgin'. He showed himself to be unusually gifted from childhood and as he grew older, went around the islands of the Eastern Mediterranean to study among the most learned Greeks of the period. It was Thales, usually considered the first Greek philosopher and himself a student in Egypt for seven years, who encouraged Pythagoras to travel to Egypt for further education. Since he came from a prominent family, and though but a youth of 18, possessed a brilliant reputation, Pythagoras had no trouble securing a letter of introduction and recommendation from Polycrates the tyrant of Samos who, on account of a thriving mercantile relationship, was a personal friend of the Pharaoh Amasis. Upon seeing the introductory letter from Polycrates, Amasis provided the young Pythagoras with a letter of his own, bidding the priests of Heliopolis to accept the young Samian postulant into the temple for instruction. Greeks had been trickling into Egypt for some time seeking higher knowledge. Orpheus, the acknowledged, semi-legendary originator of the Greek religious system, was said to have studied in Egypt. The most famous epic poet in history, Homer, is also reported to have traveled to Egypt, as did Solon, the Athenian political reformer and law-giver. But, as already noted, the priests of the temple were in no way welcoming to the unlettered interlopers from the Grecian isles, in fact telling Solon, 'you Greeks are but children, there is no such thing as an old Greek.'[53] Hoary tradition, in fact, forbade initiation of foreigners in Egypt. But after 600 BC, Egypt's political circumstances had changed drastically, and after his accession in 570 BC, Pharaoh Amasis, like his Saitic predecessors, depended on Greek mercenaries to fill his military ranks and Greek seafaring cities for much-needed trade. He must not have wanted to offend Polycrates, hence his readiness to give Pythagoras a letter recommending him for temple instruction.

The priests of Heliopolis could not reject the pharaonic command outright, but they hit upon the stratagem of 'passing the buck.' Insisting that all of their learning had been lost and their temple instruction was now at a very low ebb, they sent Pythagoras to the Temple of Ptah in Memphis. These priests were no more welcoming than their confederates in the Temple of Rā had been and, continuing the ruse, insisted that they too no longer possessed any significant knowledge, sending Pythagoras south to the Temple of Amon at Karnak. The priests of Amon, no more eager than their brethren to take in this presumptuous foreigner, realized that they could not pass him along anywhere else without potentially raising the ire of pharaoh. They decided just to discourage him, for a solid year setting him to do meaningless and demeaning tasks such as digging holes then filling them in again. Everything was done to make life as

53 Plato, **Timaeus and Critias**, translated by Desmond Lee (New York: Penguin Books, 1979) p. 35.

uncongenial and unfulfilling as possible. But they had not reckoned with the man: not only did Pythagoras do everything we was told, he did so with an efficiency and cheerfulness that astounded the priests. He would not give up, desist, nor be discouraged; he accepted every humiliation with a joyful spirit. Finally the priests of Amon recognized his extraordinary personal qualities and admitted him to the temple for initiation.

Pythagoras spent 22 years studying in Egypt, traveling to all the major temples and learning from the most celebrated sages and priests in the land. No other Greek was ever allowed to study in Egypt for so long, and doubtless Pythagoras would have stayed and studied longer if he had not been taken as a captive to Chaldea when the Persians overran Egypt (525 BC). He would stay in Chaldea another seven years (some say 12) where he continued to receive instruction under the Chaldean magi. Thus, Pythagoras went higher and farther as a man of knowledge than any Greek before or after his time. He was the quintessential philosopher and in fact coined the term *philosopher* to describe himself as a 'lover of wisdom.' It can be said that all Greek philosophy descends from Pythagoras. Eventually he would open a famous school in southern Italy at Croton and his students after him seeded the entire Greek world with the Pythagorean system. However, about his 100th year, his school was attacked, sacked, and burned by a local mob led by a spurned applicant. Some sources say that Pythagoras died in the fire, others that he escaped only to allow himself to starve to death in Tarentum.[54]

The *entente* among the Lydians, Babylonians, and Egyptians did not, in the end, stem the tide of events. In 546 BC, Croesus, King of Lydia, was finally conquered by the Persian emperor, Cyrus II, and in 539 BC, Babylon was the next to fall to the Persian onslaught. Cyrus had managed to create the largest empire ever seen up to that time and he had set his eventual sights on Egypt when he was killed in battle in 529 BC. This death only delayed the inevitable, but Amasis, called the most *philhellenic* of the pharaohs, did not live to see it, his life coming to an end after a reign of 44 years in 526 BC. He was succeeded by Psametticus III.

---

54 See Edouard Shuré, **The Great Initiates**, translated by Gloria Rasberry (Blauvelt, New York: Rudolph Steiner Publications, 1960), pp. 265 – 369 for an extended discussion of the life, times, and mission of Pythagoras and his school.

Enterprising as he was, Amasis could not fail to initiate numerous building projects all over the land, commissioning constructions and renovations at Karnak, Abydos, Memphis, Bubastis, Athribis, and Thmuis. He did not neglect his native city of Sais, and the temple of Neith was enlarged and beautified with an additional court, statues, and sphinxes. Generally speaking, the temples everywhere thrived under his patronage. His benefactions extended to sites beyond Egypt, sending money to Delphi for the re-building of the temple of Delphos, the eponymous deity of the oracle city, dedicating a statue of Athene to her temple in Cyrene, and donating two additional statues of Athene to the temple in Rhodes.

Psametticus III (526 BC–525 BC)

When Psametticus III ascended to the throne, he was clearly too weak to meet the Persian threat. Cyrus's heir, Cambyses II, wasted little time following the death of Amasis launching an invasion of the Nile Valley. Psamettichus met Cambyses at Pelusium only to have his army utterly crushed. Retreating to Memphis, Psamettichus was besieged there by the Persian army and, once again, the city, the traditional bastion against foreign invasion, fell. Once again Psamettichus effected an escape but was soon overtaken and captured by Cambyses's army. He was put in chains and deported to Susa, the capital of the Persian empire. Egypt now became a satrapy of the Persian empire. Though experiencing brief periods of independence over the next century, Egypt's fortunes would ever after be in the hands of foreign conquerors.

Assessment of the 26th Dynasty

There is a persistent tendency among historians of ancient Egypt to see the Saitic Dynasty as the last brilliant flash of Egyptian civilization compared to all that had come before since the end of the 20th Dynasty. This attitude of mind lumps the 25th Dynasty with the decline of Egypt evident since at least 900 BC. This attitude is especially pronounced in the writings of James Henry Breasted as the following passage attests:

> In the suppression of the mercenary lords and local dynasts, Psamtik made an end of the intolerable conditions of semi-anarchy which had so long blighted an unhappy land.[55]

While the outstanding achievements of the Saitic 26th Dynasty are not to be downplayed, it is clear from an unprejudiced examination that it was instead the 25th Dynasty from Cush that rescued Egypt from anarchy, restored order and settled government, and ushered in a kind of Renaissance on which the 26th Dynasty pharaohs were able to capitalize and amplify. It was not the Saitic pharaohs who had to bear the brunt of the war against Assyria; they were quite willing to stay out of the conflict with the invader in order to enhance their own political prospects. The Assyrio-Cushitic war, in the end, benefited the Saitic dynasts and them alone. The Assyrians managed to push Cush out of Egypt but shortly thereafter were themselves compelled to withdraw, probably exhausted by their long, drawn-out victory, leaving Egypt and the throne open to Psamettichus I. Breasted's assessment of Psamettichus is a veritable panegyric, actually ranking him a more important pharaoh than either Amenemhet I, founder of the 12th Dynasty or Ahmose I, conqueror of the Hyksos.[56] Given his unwillingness to give due credit to the pharaohs of the 25th Dynasty, one can say quite categorically that Breasted's enthusiasm on this point is excessive.

Having made these points, there is no doubt that the Saitic Era of the 26th Dynasty was a period of great cultural brilliance and prosperity. Art and architecture, already in revival during the 25th Dynasty, continued to flourish in a manner not seen since the 19th Dynasty. Some of the finest portrait art and bronze casting ever seen in Egypt, or indeed the world, was produced during this period. There was a kind of fossilization, however, that crept into religious observance. The sacred animals and other outward manifestations of the deities came to be increasingly venerated till there came a time when killing an animal such as a cat or bull, even accidently, meant instant death for the perpetrator. The cult of Osiris and Isis rose to supremacy, just as that of Amon was fading (except in Cush), and in the end, Isis would outstrip even Osiris in the religious sentiments of the people. Imhotep, now deified

55 Breasted JH, **A History of Egypt**, New York: Charles Scribner's Sons, 1909/1937, p. 567.
56 Ibid.

as a god of medicine, also became a much-favored deity. It is during the 26th Dynasty that a version of the ***Book of the Coming Forth By Day*** was revised and re-published, eventually becoming known as the 'Saite Recension' about which Budge says,

> The Saite Recension includes four chapters which have no counterparts in the papyri of the older period, and which are remarkable for containing a large number of foreign names and words, thought to be of Nubian origin; these, no doubt, crept into the work through the influence of the priest of Amen at Napata.[57]

One begins to get the impression that, at least in domestic affairs, the 26th Dynasty in some domains was merely maintaining policies and influences earlier shown in the 25th Dynasty.

The 26th Dynasty continued and amplified a trend already clearly evident in the 25th Dynasty: a 'psychological' return to the Old Kingdom. Old Kingdom names and titles were revived and deities who were pre-eminent in that archaic period enjoyed new prominence, along with Osiris and Isis. And, like the tomb architecture of the 25th Dynasty, that of the 26th Dynasty re-incorporated Old Kingdom motifs and mortuary inscriptions from the Pyramid Texts of the 6th Dynasty. There was a national feeling, carried over from the 25th Dynasty, that it was necessary to hearken back to the first dynasties to reclaim the 'true soul' of Egypt.

It was in the economic sphere, however, that the policy of the Saitic pharaohs changed the course of Egyptian history forever. They pursued mercantile relationships with Mediterranean cities and nations with a zeal and single-mindedness never before seen in Egyptian history. Foreigners, especially Ionian Greeks, poured into the Delta as never before as merchants and mercenaries, the latter becoming the backbone of the armies of the 26th Dynasty. Breasted describes these new mercantile-driven developments as follows:

> [Psamettichus] had personally seen the great arteries of trade throbbing from one end to the other of the vast Assyrian Empire; he comprehended the great economic value of foreign trade to the nation he was

57 Budge, op. cit., p.124.

> building up; nor did he fail to perceive that such traffic might be variously taxed and made to yield very considerable revenue for his own treasury. He therefore revived the old connections with Syria; Phoenician galleys filled the Nile mouths, and Semitic merchants...thronged the Delta. If Psamtik was able to employ the Greeks in his army he found them not less useful in the furtherance of his commercial projects.[58]

Egypt became enmeshed in an international web of commercial relations and Sais became a world-class city resplendent with magnificent temples, monuments, and palaces. Egypt as a whole, especially the Delta region and the pharaohs, accumulated wealth such as hadn't been seen since the height of the New Kingdom. The Delta now supplanted the Thebaid (Upper Egypt) as the dominant epicenter of Egyptian cultural, political, and economic life; Sais became the most brilliant city in the realm as the star of Thebes receded. Among the Egyptians themselves, only the upper echelons of the royal house, aristocracy, and merchant class embraced this brave new world; the bulk of the population from peasant to priest, held themselves aloof from the foreigners, especially the Greeks, and their influences. This disdain for the foreigner was so sharp that most Egyptians considered themselves ritually contaminated if ever touching one, even inadvertently. In such an instance, it was necessary to bathe from top to bottom to rid oneself of the taint. If entertaining a Greek became unavoidable, afterwards all the dining ware used by Greek guests were broken and buried.[59] But the Greeks were in Egypt to stay. Not even the Persian conquest could dislodge them. And after the end of the seventh century BC, increasing numbers of Greek learned men followed the mercenaries and merchants into the lands of the Nile seeking to drink from the seemingly inexhaustible fount of Egyptian knowledge. The Egyptian orientation in world affairs shifted dramatically away from Africa—Nubia and Cush—and irrevocably toward the countries and city-states of the northern and eastern Mediterranean and the Fertile Crescent. Many Egyptians, as they contemplated this shift, began to feel that the country and the people had lost their soul, no matter how outwardly prosperous Egypt appeared to the outside world.

58 Breasted, op. cit., p. 577.

59 Herodotus, op. cit., p. 145.

Chapter 10:

Egypt Under the Foreign Dynasties

I. The 27th Dynasty—The Persian Rulers of Egypt (525 BC–405 BC)

Cambyses II (525 BC–522 BC)

With the defeat of Psamettichus III by the Persian emperor Cambyses II, a son of Cyrus the Great, it could be said that in Egypt, 'the chickens had come home to roost'. Greek alliances, so carefully nurtured for the previous 130 years, fell apart at the critical moment, with crucial Greek rulers, whom the Saitic pharaohs had supported and helped to enrich, going over to the Persians in their campaign against Egypt. The Bedouin sand-farers, so-called—never friendly—led the Persian troops across the Sinai desert. The Jewish community in Elephantine also welcomed the Persian conquerors, probably because Cyrus, the first Persian emperor and creator of the vast empire, had given Jews in Babylon leave to return home and re-build the temple. Jews in Babylon generally had come to feel at home there since most of them stayed instead of returning to an uncertain future in Judea. They continued to thrive under the rule of the Persians and, in any event, Cyrus and his successors maintained a good reputation among them.

Nicolas Grimal insists that certain elements of the Egyptian nobility were also quite congenial to the rule of Cambyses, quickly reaching an accommodation with their new overlords.[1] The Egyptian elite so easily coming to terms with the new Persian masters seems to have been from Sais if the career

1 Grimal, op. cit., pp. 367-8.

of *Udjahorresnet*, a Saite doctor, priest, and naval admiral is any indication. He was engaged by Cambyses to instruct him on the rituals and ceremonies appropriate for a pharaoh as well as serve as Chief Physician. The Saites had already had a history of interfacing on cordial terms with the Greeks that had come into Egypt; it could not have been a long leap to do so with the Persians. Udjahorresnet must have made a favorable impression on his new overlord since he was able to prevail upon Cambyses to rid the temples of Neith in Sais of the many impious foreigners making their home on the precincts.[2] But Cambyses did more than that as Budge relates:

> ...the temple [of Neith] was purified, its priests reinstated, its revenues restored, and his majesty decreed that the appointed festivals and ceremonies should be duly celebrated and performed as in days of old.
>
> When the cleansing of the temple was finished Cambyses went into it in person, and he performed an act of worship after the manner of the old kings of Egypt, and poured out a libation to the goddess Neith, and made gifts to her temple.[3]

Adopting a policy afterward followed by every foreign conqueror of Egypt up to the time of Constantine, Cambyses took pains to establish himself as the reigning pharaoh. He assumed a pharaonic throne name, 'Horus, the Unifier of the Two Lands', and not only did he remove all of the profane squatters from the temples of Neith but went himself with Udjahorresnet to prostrate himself before Neith while making numerous offerings to her.[4] Contrary to the testimony derived from the anti-Persian propaganda of the later Greek writers, Cambyses, at least initially, scrupulously respected all the Egyptian gods and made benefactions to many temples. Moreover, Udjahorresnet gave a good account of himself, using the patronage of Cambyses to help the poor and the needy and, during the reign of Darius, successor to Cambyses, set up a school to educate boys in the profession of scribe.[5]

2 Lichtheim M, **Ancient Egyptian Literature**, Vol. III, Berkeley: University of California Press, 1980, pp. 37-8.

3 Budge, op. cit., p. 46.

4 Ibid.

5 Ibid., pp. 46-7.

Herodotus reports on two terrible military disasters to befall Cambyses as a consequence of his attempt to conquer Ethiopia, described as the country 'on the coast of the Indian Ocean'.[6] This area seems to conform more to parts of modern Ethiopia (or ancient Axum) and Somalia, e.g., the Horn of Africa, than it does of Napatan Cush proper. Cambyses sent men to Ethiopia—'fish-eaters' from Elephantine—posing as ambassadors of good will who were in reality spies tasked with obtaining as much intelligence about the country and its capacities as possible, preparatory to an invasion. However, the Ethiopian king, ruler of a country where the people were reputed to be the tallest and best-looking people in the world,[7] was not deceived by the false embassy. He sent the spies away with a warning:

> ...take him [Cambyses] this bow, and tell him that the king of Ethiopia has some advice to give him: 'when the Persians can draw a bow of this size thus easily, then let him raise an army of superior strength and invade the country of the long-lived Ethiopians. Till then, let him thank the gods for not turning the thoughts of the children of Ethiopia to foreign conquest'.[8]

Herodotus reports that Cambyses was so enraged by this retort from the King of Ethiopia that he immediately led his army southward, poorly-provisioned and ill-prepared. But before the Persians could arrive in the country of Ethiopia, the army, victimized by the poorly-organized campaign, started to run out of food, succumbing to disease and cannibalism. Cambyses was obliged to retreat without hazarding a battle. Herodotus's account of this ill-fated Ethiopian campaign of Cambyses stands alone; no other corroborative evidence either from literature or archaeology confirms the episode. There is probably no reason to doubt that some sort of military thrust toward Ethiopia—or Cush—was in fact attempted by the Persians and though it obviously failed, it is hard to credit all aspects of Herodotus's account. Successful conquest or not, Persian emperors always listed Cush as part of their domains, a familiar royal ploy in ancient times of claiming rulership over lands completely independent. Some

6 Vid. Herodotus, op. cit., pp. 210-4.

7 Ibid., p.211.

8 Ibid., pp. 211-2.

40 years later, during the reign of Xerxes, contingents of Cushitic mercenaries were incorporated into his army.

But the botched invasion of Ethiopia was not even the worst disaster to befall Cambyses's army. While on his way to Ethiopia, he detached 50,000 of his troops to march against the Oasis of Siwa, home to the Oracle of Amon and the people Herodotus calls the *Amonians*, which to that point had not come under the sway of Persia. The detachment never reached its destination, and not one of the 50,000 soldiers was ever seen again.[9] The entire army seems literally to have been swallowed up by the desert, probably from a fierce sandstorm that, in the Sahara, can easily bury thousands of men in a matter of minutes. For a long time, historians believed that the story was a fanciful tale told by Herodotus, but over the last decade, bits of ancient metal resembling weapons and human remains have turned up in the Western Desert suggesting to some that these finds might represent traces of Cambyses's lost army.

Cambyses died under mysterious circumstances. The most common story is that he was accidently wounded in the thigh while marching against Bardiya, a usurper who may have been his brother, and the wound turned gangrenous, killing him 11 days later. Darius I, Cambyses' lance-bearer, then seized the throne, defeating Bardiya, and executing him.

There are numerous stories concerning the atrocities and savage cruelties committed by Cambyses against the priests, the temples, and the gods of Egypt, all recounted by historians such as Herodotus, Diodorus, and Stabo. These stories seem to be completely at odds with evidence that Cambyses behaved with perfect decorum and respect toward the Egyptian gods, temples, and priests, though it is said that, in later years, he was afflicted by fits of madness that might account for the drastic change in character. Petrie in fact thinks the madness of Cambyses was precipitated by the disasters that overtook his army on the ill-fated campaign to Ethiopia.[10]

9 Ibid., p. 214.
10 Vid. Petrie, op. cit., p. 363.

Darius I (the Great) (522 BC–486 BC)

Darius was a member of a collateral branch of the royal Persian line, thus not a direct descendant of Cyrus the Great, founder of the empire. He, with six co-conspirators, managed to seize the throne after attacking and killing the occupant, Gaumāta, who by Darius's account was a usurper. However, he married Atossa, daughter of Cyrus the Great, thereby solidifying his royal claim. One of his first acts was to appoint the satrap Aryandas to govern Egypt, an appointment that turned into a disaster. In fact, it is assumed that the generally bad retrospective reputation that the Persians had in later times in Egypt is in large part traceable to the policies of Aryandas. He inaugurated a nine-month siege of the city of Barca on the coast of Libya on his own initiative though at the behest of Pheretime, Queen of Cyrene. Apparently flushed with this success, Aryandes began striking coins in his own image and, worse from the Egyptian perspective, showed a total disregard for the local customs that previous Persian rulers had honored. As if to expand his own mini-empire, he captured Libyan Cyrene the moment it rose up against their Dorian rulers from the Grecian mainland. But Aryandas's self-aggrandizing policies eventually caused enough concern to Darius that the emperor had him arrested and executed in 517 BC.

To his credit, Darius, in the aftermath of the hated rule of Aryandas, launched a number of good-faith efforts to restore the good will of the Egyptian populace. He appointed Pherendates as the new satrap of Egypt. Depending on who is telling the story, Darius either put the finishing touches on or completed the canal between the Nile's Pelusiac branch and the Red Sea. Egypt, as it would continue to be for all later foreign conquerors, was the wealthiest of Persia's satrapies and an operational canal to the Red Sea magnified the revenues derived from sea-borne trade with Arabia, East Africa, and India. The Saitic Mandarin Udjahorresnet still served the Persians in the reign of Darius and was still considered a valuable civil servant who was taken to Persia for a brief period, presumably to learn more about the functioning of the Persian state. He was able, apparently, to undo much of the damage caused by the ill-fated satrap Aryandas.

Darius, in his campaign to pacify his Egyptian subjects, restored many of the privileges and revenues of the temples. He undertook restorations at Busiris and El Kab, re-opening the quarries at Wadi Hammamat. His most striking architectural legacy was the building of a temple dedicated to Amon which came to be called the Temple of Hibis near 'The Great Oasis' at Al-Kậrga. A hymn found in the temple's second chamber calls Amon-Rā 'the One God' of whom all other gods are considered to be forms or phases.[11] Statues carved by Egyptian sculptors that Darius commissioned were taken by him to Susa where they were unearthed 2,500 years later by archaeologists. He revamped the bureaucracy, introduced a new legal code, and began to mint coinage locally. Darius's reign inaugurated a period of peace and prosperity for Egypt as Persia's most important and economically viable satrap. According to Budge, he made a good impression on the Egyptians generally:

> He [Darius] held converse often with the priests of Egypt, and learned their theology, and made himself acquainted with the things which were written in their books, and he emulated the ancient kings of Egypt in showing kindness to the people.[12]

However, even this tranquility could not last as Persia's increasing preoccupation with the conquest of Greece suffered a tremendous reverse at Marathon where, in 490 BC, a smaller Athenian army decisively defeated Darius. Avenging this stinging defeat became the sole obsession of Darius and his lack of attention to affairs in Egypt emboldened the Delta cities, yet again, to rise up against Persia in 486 BC under the leadership of *Khabbesha*, about whom little is known but who was probably the scion of a princely Saitic family. Before Darius could lead his army back into Egypt to put down the revolt, he died leaving his son Xerxes as his heir.

Xerxes (486 BC–465 BC)

Xerxes was the son of Darius and Atossa, and the direct line of descent through his mother from Cyrus the Great probably accounts for Darius's choice of him as his successor instead of an older son according to normal custom. Xerxes was

11 Budge, op. cit., p. 67.
12 Ibid., p. 65.

determined to crush the Egyptian revolt once and for all and he did exactly that with maximum force in the second year of his reign. He made his son Achaemenes satrap of Egypt and he carried out his father's mandate to expunge the last bit of rebellion from Egypt with the most stringent of measures. Later Egyptians neither forgot nor forgave the punitive exactions of Achaemenes and in after centuries, the name Xerxes was always written with an insulting determinative reserved for no other foreign ruler, Persian or otherwise. Few inscriptions bearing the name of Xerxes can be found in Egypt and, unlike his predecessors, he seems to have left no monuments or buildings of any kind. Beneath the seemingly unconquerable domination of Persia, Egyptians seethed and waited for events to turn in their favor.

The Persians had never reconciled themselves to their defeat at Marathon, and in 480 BC launched an attack on the Athenians by sea with a vast navy. At first, Persian arms were successful, at Thermopylae against the Spartan king Leonidas, then against Athens, a city deserted by its inhabitants which was subsequently burned to the ground. Achaemenes led 200 Egyptian ships to join the Persian navy but, despite the immense advantage in men, materièl, and ships, the Persian navy was defeated at Salamis by an Athenian-dominated coalition of Greek navies. As with Marathon, it was a military disaster for the Persians of epic proportions, and with additional defeats at Plataea and Mycale, the Persian military machine was sent reeling back to the homeland with Greece unconquered. From that point on, the history of the world changed completely, and it would be the Greeks who would take the geopolitical initiative in international affairs, culminating in Alexander's campaign of world conquest in the next century that would bring an end to the Persian empire. Fifteen years later (465 BC) Xerxes was assassinated by Artabanus, a member of the royal guard.

Artaxerxes I (465 BC–424 BC)

Artaxerxes I was the son of Xerxes and ascended the throne after having seized and executed his father's assassin *Artabanus*. With the death of Xerxes and the ensuing struggle for the Persian throne, the Egyptians, under the leadership of

Inaros once again rose up against Persian rule. Inaros, of Libyan descent, was the son of Psamettichus, the last native king of Egypt, and was able to gather under his leadership the disaffected princelings of the Delta. His most important ally in this attempt at re-unification under native rule was *Amyrtaeus* who, like Inaros, was a Saite. Assisted by Athenian mercenaries, Inaros and Amyrtaeus seized control of all Lower Egypt up to Memphis. The first battles against the Persian army of Artaxerxes were decided in favor of the Egyptians and resulted in the death of the hated satrap Achaemenes. But the string of victories did not last and Artaxerxes's Persian army and navy, consisting of more than 300,000 men under arms, eventually overcame the Egyptian opposition, routing the Athenians and capturing Inaros in 460 BC who was finally executed 11 years later in Persia. The Greeks, who had been warring against the Persians for nearly 40 years, made peace with their still-formidable imperial enemy.

Arsames replaced Achaemenes as satrap of Egypt and for the next 30 years, Egypt was free of war and rebellion. It is during this period of stability and truce that Herodotus visited Egypt (c. 450 BC) where he collected the material that would comprise *Book Two* and *Book Three* of his famous **The Histories**. These chapters would serve as the most important written source about ancient Egypt for the next 23 centuries. Even after nearly 200 years of systematic research, excavation, and investigation into the history and civilization of ancient Egypt since the decipherment of the Rosetta Stone in 1822, it has been impossible to dispense with Herodotus's work, however much certain details have been criticized and debunked. Indeed, most of the histories written about the 26th Dynasty and the Persian domination in modern times are largely recapitulations of Herodotus's narrative.

Though Inaros was executed for having fomented rebellion, the satrap Arsames, clearly with the approval of his sovereign, allowed the sons of Inaros to maintain their rulership of the nomes where they had been established, a policy that seems to have been unchanged from Assyrian times. He took care not to inflame Egyptian cultural and religious sensibilities and, in fact, Persian officials became gradually more Egyptianized, even taking Egyptian names. But rebellion died hard in the country with the oldest and longest-lived civilization in the world; Egyptians could not get used to being merely a province in someone else's empire. Artaxerxes died in 424 BC and the predictable fratricidal struggle surrounding the next Persian accession re-ignited the undercurrents of Egyptian revolt. However, Darius II emerged as the new emperor and managed to hold off any further outbreaks during his reign.

Like Xerxes before him there is nearly nothing in the inscriptions of Egypt about Artaxerxes and his reign. And like his father, he did no building in Egypt, showing no interest in serving as a pharaoh but only as the Great King of Persia.

Darius II (423 BC–405 BC)

Artaxerxes I was succeeded by his son Xerxes II, but seven weeks later, Xerxes II was murdered by his brother *Sogdianus*. His illegitimate brother, *Ochus*, satrap of Hyrcania, rebelled against Sogdianus and after a brief battle killed him when three of Sogidanus's most able generals deserted to him. But Ochus had to crush the attempt of his own brother *Arsites* to imitate his example and Ochus speedily executed him. The rebel's troops were won over to Ochus by monetary gifts. Ochus adopted the throne name of Darius, becoming Darius II.

Darius continued the policy of pacifying the Egyptians in every way possible. The temple of Hibis in the Al-Khârga oasis in the western desert of Upper Egypt, 125 miles west of Thebes, was decorated and beautified to an even greater extent than previously. The temple was dedicated to the Amonian triad at Thebes—Amon, Mut, and Khonsu—built in the mid-6th century BC by the Saitic pharaohs but refurbished and improved by Darius I (the Great). In fact, the oldest of the temple ruins date it to the reign of Darius the Great. Darius II continued the process of improving the temple, a probable gesture to Amon and his priesthood who while lacking influence in the northern part of the country, were still a power in Upper Egypt. But this gesture of conciliation and good will was apparently lost on the Egyptians, especially since the Jewish community in Elephantine was, and had been, wholeheartedly in support of the Persian regime, much to the chagrin of Egyptian nationalists. The Egyptians seem to have destroyed the temple at Hibis themselves in 407 BC since, though dedicated to Amon, it was considered a symbol of the hated Persian conqueror. By this time, a subterranean rebellion was being carried out in Egypt with the support of Greek contingents from Sparta who, as usual, were enlisted in the cause by Sais. In 405 BC, Darius II died and the Saite Amyrtaeus proclaimed himself king of Egypt. A year later, Egypt was again in open revolt against Persia. Amyrtaeus inaugurated the 28th Dynasty that consisted only of his reign. Darius was the last Persian king to leave behind any monumental evidence of his reign in Egypt.

The Last Native Dynasties (404 BC–343 BC
II. The 28th Dynasty

Amyrtaeus (404 BC–398 BC)

This 'dynasty' consisted of a single king, Amyrtaeus. As was the custom of the dynasts of the Delta petty kingdoms, especially the Saites, Amyrtaes took advantage of the Persian interregnum created by the death of Darius II to successfully declare himself king, extending his rule all the way down to Elephantine. He had assisted the short-lived, ill-fated rebellion of Inaros and when that attempt at independence was crushed, Amyrtaeus fled to the island of Elbo, located in the northern Delta but whose location was a complete secret to the Persians and indeed most Egyptians. Biding his time, he was able to exploit the Persian interregnum after the death of Darius II to gather an army around him, including the inevitable Greek mercenaries, and proclaim himself king. Almost nothing is known about him or his reign since not a single monument, if any were erected, survives from his brief occupancy of the throne of Egypt. However, he is significant for being a native king; the first of a mere a handful more of such rulers before Egypt fell permanently under the control of foreign powers. The Persian throne was in such disarray because of the disputed succession that there was no effort to dislodge Amyrtaeus. He died, however, barely six years after having seized power and his all-too-brief dynasty died with him.

III. The 29th Dynasty

Nepherites I (399 BC–393 BC)

This dynasty was also of short duration and Nepherites, evidently a military man from the city of Mendes, is thought to be of Libyan extraction. A single document, written in Aramaic, the lingua franca of Western Asia, describes a war launched by Nepheritis against Amyrtaeus resulting in the capture and execution of the latter. It is the only surviving record of such a war but it would account for the brevity of Amyrtaeus's reign, the abrupt way it ended, and lack of any contemporary documentation of it. In order to establish his legitimacy, Nepherites had himself crowned at Memphis but established Mendes as his capital. His reign of six years was hardly longer than that of the man whose throne he had usurped but, unlike Amyrtaeus, he managed to leave behind monuments that testified to the renewed building activities of his rulership, including some constructions and restorations at Karnak. The prestige of that ancient Vatican of Egypt was still sufficient to induce a number of pharaohs from the 26th Dynasty on to carry out building activities there. When the Spartans once again made war on the Persians, Nepherites sent them 100 ships and 500,000 bushels of wheat. But when the fleet with the provisions made port in Rhodes, their admirals were unaware that Rhodes had gone over to the Persians and the Egyptians were captured handily. No Egyptian material support ever reached the Spartans on this account.

Achoris (393 BC–379 BC)

Achoris was actually preceded by Muthis, son of Nepherites, and his rival Psammuthis who drove him from the throne. The two reigns together hardly lasted a year and Achoris rose up and overran Psammuthis, seizing power for himself. He became so dominant that he actually folded the two earlier ephemeral reigns into his own, reckoning his first regnal year from the death of Nepherites. However, even in his fleeting time on the throne, Psammuthis had managed to continue the work of Nepherites at Karnak. Nonetheless, Achoris considered himself the only valid successor to Nepherites and the one continuing the dynasty. There might be cause for supposing that he was related to or perhaps descended from Nepherites but the matter is debatable.

Like any newly-crowned pharaoh Egypt, Achoris assiduously promoted his bona fides by a vigorous building program in the time-honored fashion of Egyptian pharaohs from the dawn of its history. He left evidence of his constructions at Karnak, Medinet Habu, Elkab, Medamud, Elephantine, the Serapeum, and Hibis in the Khârga Oasis, the latter evidently rebuilt after being torn down by anti-Persian Egyptians toward the end of the 27th Dynasty. Artifacts with his cartouche emblazoned on them have been found in the ancient ruins of Phoenicia, indicating that Egypt's presence on the international front had at least partially rebounded. Despite a seemingly flourishing Egypt once again under the rule of native pharaohs, the country was no longer a major power, having to form alliances with the Greeks and other Mediterranean nations as a bulwark against the Persian empire, still large, still powerful, still seeking to regain lost territory and expand the existing territory under its control. These alliances, such as they were, did not mean that Egypt took the field against the Persian army; the most that it would attempt under Nepherites, as seen above, was supply Sparta with arms and materièl in its continuing battles against Persia, but even this effort came to naught as the consignment fell into the hands of Rhodes in transit which had abruptly allied itself with Persia.

The situation played to the Egyptians' advantage when Cyprus, aided by Athens, took up arms against Persia in 390 BC, drawing Persia away from Egypt. In 389 BC, Achoris concluded a treaty with Athens which gave him enough of a respite to build up his army. The Greek wars against the Persians came to a temporary end in 386 BC when a peace treaty prevented all the Greek cities from taking up arms against the Persian king. The Great King of Persia at this time was Artaxerxes II and, freed from the ongoing war against the Greeks, his satrap Pharnabazes could now turn his attention to Cyprus and Egypt. But Achoris was equal to the task of defending Egypt, having united the country, strengthened the army, and promoted Egyptian naval power. In addition, there was still a cohort of Greek mercenaries at his disposal, and the Athenian general Chabrias protected Egypt from invasion through the Sinai by his strong defense of the Delta region in and around the Pelusiac branch of the Nile. The Persians could make no headway against Egypt under these circumstances and the ruler of Cyprus, Evagoras, began to harass the Persians in the eastern Mediterranean gaining control as far east as Tyre.

Prudently deciding that they could not fight a two-front war, the Persian war leaders, Tiribazes and Orontes, broke off hostilities with Egypt in 381 BC to focus their efforts entirely on Evagoras and Cyprus. It turned into a back-and-forth kind of war. Evagoras was able to interdict Persian supply lines making their land forces completely ineffective. However, a series of battles with the Persian navy led to a Cypriot defeat, forcing Evagoras to not only withdraw to his own city but flee even further to Egypt itself. Anchoris, having contributed heavily to the Cypriot war effort, could offer little further assistance, but Evagoras was able to recapture Salamis, lost to the Persians during the previous naval campaign. At this juncture, the two Persian generals, Tiribazes and Orontes—providentially for Evagoras—were mired increasingly in internecine struggles between themselves, and it proved a strategically propitious moment for Evagoras to sue for peace which he accomplished successfully to the complete advantage of Cyprus. Having neutralized one enemy, it remained for the Persians to turn their attention back to Egypt, considered by them merely a rebellious satrapy, though the wealthiest and most important one of the empire. The moment seemed especially opportune when Achoris died in 380 BC, throwing Egypt into another of its by now recurring interregnal struggles for power.

IV. The 30th Dynasty

Nectanebo (380 BC–362 BC)

Nectabebo was the son of Tachos, the petty ruler of the Delta principality of Sebennytos. Nectanebo was unquestionably the most dynamic ruler among the Delta states and it took him hardly any time at all to depose the son of Achoris and establish himself as the succeeding pharaoh. Nonetheless, he was faced with potentially dangerous challenges, including a temporary weakness in Egypt's external defenses, and the departure of Chabrias, the Greek general who earlier had provided able assistance to the Egyptians against the invading Persians. The *détente* between the Persians and Greeks led to the recall of Chabrias by the Athenian government. Worse, the Athenians—constantly

Nectanebo I—1st Pharaoh of 30th Dynasty

shifting their allegiances according to the fortunes of war—sent another general, Iphicrates, with a contingent of Greek soldiers to assist the Persians in their campaign to reconquer Egypt. As long as the Persians were not threatening Greece, these latter were perfectly willing to participate in Persian empire-building elsewhere, even among erstwhile allies. Even so, the expected invasion was delayed another six years due to escalating mistrust between the Persian satrap Pharnabazes and Iphicrates. Finally, in 373 BC, the Great King was able to launch a two-pronged attack on Egypt by land and by sea.

Nectanebo had fortified the Pelusiac Nile branch, the expected route of invasion. However, Pharnabazes and Iphicrates declined to advance up that branch of the river and instead pursued their attack up the Mendesian mouth, a poorly defended section further to the west. The Great King's expeditionary force captured Mendes easily and the route to Memphis lay open down the Mendesian branch. Here again, the innate mistrust between Persian and Greek saved the Egyptians. Iphicrates, a bold and resourceful general, wanted to push forward with all deliberate speed to capture Memphis, the key to the rest of Egypt, but Pharnabazes feared that if the Greeks succeeded, they would simply take Egypt for themselves. Consequently, he refused the advance until the main body of the Persian army could rendez-vous with them in Mendes. Another delay ensued, giving Nectanebo all the time he needed to rally his troops for a direct assault on the invaders aided by the Egyptians' superior knowledge of the terrain, especially after the advent of the flood season making it difficult to maneuver an army by anyone not familiar with the marshy landscape. The army of the Great King, after being poised to defeat Nectanebo and re-take Egypt, now had to undertake an ignominious retreat. Greek might fight with Persian but neither ever trusted the other enough to carry the campaign through to victory. Iphicrates now feared that the Persians might turn on him and, holding him responsible for the defeat, execute him. He wasted no time returning to Athens where he was given command of the Athenian fleet, much to Persian displeasure. Egypt would enjoy a 30-year respite from Persian attacks.

There was no one to stand with Egypt against the Persian threat for the next seven years after Nectanebo pushed the army of the Great King out of Egypt. There was certainly no help to be expected from the Greeks and another attempt at re-conquest seemed inevitable. But again, Egypt was spared the next invasion for the time being because the Persian empire, exacerbated by the advancing age of Artaxerxes II, had become so unwieldy that mounting another major military expedition against Egypt was beyond Persian capacity. Satrapies on the empire's western borders grew increasingly independent as the central authority started to fray, and soon vassal states began to rebel openly with the ever opportunistic Greeks—Sparta and Athens—joining the rebellious provinces in the effort to throw off the Persian yoke. The empire of the Great King was not ready to disintegrate *in toto* but the disarray at its western fringes protected Egypt.

In 365 BC, Nectanebo, as if to revive a lapsed ancient custom, made his son *Tachos* co-regent. Such a dynamic ruler could not fail to carry out building projects, and Nectanebos monuments and temple constructions are found at Bubastis, Abydos, Edfu, Memphis, Hiblis, and Karnak. The famous Cippi of Horus, also known as the Metternich Stele, was carved in this reign. The Cippi of Horus tablet conferred magical protection against the bites of venomous snakes and the attacks of crocodiles. Nectanebo is noted for having revived the custom of building obelisks. He died in 362 BC and Tachos succeeded him without a dynastic struggle.

Cippi of Horus
(The Metternich Stele)

Tachos (362 BC–360 BC)

Tachos had spearheaded Nectanebo's policy of assisting those who were rebelling against Persia. After his accession he took it a step further by preparing to invade Canaan as a way of recovering Egypt's long-lost northern territories and restoring a measure of the ancient imperial grandeur. For this campaign he re-enlisted the Greeks—despite their demonstrated unreliability in the face of adversity—which included Chabrias, chief admiral of the Greek fleet and an erstwhile ally of Egypt, and Agesilaos, king of Sparta. It appeared that the Greeks would never rest until Persia was either permanently banished to its own borders or brought down altogether. However, to pay the Greeks, it was necessary to impose a heavier burden of taxation on the populace, a measure that could not endear him to his subjects. Predictably, this would soon to lead to yet another dynastic struggle. At first, Tachos, whose army and navy were sweeping toward Phoenicia, met with military success. Leading the military forces himself, Tachos had left his own son *Tjahepimu* in charge of the government during his absence, while his grandson Nectanebo accompanied him on the push north. Here, the machinations for supreme authority became decidedly murky and convoluted. Tachos had made himself unpopular on account of increased taxation but he had naturally assumed that the loyalty and fidelity of his own son, Tjahepimu, could be counted on. Instead, perceiving that a regime change was indeed possible, Tjahepimu turned on his father and declared that Nectanebo, leading the infantry of Tachos's army, was now king, making him Nectanebo II. The troops abandoned Tachos and rallied around Nectanebo II, as did the Spartan commander Agesilaos. Left without an army, allies, or indeed a kingdom, Tachos then fled to the court of his enemy, the Great King of Persia, Artaxerxes II. By now, the cumulative effect of events in the Mediterranean, North Africa, and Western Asia over the previous 160 years had compromised all geopolitical loyalties, allowing rulers and generals to switch sides at a moment's notice then back again without qualm or scruple. Egypt's ever-heavier reliance on Greek mercenaries since the beginning of the 26th Dynasty, combined with its obsession to regain its lost northern empire, exacted a terrible cost because of these tenuous alliances. None of the rulers, succeeding one upon the other, ever seemed to derive the relevant lessons from the ever-shifting events. Not only that, but the ancient reverence for one's father and royal predecessor evident among the pharaohs of Egypt's golden ages had clearly been abandoned in favor of naked self-interest. Egyptian rulers were now no better off than the Persian Great Kings who were constantly having to fend off usurpations from within their own family.

Nectanebo II (360 BC–343 BC)

The usurper Nectanebo II had one hold-out against him with whom he had to contend: the prince of Mendes, a descendant of the kings of the 29th Dynasty. The necessity of returning to Egypt to crush the revolt meant that Nectanebo II had to turn away from his victories in Western Asia which, as it turned out, represented the last important Egyptian attempt to renew its empire there. Ably assisted by the Spartan ruler Agesilaos, Nectanebo II conquered all opposition and the former, having collected the monies owed the Spartans for their services, returned home leaving Egypt entirely in Nectanebo's hands.

Though he could not know it at the time, Nectanebo II would be the last native Egyptian ruler of any consequence and he lent himself vigorously to the process of national renewal. He still relied heavily on foreigners to handle much of the administration of government but, on the other hand, he assiduously promoted the good will and the position of various priesthoods. Nectanebo II began his reign auspiciously enough by presiding over the funerary rites of the Apis Bull at Memphis—maybe the most important sacred event in the entire country—and, additionally, made every attempt to provide material support to every major temple in Egypt. He left evidence of his benefactions at more than 100 sites throughout the country.

Nectanebo II—Last Native Pharaoh of Egypt

Persia, while still casting covetous eyes toward Egypt, remained preoccupied with various internal problems besetting the empire, especially in Asia Minor. After bringing the region back under Persian control, the Great King, Artaxerxes III, essayed in 350 BC yet another attempt to accomplish a victory in Egypt, but was beaten back. This defeat provoked another rebellion against Persian rule by Cyprus and Sidon, one of the Phoenician cities, in 346 BC. Nectanebo did not join the fray directly but did send a contingent of Greek mercenaries to the aid of Sidon. An initial victory against the Persians could not be sustained; in 344 BC, Artaxerxes III not only defeated the Cypriots but marched on to Sidon, augmented by a force of Greek mercenaries, recruited primarily to fight against Egypt. No matter how many times Greeks fought with the Egyptians against the Great King, they were always ready to switch sides and fight against Egypt—or anyone else—for enough gold, Persian gold in this case. In the case of Sidon, its own king treacherously turned on his own city rather than fight the Persians, though his only reward he got was to be executed anyway. The city refused to surrender, though its cause was hopeless. Sidon was burned and all its inhabitants incinerated. The fate of Sidon persuaded the other Phoenician cities to submit to Artaxerxes.

Nectanebo made ready for the next Persian invasion but this one had a decidedly different outcome. Learning the lessons from the previous debacle against Egypt, the Persians put their Greeks, many of whom had already served in Egypt, in tactical command of the march through the Delta. These Greeks were well versed in Egyptian fortifications and employed the tactic of using captured Delta farmers to guide the army through the Delta. Also, the Persians and Greeks on this occasion picked an invasion season outside of the flood-time so the army was not hindered by the marshy conditions that had made progress impossible during the previous campaign. One by one, the fortified cities of the Delta fell to the Greco-Persian army of Artaxerxes III and it became clear to Nectanebo, who had taken refuge in Memphis, that his position was completely untenable, forcing him to flee further south away from the pincers of the advancing army. In order to stay totally clear of the Persians, Nectanebo seems to have decamped as far south as Nubia. With his Nubian ally, Khababash, Nectanebo might have fought back for a period of time:

> The Ptolemaic tradition claims that Khababash launched an anti-Persian campaign into the Delta which may have lasted until as late as the winter of 336/335 BC.[13]

But even if there was a temporary push-back emanating from the south, clearly it was over, for Nectanebo II and, after 4,000 years, for Egypt itself. The country would never again exist as a sovereign entity under native rule.

13 Grimal, op. cit., p. 381.

Second Persian Period—The 31st Dynasty (343 BC–332 BC)

Artaxerxes III (343 BC–338 BC)

Artaxerxes III exacted his revenge against the Egyptians by demolishing all their fortifications and robbing the temples of all the riches acquired during the previous reign. Greek written tradition records that he committed all manner of atrocities against the priests and the local populace, including the slaughter of the Apis Bull which, if true, would have been tantamount to deicide in Egypt of the time. But much of that may be anti-Persian Greek propaganda after the fact. *Pherendates* was installed as the satrap of Egypt while Artaxerxes returned to Susa, the capital of the Persian empire and Egypt was once again a mere satrapy of the Great King. Artaxerxes III had won the throne by a campaign of murder against his own male relatives so the atrocities of which he is accused were well within the possibilities of his character. However that may have been, within two years after his supreme triumph, Artaxerxes and his family were poisoned to death by *Bagoas*, the very general who had led the successful invasion of Egypt.

Arses (338 BC–336 BC)

Arses appeared to have been a mere puppet of Bagoas who had also killed all the brothers of Arses to remove any possible rival claimants. Arses managed to sit on the throne for a mere two years before being put to death by Bagoas. He was replaced by Darius III who managed to have Bagoas himself poisoned as a way of protecting himself from further regicide.

Darius III (336 BC–332 BC)

Darius III supplanted Arses but couldn't possibly have known then that his fate—and that of the empire—was sealed. In 334 BC an impossibly young Macedonian king and general by the name of Alexander crossed the Hellespont into Asia Minor, beginning a campaign of conquest without precedent in the world up to that time. In two years, the entire Persian empire, including Egypt, after the decisive battle at Gaugamela[14] was in Alexander's hands and two years after that—330 BC—Darius III was killed by his own generals. Never had—and never would—a single military leader conquer so much territory until the time of Ghengis Khan 15 centuries later. Alexander never lost a battle and in 332 BC when he entered Egypt, he was feted as a liberator, so deep was the hatred of the Persians. Though Alexander accepted the homage and adulation of the Egyptians, made a famous 10-day pilgrimage across the western desert to the Oasis of Siwa to be consecrated as the Son of Amon, and built his capital Alexandria on Egyptian soil, he never ruled Egypt as such. He died at age 33, having conquered half the known world, and Egypt was left to his general *Ptolemy* who founded the Ptolemaic Dynasty.

Overview of Persian Domination

From the point of view of their impact on Egypt and Egyptians it can be fairly said that the Persians had a mixed record. At least two of the Persian Great Kings—Cambyses and Darius I— were reported to have gone out of their way to reconcile Egypt to Persian rule by showing respect to their culture and customs and devoting expenditures to the maintenance and upkeep of certain temples. However, though Cambyses began his rule of Egypt auspiciously enough, his mind seemed to have become unhinged by the humiliating failures of the double campaign against Ethiopia and the Oasis of Siwa, sacred to Amon, and afterwards his policies toward Egypt's priests and temples were that of an unrestrained tyrant. Most of the Great Kings exercised a certain restraint in their rule of Egypt but, from time to time when Egyptian rebellion flared anew, satraps over Egypt would be appointed whose administration was starkly repressive, giving a harsh and negative cast to Persian overlordship not mitigated by the regimes of milder rulers. Indeed, Egyptians never reconciled themselves to the Persian conquest and constantly sought the ways and means to regain their independence and sovereignty, usually aided by Greeks and

14 Gaugamela was considered one of the 15 Decisive Battles of the world up to 1851, that is to say, one of the 15 battles that changed the course of world history.

Cypriots, unreliable allies though they may have been. The Persians on their part were equally determined to hold fast to Egypt and keep it integrated into the empire. The Persians, however, were frequently handicapped by recurring wars with the Greeks—on several occasions resulting in unmitigated disasters for the military machine of the Great King—so that they could never fully consolidate their rule over Egypt. Exacerbating not only rule over Egypt but control over the empire were the incessantly murderous intra-family conflicts in Persia when a Great King died or was assassinated. Nevertheless, the empire was sufficiently powerful and well-organized to rule Egypt for a total of 131 years, overcoming a 62-year period when aggressive native rulers were able to take Egypt back. The Persian era in fact marked the end of Egypt as a sovereign nation ruled by native pharaohs and has caused some historians to end the chronology of ancient Egyptian history at the Persian conquest. But as noted above, Persia itself would fall to a conqueror even greater and more ambitious than Cyrus the Great, e.g., Alexander the Great. This Persian defeat put Egypt in the hands of the Macedonians under the 300-year Ptolemaic Dynasty.

Chapter 11:

The Macedonian Dynasty (332 BC–30 BC)

Alexander the Great (332 BC–323 BC)

Alexander the Great in Egypt

As already noted, Alexander the Great was one of the two greatest conquerors ever and one of the most celebrated men in history. His life was and is the stuff of legend since his career of unprecented empire-building encompassed a mere span of 12 years, beginning when he was 21 and ending with his death at age 33. He never lost a battle and when the epic of conquest was over, his empire stretched from Greece to India. Though the empire that he won by force of arms could not be held together after his death, evidence of his influence and that of Macedonian Greek culture in those conquered lands stretching into India persists to this day.

Alexander had already defeated the Persians three times when he marched into Egypt in 332 BC. The universal report by observers in antiquity was that the populace was ecstatic; Alexander was universally regarded in Egypt as the country's deliverer from the hated Persian. And in fact, when his general Ptolemy inaugurated his own dynasty in Egypt after Alexander's death, there was never a single national uprising in Egypt against the Ptolemaic pharaohs—apart from a few unsuccessful riots in Upper Egypt—for the three hundred years of their rule. It's as if the spark of revolt in Egypt had been permanently extinguished and the country was more or less content to be ruled by the Ptolemies if only because it brought peace and stability.

By the time Alexander arrived in Memphis the Egyptians were ready to crown him pharaoh forthwith. A legend had sprung up that somehow made Alexander the clandestine son of Nectanebo II, a fiction that the young conqueror heartily embraced as he was being crowned pharaoh. He wasted no time further endearing himself to the Egyptians by offering sacrifices to Apis and others of the Egyptian gods. Alexander began making visits to various parts of Egypt but none more celebrated than his expedition to the Oasis of

Alexander the Great Embraced by Two Egyptian Goddesses

Siwa, northern home to Amon. This 15-day trek to Siwa was apparently suggested to him by the priests he met who had no qualms assuring him that, in reality, he was a son of Amon. Again, Alexander readily accepted his place in the divine pantheon of pharaohs, nearly all of whom since the beginning of the New Kingdom, considered themselves sons of Amon. In the event, the journey to Siwa was of legendary portent; less than one-third of the way there, the water began to give out, but a rainstorm arose in a most remarkable manner for such a desert environment, enabling the expedition to replenish its water. It is said that at that point, the new pharaoh's progress was guided by a line of crows leading the way across the desert expanses to Siwa.

Alexander finally arrived at Siwa and spent several days there in communication with the priests, guardians of Amon:

> The form of the god Amen worshipped at Siwa was a ram which was inlaid with emeralds and other precious stones, and which was carried about in a boat; it directed the priests and made known its wishes by movements of its head.[1]

Alexander was formally and ritually acknowledged as the 'Son of Amon', reportedly by Amon himself through his oracle. Well-pleased with the outcome of his pilgrimage, Alexander bestowed suitably rich gifts on the temple and returned to Memphis, fully consecrated as pharaoh.

However, he had one more task to perform, the founding of his own 'sacred city' to be named 'Alexandria', the first of nearly 20 cities he would found bearing that name. But the first Alexandria was to become one of the most culturally brilliant cities in the ancient world, renowned for its stunning architecture, matchless library, and magnetic religious attraction well into the Christian era. Only Rome would eventually compete with it as a cosmopolitan city populated by a thriving population of diverse ethnic and religious groups. Up to the 4th century, Alexandria would be the major epicenter for emerging Christianity.

The common explanation for the founding of Alexandria is that the new pharaoh desired to have a Mediterranean location for the purpose of creating a home port for his merchant marine and navy. Certainly Alexandria's location, on the coast of the western edge of the Delta is ideal for the purpose. But there is another aspect of Alexandria entirely missed by nearly all writers of ancient history: Alexander chose the site of his new Egyptian capital for geodetic purposes. To understand this premise fully it is necessary to peruse Charles

1 Budge EAW, **A History of Egypt**, Volume VII, Oosterhout N.B.: Anthropological Publications, 1902/1968, p. 148.

Hapgood's **Maps of the Ancient Sea Kings,**[2] a full and detailed investigation of the famous *Piri Re'is Map*. The Piri Re'is Map, compiled by the Turkish admiral Piri Re'is in 1513, 21 years after the Columbian voyages, is the most accurate surviving map drawn up to the 19th century, revealing a knowledge of longitude and of the earth's land surfaces that was not supposed to have been discovered until centuries later. It was originally a map of the world the surviving portion of which depicts the western promontory of Africa, the eastern tip of South America, the north coast of Antarctica, and Spain. The Piri Re'is Map was compiled from 20 source maps some going back to the time of Alexander. As a result of the Hapgood team's exhaustive researches, it was determined that the center of the original map, i.e., the 'center of the world', lay at 30° East Longitude and 23°51' North Latitude. We find that 30° E. Longitude defines the western border of the Egyptian Delta and 23°51' North Latitude the Tropic of Cancer in Alexander's time, putting the center of the Map about 100 miles west of Aswan, the southern boundary of ancient Egypt. But the striking fact about the location of Alexander's capital is that it is situated at 29°54'E. only 6' from the 30°E. meridian on which sits the center of the Piri Re'is Map. The author has dealt with this remarkable finding in an earlier book:

> ...Alexander chose the particular location he did for his capital because it lay on the meridian that defined the western boundary of the Delta, i.e., of Lower Egypt. Clearly, Alexander and his Ptolemaic successors meant for Alexandria to be the new geodetic center of Egypt and so made the meridian on which it sat the new prime meridian. What better location, according to the thinking of the time, to locate the center of a new imperial map than at the junction of the Alexandrian meridian and the Tropic of Cancer.[3]

Concerning who actually built Alexandria, Wallis Budge says:

> The architect of the city was Deinocrates, and his plans were carried out by

2 Vid. Hapgood CH, **Maps of the Ancient Sea Kings: Evidence of Advanced Civilization in the Ice Age**, New York: E.P. Dutton, 1979, passim for a full discussion.

3 Finch CS, **The Star of Deep Beginnings: The Genesis of African Science and Technology**, Decatur: Khenti, Inc., 1998, p. 229.

> Cleomenes of Naucratis, who was assisted by Heron (a Libyan), Krateros, Hyponomos, and others.[4]

It is the 'and others' in the above quote that demands closer scrutiny. The Greeks did not possess the scientific, mathematical, or technical knowledge to have laid out Alexandria according to a geodetic system that relied on a knowledge of astronomy and world geography such as was demonstrated by the placement of the city virtually on the 30th Meridian East. The priests of Egypt who, once accepting Alexander as pharaoh, undoubtedly advised him on the manner of laying out Alexandria according to a geodetic system they had maintained for millennia. It is likely that they trained a cohort of Greeks in the technical aspects of the matter but the geodetic layout of Alexandria—and the maps that would serve as the source maps for Piri Re'is more than 18 centuries later—were derivable only from knowledge held by the priests. The Greeks had surveyors and builders capable of city planning, but for advanced geodesy, they would have had to rely on the priestly knowledge of the temples.

Alexander spent five months in Egypt and while the initial foundations of his new city were being laid, he set about settling the governance of his Egyptian dominions, appointing a viceroy, provincial governors, garrison commanders, local army generals, and naval admirals. The new viceroy of Egypt, as it turned out, was *Doloaspis* the Persian, in keeping with Alexander's policy of employing talented and experienced men from all over his expanding empire in the administration of it. Doloaspis was especially adept at raising revenue, a handy skill on which Alexander would increasingly depend in all his newly-acquired domains. When Alexander left Egypt to continue his conquering march across the known world, he would never return to it alive. He died at Babylon (age 33) on the return march from India and immediately a dispute arose as to the disposition of Alexander's body. His general Ptolemy hit on the solution of consulting the oracle of the Babylonian Zeus. The reply of this oracle was that Alexander's remains be taken back to Egypt to be interred. Apparently, all or most of the contending parties accepted this judgement and after embalmment, the dead Alexander was duly returned to Egypt. A suitably lavish tomb was

4 Budge, op. cit., p. 151.

built for him in Alexandria and an equally lavish funeral procession was led by Ptolemy who laid his body to rest in the tomb built for first Macedonian pharaoh.

As was to be expected, upon Alexander's death, murderous strife broke out among those wishing to succeed him. There were two offspring of Alexander with a claim to his throne, one of them still unborn by his favorite wife *Roxane.* She allied herself with Alexander's most powerful and cunning surviving associate *Perdiccas* who assumed effective rule over Macedonia. Their first order of business was to lure Alexander's last wife and his sister into their presence in Babylonia by a forged letter and once in Roxane's power, they were speedily done away with. However, it was necessary for someone to at least nominally rule the empire until Roxane's child could be born and grow to maturity and, after terrible violence and murder, *Philip Arrhidaeus*, half-brother of Alexander, was set on the throne as Philip III of Macedon and Philip I of Egypt. Perdiccas became Philip III's chief minister. As already noted, it was necessary to portion out the existing empire in 10 parts—no one but Alexander himself could have held such a vast empire intact—with the general Ptolemy receiving Egypt and northern Libya to govern. Nonetheless, Ptolemy—probably shrewdly—did not try at first to assume for himself a royal title but preserved the fiction of ruling on behalf of Alexander's successor.

Alexander's son by Roxane was duly born and named Alexander IV. For the time being, Arrhidaeus was content to serve as regent for Alexander IV and the whole arrangement was reasonably well-managed by Perdiccas. But Perdiccas died in 321 BC and the 'coalition' of competing interests rapidly fell apart as Arrhidaeus and his partisans returned to Macedonia, increasingly threatening the child Alexander's position. Roxane and her son departed for Epirus, the residence of Olympias, mother of Alexander and grandmother of his heir. Conniving with the King of Epirus, Roxane arranged to have Arrhidaeus assassinated in 317 BC, six years after he had been set on the throne. Though Arrhidaeus never visited Egypt, Ptolemy, the loyal subaltern, caused his name to be carved in cartouches in several locations in Egypt along with an elaborate relief dedicated to Arrhidaeus in a red granite sanctuary built inside the precincts of Karnak.

The assassination of Philip Arrhidaeus seemed to have cleared the way for Alexander IV (Alexander II of Egypt) to rule unopposed with his mother and grandmother serving as regents. But there will still too many powerful factions conspiring for power and the leader of one, Cassander, made a bid for the throne first by instigating the strangling of Olympias. It took a little while longer to remove Roxane and Alexander but by 311 BC, they had been imprisoned and their executions carried out, again by the command of Cassander. Alexander had managed to survive just six years after being set on the throne, though in Egyptian annals his reign is reckoned from his birth. He also never visited Egypt. But true to form, Ptolemy caused reliefs, statues, and cartouches of the boy-king to be carved all over Egypt in the manner of a pharaoh. Even so, the entire time that Ptolemy was the Macedonian satrap of Egypt—12 years—he was systematically consolidating his position and winning over the allegiance of the priesthood. With the death of Alexander IV, there was no one to prevent Ptolemy from assuming the throne of Egypt, though he waited until 305 BC to formally declare himself pharaoh.

Egypt Under the Ptolemies (311 BC–30 BC)

Ptolemy I (311 BC–283 BC)

Ptolemy I—Soter

Ptolemy I, more commonly known as *Ptolemy Soter*, was the son of *Arsinoë* by either the commoner Lagus or by Philip II. It is commonly supposed that Philip was his father because Arsinoë was one of his concubines prior to marriage to Lagus. Thus there is the real possibility that Ptolemy was half-brother to Alexander which may account for his high position in Alexander's army. He was one of Alexander's most trusted companions and the king turned to Ptolemy frequently to handle the most dangerous and delicate missions. Ptolemy's eventual acquisition of Egypt and Libya at the time of the division of Alexander's empire was accomplished without opposition or objection and once acquired, Ptolemy moved swiftly to establish himself as Egypt's supreme viceroy under Alexander's successors.

Though, as already seen, Ptolemy handled his office with great shrewdness he still ran afoul of Perdiccas, the *de facto* ruler of Macedonia, who schemed to remove him from his position in Egypt. But Ptolemy possessed a charismatic personality and great organizing ability winning favor not only with the local populace and priests but also with a substantial army of mercenaries who flocked to his banner. Moreover, Ptolemy had not survived the intrigues surrounding Alexander in life and after death without possessing the necessary ruthlessness. Upon arriving in Egypt, he speedily removed the reigning satrap, *Cleomenes* who had amassed great wealth by looting the country, making himself irredeemably unpopular. More damning, Cleomenes was an ally of Perdiccas; his execution at Ptolemy's order came swiftly. By 321 BC, Ptolemy and Perdiccas were open enemies, exacerbated by Ptolemy's success in getting Alexander's body buried in Alexandria instead of Macedonia. For Perdiccas it was a sufficient *casus belli* to provoke him to invade Egypt by way of the Pelusiac branch of the Nile, the customary pathway for northern invaders to enter Egypt. But Perdiccas's campaign was visited by one catastrophe after another precipitated by the Nile floods that caused him to lose a large portion of his army. Numerous soldiers deserted to Ptolemy. When the battle was finally joined, a disastrous attempt at a river crossing resulted in further losses—1,000 by crocodiles according to one report—causing the army to lose all confidence in Perdiccas. Finally, a body of men went to Perdiccas's tent and killed him without further ado.

For the next nine years Ptolemy was engaged in protecting his newly-acquired domains in a series of engagements in Syria, Cyprus, and Cyrene against Macedonian generals determined to wrest away his territories from him. His most persistent enemies were Antigonus and his son Demetrius. Ptolemy suffered a serious naval reverse at Salamis at the hands of Demetrius in 308 BC and the situation looked dire for Ptolemy as Antigonus, thinking the time was propitious for another invasion attempt of Egypt, gathered together a sizable army and navy for this purpose. But again the invaders were thwarted by a combination of Ptolemy's cunning, coaxing many of the mercenaries from the expeditionary force over to his side with the enticement of higher pay, and the fortification of the various access points into Egypt through the swampy Delta making it impossible for Antigonus's army to break through into the country.

In 305 BC, 18 years after becoming the viceroy of Egypt, Ptolemy took the title of king and also *Soter*, meaning 'savior'. His wars, however, were not quite finished. Antigonus and Demetrius now invested the island of Rhodes with 40,000 soldiers and 370 warships in revenge for having sided with Egypt during the previous hostilities. But Ptolemy sent food and reinforcements to the besieged Rhodians, as did other allies, and this assistance was sufficient to force Demetrius to raise the siege and return home. Four years later, a final battle took place between Ptolemy and Antigonus at Ipsus and Antigonus was not only defeated but killed. After the demise of his most determined foe and the recapture of Cyprus in 295 BC, Ptolemy engaged in no further military campaigns, spending the rest of his reign consolidating his hold on the kingdom. Ptolemy, who married four women, installed his son by *Berenice*, also called Ptolemy, on the throne in 285 BC, dying two years later at the age of 84 after a reign of 28 years.

Ptolemy was a very capable ruler. He expended great effort beautifying Alexandria and establishing its cultural pre-eminence by founding the justly famous Library of Alexandria. At its height, the Library housed 700,000 scrolls, many taken from the vaults of Egypt's temples as well as from the learned sites of other lands. It made Alexandria the intellectual capital of the ancient world, a magnet for students and scholars from every part of the Mediterranean and beyond. The Library was home to a host of international scholars whose maintenance and upkeep were underwritten by the Ptolemies with travel, lodging and stipends for support of their whole families. New works in mathematics, astronomy, physics, and the natural sciences abounded; important scholarly scrolls were copied and made available for a price to scholars and collectors from everywhere serving as a source of income for the Library. Associated with Library was the Museum which was in fact a university, hosting astronomers, scientists, philosophers, and mathematicians of the stature of Euclid, Archimedes, Eratosthenes, Herophilus, Erasistratus, and Hipparchus, among others. It is with the founding of the Museum and Library of Alexandria that what has been called 'the Greek miracle' truly begins, the fount of Greek learning, science, and scholarship that would amaze the world in after centuries. It is Egypt's learning, hoary with antiquity, that makes possible this 'miracle' under the tutelage of the first Ptolemies.

Ptolemy Soter established a cosmopolitan atmosphere that made Alexandria a congenial environment for diverse peoples, not the least of which were Jews. He is reported to have brought many of them to settle there after taking Jerusalem by surprise, and, given the tolerant attitude towards them, many more followed of their own accord.[5] The numbers of Jews in Alexandria rose to an estimated 120,000 and Alexandria in fact became a center of Jewish learning rivaling Babylon; it was there that the *Septuagint*, the translation of the Hebrew Torah into Greek, took place in the reign of Ptolemy II (*Philadelphus*). Not only that, but it was the home of *Philo Judaeus*, the Jewish exegete in the decades just prior to the Christian era who attempted a reconciliation between Jewish theology and Greek philosophy.

It was under Ptolemy Soter that the cult of *Serapis* was first established. Serapis represented the deliberate fusion of Hades (the Greek god of the underworld), Osiris (also an Underworld deity), and Apis. Ptolemy and his successors wished to set up a deity that could appeal to both Greek and Egyptian, and the tireless promotion of the new cult succeeded greatly on this account. To the Greeks he was represented as a bearded deity covered with Egyptian paraphenalia; to the Egyptians he wore the head of the Apis Bull surmounted by the sun disc and uraeus. All of the ancient rites and ceremonials were celebrated under Serapis. Eventually his worship spread throughout the Roman empire and he came to supplant Osiris as the Consort of Isis. Egyptians knew, by this time, that there would never again be a native king of Egypt, so they accommodated themselves to the rule of Ptolemy. He was the best prospect they had, especially since he was making a concerted effort to establish common ground between Greek and Egyptian and allowing the populace to continue its ancient ways. Also, Ptolemy won favor because he had managed to re-establish the Egyptian empire in the

5 Whiston W, translator, **Josephus: Complete Works**, Grand Rapids: Kregel Publications, 1867/1981, p. 245.

north and west by his rule over Syria, Palestine, Cyprus, Libya, and Cyrene. At this time in history, it was as good as it was ever going to get for Egypt. Budge gives probably the most cogent assessment of Ptolemy as pharaoh of Egypt:

> ...Ptolemy was a brave soldier, a prudent general, and a wise and sympathetic administrator, who allowed the various peoples to enjoy their own religion and customs, and such a measure of freedom as was consistent with the security of his rule; he was both humane and generous, and his genial manners and sympathy made him popular with all classes.[6]

Ptolemy II (283 BC–247 BC)

Ptolemy II - Philadelphus

Ptolemy II, who took the cognomen *Philadelphus* ('brotherly love'), was the son of Ptolemy I and Berenice. He was co-ruler with his father during the last two years of his father's life, another ancient custom of Egypt revived by Ptolemy Soter. Soter promoted Philadelphus over two older brothers by his wife *Eurydice* and, on this occasion at least, the *fait accompli* was accepted by all parties. Ptolemy II married two women named Arsinoë, the first one eventually banished to Upper Egypt on suspicion of conspiracy and the second one being his sister whom he married—in the time-honored fashion of the ancient pharaohs—after the death of her first husband.

6 Budge, op. cit., p.188.

A pattern began early in the reign which would set its unfortunate imprint on the rest of the Ptolemies in the dynasty: two brothers were executed on suspicion of planning usurpations. Another half-brother, *Magas*, appointed governor of Cyrene under Ptolemy I, broke away from Ptolemy II's authority and allying himself with Seleucus, the post-Alexandrian Macedonian king of Babylon, made plans to invade Egypt. The first planned attack was forestalled by other matters occupying Magas's time and energy but an invasion was launched several years later. The march on Egypt was at first successful until Ptolemy found a way—probably through bribery—of luring *Antichuss II*, a major ally of Magas, to his side, thereby interdicting any further progress of the invasion. The two brotherly combatants, constrained by circumstances, reached an accommodation and to seal the *concordat* between the two sovereigns, a marriage was contracted between Berenice, daughter of Magas, and Ptolemy III, son of Philadelphus.

In spite of these seemingly bellicose incidents, Ptolemy II never committed himself to any full-scale wars, however much he participated in intrigues among the Greek city-states. He could see that Rome was an emerging power, and he cultivated cordial relations with this increasingly expansionist state. He did, however, continue the work of his father in subsizing and promoting literature, science, and culture especially through his unstinting patronage of the Museum and its linked Library. As with Ptolemy I, the professors and intellectuals associated with these two linked institutions were paid liberal stipends by the state and the Library's collection of scrolls continued to grow for the next two hundred years. Again, because of the enlightened policies of the first two Ptolemies in the sphere of scholarship, Alexandria had rapidly become the intellectual capital of the ancient world. It was during the reign of Ptolemy II that Manetho, an Egyptian priest, wrote his world famous ***History of Egypt*** in Greek making the history and culture of ancient Egypt as gleaned from primary sources and written by a learned Egyptian available to a Greek-reading public for the very first time. Even though only the *Epitome* of Manetho's ***History*** survived the ravages of time, with its pharaonic chronology it remains perhaps the most important document from antiquity bearing on ancient Egypt's history; only *Book 2* of Herodotus's ***The Histories*** compares with it in importance for the later study of ancient Egypt. The composition of the already-mentioned **Septuagint**, representing the Torah translated into

Greek by 72 Hebrew scholarly rabbis, was also undertaken during Ptolemy II's reign. In later centuries with the rise of Christianity, the **Septuagint** became the Old Testament and therefore the foundation of a new, expansive religion. In order for the translation to take place, an epistle was sent by Ptolemy to the Jewish high priest in Jerusalem. He was to send six men from each of the 12 Hebrew tribes, each one learned in the Law, to come to Egypt to be supported with a stipend by the king for the purpose of accomplishing the translation. Seventy-two such men came to Egypt and during the reign of Ptolemy completed the translation of the Five Books of Moses[7]. The remainder of the Torah was translated in the succeeding generations.

Ptolemy did not stint on construction efforts either, completing the construction of the Lighthouse of Pharos begun by his father in Alexandria's harbor, rising to more than 400 feet in height. A marvel of engineering and connected to the mainland by a causeway, it was considered one the Seven Wonders of the Ancient World. Its beacon could be seen 29 miles out to sea. Ptolemy finished the tomb of Alexander and those of his parents, Ptolemy I and Berenice. Moreover, he had built numerous temples to Greek and Egyptian gods all over Egypt.

Though not engaged in any major wars, Ptolemy nonetheless employed a sizable army of 250,000 soldiers and quite a large fleet besides. He revived Egypt's overseas trade to a level that exceeded even that current in the most prosperous days of the 26th Dynasty. Merchants from every corner of the known world flocked to Alexandria's teeming markets; Jews in particular seemed to have prospered greatly in this environment. The merchant marine, protected where necessary by powerful warships, sailed down Africa's coast in search of the exotic luxury items, still so much coveted in Egypt, as well as to Arabia and India. The founding of a fortified port town named *Ptolemais Epithêrus* on the northeastern coast of present-day Sudan testifies to the importance of this trade on the eastern side of Africa. The war elephants in Ptolemy's army were captured and brought from this region. The same merchant marine was ever-present throughout the entire Mediterranean:

> Commerce between Egypt and Greek and other settlements on the Mediterranean sea-coast was both brisk and profitable, for the ma-

7 Josephus/Whiston, op. cit., p. 247.

> terial condition of the country being flourishing the merchants and bankers of the period had no hesitation in investing their capital in concerns which were safe and lucrative especially when there was no war to shake the public confidence, and when the interests of the country were protected by a powerful army and a fleet of warships.[8]

The benefactions that Ptolemy settled on the gods and temples of Egypt were generous to the point of extravagance. The temples in the Two Lands of Egypt received on a yearly basis 10,050,000 pieces of silver which did not include the taxes the temples could levy on the households and individuals of their districts which amounted to another 100,000 pounds of silver for all temples. He paid special attention not only to the Apis Bull but the Sacred Ram of Mendes where he erected a stele showing himself and his wife making offerings to the Ram. The Mendesian Ram was almost as important as the Apis Bull and he attended the enshrinement of a succession of sacred rams at the temple built and dedicated for the purpose. Other temples that were especially favored by his time, attention, and generosity were those sacred to Sebek in the Fayum where he also built a new city named Arsinoë, the Temple of Isis at Philae, and of course Karnak. Clearly he was eager to cultivate the good will of the priests and to become in all things a true pharaoh of Egypt, even to the point of marrying his sister, a most un-Greek of customs. Most of the Ptolemies who came afterwards also adopted the practice. Ptolemy II died in 247 BC.

Ptolemy III (247 BC–222 BC)

Ptolemy III, surnamed *Euergetes*, a word meaning 'benefactor', was the eldest son of Ptolemy II and Arsinoë who was associated with his father on the throne prior to the latter's death. He was also known as *Physicon*, a word meaning 'fat', because of his obesity. His above-mentioned marriage to his cousin Berenice, daughter of Magas, brought Cyrene under his rule once he succeeded his father. The early part of his reign was occupied by a long military campaign precipitated by the murder of his sister and nephew by *Laodice* with the connivance of her son

8 Budge, op. cit., pp. 194-5.

Seleucus II. Laodice had been the original wife and queen of Antiochus of Syria but was supplanted by the daughter of Ptolemy II, also named Berenice, who was set on the throne next to Antiochus in her stead. When Ptolemy II died, Antiochus, unwisely as it turns out, brought Laodice and her children back from exile whereupon he was speedily poisoned to death by her and replaced by Seleucus II. The murder of Berenice and her infant son followed rapidly.

This murder was the *casas belli* that set in motion a large expeditionary force, by land and sea, commanded by Ptolemy III. His forces swept through Syria capturing Antioch without much resistance. However, this spectacular victory did not, apparently, result in the capture of either Seleucus or his homicidal mother Laodice because, instead of pursuing them, Ptolemy continued his march eastward where he conquered Mesopotamia, Babylonia, Susiana, Persia, and Media. Having accomplished these conquests so brilliantly, he ransacked Susa and other cities in Persia not only for loot and treasure but for all of the religious artifacts of Egypt previously carried there by Cambyses in the time of the Persian conquest of Egypt. The entire campaign lasted nearly three years, ending toward the end of 245 BC, only curtailed by urgent matters demanding attention back in Egypt. However, it was counted a huge success in Egypt because of the vast spoils brought back by Ptolemy and the return of so many divine icons previously removed from the country. However, Ptolemy, in spite of his victories, did not attempt to incorporate the conquered lands into his own empire and the Seleucids who had provoked the war in the first place regained control of the countries previously under their rule, with the exception of Syria where Egyptian hegemony was more firmly established. His only other military conflict afterwards was a naval battle against Antigonus Gonatas resulting in the defeat of the latter. There were no battles for Ptolemy for the rest of his reign.

Like his predecessors, Ptolemy III expended much time, effort, and money building and renovating temples, thereby continuing to win favor among the priesthood and more deeply reconciling them to Ptolemaic rule. In fact in 238 BC, priests from all over the realm gathered in Canopus to solemly and ritually celebrate Ptolemy's birth, accession, and reign. Nothing more fervently won the admiration and gratitude of the priests than Ptolemy's campaign into Persia that resulted in the restoration of so many sacred icons previously carried away by the original Persian conquerors. Moreover, Ptolemy had purchased grain from abroad to feed the populace after a low Nile threatened the land with famine. It has to be admitted that Ptolemy III, like his predecessors, went out of his way to govern Egypt wisely, magnanimously, and in accord with the traditions of the ancient pharaohs. It was at this time that the calendrical modification of the civil year that created the first 'leap-year'—actually a 'leap-day'—was instituted, an innovation that has been carried down to the present moment. This 'reform' affected the civil calendar of 365 days for the first time which previously had been recalibrated every 1,460 years by cycling it continuously with the Sothic Year of 365¼ days based on the heliacal rising of Sirius every year at the summer solstice. This change was effected so that the festivals would not 'slide' through the civil year as they had been doing but would occur at the same time and season every year. Every fourth year, as is true today, the year was counted as 366 days long instead of 365.

Several of the more famous temples in Egypt were built from the ground up by the Ptolemies. The Temple of Isis at Philae was started by Ptolemy II and completed by Ptolemy III. The Temple of Horus at Edfu was begun by Ptolemy III in 237 BC but not completed until 180 years later. Other Ptolemaic temples were built at Esneh and Canopus. The Horus temple at Edfu is renowned for being the only completely intact ancient Egyptian temple surviving to present times owing to the fact that, over the centuries, it had been gradually buried *in toto* by the mud from the houses of peasants who built around it and on top of it over and over again after the Arab conquest of Egypt in 642 A.D. None of these temples were, strictly speaking new; they were built exactly in the same place and even on the foundations of older temples dedicated to the same gods. Norman Lockyer demonstrated this fact over and over again in his landmark book on the astronomical orientation of Egyptian temples.[9]

Ptolemy Euergetes continued to enlarge the Library Alexandria appointing as the Head Librarian *Erastosthenes*, a native of Cyrene who was one of the most famous astronomers and mathematicians of late antiquity. He is credited as being the first to ascertain the circumference of the earth, inventing latitude and longitude, and measuring the distance between the earth and the sun. Though Erastothenes was undoubtedly an exceptionally talented polymath, the

9 Lockyer N, **The Dawn of Astronomy**, Cambridge: The M.I.T. Press, (1894), 1964, passim.

idea that he was the author of any of one of those discoveries credited to him is just another of those comfortable fictions about the uniqueness of Greek genius that on closer examination are without foundation. It is beyond the scope of this writing to delve deeply into this contentious subject which has been treated elsewhere[10] but it, again, testifies to the curious unwillingness of the modern antiquarian to link the great Greek scientific discoveries to the founding of the Library of Alexandria whose core collection came from the archives of Egyptian temples. Having said that, it is clear that Ptolemy Euergetes was a great patron of art, literature, and philosophy of both the Egyptian and Greek kind. He was known for being a magnanimous humanitarian, sending abundant amounts of money, grain, and supplies in support of the people of Rhodes who suffered terribly from the effects of a devastating earthquake in 224 BC.

Though of Macedonian descent and a grandson of one of Alexander's best and most trusted generals, by the time Ptolemy Euergetes came to the Egyptian throne, Macedonia and Egypt were enemies. Ptolemy never failed to give money and support to any coalition of states opposing the rising power of Macedonia though he never committed Egypt to a direct military confrontation with his ancestral home. He even gave sanctuary to Cleomenes, King of Sparta, who was defeated by the Macedonians at the battle of Sellasia. Macedonia declined to bring the war to Egypt and Ptolemy was content to allow the status quo to prevail. Ptolemy died in 222 BC and was succeeded by his son, the fourth Ptolemy.

Ptolemy IV (222 BC–205 BC)

Ptolemy IV, also known as *Philopator*, meaning 'lover of father', succeeded his father on the throne without having served as co-ruler as his predecessors had done prior to their accessions. However, he continued the custom of marrying his sister, also named Arsinoë as her female forbears and previous queens had been so named. A brother, Magas, was put to death by Philopator upon gaining the throne, continuing another practice from earlier reigns. In fact, Philopator was of an entirely different caliber from his predecessors. He was profligate,

10 Vid. Finch, op. cit., pp. 101-65 and 203-33

Ptolemy IV - Philopator

feckless, and indifferent to the day-to-day demands of governmental administration. He seemed to live in a perpetual state of drunkenness and riotous living, aided and abetted by his chief minister *Sosibius*. Inevitably, his utter unsuitability to rule began to induce plots to supplant him. Sosibius, taking over more and more of the reins of government, began to systematically liquidate plotters and suspected plotters, starting with Cleomenes, the Spartan king who had been under the protection of the Ptolemy Euergetes before his death. Also included were Lysimachus, Philopater's uncle, his mother Berenice, and his sister-wife Arsinoë.

Alexander's empire had been broken up into several pieces; that piece that included Asia Minor, and Greater Syria was ruled by the Seleucids, of Macedonian origin like the Ptolemies. Despite their common origin, the various kingdoms carved out of the Alexandrian empire became mutually hostile to one another, mostly because they were eager to add territory to their own kingdoms by slicing pieces from that of their post-Alexandrian neighbors. Antiochus III was the Seleucid contemporary of Ptolemy IV and thought he saw an opportunity to take Egypt, or at least a hefty portion of it, away from the indolent, debauched Ptolemy Philopator. In 220 BC he launched an attack on Egypt by way of the Pelusiac branch of the Nile, only to find that the Egyptian army was well-ensconced at the fortified garrisons in Pelusium. Rather than take on the Egyptian army, Antiochus instead started to capture the towns and cities in northern Syria that were under the rule of the Ptolemies. He found an ally in Theodotus, the Ptolemaic governor of Coele-Syria[11] who was completely alienated by the dissolute behavior of Philopator who, in addition, had completely ignored Theodotus and the work he was doing governing Coele-Syria. Antiochus first conquered the city of Seleucia, controlled by an Egyptian garrison, on the Orontes River in southern Anatolia. Not to do so while trying to conquer Coele-Syria would have left an Egyptian force to his rear that could threaten his entire invasion plan. Having captured Seleucia, Antiochus was now free to move against the Phoenician towns of Tyre and Ptolemais. With these disasters befalling the Ptolemaic empire, even Philopator could no longer remain unmoved and indigent; the danger of the conquest of Egypt grew with every victory by Antiochus.

Two individuals now took over matters in Egypt, Sosibius and *Agathocles*. Their first task would be to cause a sufficient delay in the active hostilities to allow Egypt to prepare adequately for war. Messengers were sent to Antiochus proposing a peace conference, an entirely bogus gesture meant to deflect, for the time being, Antiochus's march south. As negotiations continued for the proposed peace conference, Sosibius and Agathocles retired to Memphis to build up an army and produce the necessary weapons of war. A rather polyglot army of native soldiers, mercenaries, and auxiliary troops was raised totaling 73,000 men under the general *Nicolaus* plus a large fleet under *Perigenes*. In 218 BC, the army was at last ready; negotiations were broken off, and Nicolaus advanced out of Egypt at the head of the army confronting Antiochus at Porphyrion in what is now Lebanon. He was soundly defeated by Antiochus and when Perigenes was apprised of what had happened to the army, he withdrew the fleet to Sidon where the defeated army of Nicolaus also retreated. With no Egyptian army to oppose him, Antiochus proceeded to overrun seven cities in Coele-Syria.

In 217 BC, the two armies once again prepared to face one another, this time with Ptolemy Philopator at the head of the Egyptian army. Both armies had large contingents of war elephants among their 'live' weapons and the battle took place at Raphia, beginning on each side with a charge of the elephants.

11 *Coele* is a word that means 'all of' or 'the whole of'. Coele-Syria refers to 'the whole of Syria'.

This time, however, it was the Egyptian army that was victorious even though Antiochus managed to kill or capture all of Ptolemy's war elephants. Though winning this battle, Philopator was no real warrior and made no move to follow up his victory by pursuring Antiochus. He was content to send the ever-present Sosibius to negotiate peace terms with Antiochus and having regained control of at least Coele-Syria, Philopator was happy to return to Alexandria and resume his life of luxury and dissipation.

Though given over to sloth, Ptolemy Philopator continued the ready patronage of the Library of Alexandria and Museum inaugurated by his royal ancestors. He was a lover of the Homeric epics and dedicated a temple to the legendary Grecian epic poet. He also continued the policy of building and endowing temples dedicated to both Greek and Egyptian deities. He completed the construction of the Temple of Horus at Edfu, though the carving of the wall reliefs continued for another four years, and the Temple of Isis at Philae. There are also inscriptions at Philae commissioned by a Meroitic Cushitic king that Diodorus calls *Ergamenes*. There continues to be debate as to whether Ergamenes was a contemporary of Ptolemy II or Ptolemy IV; in either instance it would seem that his political reach extended all the way to Philae. Ergamenes is also credited with building a temple at Dakka, 70 miles south of Philae to which Ptolemy IV added a hall. Clearly, Ergamenes—to whichever Ptolemy he might have been contemporaneous—was treated as a sovereign of equal stature and whose northern jurisdiction to the south end of Aswan (Philae) was accepted and recognized:

> The remains of the temple of Ptolemy IV at Philae, and the temple at Dakkeh do, however, prove that the king of Egypt was obliged to treat Ergamenes as a friend and equal.[12]

Ptolemy IV was the first of the Ptolemies to persecute Jews, and much of his evil reputation is due to the later reports of his actions by the Jews of Alexandria. The reputed reason for turning against the Jews derives from an incident in Jerusalem where he visited after the victory at Raphia. He desired to enter the the holy sanctuary of the Temple in Jerusalem but was denied admission by the

12 Budge, op. cit., p. 242.

Jewish high priest because no non-Jew—in fact no non-priest—was allowed into such a sacred space. Accordingly, Philopator grew furious at this perceived insult and took his revenge on the Jewish population of Alexandria. Whether such an incident actually happened has never been independently verified, but, whatever the cause, Philopator raised their taxes and put severe restrictions on Jewish religious observances. The atrocities against the Jews attributed to him as described in the ***Book of Maccabees***, written fully a generation after Philopator's death, are clearly Jewish inventions designed to besmirch as much as possible Philopator's reputation, though his proscriptions against them were real enough.

In the last four years of his reign, Philopator named his son Ptolemy V, a.k.a. *Epiphanes* ('divine manifestation'), as co-regent who was but two years old at the time of his co-accession and less than six years of age when his father died and he ascended the throne. It was during the co-regency that a revolt against the regime broke out in Upper Egypt, assisted by an alliance with the Nubians, which continued unabated after Philopator's death and into the reign of Epiphanes.

Ptolemy V (205 BC–182 BC)

Ptolemy V or Epiphanes was the son of the brother-sister consort pair of Ptolemy IV and Arsinoë. The manner in which he came to the throne is recounted in the history written by Polybius as cited by Budge:

> …three or four days after the death of Ptolemy Philopator Agathocles and Sosibius caused a platform to be erected, and summoned a meeting of the foot-guards and the household, as well as of the officers of the infantry and cavalry. Mounting the platform they announced the deaths of the king and queen, and proclaimed the customary period of mourning for the people. They next placed a diadem upon the head of the child Ptolemy Epiphanes, and proclaimed him king, and read a forged will, in which the late king nominated Agathocles and Sosibius guardians of his son…[13]

13 Budge EAW, **A History of Egypt**, Volume VII, Oosterhout N.B.: Anthropological Publications, 1868, p. 2.

Ptolemy died a natural death; Arsinoë did not and there can be no doubt that Agathocles and Sosibius were the instigators of her premature death, though the assassination was actually carried out by one of their henchmen, *Philammon*. Agathocles then set about putting other minions in key positions throughout the realm to ensure his control. The assassin Philammon was made governor of Cyrene, *Pelops* was sent as ambassador to the court of Antiochus, Ptolemy, son of *Agesarchus* went to Rome in charge of the Alexandrian embassy there, and Scopas was dispatched to Greece to recruit more mercenaries for the army. Agathocles put the boy king Ptolemy Epiphanes under the care and supervision of his own mother, *Oenanthe*, and his sister *Agathocleia* who, as the mistress of the late emperor, had exercised extraordinary influence over him.

Having thus settled the affairs of the kingdom to his own satisfaction, Agathocles proceeded to follow the example of Ptolemy Philopator by succumbing entirely to a life of degeneracy and excess. It was said that no woman—be she wife, mother, or virgin daughter—was safe from his predatory sexual assaults, often in the most public fashion. For the first time since the beginning of Ptolemaic rule, seething discontent became widespread among the populace. The one man who became the lightning rod for this discontent and the best potential counterfoil to the depredations of Agathocles and his sister was *Tlepolemus* who, on the death of Philopator, became governor of Pelusium, a post he had previously held but from which he retired to get himself out of harm's way. Sensing the public mood, Tlepolemus began to create his own private army and to publicly undermine Agathocles and his sister at every opportunity. Agathocles on his part tried hard to turn the tables on his rising enemy by spreading vicious slanders concerning the treason of Tlepolemus, but by this time, he had so inflamed the general hatred against him that nothing he said or did could induce anyone to take him seriously. In fact, his actions grew more desperate and, as such, inspired more ill feeling against him; he arrested the mother-in-law of Tlepolemus, dragged her through the street, and threw her into prison. Tlepolemus marched toward Alexandria. The closer he got, the more riotous and anarchic the mood and behavior of the citizenry became. Moreover, the Macedonian soldiery themselves had had quite enough of Agathocles and were ready to turn against him *en masse*. Agathocles tried to appeal to the sentiments of Macedonians and the populace by bringing the child-king forward while posing as his designated guardian. To no avail. The Macedonian palace guard took the boy Epiphanes away from Agathocles and at that point his fate was sealed. Agathocles, his three sisters, including Agathocleia, their mother Oenanthe, and all their relatives were dragged out before the crowd, and, according to the report of Polybius, all were literally torn limb from limb, except for Agathocles himself who, mercifully, was stabbed to death the moment he was taken prisoner. Philammon, the murderer of Queen Arsinoë, did not escape the vengeance of the Alexandrians. A crowd of young women rushed to his house, found him, beat him to death with sticks and stones, strangled his infant son, and killed his wife publicly in the street after tearing off all her clothes. The whole business was savage in the extreme but Agathocles, his family, and his henchmen could truly be said to have brought it on themselves.

Tlepolemus now assumed the role of prime minister and guardian of the young king. Though a capable general and beloved by his soldiers, he possessed scant talent as an administrator. He too was fond of amusements, squandered money, and showered his soldiers with extravagant gifts. He seemed to offer no objection when the elderly mandarin *Aristomenes* assumed the reins of government and did much to set affairs in order. The Seleucid king Antiochus III, already established as a persistent nemesis of the Ptolemies, decided, along with Philip V of Macedon, that the time was once again propitious to carve off slices of Egypt's Western Asiatic empire. Philip began by taking control of the Cyclades, an archipelago of islands in the Aegean southeast of mainland Greece that, up to then, were considered collectively to be a Ptolemaic protectorate. Antiochus on his part renewed his campaign to capture Palestine and Coele-Syria. The Egyptians, under Tlepolemus and Aristomenes, roused themselves sufficiently to send an army to oppose him under the leadership of Scopas. Though Scopas won a few small initial victories, he was soundly defeated by Antiochus at the Battle of Pannium who now rolled through Palestine and Coele-Syria capturing town after town, including Jerusalem (198 BC). Thus all of the Ptolemaic possessions in Syria and Palestine were lost to Antiochus. The response of the young Epiphanes and his advisors was to send an embassy to Rome seeking an intervention against Antiochus. It was a momentous precedent whose consequences would, again, 'come home to roost' 150 years later. Rome, ever seeking to exand its power and influence, did indeed send envoys to Antiochus to 'counsel' him not to attack Egyptian imperial territories any further. But these negotiations were apparently rendered moot by the Syrian king who, in secret parleys with Epiphanes' councilors, agreed to not only betroth his daughter to the young king, but restore Coele-Syria, Samaria, Judaea, and Phoenicia as Egyptian protectorates.

Aristomenes continued to govern Egypt on behalf of Ptolemy Epiphanes and, capable administrator that he was, brought prosperity and order back to Egypt. However, the general Scopas, a man notorious for his exceeding avarice and corruption and leader of the ill-starred campaign against Antiochus, endeavored to lead a revolt against Aristomenes, presumably because his previous ability to loot the public coffers was now blocked by Aristomenes's scrupulous governance. Scopas was no more successful in this misbegotten endeavor than he had been against Antiochus, and all he accomplished was to have himself, his friends, and his family speedily thrown into prison where they were all poisoned without delay.

It was becoming obvious to the councillors of the still-young monarch that the lack of a ruling king was encouraging all manner of plots and intrigues both from within the country and without. Though Ptolemy V (Epiphanes) at age 12 was still too young to sit on the throne as the reigning monarch, the disadvantages of not having him reign outweighed the considerations of extreme youth. Thus, on March 27, 196 BC, Ptolemy V—in the solemn priestly 'festival of proclaiming a sovereign'—was formally crowned pharaoh of Egypt and its empire[14] with sacerdotal representatives from every major temple of Egypt present. The investiture took place in Memphis and the decree was inscribed on a black granite stone, originating from a granite quarry near Aswan, in three scripts—hieroglyphics, demotic, and Greek. After the Ptolemaic era, the stone was lost to history but rediscovered in 1799 by a soldier in Napoleon's army near the Delta town formerly named Rosetta, hence the name of the stone, the Rosetta Stone. Through the indefatigable labors of Thomas Young in Great Britain and, more successfully, Jean-François Champollion in France, using the Greek and Demotic texts as templates, an authentic decipherment of

14 Ibid., p. 13.

the hieroglyphic text was accomplished which, in the coming years, launched modern Egyptology. It was the first time in nearly 15 centuries that the Egyptian hieroglyphics could be read. Concerning the inscribed text itself:

> The stele is a late example of a class of donation stelae, which depicts the reigning monarch granting a tax exemption to the resident priesthood. Pharaohs had erected these stelae over the previous 2,000 years, the earliest examples dating from the Egyptian Old Kingdom. In earlier periods all such decrees were issued by the king himself, but the Memphis decree was issued by the priests, as the maintainers of traditional Egyptian culture.[15]

The name "Rosetta Stone" became—and remains—a universal by-word for a decipherment key.

Epiphanes's other benefactions included quantities of silver and grain given to the temples, the construction of a dam during a period of high flood to protect the fields of the peasant farmers, and a general amnesty to prisoners. All of the Ptolemies, at least those concerned about stability in the kingdom, went to great lengths to maintain good relations with the native priesthood because it was the one institutional body that claimed the unconditional loyalty of the local populace. It was in the best interests of all concerned that the native Egyptians stay reconciled to the Ptolemaic regime and that required the good will of the priests.

When he was 15, the new pharaoh traveled to Raphia in Syria to meet and marry his intended bride *Cleopatra*, meaning 'glory of her father', who was the daughter of Antiochus. As a gesture of good will, Antiochus 'returned' Coele-Syria and Palestine to Egypt as part of his daughter's dowry but garrisoned these territories with his own troops, thereby retaining effective control over the region. Egypt would never regain these provinces. As his reign wore on, Epiphanes chafed more and more under the guidance of Aristomenes who had been a good and faithful steward of the country during the minority of the king, but who undoubtedly continued to try to govern the kingdom on behalf of Epiphanes even after the latter was installed in the fullness of power as pharaoh. Epiphanes, following the unsavory example of at least two

15 From the ***Wikipedia***, *The Rosetta Stone*

of the earlier Ptolemies, increasingly surrounded himself with fawners and flatterers who, of course, encouraged and reinforced his widening penchant for self-indulgence. More and more, he found even the presence of the rather upright Aristomenes irksome and finally ordered him to commit suicide. He replaced Aristomenes with Polycrates, a former general under Ptolemy IV and erstwhile ally of the ill-fated Aristomenes, who, intent on ruling Egypt himself, actively encouraged Epiphanes in his decadent gratifications, making it impossible for him to actually govern. A Nubio-Theban rebellion in Upper Egypt, that began in the reign of Ptolemy IV, continued well into the reign of Epiphanes, lasting a total of 28 years. The Cushite king, Årq-Åmen, from his capital in Meroë, was able, during this time to establish his authority as far north as Thebes, though there are records of two kings of Thebes in this period named *Heru-khuti* and Ānkh-em-khu. In the event, Epiphanes commissioned precious few building programs, among these were restorations to the temple of Isis at Philae, additions to the temple of År-hes-nefer, and the completion of the temple of Imhotep, also on the island of Philae. At this time, the island of Philae with its temples seemed to be under the joint jurisdiction of Egypt and Cush.

Predictably, in a king given over so completely to depravity and decadence, Epiphanes showed himself to be totally capricious, untrustworthy, and vicious in his dealings with underlings and subjects. Under his reign, a series of revolts took place in different parts of the country, only brought to an end by negotiation in which solemn promises were made not to punish the rebels. In every instance, Epiphanes ignored the promises made, torturing and killing the men who were supposed to be under his royal protection. Not surprisingly, Epiphanes came to be widely hated. In 182 BC, he prepared to launch a war against Seleuces IV, a.k.a. Philopator, son of Antiochus in a bid to re-take the lost possessions in Coele-Syria and Palestine. This new war meant, of course, that money would be extorted from the citizens of the country once again, and a body of men, deciding they could bear this oppressive despotism no longer, rose up and had Epiphanes poisoned at age 28. He left behind two sons and a daughter.

Ptolemy VI (182 BC–182 BC)

Called *Eupator* ('of a noble father'), he was one of the sons of Epiphanes. He didn't manage to survive the year and the record of his life and reign is totally blank.

Ptolemy VII (182 BC–146 BC)

Ptolemy VII, with the cognomen *Philometor* ('loves his mother'), was the second son of Ptolemy V and Cleopatra of Syria. His mother ruled as regent for his short-lived brother and himself, both of whom were underaged upon ascending the throne. She appears to have been very competent in governing Egypt, staying on friendly terms with kings of surrounding countries and maintaining the prosperity level in Egypt itself. Meanwhile, intrigues continued among the Seleucids of Syria that would eventually have an impact on the Ptolemaic domain in Egypt. After the *Treaty of Apamea* of 188 BC—following the disastrous war of Antiochus III with the Roman Republic—his son, Antiochus IV, was sent to Rome as a hostage, to guarantee the good behavior of the Seleucids. In 175 BC, an exchange was made that sent Demetrius, son of the sitting Seleucid king Seleucus Philopator, to Rome, enabling the release of Antiochus IV (Epiphanes), who was set free after 13 years as a Roman hostage. However, before he could arrive in Syria, a minister of Seleucus Philopator named Heliodorus, who had just looted Jerusalem of its gold, assassinated Philopator and seized the throne. But within a matter of months, Antiochus was able to rally enough forces to his banner to defeat Heliodorus and execute him, ascending to the throne now on his own behalf.

Within two years of these events, Cleopatra relinquished power in Egypt and formally had her son Ptolemy Eumator crowned pharaoh. She died very shortly after this accession in 173 BC. Mindful that Cleopatra's original dowry had included Coele-Syria and Phoenicia, Eumator and his councilors quite naturally expected that the flow of the revenues from these countries into Egypt continue. Antiochus IV clearly had other ideas, and the two sides prepared for war. However, while Eumator was organizing his forces, Antiochus seized the initiative, overrunning the disputed lands and engaging the Egyptian army in a full-scale battle near Pelusium that resulted in an utter defeat for the Egyptians. Eumator himself barely escaped the battle with his life. Pursuing his advantage, Antiochus swept up river into Memphis, proclaiming himself Egypt's new king, the first time a Seleucid had actually managed to conquer Egypt after several previous attempts. Ptolemy VII became Antiochus's prisoner but was treated with every courtesy by his captor. However, another brother, also named Ptolemy, resided at Alexandria and lost no time collecting an army and shoring up his defenses while proclaiming himself king of Egypt. Antiochus in due course attacked Alexandria, but on this occasion was beaten back by the army of the younger Ptolemy, later known as Ptolemy IX or Ptolemy *Physcon*, ('the heavy one'). Though having proclaimed himself king of Egypt, after the reverse at Alexandria, Antiochus must not have felt entirely confident of his position in the country, especially with respect to the rest of his realm, because he named the captured king, Ptolemy VII, as his viceroy in Memphis, stationed a Syrian garrison at Pelusium, and returned to Syria. These actions created the bizarre circumstance of two potentates named Ptolemy ruling in Egypt at the same time.

With Antiochus having retired to Syria, the two Ptolemies reached an accommodation with one another, an accord which prompted Antiochus to attack Egypt once more. This time, however, he was told to desist by the Roman ambassador to the Seleucids, *M. Popillius Laenas*. By now (c. 172 BC), Rome was simply too powerful in the Mediterranean to be ignored. Antiochus acquiesced to this Roman demand, leaving Egypt in the hands of the two brothers who, in 170 BC, agreed to rule jointly. However, power-sharing fraternal amity could not continue indefinitely, and by 163 BC, the two brotherly co-rulers were locked in a dire quarrel. Ptolemy Physcon drove Ptolemy Philometor out of Alexandria who straightaway took the first ship to Rome. The Roman senate returned him to Egypt with envoys with the full power of Rome backing them to re-install him on the throne. They gave Physcon the 'consolation prize' of Cyrene. Not content with such a restricted territory, he made his own trip to Rome to persuade the Senate to make him master of Cyprus as well. Convoluted negotiations continued among the three parties, and while Physcon was waiting to formalize his control of Cyprus, preparing to attack Egypt again to enforce his claim, he was obliged to put down a revolt in Cyrene. Another trip to Rome by Physcon won for him a envoy escort to Cyprus to take control of the country but upon arriving, Philomator was already there and in possession of the island with a large army. Philomator forced Physcon to return to Cyrene without having won control of Cyprus in 155 BC.

A clear pattern had emerged early in the second century BC and was only intensified as the decades wore on: Rome had become the *de facto* arbiter of all disputes between the royal descendants of Alexander's generals, the Seleucids and the Ptolemies. Rome, even before the destruction of Carthage (146 BC), was the strongest individual power in the Mediterranean, with an ever-expanding empire, and was in a position to compel adherence to its rulings. Again and again, princes and kings contending for power in the kingdoms of Western Asia and Egypt sought Roman intervention on behalf of their claims and schemes. Rome kept its eyes firmly fixed on the intrigues and plots of the eastern Mediterranean, gradually acquiring decisive influence there which would have dramatic geopolitical consequences in the following century.

Tortuous intrigues continued among the Ptolemies and Seleucids despite the periodic Roman interventions. The king of Syria, Demetrius Soter, endeavored to claim more island territories for himself while Ptolemy VII was preoccupied with matters in Cyprus. Once his rulership of Cyprus had been settled, the latter then made an alliance with Demetrius Soter's enemy *Alexander Balas*, a pretender to Seleucid throne by virtue of a purported descent from Antiochus IV. Balas was able to make good on his royal claims and, to solidify the alliance, Ptolemy betrothed his daughter to him in 150 BC. Demetrius, meanwhile, had organized an army by which he meant to depose Alexander Balas, and Ptolemy marched north with his army to support his beleaguered son-in-law. When he arrived at Ptolemaïs, modern-day Acre in Israel, an assassination attempt was made upon him by Ammonius, a close friend of Alexander Balas, who refused to indict or punish the would-be assassin, thereby confirming Philometor's suspicion that Balas, if not party to the assassination attempt, was at least aware of it. Why Alexander Balas would countenance the murder of the one ally capable of helping him stay on the throne is impossible to fathom. Philometor changed allegiances totally, siding now with the son of Demetrius Soter, also named Demetrius II. He retrieved his daughter from Balas's camp, and gave her as wife to Demetrius II. Demetrius II was re-established on the throne of Syria and now had Philometor solidly with him as he confronted anew the army of Alexander Balas in 146 BC. Though the allied armies were victorious against Alexander Balas in the Battle of Antioch, Ptolemy Philometor was thrown from his horse during the battle, suffering a skull fracture severe enough to eventually kill him. However, in defeat, Alexander Balas was obliged to flee to the Nabataeans (Jordan) whose prince summarily executed him, sending his head to Ptolemy Philometor who, by this time, was himself dead.

The reign of Ptolemy VII saw another large influx of Jews from Judea, owing to the rather savage persecutions of Jews by Antiochus IV who had conquered Judea during his invasion of Egypt (167 BC). He committed many blasphemous acts against the Jewish religion and its great temple, even ordering the execution of as many as 40,000 Jews who resisted his outrages. He took 10,000 citizens away as captives to be enslaved—some say 40,000—and destroyed much of Jerusalem. As many Jews as could got away from the depredations of Antiochus and found their way into Egypt, They they were given refuge by Ptolemy VII. One such person was *Onias*, the son and nephew of the Jewish high priest who had been slain by Antiochus. Onias, on account of his high standing in Jerusalem, was able to win an audience with Ptolemy. He petitioned to be allowed to build a Jewish temple in Egypt that, among other things, would bring the Jews as a body over to Ptolemy's side in his continuing struggle with Antiochus IV specifically, and the Seleucids generally. Ptolemy granted this request and in due course, the temple was built on land donated some 22½ miles from Memphis at a place called *Onion* ('O-**ni**-on'), eponymously named after the man who was able to prevail upon Ptolemy's generosity.[16] The site of Onion was situated at or near *Leontopolis*, 'the Lion City,' dedicated in all probability to the lion-goddess Sekhmet and Atum in his lion-headed form. Many centuries later, after its destruction during the Jewish Revolt of 70 AD when the Temple in Jerusalem was destroyed a second time, Onion itself was closed down and its Jewish inhabitants dispersed. It eventually became known as *Tell el-Yahûdîyeh*, 'the Mound of the Jew'. One notices a peculiar circumstance concerning the Jewish attitude toward Egypt:

16 Josephus, Whiston, po. Cit., p. 604, *Book VII*, Paragraphs 2,3.

the Torah anathemizes Egypt and her pharaohs as Hebrew persecutors and enslavers, but within 600 years after the Exodus dates, Jews are trickling back into Egypt and settling there permanently in increasing numbers. It can be said that they thrived in the Egyptian environment, at least until the later Roman persecutions and proscriptions against them during the Jewish revolts in the first and second centuries AD, forced their dispersal ('diaspora') throughout the known world.

Ptolemy Philometor's building activities seemed to have been mostly concentrated in Upper Egypt at Karnak, Esneh, Edfu, Kom Ombo, Philae, and Dêr al-Medinah. As other Ptolemies before him, Philometor seems to have collaborated in building and decorating temples in Lower Nubia with the reigning king of Cush at the ancient city of *Parembole* or *Ta-Het*, 13 miles south of Philae.

Ptolemy died in 146 BC, the same year Carthage was destroyed by Roman legions removing the last major power capable of rivaling and opposing Roman imperial ambitions.

Ptolemy VIII (146 BC)

Ptolemy VIII, known as *Eupator II*, was the son Ptolemy VII and his sister-wife Cleopatra who came to the throne on the death of his father though still a child. Cleopatra wasted no time having her son proclaimed king and herself regent ruling in his name. The brother of the late king, Ptolemy IX, languishing in Cyrene and having been denied the throne once before, was not prepared to accept this state of affairs. Speedily, he marched on Alexandria with his army. He met no resistance, and once again the powerful Roman ambassadors intervened, awarding the throne to Ptolemy IX while insisting that he marry his brother's widow to stabilize the situation. Both parties agreed to this arrangement but Ptolemy IX, not one to allow a lingering potential threat to his position exist so near to him, executed his nephew almost immediately. There are no monumental inscriptions making any reference to Eupator II.

Ptolemy VIII (IX)[17] (146 BC–117 BC)

Ptolemy IX, surnamed *Euergetes* II, ascended the throne of Egypt at the behest of the Romans and the greater number of prominent Alexandrians. Some refer to him as Ptolemy VIII since his nephew never effectively sat on the throne. In the event, Euergetes II had apparently accepted his lot of ruling solely in Cyrene, but the simmering ambition was re-ignited once again when his brother died leaving only a young son to succeed him. As already noted, once installed on the throne and married to his brother's widow, he wasted little time killing his nephew, clearly a potential rival. However, Euergetes II did not stop there, killing any and all who had opposed his previous attempts to claim the kingship and plundering their property. An unsuspected streak of cruelty manifested at every turn, and the situation in Alexandria deteriorated to such an extent that many fled the city in fear of their lives. Those who didn't flee were expelled, including most of the city's foremost intellectuals, scholars, philosophers, mathematicians, musicians, painters, teachers, and physicians. It had the effect of benefiting other lands while improverishing Alexandria. Like other Ptolemies, he gave himself over to a life of debauchery, and the cumulative effect of all these acts was to make himself universally reviled. Everyone who had supported his ascension to the kingship after the death of his brother now had cause to regret their advocacy of his cause. He divorced his official wife, Cleopatra (II), and married her daughter, his niece in her stead, also named Cleopatra (III). Fifteen years of undiminished atrocities finally precipitated an open revolt in Alexandria (130 BC) which led to the burning of his palace and his hasty flight to Cyprus with his his niece-wife Cleopatra III and his son *Memphites* by Cleopatra II.

In the meantime, Cleopatra II took over the reins of government and declared her son Memphites the new pharaoh of Egypt. This act unhinged Ptolemy so greatly that he summarily killed Memphites, his own son, and sent his head back to Cleopatra II in Alexandria. This woman thus had the unfortunate distinction of having had both her sons killed by her brother-husband. This new barbarity

17 A discrepancy emerged among historians about Ptolemy Eupator. Some do not consider him to have been truly a king at all and don't include him in the Ptolemaic line. E.A.W. Budge, on the other hand, does include him. The author, therefore, enumerates and discusses all subsequent Ptolemies without regard to the place of Ptolemy Eupator while putting Budge's regnal numerals in parentheses at the introduction of each new Ptolemy.

provoked a fury among the Alexandrians who now prepared for war, but they could not prevail against Ptolemy who, by 128 BC, had recaptured Alexandria and regained his throne. Cleopatra II now sought refuge in the court of Demetrius II, king of Syria, whose family had long been an adversary of the Ptolemies. He agreed to help her against Euergetes. His army decamped to Pelusium but met with no better success against Euergetes than had the rebellious Alexandrians. Ptolemy, ever vengeful, now threw his support behind a pretender to the throne of Syria named *Alexander Zabinas* which was sufficient to cause the ouster of Demetrius. At this point, the twists and turns of events become muddier than ever. Zabinas managed to anger Euergetes sufficiently to lose his backing. Euergetes undertook to elevate *Antiochus Grypus*, son of Demetrius (Demetrius was the king whose ousting Euergetes engineered) onto the throne at the expense of Zabinas, now out of favor. Euergetes even contrived to have one of his daughters by Cleopatra II, *Tryphaena*, marry Antiochus, now known as Antiochus VIII Philometor. By 127 BC, he had gained the throne with help of Euergetes's army. As if these machinations weren't labyrinthine enough, Cleopatra II and Euergetes—the latter of whom was the murderer of her sons—now became reconciled, and she was welcomed back to Egypt in her old position in 124 BC. In describing the bizarre permutations of these events, the word, *Byzantine*, is the only word that fits—a by-word for complex, devious plotting and intrigue.

Though Euergetes had made numerous enemies, both within the country and without, his last years were spent in relative quietude, apart from the petty revolts that continued to break out everywhere in Egypt without making much impact on the regime. He died in 117 BC, leaving behind, besides his sister-wife, two sons and three daughters.

Like nearly all the Ptolemies, Euergetes conducted extensive renovations and restorations of Egypt's temples. He created a memorial chapel to *Ipet* at Karnak, the hippopotamus goddess who was the original divine inhabitant of the site that became dedicated to Amon at Karnak, hence its earlier name *Ipet-Isut*. He had inscriptions carved at Medînet Habu, and at Edfu, completed the ornamentation of the Temple of Horus whose construction was begun nearly a century earlier. As with all Ptolemaic temples, the Horus temple at Edfu was constructed in exactly the same place and position as a much older Horus temple probably dating back to or before the first dynasties. Renovations and restorations were continued also at Kom Ombo and Philae. Philae at this time was the destination of the most popular religious pilgrimage in Egypt; so many officials and other high-placed persons presumed on the hospitality of the priests without offering compensation, that these latter were forced to petition the king for redress. Euergetes thereupon promulgated a decree forbidding such abuses at the temple by anyone no matter how highly placed. And finally, he did not neglect the Lower Nubian temple of Arq-Amen at Dakkeh whose care and upkeep had been carefully maintained by his predecessors. Though he had, early in his reign, exiled most of the intelligentsia of Alexandria, at a later date, he must have relented on this policy because he was known to have supported the Library and Museum as generously as had the earlier Ptolemies. He seems to have created an atmosphere sufficiently favorable to the arts, learning, and science to induce the great minds of Alexandria to trickle back into the city. He was a man with a certain amount of writing and scholarly ability, having published 24 books of Memoirs.

In the main, Ptolemy VIII (IX) was detested by the great majority of people, at least among the Greeks and Macedonians, for his wanton cruelties and unmitigated debaucheries. Budge, quoting Polybius, says,

> ...he had almost exterminated the native Alexandrians, for, being troubled with seditions, he frequently exposed the common people to the fury of the soldiery and caused their destruction.[18]

As an aside, this same Polybius refers to the native Egyptians as 'an acute and civilized race', comparing the common run of Alexandrian Greeks unfavorably to them. Furthermore, as Budge states,

> ...the descendants of Lagus had occupied the throne of Egypt for about 140 years, and whilst their followers had remained Greeks they themselves had with each generation become more and more like the Egyptians...the gods of Greece were assimilated with those of Egypt, and that the temples which he [Euergetes] built or restored were erected in honour not of Greek but of Egyptian gods.[19]

18 Budge, op. cit., p. 56
19 Ibid., p. 58.

Egypt was like China, the great, long-lived civilization in the Far East, in that its conquerors, if they stayed in place long enough, were inevitably Egyptianized. The cultural power of the people and nation was simply too potent. The Romans would steadfastly counteract this tendency in after years but even one or two of their emperors would find the lure of Egyptian civilization irresistable, including the 'Divine Julius' himself. Nor is it to be forgotten that the cult of Isis eventually became so strong in Rome as to rival that of Jupiter, the reason why several emperors attempted to proscribe her worship but to no avail.

Ptolemy IX (X) (117 BC–89 BC)

Ptolemy IX (or X), a.k.a. *Lathyrus*, 'grass pea', was the son of Ptolemy Euergetes by his niece, Cleopatra III. The contorted events attending the rule of the previous Ptolemies continued under Ptolemy IX. His mother Cleopatra III had been able to convince her husband Ptolemy VIII to arrange for the transfer of royal power into her hands after his death. With the apparent consent of the citizens of Alexandria, Cleopatra after Ptolemy VIII was able to rule Egypt as regent. She attempted to set up her youngest son Ptolemy X as co-regent and eventual pharaoh but this state of affairs ran into such stiff opposition that she was obliged to accept her oldest son, *Ptolemy Lathyrus* as co-regent instead. Lathyrus, like all the Ptolemies, had married his sister, another Cleopatra, but her mother had her set aside in favor of her younger sister named *Selene*, ('the moon'). The 'consolation prize' for the rejected Ptolemy X was the complete rule of Cyprus.

For a period of time, Cleopatra and Lathyrus sustained a *modus vivendi* and governed Egypt together without incident. Inevitably, the suppressed tensions between the two co-rulers began to surface over the favoritism shown by Cleopatra towards two Jewish generals in the Ptolemaic army, *Chelcias* and *Ananias*, and, by extension, the Jewish population generally. Chelcias and Ananias were the sons of Onias whom the previous Ptolemy had allowed to build a temple at Onion. Lathyrus, on the other hand, was a fervent supporter of *Antiochus Cyzicenus*, who was then at war with the Jews in Syria; however, the son was no match for the machinations of the mother. She won the loyalty of the citizens of Alexandria by persuading them that Lathyrus was plotting to kill her. Lathyrus was duly exiled to Cyprus and the younger brother, Ptolemy X was installed as co-regent, which accorded with Cleopatra's original wishes. The exiled elder Ptolemy made himself king of Cyprus and from that vantage point, fended off all attempts by his mother to de-throne him.

Not content to merely rule in Cyprus, Ptolemy IX became embroiled in conflicts on the Western Asiatic mainland when the citizenry of Ptolemaïs sought his aid against the Jewish king *Alexander Jannaeus* who had invested the city with his army. In good time, Lathyrus landed near Ptolemaïs with an army 30,000 strong on the coast of Syria. He was apparently undone by the perfidy of the citizens of Ptolemaïs who had been persuaded by one of their own (named Demetrius) to reverse their original embassy and reject any assistance from Lathyrus. Jannaeus raised the siege and withdrew nonetheless, endeavoring to defeat Ptolemy through deceit and trickery. On the one hand, he sent a secret communication to Cleopatra asking her to attack her son's army. He then paid Lathyrus 400 talents of silver to turn against one of his allies, *Zoilus*, driving him from the field and leaving his lands open for Jannaeus's army. From the point of view of sheer duplicity, it was a good plan, ruined by Lathyrus's discovery of it. Lathyrus immediately invaded and laid waste to Judea, at the same time investing Ptolemaïs. Lathyrus continued his campaign by conquering the Galilean city of Asochis, carrying away 10,000 people to be sold as slaves, and, following that, attacked another Galilean city Sepphoris. That attack was repelled with great loss to Lathyrus's army, but he did finally meet Jannaeus's army, in a full-scale battle at Saphoth in 103 BC. This was a hard-fought battle, but in the end, Lathyrus's soldiers were able to drive the Judaean army from the field. It turned into an all-out rout of Jannaeus's army, attended with great slaughter amounting to the loss of at least 30,000 men. Lathyrus finally took Ptolemaïs and proceeded to cut a destructive swath through the Judaean country-side.

In Egypt, Cleopatra began to fear an invasion of Egypt by the victorius Lathyrus and sent an army to conquer Ptolemaïs. This did not prevent Ptolemy Lathyrus from marching on Egypt, but the subsequent attack failed, forcing him to retreat all the way back to Cyprus. Nonetheless, this intra-family war was briefly carried on by proxy in Syria where two Seleucids were locked in a mortal struggle for the throne, *Antiochus Grypus*, ally to Cleopatra, against *Antiochus Cyzicenus*, allied to Ptolemy Lathyrus. The Ptolemid family had by now acquired the habit of murder to sort out their personal and political disputes, and in 101 BC, Ptolemy X killed his mother Cleopatra to pre-empt what he considered a certain fate of death by her order. Whether for this cause or some other, the Alexandrians rose up against Ptolemy X in 89 BC driving him first to Lycia in southern Anatolia and then to Cyprus. But a pursuit force from Egypt caught up to him either by land or sea and Ptolemy X lost his life in the subsequent battle. It is pertinent to note how the fortunes of any Ptolemaic ruler could now be controlled by the mood of the citizens of Alexandria. They raise to the throne any Ptolemy whom they favor and drive from the throne any Ptolemy who displeases them. This same pattern would re-emerge after Rome rose to world power when the feelings and incitements of the urban Roman mob often dictated the fate of consuls during the Republic—and emperors after the institution of imperial rule by Augustus.

After the death of Ptolemy X, Ptolemy IX was recalled to the throne of Egypt from Cyprus by the Alexandrians. Ptolemy IX ruled until 81 BC and in what remained of his rule, the spark of revolt in the Thebaid was re-ignited anew. It was, no doubt, instigated by the kings of Cush, two of whom, Årq-Āmen and Åtchakhar, still called themselves 'King of the North and South'—a title that the Ptolemies had claimed for themselves. It testifies to the expanded power of Cush that its kings were wielding ever-greater influence in Upper Egypt to the detriment of Ptolemaic power there. The center of the revolt was Thebes itself, and for two years the Thebans fought Ptolemy's army to a standstill. Yet by the third year of the conflict, Ptolemy's forces prevailed and, in effect, slaughtered the population and destroyed Thebes. Once the center of world power, Thebes was now reduced to dust and ashes.

Ptolemy XI (XII) (81 BC–80 BC)

Ptolemy XI, or Ptolemy Alexander II, was the son of Ptolemy X, born 105 BC. The name and history of his mother are totally unknown. At about age three his grandmother, Cleopatra III, sent him away from Alexandria to the

Island of Cos in the Aegean with the bulk of her treasure because she feared an attack on Egypt by her son Ptolemy IX. In 88 BC, Cos was captured by King *Mithridates*, king of the Black Sea kingdom of Pontus and Armenia with outsized imperial ambitions that were leading him to an inevitable and decisive conflict with Rome. Though treated with respect and courtesy, the 17-year old Ptolemy XI escaped his captor at the first opportunity and fled to Rome, putting himself under the protection of the Roman dictator Sulla. He stayed in Rome until the death of Ptolemy IX (Lathyrus). However, in the short term, Cleopatra-Berenice III, daughter of Ptolemy IX, assumed the throne on her own behalf. This state of affairs did not sit well with a large and influential body of citizens. Thereupon, they sent a delegation to Sulla in Rome seeking his intervention to install Ptolemy Alexander on the throne. Sulla agreed to this proposal but with the stipulation that Ptolemy Alexander marry his stepmother, Cleopatra-Berenice. Upon arriving in Egypt, Ptolemy Alexander duly married his stepmother, but less than three weeks later had her summarily murdered. This rather impetuous, not to say murderous, power grab was to prove his undoing because it enraged the soldiery. They seized Ptolemy XI, dragged him through the streets, and slaughtered him without a second thought.

This violent end to the lives of both Cleopatra-Berenice III and Ptolemy Alexander II, in effect, meant that there were no longer any legitimate heirs to the Ptolemaic throne, leaving it open to Ptolemaic offspring by non-royal mothers. There is a persistent tradition that either Ptolemy X or Ptolemy XI actually 'willed' Alexandria and Egypt to the Roman empire as part of their post-mortem testaments. In 80 BC, when Ptolemy XI was executed by his own troops, Rome elected not to exercise this 'deeded' sovereignty over Egypt, perhaps because it was too preoccupied with its own internal strife to accept and exercise effective control over the domain of the Ptolemies. Its opportunity was coming, and all Rome had to do was wait for the more propitious moment that, by now, was not far in the future.

Ptolemy XII (XIII) (80 BC–51 BC)

Ptolemy XII had perhaps the longest surnames of all the Ptolemies—*Philopator Philadelphus Neos Dionysus*—but was called *Auletes*, 'the piper', by his subjects because of his love of that instrument. He was a natural son of Ptolemy IX by a non-royal concubine. He would have had no claim to the throne at all had all the legitimate heirs not been murdered. A influential body of Alexandrians came to his support and managed to get him placed on the throne. He was born in 95 BC and ascended the throne when he was 15. He married two women, one being his sister Cleopatra V Tryphaena, and the other being a woman whose name remains unknown to subsequent history. With the two wives, he sired a number of progeny—by his sister, Cleopatra VI Tryphaena and Berenice IV; by his second wife, Arsinoë IV, Ptolemy XIII, Ptolemy XIV, and Cleopatra VII, eventually to become world-famous for her amorous intrigues with Julius Caesar and Marc Antony coupled with her geopolitical machinations to maintain Egyptian sovereignty against the irresistible expansionist pressure of Rome. She may be the most celebrated queen of ancient times.

Typical of all the later Ptolemies, Auletes, upon assuming the kingship, undertook to induce Rome to ratify his position. The Romans—playing it cagy with a succession that existed on the most tenuous of grounds—were in no hurry to put the Roman imprimatur on Auletes's position. Auletes resorted to bribery, paying out huge sums of money to influential men in Rome to shore up his position. This policy grievously undermined his position in his own country because in order to raise money for these massive bribes he had to extort greater taxes from the populace. The popular hatred against Auletes became so pronounced that he was obliged to flee to Rome in fear of his life. In the aftermath of this desperate flight, a rumor spread that Auletes had died. Sufficient credence was given for the Alexandrians to place his daughter Berenice IV, whose mother Cleopatra V Tryphaena had already died, on the throne as queen in 57 BC. Very soon however, it was realized that Auletes was very much in Rome alive and attempting mischief against the people who had deposed him. A delegation of 100 envoys was sent to Rome to plead the Alexandrian case against Auletes who, when apprised of the coming delegation, set about to kill every one of them before they had a chance to state the case against him. He succeeded in causing the assassinations of most of the party; those who escaped simply abandoned the embassy rather than risk death at Auletes's hands.

Such a mass murder on Roman soil could not go unnoticed, and when the deadly toll of Alexandrians was revealed, a Senatorial inquiry was launched led by Marcus Favonius. But Favonius's efforts were largely stymied by Auletes's continued bribes to influential senators. Some of the assassins were brought to justice but most escaped, including Auletes who, by this time, had made allies of Caesar, Pompey, and Cicero, three of the most powerful men in Rome. Cicero, a renowned orator, was able to persuade the Roman Senate to order his restoration. However, this seeming victory for Auletes was forestalled by the Sibylline Oracle that predicted trouble for Rome should troops be sent to Alexandria to enforce Auletes's re-enthronement. A Roman of any class or station ignored the pronouncements of the Sibyllines at his peril. Some adherents desiring to support Auletes proposed sending him back to Egypt with two lictors (guards of Roman magistrates) and Pompey to re-instate him, however, there was sufficient reluctance for the Senate to provide any material support to Auletes. The best that Auletes could do was to move to Ephesus and take up residence in the Temple of Diana. Berenice, his daughter, continued to rule in Egypt with her second husband Archelaus, the son of a general of Mithridates.

Auletes, however, did not remain idle. Supported by Pompey, he entered into an alliance with Aulus Gabinius, Roman proconsul of Syria. Acting independently of the Roman Senate, Pompey instructed Gabinius to invade Egypt with the aim of restoring Auletes to the throne. In due course, Gabinius invaded Egypt through Pelusium, and in a series of three battles—one at sea—defeated the Egyptian army sent against him. Berenice's husband, Archelaus, was killed in battle, and Gabinius became the latest conqueror of Egypt, losing no time in restoring Auletes's throne to him in 55 BC. Gabinius was rewarded with 10,000 talents of silver—an astronomical sum considering that it represented 75 tons of silver extracted, of course, from the Egyptian people. Auletes's first order of business was to exact revenge on those prominent Alexandrians who had opposed him, first killing Berenice, his own daughter, then numerous other leading citizens. This execution of so many wealthy men in Alexandria meant that Auletes could confiscate their wealth which was needed to pay Gabinius and other Romans to whom he was indebted. Gabinius left a contingent of his army in Egypt, called the *Gabiniani*, and they were sorely needed to put down the numerous revolts that broke out under Auletes's atrocious rule. He was another of the debauched and drunken Ptolemaic pharaohs of Egypt and the historian Strabo considered him one of the three worst Ptolemies, the other two being the fourth and seventh.[20] Auletes was an avid player of the flute and, like Nero with his lyre more than 100 years later, loved to enter contests with the finest flautists in the land.

Though Auletes's effective rule over Egypt following his murderous restoration lasted just over three years, he did not neglect work on the temples. He decorated crypts at Denderah, dedicated a black basalt altar to the god Min in Coptos, commissioned inscriptions on the walls of the temple of Amon at Karnak, and added a pylon to the temple of Isis at Philae. Ptolemy Auletes died in 51 BC leaving the country jointly in the hands of the celebrated Cleopatra VII and her brother-husband Ptolemy XIV. Predictably, complications ensued.

Cleopatra VII Tryphaena (51 BC–30 BC)

Cleopatra VII was, by any measure, the most famous and notorious of the Ptolemaic rulers of Egypt who became and remains, more than 2,000 years later, a popular icon. Playwrights like Shakespeare and Shaw, painters like Gerome and Ford, and film makers like DeMille and Mankiewitz all used Cleopatra as an artistic subject. No other queen in antiquity commanded such fascination. That she inspired the devotion and adoration of both Julius Caesar and Marc Antony, the two most powerful and dynamic Romans of their time, only intensifies her allure and appeal to historians and the public.

20 Strabo, **Geography**, *Book 17, Chapter 1, Paragraph 11*, translated by H.L. Jones, Cambridge: Harvard University Press, 1932/1982, p. 45.

Cleopatra VII—Last
Pharaoh of Egypt

Cleopatra—Conqueror of
Caesar and Antony

Cleopatra VII was the daughter of Auletes by, again, an unknown mother. A number of the Ptolemies were born to mothers whose names and antecedents are unknown. There is reason enough to believe that these mothers, including that of Cleopatra VII, were not Macedonian but, in all probability, native Egyptian. J.A. Rogers addresses this matter directly:

> The earliest Ptolemaic rulers are in appearance white; but as time went on their physiognomies changed more and more towards the Negro one. The Negro strain in Alexander II is apparent, and still more so in Ptolemy VIII (sic), the flute-playing father of the most celebrated of the Cleopatras… Cleopatra, herself, is known through tradition as having been of a tawny, or mulatto color, and is so described by Shakespeare. Greek and Egyptian intermarried freely and brought another change of physiognomy to the population.[21]

Thus it can be inferred that Cleopatra was a mixed-race ruler of Egypt as were probably all the Ptolemies after Ptolemy V. She was a remarkably attractive

21 Rogers JA, **Sex and Race: The Old World**, Vol. I, Rogers: New York, 1952/1967, p. 57.

woman and intellectually one of the most accomplished women of the era. She was said to have spoken seven languages fluently, including flawless Latin and equally flawless Egyptian, the only one of the 13 Ptolemies who ever deigned to learn the native language of the country. More than any of her predecessors, Cleopatra thought of herself primarly as an Egyptian ruler instead of a Macedonian one. And indeed, if her mother was a native Egyptian as seems likely, it would explain both her fluency in the Egyptian tongue as well as her more thorough-going identification with Egypt itself instead of Macedonia.

Cleopatra's abilities must have profoundly impressed her father Auletes. Before his death, he made her joint ruler of Egypt with her brother Ptolemy XIII, whom in accordance with custom, she was obliged to marry. Also in his will he made the Senate of Rome his executor; but a copy of it never actually got to Rome, and instead ended up in the hands of the Roman general, Pompey. Cleopatra was 17 when she ascended the throne as co-regent. Far more gifted and dynamic than her brother-husband who was nine years her junior. She soon took steps to marginalize him so that all effective power could be concentrated in her hands. Ptolemy XIII was duly placed under the tutelage of *Achillas*, who took charge of his education, and the eunuch Pothinus who was to manage Ptolemy's financial affairs. Not surprisingly, in three years, an irreconciliable conflict broke out between Cleopatra on the one hand and the guardians of Ptolemy on the other, particularly Pothinus. The three years of the co-regency had been difficult ones exacerbated by low Nile floods, famine, and economic stress. Ptolemy, probably chafing from the necessity of sharing power with his sister-wife, sided with Pothinus. Cleopatra's position became untenable and she was obliged to seek refuge among allies in Syria. While there, using the considerable wealth she managed to bring with her, Cleopatra raised an army to attack Egypt.

With Cleopatra threatening the regime, Ptolemy and his advisors mobilized their own army, marching to Mount Casius on the border between Egypt and Syria to await the advance of Cleopatra. Many of the Gabiniani, who had been left in Egypt by Gabinius to prop up the regime of Auletes, were among the soldiers of Ptolemy's army. The Gabiniani killed the sons of the Roman governor of Syria, *Marcus Calpurnius Bibulus.* They did the killing when they came to Egypt to demand the recall of the Roman soldiers there as a way of weakening the political position of Pompey, Bibulus's enemy, in the region. Cleopatra, however, handed the murderers over in chains to Bibulus, whereupon the Gabiniani turned into bitter enemies of the queen. The Gabiniani had at one time been among Pompey's troops, and Pompey, having lost a decisive battle against Caesar at Pharsalia for control of the empire, evidently thought he would find a safe haven in Egypt under the protection of Ptolemy. Escaping with his wife from the military disaster against Caesar, Pompey sailed for Pelusium with 2,000 of what was left of his army, sending envoys ahead seeking asylum. But instead of being welcomed in recognition of all the services Pompey's legions had performed for Auletes, Ptolemy XIII's father, a treacherous plot was hatched to lure Pompey ashore for the purpose of assassinating him. Pompey—oblivious to the deadly plot building up around him—allowed himself to be coaxed into a small boat carrying Achillas, Ptolemy's tutor, and *Lucius Septimius*, a Roman soldier who previously had been one of Pompey's sub-commanders. Even before reaching shore, Septimius stabbed Pompey, and the remaining occupants finished hacking him to death, his head cut off to present as a trophy to Caesar. Ptolemy actually watched the murder being carried out from a seat on the shore. Clearly the Machiavellian deed, on the advice of *Theodotus* of Samos, was done to curry favor with Caesar, now the most powerful Roman in the empire, but it had the opposite effect. When Caesar arrived in Egypt with his army, his first order of business was to execute the conspirator Pothinus. Theodotus was eventually captured in Asia and suffered death by torture. Achillas, commander of the Egyptian army, managed to escape death at Caesar's hands only to run afoul later of Arsinoë and Ganymedes.

Caesar now seized the moment to become the sole arbiter of the dispute between Ptolemy and Cleopatra, evidently not feeling yet strong enough to execute the 13-year old boy-king who was as culpable as any other of the conspirators in Pompey's death. Never one to lose an opportunity, Cleopatra became determined to have a private audience with the one Roman who by now did seem to 'bestride the world like a Colossus'[22]. What happened next, though vouched for by the reliable Plutarch, seems more like a mise-en-scène

22 *Why, man,* **he doth bestride the narrow world** *like a Colossus, and we petty men walk under his huge legs and peep about to find ourselves dishonourable graves.* ***Julius Caesar,*** by William Shakespeared, Act 1, Scene II.

from a particularly melodramatic play: Cleopatra had herself wrapped up in a beautiful carpet and carried past Ptolemy's palace guards by a brawny servant, *Apollodorus* the Sicilian, who, when admitted into Caesar's presence, unrolled the carpet and with it, Cleopatra herself. Her flair for the dramatic seems to have outstripped even that of Caesar himself who had made a career out of the dramatic gesture. Caesar, evidently, was duly impressed and charmed by her audacity and panache. Almost immediately, he became Cleopatra's paramour and partisan, meeting for the first time a woman whose dash and daring matched his own. Within nine months, their son Cesarion was born.

Ptolemy XIII, quite naturally, became infuriated with this turn of events. There now began a struggle from which Caesar only barely managed to escape with his life. The Alexandrians rose in a body in defense of their king and besieged Caesar in the palace. It was with difficulty that Caesar calmed the angry Alexandrians. He convened a meeting and read the will of Auletes, father of Cleopatra and Ptolemy XIII. In the will, Cyprus was bequeathed to their sister Arsinoë and brother Ptolemy XIV, with Ptolemy XIII and Cleopatra once again sharing the crown as co-rulers. However, these maneuvers did nothing to stymie the intrigues because the eunuch Ganymedes, the tutor of Arsinoë who had the general Achillas executed, took over command of the Egyptian army. Renewed fighting broke out in Alexandria, and Caesar himself became so hard-pressed once again in the palace that he was only able to escape by jumping into the sea and swimming to a Roman ship. The fighting continued with two major naval engagements between Ganymedes's superior fleet and the Romans, both of which ended in defeat for Ganymedes. After continued conflict, a final battle was fought on the banks of the Nile resulting in a total rout of Ganymedes's forces. The boy co-pharaoh, Ptolemy XIII, drowned in the Nile in a bid to escape the pursuing Romans. Ganymedes himself perished soon after.

The country was now completely in the hands of Caesar and Cleopatra after nine months of war and intrigue. The two celebrated by taking a river cruise up the Nile escorted by 400 ships. Upon return, Cleopatra was married to her other half-brother, Ptolemy XIV, but this was but a *pro forma* arrangement that left Cleopatra effectively as the sole reigning monarch of the country. Caesar continued to act as Cleopatra's principle advisor and confidant and when it came time for him to return to Rome in 46 BC, he invited Cleopatra to join him. In the triumph accorded him in Rome, Cleopatra's usurping half-sister Arsinoë was made to walk in the procession as a royal prisoner. She managed to avoid death by strangulation, the usual fate of captured monarchs, and was, instead, sent to live in the Temple of Artemis in Ephesus in southwestern Asia Minor.

Cleopatra, with all the pomp and ceremony of an Egyptian queen, did indeed go to Rome with her son Cesarion on Caesar's invitation and stayed in Rome for two years, until Caesar's assassination in the Roman Senate in 44 BC. It is said that the 60 Senatorial conspirators were motivated by the prospect of Caesar becoming king and absolute ruler, thereby bringing an end to the Republic. A secondary motivation may have been the fear of Cleopatra becoming Queen of Rome once Caesar's power had been consolidated. Cleopatra definitely wanted her son Cesarion to be named as Caesar's heir but Caesar named his grandnephew *Octavian*—later *Augustus Caesa*r—as his heir, forestalling any ambition Cleopatra might have had for her son, at least for the time being. Caesar's death put an end to all speculation Cleopatra might have had on Cesarion's behalf, forestalling any possibility of Cleopatra coming to rule both Egypt and Rome with Caesar.

Cleopatra returned to Egypt with her son, taking up the cause of *Publius Cornelius Dolabella*, a Roman general who, though nominally allied with Brutus, one of Caesar's principle assassins, switched his allegiance to Marc Antony when offered command of the expeditionary force against the Parthians and the governorship of Syria. In the end, however, Dolabella was defeated by Cassius and ended his life by suicide in 43 BC. Cassius made ready to march on Egypt, but with Marc Antony and Octavian threatening Brutus, Cassius had no choice but to join Brutus in Asia Minor to meet the threat, thus sparing Egypt another military confrontation with a Roman army. A year later, both Brutus and Cassius were dead by suicide after defeats by the combined forces of Octavian and Marc Antony.

Cleopatra's brother-husband, Ptolemy XIV, had conveniently died, probably poisoned on the instigation of Cleopatra, following which she made her son Cesarion her co-regent and heir. Cleopatra, though she had known him during her association with Caesar, now attracted the attention of Marc Antony. In 41 BC, Marc Antony sent *Quintus Dellius* to Egypt to summon Cleopatra to Asia

Minor to explain what seemed to have been some acts of questionable loyalty to the prevailing regime. However, this reasoning was apparently just a ploy; what Antony really sought was support from Cleopatra in the on-going war against the Parthians. Cleopatra took her time replying, and in fact, more than one summons was issued demanding her presence. However, when she deigned to accept the 'invitation' she did so in a manner calculated to excite the wonder and admiration of Antony, for she

> ...sailed up the Cydnus [River] in a vessel with a gilded stern, with purple sails spread, and rowers working with silver oars to the sound of the flute in harmony with pipes and lutes. Cleopatra reclined under an awning spangled with gold, dressed as Aphrodite is painted, and youths representing the Cupids in pictures stood on each side fanning her. In like manner the handsomest of her female slaves, in the dress of Nereids and Graces, were stationed some at the rudders and others at the ropes. And odours of wondrous kind from much incense filled the banks.[23]

Cleopatra possessed nothing if not matchless style, always playing to the psychological whims of the men she was intent on seducing and winning. When invited to Antony's lodging for the evening supper, she declined, inviting him instead to her pavilion. When Antony arrived, he professed himself astonished not only at the variety and delicacy of the foods served, but at the splendor of the entertainments, as well as the beauty of an ever-changing décor. When she consented to dine with him the following evening, it became quickly apparent that his hospitalities were rustic and crude compared to what he had sampled at her table. The deed was done. Like Julius Caesar before him, Antony rapidly became besotted with Cleopatra. Though the Parthians were threatening Syria and trouble was brewing in Rome, he, like Caesar previously, sailed off to Egypt with Cleopatra, whiling away his time totally and completely with her.

To say that Antony was amorously enslaved by Cleopatra seems clichéd, but it is the only way to describe his attachment to her. While in Egypt with her, he was provided with every luxury and indulgence imaginable; Cleopatra

23 Budge, op. cit., p. 97, quoting from Plutarch's *Life of Antonius*, Chapter 26.

never left his side day or night, prompting Octavian to say upon receiving reports on Antony's behavior, 'I well believe that he has been bewitched by that accursed woman'.[24] They played at dice, hunted, and she watched him during his martial exercises. Antony liked to mingle with the common crowd. Cleopatra accompanied him even on these forays into the streets of Alexandria, though disguised as a slave since it simply wouldn't do for the pharaoh queen of Egypt to be seen openly in public. He engaged in an endless round of ribaldries with ordinary citizens who treated him rather like a comic actor. But more ominously, Antony enabled Cleopatra to have free rein in removing anyone whom she deemed a threat or potential threat, one-by-one killing off her sister Arsinoë, *Serapion*, prefect of Cyprus, Ptolemy XIV, and her brother-husband Ptolemy XV. Antony cared not, and at last there was no one left to challenge or threaten Cleopatra's rule.

At last, events at home conspired to extract Antony from Cleopatra's clutches. His wife Fulvia was obliged to flee Rome under pressure from Antony's enemies there. Additionally, the Parthians, Rome's most determined enemy, had invaded Syria. Letters from his hard-pressed wife finally reached him, and he disembarked for Rome commanding a fleet of 200 ships. In the event, Fulvia died suddenly at Sikyon to where she had fled, and the chain of events unfolded in such a way that Octavian and Antony made peace with one another, dividing the rule of the empire between them. To seal the concordat, Antony married Octavian's sister Octavia, and with half of the world's largest empire to rule, he made a concerted effort to put the interlude with Cleopatra behind him to settle down with his new wife. He managed to do so for a number of years, long enough to sire two children with Octavia. However, unable to settle in one place for long, he turned the guardianship of all his children by his two wives over to Octavian, setting sail for Western Asia, ostensibly to carry the war to the Parthians and wrest Syria away from them. But in fact, he had not even set foot in Syria before he was sending messengers to Egypt to bring Cleopatra to him. Presumably to curry further favor with her, Antony bestowed large territories on her—Phoenicia, Coele-Syria, Cyprus, and parts of Cilicia, Judea, and Arabia Nabathea.

---

24 Ibid., p. 98, quoting from Dion Cassius, 1.26.

Antony wound up a successful campaign against Parthia and repaired to the Phoenician coast to await the arrival of Cleopatra, who took her time arriving with new supplies for Antony's cohorts. Typically, as these events played out, plots encircled plots because Octavian arranged for his sister, Antony's wife, to join him in Phoenicia, apparently with the expectation that Antony's re-ignited connection to Cleopatra would cause sufficient insult to Octavia to justify Octavian declaring war on Antony. To forestall this outcome, Antony sent a message to his wife to stop in Athens where he would meet her forthwith. Cleopatra saw immediately that this plan would jeopardize her position with Antony, probably permanently, and bent all of her efforts to beguiling Antony sufficiently to prevent him from making the rendez-vous with his wife. Not surprisingly, the gambit was successful. Antony returned to Egypt with Cleopatra after cementing the treaty with Parthia by betrothing one of his sons by Cleopartra to one of the daughters of the Parthian king.

Soon after his return to Egypt, Antony left Cleopatra's side long enough to campaign in Armenia and after his victories there, went back to Egypt and Cleopatra to resume a life of unrestrained indulgence, while catering to Cleopatra's every whim. He had two golden thrones erected on a tribunal for himself and Cleopatra, confirming her rule over Egypt, Cyprus, Libya, and Coele-Syria with the title 'queen of kings'. Caesarion, son of Cleopatra by Julius, was officially made her heir. More and more, Cleopatra dressed and comported herself in the manner of the goddess Isis and was in fact now called 'the new Isis'. She induced Antony to dress as Osiris and the two of them were wont to perform mystery-plays as Isis and Osiris respectively. Cleopatra may have been a Ptolemaic, and of (partially) Macedonian descent, but Egyptian manners, customs, and religious observances were becoming her especial preoccupation. In any case, as Dion Cassius reported, '...she bewitched everybody'.[25]

If Octavian had contrived to use his sister to stir up opposition against Antony and Cleopatra, he succeeded. Since Antony clearly had no intentions of rejoining her and was totally in the thrall of Cleopatra, there was nothing to do for his legitimate wife except return to Rome. It was enough for Octavian who promptly took the case to Roman Senate and created sufficient outrage against

25 Ibid., p. 102.

Antony's behavior as to provoke a declaration of war against Cleopatra, seen as the real villainess of the drama. Without hesitation, Antony, too, prepared for war and with 800 ships and Cleopatra, sailed to Greece where, unaccountably, he conducted lavish entertainments on the island of Samos and Athens. Adding insult to injury, he sent agents to Rome to evict Octavia from his house. Finally the battle, a naval engagement, was joined at Actium off the coast of western Greece in 31 BC.

The battle of Actium, a decisive one for the history of Rome and Egypt, was, at the outset, an evenly fought contest, with no side gaining the upper hand until, incredibly, Cleopatra pulled sixty of her ships out of the battle to sail back to Egypt. There has never been a satisfactory explanation of why she did so because the tide of the battle had not turned in either direction. Equally baffling, Antony, instead of prosecuting a battle in which victory was still possible, abandoned his troops and sailed haplessly after Cleopatra who slowed long enough to take him on board. Thus, the issue was not decided by a triumph of arms by Octavian's forces but by an act of cowardice by Cleopatra on the one hand and abject love-struck passion by Antony on the other. It would seem that abandonment by Cleopatra was simply too much for Antony to bear. Upon arriving on the coast of Libya, Cleopatra went on to Egypt and Antony stayed behind with the intention of doing away with himself. Those around him, however, prevented it and sent him on to Alexandria.

Cleopatra at first designed to escape the pursuing Octavian by dragging ships to the Red Sea over the Isthmus of Suez but this plan was thwarted when hostile Bedouins summarily burned the ships. Instead, she began to build up her defenses in Egypt against the coming invasion. In order to obtain allies against Octavian, she beheaded *Artavasdes*, the king of Armenia in Egypt as a hostage of Antony, and sent his head to the mortal enemy of Armenia, the king of Media. Antony duly arrived, now an entirely useless character, began another round of banquets, drinking bouts, and general debaucheries as if determined to exhaust all his participation in earthly pleasures as the end drew near. Cleopatra, somewhat more cool-headed, began to collect fatal poisons and venomous animals, testing them on condemned prisoners to determine their efficacy and comparative ease of death. It is by this means that the asp, the Egyptian cobra, was selected as the instrument of suicide should it become necessary. While doing so, Cleopatra sent envoys to Octavian to request that her children inherit Egypt and Antony be permitted to live as a private citizen in Athens. Octavian's reply: kill Antony and any reasonable request will be granted. Whether Cleopatra actually considered this course of action is unknown; in the event, she made no concerted move against Antony, at least not then.

Soon enough, Octavian crossed through Syria and into Egypt and as this was happening, Cleopatra collected all her private wealth—a vast store of gold, silver, emeralds, pearls, ebony woods, and ivory—and deposited it in a sumptuous tomb already built for her near the temple of Isis, presumably for the purpose of immolating herself, the tomb, and everything in it after death. Antony, on his part, was not quite finished, seeking yet another military confrontation with Octavian. The way the story is told, Cleopatra still trying to find a way out of her difficulties with Octavian, secretly bribed the army to desert Antony as the battle loomed, while shutting herself up in her mausoleum. The upshot of all this was that Antony, finally undone by this latest betrayal by his paramour, ran himself through with his own sword since none of the men around him would heed his plea to kill him to put him out of his misery. Again, as if playing the death scene in the dénouement of a Greek tragedy, Cleopatra sent bearers to collect the dying Antony to bring him to the tomb. Not wishing to open the door, Antony was actually lifted up to her tower by two cords. All her emotions came over her in a rush whereupon she beat her breasts, tore her garments, and smeared her body with his blood. Antony, asking for a last cup of wine, drank it, said his farewell to his queenly concubine and died on the spot. It is said that Octavian, upon receiving the news, retired to his tent and wept. They were mortal enemies but once had been comrades-in-arms, co-rulers of the Roman empire, and intimate companions of Julius Caesar who had dominated both of their lives.

Octavian next sent a trusted confidant, *Procleius*, with a contingent of men to take Cleopatra alive, for the treasure and to display her in his coming triumph in Rome. Procleius in some manner managed to gain entrance to the tomb where he was just in time to prevent Cleopatra from plunging a knife into her heart. Octavian allowed Cleopatra to bury Antony with all the pomp and circumstance of royalty. Finally, Octavian came to visit and Cleopatra one last time resorted to a variety of histrionics to try to prevail upon Octavian in the way she had his predecessors. Octavian, fully conscious of her 'fatal allure', simply refused to look at her during the entire interview, saying very little. When he departed from Cleopatra's chamber, he put her on a suicide watch with a trusted aide *Epaphroditus*.

From this point on, Cleopatra's entire manner changed. She livened up and carried out her daily activities with complete normalcy, inducing everyone, including Octavian, to believe that she was resigned to her fate. After a final visit to the tomb of Antony, authorized by Octavian, she returned to the palace, bathed in waters scented with rare perfumes, and ordered up a truly royal repast for herself and companions. At the end of the banquet, a peasant brought into her a basket of figs in which was hidden the asp of legend. Cleopatra composed a final message to Octavian on a tablet, sealed it, and sent it to him by one of her royal couriers. She cleared the room of all but two of her most faithful servants, *Eiras* and *Charmion*. The final act of her life has been clouded with some uncertainty since no one really knows whether she simply swallowed poison or pulled the cobra out of the basket and, by irritating it, induced it to bite her either on the breast or arm. Posterity usually assumes death by the bite of the asp, and though Octavian immediately sent a contingent to her residence to rescue her, upon arrival she was found dead lying on a golden couch in her most queenly finery. Her servants, determined to follow her in death, had themselves partaken of poison but, taking longer to die, made sure that their queen was properly arranged on her death-bed. They were still fussing about her as the Romans arrived but expired shortly thereafter. Uniquely dramatic to the last, only Cleopatra would have thought of doing away with herself by clasping a cobra to her bosom.

Cleopatra reigned 22 years, dying at age 39. With her demise the Ptolemaic Dynasty and Egypt as a sovereign nation come to a permanent end, relegated thenceforth to the status of a mere province, though a rich one, in the Roman empire. With Antony dead, Octavian reigns supreme and unchallenged in Rome, changing his name to Augustus ('Magestic') Caesar and soon becoming Rome's first emperor. The Roman Republic is dead, never to be revived, but the Roman empire emerges more powerful and dominant than ever. Cesarion, son of Julius and Cleopatra, is executed by Augustus who could not risk a son of 'the Divine Julius' living and potentially challenging his rule. He also had killed *Antylles*, the eldest son of Antony and Fulvia but allowed all the children born to Cleopatra and Antony to live and be raised in manner suitable to their rank.

The posterior reputation of Cleopatra is, as can be surmised, decidedly mixed. No one can deny her capacity for deceit, intrigue, and the unrestrained use of political murder to achieve her ends, though in these things, she was no different from any sovereign bidding for and protecting his power in late antiquity. She was also a remarkably accomplished woman, and while there are differing reports on her physical beauty—some deny that she was beautiful at all while others claim she was the most beautiful queen of her era—no one can gainsay her captivating magnetism. She did, after all, completely mesmerize two of the most dominant personalities in Roman history and, through them, came very close to becoming queen not only of Egypt but Rome itself. That she was vain, self-serving, and ruthless beyond measure is plainly evident, but it can also be said that what she did she did for Egypt, as if to use her considerable wiles to preserve Egypt's place in the world and, if possible, revive its power. As Budge says of her:

> That she was cruel and arrogant on occasions, and allowed nothing to stand in the way of gratifying her ambition is well known...in her ambition to gain power over Octavian she betrayed Antony, though she loved him dearly...no wealth could satisfy her, and that her passions were insatiable...[26]

She remains a fascinating character study to the present day, in this regard, the equal of both Caesar and Antony. Love her or hate her,

> All writers agree in their descriptions of the charm of her conversation, and refer to the subtle and seductive effect of her sweet, soft voice upon her hearers; but the ready wit of her words was as enticing as their persuasiveness, and while her grace of manner was irresistible, her charming audacity led captive all who had the opportunity of becoming well-acquainted with her.[27]

It is no wonder that Octavian on his first and only interview with her refused to look her in the eye or engage in anything but limited conversation. She was the fifth of Egypt's women pharaohs and the last ruler of a sovereign Egypt.

26 Ibid., pp. 114-5.
27 Ibid., p.115.

The Ptolemaic Dynasty—Overall Assessment

Under the first four Ptolemies after the death of Alexander in 323 BC, Egypt, though now under the rule of a foreign dynasty of pharaohs, once again became a world power. It was pulled irresistibly into the orbit of the Hellenic world, and by Roman times, Greek was the dominant language of state. Native Egyptian was used only in religious ceremonials by the native priests and by the large bulk of the common people. Thus it was that the superstructure of a Greek state was imposed over the large, numerically dominant substratum of native Egyptians who held fast to their ancient traditions, beliefs, and lifeways. But in fact, this 4,000 year-old civilization sedulously over time began to Egyptianize their Macedonian Greek rulers however much the Hellenic influence permeated that part of northern Egypt dominated by Alexandria. The Ptolemies and the Macedonians who settled in the Egypt with them found themselves worshiping Egyptian gods and, on many occasions, affecting Egyptian attire. More tellingly, the Ptolemies, contrary to Greek custom, married their sisters in the time-honored fashion of Egyptian pharaohs. However Greek they may have been, the Ptolemies wanted to be seen and treated as 'authentic' Egyptian pharaohs. They paid honor and homage to their pharaonic predecessors and built or re-built numerous temples throughout the land on the exact foundations of ancient structures, scrupulously maintaining the architectural and artistic canons associated with such temples. Two of the best known and best-preserved temples in Egypt are the Temple of Horus at Edfu and the Temple of Isis at Philae, both in Upper Egypt, both built during Ptolemaic times.

Temple of Horus at Edfu

Temple of Isis at Philae—
Egypt's Southern Border

From the beginning of the dynasty, the Ptolemies reach an accommodation with the Egyptian priests, settling large endowments on their temples and publicly following traditional religious customs. They were anxious to keep the populace pacified and reconciled to their rule, best achieved through their 'alliance' with the priesthood. Having said that, Thebes and the priesthood of Amon have long ceased to be the major sacerdotal power in Egypt. In fact, the city of Thebes, though inspiring a certain amount of veneration in the Greeks who called it *Diopolis* ('the city of God'), had fallen into a kind of dereliction consistent with the diminution of the power and influence of the Amonian priesthood. Only in Napata, 700 miles to the south in Cush, was a vibrant Amonian faith sustained.

Casting about for ways of forging some kind of common bond between Greek and Egyptian, the first two Ptolemies, with the aid of priestly counselors such as Manetho, created the composite deity Serapis, a fusion of Hades, Osiris, and the Apis Bull. He was accepted as legitimate by all and thenceforth replaced Osiris in the pantheon, though Isis not only held her place unmodified, but gradually began to assume greater sacerdotal importance than either Serapis or Osiris. She would be the one Egyptian deity to survive and prosper outside Egypt even when the rest of the pantheon slid into a kind of oblivion. What cemented the acceptance of Ptolemaic rule, at least by the priesthood, were the

Isis—Goddess of the World

Black Madonna & Child—
Isis Christianized

conquests of Ptolemy III (Euergetes) whose successful military campaigns carried him as far east as Persia and Mesopotamia. Among the vast spoils he brought back with him were precious sacred relics and icons that had been carried away from Egypt by the Persians under Cambyses.

Though the Ptolemies went out of their way to ingratiate themselves with the priests, the latter had no say in administrative or governmental matters; it was an entirely Greek regime that ran the country. Moreover, though the Egyptians on the whole resigned themselves to Ptolemaic rule, they held tenaciously to their own culture, language, religion, and lifeways. They interfaced on a personal level as little as possible with Greeks whom they deemed ritually unclean. Upper Egypt, always the bastion of traditional Egyptian culture, sometimes broke out into open revolt against the established regime, one such revolt lasting on and off for 28 years, but it, too, was put down with great loss of life and the destruction of Thebes. But Egypt was now a Greek-dominated nation who perforce had to participate in the wider Mediterranean 'commonwealth' of nations as a fully functioning member with Greek leadership. Still, Budge has this to say about the 'binding force of the Greek element' that knitted together this Mediterranean 'commonwealth':

> In Egypt this element does not come so much to the fore as in the other Hellenic lands, because of the dominating force still possessed by the ancient civilization of the country, which Greek culture could, and did modify to some extent, but could never radically alter, far less subdue.[28]

It is still important to emphasize that Ptolemaic Egypt, for at least 100 years after advent of the dynasty, was probably the most powerful country in that part of the world. Under Ptolemy II, Egypt was by far the wealthiest nation in world, and Alexandria boasted a court whose luxuries and splendors were enough to incite gasps from visiting dignitaries from abroad. Moreover, it has already been seen the manner in which the third Ptolemy, at least for a time, revived the conquering impetus of the 18th Dynasty. Even when the empire was pared down to its smallest limits, the Ptolemies still controlled Cyrene, Cyprus, Coele-Syria, and Palestine. Alexandria became the most

28 Ibid., pp. 126-7.

cosmopolitan city in the known world, welcoming visitors and settlers from all over the Mediterranean and Western Asia; Jews, especially, took advantage of Alexandrian tolerance to emigrate there in large numbers, establishing a large and influential Jewish colony in the city, before spreading out into other parts of the country. They prospered as tax-farmers, merchants, and money-lenders, and not a few of their leading citizens, exemplified by the career of Philo Judaeus, became increasingly Hellenized. It was in Alexandria that the Hebrew Torah was translated into Greek as the Septuagint, later known by emerging Christianity as the Old Testament. But the notorious ethno-religious aloofness of the Jews often incited popular hatred against them, and at recurring intervals anti-Jewish riots broke out. In every major town in Egypt it is said that the merchants were Greek and the money-lenders Jewish.

With the establishment of the Library and Museum of Alexandria, the city becomes the intellectual capital of the ancient world. In fact the so-called 'Greek miracle' is coincident with the establishment of the Library and Museum for nearly every Greek scholar, philosopher, scientist, and mathematician spent time studying in these two centers of higher learning. The Library was built up from a core of scrolls and papyri collected from the temples of Egypt. Since by Ptolemaic times, few, apart from a small group of priestly scribes, could still read the the hieroglyphics, Demotic would have been the script in which the native literature of the country was written. Either the Greeks scholars were compelled to learn Demotic or, more likely, the Demotic manuscripts were translated into Greek. Possibly, some instruction was conveyed orally by Greek-speaking Egyptian priests. It is, after all, under the second and third Ptolemies that Manetho, an Egyptian priest capable of speaking and writing in Greek, wrote his ***Aegyptiaca***, better known as **History of Egypt**, whose dynastic lists from the ***Epitome*** still guide all reconstructions of Egyptian royal chronology. Literary, philosophic, and scientific works from all over the Hellenic world were added to the initial collection amounting, by the end of the dynasty, to 700,000 volumes.

From the reign of Ptolemy V onward, the dynasty shows a definite and inexorable decline, becoming mired in decadence, intrigue, and political murder, the latter of which seems to have become the preferred method of seizing and securing power. There was a progressive weakening in the ruling line, all of whom were named Ptolemy, until the accession of Cleopatra VII, the last of the pharaohs. It was somehow both ironic and fitting that a woman should rule Egypt as its terminal pharaoh, and she proved herself the most able of the Ptolemaic pharaohs since the reign of Ptolemy III. It might be speculated that Cleopatra was decidedly more vigorous than her predecessors because she was not the product of an incestuous marriage. However it might be, she maintained Egypt's independence and kept herself in power and by her successful seductions and manipulations of both Caesar and Antony. Though she came close to pulling off a 'bedroom coup' that would have made her both pharaoh of Egypt and queen of Rome, her own idiosyncrasies and flaws of character undid her in the end. Egypt's 4,000-year dynastic epic was at an end.

Ancient Egypt carried on through religious influence, chiefly in the person of Isis. Her worship was transmitted to Rome and won such a following there as to rival that of Jupiter. Roman legions carried her icons with the child Horus all over Roman Europe. So tenaciously did they take root there that when prosyletizing Christian priests traveled in Europe bent on conversion, instead of destroying the icons of Isis and Horus—always depicted in black coloring—they simply turned them into the Black Madonnas and Child, 400 of which still exist in Europe. At Philae, worship of Isis continued unabated until 540 A.D. when the Emperor Justinian sent his legions south to close the temple and abrogate her worship, persecuting her thousands of local devotees in the process. Ancient Egypt, surviving only through her last remaining goddess, now ceases to exist in every way.

APPENDIX I:

From the Nile to the Niger: The Antiquity of African Spiritual Concepts

I. Introduction

In the parlance of alchemy, each life has, *in potentia*, a *Magnum Opus* or a "Great Work" to accomplish. For Cheikh Anta Diop, the Great Work was to repair that ruptured cord that tied contemporary West African history to that of ancient Northeast Africa, i.e., to the Nile Valley civilizations whose origins were traceable back to 10,500 BC and possibly earlier. Much was achieved by Diop and others re-forging those linkages in the domains of language, culture, manners, customs, and material artifacts. Though the domain of religious ideas was not ignored, more work remains to be done to re-establish that indelible connection linking the theology, symbols, and spiritual conceptions of the ancient Nile to those of West African cultures, particularly those now situated in areas lying between the Senegal River and the confluence of the Niger-Benue Rivers. It is here that the traditional West African world-systems, carefully examined, reveal numerous and unmistakable parallels to ancient Nile Valley thought and religion. It has become ever more important to re-establish the continuity of African history, as the calls for an African Renaissance, first sounded by Diop in 1948, have become ever more insistent. Since there is absolutely no prospect for such a renaissance without a revival of the most dynamic and empowering of African spiritual values, a study looking at the comprehensive universe of African spiritual meaning in time and space is an indispensable undertaking.

II. Neteru: The Divine Powers of the Ancient Nile Valley

The word *neter* (pl. *neteru*) as used by the ancient Egyptians is usually translated as "god" or "deity," but E.A. Wallis Budge maintained that the word meant or implied "self-existence" or "eternal renewal." It may have been related to the Egyptian name of the Saitic Neith, i.e., *Net*, meaning "that which is." R.A. Schwaller de Lubicz stated that *neter*, in effect, meant "power" or "principle;" and the symbol of the *neter* seemed to have been the stone axe. The reason for this tool symbolizing the *neter* is obscure, though in other parts of Africa, the hatchet is associated with certain divinities, to wit, Shango, *orisha* of thunder and lightning among the Yoruba.

Though the entire Egyptian pantheon was eventually to consist of some 2,000 *neteru* or deities, the concept of a single creative power, i.e., of a supreme being, is present from the very beginning. This being was called *Uā*, "The One", or *Neter uā*, i.e., "God One". The *neteru* thus came to be seen as the active powers or principles of the One. It could therefore be said that the Supreme Being was The One whose Powers (*neteru*) were many; thus "monotheism" resolved into "polytheism" and vice-versa.

III. The Primordial Manifestations of the Creator and the Created

Several categories of *neteru*; are discernible in the ancient Egyptian pantheon, in the same way that the Greeks distinguished between the titans, the gods proper, and the demi-gods. Among the ancient Egyptians, there is clearly an older cycle of *neteru* and they represent the cosmic powers of primordial creation and ordering of the universe. They inspired deep reverence and awe among the dynastic Egyptians, for everything in the universe including all the other *neteru* was said to have sprung from them. They represent the oldest concepts of deity known to the ancient Nile dwellers.

Ta-Urt or *Ta-weret*, appears to be the oldest identifiable deity in the pantheon. She is a hippopotamus goddess (*netert*), often represented as standing on her hind legs, belly protruding, hands cupping her breasts. Her figurines are the oldest yet found, dating back to the pre-dynastic period. In her name, *Ta* means "earth" and

Urt means "great," which makes her the zoomorphic form of the "great earth." Hippopotami are obese, aquatic animals floating in the waters of Africa; the earth was also imagined as "the Great Round," floating in the waters of Heaven. Ta-Urt is the primordial Great Mother deity, one of the earliest concretized forms of divinity. In Greece she was called *Gaia*, i.e., "Mother Earth."

Nun (or *Nu*) was the "initial un-creation," the *primum materium* of existence. Théophile Obenga has shown that the Pyramid Texts posit a "pre-created" material state known as *Nun*, the primal or abyssal "waters" out of which all created things emanated. This watery Matter becomes conscious of itself and projects outward, igniting creation. Atum, in the form of a serpent or a rising mound, was the upsurge out of *Nun* that presaged creation. All potentialities and possibilities are contained in this Primal Matter called *Nun*. They begin to manifest at the first moment of creation, i.e., the "Beginning of beginnings" or "First Occasion," called *Tep Sepi*, by the Egyptians. In ancient Egypt, then, there existed a speculation about what existed before the beginning of the universe, a state that modern physics assumes is impossible to imagine. *Nu* or *Nun* would be *Ouranos* (*Uranus*) in the Greek pantheon.

The Cosmic Egg was the universal egg containing the divine breath of life and was an image of that out of which all creation emerged. The Great Cackler, *Geb*, was he out of whom the Cosmic Egg came. It is of interest that astro-physicists have found evidence that the Universe is closed; since it curves elliptically, it could be said to take the form of an infinitely vast "Egg." In Greek mythology it was referred to as the "Orphic Egg."

The Four Primordial Pairs represent the fundamental state of things just before the creation of space-time, thus, of existence prior to the existence of the universe. They were paired as follows:

> *Nu(n)* and *Nut*: the male/female aspects of the Primal Waters. Nut became the personification of the heavenly ocean.
>
> *Hehu* and *Hehut*: the male/female aspects of Timelessness or Infinity.
>
> *Keku* and *Kekut*: the male/female aspects of the Primal Darkness.

Amen or *Kerh* and *Ament* or *Kerhet*: the male/female aspects of the Hidden/Invisible, or Inactivity/Inertness. The Great Invisible also connotes latency and potentiality.

Thus the pre-created state, according to Egyptian thought, was a watery Void, infinite, dark, and invisible. A similar state is postulated in the opening chapters of *Genesis*.

IV. The Divine Triads of Egypt

By the advent of dynastic times, circa 4,268 B.C., in each of the 24 original nomes of Egypt, there was established a well-delineated cycle of divine triads. Indeed Egyptian religion as a whole, with its rites, ceremonies, and conceptions of deity, is already well-advanced. It seems likely that in earlier times, each district worshiped its own divinities—all incorporated into the body of Egyptian religion by the integrative trend evident in the period leading up to the unification of Egypt by Aha Menes 4,268 B.C. Several of the more prominent local triads became worshiped nationally, and their symbols, attributes, and liturgies became important generally throughout Egypt.

A. *The Triad of Annu* (Heliopolis) consisted of *Atum, Kheper,* and *Rā*. *Atum* was the first *neter* of Annu and the earliest of the *neteru* to be represented in the form of a man. *Atum* rose out of Nun at the onset of creation and, not finding a place to stand, created the firmament. *Atum* was frequently represented as a serpent in this capacity. By a kind of divine "onanism," Atum created Shu and Tefnut who then brought forth humanity. Atum is thus the Man-god, creator of the firmament, and father of humanity. He is also a lion-god and the god of twilight or the setting sun, making him, in this capacity, a fore-runner of Osiris. Moreover, he is the prototype of *Adam* in *Genesis*.

Kheper was the scarab beetle who was the personification of "becoming," so that, in one interpretation, creative action takes his form. He is often shown pushing the sun disk across the sky in the same way that natural scarabs push their spherical balls of dung, containing their eggs, along the ground. *Kheper* was also known as *Apur*, that is, "the flier up," in recognition of the beetle's capacity for flight. As *Apur*, he becomes *Apollo* among the Greeks.

Rā became the dominant *neter* at Annu beginning in the 5th Dynasty (c. 3000 BC). He is represented as the noon-day sun, i.e., the sun at its full strength and glory. Zoomorphically, his form is the golden hawk. Rā became the supreme *neter* of the Egyptian state pantheon for the remainder of Egyptian history. The pharaohs were ever after styled "sons of Rā." In Greece, Rā was known as *Helios.*

The female triad at Annu was *Iusaaset, Nebt-hetep* ("Lady of Peace"), and *Rāt. Iusaaset* and *Nebt-hetep* were consorts of Atum. *Rāt* was the consort of *Rā* and seemingly crossed over into the solar worship of pre-Islamic Arabia as *Ilat.*

B. *The Triad of Men-nefer* (Memphis) was comprised of *Ptah, Sekhmet,* and *Nefer-Tem,* later *Iu-em-hept* (Imhotep). *Ptah's* name derives from the Egyptian word meaning "to open" and Gerald Massey asserts that *Ptah* was the "opener of Amenta." He was the divine sculptor, fashioner, engraver, carver, i.e., the Great Craftsman *par excellence.* He is often shown fashioning the Egg of the World on a potter's wheel. Ptah was closely identified with both *Kheper* and *Nun,* and one of the forms of Ptah was as *Ta-Tanen,* an earth-god. But *Ptah* was primarily the Demiurge, i.e., the Great Artificer or Architect of the Universe. He was the patron of all builders, masons, and artisans and was usually represented as standing on a cubit, the measure that symbolized building. It was no coincidence that the height of pyramidal construction was attained during the ascendancy of Ptah in the Old Kingdom near his sacred city, Memphis or *Men-nefer.* Since he was the "opener of the earth," he was also sometimes represented as a dwarf or pygmy, reputed to know the secrets of the minerals of the earth. Ptah was thus the patron of mining and metallurgy as well. Another form of Ptah was as *Seker,* the deity of darkness and the underworld; as Osiris gained prominence, he assumed most of the attributes of Ptah-Seker. Ptah's zoomorphic symbol was the bull; in this guise, Ptah was related to Hapi or Apis. The Greeks identified him with their own *Hephaestos,* the Divine Metal-Worker.

Sekhmet was lion-headed goddess who was the sister-wife of Ptah. As a lion-figure, she was identified with Tefnut, the sister of Shu and lion-headed as well. Hathor also seems to have been identified with Sekhmet. Her name may derive from a word meaning "fire" and she represented the fiery heat of the sun and also the fire of sexual passion. Like many of the *neteru,* Sekhmet seems to have had a Nubian or Sudanese provenance. With Hathor, she was identified with the Eye of Rā and in this capacity Sekhmet was a Destroyer by bringing disease, pestilence and fever. Sekhmet was, nonetheless, the patronness of the *sunu*, the priest-physicians of ancient Egypt, presumably because she could ward off disease as well as bring it on.

Nefer-Tem was the son of Ptah and Sekhmet and like his mother, was zoomorphically represented as lion-headed. Nefer-Tem was probably a form of Atum that Gerald Massey thinks was preceded by, and therefore sprung from, Ptah. He was most often shown either holding a lotus plant or sitting on top of one. Like Horus, Nefer-Tem was the god of the rising sun and new life; the lotus, arising out of the depths of the waters atop a long stem, is an "umbilical" image.

Iu-em-hetep (Imhotep) was a late form (6th century BC) of the son of Ptah who superseded Nefer-Tem. He was the deified form of the 3rd Dynasty physician Imhotep. His name meant "he comes in peace." Imhotep was venerated by the Greeks as their own *Asclepios*, god of medicine.

C. *The Triad of Khemennu* (Hermopolis) consisted of *Tehuti* (Thoth), *Ma'āt*, and *Sesheta*. In some ways Tehuti was unique among the *neteru* for he is the Divine Messenger who is also personifies the Mind, Will, and Intelligence of The One. He is the Master of the Word, i.e., of Divine Speech, and the patron of all learning. Tehuti is also considered the "Measurer," particularly of time, and is one of the earliest masculine deities associated with the moon. It is noteworthy that the early inhabitants of the Nile Valley followed the lunar calendar. He is also the "Balancer" and is featured prominently in the "weighing of the heart" in the funerary ritual. In this capacity Tehuti is the Great Arbiter, and he re-equilibrated the relationship between Set and Horus at the conclusion of their titanic battle. Tehuti has two important zoomorphic representations: the ibis and the cynocephalic ape (baboon). The ibis, in nature, appears to give enemas to itself, making it a natural image of the physician. The cynocephalic ape is the "herald of the sun" because of its propensity to chatter at dawn. The Greeks gave Tehuti the title *Trismegistos*, "three times great," and identified him with their own Thrice Greatest Hermes, the source of all wisdom and learning. The Hermetica, encompassing all arcane subjects such as alchemy and astrology, is traceable to Tehuti.

Ma'āt was the consort of Tehuti and was always symbolized by the ostrich feather. Her name literally means "that which is straight," and she personified all that connoted right, order, balance, and truth. In one way, she was supreme over all *neteru* because all were subject to the rule of universal law she personified. Her feather, representing all righteousness and justice, was the balance against which the heart was weighed in the judgement scene. The modern image of Justice, a woman holding a balance scale, comes down directly from the ancient image of Maāt.

Sesheta, the third member of the triad, was a goddess associated with Tehuti as the inventor of letters and the patroness of books. She was also the keeper of time since she is seen holding a palm branch, symbol of time, and counting off the years. Sesheta is thus the one who presides over history and its recording. The Greek muse *Clio* descends from Sesheta.

D. *The Triad of Waset or Ta-Apt* (Thebes) was composed of *Amon, Mut,* and *Khonsu*. Amon, was one of the Primordial Eight *neteru*, who, with his sacred city Waset or Thebes, rose to prominence at the onset of the Middle Kingdom around 2,200 BC Thebes was first dedicated to *Apt*, a form of the hippopotamus goddess Ta-Urt, before becoming the center of the worship of Amon. Thus an early name for the place, *Ta-apt*, later became hellenized to *Thebes*. The word *amon* means "hidden" and it is also a name for "the west." Its root *men* means "to be permanent." Amon became fused with the supreme state deity *Rā* as *Amon-Rā* and was the ruling deity of Egypt for 2,000 years. Amon is repeatedly said to come forth from the land of the *Medjay* and from *Punt*, that is to say Africa south of Egypt. This reference to Amon's southern origin is perhaps another reason why Napata in Cush (Ethiopia) became such an important center of his worship beginning in the 18th Dynasty (1,570 BC). Amon's zoomorphic symbol was the ram. To the Greeks, Amon was their own king of the gods, *Zeus*, also zoomorphically linked to the ram.

Mut was Amon's consort and her name means literally "mother." As Wallis Budge says, she was the "World-Mother" from which all existence sprang. The word *mut* may be etymologically related to our own word "mother." She was identified with Apt, the earliest goddess of Thebes. In Greek times, Mut was called *Hera*, queen of the gods and wife of Zeus.

Khonsu was a moon deity and the son of Amon and Mut. His name means "traveler," a reference to the changing phases of the moon and to its movement across the nighttime sky. Like Thoth, he became, because of his movements, a type of messenger and also time-keeper. Among the Greeks, *Khonsu* would have been a type of the youthful *Hermes*.

E. To the *Triad at Abu* (Elephantine) belonged *Khnum, Satit,* and *Anqet*. *Khnum* was the guardian of the cataract and regulator of the flow of the Nile waters. The word *khnum* means "to unite, join, or build." Like Amon, his symbol was a ram but of the flat-horned variety; like Ptah, he was a fashioner, molding human beings out of clay on the potter's wheel. As the regulator of the Nile flood, Khnum was the deity to whom appeals were directed when famine threatened because of low waters. As with Amon, Khnum was profoundly venerated by Nubians and, with his two consorts, seems to have been of Nubian origin.

Satit was the consort of Khnum and her name derives from the word *sat* or *sati* meaning to "shoot, eject, throw, or pour out." Her name suggests that at an early time she was a goddess of the hunt like *Artemis-Diana* of Greco-Roman mythology. She is often depicted with a bow and two arrows. In dynastic times, Satit was probably associated with the flood waters shooting forth over the cataracts during flood season in the Nile Valley.

Anqet was the second consort of Khnum whose name derives from the word *anq* meaning "to surround, to embrace." Her name refers to the flood waters "surrounding" or immersing the fields, thus re-generating them. Anqet was worshipped throughout Northern Nubia.

V. The Osirian Cycle

With the Egyptian pre-occupation with resurrection and immortality, with "not dying a second time", it is no wonder that the cult of Osiris, the god of eternal life, should hold such a commanding place in Egyptian spiritual sensibilities for so long. It is in the Drama of Osiris, the archetype of the Christian dispensation, that the authentic soul of ancient Egypt is to be found.

A. The position of *Asar* or *Osiris* was unique in the pantheon of Egypt. His name, a compound of *As(t)* or *Isis* and *ar*, meaning "born of or created of", means literally "created of Isis", making him at first a type of Horus as the son of Isis. Only later does Osiris become the brother-consort of Isis. He is the god-man who ruled as King, died (at the hands of Set), and was resurrected (by Isis), thus emerging as the type and symbol of resurrection after death and of life everlasting. The prominence of other *neteru* rose and fell over the course of Egyptian history but Osiris maintained his central position in the religious sensibilities of all Egyptians for a period spanning 4,000 years. He assumed the attributes of many preceding *neteru*, especially those of Ptah, Seker, and Atum and was represented by a slew of symbols. Osiris was the personification of the growing grain that was cut down at harvest, eaten as the bread, and then resurrected in the growth of new grain. He was also represented as presiding over the growing of grapes and the making of wine that was in some sense his "blood" and "spirit." For this reason, the Greeks considered Osiris as their own *Dionysus* who was thought to have been born in North Africa. Osiris was also the growing tree, indeed all growing green things. Osiris had a lunar aspect as the waxing moon and was the sun that had set, i.e., the sun by night, making its perilous journey through *Amenta*, the "Hidden Land." He was zoomorphically represented by the bull and considered to be the Lord of Eternity and the Judge of the Dead. The souls of all the deceased had to be justified before Osiris at the "Weighing of the Hearts," presided over by Thoth or Anubis. In his mummified form, the emblem of resurrection, Osiris was the *keres(t)*, that in the Ptolemaic period yielded the Greek word *kristos*, meaning "anointed." This word *kristos* is the very word *christ* that became indelibly linked with the name of Jesus. The Djed Cross was considered the 'backbone of Osiris' and the raising of the Djed was emblematic of the resurrection of Osiris. Thus, both Jesus and Osiris were resurrected upon the Cross.

B. *Ast* or Isis was the sister-consort of Osiris and her name means "seat, throne, abode, womb, tomb." She became the most exalted of the great goddesses of Egypt and, like Osiris, her attributes were many. She was the feminine grain in its nourishing aspect and presided over beer-making as well. In Greek times, she was linked with the goddess *Demeter*, goddess of home, hearth, and horticulture. She was the full or pregnant moon whose zootype was the cow. She was identified with the star Sirius, the herald of the sun and harbinger of the flood. The flood was said to begin with a teardrop of Isis so she was also known as *Remi*, "the Weeper." Isis was styled the "Queen of Heaven" and was the one who reconstituted the dismembered body of Osiris, re-animating it with the breath of life. Finally, Isis was the Virgin Mother of *Heru* (*Horus*) and one of her names was *Meri-f-uā*, i.e., 'his beloved one'. Isis was identified with nearly every goddess in the pantheon but most closely with *Hathor, Bast,* and *Serqet.* The cult of Isis was the one to move beyond the confines of Egypt and sustain itself for more than 500 years. She became one of the most venerated goddesses in the Roman Empire and her statuettes in her shrines in Europe were, during the period of Christianization, transformed into the Black Madonna.

C. *Heru* or Horus was the son of Isis and Osiris. His name means "face" as in "the face of heaven," because Horus was originally a sky-god. He was represented as the Divine Son of Isis but, in another manifestation, as the son and consort of *Het-her* or *Hathor.* Early on, Horus was a complementary twin to *Set,* however he and Set eventually became antagonists and evolved into the warring twins of light and darkness. In dynastic times, Horus was the son and avenger of Osiris, meaning that he was Osiris re-born. Horus became an image of the rising sun conquering the "dragon of darkness," i.e., Set or Apep. His birthday was December 25th, the day the sun begins to rise on the ecliptic in the northern hemisphere. It is in this role as the "conqueror of the dragon" that Horus may have lent his Egyptian name *Heru* to the Greek word *hero.* As *Heru-khuti*, Horus was the prototype of the quintessential Greek hero *Hercules*; Horus was also the forerunner of the mythic Christian hero and dragon-slayer, *St. George.* Horus was zoomorphically shown as the Golden Hawk and in this aspect was fused with Rā. Horus was said to have come into Egypt from the south with a group of blacksmiths known as the *mesniu* and called "the followers of Horus". The pharaohs were considered human incarnations of Horus and likewise would have been linked to the metallurgical craft. As the Divine Infant cradled in the arms of Isis, Horus became part of the widespread worship of Isis and thus the prototype of the Madonna's Child, i.e., the Infant Jesus.

D. *Set* is the fourth and most enigmatic "actor" in the divine drama of Osiris. Set is undoubtedly one of the oldest if not the oldest of the Nile Valley masculine *neteru* and is represented in the most diverse guises of any of the *neteru* in the pantheon. Set, in his numerous zoomorphic forms, was variously the serpent, the jackal, the hippo, the raven, the ass, the boar, the goat, or the antelope. He was undoubtedly a *neter* that originated to the south of Egypt and early on was entirely benevolent. The word *set* has a variety of meanings: "tail, earth, fire, shoot, eject, bow, quake, seat, cut." By early dynastic times, Set had become the Great Adversary, the murderer of Osiris, and the personification of death, drought, and destruction. In one of his aspects, he was the light of the solar fire and thus the prototype of *Lucifer* whose name means "light-bringer." Set eventually becomes *Satan* as *Set-an*, i.e., "the second manifestation of Set." Whereas Osiris was *Kem-Wer*, "the Great Black One," Set was *Teshert*, "the Red One." Set and Horus engaged in a titanic battle for supremacy, reflecting the contest between Darkness and Light, that Horus appears to win, though the relative positions of the two are re-established in a dynamic equilibrium by Thoth. There are obscure hints that Set and Aset (Isis) were formerly connected, though if so, Set was supplanted in this arrangement by Asar (Osiris). Despite his change of status in the pantheon, Set and his worship remained a powerful factor throughout the history of dynastic Egypt. To the Greeks, Set was both *Typhon*, the Dragon of Destruction, and *Ares*, the god of war and conflict.

VI. Other Important *Neteru* of Egypt

A. Anup or *Anubis* is among the more shadowy *neteru*, always depicted in the form of a black jackal. Anubis is invariably associated with the dead and everything to do with mortuary practices, undoubtedly because of the jackal's role as the eater of carrion. This characteristic of the jackal may explain the name of Anubis which may derive from either *anep* meaning "to decay," or *anp* meaning "to swathe," in reference to Anubis's role as mummifier. Anubis most probably emanates from Set and is therefore older than either Thoth or Osiris, two *neteru* with whom he is closely associated. Anubis precedes Thoth as the "guide by night," taken from the jackal's nocturnal propensities. Mythically, he is the son of *Nepthys*, sister of Isis, by either Set or Osiris. As the mummifier of the dead and the balancer of the scales before Osiris, Anubis is, after Osiris himself, the most important *neter* in the funerary ritual. Other manifestations of Anubis are *Wep-wat*, the jackal or wolf *neter* who is the "Opener of the Way," and *Sab*, a jackal whose name means "Judge." These facts give clear indications that Anubis was Judge of the Dead prior to Osiris. The current pole star *Polaris* is in the *Little Bear* constellation, known in the Egyptian planisphere as the *Jackal*. In Greek myth, Anubis, Wep-wat, and Sab appear as the three-headed hound *Cerebrus*, who guards the entrance to Hades.

B. *Aten* or *Aton* was the disc of the sun and therefore coeval with Rā. He seems also to have been related to Set since he was said to have emerged from his head. Aton becomes briefly pre-eminent during the reign of Akhenaton (c. 1330 BC) who raised him to the position of sole deity. The name *Aton* may be the source of the Semitic *adon*, meaning "lord."

C. *Geb* is the Egyptian earth-god who was the consort of the sky-goddess *Nut* and Chief Magistrate of the *neteru*. In dynastic times, Geb was accounted the father of Osiris, Isis, Set, Nepthys, and the Elder Horus. His zoomorphic form was the Goose known as "the Cackler." To the Greeks, he was Father *Cronos*, whom the Romans called *Saturn*. In her aspect as wife of Geb, Nut in Greek mythology would have been *Rhea*.

D. *Hapi* was the personification of the Nile. In human form, he was depicted as a man, with one female breast, pouring out water from two vases, representing the Upper and Lower Niles. Around 320 BC, he is fused with Osiris as *Serapis*, the pre-eminent deity of Ptolemaic times. The *Apis* Bull was sacred to *Hapi* and the name *Apis* derives from *Hapi*. In the Greek Zodiac, Hapi became *Aquarius*.

E. *Het-Her* or *Hathor* was a very ancient goddess. Her name means "mansion of Horus," making her an early mother-consort of Horus and identifying her with Isis, who may be later than Hathor. In addition to Isis, Hathor is identified with Nut and Sekhmet. As *Hathor-Nehsi*, i.e., Hathor the Nubian, she too originates in the south and she is often shown and referred to as black-skinned. Like Isis, she is zoomorphically the cow and related to the moon. She is, with Nut, "Lady of the Waters" and "Lady of the Sycamore." Hathor presides over love, marriage, sensuality and merry-making and the Greeks identified her with their *Aphrodite*. Her son *Ihy* is the Egyptian prototype of *Eros (Cupid)*. In one aspect, Hathor is a sun-goddess who also had a "terrible" aspect as the "Eye of Rā" who brought destruction upon an impious human race. She had seven major shrines with seven personifications referred to as the "Seven Hathors."

These Seven Hathors—the Seven Divine Cows—are the prototypes of the Seven Cattle seen in pharaoh's dream interpreted by Joseph.

F. *Net or Neith* was yet another very ancient Egyptian cosmic goddess whose sacred city was Sais. Her name had several meanings: "water," "weave," and "that which is." In effect, Neith represented the very fabric of the universe and across the lintel to her temple were inscribed the words: "I am all that has been and shall be. No mortal may lift my veil." Like Satit, she was depicted with two crossed arrows and the Greeks derived their own *Athene* from her. She was very probably a form of the sky-goddess Nut.

VII. The Period of Transition

Between 1,680 and 660 BC, Egypt experienced one significant era of conquest, e.g., that of the Hyksos or Shepherd Kings from 1,680 to 1,580 BC. The Hyksos were probably nomadic peoples of the eastern desert, between the Nile and the Red Sea, who took advantage of a period of inner turmoil and weakness in Egypt to overwhelm the country, almost without a fight. They would have had religious and cultural links to the Canaanitic peoples and it is during the period of Hyksos rule that a small, marginal band of shepherds led by their patriarch Jacob, a.k.a. Israel, migrated into Lower Egypt. After driving out the Hyksos, native Egyptian kings from Upper Egypt established their rule, and the storied 18th Dynasty at Waset, or Thebes (Luxor), began a campaign of conquest that eventually resulted in an empire stretching from the Blue Nile (Khartoum) to Anatolia (Turkey). During this period, known as the New Kingdom, Egypt reaches the zenith of her imperial power, wealth, and glory which more or less continues through the 19th dynasty, i.e., from 1,580 to 1,200 BC At the end of the 19th Dynasty, Egypt, under Rameses III, must repulse an invasion from a powerful coalition of northern Mediterranean pirate nations known as the Sea Peoples. Though Egypt is completely victorious against the Sea Peoples, from the 20th dynasty on, a slow but inexorable decline is noticeable, so that by 750 BC, Egypt has come under the overlordship of its powerful neighbor to the south, Cush. In fact, Cushite pharaohs lead their armies north to restore order in a rapidly disintegrating political environment in Egypt and by 716

BC have established the 25th dynasty. There is a mini-Renaissance in Egypt that flourished briefly during the 25th Dynasty; but within 40 years, Egypt is menaced by a non-African aggressor for the first time in 500 years: the Assyrians.

The Assyrians, after a succession of battles stretching over 20 years, defeat the 25th Dynasty pharaoh Taharka in 660 BC, forcing the Cushites to retreat to their capital at Napata. Though the Assyrians' domination of Egypt is short-lived, their victory against the 25th Dynasty pharaohs seems to set off a series of invasions of Egypt from outside Africa that will continue in waves for the next 1,300 years. One after another, warlike nations bent on empire—the Persians, Macedonians (Greeks), Romans, and Arabs—follow the Assyrians and wash over Egypt until at last, Egypt of the pharaohs vanishes from history.

The invasions of the Nile Valley have repercussions beyond the borders of Egypt itself; they are in fact felt along the Nile all the way to the confluence of the Blue and White Niles at present-day Khartoum. What is not sufficiently appreciated is that the lower (northern) two-fifths of the Nile was united by ties of history, culture, and the geo-political overlordship of both Egyptian and Cushitic rulers into one great geo-cultural complex. It is thus possible to speak of Nile Valley culture in exactly the same way one might speak of European culture. Thus when Egypt and Nubia are assaulted by the shock waves of invasion and conquest, the whole region trembles. These invasions set in motion events that will decisively and permanently impact West African history.

Professor Boubacar Lam, a Senegalese historian and disciple of Cheikh Anta Diop, in the 1980s made a startling discovery, or more precisely, re-discovery. There exists a Senegalese oral history, published by Delafosse and Gaden in 1913, but collected and compiled by Yoro Dyâo, a scion of Tuculor nobility in northern Senegal, that details and documents migrations into West Africa from the Nile Valley. Yoro Dyâo died in 1919 and his chronicle more or less disappeared from scholarly notice for the next 64 years until unearthed by Professor Lam. From the Senegal River in the north to the Niger Delta in the southeast, the major ethnic groups virtually without exception preserve traditions of an eastern origin. These traditions have been commented on by ethnologists and historians; some, such as the Yoruba antiquarian J.O. Lucas, author of **The Religion of the Yorubas**, have gone so far as to link some these ethnic groups to ancient

Egypt itself. Reverend Samuel Johnson, also of Yoruba extraction and the 19th century author of **The History of the Yorubas**, asserted that the Yorubas, at the very least, can trace their remote origins to Nubia. Moreover, Cheikh Anta Diop himself used comparative linguistic analysis to demonstrate the manner in which several Senegalese ethnic groups, e.g., the Wolof, Serer, Peul, Tuculor, and Djola, all migrated into Senegal from an area where the Egyptian language was spoken or had influenced the local languages. However, Professor Lam found an extraordinary oral record whose existence had all but been forgotten. Even the master himself, Cheikh Anta Diop, seems not to have been aware of the oral chronicles compiled by Yoro Dyâo. These Senegalese sagas describe no fewer than *six* migrations from northeast Africa. Though far from certain, the first one may have begun as early as the mid-7th century BC, at or soon after the time of the Assyrian conquest of the Cushite 25th Dynasty (c. 653 BC), and the last one in the mid-6th century AD Though the oral chronicles compiled by Yoro Dyâo pertain to the ethnic groups of Senegambia, they are powerful evidence that the ethnic traditions along 2,500 miles of the West African coast that link dozens of peoples to Nile Valley culture are based solidly on historical fact. Moreover, dozens of inland peoples of the Western Sudan, e.g., the Dogon, have equally strong historical links to the ancient Nile Valley.

It would require detailed ethnographic work, including careful analyses of oral histories, to determine which of these peoples moved into West Africa when. However, it should be possible to determine which peoples were sent migrating west as a consequence of which invasion of the Nile Valley, going back at least to the Persian invasion of the 6th century BC and probably to the Assyrian invasion of the 7th century BC As has been noted elsewhere, Diop asserted that the present-day Berbers are descended from the defeated Sea Peoples of the northern Mediterranean who were sent fleeing north and west by the victorious navies and armies of Rameses III in 1,178 BC Thus the Berbers' ancestors would have permanently abandoned seafaring and taken up a pastoral mode of life as they spread westward across northern Africa. But so saying, there is in fact one Western Sudanic people, as already noted, for whom there are reasonably reliable dates for their migrations west that can serve as a case study of the peopling of Western Africa from the cultural regions of the Nile Valley: the Dogon.

VIII. The Dogon: A West African Link to the Ancient Nile Valley.

The Dogon, currently inhabiting the area abutting the Bandiagra cliffs in southeastern Mali not far from the Niger River city of Mopti, state categorically that they originally came *from the northeast.* According to their most important ethnographer, Marcel Griaule, they would have left their original home in northeast Africa about 1,400 years ago, eventually settling in Mali. Ethnically and linguistically allied with the Bambara and the Borzo (the fisher people of the Niger), they would have lived in proximity to these peoples until 700 years ago. Then, under the pressure of an advancing and militant Islam, they made, as a people, a calculated decision to migrate en masse to the Bandiagra cliffs region, very remote from the main population centers and caravan routes, a place no one wanted enough to bother conquering.

Of all the groups that can trace their ethnic and cultural origins to the Nile Valley, the Dogon seem to have been the one group that preserved most faithfully the cultural and spiritual legacy they carried with them when they began their migrations. Far fewer corruptions seem to have crept into their world system than in others in West Africa. That they did indeed see themselves as preserving a precious legacy is indicated by their determination to maintain their traditional way of life, complete with its symbols, ceremonies, rites, and knowledge, against the rising, almost irresistible threat of Islam. They could not fight the armies of the empire-building, Muslim, West African kings, but they could remove themselves to a place where few cared to follow. In exploring the Dogon system, clear and abundant parallels identified with ancient Egyptian thought are to be found, far too many to be dismissed merely as "coincidences". However, it is a singular fact that the Dogon did not play the role of mere preservers but amplified and augmented the system that they brought with them from Northeast Africa. Having said that, we will find in the table below the linkages that can be delineated between Dogon and ancient Egyptian thought.

THE DOGON: A WEST AFRICAN LINK TO THE ANCIENT NILE VALLEY		
	Dogon	*Egyptian*
1. *Calendars*	360 days, 12 months, 30 days/month, 5-day weeks	360 days, 12 months, 30 days/month, 10-day weeks
2. *Complementary Social Groups*	Masculine/Feminine, Initiates/ Non-initiates, Elders/Youth	Men/Women, Priests/ Laypersons, Old/Young
3. *Occupational Castes*	Farmers, Metal Workers, Wood Workers, Fishers, Leather Workers, Griots	Agricultural Peasantry, Artisans, Metal-Workers, Boat Men, Stone-workers, Praise Singers
4. *Theocratic governance*	Hogon (Priest-ruler), Totemic Priests, Council of Elders, Administrators	Pharaoh (priest-king), Sacerdotal Priests, Royal Administrators, Scribes
5. *Lineage*	Patrifocal system superimposed on a kinship system through the female line	Patriarchal superstructure under-girded by matrilineal family succession
6. *Role of Women*	In charge of home, control farm produce, fashion handiwork for sale, run the marketplace, possess own secret societies and priestesses, have right to divorce	Controlled home, pass surnames to children, own farms, produce handicrafts for market, controlled royal inheritance, maintained own priestesshoods, trained in certain professions
7. *Spiritual Personality*	Nine components to the Self	Seven components to the Self
8. *Names*	Each person has four names representing his/her 'power'	Names are considered 'words of power'
9. *Higher Powers*	Called *Nommo* and control the workings of the universe as active agents of the Creator	Called *Neters* and rule the universe as the active principles of the Creator
10. *The Creator*	Called *Amma* which means 'to hold firmly' or 'to keep in the same place'	Called *Amen*, meaning 'to make firm' or 'establish permanently'
11. *The Creation*	Before creation, *Amma* had no place to stand	Before creation, *Amen-Rā* had no place to stand
12. *World Egg*	*Amma* brought forth an Egg, containing the Cosmos	The Egg of the World was fashioned by *Ptah* on the Potter's Wheel
13. *The Mind of the Creator*	The universe came forth as a thought in the Mind of *Amma*, who then uttered the Creative Word	The *neter Thoth* is the Mind of Amen-Rā where the universe is formed before it came forth as the Word

THE DOGON: A WEST AFRICAN LINK TO THE ANCIENT NILE VALLEY		
	Dogon	*Egyptian*
14. *Spittle & Breath*	*Amma* created life on Earth from his spittle and breath	*Atum* created *Tefnut* from his spittle and *Shu* from his breath as the ancestors of living beings
15. *The Original Powers*	There are 8 *Nommo* or Primordial Ancestors of Man	There are 8 Primeval *Neters*
16. *Opening of the Eyes*	The creation of the universe begins when *Amma* 'opens his eyes'	Light is produced from the primeval darkness when Rā opens his two eyes
17. *The Original Twins*	*Amma* created the original Male/Female Twins as the *po* (primal seed)	*Atum* created the original Male/Female Twins, *Shu* and *Tefnut*
18. *The Seat and the Seeds*	Within *Amma* is the 'seat' which is the womb where the primordial seeds germinated	*Isis* is *Ast* whose name means 'seat' and 'womb'; She is the source of grains and seeds
19. *Fermentation & Resurrection*	*Amma* caused things in evolution to 'ferment' which is a 'resurrection' of cereal grains destroyed in the brewing process	*Osiris* represents the harvested grain and through him grain and grapes are fermented to produce spiritous liquors; it is another form of his resurrection
20. *The Fish-Being*	The *nommo Anagonno* is a fish-being who is the precursor of Man; *Ana* means 'rain' and 'man'	*An* is the Great Fish who was the harbinger of the Nile flood, 'the tears of Rā'
21. *The Serpent of Time*	*Nommo Sizu* is the Serpent who symbolizes immortality	The Serpent *Sata* dies and is re-born each day
22. *The Lotus*	"For it is said of the water lily (lotus) that it is the `eye of the pond', that is, of the water and of him who resides there, O *Nommo*, creature of *Amma* and begetter of humanity"	The neter *Nefer Tem* is associated with the lotus plant growing out of a pool of water, out of which emerges the head of the resurrected deceased
23. *The Creative Water*	*Amma* began his creation with Water	*Atum* began his creation in the Primordial Waters of *Nun*
24. *Disorder and Chaos*	*Ogo*, the Fox, is the universal principle of disorder, disorganization, opposition, and diversification	*Set/Anubis*, the Jackal or Wolf, is the author of all rebellion & conflict; he leads the 'Children of Revolt'

THE DOGON: A WEST AFRICAN LINK TO THE ANCIENT NILE VALLEY		
	Dogon	*Egyptian*
25. *Prematurity & Incompleteness*	*Ogo* was the premature being who stopped his own gestation and burst from his mother's side, dooming himself to incompleteness	*Set* tore himself prematurely from his mother's womb, emerging from her side, and is sometimes shown lame and imperfect because he is incomplete
26. *Primordial Incest*	*Ogo* committed a primordial act of incest with his Mother, the Earth	*Geb* the Earth-god, committed incest with his Mother
27. *Celestial Ladder*	The 'chain of *Ogo*', also called his 'ladder', connects earth and sky	The 'ladder of *Set*' connected heaven and earth
28. *Thief of Light*	*Ogo* stole the sun's fire	*Set* stole the sun's light
29. *Power comes from the South*	*Ogo* emerged from *Amma's* womb to the south	*Set* comes from and is identified with the South
30. *Opener of the Way*	*Amma* made *Ogo* the Fox descend to the World after an 'unauthorized ascent' to 'show the way' for all future descents of the beings created in his womb	The Jackal *Wep-au-wat* is the 'Opener of the Way' for all those souls descending into *Amenta*, 'the Hidden Land'
31. *The Turning of the Earth*	The Earth turns by the movement of the Paws of the Fox (*Ogo*); it is said, 'The Fox has turned with his tail; the Earth has turned on its axis'.	In the Egyptian planisphere, the north polar axis, upon which the Earth turns, points to the constellation of the Jackal (*Ursa Minor*)
32. *Sacrifice of the Twin*	*Nommo Anagonno*, the Twin of *Ogo*, who personifies the seeds and growing plants, will be sacrificed then resurrected to bring back order into *Amma's* creation. However, the equilibrium between order and disorder will be maintained in *Amma's* universe	*Osiris/Horus*, the Twin of *Set*, personifies all growing things; his death and dismemberment by *Set* leads to his resurrection then a victory over Sethian disorder. *Thoth* restores the balance between *Osiris/Horus* and *Set*, i.e., between order and disorder
33. *Humanity's Guardian*	*Nommo Anagonno* is humanity's ancestor, provider of spiritual principles, and protector	*Osiris/Horus* is the ancestor of human beings, the agent of their spiritual resurrection, and their guardian

THE DOGON: A WEST AFRICAN LINK TO THE ANCIENT NILE VALLEY		
	Dogon	*Egyptian*
34. *The Sacrifice of the Phallus*	*Nommo Anagonno*, the Fish-Being who is the Image of Man, was separated from his penis at his sacrifice which was swallowed by a fish	*Osiris* at the time of his death and dismemberment was separated from his penis which was swallowed by a fish
35. *The Crucified Victim*	*Nommo Anagonno* is the sacrificed victim who will be resurrected; he is tied to a tree standing up, arms outstretched, and attached to two branches extending at right angles from the tree	*Osiris* is principle of sacrifice and resurrection who is raised upright on the *Djed* cross, the symbol of a tree; the raising of the *Djed* cross is the act of resurrection
36. *Feeding Mankind*	*Nommo Anagonno* 'shared his body among mankind to feed it'	*Osiris*, in dying, gives his body as harvested grain to humanity for food
37. *Removal of the organs of the Body*	*Amma* takes the body of the sacrificed *Nommo Anagonno*, removes the 7 organs, and preserves them for the restoration of the *Nommo* at the time of his resurrection	During the mummification of the osirified deceased, 4 organs are removed from the body, placed in 4 Canopic jars for preservation, then restored to the deceased at the time of resurrection
38. *Restoration of the Body*	*Amma* cuts up the body of the sacrificed *Nommo*, disperses them, then re-gathers them, re-knits the body with all the organs replaced, and brings the *Nommo* back to life. In some versions it is *Ogo* the Fox who performs these functions	*Set*, after the death of *Osiris*, dismembers the body and scatters the parts. Isis then gathers the parts, puts them back together, and reanimates the body of Osiris. In other versions, it is *Anubis* the Jackal who re-assembles the body of Osiris and mummifies it
39. *Weaving the Word in the Water*	In the formation of *Amma's* second universe, the *Nommo* will weave the word in the primordial water, creating the 'cloth of existence'	*Neith* is *Net* (Eg.) whose name means 'water', 'weave', and 'that which is'

THE DOGON: A WEST AFRICAN LINK TO THE ANCIENT NILE VALLEY		
	Dogon	*Egyptian*
40. *The Sirian Calendar*	The heliacal rising of Sirius is a major event in the Dogon year and of prime importance in their Sirius-based long calendar	The ancient Egyptians discovered the calendar of 365 ¼ days based on the heliacal rising of Sirius and rectified their civil calendar of 365 days every 1,460 years by reference to the Sirian calendar
41. *Orion*	The Dogon say that the 3 stars of Orion's Belt represent the sacrificed *Nommo*	The ancient Egyptians called Orion *Sahu* which is the spiritual body of Osiris (the sacrificed *neter*)
42. *The Beneficent Sun*	The Dogon depict the sun with each of its rays ending in an open hand representing *Amma's* power over all creation	The pharaoh Akhenaten installed the sun disk Aten as the single deity of Egypt with his rays ending in open hands

This table does not exhaust the close cross-cultural correspondences between the Dogon and Egyptian world-systems but does provide clear proof that the Dogon, in their new Western Sudanic home, re-created their society on the foundation of ancient Nile Valley cultural and spiritual values. In point of fact, they carried away from the Nile Valley and dedicated themselves to preserving a legacy that was increasingly under attack from the outside. In examining their world-view and mode of life, ancient Nile Valley civilization can still be seen to be alive and vibrant.

APPENDIX II:
The Ancient African Sources of Greek Myth

In historical times, the world has probably never seen the emergence of a "single source" culture. In fact, the dynamism of any culture arises out of a synthesis of disparate influences. Nowhere is this truism more strongly implicated than in Greek myth. As classical Greek religion evolved, complete with its myths and rites, it welded influences from outside the Greek world. Therefore, it only becomes intelligible by a cogent examination of these extra-Hellenic roots. It is therefore possible in a preliminary way to clarify some of the source currents of Greek myths by reference to their progenitors in Africa.

We can delineate clear and tangible connections between African and Greek myths by relying almost entirely on internal evidence. The Greeks were not reticent about acknowledging their debt to Africa as a source of myth, philosophy, and religion; they make so many references to this African cultural wellspring that the Aryanists of the 19th century spent a good deal of time creating the impression that the Greeks' inexplicable romanticization of Africa—Egypt and Ethiopia in particular—made them unreliable as sources for investigations into the roots of their own myths and religion. In effect, Greeks were deemed the most laudable and creative of men in almost every human endeavor *except* as concerned their "incongruous" admiration of African civilizations. Martin Bernal reports that there is even a name for it: *besserwisserei. Besserwisserei* means that modern scholars know the ancients better than the ancients knew themselves.

Many Greek writers and mythographers appeared to have been unabashed Egyptophiles, and among these were Plato, Herodotus, Plutarch, and Diodorus.

Such detractors as Juvenal and Lucian were late and Latin, at a time when Egypt was no longer an independent nation but merely a Roman province and therefore no longer capable of inspiring the awe that Egypt inspired in the classical Greeks. But Herodotus was quite categorical in his declaration that all the Greek gods and goddesses and their rites had originated in Egypt. Herodotus, from classical times to the present, has been severely berated for his credulity and uncritical acceptance of certain kinds of evidence, but many others more or less echoed his opinion regarding the origin of Greek myths and religion. Moreover, at least one modern mythographer, Robert Graves, took the ancients at their word and, armed with data from cultural anthropology, several times asserted that North and East Africa had provided Greece with many of her myths and rituals.

In order to unravel the threads leading from African myths to the Greek ones, we have to clarify some toponyms ("place names"). For example, there were several Greek terms for continental Africa: *Libya, Ethiopia,* and *India*. What is confusing is that these terms were also used to designate specific countries or regions. Thus *Libya*, depending on the context, could be the North African seaboard or Africa itself; *Ethiopia* could designate ancient Cush/Nubia as well as Africa as a whole; *India* could refer to East Africa as well as the Asian subcontinent now known by that name. Moreover, though the term *Ethiopian*, meaning "sunburnt," was the most common word describing a black African, it was sometimes used synonymously with *Egyptian, Libyan,* or *Indian*. Each of these terms could be used to specify a "black African" and were also interchangeable with the others. As an example of the confusion, the Greek god Dionysus, whom the Greeks identified with the Egyptian Osiris, was said to have been born in Nysa, variously located in southwestern Arabia, Libya, or India. Most assume that this *India* refers to the Asian subcontinent; when it is more plausible to assume that it refers to Africa, which, as we have noted, was frequently called *India*.

When relating Greek deities and mythical figures to their counter-parts in Africa, the question that arises is which ones were adopted by the Greeks directly from Africa and which were "indigenous" Greek types who were merely identified with their African counterparts without any "genetic" relationship. If Herodotus is to be believed, the question is not even meaningful since there is no Greek deity that did not come from Africa, through Egypt.

After Hesiod in the 9th century BC, Greece's next important mythographer was her greatest epic poet, Homer, who made statements about the Ethiopians which continue to astound classicists: when Zeus chose to mingle among mortals, he led his Olympian entourage to feast among "the blameless Ethiopians." This statement is most remarkable because it shows that when Greek gods came down from their lofty Olympus, they did not seek the company of their worshipers in Greece but that of a people even more pious, the Ethiopians. To the Greeks, the Ethiopians were a people hardly less renowned and admirable than the Egyptians; some, like Homer, insisted that they even excelled the Egyptians in piety. In point of fact, Egyptians and Ethiopians were usually linked in the Greek mind and more than once, as we have indicated, their names were used synonymously.

That Zeus should find the company of Ethiopians the most congenial among mortals is not surprising when we consider that the origin of this supreme Greek god is the Nile Valley. He is derived from the Egypto-Ethiopian god Amon, the "Hidden One," whose zootype is the ram, the same as Zeus. Whether Amon is purely an Egyptian god or originated in Cush ("Ethiopia"), as so many Egyptian gods did; by the time Homeric Greece appears on the world stage in the 8th century BC, the most important center for the worship of Amon was Napata, the capitol of Cush. Some of Egypt's most conscientious and humane pharaohs ruled during the short-lived 25th or Ethiopian Dynasty from Napatan Cush and their reputations for justice and piety found their way into the annals of various Greek writers. This, then, may be a source of the Homeric tradition relating to the Zeus feasting among his "blameless Ethiopians."

The connection between Zeus and Amon resulted in the founding of a famous oracle at Siwa in Egypt's western desert that came to be known as the Oracle of Zeus-Ammon. Herodotus tells us that this oracle established itself also at Dodona in Greece; it was dedicated to Zeus and apparently founded by a black priestess. The late Martin Bernal, author of **Black Athena**, asserted that the totally non-Greek word *Dodona* might well have been derived from *Dedun*, the name of a wholly Nubian god worshiped in Upper Egypt who was probably related to Khnum of Upper Egypt, another ram-headed deity.

Robert Graves has delineated three main creation stories that found their way into Greek mythology. Chronologically these were: (1) the Pelasgian, (2) the

Orphic, and (3) the Olympian. The Pelasgians were the indigenous inhabitants of Greece, and it was during Pelasgian times that the first Egyptian rites were brought into Greece, according to Herodotus. The Oracle of Dodona, Greece's oldest, was founded then.

With respect to the Olympian creation myth, Graves relates that a persistent tradition makes the titan Garamas the first humanlike being created by Mother Earth. Graves says that Garamas is the eponymous ancestor of the Garamantes, an African people living south of the Fezzan in Libya who founded the settlement in eastern Libya (Siwa) that became the site of the shrine of Zeus-Ammon. It is well known that the Amonians—and therefore the Garamantes—were a black people. Greek authors recorded, and largely accepted, the Egyptian and Ethiopian claim to being the world's oldest peoples; the position of Garamas as (effectively) the first man is consistent with this tradition. It is also one of the many strands of evidence pointing to an African provenance for Zeus, originally as Amon.

Among the early goddesses, probably none was so indelibly linked to Africa in the Greek mind as Athene. Appollonius of Rhodes reported the tradition of the Pelasgians that Athene was born by Lake Tritonis in Libya; Apollodorus and Pausanias relate that she came into Hellas by way of Crete, as so many Afro-Egyptian deities and religious customs did. She seems quite clearly to have been a form of the Egypto-Libyan goddess Neith of Sais who was the goddess of weaving like Athene. Plato in **Timaeus** tells us that Athens, the city of Athene, was related to—or founded by colonists from—Sais, the city of Neith. Herodotus describes the typical garment of Athene, decorated with the *aegis*, that he says was borrowed by Greek women from Libyan women. Graves tells us that Ethiopian women still wear this costume ornamented with cowries.

Several Olympian goddesses were depicted in Ethiopian guise, including Hera, Artemis, and Aphrodite, and all were identified with Egyptian goddesses. Aphrodite was Hathor, a very popular Egyptian goddess who was the mistress of love, beauty, marriage, and merrymaking. Hathor was sometimes known as Hathor-Nehsi, which, since *Nehesi* meant "Nubian," showed her to have originally been a black Sudani goddess probably allied to Bes. In her various guises, Hathor was both mother and consort to Horus and sometimes to Rā. Certain epithets attached to Aphrodite evoke this Sudani Hathor, for Aphrodite was variously known as *Melaenis*, meaning "black one," and Scotia, meaning "dark one." Hathor and Isis were closely identified, of course, and the son-consort of Isis was Osiris. This connection finds a parallel in the relationship of Aphrodite to Adonis who was, as James George Frazer has shown, an eastern Mediterranean version of Osiris.

A Greek god more directly derived from Osiris was Dionysus who many have noted was the "least Greek" of all the Olympians, and in fact was never completely "at home" on Olympus, according to Graves. There are a number of identical features that he shared with Osiris: (1) Dionysus was dismembered and then resurrected by the mother-goddess, (2) he was the god of the vine and wine, (3) his animal types were variously represented as bull and ram, and (4) he wandered all over the world spreading his cult. Dionysus seems to have been born and raised at Mount Nysa, which has been located at various places, including Libya. Graves confirms the Libyan provenance for Dionysus. Several ancient mythographers also noted his connection to Africa: they relate that he visited the Egyptians and the Libyan Amonians where his worship became well established. That Dionysus was Osiris was accepted by most of these mythographers as a matter of course; when writing about Osiris, they most often referred to him as Dionysus. Later Greek philosophers found the orgiastic aspects of the cult of Dionysus distasteful and therefore preferred Apollo, their tutelary genius. This was especially true of the Orphic priests who nonetheless, according to Graves, wore Egyptian costume and sacramentally ate bull's flesh that they called "Dionysus." The bull, of course, was the most important zootype of Osiris.

Few triads of Greek deities demonstrate so obvious an Ethiopian origin as that of Helios, Eos, and Selene—the Sun, the Dawn, and the Moon. To the Greeks, Ethiopia represented, literally, the ends of the earth and the sun god Helios, identified with the Egyptian Rā, was said to be quartered there. He and his two sisters were children of the titan Hyperion and Theia who at other times was known as *Melaena*, "the Black Goddess." She is also the mother of Delphos, for whom the Oracle of Delphi is eponymously named, and Delphos is frequently represented as a Negro. Moreover, the son of Helios is Phaeton whose native country, Ovid tells us, is Ethiopia. The mother of Helios is sometimes known as the "cow-eyed." This can only refer to Hathor, who as "is also the mother of Rā (i.e., Helios)" represented as the celestial Cow. She is also the mother of Rā (i.e., Helios.) Eos is the consort of the mortal Tithonus and by him the mother of Memnon, renowned in antiquity as king of Ethiopia.

A cycle of mythic figures also demonstrating a distinct Egypto-Ethiopian provenance is that of Io, Epaphus, Libya, Agenor, Belus, Aegyptus, and Danaus. In fact these mythotypes appear to come from Africa into Greece virtually unmodified. Io, though she is given many adventures taking her into numerous lands, is shown at last to be Isis herself in her familiar cow-form. This reference to her travels probably pertains to the spread of the Isaic cult itself out of Egypt, a process that became intensified during the Ptolemaic period. Epaphus, Io's son by Zeus, is Hapi, the Egyptian Nile god who was identified with the Apis bull. The daughter of Epaphus was Libya who is no more than the feminine personification of Africa itself—and was so represented. By Poseidon, she gives birth to the twins Agenor and Belus. Agenor was considered ancestral to the Canaanites and Robert Graves states quite frankly that many Canaanite customs point to an East African source. Graves was of the opinion that the ancestral Canaanites may have reached Canaan from Uganda via Lower Egypt. From what we know about the Negroid skeletal remains of the Natufian people of Western Asia, who dominated the region from about 10,000 to 8,000 BC, Graves's reasoning is entirely plausible. The genealogy of Noah also supports this contention.

Agenor's brother was King Belus, ruler of Upper Egypt at Chemmis, whose wife, the daughter of the Nile, bore him the twin sons Aegyptus and Danaus. Aegyptus and Danaus were considered to be the founding ancestors of the Libyans, Ethiopians, Egyptians, Phoenicians, and Arabians. Aegyptus and Danaus, with their immediate progeny, became antagonists, but in **Suppliants**, Aeschylus makes it clear that all these *dramatis personae* were black Africans. The 50 daughters of Danaus, known as the Danaids, fled to Greece to escape a forced group marriage to their 50 male cousins, the Aegyptiads. Pursued by the Aegyptiads, they succeeded in murdering all but one on the night of a sham wedding. It was Danaus and his Danaids who came to rule the Pelasgians of early Greece. In the end, these Pelasgians called themselves Danaans. Among other things, these African Danaans instituted the Eleusinian mysteries that they had brought with them. The Pelasgian creation myth was undoubtedly inspired by the teachings of these remote Danaid ancestresses. Mythographers in antiquity—and Graves in modern times—accepted this Danaid cycle as representative of a real series of historical migrations into Greece from Canaan and Africa. Thus, few learned Greeks questioned the assumption that certain streams of Greek aboriginal people with their mythology and religion flowed directly out of Africa and into early Greece.

We have not exhausted this subject for there are many more strands we could follow that would lead us—like Theseus in the Labyrinth—back to the sources of Greek myth in Africa. To follow such threads is an important function of Martin Bernal's much-discussed—and much-criticized—"Revised Ancient Model," in two volumes of **Black Athena**, a revisionist paradigm of ancient history that has served as a much-needed corrective to the conceit that Greek culture created itself without any contribution from the surrounding, pre-existing civilizations of Africa and Western Asia. The dominant Aryan Model of the 19th and 20th centuries pre-supposed that Greek culture appeared *deus ex machina* on the world stage as the unique product of an exclusive genius. Were we to persist in this gross misperception and falsification, we might never arrive at a correct understanding of Greece's—or Africa's—place in the history of world civilization.

References

1. Bernal, Martin, **The Black Athena: The Afroasiatic Roots of Classical Civilization**, London: Free Association Books, 1987.
2. Budge, E.A. Wallis, **The Gods of the Egyptians, Studies in Egyptian Mythology, Vols. 1 and 2**, New York: Dover Publications, 1969
3. Diodorus Siculus, **On Egypt**, translated by Edwin Murphy, London: McFarland & Company, Inc., 1985.
4. Diop, Cheikh Anta, **Civilization or Barbarism, An Authentic Anthropology**, Brooklyn, NY: Lawrence Hill Books, 1991
5. Graves, Robert, **The Greek Myths**, Two Volumes, New York: Penguin Books, 1955, 1977.
6. Herodotus, **The Histories**, translated by Aubrey de Selincourt, New York: Penguin Books, 1954, 1979.
7. Hesiod, **The Homeric Hymns and Homerica**, translated by Hugh G. Evelyn-White, Cambrige: Harvard University Press, 1914, 1970.
8. Homer, **The Iliad**, translated by Robert Fitzgerald, Garden City: Anchor Press/Doubleday, 1974.
9. Massey, Gerald, **Ancient Egypt, Light of the World, Vols. 1 and 2**, New York: Samuel Weiser Inc., 1970
10. Ovid, **The Metamorphoses**, translated by Horace Gregory, New York: Viking Press, 1958.
11. Plato, **Timaeus and Critias**, translated by Desmond Lee, New York: Penguin Books, 1965, 1971.
12. Plutarch, *Of Isis and Osiris*, translated by G.R.S. Mead, in **Thrice Greatest Hermes**, by G.R.S. Mead, London: John M. Watkins, 1906, 1949.

13. Schwaller de Lubicz, R.A., **The Temple in Man, The Secrets of Ancient Egypt**, Brookline, MA: Autumn Press, 1977

14. Snowden, Frank M., **Blacks in Antiquity**, Cambridge: Harvard University Press, 1970.

Index

B

C

D

E

F

G

H

I

J

K

L

N

O

P

S

T

U

V

W

X

Y

Z